PRACTICAL IMAGE PROCESSING IN C

PRACTICAL IMAGE PROCESSING IN C

- **Acquisition**
- **Manipulation**
- **Storage**

Craig A. Lindley

JOHN WILEY & SONS, INC.
New York   Chichester   Brisbane   Toronto   Singapore

In recognition of the importance of preserving what has been written, it is a policy of John Wiley & Sons, Inc., to have books of enduring value published in the United States printed on acid-free paper, and we exert our best efforts to that end.

Library of Congress Cataloging in Publication Data

Lindley, Craig A.
    Practical image processing in C : acquisition, manipulation and storage : hardware, software, images and text / by Craig A. Lindley.
      p. cm.
    Includes bibliographical references and index.
    1. Turbo C (Computer program) 2. Image processing—Digital techniques—Data processing. I. Title.

TA1632.L56 1990
621.36′7—dc20   90–41054
ISBN 0-471-53062-X   CIP
ISBN 0-471-53240-1 (Disk)
ISBN 0-471-54377-2 (Book–Disk Set)

Printed in the United States of America

10 9 8 7 6 5 4 3 2 1

Contents

Figures

Images and Image Sequences

Program Listings

Preface

Image acquisition and processing were once performed exclusively by industry. Image processing has been used for the processing of pictures returned from deep space, as a tool for investigations of Earth's resources, for Earth-based astronomy, for weather prediction, for automated inspection, and for robotics—to name just a few applications. The acquisition, manipulation, analysis, and display of images have up to now required computers and graphics devices well beyond the means of individuals. Hardware issues aside, image processing also required an extensive mathematical background to understand and apply the complex algorithms to which image data was typically subjected. When code was available to study, in an attempt to understand the algorithms, it was generally uncommented, convoluted FORTRAN. Learning in this environment was difficult.

All of this is changing. Image processing at the desktop with a personal computer is now not only possible but is becoming a thriving industry. No longer does one have to be employed by a large corporation to utilize the techniques of image processing. Note the flood of ads for fax machines, video digitizers, flat-bed scanners, hand scanners, color scanners, and other image input devices that are now accessible by everyone. This technology is possible because of increasingly higher performance levels of the personal computer, high-resolution graphics adapters, and the low cost of digitizer hardware. What was once performed only in the labs of major corporations can now be done on one's personal computer. The well-used cliché "a picture is worth a thousand words" is finding renewed application in today's desktop publishing industry. Personal imaging technology has indeed progressed since the advent of digitized T-shirts at the amusement park.

With imaging and graphics becoming such an important aspect of the world around us, people from many diverse disciplines are working together for the first time. Electronic engineers, graphic artists, video technicians, layout artists, document processing professionals, and computer graphics programmers—all are affected by the video revolution. People in these fields are expanding their horizons into this new and exciting area. All of them may learn something from the information and techniques presented in *Practical Image Processing in C*.

In support of this revolution in imaging technology, the goal of this book is to bring image-acquisition and processing capabilities within the reach of the individual. Toward this end, presented here is what might be the world's lowest-cost video digitizer input device for a PC. This device allows still video images to be imported into a PC from a low-cost television camera for display and/or manipulation. The hardware design and fabrication of this video digitizer comprise a major portion of this book. During the discussion you'll learn the basics of video, which will allow you to understand how the digitizer works. At the end of the discussion you'll better understand how television sets and television cameras work.

In Part One, after the hardware theory and design are explained, the book discusses the software necessary to make the digitizer produce various resolution images and how to display the images on a PC. The book even demonstrates how beautiful full-color images can be produced using only a monochrome television camera. The discussion is enhanced by practical example programs that illustrate the concepts presented. Images produced by the digitizer are provided throughout the book to illustrate the capabilities of the working digitizer. Information is presented incrementally to avoid overwhelming the reader with all the details at one time.

Digitized images by themselves have limited usefulness. To become useful they must first be put into a form in which they can be manipulated by other application programs. For this reason, a chapter is included on the PCX and TIFF graphics file formats used by many PC application programs. The images digitized by the video digitizer can be saved in either of these formats. They can then be imported into Paintbrush® or desktop publishing programs for incorporation into presentations, reports, and newsletters. Not only are the graphics file formats discussed in detail but C code is given to read and write each format. Where appropriate, the complete specifications of the file formats are also provided. Finally, a view program is presented that can display image files in either of these formats.

Converting images displayed on a video monitor to images on paper requires some rather specialized techniques, and therefore Chapter 7 is devoted entirely to the production of hardcopy images. Both photographic and printer techniques are discussed at length, and an example program is provided that will allow graphic images to be produced on a line printer utilizing two popular printing algorithms.

Part Two examines classical image processing. In this section a practical rather than rigorous mathematical approach is utilized. Each major class of image processing algorithm is illustrated with example C code and images that show the effect of the algorithm. The information provided in these chapters has applications in machine vision, automated inspection, image enhancement, robotics, and so on.

Requirements

To utilize the code provided in this book (and available on the companion disks), it is necessary to have access to the following items:

a. A Turbo C® C compiler version 1.5 or newer. The code can be made to work with other brands of C compilers as well. The use of the Microsoft® C compiler is discussed at length, for example.

b. An 80×86 assembler such as MASM® from Microsoft and/or IBM® or TASM® from Borland.

c. An IBM-compatible PC with a VGA graphics adapter, color monitor, and printer port.

Notice that the video digitizer is not listed as a required tool. The code presented in this book, for the most part, is input device independent and does not require the digitizer to be useful. The algorithms presented can process input data provided by hand scanners, frame grabbers, and most other graphics input devices. The digitizer is just another source of graphics input data. It provides a very-low-cost, entry-level device to promote experimentation by the widest possible audience.

All code has been extensively tested on both the IBM PS 2 Models 60 and 70 with 1 megabyte of RAM, VGA graphics adapter, and serial and parallel ports. The digitizer image-acquisition routines will work on any IBM-compatible PC, even the original 4.77 MHz 8088 machine. The images must be displayed, however, on a VGA-equipped PC.

This book assumes a general knowledge of assembly language programming for the 80×86 family of Intel processors and some C programming experience; it does not pretend to teach either. All code is well documented and should be easy to understand even for a beginner. Please note that the performance of the code was considered a more important criterion than its portability. Even with today's powerful PCs, image processing requires an impressive amount of computing power. The more powerful a PC put to the task the better. This does not mean the code is nonportable. On the contrary: Given the motivation, the code could be moved onto any platform. Companion disks are available that contain all of the source code developed in this book along with a few images for your viewing and processing pleasure.

Again, the most important goal of this book is to introduce you to the fascinating world of image processing. You'll find that not only does image processing have many tangible uses but it can also provide hours upon hours of entertainment. To this end, I hope you will have fun with your video digitizer and with experimenting with image processing. Remember, a digitized image is worth at least 32,000 words (or 64,000 bytes) of computer memory.

Live long and prosper,

CRAIG A. LINDLEY

Manitou Springs, Colorado
November 1990

Acknowledgments

This book is dedicated to my wife Heather Hubbard, who was patient enough to proofread this book and wise enough not to let me burn myself out writing it, and to my Mom and Dad, Merrill and Neva Lindley, who taught me that self-motivation is a positive personal attribute. To you all I give thanks!

A special thanks goes to the following individuals and companies who assisted in the production of *Practical Image Processing in C*. Without their help this book would not have been completed.

Diane Cerra and Terri Hudson of John Wiley & Sons for helping me with the business of book publishing. Dennis and Kathy Stockton for assistance with the photographic equipment. ZSoft Corporation for providing an advanced copy of its excellent product, PC Paintbrush IV Plus, to help debug the TIFF library and for providing the specifications for the PCX file format. The Aldus Corporation for allowing me to include the TIFF 5.0 specification. *Gourmet* magazine for granting permission to use a photograph from the cover of the magazine. And finally, Steve Ciarcia for his electronic wizardry.

All images in this book are from photographs taken by Heather Hubbard, the author, or other public domain sources. Other images were used by permission.

C. A. L.

PART ONE

THE VIDEO DIGITIZER PROJECT

1

Background Information

In this chapter you will learn about:

- The limitations of programs written for MSDOS®
- The architecture of the Intel® 80 × 86 processors
- The capabilities and limitations of PC graphics adapters
- EGA/VGA palette, color, and color register operations
- How to access the VGA graphics adapter's capabilities
- How the printer port works on the PC
- How to deal with memory segments and memory models
- How data is shared between assembler and C code

Introduction

In the study of any new subject, be it image processing, auto mechanics, or gardening, some time must first be spent trying to understand the fundamental concepts upon which the subject is based. Reviewing basics may not always be interesting, but in many cases it is necessary. This first chapter spends some time discussing subjects not directly related to image acquisition and processing. The discussion centers on the fundamentals necessary to fully understand and apply the imaging techniques discussed later. Because the digitizer project presented in this book is specific to the IBM® PC (or compatibles), a good part of the discussion is about PC hardware and the software development tools used for code generation. As mentioned in the Preface, this book does not try to teach programming. Therefore, only the aspects of the programming languages we actually use are discussed. A generalized coverage of C and assembler language programming is *not* provided. Some of the topics covered are complex and are therefore given an appropriate treatment. See the list of excellent books provided in "References and Additional Reading" for further information on programming.

Information provided in this chapter is a prerequisite for upcoming chapters. If discussion of a topic seems to be missing in a later chapter, it is likely to be found here. Advanced PC programmers (and all others who are anxious to dive directly into the topic of imaging) may wish to scan this chapter on first reading and come back to it later as required.

PC Hardware Issues

CPU Issues

The central processing unit (CPU) is the heart of any computer system. All computation is performed within the CPU. The majority of the hardware devices inside of a PC are there to support the functions of the CPU. Throughout this book the terms *CPU, processor*, and *microprocessor* will be used synonymously to describe this single processing element.

The Intel 80×86 family of processors are used in IBM and IBM-compatible PCs. This family spans orders of magnitude of performance—from the 8088 used in the original PC to the 80486 "desktop mainframe." All the family members share a common heritage—the 8086 processor. Each of the new processors is *backwards compatible* with the previous generation of processors. This means that code written for the 8088 will run without modification on the 80486 processor, only faster. However, code written in the "native mode" for a new processor will not run on the older processors.

Code compatibility is both a blessing and a curse. Backwards compatibility is a plus in that old software still runs when a PC is replaced with a new, faster one. Compatibility is sometimes bad, however, because all applications are generally written for the lowest common denominator, the 8088 processor, and therefore do not take advantage of the advanced features of the newer generation of processors. Take the preparation of this book, for example. The text was prepared using an old version of WordStar that was originally written for the 8088 processor used in the original PC. This old version of WordStar® was run on a 80386 processor in a PS/2 Model 70. The good news is that the software executes without a hitch. The bad news is that, although it executes faster on the new computer, the features available are not expanded in proportion to the performance of the new processor. The document buffer size, for example, does not change when executed on the new processor.

The use of the "real mode" operating system, PCDOS® (PCDOS and MSDOS are two other terms that will be used synonymously in this book), is another reason why new features on the newer processors are not available. This operating system was originally developed for the 8088/86 processors utilized in the original PC. When MSDOS executes, it assumes the underlying processor is an 8088-type device and therefore does not initialize the new processors for execution in their native and more efficient mode of operation. Many different versions of PCDOS/MSDOS exist. The original version was 1.0, the newest is 4.1. Many improvements have been made in the various versions of this workhorse operating system.

None of the versions, however, make any attempt to operate in any but the "real mode" (8088/86 emulation mode) of operation.

Newer operating systems such as UNIX®, AIX®, and OS/2® take advantage of the native mode of operation provided by the more modern processors. These operating systems can provide more features and functions to application programs written to run on top of them. Notably, these operating systems provide:

a. Hardware support for multitasking
b. Memory protection for errant task isolation and debugging
c. A much larger address space for program code and data

These operating systems provide enhanced features with the limitation of not being able to be run on the older 8088/8086 processors. An Intel 80286 processor, at a minimum, is required to run these operating systems. A new version of OS/2 will be available shortly (named possibly OS/2 386 or OS/3) that will run only on 80386/486 processors. This is because it will utilize 386 specific features not available on even the 80286 processor.

Because of its wide availability and acceptance, all of the programs in this book are designed to run under the ubiquitous MSDOS operating system. Not only does this force the processor into the 8088/86 mode (real mode) of operation, it also places some limits on the resources available for our imaging programs. Namely,

a. The total amount of memory that can be addressed within an applications program is 640KB. This is a severe constraint, because some of the individual images are 300KB in size.

b. Multitasking is not available.

There are ways to get around each of these limitations, but they are somewhat application-specific and will not be discussed or used in this book. To allow the widest possible audience, unassisted MSDOS will be used exclusively for the imaging programs. It would do little good to provide other versions of the example programs for other operating systems until more people are running those operating systems.

The 8088/86 processor model, forced by the use of MSDOS, can be characterized as follows:

a. The CPU has the ability to address 1 megabyte of memory total in 64-KB segments.

b. Four special segment registers are used to manage the segmented memory architecture. They are the DS or data segment register, the CS or code segment register, the SS or stack segment register, and finally the ES or extra segment register.

c. Segments start on paragraph boundaries. A paragraph is 16 bytes in length. A paragraph boundary is any address evenly divisible by 16.

d. The notation used to identify a memory location is segment:offset. Segment points to the start of an area of memory and the offset contains the difference between the start segment address and the address of interest. Since segments can overlap, each memory location can be specified by more than one segment:offset pair. In other words, each segment:offset specifies a unique memory location; other segment:offset pairs may also specify the same location. Since the offset is a 16-bit quantity, each segment is a maximum 64KB in length.

e. All four of the segment registers can point to the same area of memory. Turbo C's tiny memory model, which will be discussed shortly, is an example of this.

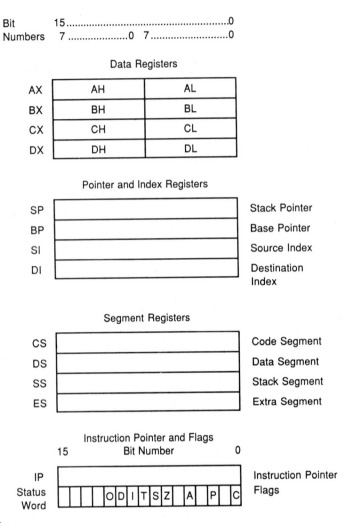

Bit   15..0
Numbers   7 ....0 7..........................0

Data Registers

AX	AH	AL
BX	BH	BL
CX	CH	CL
DX	DH	DL

Pointer and Index Registers

SP   Stack Pointer
BP   Base Pointer
SI   Source Index
DI   Destination
                                                Index

Segment Registers

CS   Code Segment
DS   Data Segment
SS   Stack Segment
ES   Extra Segment

Instruction Pointer and Flags
        15   Bit Number   0

IP   Instruction Pointer
Status |O|D|I|T|S|Z| |A| |P| |C| Flags
Word

Notes
Flag bits: C is carry, P is parity, A is auxiliary carry, Z is zero, S is sign, T is trap flag, I is interrupt enable, D is direction, and O is overflow. All other bits are reserved by Intel for future use.

Figure 1.1   8086/88 Processor Register Model

Figure 1.1 gives the programmer's model of the CPU registers.

In actuality, the segmented architecture of the Intel processors (while executing in real mode) is not ideally suited for manipulation of graphic images. Some of the images produced by the digitizer detailed in this book occupy much more memory than can be contained in a single data segment. Additional code is required to access image data that cross segment boundaries. This extra code extracts a performance penalty for the Intel processors. The Motorola® 68000 series of processors, with their large linear address space, would be a better choice for an image processor. However, since the Intel processors are ubiquitous, we will utilize them for our purpose.

One note on processor performance. Image processing is a numerically intensive computational activity. Serious amounts of image processing can consume most PCs put to this task. The more raw horsepower available for image processing the better. While all of the programs developed for this book will run on the 8088, 4.77 MHz original PC, the results will be available much sooner on a 20 MHz 80386 processor.

PC Graphics Adapters

Introduction. A graphics adapter is the hardware circuitry internal to a PC that gives the PC the capability of displaying graphic images in addition to text. Graphic images are composed of a series of dots and lines that can be placed anywhere in the display area of the attached monitor. Graphics frees the programmer from the constraints of the text mode of operation. When the term *graphics adapter* is used, it implies the availability of both text and graphics modes of operation. In industry, the term *display adapter* may imply text modes only. In this book both terms are used to mean the same thing: the ability to display both text and graphics.

The graphics display capabilities of IBM PCs and compatibles have steadily increased over the years. The first graphics display adapter, the Color Graphics Adapter (CGA), could display a 320- by 200-pixel screen in four colors or a 640 by 200 screen in two colors. Contrast that with the current Video Graphics Array (VGA) display technology, which can support screen resolutions of 640 by 480 in 16 colors or 320 by 200 in 256 colors. Advances in graphics display technology have been driven by:

a. Lower hardware costs (especially DRAM memory chips)
b. The demand for graphical user interfaces (GUIs)
c. Imaging and desktop publishing applications

The trend toward high-resolution and higher-performance graphics hardware is not abiding. Already, the widely touted VGA championed by IBM is being eclipsed. Megapixel resolution display hardware with a reasonable cost is already appearing on the horizon, and 1024 by 1024 display hardware will probably be provided on the personal computers and workstations of the mid-1990s. This resolution, coupled with 8- to 12-bit planes of color memory, will provide photographic-quality image display on the desktop. Apple® Corporation has already introduced its QuickDraw 32® software which provides nearly those capabilities now.

In contrast to Apple, IBM has never been known for providing stunning graphics capability. IBM's focus has been the business and presentation graphics markets. VGA is an attempt by IBM to keep up in the rapidly accelerating graphics hardware race. Endorsed by IBM, VGA is destined to become a graphics standard, as did CGA and Enhanced Graphic Adapter (EGA).

In the IBM and compatible world, there are no fewer than eight display adapter standards available:

a. MDA (Monochrome Display Adapter)
b. HGA (Hercules® Graphics Adapter)
c. CGA (Color Display Adapter)
d. The display adapter in the IBM PC Jr.
e. EGA (Enhanced Graphic Adapter)
f. MCGA (Multi Color Graphics Array), which is available on the Model 25 and 30 IBM PS/2 computers
g. VGA (Video Graphics Array), which is available on the Model 50, 55, 60, 70, and 80 PS/2® computers
h. 8514/A adapter card and IBM 8514 monitor

It is interesting to note that all of the display standards on the above list, with the exception of the Hercules Graphics Adapter, were developed and promoted by the IBM Corporation. There are, however, many other non-IBM graphics adapters available on the market today, some of which have specifications greater than even the 8514/A. These are not listed because they have yet to gain the status of a "standard." Many of the third-party display adapters simply emulate one or more of the standards listed above.

Modes and Resolutions. High-quality image display demands a certain minimum acceptable level of graphics adapter functionality. Certainly a fixed, four-colors-on-the-screen-at-a-time graphics adapter such as the CGA does not provide acceptable performance for anything but black and white or two color images. The display of color images with the CGA adapter is poor at best. The question becomes, What is the minimum graphics adapter functionality required for acceptable (a subjective criterion) image display? Figure 1.2 details the graphics capabilities of most display adapters, to help in making this determination. Text modes available on the various display adapters are not as important as the graphics modes for image applications and are not shown in the table.

All of the imagery in this book falls into one of two categories: continuous-tone images and color images. Continuous-tone images are displayed in resolutions of 320 by 200 in either 16 or 64 levels of gray, in 640 by 200 resolution with 16 levels of gray, and in 640 by 480 resolution with 16 levels of gray. Color images can be displayed only in 320 by 200 resolution using 256 colors.

To display multilevel gray-scale or color images, configurable palettes and color registers are required. To provide the proper color balance for realistic image display, the RGB components of the color registers must be set directly. Although the EGA provides 16 simultaneous colors out of a palette of 64, its lack of configurable color registers makes it of limited usefulness in imaging applications. Dot dithering can be used to increase the number of apparent colors an EGA can display, at the expense of lowering the display resolution (see Chapter 7). Since photographic realism is the goal of the digitization process, trading resolution for pseudocolors on a display monitor does not seem a suitable trade-off.

The answer to the question, "What is the minimum graphics adapter functionality required for acceptable image display?" should now be obvious. VGA has all the capabilities required for the imaging work done in this book. (*Note*: VGA has the *minimum* capability

	Resolution	Colors	C G A	P C J r	E G A	M C G A	V G A
1.	320 by 200	4	*	*	*	*	*
2.	640 by 200	2	*	*	*	*	*
3.	160 by 200	16		*			
4.	320 by 200	16	*	*			*
5.	320 by 200	256				*	*
6.	640 by 200	4		*			
7.	640 by 200	16			*		*
8.	640 by 350	2			*		*
9.	640 by 350	4			*		
10.	640 by 350	16			*		*
11.	640 by 480	2				*	*
12.	640 by 480	16					*
13.	Configurable Palette			*	*	*	*
14.	Configurable Color Registers					*	*

Notes

1. The HGA is not listed because it will not do color. MDA is not listed in the table because it does not support graphics. 8514/A is absent because with its prohibitively high cost, few people will have access to it.
2. A configurable palette allows the collection of colors displayed on a screen to be selected from a larger number of possible colors.
3. A color register is configurable if its individual RGB (red, green, and blue) components can be altered with software.

Figure 1.2   Display Adapter Graphics Capabilities

required for experimentation with imaging. Anything less than VGA capability will not produce satisfactory results. Capabilities beyond VGA, however, are desirable.) For this reason, all of the imaging programs in this book assume the existence of VGA adapter. To fully utilize the programs in this book requires a VGA adapter. No support for other graphics display adapters is provided. A VGA adapter is standard equipment on the PS/2 Model 50s and higher and is also available from IBM and other manufacturers as a plug-in graphics card for older PCs. An investment in a VGA adapter and monitor is a prerequisite for doing serious imaging work on PC and PC-compatible computers.

Only the standard VGA modes and resolutions provided by PC's BIOS (Basic Input/ Output System) are utilized in this book. All access to VGA is through the Turbo C's® graphics library, except for the 256-color 320 by 200 mode. This mode is supported via assembler language and C functions because Borland, the developers of Turbo C, chose not to support this graphics mode. The IBM VGA hardware is capable of many "nonstandard" modes of operation, including 256 colors at resolutions up to 360 by 480. The excellent articles by Richard Wilton (see "References and Further Reading") have information on how these nonstandard modes are accessed. The use of Turbo C's graphics procedures will be discussed shortly.

Palettes. A *palette* is defined in the dictionary as a thin board with a thumbhole at one end used by painters for holding and mixing colors. It is also defined as the set of colors on such a board. In computer graphics terms, the palette is the collection of colors available for simultaneous display on a color monitor. The various graphics adapters use different mechanisms for placing colors on a monitor. Three such arrangements are shown in Figures 1.3, 1.4, and 1.5. Each will be discussed separately.

Figure 1.3 shows the palette configuration for an EGA. EGA is discussed here so that the VGA capabilities can be contrasted with it. With EGA, the four bits of data stored in the video memory form an index into the palette data structure. The four video data bits result in

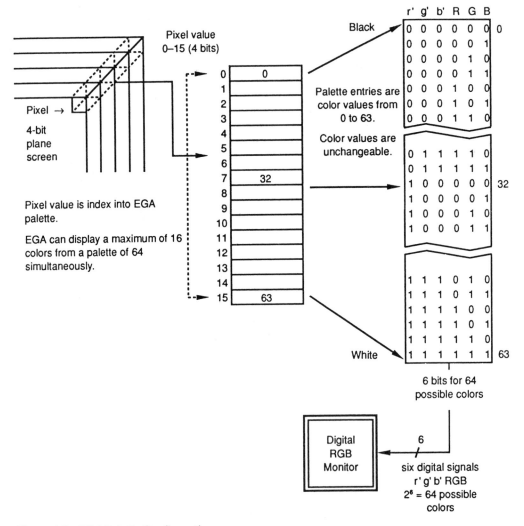

Figure 1.3   EGA Palette Configuration

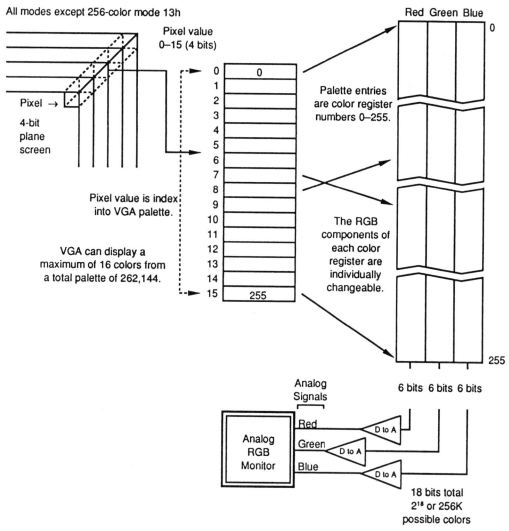

All modes except 256-color mode 13h

Pixel value
0–15 (4 bits)

Pixel →
4-bit
plane
screen

Pixel value is index
into VGA palette.

VGA can display a
maximum of 16 colors from
a total palette of 262,144.

Palette entries
are color register
numbers 0–255.

The RGB
components of
each color
register are
individually
changeable.

Red Green Blue

6 bits 6 bits 6 bits

Analog
Signals

Analog
RGB
Monitor

Red

Green

Blue

D to A

D to A

D to A

18 bits total
2^{18} or 256K
possible colors

Note
1. D to A is digital to analog converter.

Figure 1.4   VGA Palette Configuration

16 possible color index values, ranging from 0 to 15. All of the 16 entries in the palette structure are 6-bit color numbers. The color specified by the color number is fixed; it cannot be altered. Each entry in the palette, however, *can* be altered—to any one of the 64 possible color numbers. This results in the capability of displaying 16 simultaneous colors out of a total palette of 64 possible colors. Note that the monitor used for EGA display is digital (as is the monitor used for CGA display). The six bits of digital color information, r′g′b′RGB,

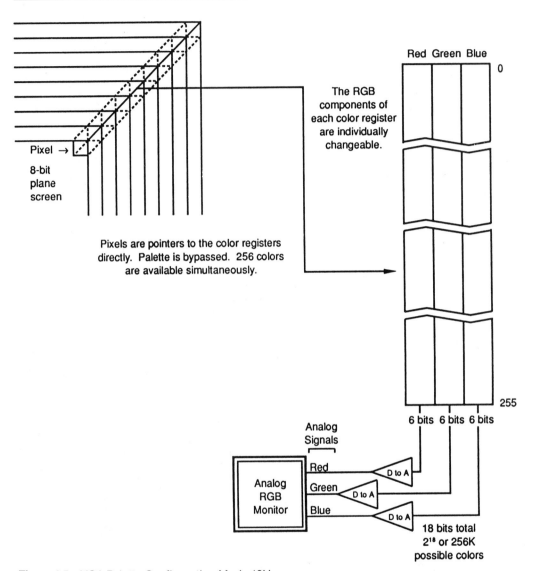

Figure 1.5   VGA Palette Configuration Mode 13H

drive directly out of the display adapter into the equivalent inputs on the monitor. From basic digital theory, 6 digital color bits represents 64 or 2^6 total combinations or colors available.

On initialization of the EGA, the palette is filled with colors that are CGA compatible. This was done to assure backwards compatibility with the large base of software written for CGA. Figure 1.6 shows the default values stored in the EGA palette data structure.

To place a light magenta pixel on an EGA screen, the value of 13 decimal would be poked into the appropriate address in video memory. In actuality, Turbo C's "putpixel" graphics function would be called and passed 13 as the requested color.

Palette Index	Color	Palette Entry
0	Black	0
1	Blue	1
2	Green	2
3	Cyan	3
4	Red	4
5	Magenta	5
6	Light Gray	7
7	Brown	20
8	Dark Gray	56
9	Light Blue	57
10	Light Green	58
11	Light Cyan	59
12	Light Red	60
13	Light Magenta	61
14	Yellow	62
15	White	63

Figure 1.6   Default EGA Colors

As changes are made to the content of the palette, all pixels mapped to the index being changed will automatically assume the new color. Once a screen is painted with an image, bizarre special effects can be produced by altering the color numbers stored in the palette. Some of these effects are quite striking.

The VGA graphics adapter uses two different methods for the handling of palettes. The method depends upon the graphics mode being utilized. All graphics modes—with the exception of mode 13H (13 hex), the 256-color 320 by 200 mode—use basically the same mechanism as does the EGA. The EGA-compatible VGA palette mechanism is shown in Figure 1.4. The difference in the VGA mechanism is that the entries in the palette contain pointers to one of 256 color registers instead of the 63 set color numbers used by EGA. The bigger difference in the two graphics adapters is that the individual red, green, and blue (RGB) components of the color registers can be configured in the VGA adapter and are fixed in the EGA. Given that each of the color components, red, green, and blue, utilizes 6 bits of information, a total of 2^{18} possible different colors are available. This works out to be 262,144 different color possibilities, 16 of which can be displayed simultaneously.

To display this many colors, analog RGB monitors must be used. As shown in the figure, digital-to-analog converters (three) are necessary to convert the 18 bits of digital color information into the analog signals required to drive the monitor. This makes the VGA more expensive than the EGA (both the graphics adapter itself and the display monitor) but the increased color capabilities make up for the price differential.

VGA mode 13H is a special color mode. In this mode, a low-resolution image (320 by 200) with a total of 256 different colors can be displayed. Figure 1.5 illustrates the palette mechanism used for this special mode. Actually, it would be more accurate to say the lack of palette mechanism used for this special mode. With mode 13H, the display memory is segmented into eight different bit planes as opposed to the four utilized for all other modes. Having eight bit planes means that a pixel of video data can take on values from 0 to 255. In this mode, the palette mechanism is bypassed completely and the video data value directly indexes a color register. A video pixel value of 10 takes on the color defined by the RGB values of color register 10, and so on. Using this graphics mode, an image can be displayed with 256 different colors out of a total of 262,144 possible. Also, any one of the 256 colors can be any of the 262,144.

At initialization time for mode 13H, the color registers are loaded as follows. (This information is excerpted from the IBM PS/2 Hardware Interface Technical Reference manual.)

a. The first 16 color registers are loaded with values corresponding to the CGA and EGA colors shown in Figure 1.6.
b. The second 16 color registers are loaded with evenly spaced gray shades.
c. The final 216 color registers contain values based on a hue, saturation, and intensity model tuned to provide a usable, generic color set that covers a wide range of color values.

Palette Generation. To display accurately a digitized image, it is necessary to generate and install a palette that reflects the color content of the image. Continuous-tone images require a gray-scale palette, while color images require a palette that most closely matches the colors contained in the original image. Two techniques exist for palette/image matching. The first, which is used for the continuous-tone image display, forces the image to be displayed in evenly spaced shades of gray. In other words, the gray-scale palette is programmed into the VGA adapter first and the image is displayed in that palette. The palette is chosen for its breadth of gray-scale coverage and is not directly related to the content of the image. Each pixel of image data is directly mapped into the gray-scale palette by its numerical value.

In the second method of palette/image matching an algorithm is utilized to build an optimal color palette that most accurately reflects the colors in the original image. In this case, the palette used to display a color digitized image is generated from the actual colors in the image. This is in contrast to displaying the image with the closest colors in a preset palette. Extracting the palette information from the image results in a much more realistic image display. The algorithm used for palette selection for color image display will be discussed in Chapter 5.

With either matching technique, adjustability of the color registers in the display adapter is an absolute necessity. This is one area in which the VGA adapter with its adjustable color registers is vastly superior to the EGA. With the fixed colors available with the EGA, neither continuous-tone nor color images can be displayed accurately. In all cases (with the EGA), the palette used to display an image is the "closest fit" to the fixed colors that are available. This results in color distortion in the displayed image. VGA, in contrast, allows the color registers to be set to colors that accurately display the digitized image.

Evenly spaced gray-scale palettes are easily generated. Their generation is based upon the fact the color gray is made up of equal parts of red, green, and blue. Regardless of the shade of gray, if the RGB components of a color register are all equal, the result will be a shade of gray or black or white. The values to be used in the color registers depend upon the number of gray levels desired and the gamma correction factor (this will be discussed shortly) for the display monitor being used. Two different gray-scale palettes can be generated that are useful in the image processing performed in this book: a 16-level and a 64-level gray scale. Of course, the 16-level gray scale requires the use of 16 color registers, while the 64-level requires 64 color registers. The 16-level gray scale can be used in any of the 16-color VGA graphics modes, whereas the 64-level gray scale can be used only in the special video graphics mode 13H discussed above. Figure 1.7 shows the values loaded into the color registers for the 16 and 64 levels of gray-scale palette.

The generation of the gray-scale palettes that are perceived to be equally spaced is complicated by two facts: the nonlinearity of computer monitors and the nonlinearity of the human eye/brain vision system. To compensate for the monitor nonlinearity, a gamma correction factor is introduced. Gamma correction attempts to establish a linear relationship between the numerical value of the data in a color register and the resultant luminance (brightness) of the display. If computer monitors were completely linear, the gray-scale palette values would be linear. You can see from Figure 1.7 the nonlinear nature of the gamma function. The formula for the correction is

Corrected Value = exp[ln(value)/gamma power factor]

The gamma power factor of most monitors ranges from 1.8 to 2.2. A value of 2.2 was used to generate the 64-level palette shown in Figure 1.7. The values of the 16-level gray scale were taken directly from the IBM BIOS code. See the *Raster Graphics Handbook* by CONRAC Corporation for further discussion of gamma correction. An example of how palettes are installed for use with VGA will be given in the section on Turbo C graphics functions.

Color Register	16-level			64-1evel		
	Red	Green	Blue	Red	Green	Blue
0	00	00	00	00	00	00
1	05	05	05	00	00	00
2	08	08	08	00	00	00
3	11	11	11	00	00	00
4	14	14	14	00	00	00
5	17	17	17	01	01	01
6	20	20	20	01	01	01
7	24	24	24	02	02	02
8	28	28	28	03	03	03
9	32	32	32	03	03	03
10	36	36	36	04	04	04
11	40	40	40	05	05	05
12	45	45	45	06	06	06
13	50	50	50	07	07	07
14	56	56	56	08	08	08
15	63	63	63	09	09	09
16	—	—	—	10	10	10
17	—	—	—	10	10	10

Figure 1.7   Gray-Scale Palette Values

(continued)

Color Register	16-level			64-1evel		
	Red	Green	Blue	Red	Green	Blue
18	—	—	—	11	11	11
19	—	—	—	12	12	12
20	—	—	—	13	13	13
21	—	—	—	14	14	14
22	—	—	—	15	15	15
23	—	—	—	16	16	16
24	—	—	—	18	18	18
25	—	—	—	19	19	19
26	—	—	—	20	20	20
27	—	—	—	21	21	21
28	—	—	—	22	22	22
29	—	—	—	23	23	23
30	—	—	—	24	24	24
31	—	—	—	25	25	25
32	—	—	—	26	26	26
33	—	—	—	27	27	27
34	—	—	—	28	28	28
35	—	—	—	29	29	29
36	—	—	—	31	31	31
37	—	—	—	32	32	32
38	—	—	—	33	33	33
39	—	—	—	34	34	34
40	—	—	—	35	35	35
41	—	—	—	36	36	36
42	—	—	—	37	37	37
43	—	—	—	39	39	39
44	—	—	—	40	40	40
45	—	—	—	41	41	41
46	—	—	—	42	42	42
47	—	—	—	43	43	43
48	—	—	—	44	44	44
49	—	—	—	46	46	46
50	—	—	—	47	47	47
51	—	—	—	48	48	48
52	—	—	—	49	49	49
53	—	—	—	50	50	50
54	—	—	—	52	52	52
55	—	—	—	53	53	53
56	—	—	—	54	54	54
57	—	—	—	55	55	55
58	—	—	—	56	56	56
59	—	—	—	58	58	58
60	—	—	—	59	59	59
61	—	—	—	60	60	60
62	—	—	—	61	61	61
63	—	—	—	63	63	63

Figure 1.7 *(continued)*

The Printer Port

A discussion of the PC's printer port is important because this port is the hardware interface utilized between the PC and the video digitizer that we will build in Chapter 3. Only the portion of the printer port's functionality needed by the digitizer will be discussed. For a discussion of the other capabilities provided by the printer port, see the technical reference manual for your variety of PC.

The use of a printer port connection between the digitizer and the PC was chosen mainly for data throughput reasons, although there are many other good reasons for its use. By virtue of its parallel nature, the printer port can transfer data faster than a serial data connection. In a parallel connection, many bits of data are transferred simultaneously. In a serial connection, the bits are transferred sequentially and therefore more slowly. A serial digitizer connection would be possible, but the time required to move the image data samples from the digitizer into the PC would be prohibitively long. Additional circuitry would be required to serially connect a digitizer to a PC. Therefore, for throughput and cost reasons, a parallel-connected digitizer was judged best.

Another advantage of using the parallel printer port for connecting the digitizer is that this interface is a mature and stable one. It has remained essentially the same throughout the evolution of the PC. This means the digitizer can be connected to any of the PC products from the original PC to the new PS/2s, including compatibles. This opens the door for many more people to use the digitizer. It should be noted that the parallel port on the PS/2 series of computers has increased in capability while remaining backwards compatible. None of the new capabilities provided by the PS/2 parallel port are utilized by the digitizer, however. In other words, the interface to the digitizer is kept at the lowest common denominator.

Finally, the use of the printer port as the connection between the PC and the digitizer alleviates the need for an interface card inside the PC. This not only avoids the use of a card slot for the digitizer, it also means a special interface card does not need to be developed for each variety of PC bus. If an internal interface card were utilized, up to three versions would be required: one for the original PC, one for the ISA/EISA bus (extended AT bus), and one for the micro channel bus (MCA) utilized in the high-end PS/2s. As you can appreciate, connecting the digitizer to the parallel printer port simplifies things immensely.

A disadvantage of using the parallel port on a PC for digitizer connection is that the printer must be disconnected whenever the digitizer is to be used. The swapping of cables can be tedious. Two solutions to this problem exist. First, additional hardware could have been added to the digitizer to make it transparent to the connected printer. This would have driven the cost and complexity of the digitizer up, and for these reasons was not adopted. The second option is an A/B switch box for printer selection. Printer selector boxes are available from many sources and are relatively inexpensive. One switch position would select the printer, the other, the digitizer. This is by far the best solution if the swapping of cables is unsatisfactory. (*Note*: when using an A/B switch box, be sure to use very short cables. The digitizer was not designed to be attached to the PC via 12 to 15 feet of cable. The data transmission rate between the digitizer and the PC requires the use of short cables.)

The parallel port consists of a total of 12 output lines and 5 input lines that can be controlled and monitored by PC software. All of these lines are TTL (Transistor/Transistor

Logic) compatible. These I/O lines can be broken down into three different categories, each with slightly different characteristics.

The first category consists of an eight-bit output port, which is usually used to pass character data between the PC and an attached printer. These output lines are capable of sourcing 2.6 milliamperes and sinking 24 milliamperes of current. When it is connected to the digitizer circuit this output port is used to set pixel counts. These lines use positive true logic. That is, when the software sets any of these bits to a high level (or one), the output pin also goes high (to approximately five volts). An eight-bit "OUT" instruction is used to set all eight bits at one time. These signals are referred to as "+ Data Bit 0" through "+ Data Bit 7" by the IBM documentation. These output signals are available at a single output address which is given the symbolic name of "PrtPortBase" in the digitizer low-level code. A one-for-one correspondence exists between the output signal connector pins (of the printer port) and the data written to the output port as follows:

```
Data Bit    – 7 6 5 4 3 2 1 0
Pin Number – 9 8 7 6 5 4 3 2
```

The second category of I/O signals describe the remaining four output lines available in the parallel printer port interface. The lines drive the outside world with an open collector TTL driver with the outputs pulled to five volts through a 4.7-kil ohm resistor. These lines, which are capable of sinking only 7 milliamperes, utilize both positive and negative true logic, as indicated below:

Printer Port Output Signal Name	Logic Type
– Strobe	negative
– Auto Feed	negative
– Select Input	negative
– Initialize Printer	positive

Negative logic implies that when a line is set to a high level, the actual output pin goes to a low level—that is, the output signal is inverted with respect to the data.

These auxiliary output signals are available at a single output address, which is given the symbolic name of "PrtPortCont". Their organization is as follows:

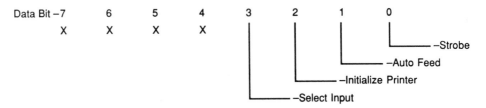

X's indicate bits we are not concerned about, or "Don't Cares".

The final group of I/O signals are the five input lines. These lines present one TTL LS load to a connected TTL signal source. When an "In" instruction is executed from the "PrtPortIn" address, the signal levels present at the input pins are latched and made available to the software. Because of hardware in the signal path between the printer port connector and the processor's data bus, the data read does not correspond with the signal levels present on the connector input pins as one might expect. These input lines or signals utilize both positive and negative true logic, as indicated below:

Printer Port Input Signal Name	Logic Type
+ Busy	negative
− Acknowledge	positive
+ P. End	positive
+ Select	positive
− Error	positive

If an input signal utilizes negative logic, a low-level signal applied from the outside world will be read as a high (or logic one) level. Positive logic implies that if the external signal is high it will be read as a high (i.e., no inversion). These input signals are organized within "PrtPortIn" as follows:

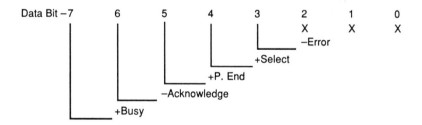

Again, X's indicate "Don't Cares".

The negative logic utilized by the + Busy signal requires special consideration in the design of the digitizer. This will be discussed in Chapter 3.

Three standard parallel port I/O addresses are defined for the IBM PCs and compatibles. They are referred to as Parallel 1, 2, and 3 in the technical reference manuals. These three different addresses allow up to three printers (or digitizers, for that matter) to be attached to a single PC without conflict. The standard address assignments for these parallel ports are as follows:

Assigned I/O Port Name	Parallel 1	Parallel 2	Parallel 3
PrtPortBase	3 BC hex	378 hex	278 hex
PrtPortIn	3 BD hex	379 hex	279 hex
PrtPortCont	3 BE hex	37A hex	27A hex

Parallel 1 is utilized in the IBM Monochrome Display Adapter/Printer interface card and as the standard parallel printer port on the PS/2 series of PCs. Parallel 2 is utilized by the IBM printer adapter card. Parallel 3 does not have a defined standard use.

As discussed above, only three I/O addresses are used for communication between the PC and a digitizer. Other hardware devices can also utilize this interface, also as long as they can function with the limited number of input and output lines available. Special multiplexing techniques were designed into the digitizer hardware to allow it to work with so few control lines. These multiplexing techniques, along with other interfacing issues, will be discussed in detail in the chapter on the digitizer's hardware and low-level software.

Software Development Tools

In this section, pertinent software development issues will be discussed. Tools and techniques for use with assembler language and C will be highlighted, as they are both used for the digitizer presented later in this book. Because of its convenience and power, C code was utilized whereever possible, while assembler code was used only where speed made it necessary. No attempt is made to teach assembler language or Turbo C. Only unique programming aspects of assembler and C that may not be apparent are discussed.

Using an Assembler

Although an attempt was made to keep the amount of assembler language code required for the support of the digitizer to a minimum, there still is a rather large amount deemed absolutely necessary. Where there were performance bottlenecks, the code was written in assembler. Meticulously coded assembler language is still faster than code generated by a C compiler, no matter how optimized the compiler is. When every processor cycle is important, assembler code must be used.

Any assembler that generates Microsoft-compatible object code can be used with the assembler language programs in this book. Both Macro Assembler/2® by IBM and MASM® by Microsoft have been used during various phases of the digitizer's development without problems. Borland's TASM® assembler could also be utilized. The assembler language source code is assembled to produce an object file, which is eventually linked with the object file(s) produced by the C compiler. If errors are detected when the assembler-generated object code is linked with the compiler-generated object code you may have to change the case sensitivity of Turbo C's linker. That will probably cure any linking incompatibility problems.

All assembler code to be linked with Turbo C must conform to a specific format. This format is comprised of special naming conventions to be used for all function names (they must begin with an underscore character) and for the code ("_TEXT") and data segments ("_DATA" and "_BSS") of the assembler code. The segment names depend upon the memory model of the C code to which the assembler code will eventually be linked. Adherence to the format provided will guarantee that Turbo C's linker will be able to resolve all references to the assembler code. It is not absolutely necessary to understand all of the subtle nuances of the assembler code format to be able to write assembler code. The format of all assembler files is basically the same and can be copied from the programs in this book. See Listing 1.1 for an example of the required assembler language code format for the small memory model. See also the *Turbo C User's Guide* for a detailed description of the formats for all memory models.

A final requirement for the successful integration of assembler and C code in the same program is an understanding of how data can be shared between them. Again, how data is shared can again depend upon the memory model being utilized by the compiler. Data sharing and parameter passing are two important topics discussed in the next section.

The assembler language code in Listing 1.1 (and available on the companion disk as file "vgagraph.asm") is part of the support provided for VGA mode 13H. This is the 320 by 200 resolution graphics mode, which supports 256 colors. This support is provided here because Turbo C release 2.0 does not provide the required support. VGA mode 13H is used throughout this book, so it was necessary to include this code. As it turns out, providing VGA mode 13H support makes the digitizer code more transportable among the various brands of C compilers. The operation of this code will be discussed in the section on the VGA function library.

Using Turbo C

Turbo C's integrated environment was used exclusively for all programs developed in this book. Its speed, flexibility, user-friendly interface, debugger, and project make facility allow applications to be produced quickly and errors to be found and fixed quickly. Project make, although not a full UNIX-style make, is sufficient for keeping the object modules that make up an image processing application organized and up to date, with little thought required from the user. See the *Turbo C User's Guide* for a complete description of the project make facility. An example project make file is shown below for purpose of discussion. This happens to be the project make file for the color video acquisition example program of Chapter 5. It is called "cvideo.prj".

```
graphics.lib
digitize.obj
vgagraph.obj
egavga.obj
pcx        (misc.h pcx.h)
vga        (misc.h vga.h pcx.h)
cvideo     (misc.h vga.h pcx.h digitize.h)
```

Listing 1.1   Video Mode 13H Assembler Language Support

```
; VGA Mode 13H -- 256 color 320x200 functions
;
; written by Craig A. Lindley
; last update: 11/29/89
;
_TEXT          segment        byte public 'CODE'
    DGROUP group _DATA,_BSS
    assume cs:_TEXT,ds:DGROUP,ss:DGROUP
_TEXT    ends

_DATA    segment word public 'DATA'
;
_DATA    ends

_BSS     segment word public 'BSS'
;
_BSS     ends
;
;
_TEXT    segment byte public 'CODE'
;
;320x200 256 Color Mode Routines
;
; Procedure _PutPixel256
;
; This procedure is used to directly access the video memory when the VGA or
; MCGA is in the 256 color mode 13H.
;
; CALL:    callable from C.
; PROTOTYPE: void PutPixel256 (unsigned Col, unsigned Row, unsigned Color);
; INPUT:   all parameters passed to this function are on the stack. The
;          stack should contain the following: Color at [bp+8], Row
;          at [bp+6] and the Col at [bp+4].
; OUTPUT: the specified pixel on the VGA screen is modified.
; USES:    and destroys AX,BX,CX,DX registers
;
        Public _PutPixel256
;
_PutPixel256    proc    near
;
        push    bp
        mov     bp,sp
```

```
        mov     cx,[bp+8]               ;get pixel color in cl reg
        mov     ax,[bp+6]               ;get Row #
        mov     bx,[bp+4]               ;get Col #
;
;compute the address of the pixel in the video buffer
;
        mov     dx,320                  ;each pixel is one byte
        mul     dx                      ;find offset
        add     bx,ax                   ;BX = x + 320 * y
        mov     ax,0A000H               ;seg of video buffer
        mov     es,ax                   ;es:BX pts at pixel in buffer
        mov     es:[bx],cl              ;update the pixel
        pop     bp
        ret
;
_PutPixel256    endp
;
; Procedure _GetPixel256
;
; This procedure is used to directly access the video memory when the VGA or
; MCGA is in the 256 color mode 13H.
;
; CALL:   callable from C.
; PROTOTYPE: unsigned PutPixel256 (unsigned Col, unsigned Row);
; INPUT:  all parameters passed to this function are on the stack. The
;         stack should contain the following: Row at [bp+6] and
;         the Col at [bp+4].
; OUTPUT: the specified pixel on the VGA screen is returned in AX.
; USES:   and destroys AX,BX,CX,DX registers
;
        Public _GetPixel256
;
_GetPixel256    proc    near
;
        push    bp
        mov     bp,sp
        mov     ax,[bp+6]               ;get Row #
        mov     bx,[bp+4]               ;get Col #
;
;compute the address of the pixel in the video buffer
;
        mov     dx,320                  ;each pixel is one byte
        mul     dx                      ;find offset
```

(continued)

Listing 1.1 *(continued)*

```
            add      bx,ax              ;BX = x + 320 * y
            mov      ax,0A000H          ;seg of video buffer
            mov      es,ax              ;es:BX pts at pixel in buffer
            mov      al,es:[bx]         ;get the pixels value
            xor      ah,ah              ;mask most significant byte
            pop      bp
            ret
;
_GetPixel256    endp

;
_TEXT   ends
        end
```

The name of an executable file produced by a project make file is the filename of the project make file without the ".prj" extension. In other words, the executable file that is generated by this project make file will be named "cvideo.exe".

Project make understands, via built-in rules, that any filename listed in a project make file without an extension is a C file. It inherently knows also that it must compile a C file before that file can be linked with other files. The line in the project make file containing "cvideo" just shown illustrates both of these rules. Further, this same line says the "cvideo.c" file depends upon all of the include files: "pcx.h", " vga.h", "digitize.h", and "misc.h". In other words, if the time stamp (the date and time when the file was last modified) on any of the include files is newer than "cvideo.c" (indicating a modification of the include files, which may impact how "cvideo.c" works), "cvideo.c" must be recompiled before it can be linked. All of the remaining files listed in this project make file indicate library files (".lib" extension) and object files (".obj" extension). These files must be linked with the "cvideo.obj" file produced by the compiler to form a complete program. The project make file will take care of the whole process automatically.

Turbo C's Graphics Features and Functions. The major reason Turbo C was chosen as a platform for image processing software development was its somewhat complete and easy-to-use graphics function library. The second, and very important, reason was that it is ANSI standard C with function prototypes (perhaps the most important new feature of ANSI standard C). The graphics library performs many important functions, such as autodetecting the video graphics hardware adapter (figuring out what type of graphics adapter the computer has on which the Turbo C program is running), initializing the correct driver for the graphics hardware, and providing a rich set of functions for the manipulation of text and graphics on the graphics output device. If these features were not provided by Turbo C, the development of graphics and imaging programs would take considerably longer.

As mentioned, in order to utilize the graphics capabilities of Turbo C, certain files must be available for linking. Namely, "graphics.lib" must be available so it can be linked with the object code produced by the compiler for a given image processing application. This file contains the code that performs all of the graphics functions. At run time, the graphics driver for the VGA video graphics adapter and all font files (of the form "fontname.chr") must be accessible. Since the VGA adapter is used exclusively in this book, only the driver file "egavga.bgi" must be around at run time (and even a way around this requirement will be presented). Fonts are not utilized in this book so the presence of font files is unimportant to the applications presented (but may be very important to your own applications).

The VGA Function Library. Graphics capabilities in addition to those provided by Turbo C are required by the various image processing programs in this book. All of these additional functions are grouped together to form the VGA function library. This function library consists of 10 functions (callable from C application programs), which provide rather specialized graphics operations. Some of these functions provide support for VGA mode 13H, which is available with VGA and MCGA graphics adapters, because Turbo C does not. Others return the current video mode or load gray-scale palettes. These functions are shown in Listings 1.1 and 1.2 and described in detail in Figure 1.8.

The functions provided in the VGA function library are used in many of the example programs in this book. To utilize these functions, an application program would need to include the file "vga.h" in its code and subsequently be linked with the file "vga.obj" produced by the compiler when the VGA function library was compiled.

In all example programs in this book, the display driver for the EGA/VGA graphics adapters is bound to the example program. This means it is linked with the example program's code at link time instead of being read from disk at run time. This is useful because it makes the example programs completely stand alone. Both display drivers and fonts can be bound to application programs in the same way. To do this, the file that contains the code for the driver or font file—for example, "egavga.bgi"—must be converted to an object file by the utility program "bgiobj.exe", included with the Turbo C package. The result is "egavga.obj", which can be linked directly with the application. Finally, the presence of the linked display driver or font code must be conveyed to the application program with a "registerbgidriver" or "registerbgifont" function call. The symbolic name of the display driver or font must be passed to these functions as parameters. In the case of the EGA/VGA display driver, the symbolic name is "EGA/VGA driver". The "bgiobj.exe" program will furnish the symbolic name when the program is finished executing. Remember to drop the leading underscore when passing the symbolic name as a parameter to the "registerbgi" functions. The "registerbgi" functions must be called before the call to "initgraph" in your graphics applications. This technique is shown and discussed in the function "InitGraphics" in the VGA function library.

Dealing with Segment Boundaries, Data Pointers, and Memory Models. There is no question that digitized images consume copious amounts of memory for storage and during manipulation. Images produced by the digitizer in this book can occupy up to 300KB of

Listing 1.2   VGA Function Library

The following is the contents of the file "vga.h".

```
/***************************************/
/*          VGA Header File          */
/*      for VGA access functions     */
/*        written in Turbo C 2.0     */
/*                by                 */
/*          Craig A. Lindley         */
/*                                   */
/*   Vers: 1.0  Last Update: 11/28/89  */
/***************************************/


/* defines for 320x200, 640x200 and 640x480 resolution VGA screens */
#define LRMAXCOLS 320      /* 320x200 256 color mode */
#define LRMAXROWS 200
#define LRVIDEOMODE 0x13   /* as returned from GetVideoMode call */


#define MRMAXCOLS 640      /* 640x200 16 color mode */
#define MRMAXROWS 200
#define MRVIDEOMODE 0x0E   /* as returned from GetVideoMode call */


#define HRMAXCOLS 640      /* 640x480 16 color mode */
#define HRMAXROWS 480
#define HRVIDEOMODE 0x12   /* as returned from GetVideoMode call */


#define SCREENWIDTHINCHES  (double) 9.500
#define SCREENHEIGHTINCHES (double) 7.125


/*
The following values are used to convert between
vertical and horizontal pixels and inches of display.
Used in aspect ratio calculations for image rotations.
Could be calculated for all resolutions, but only
low res (LR) is used currently.
*/


/*
LRPIXELSPERINCHHORIZ is LRMAXCOLS/SCREENWIDTHINCHES.
It is defined as a constant for speed in floating
point operations. LRINCHESPERPIXELHORIZ is 1 over
LRPIXELPERINCHHORIZ.
*/
```

```
#define LRPIXELSPERINCHHORIZ  (double) 33.68421053
#define LRINCHESPERPIXELHORIZ (double)  0.02968750
/*
LRPIXELSPERINCHVERT is LRMAXROWS/SCREENHEIGHTINCHES.
It is defined as a constant for speed in floating
point operations. LRINCHESPERPIXELVERT is 1 over
LRPIXELPERINCHVERT.
*/
#define LRPIXELSPERINCHVERT  (double) 28.07017544
#define LRINCHESPERPIXELVERT (double)  0.03562500
#define MAXCOLREGVAL 63


/* VGA Function Declarations */

/* Assembler Language Function Prototypes */
void     PutPixel256 (unsigned Col, unsigned Row, unsigned Color);
unsigned GetPixel256 (unsigned Col, unsigned Row);

/* C Function Prototypes */
void InitGraphics (void);
unsigned GetVideoMode(void);
void Set256ColorMode (void);
void SetAColorReg (unsigned RegNum, unsigned Red,
                             unsigned Green,  unsigned Blue);
void GetAColorReg (unsigned RegNum, unsigned *Red,
                             unsigned *Green, unsigned *Blue);
void LoadGray16Palette (void);
void LoadGray64Palette (void);
```

The following is the contents of the file "vga.c".

```
/****************************************/
/*     VGA Graphic Adapter Functions    */
/*         written in Turbo C 2.0        */
/*                  by                   */
/*          Craig A. Lindley             */
/*                                       */
/*   Vers: 1.0  Last Update: 12/04/89    */
/****************************************/

#include <stdio.h>
#include <process.h>
```

(continued)

Listing 1.2 *(continued)*

```
#include <dos.h>
#include <graphics.h>
#include "misc.h"
#include "pcx.h"
#include "vga.h"

/* equally tempered 16 level gray scale */
ColorRegister Gray16ColorPalette[MAXPALETTECOLORS] =

{ 0, 0, 0, 5, 5, 5, 8, 8, 8,11,11,11,
 14,14,14,17,17,17,20,20,20,24,24,24,
 28,28,28,32,32,32,36,36,36,40,40,40,
 45,45,45,50,50,50,56,56,56,63,63,63 };

/* equally tempered 64 level gray scale */
ColorRegister Gray64ColorPalette[MAX256PALETTECOLORS] =

{ 0, 0, 0, 0, 0, 0, 0, 0, 0, 0, 0, 0,
  0, 0, 0, 1, 1, 1, 1, 1, 1, 2, 2, 2,
  3, 3, 3, 3, 3, 3, 4, 4, 4, 5, 5, 5,
  6, 6, 6, 7, 7, 7, 8, 8, 8, 9, 9, 9,
 10,10,10,10,10,10,11,11,11,12,12,12,
 13,13,13,14,14,14,15,15,15,16,16,16,
 18,18,18,19,19,19,20,20,20,21,21,21,
 22,22,22,23,23,23,24,24,24,25,25,25,
 26,26,26,27,27,27,28,28,28,29,29,29,
 31,31,31,32,32,32,33,33,33,34,34,34,
 35,35,35,36,36,36,37,37,37,39,39,39,
 40,40,40,41,41,41,42,42,42,43,43,43,
 44,44,44,46,46,46,47,47,47,48,48,48,
 49,49,49,50,50,50,52,52,52,53,53,53,
 54,54,54,55,55,55,56,56,56,58,58,58,
 59,59,59,60,60,60,61,61,61,63,63,63 };

/* Start of VGA functions */
/* Initialize the graphics subsystem */
void InitGraphics( void )
{
    int g_driver, g_mode, g_error;

    /*
    Make sure graphic system is not already open. Whether
    it is or not, close it and open it again. Otherwise
```

```
      memory for the driver will be allocated each time this
      function is called.
      */
      closegraph();

      /* initialize graphics variables */
      g_driver = g_mode = g_error = 0;

      /*
      The call to registerbgidriver below links the display driver
      to the application program. It assumes the driver was converted from
      egavga.bgi to egavga.obj by the bgiobj converter program and
      linked into the application program. The line egavga.obj must
      be in the .prj file for the application program.
      */
      registerbgidriver(EGAVGA_driver);

      initgraph(&g_driver,&g_mode,"");
      g_error = graphresult();
      if (g_error < 0)
      {
          printf("Initgraph error: %s.\n",
          grapherrormsg(g_error));
          exit(EGraphics);
      }
      restorecrtmode();
}


/*
This function fetches the current video mode
from the active video controller.
*/
unsigned GetVideoMode( void )
{
   union REGS regs;

   regs.h.ah = 0x0F;                          /* request the current video mode */
   int86(VIDEO,&regs,&regs);
   return(regs.h.al);
}


/* Set the VGA into the 256 320 by 200 display mode. */
void Set256ColorMode( void )
```

(continued)

Listing 1.2 *(continued)*

```
{
   union REGS regs;

   setgraphmode(VGALO);                    /* go into graphic mode */
   regs.h.ah = 0;                          /* now into mode 13H for 256 colors */
   regs.h.al = 0x13;
   int86(VIDEO,&regs,&regs);
}


/* Set an individual VGA color register */
void SetAColorReg(unsigned RegNum, unsigned Red,
                           unsigned Green,  unsigned Blue)
{
   union REGS regs;

   /*
   With graphics mode set, we can load a color register
   in the DAC.
   */

   /* set a Color Register */
   regs.h.ah = 0x10;
   regs.h.al = 0x10;
   regs.x.bx = RegNum;
   regs.h.dh = Red;
   regs.h.ch = Green;
   regs.h.cl = Blue;
   int86(VIDEO,&regs,&regs);
}


/* Get the color components of a VGA color register */
void GetAColorReg(unsigned RegNum, unsigned *Red,
                           unsigned *Green, unsigned *Blue)
{
   union REGS regs;

   /*
   With graphics mode set, we can read a color register
   from the DAC.
   */
```

```
   /* get a Color Register's components */
   regs.h.ah = 0x10;
   regs.h.al = 0x15;
   regs.x.bx = RegNum;
   int86(VIDEO,&regs,&regs);
   /* store the returned values at the pointers */
   *Red   = regs.h.dh;
   *Green = regs.h.ch;
   *Blue  = regs.h.cl;
}

/* load the gray palette */
void LoadGray16Palette(void)
{
   struct palettetype palette;
   unsigned Index;
   union REGS regs;

   /*
   With a graphics mode set, we can proceed to load our palette and
   color registers in the DAC. The palette is set up in sequential
   order and the color register are set to gray scale values.
   */

   palette.size = 16;

   for (Index = 0; Index < MAXPALETTECOLORS; Index++)
      palette.colors[Index] = Index;

   /* set a block of Color Registers */
   regs.h.ah = 0x10;
   regs.h.al = 0x12;
   regs.x.bx = 0;
   regs.x.cx = MAXPALETTECOLORS;
   _ES = FP_SEG(Gray16ColorPalette);
   regs.x.dx =FP_OFF(Gray16ColorPalette);
   int86(VIDEO,&regs,&regs);

   /* install the newly created palette */
   setallpalette(&palette);
}
```

(continued)

Listing 1.2   *(continued)*

```
/* load the gray palette */
void LoadGray64Palette(void)
{
union REGS regs;

/*
This 64 level gray scale can only be loaded when the VGA is in
the 256 color mode 13h. The actual palette mechanism is bypassed
in this mode. The color registers in the DAC are loaded and accessed
directly.
*/

/* set a block of Color Registers */
regs.h.ah = 0x10;
regs.h.al = 0x12;
regs.x.bx = 0;
regs.x.cx = 64;
_ES = FP_SEG(Gray64ColorPalette);
regs.x.dx =FP_OFF(Gray64ColorPalette);

int86(VIDEO,&regs,&regs);
}
```

memory (1K = 1,024 bytes). In contrast, the code used for manipulation of the digitized images rarely consumes more than 64KB. Said another way, up to 64KB of code is used to manipulate up to 300KB of image data. Knowing the bounds of the code and data space required by our image applications allows us to select a memory model for program development. A memory model defines how much code and data space an applications program written in C will have access to and what the default types of pointer variables are.

With Turbo C, six different memory models exist: tiny, small, medium, compact, large, and huge. Each of these has various limits placed on the size of the code and data segments that make up a program. See the *Turbo User's Guide* for the exact definitions. For all of the programs in this book (except for the ''view.exe'' example program in Chapter 6), the small memory model has proven adequate. The following is from the Turbo C manual for the small memory model:

> The code and data segments are different and don't overlap, so you have 64K of code and 64K of static data. The stack and extra segments start at the same address as the data segment. Near pointers are always used. This is a good size for average application.

The VGA function library is made up of functions written in both assembler language and in C. The assembler functions are contained in the file "vgagraph.asm" and the C functions in the file "vga.c" on the companion disk.

1. Place a pixel on the 320 × 200 resolution mode 13H VGA display.

   Prototype

   void PutPixel256 (unsigned Col, unsigned Row, unsigned Color);

   Where "Col" (column) and "Row" describe the location at which to place the pixel, and "Color" is the color register number that should be used for the pixel. The proper range of "Col" values is 0 to 319, the range of "Row" values is 0 to 199, and the range of "Color" values is 0 to 255. No error checking is performed by this function.

   ## Operation

   This function, which is written in assembler language, places a pixel on the 320 × 200 resolution mode 13H display by directly accessing the VGA video memory. The video memory organization for mode 13H is a linear array of 64,000 bytes located at segment A000 hex in the PC's memory map. To place a pixel directly, it is necessary to calculate where in the 64,000 bytes of VGA memory the pixel resides and store the value of the color there. The address calculation is basically:

   VGA memory address = x coordinate + 320 • y coordinate

   This address calculation is actually the offset into the video segment of the pixel's location. With the segment and offset of the pixel known, it is a simple task to store the color value there. It is necessary to have the VGA graphics adapter in mode 13H before this function can be used. An example of the 256-color code in operation will be given in the section on color-image acquisition later in this book.

   This function was necessary for the imaging programs in this book because Turbo C does not provide mode 13H support.

2. Read a pixel from the 320 × 200 resolution mode 13H VGA display.

   Prototype

   unsigned GetPixel256 (unsigned Col, unsigned Row);

   Where all parameters are as described above.

   ## Operation

   The operation of this function is similar to "PutPixel256" above except the value of the pixel located at "Col" and "Row" is returned instead of being written. The location of the specified pixel within the VGA memory is calculated in a manner identical to that just shown.

3. Initialize the graphics subsystem.

   Prototype

   void InitGraphics (void);

   Where no parameters are utilized.

Figure 1.8 The VGA Library Functions   *(continued)*

Operation

This function initializes the graphics system of the PC. For this reason, a call to "InitGraph" is used in each of the image-acquisition and processing programs in this book. The operation of this code is straightforward, as can be seen from the listing. The first operation performed by the code is to close the graphics library. This can be done safely whether the graphics library was previously opened or not. This is necessary to prevent sequential calls to "InitGraphics" (by intention or by accident) from allocating multiple copies of the memory required for the display driver functions. Closing the library before opening it guarantees only one memory allocation is performed. Only one memory allocation is ever necessary.

Next, the display driver for EGA/VGA is registered with the graphics system. This tells the graphics system that the driver code, in this case "EGAVGA.OBJ", has previously been linked with the application's code. Registering a driver prevents it from being loaded from disk at run time when "InitGraphics" is executed. This same technique is available for use with fonts. Registering binds the display driver code (or font code) with the graphics application. (*Note*: registering a driver or font increases the size of the application program by the size of the driver or font.)

The function "initgraph" is where all of the graphics system initialization is performed. It accepts as parameters addresses of the graphics driver ("g_driver") and the graphics mode ("g_mode") variables along with a path to a directory where the graphics driver file should be found. Upon successful completion of the "initgraph" function, "g_driver" and "g_mode" will be initialized. In the code shown above, the path to the graphics driver is NULL (" ") because the driver is not loaded from disk. This is handy because the application then stands alone and does not have to search the disk at run time to find the display driver.

If an error (such as not finding a VGA adapter present) is encountered during the execution of "initgraph", an error message is output and the program terminates.

The final function call in the code above, "restorecrtmode", returns the graphics adapter to the text mode. Most of the image processing programs start out in the text mode for interfacing with the operator and later switch to the graphics mode after all operator inputs are processed. Calling "restorecrtmode" starts the program in the text mode. The function "setgraphmode" can be called later to clear the screen and place the system into the graphics mode. Use "setgraphmode" in conjunction with "restorecrtmode" to switch back and forth between the text and graphics mode.

4. Get the current video mode.

Prototype
unsigned GetVideoMode (void);

Where no parameters are utilized.

Operation

"GetVideoMode" returns the number of the current video mode being used. Currently, 20 video modes are defined for PC-compatible computers: modes 0 through 13 hex. Not all of these modes are available on all computers. For our uses in this book, three video modes are the most important. They are the 320×200 256-color mode 13 hex (13H), the 640×200 16-color mode 0E hex, and the 640×480 16-color mode 12 hex. These video modes are given symbolic names for use in the image processing programs. They are called "LRVIDEOMODE", "MRVIDEOMODE", and "HRVIDEOMODE" respectively. These symbolic names are defined in the file "vga.h". This file is shown at the top of Listing 1.2.

Figure 1.8   *(continued)*

This function, along with most others in this VGA function library, operates by stuffing the correct values into the processor register variables and executing calls to BIOS. The VIDEO interrupt (10 hex) BIOS functions are used.

5. Select the 320 × 200 256-color video mode 13H.

Prototype
void Set256ColorMode (void);

Where no parameters are utilized.

Operation
This function places the VGA (or MCGA) graphics adapter into the 320 × 200 256-color mode, 13H. As mentioned, this function is required because Turbo C does not support this graphics mode. The default palette of 256 colors is loaded into the VGA adapter as part of this function call. Palettes were discussed previously.

The call to "setgraphmode" in this function's code is necessary because it sets certain internal Turbo C variables that indicate the system is in the graphics mode. The VGALO mode does not last long, however, because mode 13H is immediately set via a call to the BIOS. The set video mode function (function code 0) is called. From this point on, the display adapter is in the special 256-color mode. It stays that way until a call to "restorecrtmode" or the graphics library is closed.

6. Set a VGA (or MCGA) color register.

Prototype
void SetAColorReg (unsigned RegNum, unsigned Red,
                    unsigned Green,   unsigned Blue);

Where "RegNum" is the number indicating which of the 256 color registers is to be manipulated and "Red", "Green", and "Blue" are the color components that should be given to that register. Each component can range in value from 0 to 63. RGB components of 0, 0, and 0 result in black, whereas components 63, 63, and 63 are white. If all three color components are equal in value, the result is the color gray.

7. Get the color components of a VGA (or MCGA) color register.

Prototype
void GetAColorReg (unsigned RegNum, unsigned *Red,
                    unsigned *Green,   unsigned *Blue);

Where "RegNum" is a number indicating which of the 256 color registers is to be read and "Red", "Green", and "Blue" are pointers to locations in which the specified color register's components should be stored.

Operation
This function performs the converse operation of the function above. It returns the RGB components of a specified color register.

Figure 1.8 *(continued)*   *(continued)*

8. Load the 16-level gray-scale palette.

Prototype
void LoadGray16Palette (void);

Where no parameters are specified.

Operation

This function loads the 16-level gray-scale palette discussed previously and shown in Figure 1.7 into the VGA adapter. It also initializes and installs the palette structure used for the 16-color video modes. The palette is initialized for straight-through mapping. That is, palette entry 0 points to color register 0, palette entry 15 points to color register 15, and so on. Recall that for the 16-color video modes, a pixel's value in display memory is an index into the palette structure that contains the number of the color register to use to display the pixel. This is why the palette structure must be initialized by this function call—to provide this mapping. The BIOS is utilized to load all 16 of the color registers (0 through 15) at one time. To do this, the processor's CX register is loaded with 16 to indicate how many color registers to load; the extra segment register ("_ES") is loaded with the segment containing the "Gray16ColorPalette" array; register DX is loaded with the offset into the segment of the array; and the video BIOS interrupt is executed. After the color registers have been loaded by the BIOS, Turbo's "setallpalette' function is used to install our initialized palette for use. When "setallpalette" is called, the palette currently being used for display by the VGA adapter is overwritten with the new palette generated by this code. All colors displayed on the screen will immediately become shades of gray: which gray shade depends upon the value of the video data. If a pixel's value were 0 the pixel would be displayed as black. If the value were 15, its display would be white. If the value were somewhere in the middle, the pixel's display would be a shade of gray. In general, the larger the numerical value of the video data, the brighter the displayed level of gray.

    Please note: the VGA adapter must be in the required graphics mode before this function is executed. Otherwise, when a graphics mode is later entered the color register values we have installed will be overwritten as part of the initialization of the new graphics mode.

9. Load the 64-level gray-scale palette.

Prototype
void LoadGray64Palette (void);

Where no parameters are specified.

Operation

This function is similar to "LoadGray16Palette" except that the 64-level gray-scale palette is loaded. In this case, the VGA adapter must be in mode 13H before this function is executed. Video mode 13H is the only mode that allows more than 16 colors on the display screen simultaneously. We need 64-color capability to display an image with 64 levels of gray scale. Video mode 13H gives us 256-color capability, not all of which is used. As you will recall, while in this video mode the video data is a direct index of a color register (the palette mechanism is completely bypassed). For example, to display a pixel with gray-scale level 0, a pixel's value would be 0. To display a pixel with gray scale 37, the pixel's value would be 37. Other than these differences, this function is identical in operation to that just discussed.

Figure 1.8   *(continued)*

A pictorial representation of the small memory model follows:

Small Memory Model Segmentation

Segment Registers		Segment Size
CS →	TEXT class 'CODE' code	Up to 64K bytes
DS → ES SS →	DGROUP: DATA class 'DATA' initialized data BSS class 'BSS' uninitialized data Heap	Up to 64K bytes
Stack → Pointer SP	Stack	
	Far Heap	to end of memory

The significance of the various partitions of memory shown in the diagram above will be discussed throughout this book. The total maximum size for a small memory model application program is 128KB. This is because both the code and the data segments can be 64KB in size and a small memory model program can have one of each. You should note that you can explicitly declare pointers or functions to be of any type, regardless of the memory model chosen.

With 64KB of data space available, how is it that we can manipulate an image 300KB in size? The answer is: The data space for an image is allocated from what Turbo C refers to as the "far heap" and does not reside in the data segment of the application program. In other words, the data segment allotted to a program contains only the program-specific data, not the actual image data. When allocating from the far heap, remember:

    a. All of available RAM can be allocated.

    b. Blocks larger than 64KB can be allocated.

    c. FAR (32-bit) pointers must be used to access the allocated blocks.

The far heap contains all of the PC memory starting at the end of the application program and ending at the 640KB limit imposed by MSDOS. Turbo's far memory allocation functions "farmalloc", "farcalloc", "farcoreleft", "farfree", and "farrealloc" are used to manage the far heap. In the small memory model, the far heap is distinct from the regular heap. For this reason, application programs must be careful not to mix memory-management methods when using the small memory model.

Although a program can allocate a large chunk of memory for an image, it is still faced with the problem of manipulating data that crosses 64KB segment boundaries. As you will recall from a previous discussion, the segmented architecture of the Intel processors (when operated in the real mode that MSDOS runs in) allows for easy access to data that is completely contained in a 64KB segment. When data crosses a segment boundary, however, additional overhead is required to access the data. This overhead slows down the execution of programs that manipulate large amounts of data or that have a large amount of code. Segment boundary checking affects both the C image application code and the low-level digitizer driver assembler language code described in Chapter 4. Turbo C has a built-in mechanism for handling large amounts of data that cross segment boundaries. The low-level assembler code has to handle this situation by itself with additional code.

The image application code gets around the segmentation problem by using HUGE pointers to access the data. HUGE pointers are a special variety of 32-bit FAR pointers. Both FAR and HUGE pointers consist of a 16-bit segment and 16-bit offset portion. HUGE pointers are different in that they are always kept in their "normalized" form. That is, the majority of the address information contained in a HUGE pointer is kept in its segment portion. Since segments always begin on 16-byte boundaries, the offset portion of a HUGE pointer is always in the range from 0 to 15, with the segment portion containing most of the address information.

To normalize a pointer, convert it to its full 20-bit address and then use the right 4 bits as the offset value and the left 16 bits as the segment value. For example, to convert the nonnormalized pointer value 3412:DF03 (this again is standard Intel segment:offset symbolism) to its normalized form:

a. Shift the hexadecimal segment value 3412 left 4 bit positions, yielding 34120.
b. Add the offset value DF03 to 34120, yielding 42023 hex.
c. The last 4 bits are the offset value, which is 3.
d. The 16 most significant bits are the segment value of 4202.

The normalized pointer value of 3412:DF03 is then 4202:0003. This normalization process is performed after each pointer manipulation and is responsible for slower program execution times.

HUGE pointers, in contrast to FAR pointers, always point to a unique memory address as a result of the normalization process. Since segments can overlap, many different FAR pointers can refer to the same physical memory address. For example, each of the following FAR pointers points at the same memory location:

```
0000 : 015A
000A : 00BA
0014 : 001A
```

The HUGE pointer equivalent, 0015:000A, is the only HUGE pointer that points at this location.

This is one advantage of using HUGE pointers. The uniqueness of each memory address makes pointer arithmetic possible. If the two FAR pointers 0000:015A and 0014:001A are compared for equality, the comparison will fail even though both pointers refer to the same physical memory location. When comparing HUGE pointers, the comparison will always perform as expected, because of the uniqueness of each pointer.

Another advantage of HUGE pointers is that they can be used to access data structures that cross segment boundaries. The normalization process described above makes segment crossing invisible to the programmer. This makes HUGE pointers perfect for image applications. To illustrate this point, consider what would happen with a FAR pointer when a segment boundary is reached. If, for example, the value of a FAR pointer was 0010:FFFF and the pointer was incremented, the new value would be 0010:0000. The offset value would roll over without incrementing the segment value. Obviously, the pointer would not end up pointing where we would expect. The use of a HUGE pointer guarantees that the segment and the offset values are incremented correctly, thereby crossing the segment boundary and allowing access to the data.

To allocate memory for an image data buffer, the FAR pointer, returned from the far heap memory allocation function, is immediately cast to HUGE before being used. A code segment follows that illustrates this technique:

```
char huge *PictureData;

printf("Allocating Picture Buffer\n");

/* allocate picture buffer and set it to zeros */

if ((PictureData = (char huge *) farcalloc(RasterSize,
    (unsigned long) sizeof(char))) == NULL)
{
    printf("Digitize Error - Not enough memory\n");
    exit();
}
```

When the program is finished using the image data buffer, the memory is given back to the system as follows:

```
farfree((char far *)PictureData);
```

The HUGE pointer "PictureData" is cast back to its original type before being used by the "farfree" function.

At the assembler language level, the manipulation of pointers is not quite as transparent to the programmer. Two methods can be used to enable pointers to correctly cross segment boundaries. The first method forces the assembler code to keep the pointer values normalized as C does. While this works correctly in all cases, it also adds overhead the low-level code cannot afford. The second method utilizes explicit checks placed in code to check for segment crossing. When segment crossing is detected, additional code is used to fix up the segment and offset value of the pointer appropriately.

In the digitizer code, the high-level C application passes a HUGE pointer to an image buffer, where the digitized image is to be stored, to the low-level digitizer driver code. As image pixels are digitized, they are stored in the image buffer and the buffer pointer is incremented. The code fragment that follows shows how the segment crossing detection and correction code is implemented. In this code, the processor's BP register contains the offset portion and the ES register contains the segment portion of the image data buffer pointer. This code is extracted from the file "digitize.asm".

```
SEGOFF                   EQU        (0FFFFH/10H)+1              ;paragraphs/segment
;
;check to see if pointer for data storage (BP register) will leave a 64K
;segment. If so the segment register must be adjusted by SEGOFF so
;offset 0 into the segment points at the next available byte of storage.
;
         cmp      bp,0FFFFH          ;at end of seg ?
         jne      gp14               ;jump if not
         mov      ax,es              ;at end of seg - get seg reg value
         add      ax,SEGOFF          ;add offset
         mov      es,ax              ;store it back
                                     ;offset will inc to 0000
gp14:    inc      bp                 ;bump offset by one byte
```

As you can see, this amounts to much less overhead than the normalization of the pointer value.

Data Sharing Between C and Assembler Code. Given that an application (such as the digitizer presented in this book) requires the use of both C and assembler language code, we will spend some time discussing how information is shared between them. Two basic techniques exist for information sharing:

 a. Data references to global data
 b. Parameter passing and returning

Global data, although not considered by some to be elegant programming, is the most direct way of sharing data between C and assembler language code. A variable can be declared in either the C or the assembler code and can be referenced as an external in any code modules that need access to it. The external declaration allows the compile or the assembly to proceed without error. The linking process, which combines both the assembler code and the C code into an executable program, resolves the references to the externally declared variable.

For example, if an integer variable, "MySum", is declared in an assembler language code module and later referenced using C, the declaration placed in the data segment of the assembler code would be as follows:

```
PUBLIC _MySum

_MySum   DW   0   ;an integer variable requires one word
                  ;initial value of MySum is zero
```

To reference "MySum" in C, an external declaration such as:

```
extern int MySum;
```

would be required. Conversely, "MySum" could be declared in C and later referenced in assembler language. The C declaration would be:

```
int MySum = 0;
```

The assembler declaration would be coded:

```
EXTRN _MySum:WORD
```

The external declaration makes the "MySum" variable visible inside the assembler language code module. To access the variable, the following could be used:

```
mov    ax,_MySum
```

This data sharing method is not utilized in the programs in this book because it was not found to be necessary. The parameter passing method, discussed next, was used instead.

Parameter passing is the second method of data sharing between assembler and C code. Parameters can be passed from the C code to a function (subroutine) written in assembler language. Conversely, when complete, the assembler language function can pass back a result to the C code. Almost all C implementations use the stack for the passing of parameters to functions. To successfully interface C to assembler language, one must be aware of the layout of the parameters on the stack. Once the stack format is understood, it is easy to retrieve any parameters passed from the C code in assembler language. The "InitializeDigitizer" function discussed in Chapter 4 illustrates the coupling between C and assembler code.

Two types of parameter passing conventions are supported in ANSI standard C: C and Pascal. The C convention is always used unless the keyword "Pascal" is included in the function's prototype. With the C parameter passing convention:

a. Parameters are pushed onto the stack in a right to left order.

b. Functions do not remove the parameters from the stack upon completion. This chore is left up to the calling code. For this reason, usage of the C convention can result in larger program memory usage.

c. All identifiers are prefixed with an underscore "_" character.

d. A variable number of parameters can be supported.

In contrast, the use of the Pascal passing convention means:

a. Parameters are pushed onto the stack in a left to right order.

b. Functions and procedures remove all parameters from the stack upon completion. This can result in a memory saving in a large program.

c. Identifiers are in uppercase only and are not prefixed with an underscore.

d. Only a fixed number of parameters are supported.

The Pascal passing convention would only be used when program memory usage was critical or when C code would be required to interface to preexisting assembler language functions that were written originally for use with Pascal. Only the C calling convention is utilized in the code provided in this book.

A diagram of the stack during the execution of an assembler language function call will help illustrate the C parameter passing mechanism. Assume for the purposes of discussion there exists an assembler language function called "Sum", which calculates the sum of two numbers and returns the result. A function prototype in C might be:

```
int Sum (int Num1, int Num2);
```

The assembler language function is as follows:

```
        PUBLIC  _Sum
_Sum proc  near
        push    bp
        mov     bp,sp
        mov     ax,[bp+4]  ;get Num1
        add     ax,[bp+6]  ;add Num2
        pop     bp         ;restore bp
        ret                ;sum returned in the ax register
_Sum endp
```

The stack, as pictured before the first instruction of the assembler language is executed, is as follows:

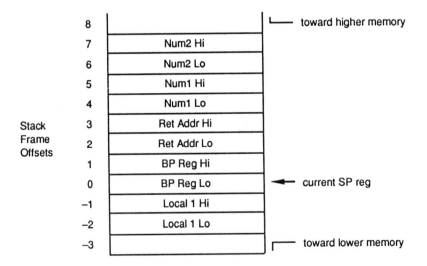

Note that:

    a. Stacks grow from high toward lower memory.

    b. The most significant byte of any word value is stored at the higher physical address.

When FAR pointers are stored on the stack, the segment is pushed followed by the offset.

c. All stack operations are done with 16-bit, 2-byte quantities. Any byte or character values are sign extended to 16 bits before being stacked.

d. Typically, with C function calls, all parameters are available as positive offsets from the base pointer register BP. All automatic or local variables are available as negative offsets from BP.

e. Specifying the BP register in an instruction automatically references the stack segment (SS) unless an explicit segment override is provided.

From the stack diagram, you'll notice that the parameters passed to the assembler language function are indeed placed onto the stack seemingly backwards, with both halves of "Num2" pushed first followed by both halves of "Num1". After the parameters are placed on the stack, a NEAR call to the assembler language function "_Sum" is performed, which places its return address on the stack under the parameters. Only the offset into the current code segment needs to be pushed because the function was declared NEAR. If "_Sum" resided in a different code segment, and was therefore declared a FAR function, the preceding stack diagram would need the following modification:

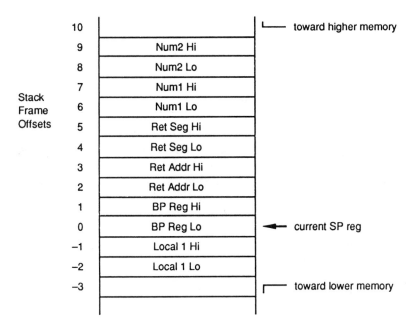

In this case, the code segment and the offset would need to be pushed onto the stack for the FAR function. After the parameters and the function return address are saved on the stack, the base pointer register BP is pushed onto the stack to save its value. This is saved so it can be loaded with the content of the stack pointer register, SP. This allows easy access to the parameters that are a constant positive offset from BP. BP and SP point to the same stack location—indicated on the diagram by a stack frame offset of 0. Once BP is loaded with SP, access to the parameters is trivial. Simply count the offset from BP to the parameter of interest and use that in conjunction with BP to access the parameter. The assembler language code shown before shows how it is done.

When execution of the assembler language function is completed, control must be returned correctly to C. This is accomplished by popping the original value of BP off of the stack and executing a return instruction. A NEAR or FAR return is required, depending upon how the function was declared. A NEAR return pops the location (offset) in the code segment at which to continue program execution into the instruction pointer (IP) register of the processor. A FAR return pops both the segment and the offset from the stack and continues from there.

Various methods are utilized by Turbo C for returning values from functions. The method used is determined by the type of object being returned. Assembler language functions must emulate these methods to properly return values to the calling C code. The three methods are:

a. The returned value is placed in the AX register if the type returned is: "char", "short", "int", "enum", or a NEAR pointer. In other words, if the type can be expressed as a 16-bit value.

b. The 32-bit values that include FAR and HUGE pointers are returned in the DX:AX register pair. The most significant 16 bits would be placed in the DX register while the least significant 16 bits would be placed in AX.

c. Structures are returned by placing the structure in a static data area and returning a pointer to it. If the structure is NEAR, the pointer will be in AX. If the structure is FAR or HUGE, it will be in DX:AX.

The "_Sum" procedure places the resultant sum of the parameters into the AX register for return to C.

One final note of caution when using assembler language functions with C. In most cases, C does not expect the processor registers to be maintained across function invocations. This means all of the processor registers with the exception of CS, SS, SP, BP, SI, and DI can be used freely within an assembler language function without saving and restoring them. Further, the SI and DI registers can be used if Turbo's use of register variables is turned off (via the Option/Compiler/Optimization menu). All of the registers can be used in an assembler function as long as the value they had on entry is restored on exit. The easiest way to accomplish this is to push the registers onto the stack, use them as necessary, and finally pop them back off before returning to C.

Conclusions

In the first part of this chapter, we discussed the graphics capabilities required for a PC to perform image processing. The modes, resolutions, and palette structures of both the EGA and VGA graphics adapters were discussed in depth. Following that, the operation of the printer port was described at the bit level, because this is the interface that will be used with the digitizer we will build. Finally, we have seen that the proper selection of a compiler memory model, data pointer types, and data sharing techniques is very important to the proper operation of image processing software. In particular, these attributes can have a significant effect on code size and code speed. In fact, they can mean the difference in whether or not our digitizer works at all.

With this discussion of background information behind us, we can concentrate on the more interesting aspects of image acquisition and processing.

2

Video Basics

In this chapter you will learn about:

- **How images are displayed on a CRT**
- **What a video signal looks like**
- **The types of "sync pulses" that define a video signal**
- **What the current video standards are**

Introduction

To understand the operation of the video digitizer discussed in the next chapter, it is necessary first to understand what video signals are and then how video signals are displayed on CRT (cathode-ray-tube) devices. The following discussion applies to the CRT devices contained in both computer monitors and conventional television sets.

To form an image on a CRT, a beam of electrons sweeps back and forth and up and down across the screen. The electrons excite dots of phosphor deposited on the back of the screen and cause them to glow. In effect, the image is painted on the phosphor by the electron beam. The intensity of the phosphor's glow is determined by the velocity of the electrons striking it. Electron velocity is in turn controlled by the applied voltage. As would be expected, the higher the voltage, the brighter the glow of the phosphor. The persistence of the excited phosphor, that is, how long the phosphor remains glowing after the electron beam moves away, gives the impression that the image is static, although in reality only a single dot on the screen is being updated at any one instant. When the electron beam stops, the image soon fades into oblivion.

Monochrome CRT devices have only a single color of phosphor deposited on the screen. When the electron beam strikes the phosphor, the phosphor glows with its characteristic color—white, amber, or green—depending upon the type of monitor. If a phosphor dot is not excited by the beam of electrons, it appears dark or black. By correct modulation of the beam of electrons, an image can be displayed in a full range of shades from black to white. Monochrome CRTs have a single electron beam source, called an *electron gun*. Magnetic fields applied to the CRT steer the beam produced by the electron gun (with magnetic deflection) so that it strikes the phosphor dots, while at the same time the intensity of the beam is being modulated to produce the various intensity levels. Magnetic fields are used to sweep the beam across the display area of the CRT screen in both the horizontal and vertical directions.

Color CRTs have three different varieties of phosphor; when excited these glow red, green, and blue. From these three primary colors, all other colors can be derived and displayed. The relative intensities of the primary colors determine what the eye perceives as the color of a pixel, or picture element, on the screen. Dots of the three phosphors are deposited close together in a matrix on the back of the screen. Color CRTs generally, but not always, have three electron guns, each aligned to excite only one color of phosphor in the matrix. By controlling the intensity and positioning of each of the three electron beams, a color image can be displayed.

The actual operation of a CRT is more complicated than the preceding discussion would seem to indicate. The key to understanding the subtle details of how CRTs work is to understand the video signals that drive them. Unfortunately, video signals are rather complex in themselves and will take a little study to completely comprehend. Please keep in mind that accurate control of the electron beam(s) both in position and in intensity, is necessary for a stable, intelligible image to be displayed. Synchronization in both the horizontal and vertical directions is required. The truth of these statements should become evident as we examine and discuss Figure 2.1.

This figure illustrates what is called *NTSC standard 2:1 interlaced video*. NTSC is one of three video standards currently in use today. Video standards will be discussed later in this chapter.

As shown, a video image is generated by two sweeps of an electron beam across the display surface of a CRT device. Each sweep is referred to as a *field*, with two fields comprising one video frame. The phosphor dots that are excited by the electron beam of a field are "interlaced" or staggered in position relative to the dots of the other field. One complete field of video is displayed before the display of the other video field is begun. Notice that each field contains a half line. Field one ends with a half line, whereas field two starts with a half line. Essentially, field one puts down the even scan lines while field two does the odd.

The dotted lines in this figure indicate times when the electron beam is turned off. This is necessary during both vertical and horizontal retrace intervals so that the image will not be corrupted while the electron beam is repositioned for the next sweep of the screen. The intervals when the beam is off are referred to as *blanking* intervals. Vertical blanking occurs at the top and bottom of the display, while horizontal blanking occurs at both the left and right sides. Understanding where the blanking intervals occur in a video signal is necessary when trying to extract the video image information required for the digitization process.

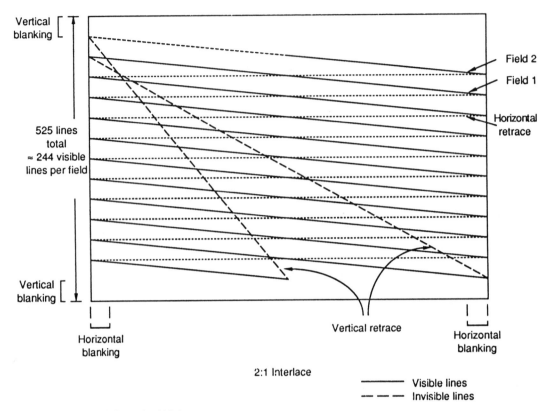

Figure 2.1 NTSC Standard Video

Standard NTSC video consists of 525 horizontal lines of video information updated 30 times a second. Since one frame occurs 30 times a second, each field requires half of that time, or 1/60 of a second, to display. Because the 525 lines are split equally between the two fields, each field is comprised of 262.5 lines. The fractional part of this number is the reason both fields of video contain a half line of display. Displaying 262.5 lines of video in 1/60 of a second means each line requires approximately 63.5 microseconds. This number is an important design parameter for the digitizer developed in Chapter 3 because it is also the length of time between vertically positioned pixels on an NTSC display.

Not all of the 262.5 lines of video information in a field are used for image display. Approximately 18.5 lines are utilized for vertical blanking and display synchronization. This leaves 244 lines per field for visible-image information. These 244 lines per field, or 488 lines per frame, make up the visible image seen on computer monitors or TVs. Of the lines used for vertical blanking, lines 17 through 20 of each field can also be used for other purposes. Applications of these hidden video lines include testing and diagnostics, cuing, and control signal transfer. Useful information that is not related to video can be conveyed in these essentially unused video lines. This information can be decoded with a properly configured receiver without impacting the normal video display.

Timing of the electron beam is very important. Timing information must be present in the video signal for:

a. Horizontal retrace timing
b. Vertical retrace timing
c. Vertical blanking
d. Horizontal blanking

Additionally, video amplitude (for a monochrome image) or color information is required to define a displayable image. Video signals that contain both timing and image information in one signal are called *composite video* signals. The EIA (Electronic Industries Association) standard monochrome composite video signal we will be most concerned with in this book is defined by the RS-170 specification, which places limits on the electrical characteristics of a video signal such that it can be exchanged between compatible video equipment without signal conversions. Composite video signals are available on most television cameras, some color computer monitors, video cassette recorders (VCRs), and some personal computers. It should be noted that the NTSC (National Television Standards Committee) color standard is a superset of the monochrome RS-170 standard and is governed by the RS-170A specification.

Figure 2.2 shows an electrical timing diagram for the RS-170A color video signal. This figure shows the relationship of control and image information in a video signal. Only the timing is shown: The video signal amplitudes will be discussed later. Ignoring for the present

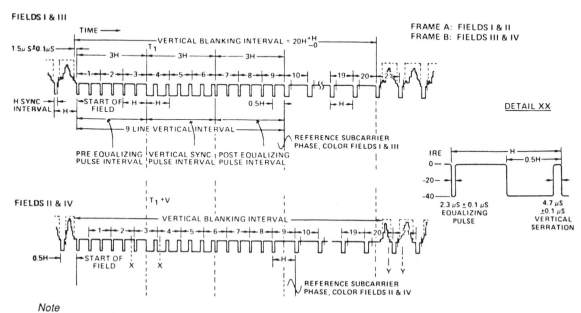

Note
The diagram includes color information. For monochrome video, fields III and IV are identical to fields I and II.

Figure 2.2 Video Frame Timing

the color attributes, all timing, also known as *synchronization*, is performed via the short sync pulses, which make excursions from what is defined as the blanking level toward the sync level. Systems, such as the one in the figure, with negative-going sync pulses are called *negative sync systems*. The composite video signal can be thought of as containing both digital and analog components. The digital component is made up of various sync pulses, whereas the analog component is the actual video signal (shown as a staircase waveform on the diagram). The sync signal locks the CRT's timing to the video source. The active video portion of the video signal modulates the intensity of the electron beam as it synchronously sweeps across the display screen's surface. The modulation causes the phosphor dots over which the electron beam passes to glow with an intensity proportional to the modulating signal. The type, width, and quantity of sync pulses are very important when trying to extract image information from a video signal. Three different types of pulses can be identified:

a. The horizontal sync pulse, which has a width of approximately 4.7 microseconds. This pulse causes the electron beam to be repositioned from the right side of the display area back to the left side in preparation for the display of a new video line. The video signal is blanked during this horizontal retrace time, so the path of the retrace is not visible on the screen.

b. The vertical sync pulse, which has a width of approximately 27.1 microseconds. This pulse causes the electron beam to be repositioned, from the bottom right of the screen back to the top left, in preparation for the display of the next field of video. Horizontal sync pulses continue to occur during the vertical retrace time interval to help keep the display device synchronized with the video source.

c. The equalizing pulse, with a width of 2.3 microseconds. These pulses are used to maintain the DC level of the video signal while supplying synchronization information to the display device.

If the total number of negative-going pulses (horizontal sync, vertical sync, and equalizing pulses) are counted in both fields of a NTSC video frame, the results are that field one has 272 pulses while field two has 271. These counts are important when a computer tries to analyze a video signal on the fly. By counting pulses in a field, software can determine which field is number one and which is number two. The digitizer presented in Chapter 3 will use this counting technique when digitizing an interlaced video signal.

Figure 2.3 shows one line of composite video. This one line of video contains both synchronization and video information. The various components of the composite video waveform are labeled and given approximate timings. Of the 63.5 microseconds of time, approximately 53 microseconds are devoted to the conveyance of image information. The remainder of the time is spent synchronizing the signal. Notice that the video signal is continuously variable within the given white/black envelope.

Signal amplitude of RS-170 compliant signals are specified in terms of IRE (Institute of Radio Engineers) units. The standard video signal of 1.0 volt peak to peak, is broken up into 140 IREs. The conversion factor is 7.1429 millivolts (thousandths of a volt) per IRE. All voltage levels between -40 IRE (the sync level) and zero IRE (the blanking level) are considered control or synchronization components of the video signal. Voltage levels between $+7.5$ IRE and $+100$ IRE contain the actual video image information. A voltage excursion to $+100$ IRE (referenced from the sync level) results in a white dot (pixel) being displayed. A

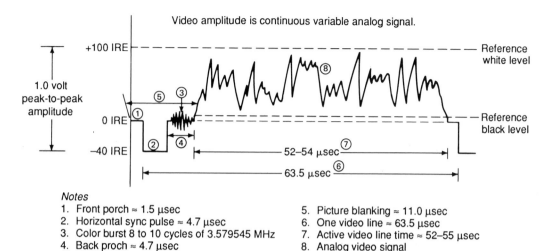

Figure 2.3 Video Line Timing

Notes
1. Front porch ≈ 1.5 μsec
2. Horizontal sync pulse ≈ 4.7 μsec
3. Color burst 8 to 10 cycles of 3.579545 MHz
4. Back proch ≈ 4.7 μsec
5. Picture blanking ≈ 11.0 μsec
6. One video line ≈ 63.5 μsec
7. Active video line time ≈ 52–55 μsec
8. Analog video signal

voltage of 0.34 volts or 7.5 IRE units is displayed as black. Voltages between these extremes result in an intermediate-intensity pixel. Voltages below the 0.34 volts black level cause the electron beam to be turned off or blanked. This voltage level is sometimes referred to as the *blacker than black* level.

All composite video signal amplitude measurements assume an impedance of 75 ohms. The RS-170 specification specifies that the impedance of a video device over the frequency range of 0 to 4.5 MHz shall be 75 ohms. Input impedance is an important design parameter for the digitizer in the next chapter.

To comply with the RS-170 standard, a video system must have a resolving power of at least 330 lines in the vertical direction and 525 lines in the horizontal direction. Resolving power is a measure of a system's ability to delineate detail in a video image. These specifications are easily met by most modern video cameras and CRT display devices. Most video cassette recorders, however, do not have the required vertical lines of resolution. Super VHS is the exception, because it has over 400 vertical lines of resolution. That is why the picture quality is improved. In general, since the number of horizontal lines of resolution is fixed by the video standard, all comparisons between video devices should be made in terms of vertical lines of resolution. The more vertical lines of resolution, the better the produced image. Unfortunately, the video devices with higher resolution also have higher prices.

Video Standards

The discussion to this point has centered on the NTSC monochrome composite video signals and standards (see Figure 2.4). In actuality, three color video standards are widely used: NTSC, PAL, and SECAM. The PAL and SECAM standards are not used in the United States and will therefore be given only a brief discussion in this section. Also, because direct extraction of color video information is not supported by the digitizer developed in the next

Video Parameter	Specification
Video signal bandwidth	0–4.5 MHz
Horizontal sync pulse frequency	15,750 Hz BW, 15,734 Hz Color
Vertical sync pulse frequency	60 Hz BW, 59.94 Color
Impedance of composite video device	75 ohms, 0–4.5 MHz
Standard video signal level	1.0 volts p-p

Key Reference Levels	
White reference level	+100 IRE or 1.00 volts above sync level
Black reference level	+7.5 IRE or 0.34 volts above sync level
Blanking level	0.0 IRE or 0.286 volts above sync level
Sync	−40 IRE or 0.0 volts

Figure 2.4   NTSC Video Specification Summary

chapter, the discussion of color-encoding schemes will only be given a cursory treatment. Additional information on color-encoding methods can be found in the articles and books listed in ''References and Additional Reading.''

NTSC

NTSC is the standard that governs all government-regulated color broadcast systems in the United States. This standard, also utilized in Japan and parts of South America, was adopted in the United States in 1953. The two other color-encoding standards were developed later. The following discussion of color-encoding methods has been excerpted from the CONRAC *Raster Graphics Handbook* and the RS-170A specification. See ''References and Additional Reading'' for the complete information on this handbook.

The basic principle underlying all three color-encoding standards is the merging of two separate image transmissions, a wide band signal carrying luminance information and a narrower bandwidth chrominance signal. The latter is added to the luminance signal in the form of a modulated sub carrier. NTSC utilizes a 3.579545 MHz chrominance sub carrier frequency while the PAL and SECAM standards use a frequency of 4.2 or 4.4 MHz.

The three primary-color signals are gamma-corrected [see Chapter 1 of this book]. The luminance signal is then generated as the sum of three color signal fractions, established by their relative contributions to the luminance of a standard ''white.'' The chrominance component is obtained by first subtracting the luminance signal from the color signals to obtain the color difference values: red minus luminance, green minus luminance and blue minus luminance. Because the luminance is also transmitted as a sum of color fractions, only two of these color difference signals must be transmitted to provide a full definition of all three primary colors.

In the NTSC system, the color difference signals are weighted, matrixed and filtered to produce a wide band orange/cyan I (in phase) signal and a narrow band magenta-green Q (quadrature) signal. The two are then used to modulate two 3.58 MHz sub-carrier signals which are 90 degrees out of phase with each other. The modulated sub-carriers are also − 57 degrees and

−147 degrees removed from the phase of a sub-carrier reference burst which accompanies each horizontal sync pulse [see Figure 2.3 in this book].

The I and Q bandwidths and representative colors take advantage of the fact that the human eye-brain system can perceive only a limited amount of color in small details and is also relatively limited in its ability to resolve magenta and green details compared to those with orange and cyan colors. The Q signal bandwidth is therefore kept to 0.5 MHz. The I signal bandwidth is nearly three times as large (1.3 MHz) but only the lower side band components outside the double side band Q signal are retained.

When the two sub carrier signals are combined, the resulting phase is a direct analog of the hue, while the amplitude of the combined signal is an indirect measure of the saturation. Thus, a zero sub carrier amplitude corresponds to zero saturation, resulting in a monochrome black and white image controlled entirely by the magnitude of the luminance signal. Timing differences also exist between the monochrome and the color encoded signals. These differences have been made small so monochrome receivers and monitors can maintain synchronization even though a color-encoded signal is being received.

PAL and SECAM

Both the PAL and the SECAM standards are designed for systems that operate at 625 lines per frame and 25 frames per second. Both are designed to avoid the color-distortion problems that can occur in NTSC systems. The PAL (*P*hase *A*lternation *L*ine) standards were developed by Telefunken and are used throughout Europe. SECAM, which stands for *S*ystème *E*lectronique *C*ouleur *a*vec *M*émoire, is a French acronym for Sequential Color with Memory. This system is used exclusively in France, the Soviet Union, and all of the eastern-bloc countries.

Conclusions

This chapter discussed video, showing how an electron beam is used to create an image on a CRT. The emphasis was on monochrome video, although a portion of the discussion dealt with color video signals. Special attention was paid to the type, number, and duration of the various sync pulses found in a video signal. These sync pulses play a key role in the development of the digitizer that will be discussed in Chapter 3.

3

Video Digitizer Hardware

In this chapter you will learn about:

- **The capabilities of commercial video digitizers**
- **The specifications of the digitizer presented in this book**
- **The host computer/digitizer interface**
- **The operation of the analog and the digital portions of the digitizer**
- **Assembling and testing your digitizer**

Introduction

Armed with the understanding of video provided in the last chapter, we can now discuss the design and implementation of a hardware device that can digitize video images and allow their importation into a PC for manipulation and display. In a crude sense, the function of a digitizer is to remove the synchronization portion of the composite video signal before converting the amplitude of the analog signal into its digital representation. The digitizer and/or host computer must have enough intelligence to understand the video signals, so image information can be correctly extracted and interpreted. An interface to a host computer must also be provided—for mass storage of the image data and possibly for image processing to be performed.

Because video digitizers come in many shapes and sizes with varying amounts of functionality, we must agree on a set of terms to be used to describe each type based upon their functional differences. The most important attributes are:

    a. Frame versus field digitizing capability
    b. Still-frame versus real-time video digitization capabilities
    c. Resolution
    d. Sample bit width
    e. Monochrome versus color capabilities
    f. On-board image processing capabilities
    g. Video output capabilities

A block diagram of a typical full-featured digitizer might appear as shown in Figure 3.1. The block diagram of the digitizer presented in this chapter is shown in Figure 3.2 for comparison.

Digitizers, also termed *frame grabbers*, allow a video signal to be digitized in real time and can digitize both fields of an interlaced video frame. Field grabbers are similar, except they ignore one of the video fields, thereby halving their possible resolution. Real-time digitization allows the object at which a video camera is pointing to move (albeit slowly) without corruption of the digitized image. This is possible as long as the complete video frame can be digitized in less than 1/30 of a second and the object does not move appreciably during the digitization period. Digitizing from a TV or VCR source is possible with a real-time digitizer because the digitizer can keep up with the update rate of the video image. Still-frame digitizers rely on the fact that the video image is stationary during the digitization process. Any movement in the object being digitized will result in distortion of the digitized image.

Resolution defines the number of pixels (picture elements) the digitizer is capable of producing. Real-time digitizers typically utilize a square pixel matrix such as 256 by 256 or 512 by 512. The image is then 256 pixels across horizontally by 256 lines vertically. Binary numbers are chosen for the matrix dimensions because of the requirement for memory in the digitizer. Memory chips are available only with storage capacities that are powers of two. Some still-frame digitizers have resolutions that are not power-of-two-related because they do not contain memory in the digitizer for image storage. Instead, they utilize memory in the host computer and are therefore not constrained by the amount of memory on the digitizer alone.

Digitizers as well as display adapters have a fixed number of bits used to represent each image sample (or pixel). Each sample represents the intensity of the image at the position where the pixel was digitized. The more bits in a sample, the more accurate the digital representation of an image. The number of bits supported determines the price of the digitizer because as the number of bits increase so does the width of the required memory and the analog-to-digital (A-to-D) conversion device. Typical sample widths are four, six, or eight bits. This results in 16, 64, or 256 possible sample intensity values. It should seem obvious that if each pixel can take on any of 256 values, it will more closely represent the original image than if sample values are limited to only 16 possibilities.

Digitizers can be monochrome only or can provide color capabilities. If a digitizer supports color, it generally has three sets of A-to-D conversion devices and three sets of image memories: one each for the red, green, and blue components of the color image. Three sets of digitizations are performed for each picture element. Digitizations can be performed

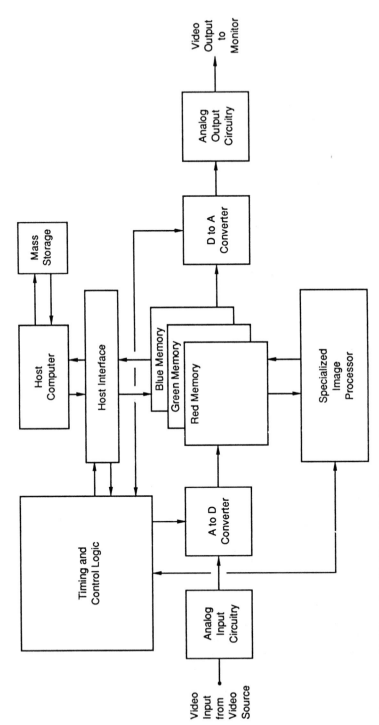

Figure 3.1 Full-Function Digitizer Block Diagram

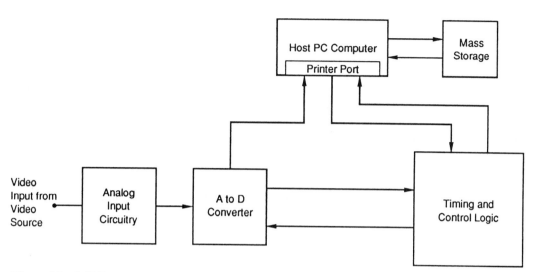

Figure 3.2   Still-Frame Video Digitizer Block Diagram

in parallel (simultaneously) or in series (one after another). Monochrome digitizers have one A-to-D converter and possibly one memory for digitized image storage. Images produced by a monochrome digitizer generally are displayed using various shades of gray to represent each possible pixel-intensity value. These images are referred to as *continuous-tone images* because the full range of gray colors from black to white are used for display.

Another feature that can distinguish one digitizer from another is whether it has an on-board image processor. With an on-board processor, various image processing algorithms can be run directly on the digitizer without burdening the host computer with these computationally intensive tasks. These image processing algorithms might also be implemented directly in hardware instead of in software. This can result in an order-of-magnitude time saving for image processing. Time can also be saved because the image data does not have to be transferred back and forth between the digitizer and the host.

Finally, many digitizers have a video output available for driving a video monitor directly. This can be used to view the effects of an image processing algorithm in near real time or more simply used to accurately set up the digitizer for operation (i.e., image positioning, etc.).

Knowing what capabilities are possible with commercial video digitizers, you might be somewhat disappointed with the specifications of the digitizer presented in this chapter. This digitizer forsakes all the bells and whistles associated with commercial digitizers in favor of *low cost*. The purpose in presenting a low-cost digitizer is to promote experimentation with the image processing techniques presented throughout this book. You, the reader, can develop creative applications faster with hands-on experimentation. A low-cost digitizer will allow more people to do this type of experimentation. With that in mind, the specifications of the digitizer hardware are as follows:

a. Frame or field acquisition capability from any standard RS-170 video source (with one caveat, see "f")

b. With a minor change, the digitizer's hardware will work with either the PAL or SECAM color video standards. It supports the monochrome NTSC standard by default.

c. Supports 320×200, 640×200, and 640×480 image resolutions

d. Six-bit A-to-D converter, giving 64 unique intensity levels

e. It can digitize monochrome images directly. Color images require extra software support (described in Chapter 5). A color video source can be used, but the resulting images will still be monochrome. The color information is removed from the composite video signal before the digitization process.

f. Only still video images can be digitized.

g. There is no on-board video processor—all processing is performed via the attached IBM or compatible PC.

h. The digitizer is a stand-alone piece of hardware that does not require a plug-in board inside of the PC. It can connect to any host computer that supports a Centronix-compatible printer port.

i. No video output is provided—images are displayed on the attached PC only.

j. The digitizer can be built for under $50.

The software provided in the next two chapters for an IBM PC or compatible computer provides:

a. Acquisition and display of monochrome images in all of the resolutions listed above. Both noninterlaced and interlaced acquisition modes are supported. Sixteen or 64 levels of gray are used to display the images on a VGA monitor.

b. A focus window updated in near real time, which is used to point and focus the attached video camera.

c. A special 256-color mode, which, with the assistance of a color wheel, can provide full-color images from a monochrome camera. The color images produced can be stored in a special image file format that makes them executable like a standard MSDOS COM file. Upon execution, these image files display themselves immediately on the VGA display screen.

d. The ability to save the digitized images in either PCX or TIFF standard graphics file formats. The images can then be imported into other applications (e.g., paint programs and desktop publishing programs). A special viewing program is provided so that the images saved in these graphics file formats can be easily displayed.

Assembly of the video digitizer is relatively straightforward. While not something to undertake as a first electronic-project, anyone with prior circuit-building experience should have no trouble. If built using wire-wrap techniques, the digitizer can be entirely assembled in approximately one day; if it is built with a printed circuit board, the assembly time is about an hour.

Most parts are standard LS TTL (Transistor Transistor Logic) integrated circuits available from any well-stocked electronics store. The only somewhat specialized parts are the CA3306C A-to-D converter and the 25.0-MHz crystal oscillator (any oscillator in the frequency range of 12.38 to 12.5 MHz could be used. The only change to the circuit would be the removal of the divide-by-two circuit placed directly after the 25.0-MHz oscillator). These parts can be acquired at most major electronics suppliers or by mail order from parts suppliers in the back of *Radio Electronics* or *BYTE* magazines.

Only two adjustments are necessary to calibrate the completed digitizer. This is because most of the digitizer is digital in design, with the analog circuitry kept to a minimum. Testing the completed project can be accomplished with only a meter, although an oscilloscope can aid in the process. If wired correctly, the digitizer should work the first time and should be reliable for a considerable length of time.

Host/Digitizer Interface

The digitizer attaches to the host PC via the Centronix-compatible printer port. A printer port connection was chosen for the digitizer instead of a serial connection or bus interface card because:

  a. Higher data transfer rates are possible with a parallel connection than with a serial connection.
  b. A unique bus interface card would be required for the original line of PCs and the new microchannel PS/2s. This card would take up a slot inside of the host PC.
  c. The Centronix printer port on the IBM PC and compatible computers has become an industry standard.
  d. The printer interface was the most compatible across the complete line of PCs. (See the discussion below.)
  e. A parallel connection as provided by the printer port requires less circuitry.

The decision to use the printer port interface was not without its problems, however. As you may know, on the pre-PS/2 line of IBM PCs, the printer port was not a true bidirectional eight-bit parallel port. Instead, it had a total of twelve output lines and five input lines, all of which were TTL compatible. The output lines were used to send control and printer data to the printer, whereas the input lines were used to monitor status sent back from the printer. When the printer port is connected to the digitizer, of course, the functions of the input and output lines change to that required by the digitizer.

One of the biggest challenges in designing of the digitizer was to be able to pass the digitized pixel data and all synchronization information back from the digitizer to the PC using only the five input lines available. Considering that the A-to-D converter was six bits wide and at least three bits of status were required, clever design was necessary to multiplex the function of the input lines into the PC. Of course, the digitizer could have been designed to work only with the newer PS/2s or PCs with a true bidirectional parallel port, but it was thought important to make it work with as many standard PCs as possible. As a result, the digitizer can be connected via the printer port to any PC from the original to a PS/2 model 70/80 386 machine and function correctly. How this was accomplished will be discussed in the section on the digital portion of the digitizer.

Figure 3.3 shows the names given to the signals that form the digitizer/host interface along with the pin numbers and signal directions. The digitizer is connected to the PC's printer port via a straight-through 25-pin cable such as a shielded RS-232 cable. This cable can be made up to six feet in length and should be shielded. Ribbon cable can be used for shorter cable lengths. (*Note*: if the digitizer is to eventually be used with an A/B switch box, the shortest possible cable lengths should be used, along with the highest quality switch box.)

Digitizer Signal Names	Pin #	Dig ← → PC Direction	PC Signal Names
Strobe	1	←	−Strobe
Pixel Count D0	2	←	+Data Bit 0
Pixel Count D1	3	←	+Data Bit 1
Pixel Count D2	4	←	+Data Bit 2
Pixel Count D3	5	←	+Data Bit 3
Pixel Count D4	6	←	+Data Bit 4
Pixel Count D5	7	←	+Data Bit 5
Pixel Count D6	8	←	+Data Bit 6
Pixel Count D7	9	←	+Data Bit 7
Pixel Data Out D2	10	→	−Acknowledge
Pixel Data Out D3	11	→	+Busy
Pixel Data Out D1	12	→	+P.End (out of paper)
Pixel Data Out D0	13	→	+Select
Sync Reset	14	←	−Auto Feed
SyncEOC	15	→	−Error
Go	16	←	−Init Printer
High/Low	17	←	−Select Input
Ground	18	←→	Ground
Ground	19	←→	Ground
Ground	20	←→	Ground
Ground	21	←→	Ground
Ground	22	←→	Ground
Ground	23	←→	Ground
Ground	24	←→	Ground
Ground	25	←→	Ground

Notes
1. All signals are TTL compatible.
2. Straight-through shielded RS-232 cable works very well.

Video Interface Cable
Male BNC to male BNC, shielded cable (75 ohm Type RG-II or RG-59 or equivalent) up to 6 feet in length.

Figure 3.3   Digitizer/Host PC Signal Connections

The block diagram of the digitizer is shown in Figure 3.2. The schematic is shown as Figure 3.4 and the parts list in Figure 3.5. These diagrams should be consulted during the discussion that follows:

The Analog Portion of the Digitizer

Only a small portion of the total digitizer circuitry is analog circuitry. This circuitry is a modified version of that originally presented by Steve Ciarcia in the June 1986 issue of *BYTE* magazine. This circuitry is copyright Steven Ciarcia and is used by permission. For those people interested in researching the original design, it may be found in *Ciarcia's Circuit Cellar*, Vol. VII (McGraw-Hill, 1990). The functions performed by this circuitry include:

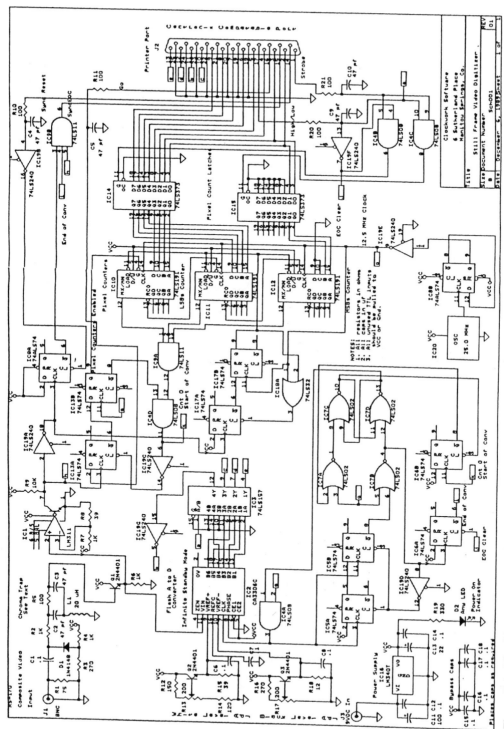

Figure 3.4 The Digitizer Schematic Diagram

61

Semiconductors

Item	Quantity	Reference	Part	
1	1	D1	1N4148	
2	1	D2	Any LED	
3	3	Q1,Q2,Q3	2N4401	
4	1	IC1	LM311 comparator	
5	1	IC2	CA3306C A to D converter	
6	1	IC3	74LS157	
7	1	IC4	74LS08	
8	4	IC5,IC6,IC13,IC17	74LS74	
9	1	IC7	74LS02	
10	1	IC8	74ALS74	
11	1	IC9	74LS11	
12	3	IC10,IC11,IC12	74LS191	
13	2	IC14,IC15	74LS373	
14	1	IC16	LM340T 5VDC regulator	
15	1	IC18	74LS32	
16	1	IC19	74LS240	
17	1	OSC	25.0 MHz Oscillator Newark Electronics Number 44F4217	

Passive Components

18	6	C2,C3,C4,C5,C9,C10	47 pf	All caps 25WVDC
19	10	C1,C6,C7,C8,C12,C14 C15,C16,C17,C18	.1 uf	or greater.
20	1	C13	22 uf	
21	1	C11	100 uf	
22	1	R1	75 ohms 5%	
23	4	R2,R4,R6,R7	1K ohms 5%	
24	2	R3,R16	270 ohms 5%	
25	5	R5,R10,R11,R20,R21	100 ohms 5%	
26	2	R8,R15	39 ohms 5%	
27	1	R9	10K ohms 5%	
28	1	R12	150 ohms 5%	
29	2	R13,R17	200 trimmer pots	
30	1	R14	120 ohms 5%	
31	1	R18	12 ohms 5%	
32	1	R19	330 ohms 5%	
33	1	L1	20 uH inductor	

Figure 3.5   Still-Frame Video Digitizer Bill of Materials

Miscellaneous Components

34	1	J1	Female BNC connector for video in
35	1	J2	Male DB25 connector
36	1	J3	Minature plug for 9VDC In
37	1	na	wire wrap board or PCB
38	1	na	Heat sink for IC16
39	1	na	9VDC wall transformer

Figure 3.5 *(continued)*

    a. 75-ohm video termination
    b. Video signal DC correction
    c. Color subcarrier rejection
    d. Signal buffering
    e. A-to-D reference voltage generation

Resistor R1 on the schematic provides the required 75-ohm termination for the video signal. This resistor is required for a proper impedance match with the video source. This resistor can be removed if a monitor is wired in parallel with the video digitizer's input and the monitor provides the proper termination.

Capacitor C1, resistors R3 and R4, and diode D1 shift the DC level of the incoming video signal to that required by the analog circuitry. AC coupling of the video is provided by C1. AC coupling is necessary to remove any DC offset that might be present in the attached video source. When AC is coupled, the sync level of the video signal floats at approximately -0.286 volts. The voltage divider formed by R3 and R4 produces an output voltage of approximately 1.06 volts. This voltage, coupled with the 0.6- to 0.7-volt voltage drop across the forward-biased small-signal diode D1, shifts the video signal by just about 0.4 volts to bring the negative-going sync excursions to just above ground level.

With the video signal shifted to the correct level, the color burst or chroma frequency can then be filtered out. This is necessary only if a color video source is used with the digitizer. This filtering is accomplished with a notch filter made up of components C2, C3, L1, and R5. This filter (with the values shown on the schematic) attenuates the NTSC 3.57-MHz color burst frequency so that its presence does not distort the digitized image. Essentially, the filter converts a color video signal to a monochrome one. If a monochrome video source will be used, the filter components can and should be removed from the circuit completely. In other words the components C2, C3, L1, and R5 can be left out of the circuit. If a "chroma trap" is not used, make sure a connection is made between R2 and the base of transistor Q1. Otherwise, the circuit will not function. If a PAL or SECAM video source is used, the value of L1 would have to be modified accordingly.

Transistor Q1 is a voltage follower and acts as a buffer for the circuitry that follows. After the video signal is buffered, it is presented to a comparator IC1 and to the analog-to-digital converter IC2. The comparator circuit changes state every time a sync pulse occurs in the video signal. The output of the open collector comparator provides a TTL-compatible output signal that interfaces to the digital portion of the digitizer circuitry. This output signal goes low (toward ground) every time the sync pulse goes low, with a pulse width equal to the input sync pulse. The reference input to the comparator is set at approximately 200 millivolts DC.

The buffered video signal is supplied to the input pin of the A-to-D converter. Other analog circuitry generates the reference voltage levels required by the converter. The A-to-D is a flash converter, which means it has comparators for each input level to be converted and an internal resistor network for setting the references for each comparator. In total, 64 comparators are inside this six-bit A-to-D converter. By connecting one end of the resistor network to the black reference voltage level (the emitter of Q3) and the other to the white reference (emitter of Q2), we can assign one of 64 possible digital values to a voltage within that range. This effectively assigns a digital number to a video amplitude level. This number is what is returned to the PC from the digitizer for each pixel digitized. Circuitry described in the next section controls the operation of the A-to-D converter. (*Note*: if more than six bits of video resolution are required, the six-bit A-to-D device (CA3306C) could be replaced with an eight-bit (CA3318C) device. Only minor modifications to the reference voltage generator circuitry and the output data multiplexing circuitry would be required.) An eight-bit A-to-D converter was not used in the original design because of the higher cost of the eight-bit device. Also, the additional bits of intensity resolution provided by the eight-bit converter could not easily be taken advantage of in the digitizer's software.

The reference voltage generators are adjustable, low-impedance, DC voltage sources that provide stable reference levels. The black voltage reference is adjusted to approximately 0.34 volts, the white level to approximately 1.0 volts. Once set, these adjustments should never have to be tweaked again.

The only other analog circuitry is the power supply. The digitizer is powered via a nine-volt DC external power supply that plugs directly into a 110-volt wall socket. The nine volts is regulated down to five volts as required by the TTL circuitry. The voltage regulator is an LM340T or equivalent device. Positive five volts is the only voltage required by the digitizer circuitry. Ample bypass capacitors are sprinkled throughout the digitizer's circuitry to lower the impedance of the power supply (to prevent high-frequency glitches from propagating through the circuitry). The voltage regulator should have a heat sink for proper heat dissipation.

The Digital Portion of the Digitizer

The digital portion of the digitizer passes synchronization information extracted from the video input signal to the PC. It also contains the timing and control circuitry that triggers the A-to-D converter to take a sample at the correct time intervals. Low level image acquisition software running in the PC coordinates the operation of digital circuitry.

All of the digital circuitry runs synchronously with the master oscillator. The frequency of this oscillator depends on the maximum number of horizontal pixels desired on a single scan line. In this case, the design criterion was to have 640 pixels digitized for each video line.

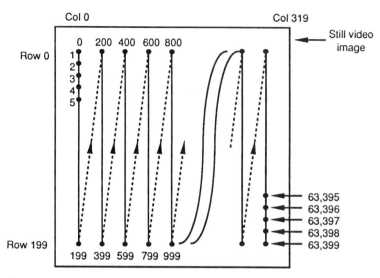

Figure 3.6 Image Scanning Sequence

Notes
1. The diagram assumes the still video image is digitized into a 320 × 200 image. There are exactly 64,000 pixels in each 320 × 200 image.
2. The direction of the digitizing process is down the image instead of across it. This is contrary to the scanning of the electron beam across the image from left to right.
3. The numbers 1, 2, 3, 4, 5, etc., show the order of pixel digitization. The first pixel digitized, number 1, is actually pixel 0.

In Chapter 2, we saw that the active portion of a video line is approximately 53 microseconds long. This equates to a sample time of approximately 80 nanoseconds. The frequency, which is calculated as one divided by this period, equates to 12.5 MHz. This then is our ideal oscillator or clock frequency. This clock frequency is derived from a 25-MHz master oscillator. IC8B divides this frequency in half for use throughout the circuit.

Obviously, it would be impossible for software running in a PC to keep up with data being acquired at the 12.5-MHz rate. For this reason, this digitizer does not attempt to acquire samples on a pixel-by-pixel basis across a video line. Instead, the digitizer acquires all samples in a column of video before moving to the next higher-numbered column to the right. This will allow 63.5 microseconds of time between samples acquired by the digitizer. In this time, a sample can be taken and transferred to the PC before the next sample is digitized. The sampling order utilized by the digitizer is illustrated in Figure 3.6.

This technique has both good and bad attributes. The good point about the technique is that no memory is required on the digitizer board, because the samples can be acquired and transferred to the PC in real time. (Large amounts of memory are required in the PC, however.) The bad point is the time required to digitize an image. Knowing that each sample requires 63.5 microseconds to acquire, the following image-acquisition times can be estimated:

Resolution	Mode	PC Memory Required	Digitizing Time Required
320 × 200	Black/White	64KB	4.06 seconds
320 × 200	Color	192KB	12.18 seconds
640 × 200	Black/White	128KB	8.12 seconds
640 × 480	Black/White	307KB	19.51 seconds

The digitization times explain why only still video images can be digitized. If there is any appreciable movement during the required digitizing time in the object being digitized, the resultant image will be corrupted. See the "Gallery of Images" (following p. 442) for an example of movement during the digitization of an image.

In order to provide the precise timing for the triggering of the A-to-D converter, hardware pixel counters are utilized. A ten-bit binary counter made up of IC10, 11, and 12 plus the latches IC14 and 15 performs this function (notice that only two of the eight bits in the latch IC15 are utilized). Ten bits are required because the counter must be able to contain a count of 640 (the total number of pixels in a line). The latches are loaded (via low-level image-acquisition software in the PC) with the number of the pixel column to be digitized. The pixel count is loaded just once by the software for each column of video. The hardware reloads itself automatically (if the Go signal from the PC is true) for each pixel in the column of video being digitized. The falling edge of the sync pulse loads the latched pixel count value into the pixel counters. The rising edge of the sync pulse, coincident with the rising edge of the buffered clock, starts the counters counting down at the 12.5-MHz rate. IC13 provides the synchronization with the clock. When the zero count is reached, a trigger pulse is sent to the A-to-D control circuitry, which causes it to digitize the video waveform at that instant. The zero count is detected with gates IC4D and IC9A. IC9A logically ANDs together the Min/Max output of each of the three 74LS191 pixel counters. When all counters contain a zero value, the output of IC9A goes high. This zero count will generate a start of conversion pulse to the A-to-D converters if and only if the counters are currently enabled for counting. IC4D prevents false triggering of the A-to-D converter during the time when the pixel counters are loaded because the counters are not enabled to count at that time. The start of conversion pulse also resets the enable for the pixel counters, stopping them from counting until retriggered. If the Go signal is false, or low, the pixel counters are prevented from operating.

In summary, the value loaded into the pixel counter determines the delay from the rising edge of the sync pulse to the exact pixel we want to digitize. As the digitization process proceeds from left to right, the values loaded into the counter get larger. When the software determines that all 640 pixels have been digitized, it knows the image-acquisition process has been completed.

Loading the pixel count latches is a multistep process. This method is required because the printer interface can only output eight bits at a time, and a total of ten bits are required by the counters. To overcome this problem, the hardware is designed such that each half of the counter is loaded separately. The eight least significant bits are loaded first, followed by the two most significant bits. The process is as follows:

a. Place the eight least significant bits of the counter value on the printer data port.
b. Drive the high/low output line low, indicating to the hardware that the lower latch is to be addressed.
c. Toggle the strobe line to latch the value into the hardware.
d. Place the two most significant bits of the counter value on the printer data port.
e. Drive the high/low output line high, indicating to the hardware that the upper latch is to be addressed.
f. Toggle the strobe line again, to latch the value into the hardware.

When this sequence is completed, the pixel counter latches contain the pixel column count.

The A-to-D control circuitry is formed by components IC5, 6, and 7. This circuit has two inputs—start of conversion and end of conversion clear—and two outputs—A-to-D clock and end of conversion. At the rising edge of the start of conversion pulse (generated by IC4D and explained above), this circuitry generates exactly two 12.5-MHz clock pulses for the A-to-D converter. When operating in the infinite standby mode as in this design, the A-to-D converter will complete its conversion in two clock periods. The conversion, which requires approximately 120 nanoseconds to complete, will be finished by the falling edge of the second pulse. The speed of the converter eliminates the necessity for a sample and hold circuit in front of the converter. The completion of the conversion also sets latch IC6A. The end of conversion status is indicated to the PC, and the software retrieves the digitized pixel data.

Transfer of the six bits (eight bits if using the CA3318C device) of pixel data to the PC is complicated because only four input lines to the PC are available. To retrieve all of the sample data, another multiplexing scheme (using IC3) must be utilized. Again, the high/low line of the digitizer is used to select which portion of the data is made available to the PC. When the high/low line is low, the four least significant bits of A-to-D data are available. To retrieve all six bits of pixel data, the controlling software must:

a. Read and save the four least significant bits of pixel data.
b. Set the high/low line high to enable the retrieval of the two most significant bits.
c. Read the two most significant bits of the pixel data.
d. Combine the data into a single six-bit value for storage.

Please note that when the high/low signal is toggled, the end of conversion latch (IC6A) is reset. Again, the lack of control signal lines made the multiplexing of this signal also necessary. This works out quite well, actually, because the software has to know the conversion is finished before it ever tries to retrieve the pixel data. The end of conversion latch is then reset as part of the normal data transfer protocol without additional software overhead. Note also the inverter IC19G in the digitized data path. It is used to compensate for an inverter in the PC printer port circuitry. It allows the software to treat all retrieved data as positive true without having to invert one of the six data bits.

The final portion of the digital hardware to be discussed is referred to as the *Sync/End of Conversion circuit*. This circuit is comprised of the three-input AND gate IC9B and a D flip/flop IC8A. IC8A is a sync pulse detector whose output will go low whenever a negative transition to the sync level is detected in the video input signal. This flip/flop is used to guarantee detection of the short equalizing pulses that might be missed if software polling was used by itself. The output of this flip/flop will remain low until the Sync Reset line from the PC is activated. The output will then return to the high state until the arrival of the next sync pulse. If the Sync Reset line is held asserted (high) by the PC, the sync detector's contribution to the Sync/End of Conversion (SyncEDC) function is disabled. This feature is utilized by the image acquisition software.

AND gate IC9B combines the raw sync signal from the sync comparator, the output if enabled of the sync detector circuit described earlier, and the End of Conversion signal from the A-to-D converter control circuitry. The output of this gate will go low if any of its three inputs are low. Each of the following scenarios will cause the "SyncEOC" line (from the digitizer to the PC) to go active (low):

a. An End of Conversion signal from the A-to-D converter control circuitry is generated, signifying a sample is ready to be moved to the PC. This output will remain low until the end of conversion latch is cleared via a transition of the high/low signal.

b. If the sync detector circuit is disabled, the output will go active for the duration of any sync pulses detected in the input video signal.

c. If the sync detector circuit is enabled, the output will go low at the negative edge of any sync pulse and remain low until both the sync reset line is asserted and the sync pulse goes away.

As is probably obvious, the information presented to the PC in the form of the SyncEOC line is context sensitive. To correctly interpret the information provided in this signal, the software must know exactly what portion of the video signal is being examined.

Finally, all of the single-bit output lines from the PC printer port to the digitizer are conditioned with a small RC circuit. This was necessary because all of the PCs used in the development of the digitizer produced small (less than 50-nanosecond) glitches if the output lines were accessed repeatedly. These glitches caused all sorts of bizarre problems during development. The RC circuits have a time constant such that these glitches cannot propagate into the digitizer circuitry. The eight data output lines to the digitizer never change rapidly, so the glitch suppressors were not required there.

Assembly of the Digitizer

Assembly of the digitizer is straightforward. Because of the relatively slow speeds involved in the circuitry, parts layout is not critical. The digitizer can be assembled using many different methods. For example, it can be wire-wrapped or soldered together on a breadboard, or a printed circuit board can be used. Image 3.1 is a photo of the wire-wrapped digitizer prototype. This prototype has never had any problems since it was built, testifying to the ruggedness of the wire wrapped construction. Some things to keep in mind while building your digitizer are:

a. Keep connections short wherever possible.

b. Keep components as close together as practical.

c. Keep analog signal wires short. Use shielded wire for the analog input connection.

Image 3.1   Digitizer Bread Board Photograph

   d. Try to wire ground connections to a single point.

   e. Use larger wire for all power and ground connections.

   f. Enclose the finished product in a metal chassis if it causes interference on nearby TVs or radios.

   g. Work slowly and carefully. It is easier and faster to wire correctly the first time then to have to redo your work.

   h. If you are wire wrapping your digitizer, use number tags that press onto the bottom of IC sockets and show the component pin numbers. This can save you many hours in assembly because you do not have to continually count the wire-wrap pins on the bottom of the sockets. These tags will also prevent confusion with pin numbers as you keep turning the wire-wrap board over and over during the assembly process.

   i. Check your work carefully before applying power. Use an ohm meter to verify every connection. Check from the top of the ICs to the top of other ICs and from the leads of the discrete components to the ICs, and so on. This checks not only the connections but the component sockets also. Make especially sure that a ground connection exists between the digitizer circuitry and the PC connector. If no ground exists, the signals will not be referenced to a common point and the digitizer will never work. Also, without a common ground, damage to the PC's printer port might be possible (though not probable), so be careful.

Testing the Completed Digitizer

Do not attempt to test your digitizer or to acquire an image until step (i) in the assembly section has been performed. It is much easier to fix a problem with the wiring than it is to try to troubleshoot a malfunctioning digitizer. Once all of the interconnections have been verified with the schematic, the following electrical checks and adjustments should be performed before trying to acquire an image. An oscilloscope can assist in making these checks, although it is not absolutely necessary. It will be necessary to power up the digitizer circuit to perform all of the following checks. Until instructed to do so in the test procedure that follows,

    a. Do not place any of the ICs into sockets on the digitizer.
    b. Do not connect your video camera to the digitizer.
    c. Do not connect the digitizer to the PC.
    d. Do not connect the wall-mounted power-supply to the digitizer circuit.

First, plug the wall-mounted power-supply into a AC outlet and verify its DC output. The voltage reading will depend upon the power-supply used but should be somewhere between 8 and 12 volts DC. If the readings are out of this range, the power-supply must be replaced.

Plug the output of the power supply into the digitizer circuit. The LED power indicator (D2) should begin to glow. With your meter, verify the operation of the voltage regulator. Five volts plus or minus 10 percent should be measured at the power-supply pins of each IC. For maximum testing effectiveness, the power-supply voltages should be measured between the power-supply pin and the ground pin of each IC socket. If all is well, power down the digitizer and install all of the ICs into their sockets. Power up the digitizer again and verify the power-supply voltage is still within tolerance.

Next, check the oscillator for 25.0-MHz operation. The test equipment, either an oscilloscope or a meter, can be connected directly between the oscillator output pin and signal ground. With an oscilloscope, the wave form produced by the oscillator can be examined to verify frequency, symmetry (Is it a square wave or not?), and the rise and fall times. Excessively long rise and fall times can inhibit the operation of the digitizer. With a meter, the oscillator operation can be verified (crudely at best) by selecting an AC voltage scale and seeing if a signal is present. If the AC reading is zero, the oscillator is probably not working. The presence of the oscillator signal should be verified at each portion of the circuit that requires the signal.

The most likely cause of a malfunctioning oscillator is improper connections. It is highly unlikely that an oscillator made by a reputable manufacturer will be faulty. Check the wiring carefully until the problem is isolated and corrected.

The next step is the calibration of the white and the black reference voltage sources. Connect a meter between the black reference input to the A-to-D converter (VREF −, pin 10) and ground. Rotate the trimmer until a reading of 0.34 volts is obtained. Next move the meter's positive lead to the white reference input to the A-to-D converter (VREF +, pin 9). Rotate the white reference trimmer until a reading of 1.0 volts is acquired. Now, go back and forth between the black and the white reference inputs, adjusting each as necessary to bring both levels into specification. There will be some interaction between these two adjustments. When the references are adjusted to your satisfaction, the trimmers can be cemented in place so that vibration does not alter their adjustments.

Connect a video cable to the video input connector J1 on the digitizer. With your meter make sure (at the camera end of the video cable) that the shield on the video connector is connected to signal ground on the digitizer, that the inner signal pin of the video connector is not connected to ground, and that no voltage is present on the inner signal pin. These checks are included to protect your video camera from damage. With these checks completed successfully, connect your video source to the input connector J1 of the digitizer. With an oscilloscope or a meter, verify that the output of the comparator IC1 changes states continually. With a scope, you can verify that the changes of state are coincident with the sync pulses in the video input signal.

These are all of the checks on the digitizer circuitry that can be performed without software support from the PC. At this point, the digitizer can be safely connected to the PC, as long as power is turned off on both units while they are connected. If the tests have been successful so far, you can attempt to digitize an image at this point. If you are successful—Congratulations! You have completed your digitizer. If not, do not feel bad. We will use some of the software developed in the next chapter to further troubleshoot the digitizer hardware. It should be relatively easy to identify the problem and correct it.

Conclusions

In this chapter we have discussed the design, construction, operation, and testing of the hardware for our video digitizer. The software discussion in the next chapter will illustrate how the seemingly unrelated pieces of hardware are coordinated to produce a pixel-perfect digitized video image.

Low-Level Digitizer Software
for Image Acquisition

In this chapter you will learn about:

- **How processor speed can effect the digitizer's operation**
- **How the "Image Request" data structure is used to control the operation of the digitizer**
- **How the hardware timers in a PC operate**
- **How the low-level digitizer support functions operate**
- **How an image is acquired by the digitizer**
- **How to finish testing your digitizer**

Introduction

With the hardware design discussed in the previous chapter behind us, it is time to look at software issues. In this chapter we will develop all of the low-level software required to produce digitized video images. The full spectrum of digitizer software will be presented in this and the following chapter; from the lowest-level bit manipulation routines of the assembler code to the somewhat esoteric median cut algorithm for producing color images. When the information presented in these two chapters has been read and understood, you will know how the digitizer works and how to modify its operation to your specification. You will also have a thorough understanding of the VGA graphics adapter (its operation and limitations) and how it is programmed.

CPU Speed Dependence

To keep the cost of this project low, it was decided that the PC would monitor and analyze the video signal to be digitized, so no additional intelligence would have to be built into the digitizer hardware. While this approach did keep the cost of the hardware down, it placed special burdens on the software running in the host PC. At one point, whether the PC could keep up with the video signal it was trying to monitor was questioned. The question boils down to whether the PC has enough processor cycles (for execution of instructions) between events in the video signal. If video events can come and go between CPU instruction execution or the execution of a tight loop, the PC would lose video information and the digitization process would be flawed. If enough CPU cycles exist, however, all video information can be acquired and a pixel-perfect digitized image can be produced. The requirements placed on the PC by the digitization process definitely place the software in the real-time category. Real-time software, by nature, must be deterministic. That is, it must execute in a predictable amount of time and that time is usually short. The real-time aspects of the digitizer have made for a very interesting project.

Of course, the real-time requirements for code execution are eased by more powerful processors or CPUs. This is for two reasons: Not only are more cycles available due to the higher clock speeds but the newer generation of processors execute most instructions in fewer cycles. Timing of the digitizer software, then, becomes less critical when it runs on the newer, faster PCs. Faster PCs have problems all their own, however, which will be addressed shortly.

Another design goal for the digitizer was to allow it to run with any IBM-compatible PC, regardless of speed. This created certain software compatibility problems, which are the focus of this section. This design goal was met because the digitizer has been used successfully with PCs ranging in performance from the original 4.77-MHz IBM PC to the 20-MHz PS/2 Model 70. Slight differences in the low-level digitizer driver software are required, however, for the various speed machines.

Before delving into how the software is modified for the various speeds of PCs, some words need to be said about what information contained in the video signal is actually monitored and what digitizer maintenance functions must be performed. This will give a qualitative feel for the work being done in the PC. Later in this chapter, when the "GetPicture" procedure is discussed, you will see how the actual work is performed. The functions of the low-level driver software that constitute the real-time processing can be categorized as follows:

   a. Sync pulse detection and counting
   b. Digital pixel data transfer
   c. Pixel counter maintenance
   d. Status latch resetting
   e. PC timer maintenance

Each of these has an impact on the real-time processing.

Three categories of timing criteria come into play when modifying the low-level digitizer driver software for use on a PC of a particular clock speed. These are:

a. I/O access timing

b. Software strobe duration timing

c. Sync detection timing

General guidelines will be given for how to modify the low level driver code for certain classes of PCs. Code is provided only on the companion disk for the PS/2 Model 70 computer, however.

I/O access timing has to do with the recovery time required between sequential accesses to I/O devices connected to the PC's bus. If sequential writes to the printer port are attempted without the required recovery, serious glitches will be output from the printer port, and the data, when it does settle, will not be what one would expect. A macro contained in the low-level driver code, "SDelay", is modified to reflect how much time is necessary between I/O operations. This small delay is required, to quote an IBM technical reference manual, because there is "not enough recovery time for some system boards and channel operations" between sequential accesses. This small delay is provided by a jump instruction to the next instruction in the code sequence, coded as follows:

```
jmp  short $+2
```

The I/O access timing problem was first identified on the PC AT class of machines and has been with the IBM PC product line ever since. From the experience gained in the development of the digitizer low-level software, the content of the "SDelay" macro depends on CPU speed and is as follows:

Computer Class	Speed	Number of Jump Instructions
original PC	4.77-MHz 8088	0
PC AT	6- or 8-MHz 80286	1
PC AT	10- to 16-MHz 80286	1 or 2
high end	16 MHz or greater	2

The number of jump instructions to place into the "SDelay" macro was found by experimentation. Further experimentation might be required on your part for your particular computer. If the image produced by the digitizer is streaked, you should increase the number of jumps in "SDelay" (up to a maximum of two) to see if it solves the problem. An oscilloscope can be used to check for the presence of glitches on any of the control lines between the PC and the digitizer. Some of these glitches are only 50 nanoseconds in duration, so a fast scope is required to see them.

As an aside, these jump instructions are also required between any I/O device access and an STI instruction. Again the IBM technical reference manual says the proper way of performing this operation is as follows:

```
out  I/O_Addr, al
jmp  short $+2
mov  al,ah
sti
```

(*Note*: on the original 4.77-MHz IBM PC (or compatible), the "SDelay" macro can be eliminated completely, because the 8088 processor is not fast enough to cause a problem with sequential I/O accesses.)

Software strobe duration timing determines how long the output control lines from the PC to the digitizer are in their asserted state before returning to the quiescent or safe state. Because strobe timing is done in software, the duration of a strobe pulse will depend on the speed of the PC. Another macro, "StbDel", controls the duration of the software strobes and therefore must be modified according to the speed of the computer. A strobe duration of two to five microseconds is required for proper operation of the digitizer circuitry. Strobes of longer duration strobes are required for longer cable connections between the PC and the digitizer. A typical instruction sequence for generating a strobe signal is:

```
mov     al, ResetSyncAndEOC
out     dx,al
StbDel
mov     al,PrtPortContSafe
out     dx,al
```

The first "out" instruction asserts the output signal while the second releases it. The duration of the output strobe signal is controlled for the most part by the "StbDel" macro.

Calculation of the time required to execute a series of instruction is necessary to determine strobe duration. Better stated, when the required strobe duration is known, instructions are put together (and placed into the "StbDel" macro) that require the given time to execute. Two items of information are required to calculate the time. First, the cycle time of the processor, which is determined by how fast the clock signal is, and second, the instruction cycle counts provided by the processor manufacturer. Figure 4.1 shows typical instruction cycle times for the Intel series of processor utilized in IBM PCs and compatibles.

Given the assumptions that memory accesses have zero wait states and no exceptions are generated during instruction execution, the elapsed time for a series of instructions is calculated by multiplying the sum of all instruction cycle counts by the processor's clock period. The clock period for a 4.77-MHz 8088 processor is 210 nanoseconds and for a 16-MHz 80386 is 62.5 nanoseconds. These raw numbers need to be modified slightly to take into consideration memory refresh, which can prevent the processor from accessing memory every time it needs to. A figure of 7 percent is taken from the IBM technical reference manual. The adjusted clock periods are then 225 and 66.9 nanoseconds respectively. These times should be utilized in all instruction duration calculations.

In summary, to develop the "StbDel" macro for a particular speed of processor, pick a series of instructions (NOPs or Pushes and Pops typically) that taken together require 2 to 5 microseconds to execute. The generated strobe duration can be checked by connecting an oscilloscope to the strobe signal output from the PC to the digitizer.

The final timing issue to be covered in this section is sync-detection timing. Accurate timing of the video sync pulses is required to allow software to synchronize to the video signal. Synchronization allows the PC to determine where the control portion of the video signal ends and the visible portion begins. Synchronization is achieved by locating a vertical sync pulse in the video signal. Once a vertical sync is located, the PC can count equalizing

Instruction		8088/8086	80286	80386
and	reg,reg	3	2	2
and	reg,immed	4	3	2
call	NEAR	19	8	8
call	FAR	28	17	22
cli		2	3	3
in	acc, immed8	10	5	12
in	acc, dx	8	5	13
je/jz		16/4*1	8/3*1	8/3*1
jne/jnz		16/4*1	8/3*1	8/3*1
jmp		15	8	8
nop		3	3	3
or	reg,reg	3	2	2
or	reg,immed	4	3	2
out	immed8,acc	10	3	10
out	dx,acc	8	3	11
pop	ax	8	5	5
push	ax	11	3	5
ret	NEAR	16	11	10
ret	FAR	26	15	18
sti		2	2	2

Notes
a. (*1) means more cycles are required if the branch is taken than if not.
b. All cycle counts are taken from Intel references and assume real address mode operation.
c. Elapsed time for a sequence of instruction is calculated by multiplying the sum of all instruction clock counts from this table by the processor's clock speed. Calculated times will typically be within 5 to 10% of actual execution time.

Figure 4.1   Intel Processor Instruction Timings

and horizontal sync pulses to determine where the visible portion of the video signal begins. Once synchronization is achieved, the digitizer hardware takes over and digitizes the video.

The identification of a vertical sync pulse is based upon its duration. Vertical sync pulses (also called vertical sync intervals) can be distinguished from horizontal and equalizing sync pulses by their duration of 27.1 microseconds. Any sync pulse that is greater than about 15 microseconds in duration can be considered a vertical sync pulse. Horizontal sync pulses are approximately 4.7 microseconds long, whereas equalizing pulses are 2.3 microseconds in duration. It is a safe bet any sync pulse greater than 15 microseconds in duration is a vertical sync pulse. This is the technique used in the low-level digitizer code to identify a vertical sync pulse. The basic algorithm is:

```
Loop
    Read SyncEOC line from digitizer
    While Sync not active (low = active)
        Read SyncEOC line from digitizer
    (Sync signal has gone active)
    Delay (for 15 microseconds)
```

```
    Read SyncEOC line from digitizer again
    If Sync still active
        Exit Loop. Vertical sync detected
EndLoop
```

As you can see, the proper operation of this algorithm is contingent upon a relatively accurate (and stable) delay being available. Two methods exist for providing this delay: a series of instructions that take 15 microseconds to execute or the use of a hardware-timer inside the PC. A third macro, "LDELAY", is defined in the digitizer code to select the delay method to be used for sync detection. For now let us say that the hardware-timer approach is the better solution, but it will work only on PCs that are relatively fast (i.e., AT class PCs and faster). This is the technique utilized in the low-level driver code presented later in this chapter. See the discussion of the "Delay" procedure for more information on the utilization of PC timers for sync detection timing.

On slower PCs, the execution of a list of instructions is the method of choice because the processors do not have extra cycles to spare interfacing with a hardware timer. NOP instructions can be used (each requiring three cycles) to generate the proper time delay. When the proper number of instructions has been determined (by performing execution time calculations as before) the instructions can be inserted into the "LDELAY" macro and the low-level code can be reassembled. For complete accuracy, the execution times of the other instructions surrounding the macro should be included in the execution time calculations.

To summarize, the speed of the PC used to host the digitizer must be taken into consideration when fine tuning the low-level driver software. Three different macros must be altered, depending upon the speed of the processor. Guidelines are given for the proper alterations of these macros.

The "ImageReq" Data Structure

The "ImageReq" data structure, which follows, is the mechanism by which the high-level C software controls the operation of the digitizer hardware. It forms the software interface between the high-level and low-level code. Manipulation of this data structure allows a wide variation in the resultant digitized image. All member items are configurable within the "ImageReq" structure. The effect of varying these items will be discussed shortly.

```
/* Image Request Structure passed between C and AL to control digitizer */

struct ImageReq
{
    enum Computer   ComputerType;   /* currently not used */
    unsigned        PrtBase;        /* base address of printer port */
    enum HorizMode  HMode;          /* low 320/high 640 resolution
    enum VertMode   VMode;          /* non interlaced 200/interlaced 480 */
    unsigned        NumberOfPasses; /* currently not used */
    unsigned long   Flags;          /* currently not used */
```

```
        char huge      *PictBuf;          /* offset/segment of image buffer ptr */
        unsigned       FirstLine;         /* 1st line of video to digitize */
        unsigned       FirstPixel;        /* 1st pixel of 1st line */
        unsigned       LastLine;          /* last line of video to digitize */
        unsigned       LastPixel;         /* last pixel of last line */
    };
```

You'll notice some of the named members of this data structure are labeled *currently not used*. They are included for future enhancements to the low-level digitizing software and will not be discussed further. This data-structure definition is found in the file "digitize.h" included on the companion disk and shown in Listing 4.1.

Listing 4.1   The Low-Level Digitizer Driver Code

The following is the contents of the file, "digitize.h":

```
/****************************************/
/*       Digitizer Header File       */
/*    for inclusion into C programs   */
/*       written in Turbo C 2.0       */
/*                by                 */
/*       Craig A. Lindley            */
/*  Vers: 1.0  Last Update: 12/07/89  */
/****************************************/

#ifndef __BYTE                     /* user defined type */
#define __BYTE
typedef unsigned char BYTE;
#endif

#define TRUE   1
#define FALSE  0
#define VIDEO 0x10          /* Video BIOS interrupt number */
#define LPT1  0x3BC         /* LPT1 base address */

typedef enum {BW,Color}                              CMode;
typedef enum {GCAL,CGAH,EGAL,EGAH,VGAL,VGAM,VGAH}    Display;
typedef enum {PC477,AT6,AT8,PS210,PS216,PS220,PS225,PS233} Computer;
typedef enum {LowRes,HighRes}                        HorizMode;
typedef enum {NonInterlace,Interlace}                VertMode;

/* Image Request Structure passed between C and AL to control digitizer */
struct ImageReq
```

```
{
    enum Computer   ComputerType;
    unsigned        PrtBase;
    enum HorizMode  HMode;
    enum VertMode   VMode;
    unsigned        NumberOfPasses;
    unsigned long   Flags;
    char huge       *PictBuf;
    unsigned        FirstLine;
    unsigned        FirstPixel;
    unsigned        LastLine;
    unsigned        LastPixel;
};


/* function declarations */
unsigned InitializeDigitizer (struct ImageReq *);
void     SetPixelCount (unsigned short);
unsigned short SyncsPerField (void);
unsigned GetPicture (void);
```

The following is the contents of the file, "digitize.asm":

```
;Generic Video Digitizer Routines in Turbo C - Computer Independent
;
; This version utilizes the 8253 timer/counter to time the sync pulses
; and should therefore be somewhat PC independent.
;
; written by Craig A. Lindley
; last update: 05/17/89
;
;NOTE: most code in this file is written as inline code for speed reasons.
;       Any change to this structure might stop the digitizer from working.
;       Any change in register usage might also cause it to stop working.
;       Be careful changing the parameter passing linkage with C.
;
_TEXT segment     byte public 'CODE'
      DGROUP      group  _DATA,_BSS
      assume      cs:_TEXT,ds:DGROUP,ss:DGROUP
_TEXT ends

_DATA   segment word public 'DATA'
;
```

(continued)

Listing 4.1 *(continued)*

```
Field1Found      DW      False     ;True after field 1 of video located
Field1Done       DW      False     ;True after field 1 has been digitized

PrtPortData      DW      0         ;data output port
PrtPortIn        DW      0         ;data input port (5 bits)
PrtPortCont      DW      0         ;cont lines output port
ImageReqPtr      DW      0         ;ImageReq structure pointer passed from C
DigitInit        DW      False     ;True when digitizer has been initialized
CompType         DW      0         ;Holds type of PC configured
;
;these variables are only used when digitizing an Interlaced image. They
;contain the address of where the next column of digitized video will be
;stored. they are necessary because Interlaced data in a single frame must
;be stored in sequential locations in the picture buffer. because two passes
;through the picture buffer are necessary it is necessary to save when the
;next column of video should be stored when we get to digitizing it.
;
PColSeg          DW      0         ;Segment for storage for this column of video
PColOff          DW      0         ;Offset in PColSeg for this column storage
;
_DATA    ends


_BSS     segment word public 'BSS'
_BSS     ends
;
;
;General Definitions
;
True             EQU     0FFH      ;all ones is true
False            EQU     0         ;all zeros is false
SegOff           EQU     (0FFFFH/10H)+1  ;paragraphs/segment
;
;PrtPortCont bit definitions
;
Strobe           EQU     1         ;used to latch pixel count data
SyncReset        EQU     2         ;reset for sync latch
Go               EQU     4         ;starts pixel counter
HighLow          EQU     8         ;selects highlow pixel count latch
                                   ;and highlow output data
PrtPortContSafe  EQU     0BH       ;when written to PrtPortCont
                                   ;forces all bits (4) to zero. Go bit
                                   ;is special because it has inverter
                                   ;in the hardware.
```

```
;Bit combinations
;
SetGo                   EQU     PrtPortContSafe OR  Go
SetStrobe               EQU     PrtPortContSafe AND NOT Strobe
SetHighLow              EQU     PrtPortContSafe AND NOT HighLow
SetHighLowAndGo         EQU     PrtPortContSafe AND NOT HighLow OR Go
SetSyncReset            EQU     PrtPortContSafe AND NOT SyncReset
SetHighLowAndStrobe     EQU     PrtPortContSafe AND NOT HighLow AND NOT Strobe
SetSyncResetAndGo       EQU     PrtPortContSafe AND NOT SyncReset OR Go
ResetSyncAndEOC         EQU     PrtPortContSafe AND NOT SyncReset AND NOT HighLow
;
;PrtPortIn bit definitions
;
SyncEOC        EQU      8       ;bit monitored to detect sync
                                ;and end of conversion (EOC).
;
;Video specific definitions
;
HBlankingOffset EQU     47      ;additional count required for horiz
                                ;blanking. 3.81 usec from rising edge
                                ;of sync pulse at 12.38 MHz.
VBlankingOffset EQU     16      ;sync pulses to consume before active
                                ;video in field.
SyncsField1    EQU      272     ;Number of sync pulses in field 1
SyncsField2    EQU      271     ;ditto for field 2
;
;ImageReq definitions
;
;This structure is sent to this code from the high level C code to tell the
;digitizer what to digitize. This declaration does not allocate space, it
;just defines the offsets of the various fields. It must correspond exactly
;with the C structure ImageReq defined in the file gvideo.h for things to
;work properly.
;
ImageReq  struc
;
ComputerType    DW      0       ;used to adjust delays according to CPU speed
PrtBase         DW      0       ;printer port to use with digitizer
HMode           DW      0       ;low or high resolution mode selector 320/640
                                ;pixels per line.
VMode           DW      0       ;non Interlace or Interlace mode. 200/480
                                ;lines per frame of video.
NumberOfPasses  DW      0       ;determines number of passes across video
```

(continued)

Listing 4.1   *(continued)*

```
Flags             DD      0       ;misc flags
PictBufOff        DW      0       ;Offset/Segment of picture buffer
PictBufSeg        DW      0
FirstLine         DW      0       ;digitized portion of video selectors
FirstPixel        DW      0
LastLine          DW      0
LastPixel         DW      0
;
ImageReq    ends
;
;The following are the equates for the various PC types. The delay MACROs
;must be adjusted to the speed of the PC. These are used to decode the
;configured type of PC and adjust the delay MACROs accordingly. These are
;all possible entries into the ComputerType field of the ImageReq.
;
PC477             EQU     0
PCAT6             EQU     1
PCAT8             EQU     2
PS210             EQU     3
PS216             EQU     4
PS220             EQU     5
PS225             EQU     6
PS233             EQU     7

LowRes            EQU     0       ;320 pixels/line
HighRes           EQU     1       ;640 pixels/line
NonInterlace      EQU     0       ;acquire a single field of video
Interlace         EQU     1       ;acquire a frame of video
;
;
;8253 Timer Definitions
;Timer 2 is used for the timing of the sync pulses. This is a more accurate
;method than a software loop. All PCs have this timer/counter available
;it is normally used to produce the beep for the keyboard.
;
;The following are timer and I/O port addresses
;
Timer2CountReg EQU      42H      ;used to set counter values
TimerCmdReg    EQU      43H      ;used to send mode cmds to timer chip
Timer2GateReg  EQU      61H      ;gate reg 8255s address
TermBitReg     EQU      62H      ;term bit reg 8255s address
;
```

```
;The following are bit assignments, masks and mode bytes
;
TimerCount      EQU        18   ;at 840 nsec period =~ 15 usec
Timer2GateBit   EQU       01H   ;gate is bit 0 of 8255 port
TermCntBitMask  EQU       20H   ;term bit is bit 5 of 8255 port
Timer2Mode      EQU       0B2H  ;timer 2 select; load LSB then MSB
                                ;counter mode = 1; binary counter
;
_TEXT   segment byte public 'CODE'
;
;Delay MACROs
;
;Short delay. This is used to allow the computers bus to recover between
;sequential accesses of the same I/O port.
;
SDelay  MACRO
        jmp     short $+2
        jmp     short $+2
        ENDM
;
;Strobe delay. This is used to make sure the software generated strobes are
;long enough for the hardware to see.
;
StbDel  MACRO
        push    ax
        pop     ax
        push    ax
        pop     ax
        push    ax
        pop     ax
        push    ax
        pop     ax
        ENDM
;
;Start of Assembly Language Procedures
;
;
; Procedure InitializeTimer2
;
; This procedure sets up the 8253 timer for use as a sync timer. Mode 1 of
; the counter is utilized. In this mode, when the gate signal transitions
; from a low to a high level, the counter is loaded with a previously set
; value and the counter starts counting down towards zero. When zero is
```

(continued)

Listing 4.1 *(continued)*

```
; reached, the terminal bit goes from a low to a high level. This procedure
; sets the mode for timer 2 and sets in the count for use by the Delay
; procedure.
;
; INPUT:  none.
; OUTPUT: none but timer 2 is initialized and the count is loaded.
; USES:   ax register.
; CALL:   not callable from C.
;
;
InitializeTimer2  proc  near
;
        mov     al,Timer2Mode       ;load mode value
        out     TimerCmdReg,al      ;send it to the 8253

        SDelay

        mov     ax,TimerCount       ;get the timers count
        out     Timer2CountReg,al   ;set the LSB of the count

        SDelay

        mov     al,ah               ;get the MSB of count
        out     Timer2CountReg,al   ;set the MSB of the count

        ret
;
InitializeTImer2  endp
;
; Procedure Delay
;
; This procedure uses timer 2 to delay for approximately 15 microseconds
; time it is called.
;
; INPUT:  none.
; OUTPUT: none but timer 2 is used to produce a delay
; USES:   ax register
; CALL:   not callable from C.
;
;
Delay   proc  near
;
```

```
        push    dx                    ;save register
        in      al,Timer2GateReg      ;read the 8255 port

        SDelay

        and     al,NOT Timer2GateBit  ;set bit 0 low
        out     Timer2GateReg,al      ;set gate bit low at timer 2

        SDelay

        or      al,Timer2GateBit      ;set bit 0 high
        out     Timer2GateReg,al      ;set gate bit high at timer 2

        SDelay

Del1:   in      al,TermBitReg         ;read the terminal bit port
        and     al,TermCntBitMask     ;is the timer period over ?
        jnz     Del2                  ;if yes jmp

        SDelay

        jmp     short Del1
;
Del2:   SDelay
        pop     dx                    ;restore register
        ret
;
Delay   endp
;
;
; Procedure InitializeDigitizer
;
; This procedure initializes the digitizer hardware in preparation
; for usage. It is necessary to set the bits in the PrtPortCont latch
; to initialize digitizer. The HighLow line must be strobed to clear
; the SyncEOC line (because the EOC latch is then reset). If this is not
; done it is possible that the SyncEOC line will remain in a low state
; forever not allowing the Sync signal to leave the digitizer.
;
; INPUT:  near pointer to the ImageReq data structure.
; OUTPUT: none but the digitizer hardware is initialized.
; USES:   ax,bx,dx registers.
```

(continued)

Listing 4.1 *(continued)*

```
; CALL:    callable from C.
; PROTOTYPE: InitializeDigitizer(sturct ImageReq *)
;
;
        Public  _InitializeDigitizer
;
_InitializeDigitizer  proc  near
;
        push    bp                   ;prepare to retrieve the near pointer
        mov     bp,sp                ;to the ImageReq structure
;
;get and store the pointer from C which points at the ImageReq structure
;
        mov     bx,[bp+4]            ;bx pts at ImageReq
        mov     ImageReqPtr,bx       ;save in local var
;
;first thing to do is to retrieve the address of the printer port to use
;for the digitizer. we must know this for any communication with the
;digitizer. with the base address ,PrtBase, of the port known, we can easily
;calculate the other important port addresses.
;
        mov     ax,[bx].PrtBase      ;get port number to use
        mov     PrtPortData,ax
        inc     ax                   ;port+1= PrtPortIn
        mov     PrtPortIn,ax
        inc     ax                   ;port+2= PrtPortCont
        mov     PrtPortCont,ax
        mov     ax,[bx].ComputerType ;read the computer type
        mov     CompType,ax          ;store locally in ds
;
;now start the initialization of the digitizer hardware
;
        mov     dx,PrtPortCont       ;pt at control latch bits
        mov     al,PrtPortContSafe   ;initialize control bits
        out     dx,al                ;sent to the digitizer
;
        call    Delay                ;let things stabilize
;
        mov     al,ResetSyncAndEOC   ;set HighLow bit high
        out     dx,al                ;to clear EOC input to

        StbDel
;
```

```
        mov     al,PrtPortContSafe  ;initialize control bits
        out     dx,al               ;sent to the digitizer

        SDelay

        mov     ax,0                ;set pixel count to 0
        call    SetPixelCount       ;send to hardware counters
        SDelay

        call    InitializeTimer2    ;initialize the sync timer
        mov     DigitInit,True      ;indicate the digitizer has been
                                    ;initialized.
        pop     bp                  ;restore bp to enable a return
        ret                         ;to C code.
;
_InitializeDigitizer   endp
;
;
; Procedure _SyncsPerField
;
; This procedure counts the number of sync pulses (of all variety) that
; occur in a single field of video. It must do its counting in 1/30 of
; a second field time. Field 1 should contain 272 syncs while field 2
; should contain 271.
;
; INPUT:  none.
; OUTPUT: number of syncs in the monitored field returned in ax.
; USES:   ax,cx,dx registers. bx perserved.
; CALL:   callable from C.
; PROTOTYPE: unsigned short SyncsPerField ( void )
;
        Public   _SyncsPerField
;
_SyncsPerField  proc  near
;
        cli                         ;interrupts off
        call    SyncsPerField       ;count them
        sti                         ;ints back on
        ret
;
_SyncsPerField  endp
;
;
```

(continued)

Listing 4.1 *(continued)*

```
; Procedure SyncsPerField
;
; See discussion above
;
; INPUT:  none.
; OUTPUT: number of syncs in the monitored field returned in ax.
; USES:   ax,cx,dx registers. bx perserved.
; CALL:   not callable from C.
;
;
SyncsPerField  proc  near
;
        push    bx                  ;save register
        mov     bx,7                ;initialize count to include all
                                    ;vertical syncs will will miss
        mov     dx,PrtPortCont      ;pt at control register
        mov     al,ResetSyncAndEOC  ;hold sync latch and EOC reset
        out     dx,al               ;so only actual sync signal will
                                    ;be seen by the hardware.
        SDelay
;
;read SyncEOC line to see if it is low
;
        dec     dx                  ;pt back at PrtPortIn
spf1:   in      al,dx               ;read data in
        and     al,SyncEOC
        jz      spf1                ;jump if SyncEOC is still low.
;
;check once again. A vertical sync interval would never be high two
;reads in a row.
;
        call    Delay
        in      al,dx
        and     al,SyncEOC
        jz      spf1                ;jump if long sync. Line still low.

        SDelay
;
;when we get here a short sync interval has been detected. Now find
;the first long sync (vertical sync) interval with which to start the
;sync count.
;
```

```
        call    FindLongSync
;
;1st long sync pulse found. Advance to 1st short sync interval
;
spf2:   in      al,dx
        and     al,SyncEOC
        jz      spf2            ;jump if SyncEOC is still low.
;
;check again.
;
        call    Delay
        in      al,dx
        and     al,SyncEOC
        jz      spf2            ;jump if long sync. Line still low.

        SDelay
;
;short sync interval found again. Count up all syncs until new long sync
;is found. This indicates end of field.
;
spf3:   in      al,dx           ;read input port
        and     al,SyncEOC      ;mask all but sync bit
        jnz     spf3            ;loop until bit active (low)

        SDelay
;
;Sync latch has gone low. Reset it.
;
        inc     dx              ;now pt dx at PrtPortCont for output
        mov     al,ResetSyncAndEOC;set SyncReset high
        out     dx,al           ;do it

        StbDel

        mov     al,PrtPortContSafe;end SyncReset pulse
        out     dx,al           ;do it
;
;read again. Short syncs should be gone
;
        call    Delay
        dec     dx              ;pt back at PrtPortIn
        in      al,dx
        and     al,SyncEOC
```

(continued)

Listing 4.1 *(continued)*

```
        jz      spf4            ;we're done when long sync detected
        inc     bx              ;count the short sync
        jmp     spf3            ;continue looking for long
;
spf4:   inc     dx              ;pt at control port
        mov     al,ResetSyncAndEOC;set Sync and EOC reset high
        out     dx,al

        SDelay

        dec     dx              ;pt back at input
;
        mov     ax,bx           ;result in ax for return
        pop     bx
        ret
;
SyncsPerField   endp
;
;
; Procedure FindLongSync
;
; Assumes it is called during active video line. That is, short syncs
; are being detected. In the routine, we set the sync reset line and the
; EOC reset line (HighLow) and leave them. We are only interested in the
; detection of long (vertical) sync periods so we don't need the assistance
; of the on board sync latch IC8a. Setting these lines guarantees that only
; the actual sync pulse will be seen on the SyncEOC line. This saves us
; the time in resetting the latch inside of the loop.
;
; INPUT:  none
; OUTPUT: none but returns when long sync interval detected
; USES:   ax, dx registers
; CALL:   not callable from C.
; PROTOTYPE: none
;
FindLongSync    proc  near
;
        mov     dx,PrtPortCont  ;pt at control port
        mov     al,ResetSyncAndEOC;set both sync and EOC reset bits
        out     dx,al

        SDelay
```

```
        dec     dx                      ;pt at input port
fls1:   in      al,dx                   ;read input port
        and     al,SyncEOC              ;mask all but sync bit
        jnz     fls1                    ;loop until bit active (low)
;
;Sync latch has gone low. By the time we realize it and read port again
;all short syncs should be gone.
;
        call    Delay                   ;wait 15 usec to be sure
        in      al,dx                   ;read SyncEOC line again to be sure
        and     al,SyncEOC
        jnz     fls1                    ;loop if line is now high => short
;
;when we get here long sync interval has been detected and we're done
;
        SDelay
        ret
;
FindLongSync    endp
;
;
; Procedure SetPixelCount
;
; This procedure sets the pixel counter latch on the digitizer board to
; the 16 bit value in the ax register. The digitizer hardware only uses
; 12 of the 16 bits at this time.
;
; INPUT:  pixel count in ax
; OUTPUT: none
; USES:   ax,cx,dx registers
; CALL:   not callable from C.
;
;
SetPixelCount   proc    near
;
        mov     cx,ax                   ;save pixel count in cx reg
;
        mov     dx,PrtPortData          ;pt at output data port
        mov     al,cl                   ;get LS byte of count
        out     dx,al                   ;write LS byte of pixel count

        StbDel
```

(continued)

Listing 4.1 *(continued)*

```
    mov     dx,PrtPortCont      ;pt at control port to strobe counters
    mov     al,SetStrobe        ;start the stobe pulse
    out     dx,al

    StbDel

    mov     al,PrtPortContSafe;strobe ended
    out     dx,al

    SDelay

    mov     dx,PrtPortData      ;pt at data port again
    mov     al,ch               ;get MSB of original pixel count
    out     dx,al               ;send to pixel counter

    StbDel

    mov     dx,PrtPortCont      ;pt at control port to set HighLow high
    mov     al,SetHighLow
    out     dx,al

    StbDel

    mov     al,SetHighLowAndStrobe  ;strobe into counters
    out     dx,al
    StbDel

    mov     al,SetHighLow       ;reset Strobe leave HighLow still high
    out     dx,al

    StbDel

    mov     al,SetSyncReset     ;reset sync latch
    out     dx,al

    StbDel

    mov     al,PrtPortContSafe;HighLow now low
    out     dx,al

    SDelay

    ret
```

```
;
SetPixelCount  endp
;
;
; Procedure _SetPixelCount
;
; C callable version of above.
;
; INPUT:  pixel count
; OUTPUT: none
; USES:   ax,cx,dx registers
; CALL:   callable from C.
; PROTOTYPE: void SetPixelCount ( unsigned short )
;
;
        Public  _SetPixelCount
;
_SetPixelCount  proc  near
;
        push    bp
        mov     bp,sp
        mov     ax,[bp+4]
        call    SetPixelCount
        pop     bp
        ret
;
_SetPixelCount  endp
;
;
; Procedure _GetPicture
;
; This procedure digitizes a complete monochrome picture. It stores
; the data for the picture in a buffer whos address is passed to it from C.
; The function InitializeDigitizer must be called before this one so that
; the hardware and software are setup correctly. All instructions for how
; the digitizer should digitize a picture are contained in the ImageReq
; data structure.
;
; INPUT:  BX is a near pointer to the ImageReq structure which contains all
;         the information for the control of the digitizer.
; OUTPUT: returns True is picture data in buffer, False if error
; USES:   all registers. saves bp,si and di registers as required by Turbo C
; CALL:   callable from C.
; PROTOTYPE: GetPicture();
```

(continued)

Listing 4.1 *(continued)*

```
;
        PUBLIC  _GetPicture
;
_GetPicture  proc  near
;
        cmp     DigitInit,True      ;has digitizer been initialized ?
        je      gp1                 ;continue if so
        mov     ax,False            ;return a false indication to C
        ret

gp1:    push    bp                  ;save for use by C
        push    si                  ;save si,di in case register vars
        push    di                  ;used in C code.
;
        mov     bx,ImageReqPtr      ;get ImageReq pointer into bx for use
                                    ;all struct references use bx as ptr
        mov     es,[bx].PictBufSeg  ;point es:bp at picture data buffer
        mov     bp,[bx].PictBufOff

        mov     PColSeg,es          ;establish addr of 1st video column
        mov     PColOff,bp

        mov     Field1Done,False    ;indicate field 1 not yet digitized
        mov     Field1Found,False   ;and has not been found yet

        mov     si,[bx].FirstPixel  ;get the first pixels (column) #
        cmp     [bx].HMode,LowRes   ;320 pixel line ?
        jne     gp2                 ;jump if not
        shl     si,1                ;if 320 pixel line pixel # * 2

gp2:    add     si,HBlankingOffset  ;add in the blanking interval
;
;this is the top of the loop which digitizes a complete column of pixels
;from the video signal. CPU register si is the pixel count across a line
;whereas register di is the line count down the video image.
;
gp3:    mov     Field1Done,False    ;false until field 1 has been done
        mov     di,[bx].FirstLine   ;initialize line count to that
                                    ;specified in the ImageReq every
                                    ;time thru this loop
        mov     es,PColSeg          ;get address of this column
        mov     bp,PColOff
;
```

```
          mov     ax,si               ;get pixel count
          call    SetPixelCount       ;load hardware pixel counters
;
gp4:      cmp     Field1Found,True    ;have we located desired field before?
          je      gp7                 ;if yes just find long sync interval
;
;when we get here we need to find the start of the first field at least once
;
gp5:      cli                         ;interrupts off from now on
          call    SyncsPerField       ;locate field 1
          cmp     ax,SyncsField2      ;are we there ?
          jmp     gp6                 ;if start of field 1 then jump
          sti                         ;interrupts back on
          call    Delay               ;delay for short period
          call    Delay               ;delay for short period
          call    Delay               ;delay for short period
          jmp     short gp5           ;repeat until we find it
;
;start of first field found
;
gp6:      mov     Field1Found,True    ;indicate it was found
          jmp     short gp8
;
;when we get here we just need to find the start of every subsequent
;even or odd field
;
gp7:      cli                         ;interrupts off from here on
          mov     di,[bx].FirstLine   ;initialize line count
          call    FindLongSync        ;find vertical sync period
;
;when we get here we have located the start of a field. NOTE: both the
;Sync and the EOC reset lines are still held active because we are not
;afraid of missing a short sync. That is, we are still only interested in
;long sync intervals. In the code that follows, we will
;continuously read the input port until we see it go high indicating a
;short sync has been detected. At that point we are past all of the long
;sync pulses and can start counting out the vertical blanking interval.
;
gp8:      in      al,dx
          and     al,SyncEOC
          jz      gp8                 ;jump if SyncEOC is still low.
;
;check once more
```

(continued)

Listing 4.1 *(continued)*

```
;
        call    Delay               ;delay 15 usec to be sure its gone
        in      al,dx
        and     al,SyncEOC
        jz      gp8                 ;jump if long sync. Line still low.

        SDelay
;
;we've just found the 1st short sync interval. Its probably an equalization
;pulse. We must now consume all of the equalization and vertical blanking
;pulses to get to the start of the active video.
;
        inc     dx                  ;pt at control port
        mov     al,PrtPortContSafe;end SyncReset pulse
        out     dx,al               ;so we can use latch to find all
                                    ;syncs no matter how small
        SDelay

        dec     dx                  ;pt back at input port
;
;count off the number of lines in the field to ignore. If a full field/frame
;picture is being digitized then ignore only VBlankingOffset number. If a
;partial picture is being digitized, ignore VBlankingOffset + FirstLine number
;of lines.
;
        mov     cx,VBlankingOffset;consume this many on default picture
;
;check for field 2 digitization
;
        cmp     Field1Done,True     ;are we digitizing field 2 ?
        jne     gp9                 ;jmp if not
        inc     cx                  ;if we are consume one more sync
                                    ;pulse to get rid of 1/2 line
gp9:    cmp     [bx].FirstLine,0    ;req pict starts at line 0 ?
        je      gp10                ;jmp if so
        add     cx,[bx].FirstLine   ;else add in additional lines to ignor

gp10:   in      al,dx               ;read input port
        and     al,SyncEOC          ;mask all but sync bit
        jnz     gp10                ;loop until sync seen

        SDelay
;
```

```
;Sync latch has gone low. Reset it.
;
        inc     dx                ;now pt dx at PrtPortCont for output
        mov     al,ResetSyncAndEOC;set SyncReset high
        out     dx,al             ;do it

        StbDel

        mov     al,PrtPortContSafe  ;end SyncReset pulse
        out     dx,al               ;do it

        SDelay
;
;Sync latch is now reset. SyncEOC line should go inactive (high) shortly
;because we are expecting only short sync pulses.
;
        dec     dx                ;pt at PrtPortIn
        dec     cx                ;one less sync to consume
        jnz     gp10              ;still more ?
;
;we have now consumed all the vertical blanking sync pulses. Set Go so
;pixel counters will be triggered on rising edge of sync pulse from camera.
;
        inc     dx                ;pt at control port
        mov     al,SetGo          ;set the go bit so counters will be
        out     dx,al             ;triggered by rising edge of sync

        SDelay

        dec     dx                ;pt at input port
;
;we are now at the start of the active video line. We must now process each
;digitization in less than one line time of 63.5 usec.
;
gp11:   in      al,dx             ;look for falling edge of sync pulse
        and     al,SyncEOC
        jnz     gp11

        SDelay
;
;line started with falling edge of SyncEOC
;
```

(continued)

Listing 4.1 *(continued)*

```
        inc     dx                  ;pt at Cont port
        mov     al,SetSyncResetAndGo  ;reset sync latch and keep Go
                                    ;line high to start pixel count
        out     dx,al               ;on rising edge of every sync
        StbDel

        mov     al,SetGo            ;end SyncReset but leave Go active
        out     dx,al               ;do it

        SDelay
;
;Sync latch is now reset and pixel counters should be running.
;SyncEOC line should go active (low) shortly when the converted data becomes
;available.
;
        dec     dx                  ;pt at PrtPortIn
gp12:   in      al,dx               ;read input port
        mov     cl,al               ;copy data to cl reg
        and     al,SyncEOC          ;mask all but EOC bit
        jnz     gp12                ;loop until data ready

        SDelay
;
;we now have four bits of the video digital data in cl register as follows:
;         7 6 5 4 3 2 1 0
;         D D D D EOC X X X
;after we shift it right four places it looks like
;         7 6 5 4 3 2 1 0
;         0 0 0 0 D D D D
;
        shr     cl,1
        shr     cl,1
        shr     cl,1
        shr     cl,1
;
;prepare to retrieve the MS nibble of data from the digitizer
;
        inc     dx                  ;pt at Cont port
        mov     al,SetHighLowAndGo  ;set High/Low high to get 2 MSBs.
        out     dx,al               ;this also resets EOC

        SDelay
```

```
          dec      dx

          in       al,dx            ;get the two MSBs
          and      al,30H           ;mask all but bits of interest
          or       cl,al            ;combine to get 6 total bits/pixel
;
          mov      es:[bp],cl       ;store all 6 bits of data
;
;
gp13:     inc      dx               ;pt at Cont port
          mov      al,SetGo         ;HighLow low again leave Go active
          out      dx,al            ;do it
          dec      dx
;
;check to see if pointer for data storage (bp register) will leave a 64K
;segment. If so the segment register must be adjusted by SEGOFF so
;offset 0 into the segment points at the next available byte of storage.
;NOTE: when digitizing an interlaced picture, where it is necessary to
;skip every other location in the picture buffer, the check for segment end
;must be slightly different. To accomodate this, the code that follows is
;executed conditionally depending upon interlaced digitization or not.
;
          cmp      [bx].VMode,Interlace  ;are we in interlace mode ?
          je       gp15             ;jmp if so
;
;when we get here we are in non Interlace mode
;
          cmp      bp,0FFFFH        ;at end of seg ?
          jne      gp14             ;jump if not
          mov      ax,es            ;get seg reg value
          add      ax,SEGOFF        ;add offset
          mov      es,ax            ;store it back
                                    ;segment offset will inc to 0000
;
;check to see if we are done with a column of pixels
;
gp14:     inc      bp               ;bump the data pointer
          inc      di               ;inc the line count
          cmp      di,[bx].LastLine ;bottom of picture ?
          jb       gp11
;
          mov      PColSeg,es       ;save ptr to next storage location
          mov      PColOff,bp
```

(continued)

Listing 4.1 *(continued)*

```
;
        jmp     gp19            ;jmp to common exit code
;
;when we get here we are in Interlace mode
;
gp15:   cmp     bp,0FFFEH       ;at end of seg ?
        jb      gp16            ;jump if not
        mov     ax,es           ;get seg reg value
        add     ax,SEGOFF       ;add offset
        mov     es,ax           ;store it back
                                ;seg offset will inc to 0000
;
gp16:   inc     bp              ;bump the data pointer
        inc     bp              ;and again to leave room for data from
                                ;other field
        inc     di              ;inc the line count
        mov     ax,[bx].LastLine ;get last line of Interlaced frame
        shr     ax,1            ;divide by two for last line per field
        cmp     di,ax           ;bottom of field ?
        jae     gp17
        jmp     gp11
;
;we are now done with one field of video for the Interlaced image. Go
;back and digitize the other field.
;
gp17:   cmp     Field1Done,True ;done with this column in both fields ?
        je      gp18            ;jmp if so
;
;when we get here we know we need to go back and do the other field
;
        mov     Field1Done,True ;set flag to say we're finished on
                                ;next pass
        mov     es,PColSeg      ;reload this columns pointer
        mov     bp,PColOff
;
        inc     bp              ;bump one to miss data from other
                                ;field
        jmp     gp7             ;get next fields data
;
gp18:   mov     PColSeg,es      ;save addr of where next columns
        dec     bp
        mov     PColOff,bp      ;data should start
```

```
;
;we are now done with a column of the video display. Advance to next pixel
;or next column. This is true for both Interlace and non Interlace
;digitizations.
;
gp19:   inc     dx                      ;pt at Cont port
        mov     al,PrtPortContSafe;reset all control lines
        out     dx,al                   ;just to be safe
        SDelay
        sti                             ;interrupts back on because timing
                                        ;between frames is not that critical


        cmp     [bx].HMode,LowRes ;a 320 pixel picture ?
        jne     gp20                    ;jmp if not
;
;when we get here we know we are digitizing a 320 pixel line picture. we
;must increment the pixel count twice (two 640 pixels = one 320 pixel)
;and check to see if we are done digitizing a picture. this is complicated
;by the fact that the pixel counts are actually twice as big so we must
;compare with twice the LastPixel value.
;
        inc     si
        inc     si
        mov     ax,[bx].LastPixel ;get the final pixel count
        shl     ax,1                    ;* 2 for comparison
        add     ax,HBlankingOffset;added in blanking interval
        cmp     si,ax                   ;is the 320 pixel pict done ?
        jae     gp21                    ;jmp if so
        jmp     gp3                     ;if not do next pixel column
;
;when we get here we know we are digitizing a 640 pixel line picture. This
;is a much easier case than the 320 pixel picture shown above.
;
gp20:   inc     si                      ;bump pixel count once for high res
        mov     ax,[bx].LastPixel ;get last pixel #
        add     ax,HBlankingOffset;added in blanking interval
        cmp     si,ax                   ;is the 640 pixel pict done ?
        jae     gp21                    ;if so jump
        jmp     gp3                     ;if not do next pixel column
;
;a complete picture is now digitized. Prepare to return to C.
;
```

(continued)

Listing 4.1 *(continued)*

```
gp21:   pop     di
        pop     si
        pop     bp
        mov     ax,True          ;indicate no error to C
        ret
;
_GetPicture  endp
;
;End of video routines
;
_TEXT   ends
        end
```

Probably the most important item of data passed in the ''ImageReq'' data structure is the ''PrtBase''. This tells the low-level code to which printer port the digitizer is physically attached. The low-level code is flexible enough to work with any of the three standard printer ports supported by IBM PC. Valid values for this entry are:

```
LPT1 03BC hex
LPT2 0378 hex
LPT3 0278 hex
```

For the PS/2 model 60 and 70, LPT1 is the value used. On older PCs, the address of LPT2 is used. A digitizer could be attached to each of the three standard printer ports (if your PC has the required hardware) and the software could manage each separately. Once the low-level code receives the address of the printer port via the ''ImageReq'' structure, all other pertinent port addresses are calculated from it.

''PictBuf'' is a huge pointer to the buffer area where the digitized picture data should be stored by the low-level code. The C code treats this as one pointer value whereas the low-level code thinks of it as a two-byte segment value followed by a two-byte offset value. The definition of the ''ImageReq'' structure used by the C code and the assembler code reflect this difference.

The remaining entries in the ''ImageReq'' structure control the configuration of the acquired digitized image. Not all configurations make sense. Figure 4.2 shows some ''standard'' values for these configuration parameters and the image types produced. All configurations are based upon the standard video display modes provided by a VGA graphics adapter. For the purposes of this book, it does little good to acquire an image that we cannot display. For your reference, the maximum resolution of the digitizer is 640 × 488.

(*Note*: six bits are moved from the digitizer to the PC for each pixel sampled regardless of the resolution of the image acquired.)

Picture Type: 320 × 200 resolution acquired
                   Usually displayed as a 320 × 200 image on VGA display
                   Termed a *low-resolution* image in the text

ImageReq Member	
Name	*Value*
HMode	LowRes
VMode	NonInterlace
FirstLine	0
FirstPixel	0
LastLine	200
LastPixel	320

In this mode, 200 of the 244 visible video lines in a single video field are digitized. The last 44 visible video lines are not acquired by the digitizer (even though it is capable of acquiring them) because there are no standard video modes that can display these additional lines without impacting the aspect ratio of the image. Only one video field is digitized because "VMode" is set to "NonInterlace". All color images (without aspect ratio correction) are acquired in this resolution.

Picture Type: 320 × 200 resolution
                   Displayed as a 100 × 100-pixel image on VGA display
                   Referred to as a *focus window* image in the text

ImageReq Member	
Name	*Value*
HMode	LowRes
VMode	NonInterlace
FirstLine	50
FirstPixel	110
LastLine	150
LastPixel	210

In this mode, the digitizer acquires an image that is 100 pixels across by 100 lines down, centered in the middle of the video image. Because this smaller image can be acquired in a shorter amount of time, it can be used as a method of focusing the video camera as the acquired image is updated in near real time. Focus window software will be presented in the high-level software discussion in Chapter 5.

Figure 4.2 "ImageReq" Parameters   *(continued)*

Picture Type: 640 × 200 resolution
          Usually displayed as a 640 × 200 image on VGA display
          Termed a *medium-resolution* image in the text

ImageReq Member	
Name	*Value*
HMode	HighRes
VMode	NonInterlace
FirstLine	0
FirstPixel	0
LastLine	200
LastPixel	640

This mode is similar to the low-resolution mode shown earlier except that the resolution in the horizontal direction is doubled. Again, the last 44 lines of the digitized video field are lost.

Picture Type: 640 × 480 resolution
          Usually displayed as a 640 × 480 image on VGA display
          Termed a *high-resolution* image in the text

ImageReq Member	
Name	*Value*
HMode	HighRes
VMode	NonInterlace
FirstLine	0
FirstPixel	0
LastLine	480
LastPixel	640

This mode is the highest resolution mode supported by both the digitizer hardware and PS/2 VGA display. With interlace set, both fields in a video frame are digitized. This produces the highest-quality digital representation of the video image possible with this digitizer. Only four visible video lines in each field are not acquired while in this mode.

Figure 4.2 *(continued)*

Low-Level Support Functions

This section discusses the operation of the low-level image-acquisition software. The discussion will be kept at a relatively high level, with only the important concepts discussed in detail. Pseudocode is provided for each support function to help you visualize its operation. All of this software is written in 80 X 86 assembler language for speed. Those persons not familiar with 80 X 86 assembler language or the format of the assembler listings should seek one of the many good books available on this topic listed in "References and Additional Reading." The discussion to follow assumes some familiarity with these concepts.

The assembler code, shown in Listing 4.1, will not be discussed line by line in the text. Almost every line of assembler code is commented to provided documentation for itself. For this reason, please refer to the listing during the discussion. All of the low-level assembler code discussed in this section is included in the file "digitize.asm" on the companion disk.

Each low-level support function is called by either the high-level C code or the main low-level picture-acquisition routine "_GetPicture". These support functions interact directly with the digitizer hardware and with the hardware of the PC. This text discusses the support routines in the order in which they appear in the listing. The terms *routine, function*, and *procedure* are used synonymously throughout this discussion. They all refer to the same thing: a small section of code (assembler or high-level language) called as a subroutine that performs an operation and optionally returns a value to the calling code.

Any assembler language procedure that is prefixed with an underscore "_" (for example, "_GetPicture") is directly callable from C. Without the underscore, the linker will not be able to associate the C function call with the required assembler language function. Functions (or procedures or routines) that do not begin with an underscore can be called only within the assembler code.

The first support function, "InitializeTimer2", is used to initialize the 8253 timer/counter chip inside of the PC. Timer channel 2 of this chip is normally used to generate the audible tones produced by the PC. Since this is not a critical system function, the use of this timer channel has been preempted for use by the digitizer. Although not absolutely necessary for the operation of the digitizer, the timer provides a somewhat CPU speed-independent, 15-microsecond delay necessary for timing sync pulses. Specifically, the timer is used to distinguish the long vertical sync pulses from all of the other short sync pulses. On the slower machines (IBM PC, PC XT®, and PC AT®) use of the hardware timer is unnecessary because it takes longer than 15 microseconds to execute the instruction to access the timer. For these machines, the 15-microsecond delay can be performed more efficiently in software. See the previous section on CPU speed dependence for more information on this subject. Faster machines benefit from the use of the hardware timer.

"InitializeTimer2" places timer channel 2 into mode 1, which emulates a hardware monostable multivibrator or "one shot." In this mode, when the gate signal transitions from a low to a high level, the counter is loaded with a previously set count value and the counter starts counting down toward zero. When zero is reached, the terminal bit goes from a low to a high level. Pertinent timer information is shown in Figure 4.3. The design for this procedure is as follows:

```
Procedure InitializeTimer2 Pseudo Code
   Function - Initialize PC timer for digitizer usage
   Entry Parameters - None
   Exit  Parameters - None
   Interrupt Status - Unimportant
```

```
Begin procedure InitializeTimer2
  Get Timer2 mode value
  Output to Timer Command Register
  Get Timer2 delay count
  Output least significant byte to Timer Count Register
  Output most  significant byte to Timer Count Register
End procedure InitializeTimer2
```

"InitializeTimer2" first writes the mode word (B2 hex) for timer 2 into the timer command register (port 43 hex) and then the count (delay) value into the timer 2 count register. Timer 2 will retain this configuration until it is changed or the PC is power cycled. Given the frequency of the clock applied to the 8253 chip in the PC, a count value of 18 will yield a delay of approximately 15 microseconds. (*Note*: in a more rigorous design, the original count value and mode of timer 2 would be saved for restoration when operations with the digitizer were completed.)

The procedure "Delay" performs the actual time-delay function. Basically, "Delay" asserts the timer 2-gate bit and then enters a loop that will be exited when the timer 2 terminal coaunt bit goes active. Because this procedure is always called when the PC's interrupts are disabled, a very accurate time delay can be produced. On slower PCs, the timer may time out before the terminal bit can be examined. For this reason, the delay will vary depending on the speed of the PC. The delay will be slightly longer on slower PCs. For our application, any delay between about 5 and 25 microseconds will suffice for detecting vertical sync intervals in a video signal. The design is as follows:

```
Procedure Delay Pseudo Code
  Function - Provides approx. 15 microsecond delay
  Entry Parameters - None
  Exit  Parameters - None
  Interrupt Status - Disabled

Begin procedure Delay
  Force Timer2 gate bit low and then high to start Timer2
  While Timer2 terminal bit not set
    Read Terminal Bit Register
End procedure Delay
```

The procedure "_InitializeDigitizer" performs three basic functions. First, it retrieves a pointer to a "ImageReq" data structure from C that defines the image to be digitized. This NEAR pointer is retrieved from the stack via the standard method. A NEAR pointer, as you will recall from Chapter 1, is an offset into the data segment used by a small memory model program. A NEAR pointer can be used anytime the memory segment of the data is known implicitly, as it is in our case.

Once this pointer value is known, the second function of this procedure can be performed. That is, the extraction of the "PrtBase" value from the "ImageReq" data

a. Timer 2 in the PC is utilized for timing of video sync pulses.

b. Timer 2 is put into timer mode 1, which acts as hardware monostable multivibrator.

c. Timer 2 is clocked at 1.19318 MHz. The period is then 840 nanoseconds.

d. Bit 0 of 8255 Output Port at address 61 hex is gate control for timer 2.

e. Bit 5 of 8255 Input Port at address 62 hex is terminal count bit for timer 2.

f. Timer Command Register at address 43 hex is used to set timer mode configuration. Value used with the digitizer is B2 hex.

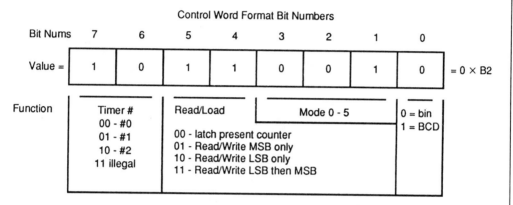

g. Timer Count Register at address 42 hex is written to in order to set the timer 2 terminal count. The least significant byte (LSB) of the count value is written first followed by the MSB of the count.

h. Timer 2 Operation Sequence
Timer 2 goes active on low to high transition of gate.
Timer 2 count value is reloaded and timer 2 starts counting toward 0.
Terminal bit goes active high when count = 0. Stays high until gate is triggered again.

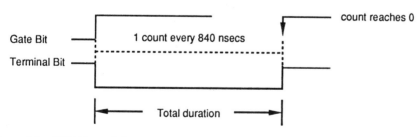

Figure 4.3 8253 Timer Information Summary

structure and subsequent calculation of the other pertinent printer port addresses. These addresses—"PrtPortData", "PrtPortIn", and "PrtPortCont"—define to which printer port the digitizer is attached and therefore how the software will interface to the hardware. These calculated values are stored locally for use throughout the digitizer low-level code.

Initialization of the digitizer hardware is the final function performed by '_Initializer''. A summary of the initialization is as follows:

a. All output control lines from the PC's printer port are placed into their nonasserted or safe state.

b. The sync detection latch and the EOC (end of conversion) latch are reset.

c. The pixel counters are initialized to a count of zero.

d. Timer 2 in the PC is initialized for use with the digitizer.

e. The flag "DigitInit" is set true, indicating that the digitizer hardware has been successfully initialized. (Actually, it indicates this procedure has been called prior to a call to the "_GetPicture" procedure.)

The delays spread throughout this procedure are there to give both the digitizer and the PC hardware a chance to stabilize after being accessed. This prevents glitches produced by the PC from propagating into the digitizer and upsetting its operation. The design of the "_InitializeDigitizer" function is as follows:

```
Procedure _InitializeDigitizer Pseudo Code
   Function - 1) retrieve ImageReq ptr from C
              2) calculate printer port addresses
              3) initialize digitizer hardware and PC timer


   Entry Parameters - None
   Exit  Parameters - None
   Interrupt Status - Unimportant


Begin procedure InitializeDigitizer
   Get NEAR pointer to ImageReq structure from C
   Get the PrtBase address from the ImageReq structure
   Calculate PrtPortData, PrtPortIn and PrtPortCont
   Safe all output lines to digitizer
   Reset sync detect and End of Conversion latches
   Safe all output lines to digitizer
   Set Pixel Counters to zero
   Initialize Timer2
   Set flag indicating initialization completed
End procedure InitializeDigitizer
```

Two versions of the "SyncsPerField" function exist. They are identical except that "_SyncsPerField" is callable from C directly and is used to verify correct operation of the digitizer. The other version, "SyncsPerField", is used by "_GetPicture" internally to locate the start of video field one. Synchronization of this procedure and the video signal is extremely time critical. For this reason, interrupts must be disabled in the PC while this code is executing. Otherwise, sync pulses might be lost while the PC serviced the interrupting devices. The number of sync pulse counted between vertical sync pulses (intervals) is returned by this function.

As mentioned in Chapter 2, field one of a video frame should have exactly 272 sync pulses, while field two should have exactly 271. For this reason, these are the only two values that should ever be returned by a call to either of the "SyncsPerField" functions. If values other than these are returned, the timing macros discussed in the section on CPU speed dependence should be varied until only these values are obtained (assuming, of course, that the digitizer hardware is working correctly).

The design of the "SyncsPerField" function is given next. It is important to understand that because vertical sync pulses are relatively long (27.1 microseconds), the sync-detector latch in the digitizer hardware does not need to be used to detect them. The code for this function reflects this fact. All other sync pulses are detected using the sync-detector hardware to avoid the possibility of missing a pulse. Equalizing pulses, for example, are 2.3 microseconds in duration. A software-only test for these short pulses might fail on slower PCs.

```
Procedure SyncsPerField Pseudo Code
   Function - counts sync pulses in a field of video
   Entry Parameters - None
   Exit  Parameters - returns count of pulses between
                      vertical sync pulses.
   Interrupt Status - Disabled


Begin procedure SyncsPerField
   Initialize return count to 7. These are the pulses which will
   be missed by this code.
   Hold the sync detector and EOC latch off so a vertical sync
   pulse can be detected directly by software.
   Find a short sync interval.
   Call FindLongSync to find the first long or vertical sync
   interval.
   Advance to the first short sync after vertical sync interval
   is located.
   While sync is not a vertical sync
      count += 1
   Return count
```

The function "FindLongSync" returns to the calling code when a long or vertical sync pulse is detected. All other shorter sync pulses are ignored. This function is used to detect the start of a new video field. The design is as follows:

```
Procedure FindLongSync Pseudo Code
   Function - Detects presence of a vertical sync pulse
   Entry Parameters - None
   Exit  Parameters - None
   Interrupt Status - Disabled
```

```
Begin procedure FindLongSync
   Hold the sync detector and EOC latch off so a vertical sync
   pulse can be detected directly by software.
   Repeat
      Read PrtPortIn
      While SyncEOC is high (no sync pulse is seen by the software)
         ReadPrtPortIn
      (sync pulse of some kind has been detected)
      Delay for 15 microseconds (all short syncs should be gone)
      Read PrtPortIn again
      (if SyncEOC still low, a vertical sync has been detected)
      (if SyncEOC high, must have been a short sync. Try again)
   Until vertical sync detected
End procedure FindLongSync
```

The function "SetPixelCount" sets the pixel count latch (actually two hardware latches) on the digitizer. The value loaded into the latch determines which column of video is to be digitized. Any count between 0 and 639 is valid. The pixel count latch is loaded by software once for each column of video digitized. The latch count is automatically loaded into the hardware pixel counters at the falling edge of each horizontal sync pulse, if the "Go" signal from the PC is active. The rising edge of the sync pulse starts the pixel counters counting down toward zero.

The pixel count latch is loaded in a two-step operation because a total of ten bits of count must be transferred over an eight-bit interface. The design given below shows how this is accomplished. This technique has also been discussed previously.

```
Procedure SetPixelCount Pseudo Code
   Function - Sets the pixel counter latches on the digitizer
   Entry Parameters - Desired pixel count to digitize
   Exit  Parameters - None
   Interrupt Status - Unimportant


Begin procedure SetPixelCount
   Output least significant byte of pixel count to PrtPortData
   output port. Data is then present on the inputs to the
   digitizers pixel count latch.
   Toggle Strobe bit to latch value.
   Output most significant byte (two bits) of pixel count
   to PrtPortData output port.
   Set High/Low bit high to select most significant
   portion of pixel count latch.
   Toggle Strobe bit again to latch value.
   Safe all output lines to digitizer.
End procedure SetPixelCount
```

The function "_GetPicture" is the main-image acquisition low-level software. It can be considered the device driver for the digitizer. Upon receiving instructions from the C code in the form of the "ImageReq" data structure, it will digitize the specified image or portion thereof and place the result into a buffer in memory. The resolution of the digitized image is controlled by parameters in the "ImageReq" data structure, as discussed previously. Each sampled pixel of the image will be given a six-bit value. Valid numerical values for a pixel are therefore 0 through 63.

Due to its flexibility, the operation of this function is quite involved. The code is not as structured as other code presented in this book because of timing constraints on the digitizing process. The listing and the pseudocode document how this codes operates. The key points of information listed here might not be obvious but are nonetheless very important to the operation of this function.

a. When digitizing in the interlaced video mode, the acquired pixel data for field one must be stored in *even* image buffer locations only. When the second field of the interlaced image is digitized, the pixel data will be stored in between the even pixel locations at the odd buffer locations. This will result in properly interlaced pixel data in the image buffer.

b. The first half line of field two of video is thrown away when in the interlaced video mode.

c. Two transfers are made between the digitizer and the PC for every pixel of digitized video. The first transfers the four least significant bits of the video data, the second transfers the two most significant bits. These are combined in software to form one six-bit pixel value, right justified in an eight-bit byte. The two byte transfers are necessary because of the lack of input lines to the PC.

d. Images digitized with a resolution of greater than 320 by 200 require more than a single segment of memory for storage. Code must be in place to manage smooth transitions between memory segments during the digitizing process in real time.

e. The digitizer handles 320 pixel lines by skipping every other sample of the video image. In other words, the digitizer does not know anything about 320 pixel lines. That mode is handled exclusively by the low-level software.

The design follows:

```
Procedure GetPicture Pseudo Code
   Function - Digitizes image described in ImageReq structure.
            Stores data in buffer indicated in ImageReq.
   Entry Parameters - None
   Exit  Parameters - None
   Interrupt Status - Unimportant


Begin procedure GetPicture
   Check for proper initialization of digitizer
   Exit if not initialized previously
   Retrieve image buffer address from ImageReq structure. Load
   into ES:BX registers and save locally.
   Indicate field one of video not yet done.
```

```
Get FirstPixel number from ImageReq
If image is LowRes (320 pixels)
  FirstPixel *= 2  (digitizer only understands 640 pixel lines)
Add Horizontal Blanking Offset to FirstPixel number
Loop (1)              (this loop digitizes a column of video)
  Indicate field one not yet found
  Get FirstLine to digitize from ImageReq
  Reload image buffer pointer into ES:BX registers from
  local storage.
  Load pixel counters with desired pixel number. This is the
  column of video to digitize.
  If field one has not yet been found
  Begin
    Loop
      Disable interrupts
      Call SyncsPerField to return sync count
      If field two located (next field will be number one)
        Exit loop
      Enable interrupts
      Delay for a time
    EndLoop
  End
  Indicate field one found
  Else field one has been located
  Begin
    Label gp7:
    Disable interrupts
    Load FirstLine of video to digitize
    Find a vertical sync pulse
  End

  (start of field located)
  Find first short sync pulse. This should be equalizing pulse
  Get Vertical Blanking Offset count
  If digitizing interlaced image and are doing field 2
    Add one to count to get rid of half line
  Get FirstLine number from ImageReq
  If FirstLine to digitize is not zero
    Add to number of lines to ignore
  While there are lines to ignore
    Wait for sync pulse
    Decrement count of lines to ignore
  Set Go line to the digitizer so pixel counters will be
  triggered on the rising edge of each sync pulse.
```

```
(now at start of active video line to digitize)
Loop (2)  (for each pixel in column of video)
  Wait for falling edge of horizontal sync pulse
  Reset sync detect latch keeping Go active
  Read PrtPortIn
  While SyncEOC line not active
    Read PrtPortIn
  (A to D is now done with conversion)
  Shift 4 LS bits of video data right four bit positions
  Set High/Low bit to retrieve 2 MS bits of video data
  Read 2 MSBs and combine with 4 LSBs to form 6 bits of
  video data.
  Store video data in buffer
  Reset High/Low bit
  (video sample now digitized and stored)
  If image is not interlaced
  Begin
    Check for byte end of memory segment in image buffer
    If at end of segment
      Bump segment value for next 64K block
    Increment data pointer into segment by 1
    Increment line counter by 1
    Exit loop (2) when LastLine digitized
    Save location in image buffer where last byte stored
  End
  Else image is interlaced
  Begin
    Check for word end of memory segment in image buffer
    If at end of segment
      Bump segment value for next 64K block
    Increment data pointer into segment by 2 to leave
    room for interlaced pixel data byte.
    Increment line counter by 1
    Get LastLine number
    Divide by 2 because of interlace
    Exit loop (2) when LastLine*2 = line digitized
    If this column in both fields not yet digitized
    Begin
      Indicate field one done
      Reload buffer pointer to beginning of data in buffer
      Bump buffer pointer by one to interlace digitized
      pixel data.
      Go to Label gp7
    End
```

```
          Else
              Store address of where next pixel should be stored
          End
      EndLoop (2)
      (done with column of video. Advance to next pixel column)
      Safe all output lines to digitizer.
      If LowRes picture (320 pixels)
      Begin
        Increment pixel count two times
        Get LastPixel count from ImageReq
        Multiply times two for comparison
        Add in Horizontal blanking offset
        Exit loop (1) if all pixels digitized
      End
      Else High Res picture (640 pixels)
      Begin
        Increment pixel count to next column
        Get LastPixel count from ImageReq
        Add in Horizontal blanking offset
        Exit loop (1) if all pixels digitized
      End
    EndLoop (1)
  End procedure GetPicture
```

Digitizer Testing Continued

With the low-level software explained, we can continue with the testing of your newly constructed digitizer. We need low-level software support to continue the testing process. As mentioned previously, the additional tests presented here are necessary only if the digitizer is not working correctly after performing all of the testing in Chapter 3. Two additional tests are offered.

The first test verifies that the low-level software in the PC can load the pixel count latch with the correct values. The symptoms of a problem with the pixel latch circuitry would be a digitized image which has portions that are repeated or that form a uniform pattern across the whole displayed image.

A program to test the pixel latch circuitry is shown in Listing 4.2 and is contained in the files "test1.c" and "test1.prj" on the companion disk. This program must be linked with the assembled low-level driver software "digitize.obj" to run successfully. This program and a meter are used to verify the correct operation of the pixel counter latch circuitry. It sequentially walks a high signal (one) across each of the ten latch outputs. The meter is used to verify the presence of the correct signal levels. When executing the program, check that the desired bit does indeed go high and all other bits are low. If all ten of the latch bits work correctly, it is safe to assume the pixel count latch circuitry is working correctly. If any of the

Listing 4.2   Digitizer Test Program One. Pixel-Count Latch Test

The following is the contents of the file, "test1.prj":

```
digitize.obj
test1          (digitize.h)
```

The following is the contents of the file, "test1.c":

```
/***********************************************************/
/***          Video Digitizer Test Program One      ***/
/***                 written in Turbo C             ***/
/***                        by                      ***/
/***                 Craig A. Lindley               ***/
/***                                                ***/
/***          Ver: 1.0    Last Update: 08/04/89     ***/
/***********************************************************/

#include <stdio.h>
#include <conio.h>

#include "digitizer.h"

#define MaxBitNum  9               /* 10 bit counter 0 .. 9 */

/*
This program is used to test the pixel count latches on the digitizer.
It will set each of the 10 bits high sequentially, so they can be
checked with a meter.
*/


void main( void )
{
   struct   ImageReq Req;          /* ImageReq structure */
   unsigned BitShift, BitPattern;

/*
   Build a structure that defines what the digitizer should acquire.
   This will be passed to the digitizer by a call to InitializeDigitizer
   function. This also tells the low level code where the digitizer
   is attached.
```

(continued)

Listing 4.2 *(continued)*

```
*/
    Req.ComputerType    = PS220;
    Req.PrtBase         = 0x3BC;
    Req.HMode           = LowRes;
    Req.VMode           = NonInterlace;
    Req.NumberOfPasses  = 1;
    Req.Flags           = 0L;
    Req.FirstLine       = 0;
    Req.FirstPixel      = 0;
    Req.LastLine        = 200;
    Req.LastPixel       = 320;

    InitializeDigitizer(&Req);          /* initialize the digitizer */

    clrscr();
    printf("Digitizer Test Program One - Pixel Counter Latch Test\n\n");
    printf("Each bit from LSB to MSB will be set to a high level\n");
    printf("with all other bits set low.\n");
    printf("The output of the pixel latches should be checked with\n");
    printf("with a meter at the following locations on the digitizer\n\n");
    printf("Bit Number - 9   8   7   6   5   4   3   2   1   0\n");
    printf("Device Pin # 1  15   9  10   1  15   9  10   1  15\n");
    printf("Device #      |IC12|  |--- IC11 --|   |--- IC10 --|\n\n");
    printf("A low is < .8 VDC and a high is > 2.5 VDC\n\n");

    SetPixelCount( 0 );                 /* set all bits to zero */
    printf("All bits of the pixel counter latch should now be low\n");

    for (BitShift=0; BitShift <= MaxBitNum; BitShift++)
    {
       printf("Press any key to continue\n\n");
       getch();
       BitPattern = 1 << BitShift;
       SetPixelCount( BitPattern );
       printf("Test bit pattern is: %x\n",BitPattern);
    }
    printf("Test Completed\n");
}
```

bits fail this test, look closely at the cable between the PC and the digitizer. Use the meter to verify the cable is straight through and that all 25 signals are present at both ends. Also make sure the cable is plugged into the printer or parallel port instead of the serial port connector.

If some of the bits work and some do not, check the wiring around the latch circuits again. If all is correct, replace the latches IC14 and IC15. If the wiring is correct and the components are good, you should not have any further problems with this circuitry. As a last resort, plug a printer into the printer port and verify that the PCs can drive the printer correctly.

The final digitizer test is shown in Listing 4.3 and is called the "SyncsPerField" test. It verifies the operation of the sync detect circuitry (made up of latch IC8 and three-input NAND gate IC9B) and the PC/digitizer interface. This test program is contained in the files "test2.c" and "test2.prj". This program must also be linked with the low-level driver software "digitize.obj".

Listing 4.3 Digitizer Test Program Two. "SyncsPerField" Test

```
The following is the contents of the file, "test2.prj":


digitize.obj
test2        (digitize.h)



The follwoing is the contents of the file, "test2.c":

/**********************************************************/
/***          Video Digitizer Test Program Two      ***/
/***                 written in Turbo C             ***/
/***                        by                      ***/
/***                 Craig A. Lindley               ***/
/***                                                ***/
/***       Ver: 1.0    Last Update: 08/04/89        ***/
/**********************************************************/
/*
This program is used to check the sync detect circuitry on the digitizer.
It continually counts how many sync pulses it detects per video field.
The timing parameters in the low level digitizer driver code, digitize.asm,
should be varied until only the values of 271 and 272 are obtained. This
program is terminated by hitting any key.
*/


#include <stdio.h>
#include <conio.h>
#include "digitizer.h"
```

(continued)

Listing 4.3 *(continued)*

```c
void main( void )
{
    struct ImageReq Req;            /* ImageReq structure */
    unsigned Done = FALSE;          /* loop terminating boolean */

    clrscr();
    printf("Digitizer Test Program Two - Sync Detect Circuitry Test\n\n");

/*
    Build a structure that defines what the digitizer should acquire.
    This will be passed to the digitizer by a call to InitializeDigitizer
    function. This also tells the low level code where the digitizer
    is attached.
*/

    Req.ComputerType    = PS220;
    Req.PrtBase         = 0x3BC;
    Req.HMode           = LowRes;
    Req.VMode           = NonInterlace;
    Req.NumberOfPasses  = 1;
    Req.Flags           = 0L;
    Req.FirstLine       = 0;
    Req.FirstPixel      = 0;
    Req.LastLine        = 200;
    Req.LastPixel       = 320;

    InitializeDigitizer(&Req);       /* initialize the digitizer */

    printf("SyncPerField Test\n");
    printf("  Hit any key to terminate\n\n");

    Done = FALSE;

    while (!Done)
    {
        printf("SPF=%d\n",SyncsPerField());
        if (kbhit())
            Done = TRUE;
    }
}
```

This program not only checks some of the digitizer hardware it also checks the timing parameters configured via the macros in the low-level digitizer driver code. Improper operation of the hardware and improperly chosen timing parameters can affect the outcome of this test program. What this test program attempts to do is to count the number of sync pulses in a video field and display the result. It does this continually until terminated by the operator. If the values 271 and 272 are continually displayed during execution, the digitizer's sync detect circuitry is working correctly. If the values are intermixed with slightly different values, the timing parameters should be modified slightly—notably, the "LDELAY" macro timing. If the test program seems to hang, look at the levels of the signals around the sync-detect latch IC8. For each sync pulse produced by the connected video source, the latch output should go low. If this is not the case, check the wiring carefully. If the output does go low and stays there, verify that the PC is outputting the "SyncReset" signal, which is used to reset this latch.

Once the correct values are returned consistently by this test program your digitizer should be working. Try digitizing an image using the programs in Chapter 5. If you still are having problems, you'll need to use an oscilloscope to further troubleshoot. Using one of the example programs from the next chapter, walk through the circuitry looking for problems during the digitizing process. Verify the following:

a. The "Go" signal from the PC goes active high (IC13A pin 2), allowing the pixel counters to continually be loaded and count down to zero.

b. The "Cnt 0/Start of Conversion" signal (IC4D pin 11) goes active high for one clock when the pixel counter reaches zero.

c. The A-to-D clock signal (IC2 pin 7) pulses twice each time the "Cnt 0" signal goes active.

d. The end of conversion latch (IC6A pin 6) goes active low after the A-to-D clock signal pulses twice.

e. All latches get reset by the appropriate signal from the PC.

Conclusions

This chapter has conveyed a great deal of important information about the digitizer hardware and low-level software. Special emphasis was given to CPU speed-dependence issues and how they affect the operation of the low-level software. The "ImageReq" data structure, which is the interface between the low-level assembly language code and the high-level C software, was discussed in detail. It was shown that the parameters placed into the "ImageReq" structure determine the type of digitized image produced by the digitizer. Finally, additional discussion on digitizer testing was provided to help ring the last bugs out of user-assembled digitizers. With the digitizer hardware now completely tested and working and the low-level software understood, it is time to discuss high-level image-acquisition software. This discussion, which begins in the next chapter, is really where the fun begins.

5

High-Level Digitizer Software for Imaging Control and Display

In this chapter you will learn about:

- How to maximize digitized image quality
- The structure of the high-level digitizer software
- How to control the digitizer
- How to acquire and display gray-scale images
- How to acquire and display color images
- How to save acquired images in a standard graphics file format

Digitized Image Quality

Before beginning the discussion of the example programs, a few words need to be said about image quality. An old adage applied to computer programs applies equally well to digitized images: "garbage in, garbage out." To produce crisp, clear digitized images requires a little forethought and preparation. Some of the factors that can adversely effect the quality of digitized images are video camera quality, video interconnection cable quality, camera focus, ambient lighting, and object movement. The equipment setup illustrated in Figure 5.1 can help maximize the quality of your digitized images by minimizing those unwanted factors just listed (see also the discussion of noise in the focus window program section for information on additional image impairment mechanisms). The video camera support structure, called a *copy stand*, with lights can be built from parts readily available at most hardware stores or can be purchased as a unit from NewTek Inc., Topeka, Kansas, 66603.

The schematic diagram in Figure 5.1 shows how the camera, video monitor, and the digitizer can be connected for maximum effectiveness. The use of a video switch will allow

120

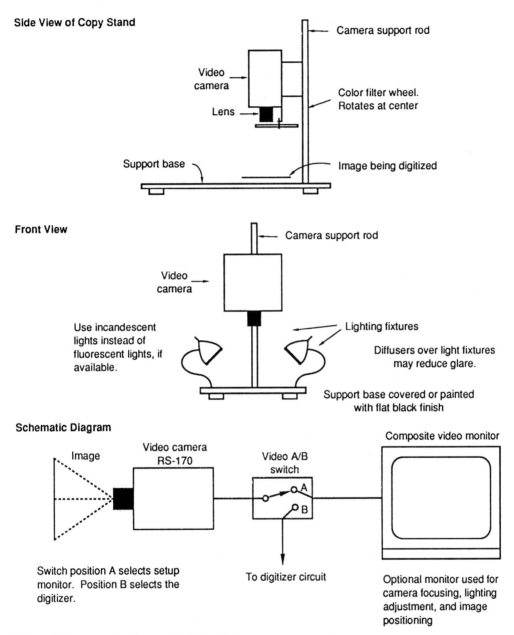

Figure 5.1 Suggested Image Digitizing Setup

the video camera to be connected directly to the video monitor while the image is positioned and the camera is focused. When the image seen in the monitor is what is desired, the video switch is flipped, thereby connecting the video camera to the digitizer circuitry. An alternative to a video switch is to manually connect and disconnect the video cable between the monitor and the digitizer. However the connection is made, once the image is framed and lighted correctly, the digitizer will produce quality digitized images. Another, much more recent, adage comes to mind: "What you see is what you get."

Structure of the High-Level Digitizer Software

As explained in Chapter 4, the low-level digitizer software does the actual acquiring of the video images. The high-level software must perform all of the less time critical but equally important housekeeping functions necessary to allow the low-level software to do its job unimpeded. The same basic housekeeping functions are required regardless of the type of image the digitizer is asked to acquire. In fact, the structure of all of the digitizing programs presented in this book is almost identical. Each program is a slight derivation of the following skeletal structure:

```
Function Acquire and Display a Digitized Image

Begin
  Initialize the VGA graphic subsystem.
  Initialize the "ImageReq" structure according to the resolution
    of the image required.
  Calculate the size of the required memory buffer(s).
  Allocate memory buffer(s) to hold the acquired image data.
  Initialize the digitizer hardware by calling the low level
    software function "InitializeDigitizer" and passing it the
    address of the initialized "ImageReq" structure.
  Call the low level function "GetPicture" to acquire the image(s).
  Optionally perform processing on acquired image data.
  Put the VGA graphics adapter into the proper mode.
  Install the VGA palette required for display.
  Display the acquired image.
  Optionally save the image as a PCX file.
  Free the memory buffer(s).
End
```

With this basic program structure, images of many different varieties can be produced. In the discussion to follow, examples of a few of the many image possibilities will be provided. In fact, the remainder of this chapter will be spent discussing nothing but example imaging programs. A wide range of example programs is provided, beginning with the most rudimentary image program possible and ending with a program that provides full-color digitized images with only a black and white video camera and a color filter wheel.

See Part Two of this book and the "Gallery of Images" (following p. 442) for numerous examples of digitized images. Every image in this book was produced by the hardware and software discussed in this and the previous two chapters. These images show the quality that can be achieved using the high-level digitizer code contained in the example programs to follow. Figure 5.2 summarizes the example programs to be presented.

Example Program 1—a Generic Imaging Program

This program acquires a 320 × 200 resolution image that is subsequently displayed with both 16 and 64 levels of gray. This program includes the "SyncsPerField" test described in Chapter 4 for testing digitizer synchronization. This basic program is ideal for testing the operation of the digitizer. The program is shown in Listing 5.1 and is included on the companion disk as files "gvideo.prj" and "gvideo.c".

Example Program 2—a Focus Window Program

This program continually digitizes and displays a small portion of an image at which the video camera is pointed. Its purpose is to provide a "focus window" display, which is updated as fast as possible to allow the video camera to be aimed and focused. The focus window image is displayed at a VGA resolution of 320 × 200 (even though the acquired image is much smaller) with 16 levels of gray. This program is shown in Listing 5.2 and is included on the companion disk as files "pvideo.prj" and "pvideo.c".

Example Program 3—the All-Resolution Image Program

This program illustrates all-possible resolutions provided by the digitizer as well as how to save the various resolution images as PCX graphics files. After the focus window is used to aim the video camera correctly, full-screen images are digitized and saved at 320 × 200, 640 × 200, and 640 × 480 resolutions. All are displayed with 16 levels of gray before the next resolution image is digitized except the 320 × 200 image, which is displayed in 64 levels of gray.

This program is shown in Listing 5.3 and is included on the companion disk as files "allvideo.prj" and "allvideo.c".

Example Program 4—the Full-Color Digitized Image Program

This program will digitize color images in 320 × 200 resolution with 256 colors. The program makes use of a color filter wheel to make color images possible. This is the most complex of the digitizer programs presented in this book. This program is shown in Listing 5.4 and is included on the companion disk as files "cvideo.prj" and "cvideo.c".

Figure 5.2 Example Imaging Programs

Generic Imaging Program

This example program (Listing 5.1) acquires a 320 × 200 resolution image from the digitizer and displays it in two ways. First, the image is displayed with a palette made up of 16 shades of gray, then it is displayed again with 64 shades of gray. As seen in the listing, this program is almost a line-by-line transcription of the skeletal structure "Acquire and Display a Digitized Image" presented earlier.

All 320 × 200 images in this book utilize the VGA mode 13H 256-color mode for display. Recall that Turbo C 2.0 does not provide support for this VGA mode, so assembler functions (detailed in Chapter 1) were developed to support this mode. This is why the display functions in this example program call the function "PutPixel256" instead of Turbo's ubiquitous "putpixel" function. "PutPixel256" is one of the assembler functions written specifically to support the 256-color VGA mode. Its function and parameter passing

Listing 5.1   The Generic Imaging Program

The following is the contents of the file, "gvideo.prj":

```
graphics.lib
vgagraph.obj
digitize.obj
egavga.obj
vga        (misc.h pcx.h vga.h)
gvideo     (misc.h pcx.h vga.h digitize.h)
```

The following is the contents of the file, "gvideo.c":

```
/***************************************/
/*    Generic Video Digitizer Program  */
/*        Digitizes 320x200 Images     */
/* Images displayed with both 16 and 64 */
/*            levels of gray            */
/*        written in Turbo C 2.0        */
/*                by                    */
/*         Craig A. Lindley             */
/*                                      */
/*    Vers: 1.0  Last Update: 09/14/89  */
/***************************************/

#include <stdio.h>
#include <conio.h>
#include <process.h>
#include <graphics.h>
#include <alloc.h>
#include "misc.h"
#include "pcx.h"
#include "vga.h"
#include "digitizer.h"

/* Global Variables */

static struct ImageReq Req;
static char huge *PictureData;

/*
This function displays the digitized image with a 16
level gray scale palette. Notice the video data in
PictData is shifted to the right twice. This scales
the 6 bit data to 4 bits as required for
```

```
a 16 color display. Notice also that this function is
driven by parameters in the ImageReq structure. That means
DisplayPictData will automatically configure itself as
the image parameters change.
*/
void DisplayPictData16Gray (char huge *PictData)
{
    register unsigned Col, Row, Color;
    unsigned ColSpan, RowSpan;
    unsigned long PixelBufOffset;

    ColSpan = Req.LastPixel - Req.FirstPixel;
    RowSpan = Req.LastLine  - Req.FirstLine;
    for (Col=0; Col < ColSpan; Col++)
    {
        PixelBufOffset = (long) RowSpan * Col;
        for (Row=0; Row < RowSpan; Row++)
        {
                Color = PictData[PixelBufOffset + Row];
            Color >>= 2;
                /* use special VGA mode 13H putpixel function */
                /* required for 320x200 images */
                PutPixel256(Col,Row,Color);
        }
    }
}


/*
This function displays the digitized image with a 64
level gray scale palette. Notice the video data in
is not scaled in this case as all 6 bits are needed
to index the correct color register.
*/

void DisplayPictData64Gray (char huge *PictData)
{
    register unsigned Col, Row, Color;
    unsigned ColSpan, RowSpan;
    unsigned long PixelBufOffset;

    ColSpan = Req.LastPixel - Req.FirstPixel;
    RowSpan = Req.LastLine  - Req.FirstLine;
    for (Col=0; Col < ColSpan; Col++)
```

(continued)

Listing 5.1   *(continued)*

```
    {
        PixelBufOffset = (long) RowSpan * Col;
        for (Row=0; Row < RowSpan; Row++)
        {
                Color = PictData[PixelBufOffset + Row];
                /* use special VGA mode 13H putpixel function */
                /* required for 320x200 images */
                PutPixel256(Col,Row,Color);
        }
    }
}
/* main digitizer program */

void main(void)
{
    unsigned Count;
    unsigned long RasterSize;

    InitGraphics();             /* initialize graphics subsystem */

    clrscr();

    printf("Generic Digitizer Test Program\n\n");
    printf("This program digitizes a 320x200 pixel image then\n");
    printf("displays it first with 16 and then with 64 levels\n");
    printf("of gray.\n\n");

    /*
    Build a structure that defines what the digitizer should acquire. this
    will be passed to the digitizer by a call to InitializeDigitizer
    function
    */
    Req.ComputerType   = PS220;
    Req.PrtBase        = 0x3BC;
    Req.HMode          = LowRes;
    Req.VMode          = NonInterlace;
    Req.NumberOfPasses = 1;
    Req.Flags          = 0L;
    Req.FirstLine      = 0;
    Req.FirstPixel     = 0;
    Req.LastLine       = 200;       /* set up 320x200 image */
    Req.LastPixel      = 320;
```

```
    RasterSize = (Req.LastLine  - Req.FirstLine) *
                 (Req.LastPixel - Req.FirstPixel);


    /* allocate picture buffer from the far heap and set it to zeros */
    printf("Allocating Image Buffer - RasterSize is %lu bytes\n\n",RasterSize);

    if ((PictureData = (char huge *) farcalloc(RasterSize,
        (unsigned long) sizeof(char))) == NULL)
    {
       printf("Digitize - Not enough memory\n");
       exit(ENoMemory);
    }


    /* place address of image buffer in the ImageReq structure */
    Req.PictBuf = PictureData;
    /* inform digitizer of image parameters */
    InitializeDigitizer(&Req);
    /* run a test of the digitizer */
    printf("SyncPerField Digitizer Synchronization Test\n\n");
    for (Count = 0; Count < 10; Count++)
       printf("SPF=%d\n",SyncsPerField());

    printf("\nPress any key to terminate image display\n\n");
    printf("Acquiring Image . . .\n");

    GetPicture();              /* acquire requested image */
    Set256ColorMode();         /* 320x200 256 color VGA mode */
    LoadGray16Palette();       /* load the gray scale palette */
    DisplayPictData16Gray(PictureData);  /* display the image */
    getch();                   /* operator terminates display */
    LoadGray64Palette();       /* load the new gray scale palette */
    DisplayPictData64Gray(PictureData);  /* display the image */
    getch();                   /* operator terminates display */
    restorecrtmode();          /* back to text mode */
    farfree((char far *)PictureData);  /* give memory back */
    closegraph();              /* close up shop */
}
```

sequence are identical to that provided by Turbo C; the difference is it supports the special video mode. The value of the parameter "Color" passed to "putpixel" is limited to the range 0 to 15, for display of 16 colors maximum. With "PutPixel256", the range of "Color" is 0 to 255, for display of 256 possible colors.

The two different display functions provided in this example program, "DisplayPictData16Gray" and "DisplayPictData64Gray", differ only in how they scale the image data they are trying to display. Both functions derive their operational parameters from the content of the "ImageReq" structure. Both accept a HUGE pointer to the image data as an input parameter, and both treat the image data internally as an array of characters. This makes manipulation of images greater than 64KB in length transparent to the programmer. This is not an issue in this example program because 320×200 images require exactly 64,000 bytes for storage. In other words, they do not cross an 80 X 86 segment boundary. In some of the other example programs, this is definitely an issue. It is *very important* to note that when a far image data buffer is indexed as an array, the index must be of type long or unsigned long! It *cannot* be cast to a long or the display functions will not work.

The digitizer, being a six-bit device, places numerical pixel sample values in the range 0 to 63 into the image data buffer "PictData". To display this data with only 16 possible shades of gray, it is necessary to scale the 0 to 63 values into the range 0 to 15. Scaling will allow the pixel data to be directly used as an index into the VGA color registers. Said another way, the scaled image data becomes the number of the color register used to display the pixel. The scaling can easily be accomplished by right shifting the image data two places as it is retrieved from the image buffer. This is the technique used by the function "DisplayPictData16Gray". Of course, it is assumed the VGA color registers zero to 15 have already been loaded with the color components of the 16-level gray scale (via a call to the function "LoadGray16Palette"). If this is not the case, the image will be displayed on the screen with rather bizarre coloration, as it will use the default colors supplied by the BIOS when VGA mode 13H is entered. This, pseudocolor technique can be used for some rather striking special effects. At this point, however, we are more interested in getting a 16-level gray-scale image displayed correctly. Fun with special effects will come later.

The second display function, "DisplayPictData64Gray", does not use any data scaling because the pixel data already is in the proper range for directly indexing the color registers. This time the first 64 color registers must be set up in advance with the 64 shades of gray for the image to be displayed correctly. This is accomplished via a call to "LoadGray64Palette".

Notice the technique used to extract the image data from the image data buffer in both of the display functions. Nested "for" loops retrieve the data in a column-by-column progression. This is necessary because sequential bytes of the image data buffer hold sequential scan lines of video data. This is the format in which the low-level digitizer code places the data into the image data buffer (please refer to Figure 3.6). By making the "Row" index change the fastest, the columns are accessed sequentially as required. This arrangement of video data in the image buffer must be understood to access (and display) the data correctly. The column-by-column arrangement of data in the image buffer forces the display functions to paint the screen in the same manner.

The "main" function in this example program is straightforward. The call to "InitGraphics" initializes the VGA graphics system and registers the inclusion of the graphics driver with the executable program. With this done, the program outputs a series of messages for the user indicating what the example program is going to do. "Req", which is an instance of the "ImageReq" data structure, is then initialized with values telling the low-level digitizer code what type of image we are requesting. The fields "ComputerType", "NumberOfPasses", and "Flags" are unused but are initialized anyway. All other fields in "Req" are pertinent to our example program and are therefore filled in with the appropriate data. Refer to Chapter 4 for an explanation of the fields in an "ImageReq" structure.

Next, the size of the required image buffer is calculated from the information in the "ImageReq" structure. In this case, the value of "RasterSize" will be 64,000 bytes. The program reports this information on the screen. A far memory allocation is attempted next for "RasterSize" number of bytes. If the memory is not available, the program will terminate with an exit code of "ENoMemory". See the file "pcx.h" for the numerical values of all exit codes.

Assuming the memory allocation was completed without error, the pointer returned by the allocation, after being converted to a HUGE pointer, is placed in the "Req" structure. The low-level code will place the digitized image data in memory starting at this address.

The call to "InitializeDigitizer" with the address of the "Req" structure as a parameter will inform the low-level digitizer code what it needs to do and will also initialize the digitizer hardware for operation. Subsequent calls to "InitializeDigitizer" are required only when any aspect of the digitizer's operation needs to be altered. Only one call to "InitializeDigitizer" is required to digitize one or a thousand of the same resolution images. See Listing 5.3 for examples of this.

Next, the "SyncsPerField" test is performed. This test was described in Chapter 4. It has nothing to do with image acquisition and could be removed completely from this example program without any detrimental effects. It is included here as a verification of the digitizer's continued operation. As explained earlier, if the digitizer is functioning correctly, the "SyncsPerField" test should return a series of ten numbers either 271 or 272 in value. This verifies the digitizer has correctly synchronized with the incoming video signal and can count the sync pulses correctly. Incorrect values returned by the "SyncsPerField" test virtually guarantee error-filled digitized images.

The innocuous call to the "GetPicture" function causes the digitizer to digitize the image the video camera is pointing at. What could be simpler? When this function returns, the image data is contained in the buffer that was specified in the "Req" structure. The acquisition portion of the example program is now completed. All that remains to do is to get the image data from the buffer and display it correctly on the VGA graphics adapter.

To display the image data, the VGA graphics adapter is first placed into the 320×200 resolution 256-color mode 13H. Next, the 16-level gray-scale palette is loaded into VGA color registers 0 through 15 by the call to the "LoadGray16Palette" function. Finally, "DisplayPictData16Gray" is called to read the image data from the buffer, scale it, and write it to the screen, pixel by pixel. The resultant 16-level gray-scale image remains on the display screen until the user hits any key.

After a key is hit, the process described above is repeated, except a palette of 64 levels of gray is loaded into the color registers and "DisplayPictData64Gray" is called to display the image in 64 instead of 16 levels of gray. Can you visually tell the difference between an image displayed in 16 and 64 levels of gray?

Program cleanup consists of switching the VGA graphics adapter back into text mode, freeing the 64,000 bytes of image memory, and closing the graphics library. The program is then terminated and control is given back to DOS.

Focus Window Program

The focus window example program (Listing 5.2) is very similar to the generic digitizer program presented as the previous example. Very little new ground is covered, but the information that is new is important. Namely, this program illustrates the control the high-level digitizer software has over the operation of the low-level code and subsequently the digitizer itself. By manipulating the parameter passed in the "Req" structure to the low-level code, a portion of a video image can be digitized instead of a full field. Notice the values given to the "Req" entries "FirstLine", "FirstPixel", "LastLine" and "LastPixel" in Listing 5.2. Please note these values are specified in terms of the resolution of the digitizer, not the resolution of the VGA display adapter, even though in this case they happen to coincide.

Consider digitizing just the center of a video image while the digitizer is in the low-resolution image-acquisition mode. In this mode, the digitizer is capable of digitizing an image with 320 pixels in the horizontal direction and 200 lines in the vertical direction. A pixel in the exact middle of the digitized video field would have pixel and line coordinates of 160 and 100 respectively. If we decide our focus window should be 100 pixels by 100 lines, the top left corner of the focus window would be at pixel 110, line 50, and the lower right corner would be at pixel 210, line 150. These are the parameters passed in the "Req" structure. Once this structure is passed to the low-level code via the call to the function "InitializeDigitizer", almost continuous images can be returned from the digitizer to our focus window. The function used to display the focus window image, "DisplayPictData", has been slightly modified from that used in the previous example to allow the focus window to be displayed anywhere on the VGA screen. Two "C #define" statements at the beginning of the program control the focus window placement.

The only further modification to this example program is the "while" loop used to acquire and display the image at the highest possible rate. As you are viewing the focus window image, the digitizer is busy acquiring the next update. When the update is ready, the focus window is refreshed and the process repeats. Hitting a key on the keyboard terminates the example program in the same fashion as the previous example program.

Two things become obvious while watching this example program operate. First, what the digitizer considers the center of the video field might differ from what a monitor connected to your camera thinks is the center. This can be compensated for by adjusting the vertical and horizontal size controls on the monitor. If these adjustments are unavailable on your monitor, the parameters passed in the "Req" structure can be offset accordingly to make monitor image center agree with digitizer image center. Experimentation can be used to determine the correct offset values to use.

The second thing that becomes obvious while watching the focus window example program is that the digitized images produced by the digitizer are not always exactly the same. The images vary slightly with every pass, sometimes resembling a slight movement of

Listing 5.2 The Focus Window Program

The following is the contents of the file, "pvideo.prj":

```
graphics.lib
vgagraph.obj
digitize.obj
egavga.obj
vga      (misc.h pcx.h vga.h)
pvideo   (misc.h pcx.h vga.h digitize.h)
```

The following is the contents of the file, "pvideo.c":

```
/***************************************/
/*    Focus Window Digitizer Program   */
/*          written in Turbo C 2.0      */
/*                 by                   */
/*          Craig A. Lindley            */
/*                                      */
/*   Vers: 1.0  Last Update: 09/14/89   */
/***************************************/

/*
This program is capable of the full utilization of the
Video Digitizer hardware. It can cause the digitizer to
digitize any portion of a video display. All aspects of
a digitized image from acquisition to display
are computed dynamically. The ImageReq structure is
passed to the low level code to command the digitizer.
*/

#include <stdio.h>
#include <conio.h>
#include <dos.h>
#include <process.h>
#include <graphics.h>
#include <alloc.h>
#include "misc.h"
#include "pcx.h"
#include "vga.h"
#include "digitizer.h"
```

(continued)

Listing 5.2 *(continued)*

```c
/*
The two defines offset the focus window so it
is displayed in the center on the VGA screen.
*/

#define ColCenterOffset 110
#define RowCenterOffset  50
/* Global Variables to this file */

static struct      ImageReq Req;
static char huge *PictureData;

/* display the digitized image */
void DisplayPictData (char huge *PictData)
{
    register unsigned Col, Row, Color;
    unsigned ColSpan, RowSpan;
    unsigned long PixelBufOffset;

    ColSpan = Req.LastPixel - Req.FirstPixel;
    RowSpan = Req.LastLine  - Req.FirstLine;
    for (Col=0; Col < ColSpan; Col++)
    {
        PixelBufOffset = (long) RowSpan * Col;
        for (Row=0; Row < RowSpan; Row++)
        {
                Color = PictData[PixelBufOffset + Row];
            Color >>= 2;
                PutPixel256(Col+ColCenterOffset,
                                Row+RowCenterOffset,Color);
        }
    }
}


/* main digitizer program */

void main(void)
{
    unsigned long RasterSize;

    InitGraphics();            /* initialize graphics subsystem */
```

```
printf("Focus Window Test Program\n\n");
printf("This program will continually digitize and display\n");
printf("a small portion of the video field\n\n");

/*
Build a structure that defines what the digitizer should acquire. this
will be passed to the digitizer by a call to InitializeDigitizer
function
*/

Req.ComputerType    = PS220;
Req.PrtBase         = 0x3BC;
Req.HMode           = LowRes;    /* 320x200 resolution mode */
Req.VMode           = NonInterlace;
Req.NumberOfPasses  = 1;
Req.Flags           = 0L;
Req.FirstLine       = 50;        /* set up focus window */
Req.FirstPixel      = 110;
Req.LastLine        = 150;
Req.LastPixel       = 210;

RasterSize = (Req.LastLine  - Req.FirstLine) *
             (Req.LastPixel - Req.FirstPixel);

/* allocate picture buffer and set it to zeros */

printf("Allocating Image Buffer - RasterSize is %lu bytes\n\n",RasterSize);

if ((PictureData = (char huge *) farcalloc(RasterSize,
    (unsigned long) sizeof(char))) == NULL)
{
   printf("Digitize - Not enough memory\n");
   exit(ENoMemory);
}

printf("Hit any key to terminate program\n\n");
printf("Acquiring Image . . .\n");

Req.PictBuf = PictureData;
InitializeDigitizer(&Req);
delay(5000);                /* allow messages to be read */
Set256ColorMode();          /* 320x200 256 color VGA mode 13H */
```

(continued)

Listing 5.2 *(continued)*

```
LoadGray16Palette();       /* load the gray scale palette */
while (!kbhit())           /* acquire a picture continually */
{                          /* until operator hits key */
   GetPicture();
   DisplayPictData(PictureData);
}
getch();                   /* empty key buffer */
restorecrtmode();          /* back to text mode */
farfree((char far *)PictureData); /* give back the memory */
closegraph();              /* close up shop */
}
```

the object being digitized. If the digitized images were always exactly the same, the updating of the focus window would be invisible. Noise in the digitizer's environment is responsible for the fluctuation of the digitized image. All video cameras produce some level of noise, which manifests itself as errors in pixel values. Electrical noise picked up by the connecting cables also contributes to the problem. To minimize the effect of the electrical noise, use good-quality shielded video cable between the video camera and digitizer. Keep the video cable short and located away from all AC power cords, including the ones for the video camera and for the light fixtures. If fluorescent lighting is used (incandescent lights are recommended) be sure the video cable is as far from the light fixture as possible. As an experiment, try moving the video cable while the program is running. Notice the images in the focus window and how they change. For another interesting effect, hold a permanent magnet near the video camera while digitizing is being performed and watch what happens. A magnet should affect only older video cameras, which use a vidicon as the image sensor. It should not affect cameras that use CCD devices. Magnetic fields (near the video camera) are considered another form of image-impairment noise with a direct effect on image quality.

All-Resolution Imaging Program

Example program 3 (Listing 5.3) is an extension of example programs 1 and 2. This program demonstrates the three image resolutions available from the digitizer. Digitized images are acquired, displayed, and optionally saved to disk as PCX files in 320×200, 640×200, and 640×480 resolutions. All images are displayed and saved with a palette of 16 or 64 levels of gray. Concepts demonstrated in this example program are:

    a. A primitive user interface via the DOS command line
    b. Changing digitizer resolution on the fly
    c. Saving images as PCX files

Please refer to Listing 5.3 during this discussion.

Listing 5.3   The All-Resolution Image Program

The following is the contents of the file, "allvideo.prj":

```
graphics.lib
vgagraph.obj
digitize.obj
egavga.obj
pcx         (misc.h pcx.h)
vga         (misc.h pcx.h vga.h)
allvideo    (misc.h pcx.h vga.h digitize.h)
```

The following is the contents of the file, "allvideo.c":

```c
/***************************************/
/*All Resolution Video Digitizer Program*/
/* Digitizes, Displays and Saves Images */
/*   in all supported digitizer modes   */
/*        written in Turbo C 2.0        */
/*                 by                   */
/*          Craig A. Lindley            */
/*                                      */
/*   Vers: 1.0  Last Update: 09/28/89   */
/***************************************/

#include <stdio.h>
#include <conio.h>
#include <dos.h>
#include <process.h>
#include <string.h>
#include <graphics.h>
#include <alloc.h>
#include "misc.h"
#include "pcx.h"
#include "vga.h"
#include "digitizer.h"

#define MaxFileNameLen 13    /* filename str length including null */

/*
The two defines offset the focus window so it
is displayed in the center on the VGA screen.
*/
```

(continued)

Listing 5.3   *(continued)*

```c
#define ColCenterOffsetAmount 110
#define RowCenterOffsetAmount  50

/* Global Variables */
struct     ImageReq Req;
char huge *PictureData;
unsigned   ColCenterOffset, RowCenterOffset;
/* display the digitized image in VGA mode 13H with 64 levels of gray */
void DisplayPictData1 (char huge *PictData)
{
   register unsigned Col, Row, Color;
   unsigned ColSpan, RowSpan;
   unsigned long PixelBufOffset;

   ColSpan = Req.LastPixel - Req.FirstPixel;
   RowSpan = Req.LastLine  - Req.FirstLine;
   for (Col=0; Col < ColSpan; Col++)
   {
      PixelBufOffset = (long) RowSpan * Col;
      for (Row=0; Row < RowSpan; Row++)
      {
              Color = PictData[PixelBufOffset + Row];
              PutPixel256(Col+ColCenterOffset,
                             Row+RowCenterOffset,Color);
      }
   }
}


/* display the digitized image in normal 16 color VGA modes */
void DisplayPictData2 (char huge *PictData)
{
   register unsigned Col, Row, Color;
   unsigned ColSpan, RowSpan;
   unsigned long PixelBufOffset;

   ColSpan = Req.LastPixel - Req.FirstPixel;
   RowSpan = Req.LastLine  - Req.FirstLine;
   for (Col=0; Col < ColSpan; Col++)
   {
      PixelBufOffset = (long) RowSpan * Col;
      for (Row=0; Row < RowSpan; Row++)
      {
              Color = PictData[PixelBufOffset + Row];
```

```
            Color >>= 2;          /* scale data to 0 ..15 */
                  putpixel(Col,Row,Color);
      }
   }
}

/*
This function provides help in the advent of operator error. Program
terminates after help is given
*/

void ShowHelp( void )
{
   printf("\nThis program digitizes, displays and optionally\n");
   printf("saves in PCX format a single digitized image in\n");
   printf("three different resolutions. Its usage is as follows:\n\n");
   printf("allvideo [-o] filename <cr>\n");
   printf("  -o creates output PCX files\n");
   printf("  filename is name given to the PCX file(s). Do not\n");
   printf("  specify a file extension, it will be provided.\n\n");
   exit(1);
}

/* main digitizer program */

void main(short argc, char *argv[])
{
   unsigned long RasterSize;
   unsigned GenPCXFile;
   unsigned FileNameCounter, ArgIndex, StrLength;
   char     *ImageFileName;
   char      ProcessedFileName[MaxFileNameLen];
   char      LRName[MaxFileNameLen];
   char      MRName[MaxFileNameLen];
   char      HRName[MaxFileNameLen];


   InitGraphics();

   clrscr();
   printf("Digitize and Display Gray Scale Images in Many Resolutions\n\n");

   /* install default options */
   GenPCXFile = FALSE;                  /* don't generate a. PCX file */
```

(continued)

Listing 5.3 *(continued)*

```
/* parse command line arguments */

FileNameCounter = 0;                 /* count of user specified filenames */
for (ArgIndex=1; ArgIndex < argc; ArgIndex++)
{
    if (*argv[ArgIndex] != '-')      /* if not a cmd line switch */
    {                                /* must be a filename */
            if (*argv[ArgIndex] == '?')   /* help requested ? */
                ShowHelp();
            if (FileNameCounter > 1)      /* only one filename allowed */
        ShowHelp();                       /* if more then error exit */
            ImageFileName = argv[ArgIndex];  /* save image filename */
        FileNameCounter++;           /* inc count for error check */
    }
    else                             /* its a cmd line switch */
    {
            switch (*(argv[ArgIndex]+1))  /* parse the cmd line */
        {
                case 'o':                 /* o or O = output files */
                case 'O':
                  GenPCXFile = TRUE;
            break;
                default:
                  printf("Error - invalid cmd line switch encountered\n");
                  ShowHelp();
        }
    }
}
if (GenPCXFile && (FileNameCounter != 1))
{
    printf("Error - single filename required for PCX files\n");
    ShowHelp();
}

/*
Preprocess any filename input from the cmd line. Strip
off any specified extension and limit the filename
length to six characters max. This will allow the
designations LR.PCX, MR.PCX and HR.PCX to be appended.
*/
if (GenPCXFile)              /* only process if necessary */
{
    strcpy(ProcessedFileName,"");    /* empty string */
```

```
        /* find filename length minus the extension */
        StrLength = strcspn(ImageFileName,".");

        if (StrLength > 6)      /* exceeds max length ? */
                strncat(ProcessedFileName,ImageFileName,6); /* cat only 6 chars */
        else
                strncat(ProcessedFileName,ImageFileName,StrLength);
        /*
        Copy the processed file name to each of the PCX
        filename storage areas and append the appropriate string.
        */
        strcpy(LRName,ProcessedFileName);
        strcat(LRName,"LR.PCX");
        strupr(LRName);

        strcpy(MRName,ProcessedFileName);
        strcat(MRName,"MR.PCX");
        strupr(MRName);
        strcpy(HRName,ProcessedFileName);
        strcat(HRName,"HR.PCX");
        strupr(HRName);
}


printf("Use focus window to focus camera. Then press\n");
printf("any key to start the digitization process.\n");
printf("Image resolutions are: 320x200, 640x200 and 640x480\n\n");

if (GenPCXFile)
{
   printf("Image filenames will be:\n\n");
   printf(" %s for the low  resolution 320x200 image\n",LRName);
   printf(" %s for the mid  resolution 640x200 image\n",MRName);
   printf(" %s for the high resolution 640x480 image\n",HRName);
}
else
   printf("PCX files will not be generated\n");

printf("\nPress any key after third image to terminate program.\n\n");
delay(4000);


/* pick largest size image buffer required */

RasterSize = 307200L;      /* big enough for 640x480 image */
```

(continued)

Listing 5.3 *(continued)*

```
/* allocate picture buffer and set it to zeros */

if ((PictureData = (char huge *) farcalloc(RasterSize,
    (unsigned long) sizeof(char))) == NULL)
{
   printf("Digitize - Not enough memory\n");
   exit(ENoMemory);
}

/*
Build a structure that defines what the digitizer should acquire. this
will be passed to the digitizer by a call to InitializeDigitizer
function. The following portion of the ImageReq structure does
not change as the image resolution changes.
*/

Req.ComputerType   = PS220;
Req.PrtBase        = 0x3BC;
Req.NumberOfPasses = 1;
Req.Flags          = 0L;
Req.PictBuf        = PictureData;      /* put buffer address into ImageReq */
/*
This portion of the structure changes with image resolution
*/

Req.HMode          = LowRes;
Req.VMode          = NonInterlace;
Req.FirstLine      = 50;  /* focus window dimensions */
Req.FirstPixel     = 110;
Req.LastLine       = 150;
Req.LastPixel      = 210;

InitializeDigitizer(&Req);/* initialize digitizer */

Set256ColorMode();        /* 320x200 256 color VGA mode */
LoadGray64Palette();      /* load the gray scale palette */

/* offset focus window to the center of the screen */
ColCenterOffset = ColCenterOffsetAmount;
RowCenterOffset = RowCenterOffsetAmount;

while (!kbhit())          /* acquire a picture continually */
```

```
{                       /* until operator hits key */
   GetPicture();
   DisplayPictData1(PictureData);
}
getch();                /* empty key buffer */

/* now digitize a full 320x200 image */

Req.HMode         = LowRes;
Req.VMode         = NonInterlace;
Req.FirstLine     = 0;
Req.FirstPixel    = 0;
Req.LastLine      = 200;      /* do a 320x200 image */
Req.LastPixel     = 320;

InitializeDigitizer(&Req);    /* initialize digitizer */

GetPicture();                 /* acquire the picture */

/* remove display offset as required for full image display */
ColCenterOffset = 0;
RowCenterOffset = 0;

DisplayPictData1(PictureData); /* display the picture */

if (GenPCXFile)               /* write out the PCX file */
   WritePCXFile(LRName,8,320,200,1,320);

/* now digitize a full 640x200 image */

Req.HMode         = HighRes;
Req.VMode         = NonInterlace;
Req.LastLine      = 200;      /* do a 640x200 image */
Req.LastPixel     = 640;

InitializeDigitizer(&Req);    /* initialize digitizer */

GetPicture();                 /* acquire the picture */
setgraphmode(VGALO);
LoadGray16Palette();          /* load the gray scale palette */
DisplayPictData2(PictureData); /* display the picture */
```

(continued)

Listing 5.3 *(continued)*

```
if (GenPCXFile)                /* write out the PCX file */
   WritePCXFile(MRName,1,640,200,4,80);


/* now digitize a full 640x480 image */

Req.HMode        = HighRes;
Req.VMode        = Interlace;
Req.LastLine     = 480;        /* do a 640x480 image */
Req.LastPixel    = 640;


InitializeDigitizer(&Req);     /* initialize digitizer */


GetPicture();                  /* acquire the picture */
setgraphmode(VGAHI);
LoadGray16Palette();           /* load the gray scale palette */
DisplayPictData2(PictureData); /* display the picture */

if (GenPCXFile)                /* write out the PCX file */
   WritePCXFile(HRName,1,640,480,4,80);

getch();                       /* wait for operator */
restorecrtmode();              /* clean up and quit */
farfree((char far *)PictureData);
closegraph();

}
```

In this program, as in Listing 5.1, there are two distinct image-display functions, called "DisplayPictData1" and "DisplayPictData2". "DisplayPictData1" is used to display an image whenever the VGA resolution is 320 × 200 and 64 levels of gray are required. In other words, whenever the VGA adapter is in mode 13H. "DisplayPictData1' is used both for the display of the focus window and for display of the full-screen 320 × 200 image. "DisplayPictData2" is used for all other VGA display modes. Specifically, it is used to display the 640 × 200 and 640 × 480 resolution images with 16 levels of gray. The operations of these image-display functions have been discussed in previous example programs. Please refer to those discussions for further details.

A new function, "ShowHelp", has been incorporated into this program as part of the user-interface mechanism. When this function is executed, it provides a short description of this program's usage and then terminates operation. A return is never made to the code that called this function. This function provides the only help available to the user of this program.

The most interesting code is located in the "main" portion of the example program.

Here you will find the code that processes the command line arguments provided by the user (the user-interface code, if you will). This code parses the command line looking for command line switches (single-character commands following a dash character) and/or a filename. As shown in the "ShowHelp" function, only a single command line switch, "-o", is supported by this program. This switch is used to tell the program that PCX (o)utput files should be generated. If -o is specified, the command line parsing code looks for a single filename also specified by the user. If a filename is not found or if more than one filename is specified, an error message will be output and "ShowHelp" will be called to remind the user of proper program usage. Notice that a question mark as a command line switch will bring up the help text also.

To summarize, this example program works two different ways, depending upon the command line typed to execute the program. First, if "allvideo" is typed without the "-o" command line switch the program will executed but no PCX output files will be created. If "-o" is included anywhere on the command line (it can be before or after the user-specified filename) three PCX image files will be created, one for each resolution displayed. If an illegal command line switch is entered on the command line, an error message will be output and the user will be provided with help.

After the command line parsing code has executed, the variable "GenPCXFile" will be set TRUE if the operator wants PCX output files or FALSE if not. "GenPCXFile" is used to conditionally execute additional filename manipulation code only if the PCX output files are to be generated. The purpose of this additional code is to generate a unique PCX filename for each resolution of digitized image based upon the filename specified by the user. Basically, the user-entered filename is stripped of an extension if one was specified and trimmed down to six characters maximum. This is necessary because the code that follows appends a unique two-character tag and "PCX" file extension to the filename. The tag is "LR" for low resolution, "MR" for medium resolution, and "HR" for high resolution. The six characters of the trimmed filename plus two of the tag equal the eight maximum characters allowed by DOS. The three unique filenames are then stored, each in its own string buffer, until needed to generate the PCX files. A few examples will help illustrate the operation of this code. If the command line specified filename was "filename.ext", the resultant names given to the PCX files would be "FILENALR.PCX", "FILENAMR.PCX", and "FILENAHR.PCX".

Notice how the string "filename" was trimmed down to the six-character limit of "filena" before the tag and the extension were appended and how the user-specified file extension was eliminated completely. Note also that each of the generated filenames are converted to uppercase character strings before being stored. If the specified filename was "junk", the resultant names given to the PCX files would be "JUNKLR.PCX", "JUNKMR.PCX", and "JUNKHR.PCX".

Note that the filename processing code in this example program does not support DOS paths. If a path is specified by the user, the program will probably malfunction.

After all the command line parsing and string manipulations are performed, memory is allocated for image storage just as in the other example programs. In this case, however, the amount of memory allocated is not computed from entries in the "ImageReq" data structure. Instead, a single buffer large enough for the highest-resolution image, 640×480, is allocated from the far heap (307,200 bytes). This buffer is used for storing all the digitized images produced by this program. The smaller images, like that used for the focus window, occupy only a small portion of this very large image buffer.

After memory allocation, the fixed portion of the "Req" structure is initialized. This portion of the data structure will not change during the lifetime of this example program. All other entries in the structure will be changed as required to produce the desired image resolutions.

From here till the end of this example program, four blocks of similar code are executed sequentially, one block for each type of image acquired and displayed. In each code block is code for initializing the "Req" structure for the resolution of image required, for acquiring the specified image, for setting up the VGA graphics adapter for display of the image, and for optionally saving the image as a PCX file. Pay special attention to the initialization of the "Req" structure. Remember, it is necessary to execute the function "InitializeDigitizer" every time a change is made to the "Req" structure.

The two lines of code:

```
if (GenPCXFile)
    WritePCXFile( ........);
```

are all that is required to save the image currently displayed on the monitor as a PCX file. If "GenPCXFile" is TRUE, the PCX files will be generated. If FALSE, they will not be generated. The parameters passed to the "WritePCXFile" function are very important for proper operation of this function. To discuss the parameters here would be getting ahead of ourselves. The operation of this and all PCX file functions will be discussed in depth in Chapter 6. The "WritePCXFile" function is part of the PCX function library presented there. All PCX questions should be saved until the next chapter. For the time being, "WritePCXFile" must be used without knowing exactly how it works.

The PCX files generated by this example program can be displayed at any time with the "view.exe" program provided on the companion disk and discussed at the end of Chapter 6. These files are also importable into PC PaintBrush® or any other graphics program that accepts PCX files. The PCX image files produced by this example program have practical use outside the digitizer's environment. As a matter of fact, all of the images used for the image processing discussion in Part Two were digitized using a slight variation of this program.

Full-Color Digitized Image Program

Example program 4 (Listing 5.4) produces full-color digitized images utilizing only the digitizer, a monochrome video camera, and a color filter wheel. This program uses equal parts of computer science, physics, and magic to produce the color images. After you see this program operate and understand how it works, you will appreciate how magic could be involved. It is gratifying to see accurate, full-color images displayed on the VGA monitor after such a short period of digitization and processing time.

Listing 5.4   The Full-Color Digitized Image Program

The following is the contents of the file, "cvideo.prj":

```
graphics.lib
digitize.obj
vgagraph.obj
egavga.obj
pcx        (misc.h pcx.h)
vga        (misc.h vga.h pcx.h)
cvideo     (misc.h vga.h pcx.h digitize.h)
```

The following is the contents of the file, "cvideo.c":

```
/************************************************************/
/***                                                    ***/
/***              Video Digitizer Program               ***/
/***      produces color images from monochrome camera  ***/
/***        utilizes the 256 color 320x200 VGA mode     ***/
/***                  written in Turbo C                ***/
/***                        by                          ***/
/***                  Craig A. Lindley                  ***/
/***       Median Cut Algorithm code developed by       ***/
/***                  Dan Butterfield                   ***/
/***                                                    ***/
/***   Usage:                                           ***/
/***   cvideo [-a -d -h -o -p -s -v -x] filename <cr>   ***/
/***        -a correct aspect ratio of image            ***/
/***        -d use Floyd-Steinberg dithering            ***/
/***        -h or ? show help                           ***/
/***        -o calculates optimum color palette         ***/
/***        -p create PCX output file                   ***/
/***        -s scales color register values to max      ***/
/***        -v displays program progress information    ***/
/***        -x create executable display program        ***/
/***         filename is name given to output files     ***/
/***                                                    ***/
/***         Ver: 1.0    Last Update: 12/05/89          ***/
/************************************************************/

#include <stdio.h>
#include <conio.h>
#include <dos.h>
```

(continued)

Listing 5.4 *(continued)*

```
#include <process.h>
#include <graphics.h>
#include <string.h>
#include <alloc.h>
#include <math.h>
#include "vga.h"
#include "misc.h"
#include "pcx.h"
#include "digitize.h"
/*
Please see chapter 12 for a complete discussion of aspect ratio
problems and correction techniques. What we will do in this
program is to acquire three 320x240 images and compress them into
three 320x200 images correcting the aspect ratio problem caused by
the VGA graphics adapter. The three corrected images will then be
used to produce a single full color aspect ratio corrected image.
The aspect ratio correction is performed in the function
AspectCorrect.
*/
#define ROWASPECTCORRECTION (double) 1.2
#define SOURCEIMAGEROWS     240


/*
Memory allocation bits used to keep track of how much far heap memory
has been allocated by this program.
*/


#define   RGBMEM       1
#define   REDMEM       2
#define   GREENMEM     4
#define   BLUEMEM      8
#define   IMAGEMEM    16

unsigned MemoryAlloc = 0;                /* variable used to keep track */

#define COLLEVELS       32               /* number of brightness levels */
#define MAXNUMCOLREGS  256               /* max num of color registers */
#define NUMCOLS        320               /* image dimensions */
#define NUMROWS        200
#define NUMAXIS          3               /* num of axes in RGB cube */
#define NUMPIXELS (long)NUMROWS*NUMCOLS /* total pixels in image */
#define SQUARE(x) (x)*(x)
```

```
union REGS regs;

char huge *Red;                     /* pts to image data */
char huge *Green;
char huge *Blue;
char huge *ImageBuf;
struct ImageReq Req;                          /* image request structure */

/*
RGBCube: Three dimensional array implemented in such a way as to work well
on a machine that has trouble with objects greater than 64K.  The indices
into this array are the color components, rgb, normalized to fit in
the range defined by COLLEVELS.  The values in the array are frequency counts
of the particular color.  The array is set up here to be an array of pointers
to smaller 2 dimensional arrays, so no object is greater than 64K.
*/

unsigned far *RGBCube[COLLEVELS];
unsigned NumBoxes;
unsigned FloydStein;
unsigned OptimumColors;
unsigned Verbose;
unsigned GenComFile;
unsigned GenPCXFile;
unsigned ScaleColRegs;
unsigned CorrectAspectRatio;
/*
Boxes: Structure holding the unsorted generated color boxes.  Includes the
low and high value along each axis of RGBCube, and the number of elements
in the box.
*/
struct Box
{
    unsigned Lo[3];
    unsigned Hi[3];
    unsigned long NumElements;
} Boxes[MAXNUMCOLREGS];

/*
Sorted version of Boxes.
*/
struct Box SBoxes[MAXNUMCOLREGS];
```

(continued)

Listing 5.4 *(continued)*

```c
/*
ColRegs: Holds the determined values of the color registers.
*/
struct Regs
{
  BYTE Red;
  BYTE Green;
  BYTE Blue;
} ColRegs[MAXNUMCOLREGS];

/*
SColRegs: Sorted version of ColRegs.
*/
struct Regs SColRegs[MAXNUMCOLREGS];

/* beginning of program functions */
/*
This function will output the message string passed to it if the Verbose
option variable is set true.
*/
void Message(char *String)
{
   if (Verbose)
     printf("%s",String);
}

/*
This function deallocates all far heap memory that has been allocated
*/
void DeAllocMemory( void )
{
   register unsigned Index;

   /* test MemoryAlloc bit to see what was allocated then dispose */

   Message("Deallocating program memory\n");

   if (MemoryAlloc & RGBMEM)
     for (Index=0; Index < COLLEVELS; Index++)
        if (RGBCube[Index] != NULL)
                farfree((unsigned far *) RGBCube[Index]);
```

```
    if (MemoryAlloc & REDMEM)
       farfree((char far *) Red);
    if (MemoryAlloc & GREENMEM)
       farfree((char far *) Green);
    if (MemoryAlloc & BLUEMEM)
       farfree((char far *) Blue);
    if (MemoryAlloc & IMAGEMEM)
       farfree((char far *) ImageBuf);
}


/*
Allocate all memory for the entire program. The MemoryAlloc variable is
used to keep track of all memory that has been allocated from the far
heap. That way DeAllocMemory can give it all back to the system when the
program terminates.
*/
unsigned AllocMemory( void )
{
    register unsigned Index;

    Message("Allocating program memory\n");

    /* create COLLEVELS number of pointer to 2 D arrays */
    /*
    Set the initial values of the RGBCube sub-array pointers to NULL,
    so we can do proper checks later to see if they have been allocated
    or not.
    */

    for (Index=0; Index < COLLEVELS; Index++)
       RGBCube[Index] = NULL;

    for (Index=0; Index < COLLEVELS; Index++)
    {
       RGBCube[Index] = (unsigned far *) farcalloc(COLLEVELS*COLLEVELS,
                       (unsigned long) sizeof(short));

       if (RGBCube[Index] == NULL)
       {
          printf("RGBCube memory allocation failed\n");
          printf("\t only %ld bytes of memory available\n",farcoreleft());
```

(continued)

Listing 5.4 *(continued)*

```
        DeAllocMemory();
        return(FALSE);
    }
}
MemoryAlloc |= RGBMEM;                    /* indicate success */

Red  = (char huge *) farcalloc(NUMPIXELS,(unsigned long) sizeof(char));
if (Red == NULL)
{
    printf("Red allocation failed\n");
    printf("\t only %ld bytes of memory available\n",farcoreleft());
    DeAllocMemory();
    return(FALSE);
}
MemoryAlloc |= REDMEM;                    /* indicate success */

Green = (char huge *) farcalloc(NUMPIXELS,(unsigned long) sizeof(char));
if (Green == NULL)
{
    printf("Green allocation failed\n");
    printf("\t only %ld bytes of memory available\n",farcoreleft());
    DeAllocMemory();
    return(FALSE);
}
MemoryAlloc |= GREENMEM;                  /* indicate success */

Blue = (char huge *) farcalloc(NUMPIXELS,(unsigned long) sizeof(char));
if (Blue == NULL)
{
    printf("Blue allocation failed\n");
    printf("\t only %ld bytes of memory available\n",farcoreleft());
    DeAllocMemory();
    return(FALSE);
}
MemoryAlloc |= BLUEMEM;                   /* indicate success */

/* allocate buffer into which all three images will be acquired */
ImageBuf = (char huge *) farcalloc(320L*240L,(unsigned long) sizeof(char));
if (ImageBuf == NULL)
{
    printf("Image buffer allocation failed\n");
    printf("\t only %ld bytes of memory available\n",farcoreleft());
```

```
         DeAllocMemory();
         return(FALSE);
      }
   MemoryAlloc |= IMAGEMEM;              /* indicate success */
   return(TRUE);
}


/*
This function forces the input data to fit in the range described by
COLLEVELS.  When it is complete, the specified array will only contain
values between 0 and COLLEVELS-1 inclusive.
*/
void Normalize(char huge *ColorData)
{
  register BYTE Min, Max;
  unsigned long LongIndex;

/* find minimum and maximum values in the array. */
  Min = 0;
  Max = 0;

  for (LongIndex=0; LongIndex < NUMPIXELS; LongIndex++)
  {
     if (ColorData[LongIndex] < Min)
            Min = ColorData[LongIndex];
     if (ColorData[LongIndex] > Max)
            Max = ColorData[LongIndex];
  }

/* Force each pixel to the range 0..COLLEVELS-1 */
  for (LongIndex=0; LongIndex < NUMPIXELS; LongIndex++)
    ColorData[LongIndex] = ((ColorData[LongIndex]-Min)*(COLLEVELS-1))/
                           (Max-Min);
}
/*
This function fills the RGBCube array with the color frequencies, and as a
side effect, counts and prints the number of unique colors in the input.
*/
void ScanColorFrequencies( void )
{
   register unsigned c, k, NumColors;
   unsigned long LongIndex;
```

(continued)

Listing 5.4   *(continued)*

```
  /* Initialize RGBCube to all zeros */
  for (c=0; c < COLLEVELS; c++)
    for (k=0; k < COLLEVELS*COLLEVELS; k++)
      RGBCube[c][k] = 0;


  /* For each pixel, count the number of pixels with that color */
  for (LongIndex=0; LongIndex < NUMPIXELS; LongIndex++)
    RGBCube[Red[LongIndex]][(Blue[LongIndex]*COLLEVELS)+Green[LongIndex]]++;


  /*
  Count and print the number of unique colors in the input by scanning the
  RGBCube array and looking for non-zero frequencies.
  */
  NumColors = 0;
  for (c=0; c < COLLEVELS; c++)
    for (k=0; k < COLLEVELS*COLLEVELS; k++)
      if (RGBCube[c][k])
            NumColors++;

  if (Verbose)
    printf("%d unique colors in image data\n",NumColors);
}


/*
This function sets the indices to the numbers of the other axes after
a main axis has been selected.
*/
void OtherAxes(unsigned mainaxis,unsigned *other1,unsigned *other2)
{
  switch (mainaxis)
  {
  case 0:
    *other1 = 1;
    *other2 = 2;
    break;
  case 1:
    *other1 = 0;
    *other2 = 2;
    break;
  case 2:
    *other1 = 0;
    *other2 = 1;
  }
}
```

```c
/*
This function takes a index value into the Boxes array, and shrinks the
specified box to tightly fit around the input color frequency data (eg.
there are no zero planes on the sides of the box).
*/
void Shrink(unsigned BoxIndex)
{
   unsigned axis,aax1,aax2;
   register unsigned ind[3], flag;

   /* Along each axis: */
   for (axis=0; axis < NUMAXIS; axis++)
   {
     OtherAxes(axis,&aax1,&aax2);

     /* Scan off zero planes on from the low end of the axis */
     flag = 0;
     for (ind[axis]=Boxes[BoxIndex].Lo[axis];
               ind[axis] <= Boxes[BoxIndex].Hi[axis]; ind[axis]++)
     {
        for (ind[aax1]=Boxes[BoxIndex].Lo[aax1];
                ind[aax1] <= Boxes[BoxIndex].Hi[aax1]; ind[aax1]++)
        {
           for (ind[aax2]=Boxes[BoxIndex].Lo[aax2];
                      ind[aax2] <= Boxes[BoxIndex].Hi[aax2]; ind[aax2]++)
             if (RGBCube[ind[0]][ind[1]*COLLEVELS+ind[2]])
             {
                flag=1;
                break;
             }
              if (flag) break;
        }
        if (flag) break;
     }
     Boxes[BoxIndex].Lo[axis] = ind[axis];

     /* Scan off zero planes from the high end of the axis */
     flag = 0;
     for (ind[axis]=Boxes[BoxIndex].Hi[axis];
               ind[axis]+1 >= Boxes[BoxIndex].Lo[axis]+1; ind[axis]--)
     {
        for (ind[aax1]=Boxes[BoxIndex].Hi[aax1];
                ind[aax1]+1 >= Boxes[BoxIndex].Lo[aax1]+1; ind[aax1]--)
```

(continued)

Listing 5.4 *(continued)*

```
        {
          for (ind[aax2]=Boxes[BoxIndex].Hi[aax2];
               ind[aax2]+1>=Boxes[BoxIndex].Lo[aax2]+1; ind[aax2]--)
            if (RGBCube[ind[0]][ind[1]*COLLEVELS+ind[2]])
            {
              flag = 1;
              break;
            }
              if (flag) break;
        }
        if (flag) break;
      }
    Boxes[BoxIndex].Hi[axis] = ind[axis];
  }
}


/* print box debug function */
void PrtBox(unsigned BoxIndex)
{
   printf("\nBox Number %d\n",BoxIndex);
   printf("Hi[0]=%d Lo[0]=%d\n",Boxes[BoxIndex].Hi[0],Boxes[BoxIndex].Lo[0]);
   printf("Hi[1]=%d Lo[1]=%d\n",Boxes[BoxIndex].Hi[1],Boxes[BoxIndex].Lo[1]);
   printf("Hi[2]=%d Lo[2]=%d\n",Boxes[BoxIndex].Hi[2],Boxes[BoxIndex].Lo[2]);
   printf("Elements %ld\n\n",Boxes[BoxIndex].NumElements);
   getch();
}


/*
This function selects the optimum colors from the color frequency data,
using the Median Cut algorithm.  It prints the number of colors used at
its termination.
*/
void SelectColorBoxes( void )
{
   register unsigned SelectedBox, c;
   register unsigned ind[3], Max, axis, TargetBox, k;
   unsigned aax1,aax2;
   unsigned long LongMax, PlaneSum, ElementSum;

   /*
   Initialize the first and only box in the array to contain the entire RGBCube,
   then discard unused zero planes surrounding it.
```

```
*/
for (c=0; c < NUMAXIS; c++)
{
   Boxes[0].Lo[c] = 0;
   Boxes[0].Hi[c] = COLLEVELS-1;
}
Boxes[0].NumElements = NUMPIXELS;
NumBoxes = 1;
Shrink(0);
/* Perform the following until all color registers are used up */
while(NumBoxes < MAXNUMCOLREGS)
{
   /*
   Pick the box with the maximum number of elements that is not a single
   color value to work with.  It will be the box we will split.
   */
   LongMax = 0;
   SelectedBox = 1000;
   for (c=0; c < NumBoxes; c++)
   {
         if ((Boxes[c].NumElements > LongMax) &&
         ((Boxes[c].Lo[0] != Boxes[c].Hi[0]) ||
         (Boxes[c].Lo[1] != Boxes[c].Hi[1]) ||
         (Boxes[c].Lo[2] != Boxes[c].Hi[2])))
      {
            LongMax = Boxes[c].NumElements;
         SelectedBox = c;
      }
   }
   /*
   If we couldn't find any box that was not a single color, we don't
   need to assign any more colors, so we can terminate this loop.
   */
   if (SelectedBox == 1000)
     break;

   /* Choose the longest axis of the box to split it along */
   axis = 0;
   Max = Boxes[SelectedBox].Hi[axis] - Boxes[SelectedBox].Lo[axis];
   for (k=1; k < NUMAXIS; k++)
   {
      if (Max < (c=(Boxes[SelectedBox].Hi[k]-Boxes[SelectedBox].Lo[k])))
```

(continued)

Listing 5.4   *(continued)*

```
    {
        Max = c;
        axis = k;
    }
}


/*
Check to see if any of our previously assigned boxes have zero elements
(may happen in degenerate cases), if so, re-use them.  If not, use the
next available box.
*/
TargetBox = NumBoxes;
for (c=0; c < NumBoxes; c++)
{
        if (Boxes[c].NumElements == 0)
    {
        TargetBox = c;
        break;
    }
}


OtherAxes(axis,&aax1,&aax2);
if (Boxes[SelectedBox].Hi[axis] != Boxes[SelectedBox].Lo[axis])
{
    /*
    Sum planes of box from low end until the sum exceeds half the total
    number of elements in the box.  That is the point where we will
    split it.
    */
    ElementSum = 0;
    for (ind[axis]=Boxes[SelectedBox].Lo[axis];
            ind[axis] <= Boxes[SelectedBox].Hi[axis]; ind[axis]++)
    {
        PlaneSum = 0;
        for (ind[aax1]=Boxes[SelectedBox].Lo[aax1];
                    ind[aax1] <= Boxes[SelectedBox].Hi[aax1]; ind[aax1]++)
            for (ind[aax2]=Boxes[SelectedBox].Lo[aax2];
                        ind[aax2] <= Boxes[SelectedBox].Hi[aax2]; ind[aax2]++)
                PlaneSum += RGBCube[ind[0]][ind[1]*COLLEVELS+ind[2]];
        ElementSum += PlaneSum;
        if (ElementSum > Boxes[SelectedBox].NumElements/2)
            break;
    }
```

```
/*
If we did not exceed half the total until we added the last plane
(such as in a case where the last plane contains the bulk of the data
points), back up so we do not create the new box as a degenerate box.
*/
     if (ind[axis] == Boxes[SelectedBox].Hi[axis])
{
   ind[axis]--;
   ElementSum -= PlaneSum;
}
/*
The new box has most of the data the same as the old box, but its low
extent is the index above the point where we needed to split, and its
number of elements is the total number of elements in this whole box,
minus the number in the planes we just summed.
*/
for (c=0; c < NUMAXIS; c++)
{
   Boxes[TargetBox].Lo[c] = Boxes[SelectedBox].Lo[c];
   Boxes[TargetBox].Hi[c] = Boxes[SelectedBox].Hi[c];
}
Boxes[TargetBox].Lo[axis] = ind[axis]+1;
Boxes[TargetBox].NumElements = Boxes[SelectedBox].NumElements -
                              ElementSum;


/*
The high extent of our old box is now cut off at the plane we just
split at and the number of elements in it is the number we just
summed.
*/
Boxes[SelectedBox].Hi[axis] = ind[axis];
Boxes[SelectedBox].NumElements = ElementSum;


/* Discard zero planes around both our new boxes */
Shrink(SelectedBox);
Shrink(TargetBox);


/*
If we used the top box in our list, we have to increment the
total number of boxes used, to make ready for the use of the next
free box.
*/
```

(continued)

Listing 5.4 *(continued)*

```
          if (TargetBox == NumBoxes)
              NumBoxes++;
      }
   }


   /* show number of display colors to be used if requested to */
   if (Verbose)
      printf("%d colors will be used for display of the image\n",NumBoxes);
}


/*
This function calculates the actual color register values for each box,
based on the weighted distribution of data in the box.  It then sorts the
color registers by brightness (using a calculation described by the VGA
technical reference for calculating brightness).
*/
void SortColors( void )
{
   register unsigned Index,c,flag,temp,r,b,g;
   unsigned indices[MAXNUMCOLREGS];
   unsigned long weightedcolor[MAXNUMCOLREGS],rsum,bsum,gsum,tmp;

   for (Index=0; Index < NumBoxes; Index++)
   {

      /* Calculate a weighted sum of the color values in the box */

      rsum = bsum = gsum = 0;
      for (r=Boxes[Index].Lo[0]; r<=Boxes[Index].Hi[0]; r++)
         for (b=Boxes[Index].Lo[1]; b<=Boxes[Index].Hi[1]; b++)
            for (g=Boxes[Index].Lo[2]; g<=Boxes[Index].Hi[2]; g++)
            {
               tmp = RGBCube[r][b*COLLEVELS+g];
               rsum += r*tmp;
               bsum += b*tmp;
               gsum += g*tmp;
            }

      /* Pick the actual color for that box based on the the weighted sum */
      ColRegs[Index].Red   = rsum/Boxes[Index].NumElements;
      ColRegs[Index].Blue  = bsum/Boxes[Index].NumElements;
      ColRegs[Index].Green = gsum/Boxes[Index].NumElements;
   }
```

```
/*
Set up for an index sort of the brightnesses by first calculating the
weighted brightness of each color (based on the calculation described in the
VGA manual.
*/
for (Index=0; Index < NumBoxes; Index++)
{
    indices[Index] = Index;
    weightedcolor[Index] = ColRegs[Index].Red  *30 +
                                    ColRegs[Index].Blue *11 +
                                    ColRegs[Index].Green*59;
}


/*
Do a bubble sort of the weighted colors via indices. Sort is done in
ascending order.
*/
flag = 1;
while (flag)
{
    flag = 0;
    for (Index=0; Index < NumBoxes-1; Index++)
        if (weightedcolor[indices[Index]] > weightedcolor[indices[Index+1]])
        {
            temp = indices[Index];
            indices[Index] = indices[Index+1];
            indices[Index+1] = temp;
            flag = 1;
        }
}
/*
Re-map the boxes and the color registers into SBoxes and SColRegs via the
sorted indices found above.
*/
for (Index=0; Index < NumBoxes; Index++)
{
    SColRegs[Index].Red   = ColRegs[indices[Index]].Red;
    SColRegs[Index].Blue  = ColRegs[indices[Index]].Blue;
    SColRegs[Index].Green = ColRegs[indices[Index]].Green;
    SBoxes[Index].NumElements = Boxes[indices[Index]].NumElements;
    for (c=0; c < NUMAXIS; c++)
    {
        SBoxes[Index].Hi[c] = Boxes[indices[Index]].Hi[c];
```

(continued)

Listing 5.4 *(continued)*

```
          SBoxes[Index].Lo[c] = Boxes[indices[Index]].Lo[c];
      }
   }
}


/* Get the color value of the specified pixel on VGA screen */
unsigned GetPixelValue(unsigned long PixNum)
{
   register unsigned Col, Row;

   Col = (unsigned)(PixNum / (long) NUMROWS);
   Row = (unsigned)(PixNum % (long) NUMROWS);
   return(GetPixel256(Col,Row));
}


/* Set the color value of the specified pixel on VGA screen */
void SetPixelValue(unsigned long PixNum, unsigned Value)
{
   register unsigned Col, Row;

   Col = (unsigned)(PixNum / (long) NUMROWS);
   Row = (unsigned)(PixNum % (long) NUMROWS);
   PutPixel256(Col,Row,Value);
}


/*
This function maps the raw image pixel data in the input array into the
new color map we've come up with in the SColRegs array.  In addition, it
may use Floyd-Steinberg dithering to reduce the error in the image conversion.
*/
void DisplayImageData( void )
{
   register unsigned c,k,goodindex, PixVal;
   unsigned long minerror,error,LongIndex;
   register int RedDif,GreenDif,BlueDif,r,b,g,i;

   /*
   Set the RGBCube array to a value that can't be a color register index
   (MAXNUMCOLREGS*2) so we can detect when we hit on a part of the array that
   is not included in a color box.
   */
   for (c=0; c < COLLEVELS; c++)
      for (k=0; k < COLLEVELS*COLLEVELS; k++)
              RGBCube[c][k] = MAXNUMCOLREGS*2;
```

```
/*
Fill the boxes in the RGBCube array with the index number for that box, so
we can tell what box a particular color index into the RGBCube array is in
by a single access.
*/
for (i=0; i < NumBoxes; i++)
    for (r=SBoxes[i].Lo[0]; r <= SBoxes[i].Hi[0]; r++)
            for (b=SBoxes[i].Lo[1]; b <= SBoxes[i].Hi[1]; b++)
                for (g=SBoxes[i].Lo[2]; g <= SBoxes[i].Hi[2]; g++)
            RGBCube[r][b*COLLEVELS+g] = i;
/* for each pixel */
for (LongIndex=0; LongIndex < NUMPIXELS; LongIndex++)
{
    /*
    If the color levels at that pixel are within proper range, and
    this particular color is inside one of the boxes, and we are not
    in optimum color mode, assign the color index for this pixel to the
    value at that spot in the cube.
    */
    if (Red[LongIndex]   < COLLEVELS &&
        Blue[LongIndex]   < COLLEVELS &&
        Green[LongIndex] < COLLEVELS &&
        (RGBCube[Red[LongIndex]][Blue[LongIndex]*COLLEVELS+Green[LongIndex]]
        !=MAXNUMCOLREGS*2) && !OptimumColors)
    {
        PixVal = RGBCube[Red[LongIndex]][Blue[LongIndex]*COLLEVELS+
                    Green[LongIndex]];
        SetPixelValue(LongIndex,PixVal);
    }
    else
    {
        /*
        Otherwise, we need to scan the array of colors to find which is
        the closest to our prospective color.
        */
        goodindex = 0;
        minerror = SQUARE(Red[LongIndex]-SColRegs[goodindex].Red)+
                    SQUARE(Blue[LongIndex]-SColRegs[goodindex].Blue)+
                    SQUARE(Green[LongIndex]-SColRegs[goodindex].Green);
        /*
        Scan all color registers to find which has the smallest error
        when it is used for this pixel.
        */
        for (k=1; k < NumBoxes; k++)
```

(continued)

Listing 5.4 *(continued)*

```
    {
       error = SQUARE(Red[LongIndex]-SColRegs[k].Red)+
               SQUARE(Blue[LongIndex]-SColRegs[k].Blue)+
               SQUARE(Green[LongIndex]-SColRegs[k].Green);
       if (error < minerror)
       {
          minerror = error;
          goodindex = k;
       }
    }
    /* Assign that register to this pixel */
    SetPixelValue(LongIndex,goodindex);
 }

 /* do dithering if requested */
 if (FloydStein)
 {
    /*
    Calculate the difference between the actual color at this pixel
    and the color of the register we are assigning it to.
    */
    RedDif = ((int) SColRegs[GetPixelValue(LongIndex)].Red) -
               ((int) Red[LongIndex]);
    BlueDif = ((int) SColRegs[GetPixelValue(LongIndex)].Blue) -
               ((int) Blue[LongIndex]);
    GreenDif = ((int) SColRegs[GetPixelValue(LongIndex)].Green) -
               ((int) Green[LongIndex]);

       /* If we are not at the right hand column of the image */
       if ((((LongIndex+NUMROWS) / NUMROWS) < NUMCOLS) &&
           (LongIndex+NUMROWS) < NUMPIXELS)
       {
          /* Diffuse 3/8s of the error to the pixel to our right */
          Red[LongIndex+NUMROWS]   += (RedDif*3)/8;
          Blue[LongIndex+NUMROWS]  += (BlueDif*3)/8;
          Green[LongIndex+NUMROWS] += (GreenDif*3)/8;

          /* if that caused the pixel to our right to wrap */
          if (Red[LongIndex+NUMROWS]   > COLLEVELS-1 ||
                Green[LongIndex+NUMROWS] > COLLEVELS-1 ||
                Blue[LongIndex+NUMROWS]  > COLLEVELS-1)
          {
             /* undo the addition on that pixel */
                Red[LongIndex+NUMROWS]   -= (RedDif*3)/8;
```

```
                        Blue[LongIndex+NUMROWS]  -= (BlueDif*3)/8;
                        Green[LongIndex+NUMROWS]  -= (GreenDif*3)/8;
           }
        }
        /* if not at bottom of image */
        if (LongIndex % NUMROWS < NUMROWS-1)
        {
           /* Diffuse 3/8s of the error to the pixel below */
           Red[LongIndex+1]    += (RedDif*3)/8;
           Blue[LongIndex+1]   += (BlueDif*3)/8;
           Green[LongIndex+1] += (GreenDif*3)/8;

           /*  If that caused the pixel below us to wrap */
           if (Red[LongIndex+1]   > COLLEVELS-1 ||
                   Green[LongIndex+1] > COLLEVELS-1 ||
                   Blue[LongIndex+1]  > COLLEVELS-1)
           {
              /* Undo the addition on that pixel */
              Red[LongIndex+1]    -= (RedDif*3)/8;
              Blue[LongIndex+1]   -= (BlueDif*3)/8;
              Green[LongIndex+1] -= (GreenDif*3)/8;
           }
        }
        /* if not on last row and not in last column of image */
        if ((((LongIndex+NUMROWS) / NUMROWS) < NUMCOLS) &&
                (LongIndex % NUMROWS < NUMROWS-1))
        {
           /* Diffuse 1/4 of error to the pixel below and to our right */
           Red[LongIndex+1+NUMROWS]    += RedDif/4;
           Blue[LongIndex+1+NUMROWS]   += BlueDif/4;
           Green[LongIndex+1+NUMROWS] += GreenDif/4;

           /* if pixel value wrapped */
           if (Red[LongIndex+1+NUMROWS]   > COLLEVELS-1 ||
                   Green[LongIndex+1+NUMROWS] > COLLEVELS-1 ||
                   Blue[LongIndex+1+NUMROWS]  > COLLEVELS-1)
           {
              /* Undo the addition on that pixel */
              Red[LongIndex+1+NUMROWS]    -= RedDif/4;
              Blue[LongIndex+1+NUMROWS]   -= BlueDif/4;
              Green[LongIndex+1+NUMROWS] -= GreenDif/4;
           }
        }
     }
   }
 }
}
```

(continued)

Listing 5.4 *(continued)*

```
/*
The purpose of this function is to partially make up
for the normalization of pixel values performed previously.
The values in the color registers are scaled upwards toward
the maximum value of 63 to increase image briteness.
*/
void ScaleColRegisters(void)
{
   unsigned Index;
   unsigned MaxVal = 0;
   unsigned Temp;

   /* Find the maximum value of any RGB component value */
   for (Index = 0; Index < MAXNUMCOLREGS; Index++)
   {
      if (SColRegs[Index].Red > MaxVal)
            MaxVal = SColRegs[Index].Red;
      if (SColRegs[Index].Green > MaxVal)
            MaxVal = SColRegs[Index].Green;
      if (SColRegs[Index].Blue > MaxVal)
            MaxVal = SColRegs[Index].Blue;
   }
   /* Scale all color register components accordingly */
   for (Index = 0; Index < MAXNUMCOLREGS; Index++)
   {
      /* temp used to prevent overflow of BYTE value */
      Temp = SColRegs[Index].Red * (unsigned) MAXCOLREGVAL;
      Temp /= MaxVal;
      SColRegs[Index].Red = Temp;

      Temp = SColRegs[Index].Green * (unsigned) MAXCOLREGVAL;
      Temp /= MaxVal;
      SColRegs[Index].Green = Temp;

      Temp = SColRegs[Index].Blue * (unsigned) MAXCOLREGVAL;
      Temp /= MaxVal;
      SColRegs[Index].Blue = Temp;
   }
}


void InstallPalette256( void )
{
   register unsigned Index;
```

```
/*
With a graphics mode set, we can proceed to load our colors
into the DAC. A palette is not used in the 256 color mode of VGA.
*/
for (Index = 0; Index < MAXNUMCOLREGS; Index++)
{
   /* set a Color Register */
   regs.h.ah = 0x10;
   regs.h.al = 0x10;
   regs.x.bx = Index;
   regs.h.dh = SColRegs[Index].Red;
   regs.h.ch = SColRegs[Index].Green;
   regs.h.cl = SColRegs[Index].Blue;
   int86(VIDEO,&regs,&regs);
}
}


/*
This function produces an executable .COM file for display of the
digitized color image. It writes a small code segment followed by
the 256 color register value followed by the image data to the
specified file.
*/
void WriteComFile(char *FileName)
{
   FILE *OutPutFile;
   char    String[80];
   unsigned Index, PixelValue, Col, Row;
   BYTE FileCode[] =
     {0xB4,0x0F,0xCD,0x10,0xA2,0x37,0x01,0xB4,0x00,0xB0,0x13,0xCD,0x10,
      0xB8,0x12,0x10,0xBB,0x00,0x00,0xB9,0x00,0x01,0xBA,0x38,0x01,0xCD,
      0x10,0xB9,0x00,0xFA,0xBE,0x38,0x04,0xB8,0x00,0xA0,0x8E,0xC0,0xBF,
      0x00,0x00,0xF3,0xA4,0xB4,0x00,0xCD,0x16,0xB4,0x00,0xA0,0x37,0x01,
      0xCD,0x10,0xC3,0x00};

   if (!strchr(FileName,'.'))          /* is there an ext ? */
   {
      strcpy(String,FileName);         /* copy filename to buffer */
      FileName = String;               /* FileName now pts at buffer */
      strcat(FileName,".com");         /* if not add .com ext */
   }
    /* open the output file */
    if ((OutPutFile = fopen(FileName,"wb")) == NULL)
```

(continued)

Listing 5.4   *(continued)*

```c
{
    printf("Cannot open Image .COM file\n");
    exit(1);
}


/* write code segment to the file */
for (Index=0; Index < sizeof(FileCode); Index++)
    if (fputc(FileCode[Index],OutPutFile) != FileCode[Index])
    {
        restorecrtmode();
        DeAllocMemory();
        printf("Error writing Image .COM code seg\n");
        exit(1);
    }

/* now write the color register rgb values to the file */
for (Index = 0; Index < MAX256PALETTECOLORS; Index++)
{
    if (fputc(SColRegs[Index].Red,OutPutFile) != SColRegs[Index].Red)
    {
        restorecrtmode();
        DeAllocMemory();
        printf("Error writing Image .COM red color reg\n");
        exit(1);
    }
    if (fputc(SColRegs[Index].Green,OutPutFile) != SColRegs[Index].Green)
    {
        restorecrtmode();
        DeAllocMemory();
        printf("Error writing Image .COM green color reg\n");
        exit(1);
    }
    if (fputc(SColRegs[Index].Blue,OutPutFile) != SColRegs[Index].Blue)
    {
        restorecrtmode();
        DeAllocMemory();
        printf("Error writing Image .COM blue color reg\n");
        exit(1);
    }
}
/* now write the actual image data to the file */
for (Row=0; Row < NUMROWS; Row++)
    for (Col=0; Col < NUMCOLS; Col++)
```

```
          {
              PixelValue = GetPixel256(Col,Row); /* read the value from display */
              fputc(PixelValue,OutPutFile);
          }

      fclose(OutPutFile);
}


/*
This function corrects the aspect ratio distortion caused by
the 320x200 VGA display mode. Essentially, a 320x240 pixel image
is acquired by the digitizer and compressed into a 320x200 buffer.
See chapter 12 of this book for details.
*/
void AspectCorrect(unsigned CorrectAspect, char huge *InImage,

                                                    char huge *OutImage)
{
    register unsigned Col, Row;
    register unsigned LowerBufferRow, UpperBufferRow;
    register unsigned UpperIntensity, LowerIntensity;
    register BYTE     Intensity;
    unsigned long     InImageBufOffset, OutImageBufOffset;
    double            FractionalRowAddr, RowDelta;


    if (CorrectAspect)
    {
       Message("Correcting Aspect Ratio of Image\n");

       /* For each column of the destination buffer (320 total) */
       for (Col=0; Col < LRMAXCOLS; Col++)
       {
              /*
              Calculate the start of the digitized video information
              in the image buffer for this column.
              */
              InImageBufOffset  = (long) SOURCEIMAGEROWS * Col;
              OutImageBufOffset = (long) LRMAXROWS * Col;
              /*
              For each rows in the destination buffer ...
              */
              for (Row=0; Row < LRMAXROWS; Row++)
```

(continued)

Listing 5.4 *(continued)*

```
{
    /*
    Which actual digitized video row out of the
    total of 240 should we accessed ? The calculated
    address will reside between two actual addresses.
    The address will be fractional.
    */
    FractionalRowAddr = ROWASPECTCORRECTION * (double) Row;
    /*
    Get the address of the row bytes just below and just
    above the calculated fractional address. Fetch the
    intensity values of each.
    */
    LowerBufferRow = (unsigned) FractionalRowAddr;
    UpperBufferRow = LowerBufferRow + 1;
    LowerIntensity = InImage[InImageBufOffset + LowerBufferRow];
    UpperIntensity = InImage[InImageBufOffset + UpperBufferRow];


    /*
    Calculate the distance the fractional address is off
    from the lower real address. This distance is required
    for the interpolation process.
    */
    RowDelta = FractionalRowAddr - LowerBufferRow;
    /*
    Interpolate for the value of the intensity to assign
    to the pixel at this row.
    */
    Intensity = RowDelta*((double) UpperIntensity - LowerIntensity) +
                                                    LowerIntensity;


    /*
    Store the calculated intensity in the destination
    image buffer;
    */
    OutImage[OutImageBufOffset+Row] = Intensity;
        }
    }
    }
}


/*
This function provides help in the advent of operator error. Program
terminates after help is given
```

```
*/
void ShowHelp( void )
{
   printf("\nThis program digitizes and displays a color image. It\n");
   printf("is envoked as follows:\n\n");
   printf("Usage: cvideo [-a -d -h -o -p -s -v -x] filename <cr>\n");
   printf("  -a correct aspect ratio of image\n");
   printf("  -d use Floyd-Steinberg dithering\n");
   printf("  -h or ? show help\n");
   printf("  -o calculates optimum color palette\n");
   printf("  -p create PCX output file\n");
   printf("  -s scales color register values to max\n");
   printf("  -v displays program progress information\n");
   printf("  -x create executable display program\n");
   printf("  filename is name given to generated display file(s).\n");
   printf("     Do not specify a file extension, it will be provided.\n\n");
   exit(1);
}


/* main digitizer program */
void main(short argc, char *argv[])
{
   unsigned FileNameCounter, ArgIndex;
   char    *ImageFileName;

   InitGraphics();
   clrscr();
   printf("Digitize, Display and Save a Color Image\n\n");

   /* install default options */
   FloydStein    = FALSE;            /* no dithering */
   OptimumColors = FALSE;            /* use best guess color approx */
   Verbose       = FALSE;            /* don't be wordy */
   GenComFile    = FALSE;            /* don't generate an .COM file */
   GenPCXFile    = FALSE;            /* don't generate a. PCX file */
   ScaleColRegs  = FALSE;            /* don't scale col reg values */
   CorrectAspectRatio = FALSE;       /* don't correct aspect ratio */

   /* parse all command line arguments */

   FileNameCounter = 0;              /* count of user specified filenames */
   for (ArgIndex=1; ArgIndex < argc; ArgIndex++)
   {
      if (*argv[ArgIndex] != '-')    /* if not a cmd line switch */
```

(continued)

Listing 5.4 *(continued)*

```
{                                      /* must be a filename */
        if (*argv[ArgIndex] == '?')    /* help requested ? */
            ShowHelp();
        if (FileNameCounter > 1)         /* only one filename allowed */
      ShowHelp();                        /* if more then error exit */
        ImageFileName = argv[ArgIndex];  /* save image filename */
    FileNameCounter++;                   /* inc count for error check */
}
else                                   /* its a cmd line switch */
{
    switch (*(argv[ArgIndex]+1))       /* parse the cmd line */
    {
            case 'a':
            case 'A':
                CorrectAspectRatio = TRUE;
        break;
            case 'd':
            case 'D':
                FloydStein = TRUE;
        break;
            case 'h':
            case 'H':
                ShowHelp();
        break;
            case 'o':
            case 'O':
                OptimumColors = TRUE;
                break;
            case 'p':
            case 'P':
                GenPCXFile = TRUE;
        break;
            case 's':
            case 'S':
                ScaleColRegs = TRUE;
        break;
        case 'v':
        case 'V':
                Verbose    = TRUE;
            break;
            case 'x':
            case 'X':
                GenComFile = TRUE;
```

```
                break;
                    default:
                        printf("Error - invalid cmd line switch encountered\n");
                        ShowHelp();
            }
        }
    }
    if ((GenComFile | GenPCXFile) && (FileNameCounter != 1))
    {
        printf("Error - single filename required for output file(s)\n");
        ShowHelp();
    }
    /* attempt to allocate all required memory */
    if (!AllocMemory())
    {
        printf("memory allocation error - program terminated !\n");
        exit(ENoMemory);
    }


    /*
    Build the structure that defines what the digitizer should acquire. This
    will be passed to the digitizer by a call to InitializeDigitizer
    function
    */
    Req.ComputerType    = PS220;
    Req.PrtBase         = LPT1;
    Req.HMode           = LowRes;
    Req.VMode           = NonInterlace;
    Req.NumberOfPasses  = 1;
    Req.Flags           = 0L;
    Req.FirstLine       = 0;
    Req.FirstPixel      = 0;
    Req.LastPixel       = 320;

    /* acquire a 320x240 image if aspect ratio is to be corrected */
    if (CorrectAspectRatio)
        Req.LastLine    = 240;
    else
        Req.LastLine    = 200;
    InitializeDigitizer(&Req);          /* tell hardware what to do */

    printf("Put Red filter in front of the camera\n");
    printf("Press a key when ready\n");
```

(continued)

Listing 5.4 *(continued)*

```
getch();
Message("Acquiring the Red Picture Data from the Digitizer\n");
if (CorrectAspectRatio)
   Req.PictBuf = ImageBuf;
else
   Req.PictBuf = Red;
GetPicture();
AspectCorrect(CorrectAspectRatio,ImageBuf,Red);

printf("Put Green filter in front of the camera\n");
printf("Press a key when ready\n");
getch();
Message("Acquiring the Green Picture Data from the Digitizer\n");
if (CorrectAspectRatio)
   Req.PictBuf = ImageBuf;
else
   Req.PictBuf = Green;
GetPicture();
AspectCorrect(CorrectAspectRatio,ImageBuf,Green);

printf("Put Blue filter in front of the camera\n");
printf("Press a key when ready\n");
getch();
Message("Acquiring the Blue Picture Data from the Digitizer\n");
if (CorrectAspectRatio)
   Req.PictBuf = ImageBuf;
else
   Req.PictBuf = Blue;
GetPicture();
AspectCorrect(CorrectAspectRatio,ImageBuf,Blue);

Message("Picture data acquired. Processing the palette data ...\n");

Message("Normalizing color data\n");
Normalize(Red);
Normalize(Blue);
Normalize(Green);

Message("Building color frequency table\n");
ScanColorFrequencies();
Message("Selecting optimum color palette\n");
SelectColorBoxes();
SortColors();
```

```
/* display the resultant color image with the proper palette */
Set256ColorMode();
DisplayImageData();
if (ScaleColRegs)
   ScaleColRegisters();
InstallPalette256();

if (GenPCXFile)
{
   /* create a PCX file for display of color image */
   WritePCXFile(ImageFileName,8,320,200,1,320);
}
if (GenComFile)
{
   /* create an executable file for display of color image */
   WriteComFile(ImageFileName);
}

/* prepare to return to dos */
getch();
restorecrtmode();
DeAllocMemory();
closegraph();
}
```

Producing color images is not a trivial task. This program, by necessity, is the most complex presented in this book. Over 6,000 lines of C and 400 lines of assembler code are required to produce and display the color images. The results, although quite spectacular, could be improved substantially with the removal of certain constraints. These will be discussed later.

General Operation

Color images are produced by making three individual digitizings of an image, each time using a different colored filter (between the video camera and the object/image). The colors of the filters are, as you might have guessed, the three primary colors: red, green, and blue. From the three different digitizings, software can determine on a pixel-by-pixel basis the color components that best describe the pixel's color. When eventually loaded into one of the 256 color registers in the VGA graphics adapter, these components will cause a color very close to that in the original image to be displayed on the screen at that pixel's location. This highly simplified explanation will be expanded upon throughout the remainder of this chapter.

Naturally, it is necessary for the object/image being digitized to remain stationary during all three passes of the digitization process. If there is movement during digitization, the image's "database" (the red, green, and blue image data buffers) will be corrupted, resulting in a less than perfect color image display. Movement can sometimes be used, however, as a special effect during the digitization process. See "Modifications, Manipulations, and Experimentation," later in this chapter, for details.

From experimental measurements it is known that the human visual system (the eye/brain system) is capable of distinguishing approximately 350,000 colors. Any natural scene we look at is made up of many colors, both striking and subtle. The eye/brain system uses the dominant colors to convey the image information to our brains, where the image is perceived. The more subtle aspects of color in the perceived image enhance the details of an image but are not absolutely necessary for recognition. Additionally, the brain will fill in details that appear to be lacking in order to make sense of an image.

Whereas the human eye is capable of distinguishing a large color space, computer and video monitors are not capable of producing anywhere near that many unique colors. As we have seen, the maximum number of simultaneously displayable colors available in a VGA-equipped system is 256—less than one-thousandth of the number of colors the eye can perceive. Yet by optimally choosing the dominant 256 colors that make up a natural scene, an accurate digitized color image can be produced. Surprisingly, displaying an image with as few as 16 unique colors gives fairly good results. Using less than 16 colors for image display, however, impacts the realism of the image dramatically.

In this example program, we will use mode 13H of the VGA adapter exclusively to provide color images with a resolution of 320 by 200 in 256 colors. This turns out to be a nice trade-off among resolution, number of colors, and memory usage. Higher resolution and more colors would be nice, but as we shall see later in "TradeOffs," it does not come without a price. It will be left to the reader to extend the example program to suit individual needs.

Most large programs, that are as complex as this example program provide options for tailoring program execution per the user's requirements. This program is no different. It extends the command line user interface of the previous example program to provide many options for program execution—all under operator control. The operation of the color digitizer program, "cvideo.exe", will become obvious after studying the command line options. Figure 5.3 shows the available options and gives a description of what each option does.

Any and all of the command line switches can be used together for a combined effect on the resultant image. Each switch must be separated from the previous switch by a space. Switches can be specified in either upper- or lowercase. It is possible to execute the program without any switches or filenames. This will result in a color image being acquired and displayed without any optional processing or output files being produced.

The process of accepting raw, three-color image data from the digitizer and converting it to a format suitable for display on a VGA graphics adapter can be described by a four-step process. The first step is sampling the image to determine its color distribution. The result of this step is a three-dimensional color histogram (the "RGBCube" in our implementation), which is needed in step 2.

The second step in this process is *color map selection*. Here, the optimal 256 colors required to display a digitized color image are extracted from the input color distribution (or

Program usage: cvideo [-a -d -h -o -p -s -v -x][filename]
Items in [ ] are optional

-a This switch causes the image acquired by the digitizer to be aspect ratio corrected. Inclusion of this switch considerably slows the operation of the "cvideo" program. See Chapter 12 for details of aspect ratio correction.

-d The inclusion of this switch causes Floyd-Steinberg dithering to be performed. Dithering attempts to correct for the errors that occur when mapping a color to one that is not an exact match by spreading the error to surrounding pixels.

-h This switch causes the program to display a concise help screen describing the operation of the "cvideo" program and each of the command line switches. The "cvideo" program terminates immediately after the help screen is displayed.

-o This switch causes the program to search for an optimum color match for each pixel instead of using the "best guess" method it uses by default. The use of this option increases image processing time from about 30 seconds to 20 minutes. The additional image quality produced by the option is of questionable value.

-p The inclusion of this switch results in the generation of a PCX image file from the image displayed on the VGA monitor. When this switch is included on the command line, a filename without extension is required. The name of the produced PCX image file will be "filename.pcx".

-s This option causes the calculated color register values to be scaled upward toward maximum value. The ratio of the color components of each color register remain intact. This option increases image brightness and generally makes for a more attractive image.

-v This option turns on the "Verbose" flag in the code, which causes the program to report its progress. In the Verbose mode, the steps required to acquire and process an image before display will be displayed.

-x This option causes a "COM" file to be created that will display the color image when executed. This feature is referred to as *autodisplay* and will be discussed in detail later in this chapter. When this switch is included on the command line, a filename without extension is required. The name of the autodisplay program will become "filename.com".

Figure 5.3 CVIDEO Command Line Switches

histogram) provided in step 1. This color distribution is the content of the original image as perceived by the digitizer. The digitizer, being a six-bit device, produces image samples within the range 0 to 63 (2^6) for each pixel. Because three different passes are made over the color image being digitized, a total of 2^{18} colors are possible ($64 \cdot 64 \cdot 64$, or 262,144). The 256 optimal colors are therefore selected from the possible 262,144 colors perceptible to the digitizer. Experience has shown that 3,000 to 5,000 unique colors are typically perceived by the digitizer when digitizing color photographs.

Many different techniques and algorithms are available in the literature for performing the three-dimensional optimization required for color map selection. Some work better with one kind of image than with others. The algorithm selected for use in this program is referred to as the *median cut algorithm*. This algorithm is the brain child of Paul Heckbert and was published in *ACM Computer Graphics Journal* in 1982. See "References and Additional Reading" for the specifics of this article. This algorithm seems to work well regardless of the type of image digitized. The C code that implements the median cut algorithm was provided by Dan Butterfield. His code was ported to Turbo C and integrated into the digitizer environment by the author. Dan has graciously given his permission to use his code in this book.

In the third step, a mapping is established between all colors that made up the original image and the closest colors contained in the color map. The mapping function is usually stored in a quantization table ("RGBCube" in our implementation) to speed the processing in step 4. In other words, the mapping between the thousands of colors in the original image and the 256 colors that will be used to display the image is developed.

After the color map has been selected in step 2 and the quantization table is created in step 3, the fourth and final step of the process is image quantization and display. In this step each pixel of the original image is passed through the quantization table (thereby mapping it to the correct color register for display) and is then stored directly in the VGA display's memory. Installation of the correct 256-color palette is the final step in the display process.

Color Filters

The only new equipment required to produce color images (in addition to the equipment required in the previous example programs) are the color filters. Three different color filters—red, green, and blue—are required. These filters can be manually held between the video camera and the object being digitized, but are more easily manipulated if arranged as a color wheel and mounted to the copy stand, as shown in Figure 5.1. A clear segment can be included in the color wheel to allow permanent mounting. The clear segment is placed in front of the camera when monochrome images are being digitized.

As one might expect, the "color properties" of the color filters play an important role in the quality of the digitized color images produced. Ideally, the filters should possess the same chromaticity as the primary colors produced by the video monitor on which the color images will be displayed. The term *chromaticity* refers to the dominant wave length and purity of a color. Unfortunately, color specifications for computer monitors are hard to come by. Monitor specifications, if available and if expressed in terms of CIE (International Commission on Illumination) color specifications, could be used to select the required red, green, and blue filters exactly. In lieu of precise monitor specifications, an experimental method was used to select the filters. The specifications of the resultant filter wheel are shown in Figure 5.4. This filter wheel has been tested with two different computer monitors (an Amiga RGB color monitor and an IBM 8512 monitor) with good results.

Trade-offs

Trade-offs are always required in real-world application programs (sometimes even in not-so-real world example programs). The trade-offs made in this example program stem from (1) the amount of memory addressable under DOS by an application program, and (2) the maximum resolution VGA display available with 256 colors.

The algorithms underlying this example program do not have any inherent limitations. Constraints must be placed on their operation, however, to allow them to run on commonly available hardware and software platforms. The 640KB memory limit of DOS is the single

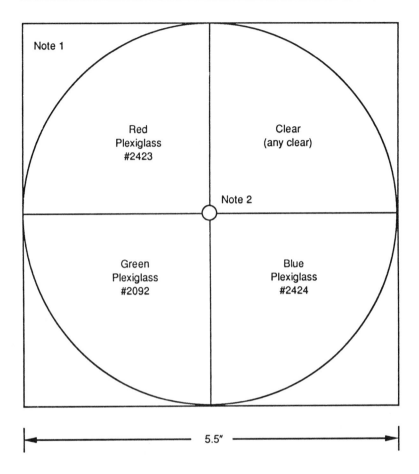

Figure 5.4 Color Filter Wheel Specifications

Notes
1. Filter can be round or square.
2. Center hole diameter sufficient for #8 screw.

largest obstacle to overcome when attempting to stretch the capabilities of this example program.

The data structures used by this program require large amounts of memory. Any attempts to minimize the amount of memory required would impact performance dramatically. A summary of the important data structures and the amount of memory they each consume follows on page 178. The numbers reflect the compromises required to permit this example program to run under DOS.

Other memory is required by the example program in addition to that utilized by its data structures in order to have a working application program. Additional memory is required by DOS itself, Turbo C's run-time library, and the example program's code. When it

Data Structure	Name	Number	Size in Bytes	Total
Box	Box	256	16	4,096
Sorted Box	SBox	256	16	4,096
Color Regs	ColRegs	256	3	768
Sorted Color Regs	SColRegs	256	3	768
Image Buffers	Red, Green, Blue	3	64,000	192,000
3D Color Array	RGBCube	1	65,536	65,536
			$32 \cdot 32 \cdot 32 \cdot 2$	

Approximate Total Memory Required 267,264

is all added up, the "cvideo" example program has just enough memory in a fully equipped system to run successfully. There is very little memory space to spare.

The first compromise made in this example program (to allow it to run in the DOS environment) is the allocated size of the 3D color array, "RGBCube". Ideally, each dimension of the cube should equal the numerical value of the largest pixel sample value plus 1, or 64. "RGBCube" should be $64 \cdot 64 \cdot 64 \cdot 2$, or 524,288 bytes in size. As you can see, if one half a megabyte of memory is required for just the "RGBCube", the program has no possibility of running in the DOS environment.

To accommodate a smaller than optimal "RGBCube", the input pixel data from the digitizer must be scaled and normalized so as to map correctly into the "RGBCube" color frequency array. This extra processing step would not be required if more memory were available. Scaling removes approximately one bit of image dynamic range, which impacts the quality of the produced images slightly.

The resolution of the processed images is also hindered by the lack of available memory. The three 320×200 image buffers currently consume 192,000 bytes of memory. If the image resolution were increased to 640×480, the total amount of memory required for the image buffers would rise to 921,600 bytes. Of course, an IBM standard VGA graphics adapter could not display 640×480 images with 256 colors anyway, but a third-party VGA graphics adapter could, and the realism is incredible: 640×480 images displayed in 256 colors look like color photographs.

The best way around the memory limitations imposed by DOS is to get rid of DOS. A version of this example program could be made to run under one of the currently available protected mode operating systems, such as OS/2 or Unix, which would not suffer the memory constraint. A third-party VGA graphics adapter card (or an IBM 8514/A card and monitor) would be the final key to higher-resolution color image display.

Color Image Acquisition

The steps this example program goes through to acquire and process full-color images are best illustrated with the pseudocode shown here. As you will see, many more steps are required in practice than were described in the theoretical discussion provided previously. The step numbers shown in parentheses correspond to the step numbers given in the theoretical discussion.

```
Function Acquire and Display Color Images

Begin
  Initialize the VGA graphics subsystem
  Parse all command line arguments. Set global variables
    accordingly.
  Allocate memory for all program data structures and image
    buffers.
  Build an ImageReq structure for acquiring 320x200 resolution
    images.
  Initialize the digitizer for the 320x200 images.
  Acquire a 320x200 resolution image through a red filter.
  Aspect ratio correct the image is requested.
  Acquire a 320x200 resolution image through a green filter.
  Aspect ratio correct the image is requested.
  Acquire a 320x200 resolution image through a blue filter.
  Aspect ratio correct the image is requested.
  Normalize the red, green and blue image data.
  Build the color frequency table (RGBCube) for the image.
   (Step one)
  Select the color map (color boxes) (Step two).
  Sort the colors by brightness level.
  Select VGA mode 13H for display of image.
  Display the image (Steps three and four).
  Set the VGA palette from the color map (Step four continued).
  Scale the palette register values if requested.
  Generate a COM file, autodisplay program, if requested.
  Generate a PCX file if requested.
  Wait for the user to hit a key
  Leave graphics mode and go back into text mode.
  Deallocate all program memory.
  Close the graphics library.
End
```

The mechanics of the median cut algorithm are best left to the original author, Paul Heckbert, for description. See his article, listed in "References and Additional Readings," and also the comments in Listing 5.4, for details.

Output Image Files

Two very different output files can be produced by this program. First, if the "-p" command line switch is used when the program is executed, a PCX image file with extended palette structure will be produced from the image on the display. The "view.exe" program, given at the end of Chapter 6, can be used to display the PCX color image at any time. PCX file format will be given a proper explanation in the next chapter.

The second variety of output file is what is referred to as an *autodisplay* file ("Auto-Display"). An autodisplay file is created when the command line switch -x is used. This is a unique file type, which contains a small code segment, the 256 color register values, and the raster data for the 320×200 color image. This file is organized into DOS ".COM" file format and given the filename specified by the user. Being a COM file means the file is directly executable by typing its name at the DOS prompt or by including the filename within a batch (".BAT") file. The autodisplay file produced by this program will display the contained image immediately, in full color, when the file is executed. Please refer to the code for the autodisplay program shown in Listing 5.5 during the short discussion to follow.

The code portion of the autodisplay program is comprised of 23 lines of assembler code. The bulk of the file is comprised of color register data and image raster data. All autodisplay COM files are exactly 64,824 bytes in length because the raster data is uncompressed. The operation of this code is best understood by examining the pseudocode shown below:

```
Function AutoDisplay

Begin
  Get the current video mode by asking the BIOS
  Save the current video mode in memory
  Set the video mode to mode 13H the 320x200 256 color mode.
  Copy the RGB values for all 256 color registers from the
     file into the VGA color registers.
  Set the CX register to the number of bytes of raster data
     stored in the file that will be moved to VGA video memory.
  Set DS:SI registers to point at the raster data in the file.
  Set ES:DI registers to point at VGA video memory located
     at A000:0000.
  Block move the raster data to video memory.
  Wait for user to hit a key (keyboard polled via BIOS).
  Get original video mode from memory.
  Restore original video mode.
End
```

The function of this code should be obvious and need no further explanation. The operation of this code can be observed by executing any of the COM files in the "images" directory on the companion disk. For a nice change of pace, try executing one of these autodisplay files from your computer's "autoexec.bat" file. Then, each time you turn your computer on, you will be greeted with a color digitized image to start your day off right.

The function "WriteComFile" in the example program is what creates the "autodisplay" file. In this function, the object code generated by assembling the autodisplay program is hardcoded into the array "FileCode". The sequence of events necessary to create an executable autodisplay program are as one would expect. First, an output file is opened in

Listing 5.5 The Autodisplay Program

The following is the contents of the file, "imagecom.asm":

```
;320x200 Color Image Display Program
;
;NOTE: this program will only work with a VGA video adapter
;
;written by  Craig A. Lindley
;Vers: 1.0   Last Update: 06/21/89
;
;This program produces a .COM file which when execute will display a
;320x200 256 color image originally produced by the video digitizer.
;
VIDEO           EQU    10H         ;video BIOS interrupt code
KEYBOARD        EQU    16H         ;keyboard BIOS interrupt code
;
IMAGESIZE       EQU    64000       ;320x200 image size in bytes
RGBSIZE         EQU    256*3       ;number of rgb bytes
GETVIDEOMODE    EQU    0FH         ;BIOS function code
SETVIDEOMODE    EQU    00H         ;BIOS function code
SET256COLORMODE EQU    13H         ;320x200 256 color video mode
SETCOLREGBLOCK  EQU    1012H       ;BIOS function/sub function code
VGAMEMSEG       EQU    0A000H      ;segment of VGA display memory
GETKEY          EQU    00H         ;wait for key function code
;
;
CSEG    SEGMENT  PARA  PUBLIC  'CODE'
        ASSUME CS:CSEG,DS:CSEG,SS:CSEG,ES:CSEG ;set by loader
;
        ORG    100H                ;com file org location
;
;NOTE: when transcribing the addresses listed in the list file to the
;      procedure WriteComFile be sure to reverse the order of the address
;      bytes otherwise the resultant .COM image file will not execute.
;
;Start of the display program
;
Start   proc   near

        mov    ah,GETVIDEOMODE     ;get the current video mode
        int    VIDEO               ;result in AL register
        mov    VMode,al            ;save video mode
```

(continued)

Listing 5.5   *(continued)*

```
;
        mov     ah,SETVIDEOMODE   ;set video mode function code
        mov     al,SET256COLORMODE;to special VGA mode
        int     VIDEO             ;do it
;
        mov     ax,SETCOLREGBLOCK ;prepare to load all 256 color regs
        mov     bx,0              ;starting with reg 0
        mov     cx,256            ;all 256 registers
        mov     dx,offset ColorRegs  ;pt at rgb[256] data
                                  ;assumes es=cs
        int     VIDEO             ;load the registers
;
        mov     cx,IMAGESIZE      ;number of bytes to move
        mov     si,offset ImageData  ;source of data to move
                                  ;assume ds=cs
        mov     ax,VGAMEMSEG      ;dest of data to be moved is VGA
        mov     es,ax             ;memory. es[di] = A000:0000
        mov     di,0
        rep     movsb             ;move the image data
;
        mov     ah,GETKEY         ;wait for key press
        int     KEYBOARD          ;ask BIOS
;
        mov     ah,SETVIDEOMODE   ;set video mode function code
        mov     al,VMode          ;to original mode
        int     VIDEO             ;do it
;
        ret                       ;ret to dos
;
Start   endp
;
;Program Data Area - stored in code segment cs
;
VMode       DB      0           ;storage for original video mode
ColorRegs   DB      RGBSIZE   DUP(0);256 rgb triads
ImageData   DB      IMAGESIZE DUP(0);image data storage 64000 bytes
;
CSEG    ENDS
        END     Start
```

binary mode with the name specified by the user on the command line and the extension ".COM" supplied by the program. The executable code is then written from the "FileCode" array to the file. The color register data is then written to the file. The RGB components of color register 1 are written, followed by color register 2, and so on. Finally, the image raster data is read directly from the VGA display with the function "GetPixel256" and written to the file. The data is written in normal line by line raster format from the top of the display to the bottom. After the raster data is written, the autodisplay file is closed, which completes the creation process.

No other new techniques are presented in this code which need discussion. The movement of data into the VGA video memory is the same technique as was presented in Chapter 1 in the discussion of the VGA assembler functions contained in the file "vga-graph.asm".

Modifications, Manipulations, and Experimentation

Once these example programs are operational, you can begin experimenting. At first you will probably be happy digitizing pictures of your family and friends; later, landscapes and arty stuff. During this first phase of experimentation, the more accurate the digitized image you can create, the better. Try the various command line switches to modify the operation of the program to see the effect each has. The scaling option, "-s", generally gives a bright image that is pleasing to look at.

After the initial newness wears off, you can try many experiments to give special effects to your digitized images. Not all will be successful, but you won't know unless you try. After all, you can see the results immediately—you don't have to wait to get the film developed, as you would with traditional film and camera. For example: Try digitizing using the wrong filters in front of the video camera. Try moving the filters while an image is being digitized. If you have access to photographic special-effect filters, these can be placed in front of the video camera to provide the same special effect for your digitized images. Digitize an image through a prism or a kaleidoscope or through rose-colored glasses. Try moving the picture being digitized slightly between filter changes. You can possibly produce a 3D effect if you offset the red and green digitization and wear those funny glasses to view the resultant image.

Another interesting effect can be seen by changing the code in the example program to reduce the number of color registers used for image display. To do this, change the statement "#define MAXNUMCOLREGS 256" to some lower number such as 16 and recompile the example program. Notice the effect this change has on image quality. Try dithering the 16-color image and observe that effect.

You might want to add code to the example program that periodically shifts the color register values. This can produce images that seem to jump out of the screen toward you. You could also scale the color register values over a short period of time to cause your image to fade in to full brightness and then fade back out when it is displayed. Nothing is sacred when it comes to image special effects. Experiment to your heart's content. Maybe your special-effect color images can be sold as digital art.

Conclusions

In this chapter, we have described how high-level code written in C is used to control the operation of the digitizer. We have also talked about how the quality of the digitized images can be enhanced. Finally, we have shown how monochrome and color images can be acquired, displayed, and saved as either a PCX file or an autodisplay program. Many examples of digitizer-produced images are scattered throughout this book. These images were produced with software identical to that presented in this chapter.

This ends the discussion of digitizer hardware and software. From this point on, we will assume your digitizer is working and that you understand how the high-level code for digitizer control can be modified for your particular application. I applaud those who built their own digitizers. I hope it has been a painless experience. In fact, I hope it has been fun.

The discussion will now shift to images and image processing in general. We will not make the assumption that all images to be manipulated were produced by our digitizer. Instead, the assumption is that any image in a standard graphics file format can be processed. To this end, the two most important graphics file formats, PCX and TIFF, are explained in depth in Chapter 6.

Graphics File Formats and Functions

In this chapter you will learn about

- **The difference between vector and raster graphics**
- **Which graphics file formats are considered the standards**
- **How PCX graphic files are organized**
- **What it takes to read and write PCX files**
- **How TIFF graphics files are organized**
- **What it takes to read and write TIFF files**
- **How "view.exe" can display both PCX and TIFF files**

Introduction

Digitized images in themselves have limited value. These images become useful when they are put into a form that can be manipulated by other applications. In order for this to occur, it is necessary to put the image data into a ''standard form'' that other applications can interpret and use. When an image can be imported into a paint program or desktop publishing program, it can be incorporated into presentations, slide shows, reports, newsletters, and so on. The image can even be used to make custom T-shirts. All of the image processing code in Part Two of this book will manipulate images stored in the standard PCX file format.

Graphics programs in general can be categorized by how image data is stored and displayed. Two categories exist: *raster format* and *vector format*. Raster format is comprised of a series of picture elements, or pixels, that cover a complete display area. Raster displays are usually generated by the periodic sweeping of an electron beam over an imaging surface with a predetermined pattern (a video camera, for example). The pixels that make up a rasterized image do not necessarily relate to each other. The concept of shape is not inherent in a raster image. Raster images are often used for presentation graphics, where artistic considerations and image quality are important.

The main advantages of raster format are:

a. It is easy to output data from a raster input device (i.e., a video digitizer or scanner) on a raster output device such as a computer monitor or graphics printer.

b. The display of raster data is usually faster than the display of vectored data because raster devices do the display and thus a vector-to-raster conversion does not have to be performed.

Vector format, on the other hand, involves the use of directed line segments instead of pixels to make up an image. A vector image is made up of shapes that are made up of line segments.

Connectedness and hierarchy are the cornerstones of vector images. With vector-formatted image data, it is easy to determine what component line segments make up any object. Vector images are used primarily in CAD applications where precision scaling and element relationships are important. AutoCAD® is an example of a program that utilizes vector graphics. Map generation and manipulation is another important application area for vector images. The relationship of objects on a map (all storm drains in a city, for example) and the ability to view only selected objects or collections of objects is often very useful.

Vector images are easily output to a plotter because a plotter is a vector type device. Vector images can also be converted to raster format for display and/or hard copy with a printer. The conversion from raster to vector, unfortunately, is much harder to perform.

The two major raster formats we will be concerned with in this chapter are the PCX/PCC format supported by ZSoft's PC PaintBrush and TIFF, which is supported by Aldus®, Microsoft®, Hewlett-Packard, and many desktop publishing application programs. Vector formats will not be discussed because of their limited usefulness in image processing applications. Both the PCX/PCC and TIFF graphics file formats will be given an in-depth discussion. C code is provided to read and write these file formats. The code will be in the form of a library of functions easily linked into other applications. A ''view'' program that can display properly formatted images in either format is included. The ''view'' program is an example of how the graphics library functions can be used by an application program.

The PCX/PCC Graphics File Format

This file format was one of the earliest attempts in the PC world to enable storage and standardization of graphic images. A standard file format was necessary, both to allow the movement of images between applications and to provide file compression to save disk storage space. The PCX/PCC graphics file format is an example of a method used in industry which became a standard by default. Because it has been around for such a long time, the PCX/PCC graphics file format is probably supported by more graphics application programs than all other (PC-compatible) graphics file formats combined.

One caveat is necessary before the discussion continues. The code provided in this

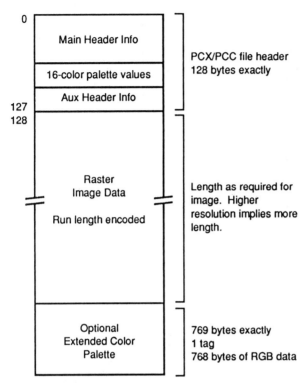

Figure 6.1 PCX/PCC File Structure

section assumes the existence of a VGA display adapter; CGA and EGA display adapters and therefore CGA- and EGA-created PCX files are not supported. The discussion to follow will touch upon how CGA and EGA files are encoded differently than VGA files, but it is left to the reader to implement changes to the code for support of these graphics adapters. The result of this is that PCX images created for graphics adapters other than VGA will not be displayed correctly by the PCX function library provided. The reasons will become obvious when PCX palettes are discussed below.

The PCX/PCC graphics file format is not very flexible with regard to the information it can contain. The file format is rigid, with a file header of fixed length followed by the raster image data, optionally followed by an extended palette structure. Figure 6.1 shows the layout of a typical PCX/PCC file. As will be discussed, a PCC file is simply a subset (or cutout) of a PCX file.

The simplicity of this file format makes the code required to support PCX easy to understand, develop, and use. The PCX/PCC function library code is contained in two files on the companion disk, ''pcx.h'' and ''pcx.c''. Both files are shown as Listing 6.1. Please refer to this listing during the discussion to follow. All information about the structure and format of PCX/PCC files was derived from documentation provided by ZSoft® Corporation for the PC PaintBrush program.

Listing 6.1   The PCX Library Functions

The following is the contents of the file, "pcx.h":

```
/****************************************/
/*          PCX Header File          */
/*     for PCX file access functions   */
/*        written in Turbo C 2.0       */
/*               by                    */
/*          Craig A. Lindley           */
/*                                     */
/*   Vers: 1.0  Last Update: 12/08/89  */
/****************************************/


#define MAXSCREENWIDTH      640
#define MAXSCREENHEIGHT     480
#define BITSPERBYTE           8
#define MAXPLANES             4
#define MAXBYTESPERSCAN     320
#define MAXPALETTECOLORS     16
#define MAX256PALETTECOLORS 256


/*
Function Control Equates.
Controls the DisplayImageInBuf function.
*/
#define INITVGALOADPALETTE  TRUE
#define NOVGAINIT           FALSE
#define WAITFORKEY          TRUE
#define NOWAITFORKEY        FALSE


/* Error Bit Definitions */
#ifndef _CompletionCode_
#define _CompletionCode_
typedef int CompletionCode;
#endif

/* Error bit definitions from PCX code */
#define NoError             0
#define EBadParms          -1
#define EFileNotFound      -2
#define EReadFileHdr       -3
#define ENotPCXFile        -4
#define ECorrupt           -5
```

```
#define EWrtFileHdr       -6
#define EWrtOutFile       -7
#define EWrtScanLine      -8
#define EPCCFile          -9
#define EGraphics         -10
#define ENoMemory         -11
#define EWrtExtPal        -12
/* Misc Error bit definitions */
#define EKernelSize       -21


/* PCX File Structures and Defines */

#define PCXHdrTag         10      /* tag in valid PCX file */
#define MaxRepCount       63      /* max # of repeat bytes */
#define PCX256ColorTag    12      /* tag for extended palette in PCX file */


/*
NOTE: compiler must generate BYTE aligned code for this structure to
contain only three bytes. Otherwise if WORD aligned the stucture will
contain four bytes and prohibit program operation.
*/
typedef struct
{
   BYTE Red;                      /* RGB components of color */
   BYTE Green;                    /* register */
   BYTE Blue;
} ColorRegister;

struct PCXFileHeader
{
   BYTE      Header;              /* marks file as PCX file */
   BYTE      Version;             /* 0 = version 2.5 */
                                  /* 2 = 2.8 with palette info */
                                  /* 3 = no palette info 2.8 or 3.0 */
                                  /* 5 = 3.0 with palette info */
   BYTE      Encode;              /* File encoding mode */
   BYTE      BitPerPix;           /* Bits per pixel */
   unsigned X1;                   /* Picture dimensions inclusive */
   unsigned Y1;
   unsigned X2;
   unsigned Y2;
   unsigned Hres;                 /* Graphics adapter Horiz    resolution */
   unsigned Vres;                 /* Graphics adapter Vertical resolution */
};
```

(continued)

Listing 6.1 *(continued)*

```
struct PCXInfo
{
   BYTE      Vmode;            /* Ignor should always be zero */
   BYTE      NumOfPlanes;      /* Number of bit planes */
   unsigned BytesPerLine;      /* Bytes Per Line in picture */
   BYTE      unused[60];       /* fills out header to 128 bytes */
};

struct PCX_File
{
   struct PCXFileHeader PCXHeader;
   ColorRegister        Palette[MAXPALETTECOLORS]; /* Max size of 48 bytes */
   struct PCXInfo        Info;
};

/* Extended palette data structure for 256 color PCX files */

struct ExtendedPalette
{
   BYTE ExtendedPalette;
   ColorRegister Palette[MAX256PALETTECOLORS]; /* Max size of 768 bytes */
};

/* Function Declarations */
void DisplayPCXFile (char *FileName,
                     int Verbose);      /* display a PCX file */

void WritePCXFile (char *FileName, unsigned BitsPerPixel,
                         unsigned MaxX, unsigned MaxY,
                         unsigned Planes, unsigned BytesPerLine);

unsigned InstallPCXFilePalette (void);  /* Install palette from PCX file */

CompletionCode ReadPCXFileToBuf (char *FileName, BYTE huge * * BufferPtr);

CompletionCode WritePCXFileFromBuf (char *FileName, BYTE huge *ImageMemory);

void DisplayImageInBuf(BYTE huge *Image, unsigned SetMode, unsigned Pause);

CompletionCode ReadRawImageFileToBuf(char *FileName,
                                            unsigned ImageWidth,
                                            unsigned ImageHeight,
                                            BYTE huge * *BufferPtr);
```

```
CompletionCode WriteRawImageFileFromBuf(char *FileName,

                                        unsigned ImageWidth,
                                        unsigned ImageHeight,
                                        unsigned Transpose,
                                        BYTE huge *ImageBuffer);
```

The following is the contents of the file, "pcx.c":

```
/****************************************/
/*        PCX Function Library        */
/*        written in Turbo C 2.0      */
/*                by                  */
/*         Craig A. Lindley           */
/*                                    */
/*   Vers: 1.0  Last Update: 11/21/89 */
/****************************************/

#include <stdio.h>
#include <string.h>
#include <process.h>
#include <conio.h>
#include <dos.h>
#include <alloc.h>
#include <graphics.h>
#include "misc.h"
#include "pcx.h"
#include "vga.h"

/* Externally Accessable Global Variables */
struct  PCX_File PCXData;        /* PCX File Hdr Variable */
unsigned ImageWidth, ImageHeight;

/* Variables global to this file only */
static FILE    *PCXFile;        /* file handle */
static BYTE     ScanLine[MAXBYTESPERSCAN];
static BYTE     PixelColorNum[MAXSCREENWIDTH];
static unsigned Is256ColorFile;
static struct   ExtendedPalette Color256Palette;

/* Start of Functions */
CompletionCode ReadPCXFileHdr (char *FileName, int Verbose)
```

(continued)

Listing 6.1   *(continued)*

```c
{
   unsigned Index;
   char     String[80];

   Is256ColorFile = FALSE;               /* initialize mode variable */

   if (!strchr(FileName,'.'))            /* is there an ext ? */
   {
      strcpy(String,FileName);           /* copy filename to buffer */
      FileName = String;                 /* FileName now pts at buffer */
      strcat(FileName,".pcx");           /* if not add .pcx ext */
   }
   /* try to open the PCX file */
   if ((PCXFile = fopen(FileName,"rb")) == NULL)
   {
      printf("PCX file: %s not found\n",FileName);
      return(EFileNotFound);
   }
   /* try to read the file header record */
   if (fread(&PCXData,sizeof(struct PCX_File),1,PCXFile) != 1)
   {
      printf("Error reading PCX file header\n");
      return(EReadFileHdr);
   }
   /* check to make sure its a PCX file */
   if (PCXData.PCXHeader.Header != PCXHdrTag)
   {
      printf("Error not a PCX file\n");
      return(ENotPCXFile);
   }
   /* Yep, we've got a PCX file OK. Display info if requested */
   if (Verbose)
   {
      clrscr();
      printf("PCX Image Information for file: %s\n\n",FileName);
      printf("\tVersion: %d\n", PCXData.PCXHeader.Version);
      printf("\tCompression: %s\n",
             PCXData.PCXHeader.Encode == 0 ? "None":"RLL");
      printf("\tBits Per Pixel: %d\n",PCXData.PCXHeader.BitPerPix);
      printf("\tX1: %d\n",PCXData.PCXHeader.X1);
      printf("\tY1: %d\n",PCXData.PCXHeader.Y1);
      printf("\tX2: %d\n",PCXData.PCXHeader.X2);
```

```c
        printf("\tY2: %d\n",PCXData.PCXHeader.Y2);
        printf("\tHoriz Resolution: %d\n",PCXData.PCXHeader.Hres);
        printf("\tVert  Resolution: %d\n",PCXData.PCXHeader.Vres);
        printf("\tVMode: %d\n",PCXData.Info.Vmode);
        printf("\tNumber of Planes: %d\n",PCXData.Info.NumOfPlanes);
        printf("\tBytes Per Scan Line One Plane: %d\n",PCXData.Info.BytesPerLine);
        printf("\nHit any key to proceed\n");
        getch();                        /* wait for operator input */

        clrscr();
        printf("Color Register Values for PCX file: %s\n\n",FileName);
        for (Index = 0; Index < MAXPALETTECOLORS; Index++)
        {
            printf("Palette Index: %2d  R = %2x G = %2x B = %2x\n",
                        Index,PCXData.Palette[Index].Red,
                              PCXData.Palette[Index].Green,
                              PCXData.Palette[Index].Blue);
        }
        printf("\nHit <Enter> to proceed - ^C to abort\n");
        getchar();                      /* wait for operator input */
    }
    return(NoError);
}

static CompletionCode ExpandScanLine (FILE *InFile)
{
    register short    BitNum;
    register unsigned ByteNum;
    register short    CharRead;
    unsigned          InPtr,RepCount,PixelsData;
    unsigned          BytesToRead,PlaneNum,ShiftCount;
    unsigned          ByteOffset, BitOffset;

    BytesToRead = PCXData.Info.NumOfPlanes * PCXData.Info.BytesPerLine;
    InPtr = ShiftCount = 0;             /* initialize vars */
    do
    {
        CharRead = getc(InFile);        /* read a byte from the file */
        if (CharRead == EOF)            /* error should never read EOF */
            return(FALSE);              /* abort picture */

        if ((CharRead & 0xC0) == 0xC0)  /* a repeat tag ? */
```

(continued)

Listing 6.1 *(continued)*

```
    {
        RepCount = CharRead & ~0xC0;    /* repeat 1..63 */
        CharRead = getc(InFile);        /* read byte to repeat */
        if (CharRead == EOF)            /* error should never read EOF */
            return(FALSE);              /* abort picture */

        while (RepCount--)              /* expand byte */
            ScanLine[InPtr++] =         /* RepCount times */
                CharRead;
    }
    else                               /* just a byte of data */
        ScanLine[InPtr++] = CharRead;  /* store in buffer */
} while (InPtr < BytesToRead);         /* expand a full scan line */


/*
When we get here, we have an array, ScanLine, which is composed of
NumOfPlanes sections each BytesPerLine long. For a normal EGA/VGA image
this works out to be 4 planes of 80 bytes each. For a 256 color VGA image
it is 1 plane of 320 bytes. For the normal image we must merge each of these
bit planes into the array PixelColorNum so that we can display the
resultant image. Each entry into this array corresponds to a pixel on
a single scan line of the monitor. For a 256 color image, the ScanLine is
simply copied into the PixelColorNum array because there is no interleaving
of bit planes.
*/
    if (PCXData.PCXHeader.X2 == 319)    /* if 256 color image */
        memcpy(PixelColorNum,ScanLine,ImageWidth);
    else                               /* normal image file */
    {
        /* clear PixelColorNum array to zeros */
        memset(PixelColorNum,'\0',ImageWidth);

        for (PlaneNum=0; PlaneNum < PCXData.Info.NumOfPlanes; PlaneNum++)
        {
            ByteOffset = PlaneNum * PCXData.Info.BytesPerLine;
            for (ByteNum=0; ByteNum < PCXData.Info.BytesPerLine; ByteNum++)
            {
                /* read 8 bits of pixel data for one plane */
                PixelsData = ScanLine[ByteOffset+ByteNum];
                BitOffset = ByteNum * BITSPERBYTE;

                for (BitNum=BITSPERBYTE-1; BitNum >= 0; BitNum--)
```

```
            {
                    if (PixelsData & (1 << BitNum))
                    {
                            /* OR in each component of the color */
                            PixelColorNum[BitOffset + (7 - BitNum)] |=
                                (1 << ShiftCount);
                    }
                }
            }
        }
        ShiftCount++;
    }
  }
/*
When we get here, the PixelColorNum array has a byte color value for each
pixel on the display. Return an indication that this operation went
smoothly.
*/

    return(TRUE);
}

unsigned InstallPCXFilePalette(void)
{
    struct    palettetype palette;
    union     REGS regs;
    unsigned Index;

    /*
    Always load the VGA palette as long as the version is not 3 which
    doesn't have palette information in the file. If version 3
    use the default palette
    */
    if (PCXData.PCXHeader.Version != 3)
    {
        if (Is256ColorFile)              /* if a mode 13h file */
        {
            /*
            When we get here, we have a mode 13h file image. In this
            VGA mode, the palette mechanism is bypassed. The color
            registers are loaded from the extended palette in the
                PCX file. The values in the file's palette are four
                times their actual values. They must be scaled before
                being used. All 256 of the color registers must be loaded.
            */
```

(continued)

Listing 6.1 *(continued)*

```
        for (Index=0; Index < MAX256PALETTECOLORS; Index++)
        {
            Color256Palette.Palette[Index].Red   >>= 2;
            Color256Palette.Palette[Index].Green >>= 2;
            Color256Palette.Palette[Index].Blue  >>= 2;
        }

        /* set a block of Color Registers */
        regs.h.ah = 0x10;
        regs.h.al = 0x12;
        regs.x.bx = 0;
        regs.x.cx = MAX256PALETTECOLORS;
        _ES = FP_SEG(&Color256Palette.Palette);
        regs.x.dx =FP_OFF(&Color256Palette.Palette);
        int86(VIDEO,&regs,&regs);
    return(TRUE);        /* indicate palette installed successfully */
}
else
{
    /*
    When we get here we have a 16 color VGA image. We must
    build a palette data structure with data loaded from the PCX
    file. The palette is set up in sequential order and the
        color register are set from values in the file. The file
        values are scaled before being installed.
    */

        palette.size = MAXPALETTECOLORS;

        for (Index = 0; Index < MAXPALETTECOLORS; Index++)
        {
            palette.colors[Index] = Index;
            PCXData.Palette[Index].Red   >>= 2;
            PCXData.Palette[Index].Green >>= 2;
            PCXData.Palette[Index].Blue  >>= 2;
        }
        /* set a block of Color Registers */
        regs.h.ah = 0x10;
        regs.h.al = 0x12;
        regs.x.bx = 0;
        regs.x.cx = MAXPALETTECOLORS;
        _ES = FP_SEG(&PCXData.Palette);
        regs.x.dx =FP_OFF(&PCXData.Palette);
        int86(VIDEO,&regs,&regs);
```

```
                    /* enable the palette we just read from the file */
         setallpalette(&palette);
         return(TRUE);          /* indicate palette installed successfully */
      }
   }
   else
      return(FALSE);            /* no palette info to load */
}


/*
This function reads a PCX file into a buffer in memory. It does not
alter the palette currently used for the VGA display.
*/

CompletionCode ReadPCXFileToBuf (char *FileName, BYTE huge * *BufferPtr)
{
   register unsigned ScanNum;          /* scan line being expanded
                                           and displayed */
   register unsigned ColNum;               /* pixel being read */
   int      PCXError;
   BYTE huge *ImageMemory;             /* memory block where image */
                                       /* will be stored */
   unsigned long PixelBufOffset;

   if ((PCXError = ReadPCXFileHdr(FileName,FALSE)) != NoError)
      return(PCXError);

   /* Header has been read, now we are ready to read the PCX image */
   /* PCC files cannot be displayed */

   if ((PCXData.PCXHeader.X1 != 0) || (PCXData.PCXHeader.Y1 != 0))
   {
      printf("Error PCC file not PCX file\n");
      return (EPCCFile);
   }

   /*
   From the header information determine the size of the buffer
   required to store the image. Set the global vars ImageWidth
   and ImageHeight are accordingly.
   */
```

(continued)

Listing 6.1 *(continued)*

```
if (PCXData.PCXHeader.X2 == 319)
{
   ImageWidth  = 320;
   ImageHeight = 200;
}
else
{
   ImageWidth = 640;
   switch(PCXData.PCXHeader.Y2)
   {
           case 479: ImageHeight = 480;
                                 break;
           case 349: ImageHeight = 350;
                           break;
           case 199: ImageHeight = 200;
                           break;
   }
}


/* allocate far memory for the image */
ImageMemory = (BYTE huge *) farcalloc((long) ImageWidth * ImageHeight,
                                   sizeof(BYTE));
if (ImageMemory == NULL)
{
   printf("Error Not enough memory for PCX buffer\n");
   return (ENoMemory);
}
/*
Proceed to unpack and store the PCX data. A scan line at
a time.
*/

for (ScanNum=0; ScanNum < ImageHeight; ScanNum++)
{
   if (ExpandScanLine(PCXFile) != TRUE)
   {
     printf("Error Scanline corrupt in PCX file\n");
          return(ECorrupt);
   }
   PixelBufOffset = (long) ScanNum * ImageWidth;
   for (ColNum=0; ColNum < ImageWidth; ColNum++)
```

```
        {
         ImageMemory[PixelBufOffset + ColNum] =
                    PixelColorNum[ColNum];
        }
    }
    /*
    Determine if the PCX file is a mode 13h extended color file by
    trying to read the extended palette record located after the
    raster data. If EOF is read then no extended palette info
    is included in the file.
    */

    Is256ColorFile = FALSE;    /* set global flag to indicate file type */

    if (fread(&Color256Palette,sizeof(struct ExtendedPalette),1,PCXFile) == 1)
        /* Extended palette read ok. Now check tag. */
        if (Color256Palette.ExtendedPalette == PCX256ColorTag)
            /*
            Tag is ok, extended palette RGB values in Color256Palette
            structure.
            */
            Is256ColorFile = TRUE;

    /* file has been read prepare to close up shop */

    fclose(PCXFile);
    *BufferPtr = ImageMemory;                /* return the buffer address */
    return(NoError);
}


/*
This function displays an image in a buffer. If SetMode is TRUE,
the graphics mode will be set and the palette will be loaded. If FALSE,
neither will be performed, the image will be displayed with current
settings. If Pause is requested, this function will wait for a key
press before returning to the calling code.
*/

void DisplayImageInBuf(BYTE huge *Image, unsigned SetMode, unsigned Pause)
{
    register unsigned ScanNum, PixelNum;
    unsigned long PixelBufOffset;
```

(continued)

Listing 6.1 *(continued)*

```
if (SetMode)
   InitGraphics();            /* initialize graphic system if required */
if (ImageWidth == 320)        /* a 256 color image ? */
{
   if (SetMode)               /* if a mode set is required */
   {                          /* set mode and load palette */
           Set256ColorMode();
           InstallPCXFilePalette();
   }
   for (ScanNum=0; ScanNum < ImageHeight; ScanNum++)
           for (PixelNum=0; PixelNum < ImageWidth; PixelNum++)
           {
              PixelBufOffset  = ScanNum;  /* done to prevent overflow */
              PixelBufOffset *= ImageWidth;
              PixelBufOffset += PixelNum;
              PutPixel256(PixelNum,ScanNum,Image[PixelBufOffset]);
           }
}
else
{
   if (SetMode)               /* if mode set required */
   {
           switch(ImageHeight) /* determine VGA mode */
           {
              case 480:  setgraphmode(VGAHI);
                              break;
              case 350:  setgraphmode(VGAMED);
                              break;
              case 200:  setgraphmode(VGALO);
                              break;
           }
           InstallPCXFilePalette();
   }
   for (ScanNum=0; ScanNum < ImageHeight; ScanNum++)
           for (PixelNum=0; PixelNum < ImageWidth; PixelNum++)
           {
              PixelBufOffset  = ScanNum;  /* done to prevent overflow */
              PixelBufOffset *= ImageWidth;
              PixelBufOffset += PixelNum;
              putpixel(PixelNum,ScanNum,Image[PixelBufOffset]);
           }
}
```

```c
    if (Pause)                      /* if pause requested wait for key */
        getch();
}


/*
This function reads and displays a PCX file.
*/
void DisplayPCXFile (char *FileName, int Verbose)
{
    register unsigned ScanNum;          /* scan line being expanded
                                           and displayed */
    register unsigned ColNum;                /* pixel being read */
    int     PCXError;


    if ((PCXError = ReadPCXFileHdr(FileName,Verbose)) != NoError)
        exit(PCXError);

    /* Header has been read, now we are ready to display the PCX image */
    /* PCC files cannot be displayed */

    if ((PCXData.PCXHeader.X1 != 0) || (PCXData.PCXHeader.Y1 != 0))
    {
        printf("Error PCC file not PCX file\n");
        exit(EPCCFile);
    }

    InitGraphics();               /* initialize graphs subsystem */

    /* From the header information determine which mode the display should
       be in. If width is 320 then its mode 13 hex 256 colors. Otherwise
       its a VGA mode with a width of 640. */

    if (PCXData.PCXHeader.X2 == 319)
    {
        Set256ColorMode();
        ImageWidth  = 320;
        ImageHeight = 200;
    }
    else
    {
        ImageWidth = 640;
        switch(PCXData.PCXHeader.Y2)
```

(continued)

Listing 6.1   *(continued)*

```
    {
       case 479: setgraphmode(VGAHI);
                          ImageHeight = 480;
                             break;
       case 349: setgraphmode(VGAMED);
                          ImageHeight = 350;
                          break;
         case 199: setgraphmode(VGALO);
                          ImageHeight = 200;
                          break;
    }
}
/* proceed to unpack and diplay the PCX file */
for (ScanNum=0; ScanNum < ImageHeight; ScanNum++)
{
    if (ExpandScanLine(PCXFile) != TRUE)
    {
       printf("Scanline corrupt in PCX file\n");
       exit(ECorrupt);
    }
    if (ImageWidth == 320) /* 256 color mode */
    {
       for (ColNum=0; ColNum < ImageWidth; ColNum++)
          PutPixel256(ColNum,ScanNum,(int) PixelColorNum[ColNum]);
    }
    else                   /* normal 16 color modes */
    {
       for (ColNum=0; ColNum < ImageWidth; ColNum++)
          putpixel(ColNum,ScanNum,(int) PixelColorNum[ColNum]);
    }
}
/*
Determine if the PCX file is a mode 13h extended color file by
trying to read the extended palette record located after the
raster data. If EOF is read then no extended palette info
is included in the file.
*/

Is256ColorFile = FALSE;   /* set global flag to indicate file type */

if (fread(&Color256Palette,sizeof(struct ExtendedPalette),1,PCXFile) == 1)
   /* Extended palette read ok. Now check tag. */
   if (Color256Palette.ExtendedPalette == PCX256ColorTag)
```

```
            /*
            Tag is ok, extended palette RGB values in Color256Palette
            structure.
            */
            Is256ColorFile = TRUE;

    /* file has been read prepare to close up shop */

    /* Install palette read from file */
    InstallPCXFilePalette();

    fclose(PCXFile);
}
/*
The following routines create a PCX file from a raster image
or a memory buffer and writes it to disk.
*/

CompletionCode WritePCXHdr(char *FileName, unsigned BitsPerPixel,
                                unsigned MaxX,  unsigned MaxY, unsigned Planes,
                                unsigned BytesPerLine)
{
    struct palettetype palette;
    unsigned    Index;
    union REGS  regs;
    char        String[80];

    if (!strchr(FileName,'.'))         /* is there an ext ? */
    {                                  /* if not ... */
        strcpy(String,FileName);       /* copy filename to buffer */
        FileName = String;             /* FileName now pts at buffer */
        strcat(FileName,".pcx");       /* add .pcx ext */
    }

    if ((PCXFile = fopen(FileName,"w+b")) == NULL)
    {
        restorecrtmode();
        printf("Could not open output PCX file\n");
        return (EWrtOutFile);
    }

    /* initialize the PCX file header info */
    PCXData.PCXHeader.Header     = PCXHdrTag;
```

(continued)

Listing 6.1 *(continued)*

```
PCXData.PCXHeader.Version  = 5;
PCXData.PCXHeader.Encode   = 1;
PCXData.PCXHeader.BitPerPix = BitsPerPixel;
PCXData.PCXHeader.X1        = 0;
PCXData.PCXHeader.Y1        = 0;
PCXData.PCXHeader.X2        = MaxX-1;
PCXData.PCXHeader.Y2        = MaxY-1;
PCXData.PCXHeader.Hres      = MaxX;
PCXData.PCXHeader.Vres      = MaxY;
ImageWidth                 = MaxX;
ImageHeight                = MaxY;
PCXData.Info.Vmode         = 0;
PCXData.Info.NumOfPlanes    = Planes;
PCXData.Info.BytesPerLine   = BytesPerLine;

/*
Initialize the palette structure in the PCX file data. The palette
will be written to the PCX file regardless of whether it is a 16
or 256 color image. If its a 256 color image an extended palette
structure will be written at the end of the PCX raster data.
The palette values must be scaled up by four before being
written to the file.
*/

getpalette(&palette);
for (Index = 0; Index < palette.size; Index++)
{
   regs.h.ah = 0x10;
   regs.h.al = 0x15;
   regs.x.bx = palette.colors[Index];
   int86(VIDEO,&regs,&regs);
   PCXData.Palette[Index].Red   = regs.h.dh <<= 2;
   PCXData.Palette[Index].Green = regs.h.ch <<= 2;
   PCXData.Palette[Index].Blue  = regs.h.cl <<= 2;
}

/* clear the unused area at the end of the PCX header */
memset(&PCXData.Info.unused,'\0',sizeof(PCXData.Info.unused));

/* now write the file header to the physical file */
if (fwrite(&PCXData,sizeof(struct PCX_File),1,PCXFile) != 1)
{
   restorecrtmode();
```

```
        printf("Error writing PCX file header\n");
        return(EWrtFileHdr);
    }
    return(NoError);
}


static CompletionCode CompressScanLine(FILE *OutFile)
{
    register unsigned OutPtr,RepCount,RepChar;
    register unsigned BytesToWrite;

    BytesToWrite = PCXData.Info.NumOfPlanes * PCXData.Info.BytesPerLine;

    OutPtr = 0;                        /* ptr to data to compress */
    do
    {
        RepChar = ScanLine[OutPtr++];    /* get byte to start compression */
        RepCount = 1;                    /* byte seen once at this point */
        while ((ScanLine[OutPtr]==RepChar) &&
                (RepCount < MaxRepCount)     &&
                    (OutPtr < BytesToWrite))
        {
            RepCount++;                  /* count all repetitions of char */
            OutPtr++;                    /* bump ptr and check again */
        }

        /* repeat sequence found or if chars has either or both MSBs set
           than must process as a repetition count and char sequence */

        if ((RepCount > 1) || (RepChar > 0xBF))
        {
            RepCount |= 0xC0;            /* set two MSBs */
            if (putc(RepCount,OutFile) == EOF) /* write count to file */
                return(FALSE);          /* if error return error */
        }

        if (putc(RepChar,OutFile) == EOF)/* write char to file */
            return(FALSE);              /* if error return error */
    } while (OutPtr < BytesToWrite);    /* until all bytes in scan
                                          are compressed */
    return(TRUE);                        /* indicate operation successful */
}
```

(continued)

Listing 6.1 *(continued)*

```
/*
This function writes a PCX file to disk contained in a buffer in
memory. The current palette being used for display is written to
the PCX file. All entries in the PCX header are from the image
which was originally read into the buffer under the assumption
that the content of the image might change but not its basic
parameters.
*/


CompletionCode WritePCXFileFromBuf (char *FileName, BYTE huge *ImageMemory)
{
    register unsigned PlaneNum, BitNum, ByteNum, PData;
    register unsigned ScanLineNum,PixelNum, Index;
    int PCXError;
    unsigned long PixelBufOffset;
    union   REGS regs;

    /* write out PCX header and palette */
    if ((PCXError = WritePCXHdr(FileName, PCXData.PCXHeader.BitPerPix,
                          PCXData.PCXHeader.X2+1,PCXData.PCXHeader.Y2+1,
                PCXData.Info.NumOfPlanes,
                PCXData.Info.BytesPerLine)) != NoError)
        return(PCXError);


/*
At this point we will read the image from the buffer a scanline
at at time. For 320x200 256 color images there is only a single bit plane
so the data read from the buffer is placed directly into the ScanLine array
for compressing. For normal VGA images, the color value returned need to be
separated into their component parts which will be compressed separately.
In essense, the single array of 640 bytes corresponding to 640 separate
pixels on the scan line is broken up into four separate arrays 80 bytes
apiece (all contained in ScanLine[]). These arrays are the i,r,g,b components
of the pixel values. The separates components or planes are then compressed.
The components are written to disk in the following order: blue, green,
red and then intensity.
*/

    for (ScanLineNum=0; ScanLineNum < ImageHeight; ScanLineNum++)
    {
        PixelBufOffset = (long) ScanLineNum * ImageWidth;
        if (PCXData.PCXHeader.X2 == 319)     /* if 256 color image */
```

```
        {
              for (PixelNum=0; PixelNum < ImageWidth; PixelNum++)
                 ScanLine[PixelNum] = ImageMemory[PixelBufOffset + PixelNum];
        }
        else                                 /* normal image file */
        {
              /* clear ScanLine array to zeros for each scan line */
              /* this is an array of NumOfPlanes * BytesPerLine bytes */
              memset(ScanLine,'\0',MAXBYTESPERSCAN);

              for (PixelNum=0; PixelNum < ImageWidth; PixelNum++)
              {
          /* get pixel value from buffer */
                 PData = ImageMemory[PixelBufOffset + PixelNum];
                 ByteNum = PixelNum/BITSPERBYTE;         /* calc byte offset */
                 BitNum  = 7 - (PixelNum % BITSPERBYTE); /* calc bit offset */
                 for (PlaneNum=0; PlaneNum < PCXData.Info.NumOfPlanes; PlaneNum++)
                    if (PData & (1<<PlaneNum))           /* if bit in plane is 1 */
                            ScanLine[(PlaneNum * PCXData.Info.BytesPerLine) + ByteNum] |=
                                    (1<<BitNum);
              }
        }

     if (CompressScanLine(PCXFile) != TRUE)   /* compress a complete scan */
     {                                        /* line */
        restorecrtmode();
        printf("Error writing a compressed scan line\n");
        return(EWrtScanLine);
     }
}


/*
Determine if the PCX file is a mode 13h extended color image.
If so, write an extended palette record to the file after the
raster data.
*/
if (ImageWidth == 320)    /* 256 color mode 13h image ? */
{                         /* yes it is */
   /*
   Read the 256 color register RGB values and store them in
   the Color256Palette structure before writing them to the
   PCX file. This structure is tagged to assure validity.
   */
```

(continued)

Listing 6.1 *(continued)*

```
     Color256Palette.ExtendedPalette = PCX256ColorTag;

     /* get a block of Color Registers */
     regs.h.ah = 0x10;
     regs.h.al = 0x17;
     regs.x.bx = 0;
     regs.x.cx = MAX256PALETTECOLORS;
     _ES = FP_SEG(&Color256Palette.Palette);
     regs.x.dx =FP_OFF(&Color256Palette.Palette);
     int86(VIDEO,&regs,&regs);

     /*
     The palette data must be scaled up by four before
     being written to the file.
     */
     for (Index=0; Index < MAX256PALETTECOLORS; Index++)
     {
            Color256Palette.Palette[Index].Red   <<= 2;
            Color256Palette.Palette[Index].Green <<= 2;
            Color256Palette.Palette[Index].Blue  <<= 2;
     }

     /*
     With all of the color register values read, write the
     extended palette structure to the PCX file.
     */
     if (fwrite(&Color256Palette,
                sizeof(struct ExtendedPalette),1,PCXFile) != 1)
     {
        restorecrtmode();
        printf("Error writing extended palette structure\n");
        fclose(PCXFile);              /* close the PCX file */
        farfree((BYTE far *) ImageMemory);  /* return buffer memory */
        return(EWrtExtPal);
     }
  }
  /* file has been written prepare to close up shop */
  fclose(PCXFile);                  /* close the completed PCX file */
  farfree((BYTE far *) ImageMemory);  /* return buffer memory */
  return(NoError);
}
```

```
/*
This function writes a PCX file to disk from the image currently
being displayed on the monitor.
*/

void WritePCXFile (char *FileName, unsigned BitsPerPixel,
                           unsigned MaxX, unsigned MaxY, unsigned Planes,
                           unsigned BytesPerLine)
{
    register unsigned PlaneNum, BitNum, ByteNum, PData;
    register unsigned ScanLineNum,PixelNum;
    int PCXError;
    unsigned Index;
    union   REGS regs;


    /* write out PCX header and palette */
    if ((PCXError = WritePCXHdr(FileName, BitsPerPixel,
                           MaxX, MaxY, Planes, BytesPerLine)) != NoError)
       exit(PCXError);

/*
At this point we will read the displayed image from the screen a scanline
at at time. For 320x200 256 color images there is only a single bit plane
so the data read from the screen is placed directly into the ScanLine array
for compressing. For normal VGA images, the color value returned need to be
separated into their component parts which will be compressed separately.
In essense, the single array of 640 bytes corresponding to 640 separate
pixels on the scan line is broken up into four separate arrays 80 bytes
apiece (all contained in ScanLine[]). These arrays are the i,r,g,b components
of the pixel values. The separates components or planes are then compressed.
The components are written to disk in the following order: blue, green,
red and then intensity.
*/

    for (ScanLineNum=0; ScanLineNum < ImageHeight; ScanLineNum++)
    {
       if (PCXData.PCXHeader.X2 == 319)     /* if 256 color image */
       {
              for (PixelNum=0; PixelNum < ImageWidth; PixelNum++)
                 ScanLine[PixelNum] = GetPixel256(PixelNum,ScanLineNum);
       }
```

(continued)

Listing 6.1 *(continued)*

```
        else                            /* normal image file */
        {
                /* clear ScanLine array to zeros for each scan line */
                /* this is an array of NumOfPlanes * BytesPerLine bytes */
                memset(ScanLine,'\0',MAXBYTESPERSCAN);
                for (PixelNum=0; PixelNum < ImageWidth; PixelNum++)
                {
                    PData = getpixel(PixelNum,ScanLineNum); /* get pixel value */
                    ByteNum = PixelNum/BITSPERBYTE;          /* calc byte offset */
                    BitNum  = 7 - (PixelNum % BITSPERBYTE); /* calc bit offset */
                    for (PlaneNum=0; PlaneNum < PCXData.Info.NumOfPlanes; PlaneNum++)
                      if (PData & (1<<PlaneNum))             /* if bit in plane is 1 */
                            ScanLine[(PlaneNum * PCXData.Info.BytesPerLine) + ByteNum] |=
                                    (1<<BitNum);
                }
        }


        if (CompressScanLine(PCXFile) != TRUE)    /* compress a complete scan */
        {                                         /* line */
            restorecrtmode();
            printf("Error writing a compressed scan line\n");
            exit(EWrtScanLine);
        }
}
/*
Determine if the PCX file is a mode 13h extended color image.
If so, write an extended palette record to the file after the
raster data.
*/

if (ImageWidth == 320)    /* 256 color mode 13h image ? */
{                         /* yes it is */
    /*
    Read the 256 color register RGB values and store them in
    the Color256Palette structure before writing them to the
    PCX file. This structure is tagged to assure validity.
    */

    Color256Palette.ExtendedPalette = PCX256ColorTag;

    for (Index = 0; Index < MAX256PALETTECOLORS; Index++)
    {
        regs.h.ah = 0x10;
```

```
            regs.h.al = 0x15;
            regs.x.bx = Index;   /* get this color reg RGB values */
            int86(VIDEO,&regs,&regs);
                  Color256Palette.Palette[Index].Red   = regs.h.dh <<= 2;
                  Color256Palette.Palette[Index].Green = regs.h.ch <<= 2;
                  Color256Palette.Palette[Index].Blue  = regs.h.cl <<= 2;
      }
      /*
      With all of the color register values read, write the
      extended palette structure to the PCX file.
      */
      if (fwrite(&Color256Palette,
                  sizeof(struct ExtendedPalette),1,PCXFile) != 1)
      {
         restorecrtmode();
         printf("Error writing extended palette structure\n");
      }
   }
   /* file has been written prepare to close up shop */

   fclose(PCXFile);                        /* close the completed PCX file */
}


/*
This function reads a raw image file into memory. The amount
of data read from the file is determined from the specified image
dimensions. Various error codes are returns in the advent
of an error reading the image file. If the read is successful,
a pointer to the image data and the NoError status will be
returned to the calling code. No assumptions are made about the
format of the data read other than that it should be stored
in sequential image buffer memory locations.
*/

CompletionCode ReadRawImageFileToBuf(char *FileName,

                                           unsigned ImageWidth,
                                           unsigned ImageHeight,
                                           BYTE huge * *BufferPtr)

{
   unsigned long RasterSize, Index;
   BYTE huge    *ImageBuffer;
   FILE         *ImageDataFile;
   int          DataRead;
```

(continued)

Listing 6.1 *(continued)*

```
/* Assigned an error value until read is completed successfully */
*BufferPtr = NULL;

/* Calculate size of buffer required to store image */
RasterSize = (long)ImageWidth * ImageHeight;

/* Check for sufficient memory for buffer */
if (RasterSize >= farcoreleft())
{
   printf("Not enough memory for image!\n");
   return(ENoMemory);
}


/* Allocate buffer from FAR heap */
ImageBuffer = (BYTE huge *)farcalloc(RasterSize,

                                          (unsigned long) sizeof(BYTE));
/* Attempt to open the raw image data file */
if ((ImageDataFile = fopen(FileName,"rb")) == NULL)
{
  printf("Cannot open image data file: %s\n",FileName);
  farfree((char far *) ImageBuffer);
  return(EFileNotFound);
}
/* With file open, read RasterSize number of bytes from file */
for (Index=0; Index < RasterSize; Index++)
{
   /* Check each read for an error */
   if((DataRead = fgetc(ImageDataFile)) == EOF)
   {
           fclose(ImageDataFile);   /* close file */
           farfree((char far *) ImageBuffer);
           return(ECorrupt);        /* return error code */
   }
   /* If all is well, store the BYTE read into the buffer */
   ImageBuffer[Index] = (BYTE) DataRead;
}
/* Everythings ok. Close file, store ptr and return NoError */

fclose(ImageDataFile);
*BufferPtr = ImageBuffer;      /* return ptr to buffer */
return(NoError);
}
```

```
/*
This function writes to a file the raw image data produced
by the digitizer. NOTE: This function will convert the column
by column image data returned by the digitizer to a row
by row raster data format if Transpose is TRUE. Otherwise,
the output file is written in the same manner as the data
returned by the digitizer; column by column.
*/


CompletionCode WriteRawImageFileFromBuf(char *FileName,

                                                              unsigned ImageWidth,
                                                              unsigned ImageHeight,
                                                              unsigned Transpose,
                                                              BYTE huge *ImageBuffer)
{
    unsigned long RasterSize, Index, Col, Row;
    FILE          *ImageDataFile;
    BYTE          WriteData;

    /* Attempt to open the raw image output data file */
    if ((ImageDataFile = fopen(FileName,"wb")) == NULL)
    {
      printf("Cannot open image data output file: %s\n",FileName);
      return(EWrtOutFile);
    }

    if (!Transpose)                 /* write data in normal format */
    {
      /* Calculate number of bytes to write */
      RasterSize = (long)ImageWidth * ImageHeight;

      /* With file open, write RasterSize number of bytes to file */
      for (Index=0; Index < RasterSize; Index++)
      {
            /* Get the byte to write */
            WriteData = ImageBuffer[Index];

            /* Check each write for an error */
            if (fputc(WriteData,ImageDataFile) != WriteData)
            {
               fclose(ImageDataFile);   /* close file */
               return(EWrtOutFile);     /* return error code */
            }
      }
    }
```

(continued)

Listing 6.1   *(continued)*

```
  else                              /* data must be in raster format */
  {
     for(Row=0; Row < ImageHeight; Row++)
             for (Col=0; Col < ImageWidth; Col++)
             {
                /* Get the byte to write */
                WriteData = ImageBuffer[(Col * ImageHeight) + Row];

                /* Check each write for an error */
                if (fputc(WriteData,ImageDataFile) != WriteData)
                {
                   fclose(ImageDataFile);   /* close file */
                   return(EWrtOutFile);      /* return error code */
                }
             }
  }
  /* Everythings ok. Close file, free buffer memory and return NoError */

  fclose(ImageDataFile);
  farfree((char far*) ImageBuffer);   /* free memory */
  return(NoError);
}
```

The PCX/PCC File Header

The best way to describe the PCX/PCC file format is to describe the content of the header portion of the file. The header contains the information necessary to allow correct interpretation of the raster data that follows it. Without the header, the image data could not be deciphered. As shown here, the header is 128 bytes in length and is made up of the following data structures taken from the file ''pcx.h'':

```
    typedef struct             /* definition of VGA color register */
    {
       BYTE Red;               /* RGB components of color */
       BYTE Green;             /* register */
       BYTE Blue;
    } ColorRegister;

    /* The PCX/PCC file header */
    struct PCXFileHeader
```

```
{
    BYTE       Header;              /* marks file as PCX file */
    BYTE       Version;             /* 0 = version 2.5 */
                                    /* 2 = 2.8 with palette info */
                                    /* 3 = no palette info 2.8 or 3.0 */
                                    /* 5 = 3.0 with palette info */
    BYTE       Encode;              /* File encoding mode */
    BYTE       BitPerPix;           /* Bits per pixel */
    unsigned X1;                    /* Picture dimensions inclusive */
    unsigned Y1;
    unsigned X2;
    unsigned Y2;
    unsigned Hres;                  /* Graphics adapter Horiz    resolution */
    unsigned Vres;                  /* Graphics adapter Vertical resolution */
};

struct PCXInfo
{
    BYTE       Vmode;               /* Ignore should always be zero */
    BYTE       NumOfPlanes;         /* Number of bit planes */
    unsigned BytesPerLine;          /* Bytes Per Line in picture */
    BYTE       unused[60];          /* fills out header to 128 bytes */
};

/* The PCX/PCC complete file structure */
struct PCX_File
{
    struct PCXFileHeader PCXHeader;
    ColorRegister        Palette[MaxPaletteColors]; /* Max size of 48 bytes */
    struct PCXInfo       Info;
};
```

The structure "PCX_File" represents the complete header portion of a PCX/PCC file. Internal to this structure, the structure "PCXHeader" represents what is referred to as the "Main Header Info" in Figure 6.1, the "palette" is an array of 16 color registers with each register containing one byte each of red, green, and blue color information, and the "Info" structure, which contains the auxiliary file information. Notice how the "Info" structure is padded to make the entire header exactly 128 bytes in length.

Each of the individual fields within the PCX/PCC header plays an important role in characterizing the contained image. The functions of some of the header fields are not intuitively obvious, as they are based on historical perspectives that today escape us. Also, various manufacturers of PCX-generating programs might use these fields in proprietary ways for their specific applications. Worse yet, other PCX programs ignore the file header completely, assuming all imported PCX files were previously written out by their application (and therefore decipherable because of the known context) as if no other PCX-producing programs exist. This means code designed to read PCX files must do the best it can deciphering so-called standard PCX files produced by some application programs. Additionally, code written to produce PCX files must accurately and completely build the PCX file header so other applications have the ability to correctly decode the resultant image files. The content of the PCX file header fields as utilized by the code in this book are now discussed.

The "Header" field in the PCX file header is used to determine if a file is a legitimate PCX or PCC file. The value read from the graphics file into this field must be equal to ten decimal for the file to be considered a PCX/PCC file. Most PCX/PCC readers will reject a file if the "Header" byte is incorrect.

The "Version" field provides the PCX revision level used to encode the contained image. The major revision levels are:

Version	PCX software revision
0	version 2.5
2	version 2.8 with palette
3	version 2.8 or 3.0 without palette
5	version 3.0 with palette

The PCX code provided in this chapter can read version 3.0 with or without palette information but writes only version 3.0 with palette information.

The "Encode" field determines if the raster image data is RLL (run length limited), encoded, or byte packed. If the image is RLL encoded, the value of this field will be nonzero. Otherwise, if the value is zero, the image data is byte packed. For all practical purposes, every PCX/PCC file is RLL encoded to save space during image storage. See "Run Length Limited Compression" for a detailed description of RLL encoding.

The field "BitPerPix" determines how many bits per pixel per bit plane are used in the image. In 16-color, 4-bit-plane VGA images, the value of this field is 1. A related field, "NumOfPlanes", in this case would be set to 4. In 256-color (VGA mode 13 hex) images, "BitPerPix" would be 8 and "NumOfPlanes" would be 1.

The fields "X1", "Y1", "X2", and "Y2" delineate the dimensions of the raster image contained in the PCX file. In PCX files, "X1" and "Y1" always equal zero and "X2" and "Y2" equal the maximum X and Y pixel values available for a display adapter in a given display mode. In other words, PCX files fill a complete display screen. PCC files, on the other hand, have "X1" and "Y1" values greater than or equal to zero and "X2" and "Y2" values less than or equal to the maximum display resolution. PCC images are partial images that do not necessarily fill a full display screen. PCC images are not supported fully by the PCX function library because it is not always possible to tell what resolution VGA screen to use to display a partial screen image from the values contained in the fields "X1", "Y1", "X2", and "Y2". Correct interpretation of the two fields "Hres" and "Vres", described next, would eliminate this problem—if the fields were correctly maintained by all PCX/PCC application programs. Unfortunately, they are not. For example, one version of PC PaintBrush always stores the value of 75 hex into "X2" and "Y2" regardless of the display mode the display adapter is in. These unrelated values do not help determine the proper display adapter mode required to display the contained PCC image.

The fields, "Hres" and "Vres" should always contain the resolution of the display adapter required to display the raster image. In the PCX function library, these fields are maintained correctly for all PCX images written. These fields are ignored when a PCX file is read with the PCX function library.

The last PCX header field to be discussed is "BytesPerLine". This value is the number of uncompressed data bytes necessary to contain a full scan line (row of data from the screen) of image data. For images with "BitPerPix" equal to 1 that are 640 pixels wide (640×200 and 640×480 images), "BytesPerLine" is equal to 80 (640 pixels/8 pixels per byte). For 320×200 images (256 colors) with "BitPerPix" equal to 8, "BytesPerLine" is equal to 320 (320 pixels/1 pixel per byte).

PCX File Palettes

Palette information is stored in a PCX file so an application that reads the PCX image data can display it in the colors in which it was originally created and therefore meant to be displayed. Without palette information, an image would have to be displayed with a default palette provided by the application program. The colors in the default palette may not reflect those of the original image. In fact, displaying an image with a default palette could completely ruin the beauty of the image. Imagine an image of the ocean displayed with orange water—not very appealing. Saving the palette information with the PCX file allows applications other than that on which an image was created to display the image correctly and accurately.

It is important to understand the distinction between the palette information stored in a PCX file and the palette mechanism used by the VGA display adapter. Chapter 1 told us a palette is no more than a collection of colors, which can be displayed simultaneously and are used to display an image. The palette information in a PCX file tells us the correct color components (what percentages of red, green, and blue make up the desired color) of each color that should be available for the image display. There must be one palette entry in the PCX file for each color used in the raster image. The order of the palette entries in the PCX file determine the pixel value required to display the described color. For example, a pixel value of 0 should be displayed in the color specified by the 0th palette entry (i.e., the first palette entry). A pixel value of 15 will be displayed in the color specified by the 15th palette entry, and so on.

To correctly display a PCX image, it is necessary to build a palette for the VGA graphics adapter and to load the VGA color registers with the proper RGB components of the required colors. The easiest way to accomplish this is to load the color registers starting at register 0 with the RGB components read from the PCX file and then create a 16-entry VGA palette containing the values 0 through 15. This will provide the required mapping of pixel value to color. Note, however, that this is just one possible mapping of many that will provide the same result. Only when the palette of colors being used by the VGA graphics adapter match the palette contained in the PCX file can an image be displayed in its proper colors (the colors it was meant to be displayed in).

Two different palette mechanisms are utilized in PCX files. The original palette mechanism is built into the header of the file. This palette is used for images that contain up to 16 colors for display. This palette structure has room for 16 color register values composed of one byte each of red, green, and blue color information. The total space allotted for this palette structure in the PCX file header is therefore 48 bytes (16 color register values·3 bytes each). How the palette information is interpreted depends upon the graphics adapter being utilized.

For normal 16-color VGA images, the first 16 color registers are set to the colors described by the RGB components in the PCX file's palette structure. The actual palette, which as you remember is nothing more than a table with which to index into the color registers, is set up in sequential order starting at 0 and ending at 15. An image pixel value of 0 will select color register 0 which most of the time is black. A pixel value of 15 will select the color in color register 15, and so on. Loading RGB values into the VGA color registers was described in Chapter 1.

Also as described in Chapter 1, an EGA display adapter is capable of displaying 16 colors on the screen simultaneously out of a total palette of 64 colors. The format of a color descriptor was given as:

r′g′b′ R G B

where the R, G, and B bits are referred to as the base color bits and r′, g′, and b′ are the alternate color bits. If a color component byte has any of the even bits set, then the base color bit is considered to be on. If any of the odd bits are set, the alternate color bit is on. If both even and odd bits are set, both the base and the alternate bits are on. To determine which of the 64 possible colors a palette entry refers to, it is necessary to apply this rule for each of the RGB bytes in a PCX file's palette entry. For example, if the hex values of the RGB components equal 55, AA, and FF respectively, the color descriptor would equal:

Descriptor	r′	g′	b′	R	G	B	
Red = 55 => odd bits only	1			0			alternate bit set
Green = AA => even bits only		0			1		base bit set
Blue = FF => even and odd			1			1	both sets
Total Color Value	1	0	1	0	1	1	= Color 43

The EGA palette for this PCX palette entry would then be set to color 43. (*Note*: an equally valid RGB palette entry for this same color would be 01, 02, 03 hex. This satisfies the same criteria with the even and the odd bits. Think about it.)

For four-color CGA images, the red component of the first palette entry divided by 16 is the background color (0 through 15), and the red component of the second palette entry divided by 32 is the CGA palette identifier (0 through 7, although standard CGA supports only palettes 0 through 3). The remainder of the palette data is ignored.

A different palette mechanism must be used within a PCX file whenever more than 16 colors are required to display an image. This alternative palette mechanism is referred to as an *extended palette*. With the PCX file header being of a fixed length and format and the palette storage area within the header limited to 48 total bytes, an entirely new palette area must be allocated in a PCX file whenever more than 16 colors are required. All VGA mode 13 hex pictures (with 256 possible colors saved in PCX file format) require an extended palette.

The extended palette is an additional data structure appended to the end of a PCX file after the raster image data. The format of this data structure is as follows:

```
/*
Optional extended palette data structure for 256 color PCX files
*/

struct ExtendedPalette
{
    BYTE ExtendedPalette;
    ColorRegister Palette[Max256PaletteColors]; /* Max size of 768 bytes */
};
```

The first field in the structure is a tag that identifies the extended palette. This tag is always equal to decimal 12 for a valid extended palette structure. Following the tag are storage positions for 256 three-byte RGB entries: 768 bytes in total. These RGB entries are transferred directly into the VGA's 256-color registers when the extended palette structure is read from a PCX file. The PCX function library supports the extended palette both in reading and writing PCX files.

The concept of the extended palette illustrates how confining a graphics file format with a fixed structure really is. The extended palette had to be tacked onto the end of the PCX file structure; otherwise it would completely change the fixed format of PCX image files. A change of this magnitude would make the new PCX files unreadable by all existing applications, effectively making them obsolete. This would create a serious problem for all application programs supporting PCX files. Placing the extended palette structure at the end of the file means all application programs that understand extended palettes can find them and those applications that do not understand them can ignore them.

Although this scheme works, it can cause a problem in PCX file readers. The "view.exe" program presented on page 259 suffers from just such a problem. That is, the absence or presence of an extended palette is not known until all of the raster image data has already been read from the file. If the raster data is moved directly onto the video display as it is being read, the image will be displayed in bizarre colors (the default palette of the display mode being utilized) until the presence of the extended palette structure is verified and its contents read and stored in the VGA adapter. Only after the complete image is written to the screen will the VGA palette be modified to the colors required by the image. Only then will the image be displayed in the proper colors.

A possible way to work around this problem would be to position to the end of the PCX file, back up 769 bytes, and try to find the extended palette tag. If it is found, the extended palette can be read into the VGA graphics adapter before the raster data is read. This will result in the image having the correct colors while it is being displayed. We have just presented a work around for a work around.

What would happen if the PCX file format needed to be extended again? The new extension would also have to be placed at the end of the file for the reasons previously stated. The 769 byte backup from the end of the PCX file to find the extended palette would no longer work; the offset would be wrong. From this discussion you should understand the implications and the limitations of fixed file formats. The TIFF format (to be discussed later in this chapter) was designed to prevent this type of problem.

To conclude this discussion of PCX file palettes, it is necessary to emphasize one more important point. That is, the RGB component values contained in a PCX file's palette (as it is stored in the file on disk) are four times their actual value. In other words, the range of color component values stored in the PCX file is 0 to 255, whereas the VGA color register values must be in the range 0 to 63. For this reason, when a PCX file is read by the PCX library functions, the palette color values are divided by four before being loaded into the VGA color registers. Conversely, the color register values are multiplied by four before being placed in a PCX palette structure in preparation for being written to a PCX file. The reason for scaling the color values in this fashion is an anachronism left over from how EGA PCX files were handled.

Run Length Limited Compression

The need for data compression becomes obvious when the amount of storage required for an image is realized. As an example, 307,200 bytes of storage are required for a 640 by 480 continuous-tone image produced by the digitizer. A page scanner with a 300 DPI (dots per inch) resolution in both the horizontal and vertical directions utilizing eight bits per pixel can produce a file in excess of eight megabytes in size. See Figure 6.2 for the storage requirements of bit-mapped images. It does not take many image files of this size to fill up the largest hard disk.

The amount of compression achieved by the RLL method is image file dependent but typically reduces the storage requirement by one half to three quarters. This is a significant reduction from such a simple compression method. Other compression methods with higher compression ratios are available (Huffman and LZW algorithms for example), but they suffer from substantial computational overhead (see the October 1989 issue of *Dr. Dobb's Journal* for an excellent article on LZW methods). RLL is a good trade-off between image size and compression/expansion times.

In RLL compression, each row of image data is compressed separately. If there are multiple-bit planes in an image, the compressed data consists of a row from each of the component planes. Up to four bit planes are supported by the PCX format. The order of the bit planes is BGRI. That is, the blue row data, the green row data, the red row data, and finally, the row intensity data. RLL compression cannot span a scan line but can and does span the color components of a scan line. If the image does not use multiple-bit planes, the image data is the index into the palette for each pixel value on the scan line. Row data is

Notes
a. The following data assumes all images are 8.5 × 11 inches.
b. The horizontal and vertical resolutions are the same.
c. The table indicates the total number of bytes required for storage of an uncompressed image at the specified resolution.

Resolution in dots/inch (DPI)	BitsPerSample			
	1	4	8	24
72	60,588	242,352	484,704	1,454,112
150	262,969	1,051,875	2,103,750	6,311,250
300	1,051,875	4,207,500	8,415,000	25,245,000

Figure 6.2   Storage Requirements of Bit-Mapped Images

compressed by replacing a repetitive sequence of bits by a repeat count byte and a data byte. A repeat count byte is identified by having its two most significant bits set (to 1). Its lower six bits specify a repeat count value from 1 to 63 for the data byte that follows. If a data byte has both of its high-order bits set, then it, too, must be encoded as a repeat count byte and a data byte. The pseudocode for RLL compression is as follows:

```
Function CompressScanLine

Calculate the total number of bytes to compress
Repeat
    Get input data byte character
    Increment input pointer
    Set repeat count to a 1
    While next input data byte is a match and
            the maximum repeat count of 63 is not exceeded and
            there is more input data bytes to compress

    Increment the repeat count
    EndWhile
    If the repeat count is greater than 1 or
        the character has 2 MSBs set then
        Set two MSBs in repeat count
        Write repeat count to the output file
    Endif
        Write the data byte to the file
    Until All bytes compressed
End
```

C code that implements the RLL compression is contained in the function "CompressScanLine" from the PCX function library. This function is shown in Listing 6.1. An assembler language version of "CompressScanLine" called "Pack" is shown in Listing 6.2.

Listing 6.2   An Assembler Language RLL Encoder

The following is the contents of the file, "compress.asm":

```
; Video Compression Routine callable from Turbo C
;
; written by Craig A. Lindley
; last update: 05/22/89
;
_TEXT segment    byte public 'CODE'
     DGROUP      group _DATA,_BSS
     assume      cs:_TEXT,ds:DGROUP,ss:DGROUP
_TEXT ends


_DATA    segment word public  'DATA'
;
_DATA    ends


_BSS     segment word public  'BSS'
;
_BSS     ends
;
;
_TEXT    segment byte public  'CODE'
;
;Scan Line Compression
;
; Procedure _Pack
;
; This procedure compresses a video line into RLL encoding. Specifically,
; the RLL encoding used by PCX graphics files. In this encoding, a repeat
; byte sequence is compressed into a repeat count followed by the byte
; to be repeated. A maximum repeat of 63 is all that is allowed because a
; repeat count byte is identified by having its most significant two bits
; set high. This also means that any single char with a value above 0BFH
; also will be encoded as a repeat count (C1) followed by the bytes value so
; the bytes value will not be misinterpreted as a repeat count.
;
; CALL:   callable from C.
; PROTOTYPE: unsigned Pack (BYTE far *, BYTE far *, unsigned Count)
; INPUT:  all parameters passed to this function are on the stack. The
;         stack should contain the following: Count at [bp+12], Output buf seg
;         at [bp+10], Output buf offset at [bp+8], Input buf seg at [bp+6]
;         and the Input buf offset at [bp+4].
```

```
; OUTPUT: the number of bytes in the packed output buffer returned in ax.
; USES:    ax,bx,cx,dx,es,si,di registers
;
        Public  _Pack
;
_Pack   proc    near
;
        push    bp
        mov     bp,sp
        push    si
        push    di
;
        mov     si,[bp+4]       ;load parms from the stack
        mov     ds,[bp+6]       ;ptr to buffer to pack
        mov     di,[bp+8]
        mov     es,[bp+10]      ;ptr to packed buffer
        mov     dx,[bp+12]      ;size of buffer to pack
;
;when we get here the actual RLL encoding is performed
;
        cld                     ;move ptrs forward in memory
pack1:  lodsb                   ;get byte from input buffer
        mov     bl,al           ;save in bl
        mov     cx,1            ;char rep count is 1
        dec     dx              ;dec # of input bytes to process
;
pack2:  cmp     dx,0            ;all input bytes compressed ?
        je      pack3           ;jump if so
        cmp     cx,63           ;at max block size ?
        je      pack3           ;jump if so
        cmp     bl,[si]         ;look at next byte
        jne     pack3           ;jump if not same
        inc     si              ;bump input ptr to next byte
        dec     dx              ;now one less
        inc     cx              ;byte same so bump rep count
        jmp     short pack2     ;try for another match
;
;we are now ready to place compressed items in the output buffer
;
pack3:  cmp     cx,1            ;rep count > 1 ?
        ja      pack5           ;jump if so
        cmp     al,0BFH         ;char > BFH ?
        ja      pack5           ;jump if so
```

(continued)

Listing 6.2 *(continued)*

```
;
;when we get here we have a single byte to place in the output buffer with
;a value less than COH.
;
pack4:  stosb                   ;put byte in output buffer
        cmp     dx,0            ;any more input chars ?
        jne     pack1           ;if so go back and start over
        jmp     short pack6     ;get ready to exit if no more
;
;when we get here, we must process a repeat count followed by a repeat byte
;
pack5:  push    ax              ;save rep byte
        mov     al,cl           ;rep count to al
        or      al,0C0H         ;set the 2 msbits
        stosb                   ;store rep count in output buffer
        pop     ax              ;get byte back
        jmp     short pack4     ;now output the byte
;
;we're done and ready to exit
;
pack6:  mov     ax,di           ;get output ptr
        sub     ax,[bp+8]       ;calc # of bytes in output buf
        pop     di              ;restore regs and exit
        pop     si
        pop     bp
        ret
;
_Pack   endp
;
_TEXT   ends
        end
```

"Pack" is included on the companion disk as file "compress.asm" but is not utilized in this book. It is included to show two different ways of accomplishing the same thing. It is slightly faster but less portable than the C version.

Because the PCX function library must be able to read as well as write PCX image files, an analogous RLL expansion function is required. The function that implements RLL expansion is called "ExpandScanLine". The pseudocode for the expansion processes is:

```
Function ExpandScanLine

Calculate the number of expanded bytes expected
Repeat
   Read data byte from file
   If two MSBs set then its a repeat tag
      Mask off the two MSBs to get repeat count
      Get next data byte from file
      Store this byte count number of times in output buffer
   Else its actual data byte
      Store data byte in output buffer
   Endif
Until all bytes are expanded
```

Single-bit-plane images get different treatment than multiple-bit-plane images. Actually, single-plane images require much less processing and can therefore be compressed and expanded much faster. See the function "WritePCXFile" for details. Images that utilize VGA mode 13 hex, the 256-color mode, are single-plane images. All 16-color VGA images in this book utilize 4-bit planes.

The PCX Function Library

The PCX function library consists of a total of 12 PCX functions, 8 of which are meant to be used externally. Figure 6.3 shows the externally available functions and gives a short description of their operation.

Example Usage of the PCX Function Library

Actually, the PCX function library was used extensively in Chapter 5 to save digitized images as PCX files. To use the PCX function library an application program must include the PCX header files "pcx.h" and "misc.h" during compilation. With the header file included, a call to "WritePCXFile" in the application program (previously linked with "pcx.obj") is all that is necessary to produce a PCX file of an image displayed on the VGA graphics adapter. The parameters passed to the "WritePCXFile" function were described earlier and are repeated in Figure 6.4 for reference.

Only three different varieties of PCX image files are required to save images produced by the digitizer. They are 320×200 resolution 256-color images, 640×200 resolution continuous-tone (16 levels of gray) images, and 640×480 resolution continuous-tone images. Figure 6.4 shows the parameters required by the "WritePCXFile" function to save PCX images in each required resolution. The 640×350 resolution mode is shown in the table because the "WritePCXFile" function supports it, even though it is never used in saving digitized images.

1. Load the palette information from a PCX file into the VGAgraphics adapter.

Prototype
unsigned InstallPCXFilePalette (void);

Where no parameters are utilized.

Operation
When executed, this function will determine if a previously loaded PCX image file contains palette information; if so, the function will load the palette and color registers of the VGA graphics adapter appropriately. The VGA graphics adapter must be in the correct graphics mode before this function is executed. Otherwise, all loaded color registers will be overwritten by the BIOS when the correct graphics mode is entered. This function supports both the normal 16-color PCX palette and the extended palette mechanisms described earlier.

2. Read a PCX image into a memory buffer.

Prototype
CompletionCode ReadPCXFileToBuf (char *FileName, BYTE huge **BufferPtr);

Where:

"FileName" is the name of the PCX file to read into memory. "FileName" must be a null terminated string of characters. Full path names are accepted. "FileName" does not require (or prohibit the use of) a file extension. Since this function calls "ReadPCX-FileHdr", any file extension specified will be stripped off and the extension ".PCX" will be used instead.

"BufferPtr" is a pointer to the storage location where the address of the image data read from the PCX file should be stored.

Operation
This function will read a PCX image file into a buffer in memory (which it allocates from the far heap) and return a pointer to the image. Upon successful completion, the variable PCXData will contain all of the image header information, and the array "Color256Palette" will contain the extended palette, if one exists. The current VGA palette and color registers are not modified directly by this function call. To display the PCX image data in the buffer a call to "InstallPCX-FilePalette" is necessary followed by a call to "DisplayImageInBuf". Various error codes (defined in "pcx.h") will be returned by this function if it is unable to load the PCX image data. This function is used extensively by the image processing code presented in Part 2.

3. Display a previously loaded PCX image from a memory buffer.

Phototype
void DisplayImageInBuf (BYTE huge *Image,unsigned SetMode, unsigned Pause);

Where:

"Image" is a pointer to where in memory (on the far heap) the image data resides.

"SetMode" determines whether or not the VGA video mode and palette need to be initialized before the image is displayed. If "SetMode" is TRUE, the video mode and palette will be initialized as appropriate for the display of the image contained in the memory buffer before image display is attempted. If "SetMode" is FALSE, this function assumes that the

Figure 6.3   The PCX Function Library

video mode and the palette are already correct and proceeds to display the image without initialization. Two constants, "INITVGALOADPALETTE" and "NOVGAINIT", are defined to aid in writing clear programs. As you might suspect, "INITVGALOADPALETTE" is defined as TRUE whereas "NOVGAINIT" is defined as FALSE.

Pause determines whether this function should wait until a user presses a keyboard key before returning to the calling program. If "Pause" is TRUE or if it is equal to the constant "WAITFORKEY", the user must press a key before this function will finish. If "Pause" is FALSE or is equal to "NOWAITFORKEY", return from this function happens immediately after the image is displayed.

Operation

This function will display a raster image contained in a buffer in memory. Four display resolutions are supported: 320×200 with 256 colors and 640×200, 640×350, and 640×480— each with 16 possible colors. It is assumed the variables "ImageWidth" and "ImageHeight" are set appropriately before this function is called. These variables would have been set up by the call to "ReadPCXFileToBuf", which placed the image into the memory buffer. This function will be used in Part Two of the book to display the result of image processing algorithms executed on raster image data.

4. Display a PCX file on the VGA graphics adapter.

Prototype

void DisplayPCXFile (char *FileName, int Verbose):

Where:

"FileName" is an ASCII filename as specified above.
"Verbose" is a variable that controls whether or not detailed image information contained in the PCX file header should be displayed. If TRUE, the image information will be displayed before the image is displayed. See the function "ReadPCXFileHdr" for details of what PCX information will be displayed.

Operation

This function loads and displays a PCX image from a disk file. All parameters required for proper image display are taken from the header read from the PCX image file. The image data is taken directly from the file and placed onto the VGA display. No intermediate image buffer is utilized. Any errors encountered in the execution of this function will terminate program operation and provide an exit code to explain the error.

5. Write a PCX file from the image contained in a memory buffer.

Prototype

CompletionCode WritePCXFileFromBuf (char *FileName, BYTE huge *ImageMemory);

Where:

"FileName" is as specified above.
"ImageMemory" is a pointer to where in memory the image data resides.

Operation

This function is similar to "WritePCXFile" (described next) except that it takes its raster data from a buffer in memory instead of from the display. The parameters that control the type of

Figure 6.3 *(continued)*   *(continued)*

PCX image written are taken from the "PCXData" structure (previously read from a PCX file) instead of from parameters passed to this function. The palette currently being used by the VGA graphics adapter is written out to the PCX file. This function supports both the normal and the extended palette mechanisms. This function, upon completion, frees the memory associated with the image buffer (previously allocated by "ReadPCXFileToBuf") after the PCX file is written to the disk.

6. Write a PCX file from the image currently being displayed on the VGA display.

Prototype
void WritePCXFile (char *FileName,   unsigned BitsPerPixel,
                   unsigned MaxX,   unsigned MaxY,
                   unsigned Planes,   unsigned BytesPerLine);

Where:

"FileName" is as specified above.

"BitsPerPixel" indicates the number of bits per pixel per bit plane for each pixel to be written to the PCX file. All supported image resolutions except 320 × 200 with 256 colors used "BitsPerPixel" equal to 1. Each of these types of images uses 4-bit planes for a total of 4 bits per pixel, or 16 color possibilities. The 256-color mode, being a single-bit plane image, uses a value of 8 for "BitsPerPixel".

"MaxX & MaxY" are the dimensions of the image to be written out as a PCX file. Generally, they equal the resolution of the VGA mode used to display the image.

"Planes" is the number of bit planes used to represent the image. The value of "Planes" is either 1 for the 256-color images or 4 for 16-color images.

"BytesPerLine" specifies how many bytes make up a single scan line of the image. For 320 × 200 images "BytesPerLine" is equal to 320. For all other images, which use 4-bit planes, it is equal to 80 (640 pixels wide/8 pixels per byte).

Operation

This function creates a PCX file from the image currently being displayed on the VGA monitor. It writes out the PCX file header followed by the raster data and optionally followed by an extended palette structure. The type of PCX file created depends upon the parameters passed to this function.

7. Read an uncompressed image file into a memory buffer.

Prototype
CompletionCode ReadRawImageFileToBuf (char *FileName,
                                      unsigned ImageWidth,
                                      unsigned ImageHeight,
                                      BYTE huge * *BufferPtr);

Where:

"FileName" is as specified above.

"ImageWidth & ImageHeight" describe the dimensions of the image and therefore the number of raw data bytes to be read from the disk file.

"BufferPtr" is a pointer to the storage location where the address of the image data read from the raw data file should be stored.

Figure 6.3 *(continued)*

Operation

This function, while not related to PCX files, is included in this function library to keep all file I/O functions in one place. It reads a raw image data file into a memory buffer it allocates for the image. The amount of data read from the file is determined from the specified image dimensions. Various error codes are returned in the event of an error reading the image file. If the read is successful, a pointer to the image data and the "NoError" status will be returned to the calling code. This function makes no assumptions about the format of the data read from the file other than that it should be stored in sequential memory locations of the image buffer. It is up to the code that processes the image buffer to make sense of the data. In other words, it is important for the code that writes the raw data to the file and the code that processes the image buffer to agree on the format of the data. If the two processes do not agree on the format, image data will never be exchanged correctly.

8. Write uncompressed image data from a memory buffer to disk.

Prototype
CompletionCode WriteRawImageFileFromBuf (char *FileName,
                                    unsigned ImageWidth,
                                    unsigned ImageHeight,
                                    unsigned Transpose,
                                    BYTE huge *ImageBuffer);

Where all parameters except for the following are as specified:

"Transpose" determines which of two output data formats shall be written to the file. If "Transpose" is FALSE, data in the file will be organized in column-by-column format exactly as the data is stored in the image buffer filled by the digitizer. If TRUE, the data will be rearranged before being written to the output file such that it is in row-by-row raster format.

"ImageBuffer" is a HUGE pointer to the image data that will be written to disk.

Operation

This function writes raw image data to a disk file from a buffer in memory. It supports two different formats of output data as determined by the parameter "Transpose" passed to this function. Which output file format to use is dependent upon the application program(s). Various error codes will be returned by this function if a problem is encountered in writing the output file. Although code is included to support them, raw image files are not utilized in this book.

The operation of the other functions provided in the PCX function library (those not meant to be called externally) are explained in detail in Listing 6.1.

Figure 6.3 *(continued)*

Resolution	Colors	BitsPerPixel	MaxX	MaxY	Planes	BytesPerLine
320 × 200	256	8	320	200	1	320
640 × 200	16	1	640	200	4	80
640 × 350	16	1	640	350	4	80
640 × 480	16	1	640	480	4	80

Figure 6.4 "WritePCXFile" Function Call Parameters

An example of displaying a PCX file is shown in the last portion of this chapter in the discussion of the "view.exe" program. Please refer to Listing 6.4 for an example of using the PCX function library to directly display a PCX image. As shown in the preceding example, displaying a PCX image file is as trivial as writing a PCX file. Again, a single line of code is all that is required.

The reading and writing of PCX files to memory instead of to the VGA display deserves further explanation. The function "ReadPCXFileToBuf" provides a method of bringing an image into memory (from a PCX file) for manipulation. After the manipulation is completed, the function "WritePCXFileFromBuf" is used to write the image back out to a PCX file. These functions will be used in conjunction with other image processing support routines in Part Two of this book. For now, however, it is necessary only to understand correct evocation of these functions. The following code fragment illustrates their usage. The comments should adequately describe the code's operation.

```
/* Important Variables */

char     *InFileName;  /* a ptr to a PCX input filename */
char     *OutFileName; /* a ptr to a PCX output filename */
BYTE huge *TheImage;    /* a huge pointer to an image */

/*
Attempt to read a PCX file into a buffer. Allocate a buffer
of the required size to hold the image. If successful, set
the HUGE pointer variable, TheImage, to point at the image buffer.
If an error occurs, treat it appropriately for the application.
*/
if (ReadPCXFileToBuf(InFileName,&TheImage) != NoError)
   exit(1);

/*
The PCX file has been successfully read into memory. Now
install the palette read from the PCX file in preparation
for displaying the image.
*/
InstallPCXFilePalette();

/* Optionally display the original image. */
DisplayImageinBuf(TheImage);

/* image processing performed here on the data in the buffer */

/* Optionally display the processed image. */
DisplayImageinBuf(TheImage);
```

```
/*
Write the processed image out as a PCX file. Again,
treat errors appropriately. This function automatically
frees the buffer memory in which the image was stored.
*/
if (WritePCXFileFromBuf(OutFileName,TheImage) != NoError)
   exit(1);
```

Loss of Image Information

It is important to realize that when a PCX image file is created from a 16-color VGA screen, some image information is lost. To understand why this is true, refer to the discussion of the example programs in Chapter 5. Remember, the image data had to be scaled from the range 0 to 63 (which was produced by the digitizer) to the range 0 to 15 to be displayed. When a PCX file is written (from the screen) using this scaled data, some of the dynamic range of the original image is lost. The produced PCX file contains 4 bits per pixel (all that is required for 16 possible colors) of image information, whereas the original data contained 6 bits.

Two techniques are available to combat this loss of image information: read and write raw image data files instead of PCX data files for 16-color images, or use the 320×200 256-color mode exclusively for saved PCX files that are to be used for image-data exchange between applications.

The functions "ReadRawImageFileToBuf" and "WriteRawImageFileFromBuf" from the PCX function library provide the capability to exchange raw, unprocessed image data between applications. In other words, 6 bits of image data written into a raw image file equals 6 bits of image data read out of the file; no reduction in image information content is incurred. The drawbacks involved in using these raw image files are (1) that no commercial applications will understand this format, and (2) that the size of the files can be prohibitive. Still, when image "fidelity" is of utmost importance and all of the application programs that utilize the images are custom (under control of the programmer), the exchange of raw image data is a reasonable technique to use.

If 320×200 resolution images will suit your application needs, then a PCX file can be used for interapplication data exchange without fear of image data information loss. This is possible because all images with this resolution (produced by code in this book) are stored with 8 bits per pixel. This means the original 6-bit content of each pixel is easily retained within the PCX's file.

The TIFF Image File Format

Introduction

The Tagged Image File Format (TIFF) was designed from the ground up to alleviate the problems associated with fixed file formats. (Some of the problems with the extendability of the PCX format were described earlier in this chapter.) The key word here is *designed*. TIFF did not evolve from a de facto standard. It was created to become the industry standard for image-file exchange. TIFF is a superset of all existing graphics or image file formats. TIFF incorporates enough flexibility to eliminate the need or justification for proprietary image file formats. As a matter of fact, it is possible to store proprietary information in a TIFF file without violating the intent of the format. TIFF was designed with an eye toward the future, not just for use in the present. The designers of the TIFF file format had three important goals in mind:

a. *Extendability*. This is the ability to add new image types without invalidating older types and to add new informational fields to the format without impacting the ability of older applications to read the image files.

b. *Portability*. TIFF was designed to be independent of the hardware platform and the operating system on which it executes. TIFF makes very few demands upon its operating environment. TIFF should (and does) perform equally well in both the IBM PC and Apple Macintosh® environments.

c. *Revisability*. TIFF was designed not only to be an efficient medium for exchanging image information but also to be usable as a native internal data format for image editing applications.

The correctness and the accomplishment of these goals is corroborated by the number of software vendors supporting the TIFF format. Every major scanner manufacturer and every desktop publishing program supports TIFF. More application programs support TIFF every day. Also, numerous translator programs that translate other image-file formats to TIFF format are becoming available.

The richness of the TIFF format solves many problems, but at the same time creates a few all its own. The TIFF file structure, is necessarily complex—more complex, in fact, than many of the proprietary file formats it was designed to replace. The added complexity of the TIFF format requires much more code to manage it than do most other image-file formats. This results in slower execution times reading and writing files and in longer TIFF code development cycles. The code provided in this book will drastically reduce your development time, however, because all of the hard work has already been done for you. To give you a relative comparison in code complexity, the PCX function library provided earlier in this chapter contains approximately 2,600 lines of C code. The TIFF function library contains approximately 13,500 lines of code. Over five times as much code is required to support the TIFF format.

The TIFF function library supports TIFF revision 5.0. The TIFF format is controlled by a specification jointly written by the Aldus Corporation and Microsoft. Many other companies in addition to these two contributed to the formulation of the TIFF format. Version 5.0 of this specification is dated April 1988 and can be found in an Appendix 2. It is included in this book with the permission of Aldus Corporation. Although the specification document itself is copyrighted by the Aldus Corporation, the TIFF format is in the public domain. This means no fees or royalties are required to use the format. The complete specification is included because of its reference value. The spec and its appendices contain a lot of valuable information about imaging topics in general, in addition to hard facts about TIFF. Because the specification document is available and because, unlike most other specifications, it is quite readable, the discussion to follow only highlights TIFF functionality. Any questions you might have about TIFF are answered somewhere in the spec.

Finally, a few good articles have been written about the TIFF file format. Information about these articles can be found in "References and Additional Reading."

The TIFF File Structure

TIFF files are made up of three unique data structures. These structures along with their functions are illustrated in Figure 6.5. Please refer to this figure during the discussion.

The first data structure found in every TIFF file is called the *Image File Header*, or *IFH*. This structure is the only portion of a TIFF file that has a fixed location. This 8-byte structure must be located at offset zero in the file. The IFH contains important information necessary to correctly interpret the remainder of the TIFF file. The first field within the IFH, and possibly the most important, is the byte-ordering field. This field indicates the byte-ordering that was used when the TIFF file was created. This is especially important because TIFF files can be moved between the IBM PC world (based upon Intel processors) and the Macintosh world (based upon the Motorola series of processors). As you may or may not know, the byte ordering (within 16-bit integers and long 32-bit integers) used by Intel and Motorola processors is quite different. Figure 6.6 shows how different it is. Without knowing the order of bytes used when an image file was created, a TIFF file reader would have little hope of recovering the image. This ordering affects any items read from a TIFF file that are longer than one byte in length.

The byte-ordering field in the IFH contains either two bytes of M's (hex 4D4D), indicating Motorola integer format, or two bytes of I's (hex 4949), indicating Intel format. Using the dual bytes allows this field to be correctly read by either type of processor. If the byte ordering utilized in the file differs from that of the computer on which the image file is being read, all subsequent 16- and 32-bit integer values will have to have their byte ordering reversed. If the byte ordering is the same, integer and long values can be read and used without modification. Luckily, all current data-compression methods utilized by the TIFF standard are byte oriented. If a word- or integer-oriented compression method were utilized, byte ordering of the image data would have to be taken into consideration as the data was read from the file. Swapping each word of compressed image data as a file was being read would be a computationally expensive process.

The version field in the IFH always contains the decimal value of 42. This field can be used to further verify that a file is a TIFF file. This number is not a TIFF software version number as one would expect. In fact, this number will probably never change. If it does, it indicates that the format of the TIFF file has changed radically and that TIFF reader programs should not even attempt to read the file. Major changes to the TIFF format that would necessitate changing the version field are in direct conflict with the philosophy of TIFF extendability.

The final field in the IFH contains the offset in bytes from the start of the file to the Image File Directory, or IFD, structure. This is the second of the three data structures contained in a TIFF file. Note that, although Figure 6.5 seems to indicate that the IFD immediately follows the IFH in the TIFF file, this is not necessarily the case. TIFF readers should never assume this but should seek to the offset value specified to find the first IFD in the image file. It may or may not follow the IFH in the file.

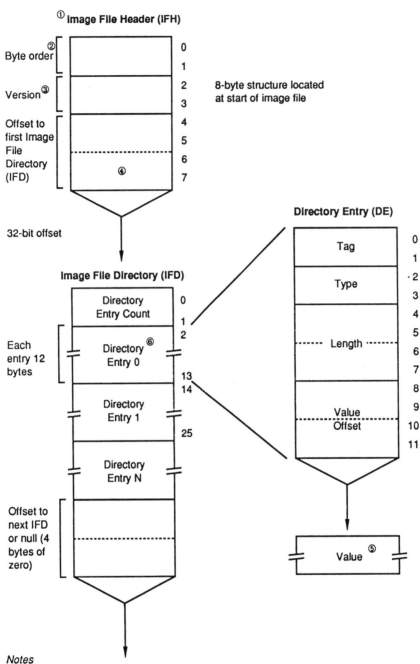

Byte order ②

Version ③

Offset to
first Image
File
Directory
(IFD)

④

	0
	1
	2
	3
	4
	5
	6
	7

8-byte structure located
at start of image file

32-bit offset

Image File Directory (IFD)

Directory
Entry Count

Each
entry 12
bytes

Directory ⑥
Entry 0

Directory
Entry 1

Directory
Entry N

Offset to
next IFD
or null (4
bytes of
zero)

Directory Entry (DE)

Tag

Type

Length

Value
Offset

	0
	1
	2
	3
	4
	5
	6
	7
	8
	9
	10
	11

Value ⑤

Notes

1. Image file header must be located at offset 0 into file.
2. Byte ordering "II" (hex 4949) is for Intel-created image file. "MM" (hex 4D4D) is for Motorola-created image file.
3. Version is always 42; (hex 2A) should never change.
4. First IFD may or may not follow Image File Header. TIFF readers must follow the pointers to find it.
5. If value can fit into Value Offset field, it will be placed there. If value cannot fit, Value Offset will contain a pointer (file offset from file beginning) to where value is located.
6. IFD entries sorted in ascending order by Tag value.

Figure 6.5 TIFF File Structure

234

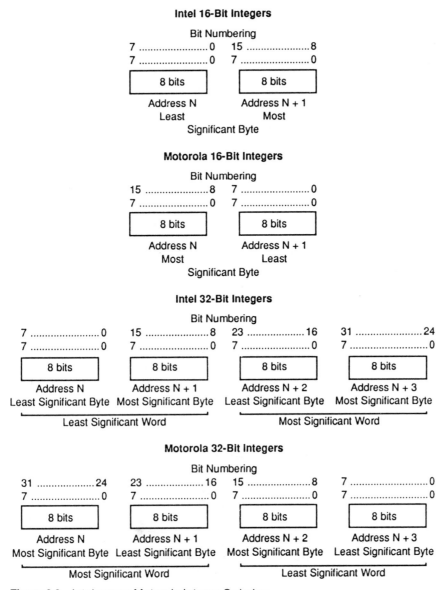

Figure 6.6   Intel versus Motorola Integer Ordering

One or more IFDs can reside in a TIFF file. Each IFD must be located on a word boundary. If more than one IFD exists, the file contains more than one image. A full-blown TIFF reader should be able to access any number of images in a TIFF file. Unfortunately, not many do. In fact, very few TIFF readers have as much capability as the TIFF code presented in this chapter

An IFD consists of a count N of the number of directory entries that follow, *N* 12-byte directory entries, and finally another offset value. The offset storage location within the IFD will contain the offset from the beginning of the TIFF file to the next IFD, or four bytes of zeros if this IFD is the last in the file. The Directory Entries (DEs) within an IFD must be sorted into ascending order by the value of the tag. This is a requirement that helps reduce overhead as TIFF files are processed.

The final data structure within the TIFF file format is the Directory Entry, or DE. It is the format of the DE's that gives TIFF its flexibility. As noted, each DE is exactly 12 bytes in length and is segmented into the four fields shown in Figure 6.5. The first field of the DE is the tag field. As the full name of this image-file format indicates, the tag is the foundation on which this file structure is based. The raster data contained in a TIFF file is defined by the tags to which it is attached. The advantages of a tagged image file are:

a. Application programs such as TIFF readers can safely ignore any tags they do not understand.

b. New tags can be added at any time without invalidating any of the older tags. In a sense, this prevents the TIFF file format from becoming obsolete.

c. Private tags can be defined to contain proprietary information within a TIFF file without affecting other application programs. The tags with values between 32,768 and 65,535 are reserved for just this purpose.

In all, 45 tags are defined in version 5.0 of the TIFF specification. These tags are summarized in Figure 6.7.

The numeric value of the tag indicates which image parameter is contained in the DE. Tag values between zero and 32,767 are reserved for use by TIFF public fields, while tags 32,768 to 65,535 are reserved for private fields. Private fields must be allocated by Aldus and/or Microsoft to prevent different software vendors from using the same tags in different ways.

Num	Tag Name	Tag Value	Tag Type	Tag Length
Basic Tags				
1.	BitsPerSample	258	SHORT	SamplesPerPixel
2.	ColorMap	320	SHORT	3*(2**BitsPerSample)
3.	ColorResponseCurve	301	SHORT	3*(2**BitsPerSample)
4.	Compression	259	SHORT	1
5.	GrayResponseCurve	291	SHORT	2**BitsPerSample
6.	GrayResponseUnit	290	SHORT	1
7.	ImageLength	257	SHORT/LONG	1
8.	ImageWidth	256	SHORT/LONG	1
9.	NewSubfileType	254	LONG	1
10.	PhotometricInterp	262	SHORT	1
11.	PlanarConfiguration	284	SHORT	1
12.	Predictor	317	SHORT	1
13.	PrimaryChromaticities	319	RATIONAL	6
14.	ResolutionUnit	296	SHORT	1
15.	RowsPerStrip	278	SHORT/LONG	1
16.	SamplesPerPixel	277	SHORT	1

Figure 6.7 TIFF Tag Summary

Num	Tag Name	Tag Value	Tag Type	Tag Length

Basic Tags

17.	StripByteCounts	279	SHORT/LONG	

Tag length = StripsPerImage for PlanarConfig = 1
SamplesPerPixel • StripsPerImage for PlanarConfig = 2

18.	StripOffsets	273	SHORT/LONG	

Tag length = StripsPerImage for PlanarConfig = 1
SamplesPerPixel • StripsPerImage for PlanarConfig = 2

19.	WhitePoint	318	RATIONAL	2
20.	XResolution	282	RATIONAL	1
21.	YResolution	283	RATIONAL	1

Information Tags

22.	Artist	315	ASCII	?
23.	DateTime	306	ASCII	20 "YYYY:MM:DD HH:MM:SSO"
24.	HostComputer	316	ASCII	?
25.	ImageDescription	270	ASCII	?
26.	Make	271	ASCII	?
27.	Model	272	ASCII	?
28.	Software	305	ASCII	?

Facsimile Tags

29.	Group3options	292	LONG	1
30.	Group4options	293	LONG	1

Document Storage and Retrieval Tags

31.	DocumentName	269	ASCII	?
32.	PageName	285	ASCII	?
33.	PageNumber	297	SHORT	2
34.	XPosition	286	RATIONAL	1
35.	YPosition	287	RATIONAL	1

No Longer Recommended Tags

36.	CellLength	265	SHORT	1
37.	CellWidth	264	SHORT	1
38.	FillOrder	266	SHORT	1
39.	FreeByteCounts	289	LONG	?
40.	FreeOffsets	288	LONG	?
41.	MaxSampleValue	281	SHORT	SamplesPerPixel
42.	MinSampleValue	280	SHORT	SamplesPerPixel
43.	SubfileType	255	SHORT	1
44.	Orientation	274	SHORT	1
45.	Thresholding	263	SHORT	1

Notes
a. Tag length is really the number of items of tag type to follow, not the length in bytes.
b. A question mark indicates a variable number of data items.
c. Some tags can be short or long according to the TIFF specification.

Figure 6.7   *(continued)*

The "type" field indicates the data type of the image parameter. Five unique data types are currently defined by the TIFF specification. Each data type is assigned an integer number which is stored in the "type" field of a DE. The data types are as follows:

Tag Type	Tag Enumeration	Type Description
BYTE	1	An 8-bit unsigned integer
ASCII	2	8-bit ASCII codes terminated with a null (hex 0) character
SHORT	3	A 16-bit (2-byte) unsigned integer
LONG	4	A 32-bit (4-byte) unsigned integer
RATIONAL	5	Two LONG values. The first represents the numerator of a fraction, the second the denominator

The DE "length" (sometimes called the "count") field contains the number of items of the specified data type provided. It is specified in terms of the data type, not the total number of bytes required for storage. A single SHORT tag (data type 3) has a length of one and not two, for example.

The final field in a DE is the "value offset" field. This field usually contains the file offset to the actual data associated with the tag. In other words, the data associated with a DE does not have to be physically stored with the DE but can reside anywhere in the TIFF file. Again, data pointers must be followed to find the actual data. If the data associated with a DE is four bytes or less in length, it can be stored in the "value offset" field directly instead of at a location pointed to by the this field. This was done to increase TIFF performance when retrieving small data items. Any data stored in "value offset" must be left justified (stored toward the lower-numbered bytes). The "type" and "length" fields must be consulted to determine if the total amount of storage required by a data item is four or fewer bytes and therefore whether it can be stored directly in the "value offset" field.

If the data type for a tag is ASCII, a null (hex 0) terminated string of characters is expected. No length byte is provided as is the case with Pascal strings. Of course, the null terminated string is exactly what C expects. The "length" field for an ASCII tag includes the null terminating character. The "length" field does not, however, include any padding of the ASCII string that may be required.

The raster data contained in a TIFF file is organized into groups of scan lines (or rows) of image data called *strips*. This organization helps reduce the memory requirements of TIFF readers because the complete image file does not have to be resident in memory all at once. Only enough memory must be available to buffer a single strip of image data at a time. Many of the early TIFF writing programs produced single-strip images that are difficult for many readers to read because of memory constraints. While this is legal according to the specification, the spec recommends that strips be limited to 8 KB (8,192 bytes) or less in length. The code provided in the TIFF function library can handle strips with lengths to approximately 60,000 bytes.

TIFF Data Compression

As pointed out in an earlier portion of this chapter, bit-mapped images required an incredible amount of memory for storage. To reduce the size of TIFF image files, the TIFF specification recommends support for four different types of data compression. A TIFF writer must support at least one of the compression methods. A TIFF reader should be able to understand all of the compression methods. The method utilized to compress an image is stored in the "Compression" tag. A TIFF reader must read the "Compression" tag to determine the type of data expansion to apply to the raster data contained in the TIFF file. Please note, data compression applies only to the image raster data. All other items of information contained in a TIFF file (the IFH, the IFDs, and the DEs) are not compressed in any way. The compression methods and their tag values are as follows:

Compression Tag Value	Compression Type
1	No compression but bytes are tightly packed
2	CCITT Group 3 1-Dimensional modified Huffman RLE
3	Facsimile compatible CCITT Group 3
4	Facsimile compatible CCITT Group 4
5	LZW (Lempel-Ziv & Welch)
32,773	PackBits (Macintosh)

The TIFF specification does not recommend storing images in noncompressed form because of the size of the file that results. The TIFF function library code supports methods 1, 5, and 32,773. Method 1 provides no compression at all. With this method, the bytes that make up a row of image data are packed tightly together with no extraneous bits except possibly at the end of the row. The LZW data compression method is described in depth in Appendix F of the TIFF specification. The PackBits method is also described in Appendix C of the TIFF specification. Appendix 2 of this book contains this specification.

TIFF Classes

As mentioned, TIFF's extreme flexibility places a burden on software developers who support this format. It requires a considerable amount of code to handle all of the options available. An application program wanting to import any TIFF image has no choice other than to handle all of the options. That is the only way to guarantee the image can be displayed exactly as it was produced. To reduce some of this burden, TIFF version 5.0 has introduced the concept of TIFF conformant classes. An application program can now handle a specific TIFF class without needing to handle all classes. It is the responsibility of the application program to advertise which TIFF classes it supports.

In general, three different categories of images can be contained in a TIFF file. These are:

a. *Black and white images*. These utilize one bit per pixel for display
b. *Gray-scale images*. These utilize between two and eight bits per pixel, which results in 4 to 256 levels of gray available in an image.
c. *Color images*. These are of both the palette and RGB varieties, with up to 24 bits of color data per pixel.

The TIFF classes quantify which image types fit into which class along with the compliment of TIFF tags required by each class. The TIFF class concept results in a small reduction in TIFF flexibility with the added benefit that TIFF writers will be able to produce images that can be read by more application programs. TIFF classes are summarized in Figure 6.8. This information has been extracted from Appendix G of the TIFF specification.

Four TIFF Classes are defined:

Class B (also called TIFF B) for bilevel, 1-bit images
Class G (also called TIFF G) for gray-scale images
Class P (also called TIFF P) for palette-color images
Class R (also called TIFF R) for RGB full-color images

A TIFF X class combines all four of the above.
    All TIFF classes are required to support the following tags:

1. NewSubfileType

2. ImageWidth

3. ImageLength

4. RowsPerStrip

5. StripOffsets

6. StripByteCounts

7. XResolution

8. YResolution

9. ResolutionUnit

Additionally, *TIFF Class B* conformant images are required to have the following tags with the following values:

1. SamplesPerPixel = 1

2. BitsPerSample   = 1

3. Compression   = 1, 2, or 32,773 (PackBits)

4. PhotometricInterpretation = 0 or 1

Figure 6.8   TIFF Classes

TIFF *Class G* conformant images are required to have the following tags with the following values:

1. SamplesPerPixel = 1
2. BitsPerSample = 4 or 8
3. Compression = 1 or 5 (LZW)
4. PhotometricInterpretation = 0 or 1

TIFF *Class P* conformant images are required to have the following tags with the following values:

1. SamplesPerPixel = 1
2. BitsPerSample = 1, 2, 3, 4, 5, 6, 7, or 8
3. Compression = 1 or 5 (LZW)
4. PhotometricInterpretation = 3
5. ColorMap

TIFF *Class R* conformant images are required to have the following tags with the following values:

1. SamplesPerPixel = 3
2. BitsPerSample = 8, 8, and 8
3. PlanarConfiguration = 1 or 2
4. Compression = 1 or 5 (LZW)
5. PhotometricInterpretation = 2

Figure 6.8 *(continued)*

The TIFF Function Library

The code provided in the TIFF function library provides support for all TIFF classes. Class B, however, is not fully supported because the CCITT compression algorithms are not provided. They are not supported because they have limited usefulness with imaging. They are specifically tailored for bilevel, black and white images only. Black and white images can be written or read using the ''PackBits'' compression method, however. If CCITT compression is desired, it will have to be added by the reader.

The code in the TIFF function library is designed to make reading and writing TIFF files as painless as possible. Most of the complexities of the file format are kept from the user/programmer. Many operations are performed automatically in the background that would have to be performed consciously by the programmer when using lesser TIFF implementations. Only the handful of functions declared in the file ''tiffintf.h'' are used to read and write any TIFF image file.

Almost all of the code that makes up the TIFF function library is part of a public domain TIFF library written by Sam Leffler of the University of California at Berkeley. The LZW compression/expansion code was also written at the University of California at Berkeley and is used with permission. The complete Berkeley copyright notice appears in its entirety in the file "lzw.c". Considerable reorganization of the TIFF library code was performed during the port to Turbo C and subsequent debugging of the original code. All of the source code was put into a format that is compatible with the other code found in this book. The TIFF function library code is in the public domain and can be used without prior permission or restriction as long as the original copyright notices remain intact.

The files that make up the TIFF function library are shown here. A short description of the contents of each file is provided.

TIFFINFO.DOC This file contains additional information about the internal functions of the TIFF function library. It should be read before attempting to utilize the library.

TIFF.H and TIFFIO.H These files define all TIFF data structures and the internal data structures used in the TIFF support code. All tags that are supported in TIFF version 5.0 are enumerated in these files.

IO.C This file contains all of the code that performs reading and writing of TIFF data to disk. It also contains portions of the code used to initialize the TIFF package.

DIR.C This file contains the code that parses the TIFF directory structure (the IFH, the IFDs, and the DEs) on reading a TIFF file and builds the directory structure when writing TIFF files. This is where the majority of the difficult code resides.

ERROR.C This file contains the functions that produce the warning and error messages that are output when improperly formatted TIFF files are read or written.

SWAB.C This file contains the code that performs all byte reordering operations.

PRINT.C This file contains a utility program which is used to dump all tag information from a TIFF file for user inspection. This code is utilized by the "view.exe" example program described shortly.

COMPRESS.C This short file contains a function that selects the compression algorithm to be used when reading and/or writing TIFF files.

DUMPMODE.C This file has the code that handles files that do not utilize data compression of the raster data. In other words, these functions read and write noncompressed TIFF files.

CCITT.C This file contains the stubs where the CCITT compression algorithms would be added to the function library. Currently, these stubs produce an error message, indicating that the TIFF function library does not support these compression methods.

PACKBITS.C This file contains the code to read and write TIFF files that utilize compression method 32773. This method is referred to as the "Macintosh PackBits" method.

LZW.C This file contains the code to read and write image raster data compressed using the Lempel-Ziv & Welch method.

Unfortunately, the files that comprise the TIFF function library just listed are too long to list in this book. These files are available in source form on the companion disk, however.

The following files were developed specifically for this book to support the specific imaging requirements of the digitizer.

TIFFINTF.H This file is an interface file to be used by all application programs wishing to utilize the TIFF library functions. It takes care of all TIFF library function declarations so the programmer does not have to. See the "view.exe" example program for an example of how to utilize this interface file.

TIFF.C This file provides the basic TIFF file access functions required to read and write TIFF files. These functions are analogous to some of the functions contained in the PCX function library discussed in the first part of this chapter. These functions are described in detail in Figure 6.9 and are shown in Listing 6.3.

---

1. Write a TIFF file from the image currently displayed on the VGA screen.

Prototype
CompletionCode WriteTIFFFile (char *FileName,unsigned BitsPerSample,
                              unsigned SamplesPerPixel,
                              unsigned ImageWidth,unsigned ImageLength);

Where:

"FileName" is the name of the TIFF output file to create. "FileName" must be a null terminated string of characters. Full path names are accepted. "FileName" does not require (or prohibit the use of) a file extension. Since this function calls "TIFFOpen", any file extension specified will be stripped and an extension of ".TIF" used instead.

"SamplesPerPixel" controls whether an image is written as a single-or multiple-plane image. Normally, "SamplesPerPixel" equals 1, and the produced image is a single plane. If "SamplesPerPixel" is equal to 4, a 4-plane image is created. Multiple-plane images require much longer to read and write from/to a disk file because of the additional processing required. Multiple-plane images are supported only because "ZSoft's PC PaintBrush 4 + " reads and writes multiple-plane images.

"BitsPerSample" should be 1 for black and white images, 4 for 16-color gray-scale images, and 8 for 64-level gray-scale or 256-color images.

ImageWidth & Image Length describe the dimensions of the image to be written to the specified TIFF file. They should contain the maximum resolution of the display mode utilized to display the image. That is, "ImageWidth" should be either 320 or 640, and "ImageLength" should be either 200 or 480.

Figure 6.9 The TIFF Library Functions *(continued)*

Operation

This function is not very flexible in its operation. It will support only the production of gray-scale and color images, not black and white images. From this you should not form the impression that the TIFF function library is incomplete. The limitation is in this function alone, not the function library. Black and white images are not supported because the digitizer does not produce single-bit-per-pixel images. All images, whether gray scale or color, regardless of the number of colors or gray levels, will be written out as a "palette" format TIFF file. This means a "ColorMap" also needs to be written to the output TIFF file so TIFF readers can recreate the original images. See the TIFF specification in Appendix 2 for details of "palette" images.

This function begins by calling "TIFFOpen", passing it a filename and the write mode flag, "w". This function will create a TIFF file with the given name and prepare it for being written. "TIFFOpen" also performs hidden initialization of the TIFF directory that will eventually be written to disk as part of the TIFF image. Any previous directory information is erased, and various default values for certain tags are installed. See the file "io.c" for more information.

Once the TIFF output file is opened, the function "TIFFSetField" is called many times to place the important image parameters into the newly initialized directory structure. As a result, tags will be placed in the output file for "SubfileType", "ImageWidth", "ImageLength", the number of "BitsPerSample", the compression type (always LZW in this code), the palette photometric interpretation, the make, the artist, the host computer, the number of "SamplesPer-Pixel", the "X" resolution, the "Y" resolution, the single-plane planar configuration, and the resolution units. Basically, tags are created for all of the mandatory tags specified in the TIFF specification.

After these tags are written, memory is allocated for a single row of image data. This buffer will be filled from the display once for each row. The address of this buffer will be passed to the TIFF library functions. The TIFF functions will compress the data from this buffer using LZW compression and write it to the output file.

Once the number of bytes that make up a row of display data is known, the number of rows per strip can be calculated. You'll recall that the length of a strip should be approximately 8KB. This function uses the 8KB target to calculate how many rows should be used to make up a strip. With this figure known, a "RowsPerStrip" entry is placed in the TIFF directory for eventual placement in the output file. Some programs will require fewer rows per strip because of memory constraints. For these programs, reduce the number of "RowsPerStrip" accordingly.

Next, the VGA color registers are read in preparation for building a "ColorMap" structure that will be written to the output file. The number of entries in the "ColorMap", as you will recall, is controlled by the number of bits in a pixel and the number of samples that make up a pixel. If there are 4 bits per sample, the "ColorMap" should contain 16 total entries. If 8 bits per sample are used, the "ColorMap" will contain 256 entries. This code is complicated by the fact that the 16-color VGA modes utilize a palette that adds a layer of indirection to the actual color register number. The 256-color VGA mode does not use a palette (see Chapter 1 for details). Whether or not a palette is used, the "RedColorMap", "GreenColorMap", and "BlueColorMap" arrays are loaded with values from the VGA color registers. These will become the "ColorMap" structure in the TIFF file. (*Note*: the VGA color register values range from 0 to 63. The TIFF "ColorMap" values range from 0 to 65,535. For this reason, the values read from the VGA color register are multiplied by 1,024 before being placed in the "ColorMap".) Once the "ColorMap" is built, a directory entry is made for it.

Finally, the image raster data is read from the screen and passed to the TIFF library function "TIFFWriteScanline" for compression and storage. How the information is read from the screen

Figure 6.9   *(continued)*

and passed to the TIFF function is determined by the number of bits utilized for each pixel and the mode the VGA adapter is in. If the image being encoded is 640 pixels in width, the code knows that 4 bits per pixel are utilized, so it packs two 4-bit pixel values together into a single byte. These bytes are accumulated for a single row of the displayed image and then are written to disk. This process continues for each row of the displayed image. A similar process is used if the image being encoded is 320 pixels wide.

After all of the image data is written to the file, the function "TIFFClose" is called. This function causes all of the tags to be created from the internal directory structure (which defines the raster image) and written to disk. It then closes the output file. After that, all memory that was allocated for this function is freed, and control is returned to the calling application program.

2. Read and display a TIFF file on the VGA screen.

Prototype
CompletionCode DisplayTIFFFile (char *FileName, unsigned Verbose);

Where:

"FileName" is an explained above.
"Verbose" controls whether detailed information about the TIFF file structure should be displayed or not. In other words, if "Verbose" is TRUE, all of the tag information from the TIFF file will be displayed on the monitor before the actual image is displayed. If FALSE, the image only will be displayed.

Operation
The operation of this function is somewhat more straight-forward than the function just described. Its first action is to open the specified TIFF file. If the file is located, the "Verbose" flag is checked to see if a detailed dump of TIFF file information was requested. If so, the function "TIFFPrintDirectory" from the file "print.c" is called to display the TIFF tag information. Next, the function "TIFFGetField" is repeatedly called to check for the presence of required tags and to retrieve the tag information. If any of the required tags are not found, this function will abort operation after displaying an error message. If some of the tags that have default values are missing, a warning message is output but the operation continues.

From the image parameters retrieved from the TIFF file, the required VGA mode for image display can be deduced. Once the video mode is decided and selected, various VGA default palettes are loaded just in case a "ColorMap" is not found in the TIFF file. The VGA palette is overwritten when a "ColorMap" structure is read from the TIFF file. Once all this preparatory work is accomplished, the actual raster data is read from the file a strip at a time and presented to the display portion of this function on a row-by-row basis. Just as before, how the row data is displayed depends upon the number of bits utilized per pixel. A separate code segment is used to process images with 1, 4, or 8 bits per pixel.

After the image is displayed, all memory allocated by this function is freed, and the TIFF file is closed. Control is then returned to the calling code. The image will remain on the VGA display until another image overwrites it or text mode is again selected.

Figure 6.9 *(continued)*

Listing 6.3   The TIFF Library Functions

The following is the contents of the file, "tiffintf.h":

```
/****************************************/
/*          TIFF Header File         */
/*    for TIFF file access functions */
/*       written in Turbo C 2.0      */
/*                by                 */
/*         Craig A. Lindley          */
/*                                   */
/*   Vers: 1.0  Last Update: 12/29/89   */
/****************************************/
#ifndef _TIFFIO_
#include "tiffio.h"
#endif
/* handy functions */
#define howmany(x, y)    (((x)+((y)-1))/(y))
#define roundup(x, y)    ((((x)+((y)-1))/(y))*(y))

/* Error bit definitions from TIFF code */
#define NoError             0
#define EBadParms          -1
#define EFileNotFound      -2
#define EReadFileDir       -3
#define ENotTIFFFile       -4
#define ECorrupt           -5
#define EWrtFileDir        -6
#define EWrtScanLine       -8
#define EGraphics         -10
#define ENoMemory         -11
#define EUnKnownCompression -13
#define EFileIOError       -14


/* TIFF Library Interface Routines */
TIFF *TIFFOpen(char *name, char *mode);
CompletionCode TIFFClose(TIFF *tif);
CompletionCode TIFFReadScanline(register TIFF *tif, char *buf,
                                        long row, unsigned sample);
CompletionCode TIFFReadStrip(register TIFF *tif, long strip);
void TIFFPrintDirectory(TIFF *tif, FILE *fd, unsigned showstrips,
                    unsigned showresponsecurve, unsigned showcolormap);
long TIFFScanlineSize(TIFF *tif);
CompletionCode TIFFGetField(TIFF *tif, unsigned tag, ...);
```

```
CompletionCode TIFFSetField(TIFF *tif, unsigned tag, ...);
CompletionCode TIFFSetDirectory(register TIFF *tif, long n);
CompletionCode TIFFWriteScanline(TIFF *tif, char *buf,
                                        unsigned row, unsigned sample);
CompletionCode WriteTIFFFile(char *FileName,
                    unsigned BitsPerSample, unsigned SamplesPerPixel,
                                unsigned ImageWidth, unsigned ImageLength);
CompletionCode DisplayTIFFFile(char *FileName, unsigned Verbose);
```

The following is the contents of the file, "tiff.c":

```
/***************************************/
/*        TIFF Function Library        */
/*        written in Turbo C 2.0       */
/*                by                   */
/*        Craig A. Lindley             */
/*                                     */
/*   Vers: 1.0  Last Update: 12/29/89  */
/***************************************/

#include <stdio.h>
#include <stdlib.h>
#include <process.h>
#include <mem.h>
#include <conio.h>
#include <string.h>
#include <graphics.h>
#include "misc.h"
#include "vga.h"
#include "pcx.h"
#include "tiffintf.h"


/*
Create a TIFF file from the image currently
being displayed on the VGA adapter.
*/

CompletionCode WriteTIFFFile(char *FileName,
                                unsigned BitsPerSample,
                                unsigned SamplesPerPixel,
                                unsigned ImageWidth, unsigned ImageLength)
```

(continued)

Listing 6.3 *(continued)*

```
{
   TIFF *tif;
   char *RowBuffer  = NULL;
   char *Message = "";
   register unsigned Col, Row;
   unsigned *RedColorMap   = NULL;
   unsigned *GreenColorMap = NULL;
   unsigned *BlueColorMap  = NULL;
   unsigned Index, ColorReg, BytesPerRow, Sample;
   unsigned RedColor, GreenColor, BlueColor;
   unsigned BitPlane, Mask;
   long      RowsPerStrip;
   struct palettetype Palette;

   /*
   Allocate colormaps arrays. Calloc clears them to zero.
   */
   if((RedColorMap = (unsigned *) calloc(MAX256PALETTECOLORS,sizeof(unsigned))) == NULL)
   {
      Message = "No memory for RedColorMap";
      goto NoMem;
   }

   if((GreenColorMap = (unsigned *) calloc(MAX256PALETTECOLORS,sizeof(unsigned))) == NULL)
   {
      Message = "No memory for GreenColorMap";
      goto NoMem;
   }

   if((BlueColorMap = (unsigned *) calloc(MAX256PALETTECOLORS,sizeof(unsigned))) == NULL)
   {
      Message = "No memory for BlueColorMap";
      goto NoMem;
   }

   tif = TIFFOpen(FileName,"w");
   if (!tif)
   {
      restorecrtmode();
      printf("Error opening output file: %s\n",FileName);
      return(EFileIOError);
   }
```

```
/* set constant tags */
TIFFSetField(tif,TIFFTAG_SUBFILETYPE,OL);
TIFFSetField(tif,TIFFTAG_IMAGEWIDTH,(long)ImageWidth);
TIFFSetField(tif,TIFFTAG_IMAGELENGTH,(long)ImageLength);
TIFFSetField(tif,TIFFTAG_BITSPERSAMPLE,BitsPerSample);
TIFFSetField(tif,TIFFTAG_COMPRESSION,COMPRESSION_PACKBITS);
TIFFSetField(tif,TIFFTAG_PHOTOMETRIC,PHOTOMETRIC_PALETTE);
TIFFSetField(tif,TIFFTAG_MAKE,"Craig's Video Digitizer");
TIFFSetField(tif,TIFFTAG_ARTIST,"Craig A. Lindley");
TIFFSetField(tif,TIFFTAG_HOSTCOMPUTER,"IBM PC with VGA graphics adapter");
TIFFSetField(tif,TIFFTAG_SAMPLESPERPIXEL,SamplesPerPixel);
TIFFSetField(tif,TIFFTAG_XRESOLUTION,72.0);
TIFFSetField(tif,TIFFTAG_YRESOLUTION,72.0);
if (SamplesPerPixel == 1)
   TIFFSetField(tif,TIFFTAG_PLANARCONFIG,PLANARCONFIG_CONTIG);
else
   TIFFSetField(tif,TIFFTAG_PLANARCONFIG,PLANARCONFIG_SEPARATE);

TIFFSetField(tif,TIFFTAG_RESOLUTIONUNIT,RESUNIT_INCH);

BytesPerRow = (unsigned) TIFFScanlineSize(tif);
/* allocate memory for single scan line from display */
if ((RowBuffer = malloc(BytesPerRow)) == NULL)
{
   Message = "No memory for RowBuffer";
   goto NoMem;
}
/* make strips approximately 8K in length */
RowsPerStrip = 8; /* (8L*1024L)/(long) BytesPerRow; */

TIFFSetField(tif,TIFFTAG_ROWSPERSTRIP,RowsPerStrip);

if ((BitsPerSample == 1) || (BitsPerSample == 4))
{
   /* read palette from VGA adapter */
   getpalette(&Palette);
   for (Index=0; Index < 16; Index++)
   {
         /*
         Even 16 color 320x200 images use VGA mode 13H
         without a palette.
         */
```

(continued)

Listing 6.3 *(continued)*

```
            if (ImageWidth == LRMAXCOLS)
               ColorReg = Index;
            else
               ColorReg = Palette.colors[Index];
            /* read color register components from VGA */
            GetAColorReg(ColorReg,&RedColor,&GreenColor,&BlueColor);
            /*
            Scale color components to range 0..255 as
            required by the TIFF spec. Normal range is
            from 0..63.
            */
            RedColorMap[Index]   = RedColor<<2;
            GreenColorMap[Index] = GreenColor<<2;
            BlueColorMap[Index]  = BlueColor<<2;
      }
   }
   else
   {
      for (Index=0; Index < MAX256PALETTECOLORS; Index++)
      {
            /* read color register components from VGA */
            GetAColorReg(Index,&RedColor,&GreenColor,&BlueColor);
            /*
            Scale color components to range 0..255 as
            required by the TIFF spec. Normal range is
            from 0..63.
            */
            RedColorMap[Index]   = RedColor<<2;
            GreenColorMap[Index] = GreenColor<<2;
            BlueColorMap[Index]  = BlueColor<<2;
      }
   }
   TIFFSetField(tif,TIFFTAG_COLORMAP,RedColorMap,GreenColorMap,BlueColorMap);

   if (ImageWidth == HRMAXCOLS)     /* a 640x200 or 640x480 image */
   {
      if (SamplesPerPixel == 1)
      {
            for (Row = 0; Row < ImageLength; Row++)
            {
               for (Col=0; Col < HRMAXCOLS; Col+=2)
               {
                  Sample = getpixel(Col,Row) << 4;
```

```
                    RowBuffer[Col>>1] = Sample + getpixel(Col+1,Row);
                }
                if (!TIFFWriteScanline(tif,RowBuffer,Row,0))
                    return(EWrtScanLine);
            }
    }
    else
    {

            /* Four samples per pixel */
            for (BitPlane = 0; BitPlane < SamplesPerPixel; BitPlane++)
            {
                Mask = 1 << BitPlane;
                for (Row = 0; Row < ImageLength; Row++)
                {
                    memset(RowBuffer,0,BytesPerRow);
                    for (Col=0; Col < HRMAXCOLS; Col++)
                            if (getpixel(Col,Row) & Mask)
                                RowBuffer[Col>>3] |= 1 << (7 - (Col % BITSPERBYTE));
                    if (!TIFFWriteScanline(tif,RowBuffer,Row,BitPlane))
                            return(EWrtScanLine);
                }
            }
    }
}
else
/*
320x200 pixel image. All 320x200 images are assumed to use
VGA mode 13H. For this reason, the GetPixel256() function
must be used to read the pixels from the image currently
displayed on the screen.
*/
{
    if (BitsPerSample == 4)
    {
            for (Row = 0; Row < ImageLength; Row++)
            {
                for (Col=0; Col < LRMAXCOLS; Col+=2)
                {
                    Sample = GetPixel256(Col,Row) << 4;
                    RowBuffer[Col>>1] = Sample + GetPixel256(Col+1,Row);
                }
                if (!TIFFWriteScanline(tif,RowBuffer,Row,0))
                    return(EWrtScanLine);
            }
    }
```

(continued)

Listing 6.3 *(continued)*

```
    else /* 320x200 8 bits/sample image */
    {
            for (Row = 0; Row < ImageLength; Row++)
            {
                for (Col=0; Col < LRMAXCOLS; Col++)
                    RowBuffer[Col] = GetPixel256(Col,Row);

                if (!TIFFWriteScanline(tif,RowBuffer,Row,0))
                    return(EWrtScanLine);
            }
    }
}
TIFFClose(tif);
free((char *) RowBuffer);
free((char *) RedColorMap);
free((char *) GreenColorMap);
free((char *) BlueColorMap);
return(NoError);

NoMem:
restorecrtmode();
printf("Error: %s\n",Message);
if (RowBuffer)
    free((char *) RowBuffer);
if (RedColorMap)
    free((char *) RedColorMap);
if (GreenColorMap)
    free((char *) GreenColorMap);
if (BlueColorMap)
    free((char *) BlueColorMap);
TIFFClose(tif);
return(ENoMemory);
}


/*
This function will display a TIFF file on the VGA
graphics adapter. It will complain about TIFF files
it doesn't understand. This code only supports a small
portion of possible TIFF images. Constraints mainly a
result of VGA limitations.
*/

CompletionCode DisplayTIFFFile(char *FileName, unsigned Verbose)
```

```
{
   TIFF *tif;
   unsigned long ImageWidth, ImageLength;
   unsigned PhotometricIntrp, Index;
   unsigned *RedColorMap, *GreenColorMap, *BlueColorMap;
   register short PixelNum;
   register unsigned Col, Row;
   unsigned MaxColors, LoadColorMap, RowByte, RowByteCnt;
   unsigned BitColor, BitPlane, LowResImage;
   unsigned long ScanlineBytes;
   BYTE *RowBuffer;
   register BYTE *RowBufferPtr;
   char *Message = "";
   BYTE *Map = NULL;
   struct palettetype Palette;

   unsigned BitsPerSample = 1;           /* install TIFF defaults */
   unsigned SamplesPerPixel = 1;
   unsigned PlanarConfig = PLANARCONFIG_CONTIG;

   /* Attemp to open the specified TIFF file */
   tif = TIFFOpen(FileName,"r");
   if (!tif)
   {
      restorecrtmode();
      printf("TIFF error: File %s not found or directory format error",FileName);
      return(EFileNotFound);
   }

   if (Verbose)
   {
      printf("\nTIFF file: %s\n\n",FileName);
      TIFFPrintDirectory(tif, stdout, TRUE, TRUE, TRUE);
      getch();
   }
   if ((RowBuffer = malloc((unsigned) TIFFScanlineSize(tif))) == NULL)
   {
      Message = "No memory for RowBuffer";
      goto bad;
   }

   /* check for the presence of the proper tag compliment */
   if (!TIFFGetField(tif,TIFFTAG_IMAGEWIDTH,&ImageWidth))
```

(continued)

Listing 6.3 *(continued)*

```
{
   Message = "ImageWidth tag missing";
   goto bad;
}
ImageWidth = MIN(ImageWidth,HRMAXCOLS);

if (!TIFFGetField(tif,TIFFTAG_IMAGELENGTH,&ImageLength))
{
   Message = "ImageLength tag missing";
   goto bad;
}
ImageLength = MIN(ImageLength,HRMAXROWS);

if (!TIFFGetField(tif,TIFFTAG_BITSPERSAMPLE,&BitsPerSample))
   printf("Warning BitsPerSample tag missing\n");

/* check for proper values */
if ((BitsPerSample != 1) && (BitsPerSample != 4) && (BitsPerSample != 8))
{
   Message = "BitsPerSample not 1,4 or 8";
   goto bad;
}

if (!TIFFGetField(tif,TIFFTAG_SAMPLESPERPIXEL,&SamplesPerPixel))
   printf("Warning SamplesPerPixel tag missing\n");
/* check for proper value */

if ((SamplesPerPixel != 1) && (SamplesPerPixel != 4))
{
   Message = "SamplesPerPixel not 1 or 4";
   goto bad;
}

if(!TIFFGetField(tif,TIFFTAG_PLANARCONFIG,&PlanarConfig))
   printf("Warning PlanarConfig tag missing\n");


if (!TIFFGetField(tif,TIFFTAG_PHOTOMETRIC,&PhotometricIntrp))
{
   Message = "PhotometricInterpretation tag missing";
   goto bad;
}
/* check for proper value */
```

```
if ((PhotometricIntrp != PHOTOMETRIC_MINISWHITE) &&
    (PhotometricIntrp != PHOTOMETRIC_MINISBLACK) &&
    (PhotometricIntrp != PHOTOMETRIC_PALETTE))
{
    Message = "Cannot handle this PhotometricInterpretation";
    goto bad;
}
/*
Figure out the max number of colors necessary for this
image. Create a mapping function, only required for
black and white images, to convert images which have
the color white as the minimum value to minimum black.
as required by the VGA adapter. The variable LoadColorMap
will be set true if this image contains a COLORMAP tag.
It will cause the palette to be loaded later.
*/
MaxColors = 1 << (BitsPerSample * SamplesPerPixel);
Map = (char *)malloc((MaxColors) * sizeof (BYTE));
LoadColorMap = FALSE;

switch(PhotometricIntrp)
{
    case PHOTOMETRIC_MINISBLACK:
            for (Index=0; Index < MaxColors ; Index++)
               Map[Index] = Index;
            break;
    case PHOTOMETRIC_MINISWHITE:
            for (Index=0; Index < MaxColors; Index++)
               Map[Index] = MaxColors - Index - 1;
            break;
    case PHOTOMETRIC_PALETTE:
            /*
            Check to see if file has COLORMAP tag. If so, load
            the three pointers to the colormap data.
            */
            if (!TIFFGetField(tif,TIFFTAG_COLORMAP,&RedColorMap,
                                                            &GreenColorMap,
                                            &BlueColorMap))
        {
                Message = "ColorMap tag missing";
                goto bad;
        }
```

(continued)

Listing 6.3 *(continued)*

```
            LoadColorMap = TRUE;
            break;
    default:
            Message = "Unsupported PhotometricInterpretation";
            goto bad;
}


InitGraphics();
/* Determine VGA mode to use for display of image */
if (ImageWidth <= LRMAXCOLS)         /* less than 320 pixels */
{
    ImageLength = MIN(ImageLength,LRMAXROWS); /* truncate to 200 */
    Set256ColorMode();                    /* VGA mode 13H */
    LoadGray64Palette();                  /* default 64 levels of gray */
}
else
{
    ImageWidth = MIN(ImageWidth,HRMAXCOLS); /* truncate to 640 pixels */
    if (ImageWidth <= LRMAXROWS)      /* 640x200 image ? */
            setgraphmode(VGALO);
    else if (ImageWidth <= MRMAXROWS)/* 640x350 image ? */
            setgraphmode(VGAMED);
    else                             /* 640x480 image */
            setgraphmode(VGAHI);

    LoadGray16Palette();                  /* 16 levels of gray palette */
}
if (LoadColorMap)
{
    /*
    Load the color registers with this palette after
    scaling the color data by 4. Scaling is necessary
    because data ranges from 0..255 and VGA accepts
    0..63.
    */
    if (!LowResImage)
            Palette.size = MaxColors;
    for (Index=0; Index < MaxColors; Index++)
    {
            if (!LowResImage)
                Palette.colors[Index] = Index;
            SetAColorReg(Index,RedColorMap[Index]  >>2,
                                        GreenColorMap[Index]>>2,
```

```
                                    BlueColorMap[Index] >>2);
      }
   if (!LowResImage)
         setallpalette(&Palette);
}
switch(BitsPerSample)
{
   case 1:
         if (SamplesPerPixel == 1)
         {
           ScanlineBytes =
             MIN(TIFFScanlineSize(tif),ImageWidth/(long)BITSPERBYTE);
           for (Row=0; Row < ImageLength; Row++)
           {
              if (!TIFFReadScanline(tif, RowBuffer, Row, 0))
                     break;
              RowBufferPtr = RowBuffer;
              for (RowByteCnt=0; RowByteCnt < ScanlineBytes; RowByteCnt++)
              {
                     RowByte = *RowBufferPtr++;
                     for (PixelNum=7; PixelNum >= 0; PixelNum--)
                     {
                        BitColor = (Map[((RowByte & (1 << PixelNum)) != 0)])? 15:0;
                        putpixel(RowByteCnt*8+(7-PixelNum),Row,BitColor);
                     }
              }
           }
         }
         else /* Samples per Pixel = 4 */
         {
           for (Row=0; Row < ImageLength; Row++)
           {
              if (!TIFFReadScanline(tif, RowBuffer, Row, 0))
                     break;
              for (Col = 0; Col < ImageWidth; Col++)
                     if (LoadColorMap && (ImageWidth == LRMAXCOLS))
                        PutPixel256(Col,Row,
                           (RowBuffer[Col>>3] & (1 << (7 - Col % BITSPERBYTE)))? 1:0);
                     else
                        putpixel(Col,Row,
                           (RowBuffer[Col>>3] & (1 << (7 - Col % BITSPERBYTE)))? 1:0);

           }
```

(continued)

Listing 6.3 *(continued)*

```
                for (BitPlane = 1; BitPlane < SamplesPerPixel; BitPlane++)
                  for (Row=0; Row < ImageLength; Row++)
                  {
                        if (!TIFFReadScanline(tif, RowBuffer, Row, BitPlane))
                          break;
                        for (Col = 0; Col < ImageWidth; Col++)
                          if (RowBuffer[Col>>3] & (1 << (7 - Col % BITSPERBYTE)))
                                if (LoadColorMap && (ImageWidth == LRMAXCOLS))
                                    PutPixel256(
                        Col,Row,GetPixel256(Col,Row) | (1 << BitPlane));
                                    else
                                        putpixel(
                        Col,Row, getpixel(Col,Row) | (1 << BitPlane));
                  }
          }
      break;
    case 4:
          ScanlineBytes = MIN(TIFFScanlineSize(tif),ImageWidth/2L);
      for (Row=0; Row < ImageLength; Row++)
      {
        if (!TIFFReadScanline(tif, RowBuffer, Row, 0))
          break;
        RowBufferPtr = RowBuffer;
            for (RowByteCnt=0; RowByteCnt < ScanlineBytes; RowByteCnt++)
        {
              RowByte = *RowBufferPtr++;
          if (LoadColorMap && (ImageWidth == LRMAXCOLS))
          {
            PutPixel256(RowByteCnt*2,Row,((RowByte>>4) & 0xFF));
            PutPixel256(RowByteCnt*2+1,Row,(RowByte & 0xFF));
          }
          else
          {
            putpixel(RowByteCnt*2,Row,((RowByte>>4) & 0xFF));
            putpixel(RowByteCnt*2+1,Row,(RowByte & 0xFF));
          }
        }
      }
          break;
    case 8:
          ScanlineBytes = MIN(TIFFScanlineSize(tif),ImageWidth);
      for (Row=0; Row < ImageLength; Row++)
```

```
        {
           if (!TIFFReadScanline(tif, RowBuffer, Row, 0))
              break;
           RowBufferPtr = RowBuffer;
                 for (RowByteCnt=0; RowByteCnt < ScanlineBytes; RowByteCnt++)
                    PutPixel256(RowByteCnt,Row,(unsigned) *RowBufferPtr++);
        }
        break;
     }
     if (Map)
        free((char *) Map);
     if (RowBuffer)
        free((char *) RowBuffer);
     TIFFClose(tif);
     return(TRUE);

bad:
     restorecrtmode();
     printf("Error: %s\n",Message);
     if (Map)
        free((char *) Map);
     if (RowBuffer)
        free((char *) RowBuffer);
     TIFFClose(tif);
     return(FALSE);
}
```

The View Example Program

The operation of the two functions "WriteTIFFFile" and "DisplayTIFFFile" described in
Figure 6.9 are exactly analogous to their PCX counterparts described early in this chapter. To
illustrate the use of the TIFF library functions and the PCX library functions in an
application program, this example program is provided. The purpose of this program is to
allow the display of properly formatted PCX or TIFF images on a VGA adapter. This
example program was very useful during the preparation of this book, as it allows images to
be displayed quickly for easy identification. The program also can be used in an "auto-
exec.bat" file to display an image for you every time you boot your computer. The program
code is shown in Listing 6.4; its operation should be discernible from the comments in the
listing.

Please pay proper attention to the project make file, "view.prj", and the code file.
These illustrate how any application program would interface to both the PCX and the TIFF
function libraries. Note also that Turbo C's "medium" memory model had to be used to

Listing 6.4 The View Program

The following is the contents of the file, "view.prj":

```
graphics.lib
vgagraph.obj -- NOTE: must use the medium memory model version of this
egavga.obj              file for the view program to work correctly !
pcx        (misc.h pcx.h)
vga        (misc.h vga.h pcx.h)
io         (tiff.h tiffio.h)
swab       (tiff.h tiffio.h)
dir        (tiff.h tiffio.h)
dumpmode   (tiff.h tiffio.h)
error      (tiff.h tiffio.h)
compress   (tiff.h tiffio.h)
ccitt      (tiff.h tiffio.h)
packbits   (tiff.h tiffio.h)
lzw        (tiff.h tiffio.h)
print      (tiff.h tiffio.h)
tiff       (tiff.h tiffio.h tiffintf.h)
view       (pcx.h tiffintf.h)
```

The following is the contents of the file, "view.c":

```
/**************************************/
/*  PCX/TIFF File View Utility Program  */
/*        written in Turbo C 2.0        */
/*                by                    */
/*         Craig A. Lindley             */
/*  Usage:                              */
/*    view [-v ?] filename[.pcx | .tif] */
/*    Vers: 2.0  Last Update: 12/11/89  */
/**************************************/
/*
NOTE:
This example program must be compiled using Turbo's medium
memory model because of its size.
*/
#include <stdio.h>
#include <process.h>
#include <conio.h>
#include <dos.h>
#include <graphics.h>
#include <string.h>
```

```
#include <io.h>
#include "misc.h"
#include "pcx.h"
#include "tiffintf.h"

#define MAXFILENAMELENGTH 30 /* max supported length of filename */

extern struct PCX_File PCXData;
/* current revision level */
unsigned Release = 2;
unsigned Revision = 0;

/*
This function provides help in the advent of operator error.
Program terminates after help is given
*/

void ShowHelp( void )
{
   printf("\nView usage: view [-v ?] filename[.pcx | .tif] <cr>\n");
   printf(" -v displays image file information\n");
   printf(" ? or -?  displays this help text\n");
   printf(" filename is name given to PCX or TIFF image file\n\n");
   exit(EBadParms);
}

void main(unsigned argc, char *argv[])
{
   unsigned Verbose = FALSE;
   unsigned FileNameCounter, ArgIndex, StrLength;
   char    *ImageFileName;
   char    FileName[MAXFILENAMELENGTH];
   char    PCXFileName[MAXFILENAMELENGTH];
   char    TIFFFileName[MAXFILENAMELENGTH];

   clrscr();
   printf("View - PCX or TIFF Image File Display Program\n");
   printf(" Version: %d.%d by Craig A. Lindley\n\n",Release,Revision);

   /* parse all command line arguments */

   FileNameCounter = 0;                     /* count of user specified filenames */
   for (ArgIndex=1; ArgIndex < argc; ArgIndex++)
```

(continued)

Listing 6.4 *(continued)*

```
{
    if (*argv[ArgIndex] != '-')      /* if not a cmd line switch */
    {                                /* must be a filename */
            if (*argv[ArgIndex] == '?')   /* help requested ? */
                ShowHelp();
            if (FileNameCounter > 1)      /* only one filename allowed */
        ShowHelp();                       /* if more then error exit */
            ImageFileName = argv[ArgIndex]; /* save image filename */
        FileNameCounter++;           /* inc count for error check */
    }
    else                             /* its a cmd line switch */
    {
        switch (*(argv[ArgIndex]+1))     /* parse the cmd line */
        {
            case 'v':
            case 'V':
              Verbose = TRUE;
              break;
            case '?':
                    ShowHelp();
              break;
                default:
                  printf("Error - invalid cmd line switch encountered\n");
                  ShowHelp();
        }
    }
}
if (FileNameCounter != 1)
{
    printf("Error: a single PCX or TIFF filename must be specified\n");
    ShowHelp();
}

printf("Press any key to terminate display\n\n\n");
delay(1000);
/*
Check for which type of file to display. This
sometimes means adding filename extensions if
one was not specified by the user.
*/
strupr(ImageFileName);                      /* Convert to upper case */
if (strstr(ImageFileName,".PCX"))           /* does it have a .PCX ext ? */
```

```
      DisplayPCXFile(ImageFileName,Verbose); /* display PCX file */
   else if (strstr(ImageFileName,".TIF"))     /* does it have a .TIF ext ? */
      DisplayTIFFFile(ImageFileName,Verbose);/* display TIFF file */
   else
   {
      strcpy(FileName,"");                         /* make storage empty */

      /* find filename length minus the extension */
      StrLength = strcspn(ImageFileName,".");

      if (StrLength == 0)                      /* no ext specified */
             strncat(FileName,ImageFileName,MAXFILENAMELENGTH); /* copy filename completely */
      else                                     /* an ext was specified */
             strncat(FileName,ImageFileName,StrLength); /* copy name only */
      /*
      Copy the processed file name to each of the
      filename storage areas and append the appropriate string.
      */
      strcpy(PCXFileName,FileName);
      strcat(PCXFileName,".PCX");
      strcpy(TIFFFileName,FileName);
      strcat(TIFFFileName,".TIF");
      /*
      Determine is files with these extensions really
      exist. If so display with appropriate
      function.
      */
      if (access(PCXFileName,0) == 0)            /* does PCX file exist ? */
             DisplayPCXFile(PCXFileName,Verbose);  /* yes then display */
      else if (access(TIFFFileName,0) == 0)     /* does TIFF file exist ? */
             DisplayTIFFFile(TIFFFileName,Verbose);/* yes then display */
      else
      {
             printf("Neither file %s nor %s found\n",
                       PCXFileName,TIFFFileName);
             exit(EFileNotFound);
      }
   }
   getchar();
   restorecrtmode();
   closegraph();
}
```

generate this example program because the code size of "view.exe" exceeds 128KB. It is interesting that only the file "vgagraph.asm" had to be modified to allow the "view.exe" example program to work with the medium memory model. The new, medium memory model version of "vgagraph.asm" is contained on the companion disk in directory "\chap6\view". The changes to this file consist of making the assembler language functions FAR and adjusting the parameter offsets, as discussed in Chapter 1. In all, over 20,000 lines of C code make up this example program.

Conclusions

This has been a rather long chapter containing a lot of important information and code. In reading it, you should have developed a good feel for the structure of image-file formats, especially the PCX and TIFF file formats. You can now appreciate how much work it is to fully support any image-file format. With the code presented in this chapter (approximately 20,000 lines of C), images of many varieties can be saved in standard formats that can be imported by other application programs; you have the ability to read image files produced by other application programs; and you also have the components of an image conversion program that can load in a PCX file, for example, and write out a TIFF equivalent.

The "view.exe" example program showed how all of the code could be combined into a coherent application program. This example program is also very handy as a stand-alone PCX and TIFF reader and file structure browser. This program will be used extensively in Part Two of this book to view the results of the image processing algorithms.

Now that we know how to save images acquired by our digitizer, let's figure out how to make hard copy from them. This topic will be taken up in the next chapter.

7

Production of Hardcopy Images

In this chapter you will learn about:

- Various techniques for producing hardcopy images
- How magazines and newspapers print images
- The techniques of thresholding, patterning, and halftoning
- How to use BIOS functions to access a printer
- How color and/or monochrome images can be printed

Introduction

Previous chapters have shown how a video image can be acquired, how to save that image in a graphical file format, and how to redisplay the saved image on a computer monitor. This chapter describes various techniques for producing a hardcopy (printed) version of a previously acquired image. Along the way, we will discuss some of the techniques used to produce pictures in books and magazines.

Photographic Hardcopy Techniques

By far, the highest-quality and lowest-cost method of producing hardcopy of computer images is photography. The desired image is displayed on a high-quality video monitor and photographed. All of the imagery included in Part Two of this book was produced in this manner. After a high-quality photograph is taken, standard darkroom techniques can be used to enhance the image as required. For example, the image can be enlarged or reduced in size to fit the requirements of its application.

Talk of photography as a method of hardcopy production in this age of the computers and laser printers probably borders on heresy. Unfortunately, not all people have access to expensive printers. Printer-type devices that produce high-resolution color images (of photographic quality) are just now possible and won't be available for general use for a few years. Until a desktop-size, photograph-quality color printer is available for under a few hundred dollars, a properly taken photograph of a color monitor will have to suffice.

The techniques for color monitor photography are relatively simple. They can be summarized as follows:

a. Shoot in a dark room with the camera positioned at least 10 feet away from the monitor.

b. Use a zoom lens. This will flatten out the curve of the monitor's screen. As a result, the photograph will appear flatter.

c. Turn down the brightness and contrast of the monitor to prevent glare in the photograph. Bright colors of high intensity will tend to bleed in the photo.

d. Set the shutter speed of the camera somewhere in the range 1/8 to 1/2 of a second. With a shutter speed of 1/4 second, start with the f/stop at f/8. You do not want to use a shutter speed faster than 1/15 of a second because that is approaching the speed at which the monitor is refreshed. Too fast a shutter speed will produce images in which the interlace pattern is evident. Be careful not to move the monitor and/or camera during exposure. Any movement with such a slow shutter speed will destroy the quality of the image being photographed.

For the best possible result, the photographic technique of bracketing should be employed. That is, several photographs of the monitor should be taken while adjusting the f/stop setting around the initial setting of f/8. This can use up a lot of film but will usually result in an optimum exposure for each photographed image. By following these guidelines, quality photographs of either continuous-tone or color images can be produced in hardcopy form.

Printer Hardcopy Techniques

Before delving into computer/printer-generated hardcopy images, it is helpful to understand the techniques used in books, magazines, and newspapers to produce images. These techniques can be lumped into the general category of *halftoning*. With halftoning, an image is produced with a series of dots printed on the paper. This can be seen if you inspect a newspaper closely with a magnifying glass. Each picture element of an image consists of a white square that encloses a black dot. The larger the black dot in the white square, the darker the picture element becomes. In other words, the area of the black dot is proportional to its darkness. To produce dark areas in an image, large regions of picture elements that are almost or totally black can be clustered. The middle range of gray values can be simulated by using picture elements in which the enclosed black dot takes up approximately 50 percent of the available space. Bright regions are produced by clusters of picture elements with little or no enclosed black dot. This is illustrated in highly magnified form in Figure 7.1.

Halftoning works because of the spatial (space) integration performed by the eye and brain. The eye integrates the fine detail in an image viewed from a distance and records only

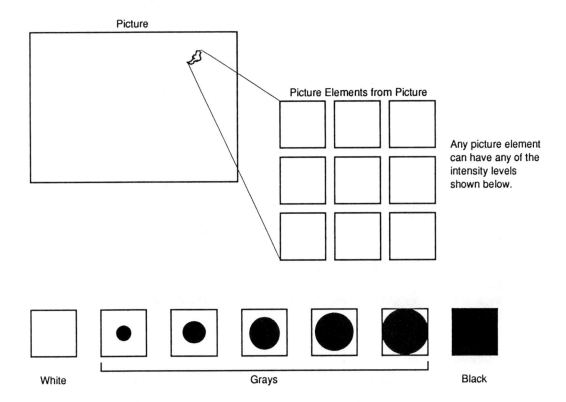

Picture

Picture Elements from Picture

Any picture element can have any of the intensity levels shown below.

White   Grays   Black

Seven different intensity levels are illustrated here. The larger the enclosed black dot, the darker the picture element. Spatial integration of the eye/brain mechanism allows this picture reproduction system to work.

Figure 7.1   Halftone Image Production

the overall intensity. The varying intensities of the black dots within the white picture elements produce a simulation of a continuous-tone image. What the eye sees is an image that ranges in color from black through gray to white. The total number of unique intensities available is determined by the number of different sizes of black dots available. Most newspapers produce halftone images with resolutions of 60 to 80 dots per inch (DPI). Books can be printed with up to 150 DPI resolution.

Unfortunately, personal computer printers do not have available an assortment of black dots of different sizes for halftoning. Without this capability, other methods must be utilized. Three of the most important methods are *thresholding*, *patterning*, and *dithering*. Each of these techniques has strengths and weaknesses, as we shall see in the discussion that follows.

Please note that we will discuss thresholding, patterning, and dithering techniques in the context of printed output. These techniques are equally applicable, however, to other types of output devices, including computer monitors.

Image 7.1   A Thresholded Image

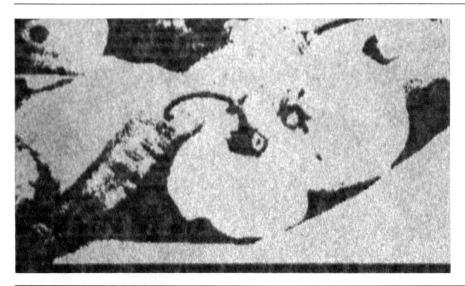

Thresholding

Thresholding is not a simulation of halftoning. Instead, it is a rather crude method of providing printed output of a continuous-tone image. It is included in this discussion only for completeness, as it is a method of generating hardcopy. The results of thresholding are generally so poor that an example program is not even included. Image Sequence 7.1 shows a portion of a thresholded image, to give you an idea of the quality of the printed output.

As you can see from this figure, all image detail is lost. The output is discernible only if you know what the image is supposed to look like. To produce a hardcopy printout of this type, the source image is scanned a pixel at a time. The intensity of each pixel is used to decide whether the corresponding picture element on the printer is engaged or not. All pixels above a certain threshold cause the printer's picture element (a pin in a dot matrix printer) to strike the paper, creating a black dot. All pixels below the threshold do not cause the printer to print. Judicious selection of the threshold level can result in a hardcopy printout that is pleasing to look at. Most of the time, however, the printout is unusable. Thresholding may have application in some form of artistic work, but for use as a generalized hardcopy technique it is unacceptable. In summary, thresholding converts a continuous-tone gray-scale or color source image to a bilevel black and white printout. The results of thresholding are usually substandard.

Patterning

Thresholding is unacceptable because the continuous-tone nature of the source image is lost completely on output. Patterning, which simulates halftoning, allows the printed output to retain some (if not all) of the gray-scale information even when printed on a bilevel device like a printer. It does this by trading resolution in the printed output for intensity values. Patterning is very useful if the output device has more resolution than that of the image being produced. If this is the case, no degradation in the hardcopy output will be experienced, and patterning will produce a very good reproduction of the source image. If the output device does not have sufficient resolution, the printed output must suffer a reduction in resolution as a cost of being printed. Why this is necessary will become clear as the discussion proceeds. In any case, the higher the resolution of the printing device the better. Higher resolution allows more flexibility in the selection of algorithms used for hardcopy output.

Patterning uses a group of picture elements on the output device (a printer in this case) to represent a single pixel of the source image. The number of picture elements within the group that are on (will be printed as a black dot) determines the relative brightness or darkness of the whole group. The picture elements within the group are used to simulate the black dot within a halftone picture element, the size of which determines the element's intensity. In this case, the number of picture elements that are on determines the intensity of the picture element group.

Picture element groups are usually in the form of a square matrix. An n by n group of picture elements can produce $n^2 + 1$ unique intensity levels. Refer to Figure 7.2 for a visual illustration of how this works. The four by four group used in the example program provided in this chapter produces 17 unique intensity levels on the printed output. This is more than sufficient for the 16-color images acquired by the digitizer. The patterning matrix shown in Figure 7.2 is attributed to Rylander and is referred to as the Rylander recursive patterning matrix.

To visualize how patterning operates, think of each pixel of the source image becoming one "big" picture element on the output device. In the case of a four by four picture element group, the output picture element is actually four by four picture elements in size. This mapping reduces the resolution of the output device by four in each direction. For example, if an output device had a resolution of 640×480, the effective resolution with patterning becomes just 160×120 with the added capability of producing 17 unique intensity levels. This is how resolution of an output device is traded for the production of intensity levels.

If a greater number of intensity levels are required on the printed output, a larger matrix of patterns must be used. The trade-off in printed resolution versus the number of intensity levels is limited by human visual acuity. In other words, patterning is no longer an acceptable solution when the picture element groups get so large that they are noticeable and distract from the printed image.

The picture element patterns that represent the various intensity levels must be carefully chosen. Improperly chosen patterns will result in distracting designs showing up in portions of images with constant intensity values. The patterns chosen usually represent a growth sequence that is recursively generated. For good results, it is imperative that each picture element considered on at a specific intensity level remain on for all greater intensity levels. Expressed mathematically, each on picture element at level J must be on for all levels $K > J$. If this criterion is not met, the properties of the growth pattern are not satisfied and the resulting printed output will be less than optimal.

Images rendered using patterning tend to have a relatively rough but constant texture.

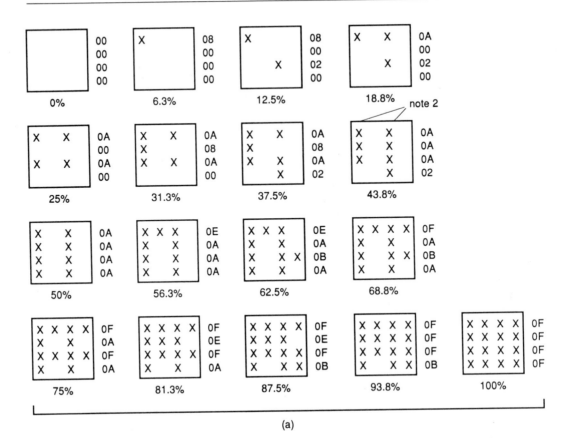

(a)

4 × 4 Patterning Matrices
Rylander Recursive Matrices

Matrix Notation

0	8	2	10
4	12	6	14
3	11	1	9
7	15	5	13

(b)

Notes
1. To display a pixel, all members of the matrix (b) are on that exceed the pixel's intensity value. All others are off.
2. X's indicate picture elements considered on. Blank spaces indicate elements that are off.
3. A 4 × 4 matrix produces $n^2 + 1$ or 17 unique intensity levels.

Figure 7.2   Rylander 4 x 4 Patterning

Patterning generates images that have less high-frequency content than dithered images and are therefore more accurately displayed on a computer monitor. If a printer is the output device, high-frequency content is not as important.

Dithering

Dithering is a technique that can be utilized for the production of gray-scale images when the resolution of the output device is the same as the image being produced or when a reduction in output device resolution cannot be tolerated. Dithered images tend to have a more even texture than patterned images. They also tend to have components of higher frequency, which, as noted previously, can plague inexpensive computer monitors. Ordered dithering techniques were developed by B. E. Bayer.

Dithering techniques are almost identical to the patterning techniques described previously. Dithering is applied to an image in a manner similar to patterning, using a matrix. Further, the content of the dithering matrix is almost identical to that of the patterning matrix. Both are shown here for comparison.

Rylander Patterning Matrix				*Bayer Ordered Dither Matrix*			
0	8	2	10	0	8	2	10
4	12	6	14	12	4	14	6
3	11	1	9	3	11	1	9
7	15	5	13	15	7	13	5

The difference between the techniques has to do with how the matrix is applied to the image. To understand how the dither matrix is applied, visualize it packed onto the source image in both the horizontal and vertical directions. Every pixel of the source image then corresponds to one element of the dither matrix. The output picture element associated with each of the source image pixels is turned on if the intensity of the pixel is greater than the dither matrix element to which it is associated. If the intensity is less than the dither matrix entry, the output picture element is turned off. The pseudocode for this procedure is as follows: Given a pixel P at point "XCoord" and "YCoord",

```
for a dither matrix of n by n
i = XCoord mod n
j = YCoord mod n
if Intensity of pixel P(XCoord, YCoord) > Dij then
   output picture element is on
else
   output picture element is off
```

where D is the dither matrix of dimension n by n and i and j are indices into the matrix.

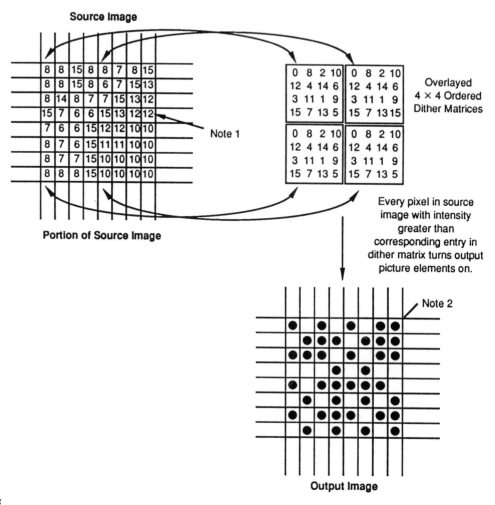

Figure 7.3 Ordered Dithering Applied to an Image

Notes
1. All source image pixels have been scaled to the range $0 \ldots n^2$. For $n = 4$ the range is $0 \ldots 16$.
2. All dots indicate output picture elements that are set to on.
3. Source and destination or output image have the same resolution.

Figure 7.3 illustrates the application of a four by four dither matrix to a small portion of an image.

Like patterning, larger dither matrices can be used if additional intensity levels are required. The total number of intensity levels available is $n^2 + 1$, just as before. Too large a dithering matrix tends to spread image information out to the point that the intensity given a picture element on the output device no longer is related to the information in the source image. A four by four dither matrix seems to be a good compromise between intensity levels and image resolution.

The Screen Print Program

Listing 7.1 reads a PCX file from disk, displays the image on the screen, and subsequently prints it on an attached, IBM-compatible dot matrix graphics printer. This program will work only with images of 320×200 resolution with 256 colors, 640×200 images with 16 colors, and 640×480 images with 16 colors. Not too surprisingly, these happen to be the image resolutions produced by the digitizer described in earlier chapters. This program is not limited to the printing of digitizer-produced images, however. Any PCX image in the supported resolutions can be printed. All printed images utilize a four by four pattern or dither matrix. This results in a total of 17 unique intensity levels that can be produced on the hardcopy output.

Before the discussion continues, please note that generalized graphics printer driver programs are very hard to write. Accurately portraying an image in hardcopy is difficult for a number of reasons, including:

a. Aspect ratio considerations, that is, trying to keep the proportions of a printed image the same as that shown on the video display. See Chapter 12 in Part Two for a detailed discussion of aspect ratios and aspect ratio correction techniques.

b. Color management on a color printer or color to black and white conversions for a bi-level, black and white printer. This is where thresholding, patterning, and dithering come in.

c. Image resolution and multiple-color management. If hardcopy is to be produced from the video display, a print driver might need to support all 19 possible video modes defined by IBM for the PC/PS2 line of computers.

d. The differences from one manufacturer's printer to the next, specifically, the available resolutions and the various printer control languages and codes.

The example program does not claim to be a generalized graphics printer driver. Providing a full-fledged program would unnecessarily complicate the information being presented. The example program, like the "graphics.com" program provided with MSDOS for screen printing displayed graphical images, can support only a small number of the possible video display modes. This is because it is very difficult to support all video display modes. Instead of a generalized approach that is workable with a wide variety of printers, this program is designed instead to work only with the variety of printer most people have access to—the ubiquitous nine-pin dot matrix, black and white graphics printer. The techniques presented, of course, can be applied to any printer, including color printers and laser printers. Laser printers that emulate an IBM graphics printer can use the provided code directly.

Other than the lack of generality, the major compromise made during the development of this example program was the lack of aspect ratio correction. The printed images produced with this example program in most cases will have an aspect ratio "close" to that of the displayed image; 320×200 images printed using patterning will have a greatly distorted aspect ratio. Images of this resolution should be printed using dithering instead. The techniques presented in Chapter 12 for aspect ratio correction on a video monitor can also be applied to printed output. The addition of code for aspect ratio correction into the example program is left to the interested reader.

The example program was used to create all of the hardcopy images (see Image Sequence 7.2) shown in this chapter. This program is made up of the files "printer.h",

Image 1

Image 2

Screen images

(a)

(d)

Patterned hardcopy images

(b)

(e)

Dithered hardcopy images

(c)

(f)

"print.c", and "print.prj" on the companion disk and shown in Listing 7.1. These files form a stand-alone application program in their present form. An application program wishing to utilize the graphics screen print portion of the "print.c" program will need to modify the code slightly. Namely, the "main()" function will need to be removed and new parameters that were passed in the example program as global variables will need to be passed to the "PrtScreen" function. With these changes made, the application program would also need to include the file "printer.h" in its code and would subsequently need to be linked with "print.obj".

Listing 7.1 The Print Screen Example Program

The file "print.prj" contents:

```
graphics.lib
vgagraph.obj
egavga.obj
vga     (misc.h vga.h)
pcx     (misc.h pcx.h)
print   (misc.h pcx.h vga.h printer.h)
```

The header file "printer.h" contents:

```
/***************************************/
/*      Graphics Print Include File    */
/*      written by Craig A. Lindley     */
/*                                     */
/*   Vers: 1.0  Last Update: 11/29/89   */
/***************************************/
#ifndef __BYTE
#define __BYTE
typedef unsigned char BYTE;
#endif

#define POSPRINT        TRUE      /* pixel over threshold prints black */
#define NEGPRINT        FALSE     /* pixel over threshold prints white */

/* printer status equates */
#define PRTTIMEOUT      0x01
#define PRTBUSYBIT      0x80      /* msb of printer status is busy bit */
#define PRINTERINT      0x17      /* printer BIOS interrupt 17H number */
#define PRTCHARCODE     0         /* int 17H print character func. code */
#define INITPRTCODE     1         /* int 17H initialize printer func. code */
#define GETPRTSTATUSCODE 2        /* int 17H get printer status func. code */
#define LPT1            0         /* printer select codes for BIOS */
```

(continued)

Listing 7.1 *(continued)*

```
#define LPT2               1
#define LPT3               2
#define PIXELSPERPASS      8        /* 8 pixel printed per print head pass */

typedef enum {LowResMode, MedResMode, HighResMode} PrinterModes;
typedef enum {BayerMatrix, RylanderMatrix} MatrixType;

/* structure for holding a half tone dot pattern */
struct DotPatterns
{
   BYTE Row1;
   BYTE Row2;
   BYTE Row3;
   BYTE Row4;
};
/* Function Declarations */
CompletionCode PrtScreen (unsigned NegPos);
```

The program file "print.c" contents:

```
/******************************************************/
/*                     print.c                      */
/*                                                  */
/*          Display and Print .PCX files            */
/*       Prints images displayed on VGA adapter     */
/*   on an IBM ProPrinter using halftone techniques */
/*             written in Turbo C 2.0               */
/*                                                  */
/* Usage: print [-v -mB/R -b(+/- 0-9) -n] filename  */
/*    -v displays info about the .PCX file          */
/*    -m selects the dither matrix to use:          */
/*       B = Bayer ordered dither                   */
/*       R = Rylander recursive halftoning          */
/*    -b alters brightness                          */
/*    -n prints negative image                      */
/*                                                  */
/*         written by Craig A. Lindley              */
/*       Vers: 1.0  Last Update: 11/29/89           */
/******************************************************/

#include <stdio.h>
#include <conio.h>
#include <dos.h>
```

```c
#include <process.h>
#include <stdlib.h>
#include <string.h>
#include <graphics.h>
#include "misc.h"
#include "pcx.h"
#include "vga.h"
#include "printer.h"

#define MAXVGAINTVAL 6300.0      /* Max VGA intensity x 100 */
#define MAXPRTINTENSITIES 17     /* 17 possible densities in 4x4 matrix */
#define MAXDENSITYINDEX (MAXPRTINTENSITIES-1)

/* Version information */
static short ver = 1;
static short rel = 0;

/* print function variables */
static unsigned Verbose, PrintMode;
static int       Brightness;
static unsigned MaxScreenRow, MaxScreenCol, Is256Colors;
static unsigned DensityTbl[MAX256PALETTECOLORS];
static unsigned N1,N2;
static union    REGS regs;
static enum     MatrixType Matrix;
/*
The following arrays define the half tone patterns used
for the printout. 4x4 dither matrices are used in
both cases.
*/

/* Bayer ordered dither matrix */
BYTE BayerMat[4][4] =
{ 0,  8,  2, 10,
 12,  4, 14,  6,
  3, 11,  1,  9,
 15,  7, 13,  5};


/* Rylander recursive halftoning matrix */
struct   DotPatterns RylanderMat[MAXPRTINTENSITIES] =
        {0x0F,0x0F,0x0F,0x0F,    /* 100.0% - all black */
         0x0F,0x0F,0x0F,0x0B,    /*  93.8% */
```

(continued)

Listing 7.1 *(continued)*

```
         0x0F,0x0E,0x0F,0x0B,    /*  87.5% */
              0x0F,0x0E,0x0F,0x0A,    /*  81.3% */
         0x0F,0x0A,0x0F,0x0A,    /*  75.0% */
         0x0F,0x0A,0x0B,0x0A,    /*  68.8% */
         0x0E,0x0A,0x0B,0x0A,    /*  62.5% */
         0x0E,0x0A,0x0A,0x0A,    /*  56.3% */
         0x0A,0x0A,0x0A,0x0A,    /*  50.0% */
         0x0A,0x0A,0x0A,0x02,    /*  43.8% */
         0x0A,0x08,0x0A,0x02,    /*  37.5% */
         0x0A,0x08,0x0A,0x00,    /*  31.3% */
         0x0A,0x00,0x0A,0x00,    /*  25.0% */
         0x0A,0x00,0x02,0x00,    /*  18.8% */
         0x08,0x00,0x02,0x00,    /*  12.5% */
         0x08,0x00,0x00,0x00,    /*   6.3% */
         0x00,0x00,0x00,0x00};   /*   0.0% - all white */

/* IBM ProPrinter Specific Printer Control Code Strings */
BYTE *OneDirection    = "\x1BU\x31";       /* ESC U 1 */
BYTE *TwoDirection    = "\x1BU\x30";       /* ESC U 1 */
BYTE *LowRes          = "\x1BK";           /* ESC K */
BYTE *MedRes          = "\x1BY";           /* ESC Y */
BYTE *HighRes         = "\x1BZ";           /* ESC Z */
BYTE *TextLineFeed    = "\x1B\x31";        /* ESC 1 - normal 7/72 text line feed */
BYTE *GraphicLineFeed= "\x1B\x33\x18"; /* ESC 3 24 -  24/216ths line feed */
BYTE *CrLf            = "\r\n";            /* graphics carriage ret line feed */
BYTE *DisAutoLf       = "\x1B\x35\x30"; /* ESC 5 0 disable auto line feed */


/* Printer Interface Functions */


/* This function initializes the line printer for operation */
void PrtInit (unsigned PrtNum)
{
   regs.h.ah = INITPRTCODE;
   regs.x.dx = PrtNum;
   int86(PRINTERINT, &regs, &regs);
}


/* This function reads the status of the line printer */
BYTE PrtStatus (unsigned PrtNum)
{
   regs.h.ah = GETPRTSTATUSCODE;
   regs.x.dx = PrtNum;
```

```
    int86(PRINTERINT, &regs, &regs);
    return (regs.h.ah);
}


/* this function prints a character on the specified printer */
BYTE PrtChar(unsigned PrtNum, BYTE Character)
{

    while(!(PrtStatus(PrtNum) & PRTBUSYBIT)); /* wait until not busy */
    regs.h.ah = PRTCHARCODE;                 /* prt a character code */
    regs.h.al = Character;
    regs.x.dx = PrtNum;                      /* select the printer */
    int86(PRINTERINT, &regs, &regs);
    return(regs.h.ah);                       /* return operation status */
}


/* this function prints a null terminated string of characters
   to the named printer */

BYTE PrtString(unsigned PrtNum, BYTE *String)
{
    BYTE PrtError;

    PrtError = FALSE;
    while ((*String != NULL) && (!PrtError)) /* do until the null or error */
        PrtError = ((PrtChar(PrtNum,*String++) & PRTTIMEOUT) == 1);
    return(PrtError);
}


/*
This function builds the DensityTbl which contain the index into the
DotDensities array that is to be used to represent the color of a given pixel
(in gray scale) when printed. The print dot density is calculated
from the value of a color register.  The intensity value for a
given color is computed from the formula:

    Intensity = Red Comp*30% + Green Comp*59% + BlueComp*11%

which corresponds to the sensitivity of the human eye to the various
color components. This formula is taken from the IBM VGA technical reference
manual.
```

(continued)

Listing 7.1 *(continued)*

With VGA, the value of the color registers are settable. This means the
color register RGB components must be read from the hardware before the
intensity calculation can be performed. Each color component has the
range 0..63. With the maximum intensity VGA color (white) the intensity
value turns out to be 63. This value will be used to scale all intensity
values into the range 0..16 as required by the DensityTbl array.
*/

```
void InitDensityTbl( void )
{
    unsigned ColorEntry, ColorNum;
    unsigned Intensity;
    struct palettetype palette;

    /* this procedure builds the DensityTbl based upon the intensity of
        the colors used in the palette to display the PCX image. The intensity
        are calculated as described above. */

    getpalette(&palette);               /* get the current palette */

    if (!Is256Colors)                   /* 16 color modes only */
    {
        /* for each entry in the palette */
        for (ColorEntry=0; ColorEntry < palette.size; ColorEntry++)
        {
            ColorNum = palette.colors[ColorEntry]; /* get a palette entry */
            /*
            because the color register values can change for VGA, the
            color components of each palette entry must be read before the
            Intensity can be calculated
            */
            regs.h.ah = 0x10;           /* get the color components of a */
            regs.h.al = 0x15;           /* color register. */
            regs.x.bx = ColorNum;
            int86(VIDEO,&regs,&regs);

            /*
                If the palette is a gray scale already, its intensity is
            just a single component. In this case Red. The intensity
                value must be scaled by 100 because it will be divided
                later when scaled.
            */
            if ((regs.h.dh == regs.h.ch) && (regs.h.ch == regs.h.cl))
                    Intensity = regs.h.dh*100;
            else
```

```
      {
         /* calculate the intensity from the color values */
         Intensity = ((unsigned) regs.h.dh*30);  /* calculate red   contribution */
         Intensity += ((unsigned) regs.h.ch*59); /* calculate green contribution */
         Intensity += ((unsigned) regs.h.cl*11); /* calculate blue  contribution */
      }
      /* scale and store intensity result */
         DensityTbl[ColorEntry] = (unsigned) (((((double) Intensity *
                                    (double) MAXDENSITYINDEX)
                                    / MAXVGAINTVAL)+0.5));
   }
}
else                         /* 256 color mode */
{
   /* for each color register */
   for (ColorNum=0; ColorNum < MAX256PALETTECOLORS; ColorNum++)
   {
      /* no palette is used in 256 color mode */
      regs.h.ah = 0x10;               /* get the color components of a */
      regs.h.al = 0x15;               /* color register. */
      regs.x.bx = ColorNum;
      int86(VIDEO,&regs,&regs);

      /*
            If the palette is a gray scale already, its intensity is
            just a single component. In this case Red. The intensity
            value must be scaled by 100 because it will be divided
            later when scaled.
      */

      if ((regs.h.dh == regs.h.ch) && (regs.h.ch == regs.h.cl))
            Intensity = regs.h.dh*100;
       else
      {
         /* calculate the intensity from the color values */
         Intensity = ((unsigned) regs.h.dh*30);  /* calculate red   contribution */
         Intensity += ((unsigned) regs.h.ch*59); /* calculate green contribution */
         Intensity += ((unsigned) regs.h.cl*11); /* calculate blue  contribution */
      }
      /* scale and store intensity result */
         DensityTbl[ColorNum] = (unsigned) (((((double) Intensity *
                                    (double) MAXDENSITYINDEX)
                                    / MAXVGAINTVAL)+0.5));
   }
 }
}
```

(continued)

Listing 7.1 *(continued)*

```
/*
This function returns a pixel from the screen. It works
differently for the 16 and the 256 color modes.
*/
unsigned GetAPixel(unsigned Col, unsigned Row)
{

   if (Is256Colors)
     return(GetPixel256(Col,Row));
   else /* is 16 color mode */
     return(getpixel(Col,Row));
}



void DitherPrintCol (unsigned PrintMode, PrinterModes PrtMode, unsigned Col)
{
   register unsigned CurrentRow, MatrixRow;
   register BYTE      Intensity, PrtByte;

   switch (PrtMode)                    /* send printer the graphic mode */
   {                                   /* control code sequence */
     case HighResMode: {

                                       PrtString(LPT1,HighRes);
                                       break;

                         }
     case MedResMode:  {

                                       PrtString(LPT1,MedRes);
                                       break;

                         }
     case LowResMode:
                default:  {

                                       PrtString(LPT1,LowRes);
                                       break;

                         }
   }

   /* tell printer how many bytes to follow */

   PrtChar(LPT1,N1);
   PrtChar(LPT1,N2);

   for (CurrentRow=0; CurrentRow < MaxScreenRow; CurrentRow++)
```

```c
{
    PrtByte = 0;
    MatrixRow = CurrentRow % 4;
    Intensity  = DensityTbl[GetAPixel(Col, CurrentRow)]+Brightness;
    if (Intensity > BayerMat[MatrixRow][3])
            PrtByte |= 128;

    Intensity  = DensityTbl[GetAPixel(Col-1, CurrentRow)]+Brightness;
    if (Intensity > BayerMat[MatrixRow][2])
            PrtByte |= 64;

    Intensity  = DensityTbl[GetAPixel(Col-2, CurrentRow)]+Brightness;
    if (Intensity > BayerMat[MatrixRow][1])
            PrtByte |= 32;

    Intensity  = DensityTbl[GetAPixel(Col-3, CurrentRow)]+Brightness;
    if (Intensity > BayerMat[MatrixRow][0])
            PrtByte |= 16;

    Intensity  = DensityTbl[GetAPixel(Col-4, CurrentRow)]+Brightness;
    if (Intensity > BayerMat[MatrixRow][3])
            PrtByte |= 8;

    Intensity  = DensityTbl[GetAPixel(Col-5, CurrentRow)]+Brightness;
    if (Intensity > BayerMat[MatrixRow][2])
            PrtByte |= 4;

    Intensity  = DensityTbl[GetAPixel(Col-6, CurrentRow)]+Brightness;
    if (Intensity > BayerMat[MatrixRow][1])
            PrtByte |= 2;

    Intensity  = DensityTbl[GetAPixel(Col-7, CurrentRow)]+Brightness;
    if (Intensity > BayerMat[MatrixRow][0])
            PrtByte |= 1;

    /*
    The off and on pins are reversed at this point. For example,
    PrtByte = 0 should print as black all pins on but will instead
    print as white (all pins off). To correct for this inversion,
    invert the sense of the PrintMode.
    */
    if (PrintMode == POSPRINT)
            PrtByte ^= 0xFF;
```

(continued)

Listing 7.1   *(continued)*

```
    PrtChar(LPT1,PrtByte);              /* send two identical bytes */
    PrtChar(LPT1,PrtByte);              /* to the printer. */

    if (MaxScreenCol == 640)           /* if in 640 pixel mode */
    {
            PrtChar(LPT1,PrtByte);         /* send two more identical bytes */
            PrtChar(LPT1,PrtByte);         /* to the printer. */
    }
  }
  PrtString(LPT1,CrLf);                /* output LfCr to printer */
}


void PatternPrintCol (unsigned PrintMode, PrinterModes PrtMode, unsigned Col)
{
    register unsigned CurrentRow;
    register int Density;
    BYTE     Row1Data, Row2Data, Row3Data, Row4Data;

    switch (PrtMode)                     /* send printer the graphic mode */
    {                                    /* control code sequence */
      case HighResMode: {
                                         PrtString(LPT1,HighRes);
                                         break;
                             }
      case MedResMode:  {
                                         PrtString(LPT1,MedRes);
                                         break;
                             }
      case LowResMode:
                default:  {
                                         PrtString(LPT1,LowRes);
                                         break;
                             }
    }

    /* tell printer how many bytes to follow */
    PrtChar(LPT1,N1);
    PrtChar(LPT1,N2);

    for (CurrentRow=0; CurrentRow < MaxScreenRow; CurrentRow++)
    {
        /* calc the average density of a group of 4 horiz. pixels */
```

```
Density  = DensityTbl[GetAPixel(Col  , CurrentRow)];
Density += DensityTbl[GetAPixel(Col-1, CurrentRow)];
Density += DensityTbl[GetAPixel(Col-2, CurrentRow)];
Density += DensityTbl[GetAPixel(Col-3, CurrentRow)];
Density /= 4;
Density += Brightness;              /* shift brightness level */
Density = (Density < 0 ) ? 0:Density;
Density = (Density > MAXDENSITYINDEX) ? MAXDENSITYINDEX:Density;

/* get dot pattern representing this average density */
/* shift by 4 because these dots will become the MS pin date */
Row1Data = RylanderMat[Density].Row1 << 4;
Row2Data = RylanderMat[Density].Row2 << 4;
Row3Data = RylanderMat[Density].Row3 << 4;
Row4Data = RylanderMat[Density].Row4 << 4;

/* calc the average density of a group of 4 horiz. pixels */
Density  = DensityTbl[GetAPixel(Col-4, CurrentRow)];
Density += DensityTbl[GetAPixel(Col-5, CurrentRow)];
Density += DensityTbl[GetAPixel(Col-6, CurrentRow)];
Density += DensityTbl[GetAPixel(Col-7, CurrentRow)];
Density /= 4;
Density += Brightness;              /* shift brightness level */
Density = (Density < 0 ) ? 0:Density;
Density = (Density > MAXDENSITYINDEX) ? MAXDENSITYINDEX:Density;

/* get dot pattern representing this average density */
/* merge with MS pin data */
Row1Data |= RylanderMat[Density].Row1;
Row2Data |= RylanderMat[Density].Row2;
Row3Data |= RylanderMat[Density].Row3;
Row4Data |= RylanderMat[Density].Row4;

/* if a reverse image is requested compliment dot data */
if (PrintMode != POSPRINT)
{
   Row1Data ^= 0xFF;
   Row2Data ^= 0xFF;
   Row3Data ^= 0xFF;
   Row4Data ^= 0xFF;
}
PrtChar(LPT1,Row1Data);          /* send 4 bytes of printer data */
PrtChar(LPT1,Row2Data);          /* to the printer. This 32 bits of */
PrtChar(LPT1,Row3Data);          /* data represent 8 bits of pixel */
```

(continued)

Listing 7.1 *(continued)*

```
      PrtChar(LPT1,Row4Data);              /* data */
   }
   PrtString(LPT1,CrLf);                   /* output LfCr to printer */
}



/*
This is the main print screen function. It will print in gray scale any
picture displayed on a VGA graphic adapter. The parameter Rev
controls the interpretation on the data on the screen.
*/

CompletionCode PrtScreen (unsigned PrintMode)
{
   int          ScreenCol;
   PrinterModes PrtMode;
   unsigned     CurrentDisplayMode;

   CurrentDisplayMode = GetVideoMode(); /* get the current mode */
   switch(CurrentDisplayMode)
   {
     case LRVIDEOMODE:
        PrtMode = MedResMode;
        MaxScreenCol = 320;
        MaxScreenRow = 200;
        Is256Colors = TRUE;
        break;
     case MRVIDEOMODE:
        PrtMode = MedResMode;
        MaxScreenCol = 640;
        MaxScreenRow = 200;
        Is256Colors = FALSE;
        break;
     case HRVIDEOMODE:
        PrtMode = HighResMode;
        MaxScreenCol = 640;
        MaxScreenRow = 480;
        Is256Colors = FALSE;
        break;
     default:
        return(FALSE);  /* unsupported video mode */
   }
```

```
/*
Calculate densities to be used to display image
*/
InitDensityTbl();


/*
Because we'll be dumping the display in a vertical fashion starting from
the right most column, we must calculate the byte counts that will be
sent to the printer from the MaxScreenRow value. The number of screen
rows will be either 200 or 480. A 200 row screen will be dumped to the
printer while it is in the 960 dot mode. This will mean that each pixel
from the display will be printed two dots wide. A 480 row screen will be
dumped to the printer while it is in the 1920 dot mode. Each pixel
will be four dots wide.
*/

if ((MaxScreenCol == 320) && (Matrix == BayerMatrix))
{
   N2 = (MaxScreenRow*2) >> 8;          /* calculate byte counts */
   N1 = (MaxScreenRow*2) & 0xFF;        /* to be sent to printer */
}
else
{
   N2 = (MaxScreenRow*4) >> 8;          /* calculate byte counts */
   N1 = (MaxScreenRow*4) & 0xFF;        /* to be sent to printer */
}

PrtInit(LPT1);                          /* initialize the printer */
PrtString(LPT1,OneDirection);           /* set printer in one dir mode */
PrtString(LPT1,DisAutoLf);              /* disable auto line feed */
PrtString(LPT1,GraphicLineFeed);        /* set 24/216 line feed as required */
                                        /* for 8 pin bit mapped printing */

/* move backward across displayed image */
for (ScreenCol=MaxScreenCol-1; ScreenCol >= 0; ScreenCol -= PIXELSPERPASS)
{
   if (kbhit())                         /* check for abort */
   {                                    /* if key hit */
     getch();                           /* consume it */
     break;                             /* and quit */
   }
   if (Matrix == BayerMatrix)
         DitherPrintCol(PrintMode, PrtMode, ScreenCol);
```

(continued)

Listing 7.1 *(continued)*

```
    else

            PatternPrintCol(PrintMode, PrtMode, ScreenCol);

    }
    PrtString(LPT1,TextLineFeed);        /* set text line feed */
    PrtChar(LPT1,'\f');                  /* do form feed when finished */
    PrtString(LPT1,TwoDirection);        /* set printer to two dir mode */
    return(NoError);
}


/*
This function provides help in the advent of operator error. Program
terminates after help is given
*/

void ShowHelp( void )
{
    printf("\nThis program displays and prints a .PCX file. Image\n");
    printf("must be 320x200 in 256 colors, 640x200 in 16 colors or\n");
    printf("640x480 in 16 colors.\n\n");
    printf("Program is invoked as follows:\n\n");
    printf("Usage: print [-v -mB/R -b(+/- 0-9) -n] filename <cr>\n");
    printf("    -v displays info about the .PCX file\n");
    printf("    -m selects the dither matrix to use:\n");
    printf("        B = Bayer ordered dither\n");
    printf("        R = Rylander recursive halftoning\n");
    printf("    -b alters brightness\n");
    printf("    -n prints negative image\n");
    printf("    filename is the name of a .PCX image file\n\n");
    exit(1);
}




void main(argc,argv)

short argc;
char *argv[];

{
    unsigned FileNameCounter, ArgIndex;
    char    *InFileName;
```

```
InitGraphics();
printf("Print Program -- Displays and Prints a .PCX Image\n");
printf("  Ver: %d.%d by Craig A. Lindley\n\n\n",ver,rel);
delay(1000);

/* install defaults */
Verbose = FALSE;                    /* not verbose */
Brightness = 0;                     /* use calculated brightness */
PrintMode = POSPRINT;               /* print whites as white */
Matrix = BayerMatrix;               /* use Bayer matrix */

FileNameCounter = 0;                /* count of user specified filenames */
for (ArgIndex=1; ArgIndex < argc; ArgIndex++)
{
   if (*argv[ArgIndex] != '-')      /* if not a cmd line switch */
   {                                /* must be a filename */
      if (FileNameCounter > 1)      /* only one filename allowed */
         ShowHelp();                /* if more then error exit */
      InFileName = argv[ArgIndex];  /* save PCX filename */
      FileNameCounter++;            /* inc count for error check */
   }
   else                            /* its a cmd line switch */
   {
      switch (*(argv[ArgIndex]+1))    /* parse the cmd line */
      {
         case 'v':
         case 'V':
           Verbose = TRUE;
           break;
         case 'm':
         case 'M':
           if ((*(argv[ArgIndex]+2) == 'r') || (*(argv[ArgIndex]+2) == 'R'))
              Matrix = RylanderMatrix; /* use Rylander matrix */
           else
              Matrix = BayerMatrix;    /* use Bayer matrix */
           break;
         case 'b':
         case 'B':
           sscanf(argv[ArgIndex]+2,"%d",&Brightness);
           if (abs(Brightness) > 9)
           {
              printf("Error - invalid brightness specified\n");
              ShowHelp();
           }
```

(continued)

Listing 7.1 *(continued)*

```
              break;
          case 'n':
          case 'N':
              PrintMode = NEGPRINT;
              break;
          default:
            printf("Error - invalid cmd line switch encountered\n");
            ShowHelp();
      }
    }
  }
  if (FileNameCounter != 1)
  {
      printf("Error - a PCX filename is required\n");
      ShowHelp();
  }

  /* Display the specified PCX file */
  DisplayPCXFile(InFileName,Verbose);

  /* Print the image displayed on the screen */
  if (PrtScreen(PrintMode) != NoError)
  {
      restorecrtmode();
      closegraph();
      printf("Unsupported video mode being utilized\n\n");
      exit(FALSE);
  }
  restorecrtmode();
  closegraph();
}
```

Screen Print Program Operation

The code in this program can be broken down into four distinct sections. The printer interface code, the intensity calculation code, the screen print code, and finally the user interface code. Each section will be discussed separately. Please refer to Listing 7.1 during these discussions.

    The printer interface code provides a software interface between the screen print code in the example program and the PC's BIOS (Basic Input/Output System). The C functions

"PrtInit", "PrtStatus", "PtrChar", and "PrtString" form this interface. Each of these functions directly or indirectly utilizes BIOS printer support for its operation. The printer BIOS functions are accessed using software interrupt 17 hex. To access a printer BIOS function, a command code is placed in the processor's "ah" register to identify the printer function required; the printer number (0 through 3 is acceptable) is placed in the "dx" register; other processor registers are loaded as required; and finally an interrupt 17 hex is executed to perform the function. The short code segment that follows illustrates the proper sequence of events.

```
BYTE PrtChar(unsigned PrtNum, BYTE Character)
{

    while(!(PrtStatus(PrtNum) & PRTBUSYBIT)); /* wait until not busy */
    regs.h.ah = PRTCHARCODE;            /* print a character code */
    regs.h.al = Character;              /* place character to print in al */
    regs.x.dx = PrtNum;                 /* select the printer */
    int86(PRINTERINT, &regs, &regs);    /* print the character */
    return(regs.h.ah);                  /* return operation status */
}
```

In this code, the command to print a character on the printer is placed in the "ah" register; the character to print is placed in the "al" register; the printer number, passed as a parameter to this code, is placed in the "dx" register; and interrupt 17 hex is executed via the "int86" function call. On return from BIOS, the printer status is contained in the "ah" register. This status is returned to the calling code with the C return statement.

The operations performed by the printer interface functions should be obvious from their names. The function "PrtInit" initializes the specified printer for operation. This places the attached printer in a known state so printing can proceed. The function "PrtStatus" returns the current status of the attached printer. The status bits returned by this function are explained in detail in Chapter 1 and illustrated here:

Bit Numbers of Processor Register "ah"

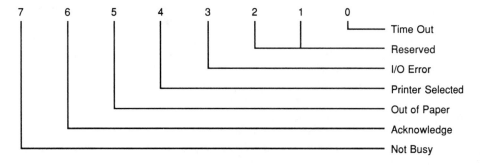

The function "PrtChar" sends a character to the printer to be printed. This function was shown and discussed earlier. The function "PrtString" sends a null terminated string of characters to the printer. This allows C strings to be sent to the printer with a single function call. The null that terminates all C strings is not sent to the printer, however. These four functions are all that are needed to interface the graphics screen print code to an attached printer.

The next step in the operation of the graphics print code is the calculation and scaling of pixel-intensity values. As mentioned, the print program is capable of producing 17 unique intensity levels on the hardcopy output. For this reason, the intensity of all possible pixel values from the source image must be scaled into the range 0 through 16. This is necessary for the patterning or dithering algorithms to work correctly. As you will recall from Chapter 1's discussion of the VGA graphics adapter, each value of a pixel on the display is not the color of the pixel but rather an index (directly or indirectly through a palette) of a color register that actually contains the pixel's color components. To find the intensity of a pixel so it can be scaled, the red, green, and blue (RGB) components of the corresponding color register must be found. If the color register represents a gray level (as it does if all three of the color components are equal), the intensity of the corresponding pixel is just the level of any one of the three individual color components. If, however, the pixel represents a color other than gray, the intensity must be calculated using the following formula extracted from the IBM technical reference manual:

Intensity $= 30\% \cdot \text{Red} + 59\% \cdot \text{Green} + 11\% \cdot \text{Blue}$

The maximum intensity of any pixel, gray or otherwise, is 63. All calculated pixel-intensity values must be scaled to the range 0 through 16. This is done by multiplying the calculated intensity value by 16 and dividing by the maximum intensity value of 63. This process is complicated somewhat in actual code because integer arithmetic was utilized. See Listing 7.1 for details.

A table called "DensityTbl" is filled with all of the scaled intensity values possible for a given number of unique colors. For a 256-color image, "DensityTbl" will have 256 entries. For 16-color images, there will be 16 entries. Each entry in "DensityTbl" will be in the range 0 through 16. To return the scaled intensity value for any pixel of the source image, the pixel's value is used as an index into "DensityTbl". The value returned from "DensityTbl" is the scaled value of the pixel's intensity. It should be obvious from this discussion that many of the colors available in the 256-color mode will scale to the same intensity value. All of the 256 colors must be printed using the same 17 intensity levels used for a 16-color image. As one would expect, 256-color images lose something when printed.

Once "DensityTbl" is built, the image can be printed. It is assumed at this point that the source image is already read from the disk and displayed on the monitor. The image will be printed from the information displayed on the monitor. For information on how to read and display PCX files, please refer to Chapter 6. For information on how to access pixels on a VGA display, please refer to Chapter 1.

An image is printed by scanning the image from right to left, each time printing a representation of a single column of source image pixels on the printer. The printed image will be at right angles to the direction of the printer paper. The right-most column of the image will be printed toward the top of the page, whereas the left-most image column will be at the bottom of the paper. The printing process is begun by calling the ''PrtScreen'' function.

''PrtScreen'' was designed for the most part to be a stand-alone function callable from any of the imaging programs in this book to produce a hardcopy representation of what is currently displayed on the VGA monitor. For this reason, ''PrtScreen'' gathers information itself about the status of the VGA display (current resolution, mode, number of colors, and so on) instead of relying on information that could be passed to it by the PCX functions that were used to load the image from disk onto the display.

The function ''GetVideoMode'' provided in the VGA function library of Chapter 1 is used to determine the current status of the video display. As stated, only three video modes are supported by the ''PrtScreen'' function. If a video mode other than those supported is indicated, an error is returned and the graphics print screen operation is aborted.

From the current video mode it can be determined how many rows and columns make up the image being displayed and whether 16 or 256 colors are being used to display the image. With the information on the number of colors available, the function ''InitDensityTbl'' is called to build the ''DensityTbl'', as described earlier. Next, the total number of bytes that the printer should expect for each column (line) of printed output is calculated. The number of bytes varies with the resolution of the image to be printed. Following this, strings of printer control codes are sent to the printer to put it into the correct mode for graphics printout. Please note that these printer control strings are for IBM-compatible printers only. If you are using a different printer, change these control codes appropriately. With the IBM Proprinter, it is necessary to put the printer in the one-direction print mode so the printed graphic dots all line up correctly. Bidirectional graphics printing results in wavy columns of graphic dots. Also for this printer, the line-feed distance must be changed from that used for printing text. Otherwise, white streaks will appear in the printed image between the rows of graphic dots.

With printer initialization completed, the program enters a loop that prints eight pixels of the source image at a time (moving from right to left). If a key is struck at the keyboard during the printing process, this loop and therefore the screen printing operation will be aborted. The method utilized to print the eight pixels of the source image depends upon the print algorithm being used. If patterning is selected, the function ''PatternPrintCol'' is utilized. If dithering is requested, ''DitherPrintCol'' is used. After all columns of the source image are printed, the printer is placed back into the text mode by sending it another series of printer control strings. A form feed is also sent to the printer to conveniently advance the printer paper so it can be torn off. If the screen print operation was successful, a ''NoError'' code is returned by the ''PrtScreen'' function.

The function ''PatternPrintCol'' utilizes patterning for generating the printed image. As stated, patterning results in the loss of image resolution unless the resolution of the output device is greater than that required by the image. In our case, the printer's resolution is four times greater than the image in the horizontal direction, but not in the vertical (paper movement) direction. For this reason, left to right resolution of the image is lost when the image is printed with patterning.

The nine-pin print head of this printer prints eight graphic dots during each pass over the paper. The correspondence between the data byte sent to the printer and the printer pins that are actuated is shown here.

Pin Number	Dot Orientation	Bit Number	Decimal Value
8	Top Pin	○ — 7	(128)
7		○ — 6	(64)
6		○ — 5	(32)
5		○ — 4	(16)
4		○ — 3	(8)
3		○ — 2	(4)
2		○ — 1	(2)
1	Bottom Pin	○ — 0	(1)

The table shows how individual graphic dots are generated. To actuate the top-most pin (number 8) of the print head, a value of 128 is sent to the printer. To actuate the bottom-most pin, a value of 1 is sent. To strike the paper with all pins engaged, a value of 255 (the summation of all of the decimal values) is sent. To advance the print head without striking the paper at all, a value of 0 is sent. In any case, the print head will be advanced to its next physical location after it prints each column of dots.

The information as to which dots (printer head pins) are to be actuated is calculated from the source pixel information. The calculation is performed on two four-pixel groups. The process is summarized in the following steps:

a. The values of the right-most group of four pixels (half of the eight image pixels printed for each call to "PatternPrintCol") are read from the VGA screen.

b. The scaled intensity values for each of the four pixels is found in "DensityTbl".

c. The average scaled intensity for this group of four pixels is found by averaging the scaled values for each of the pixels. You'll notice that here is where the resolution is lost. A group of four horizontal source image pixels are taken together to produce a single patterned four by four group for printing. This is the "big" picture element discussed previously.

d. A brightness-adjustment factor is added to the average scaled intensity value if the user input a brightness adjustment. Each increment of user-specified brightness will select the next-less-dense pixel patterning pattern from the Rylander matrix.

e. The adjusted intensity value is then used to select the proper patterning data from the Rylander matrix. The Rylander data, which is comprised of four nibbles of printer pin patterns, is shifted and loaded into the row 1, 2, 3, and 4 data variables that will eventually be sent to the printer. The data for the required intensity pattern is now loaded. It will be sent eventually to the top four printer pins.

f. Steps (a) through (e) are repeated again for the second group of four horizontal pixels. This time, however, the patterns from the matrix are merged with the previously shifted and loaded data patterns. This new data will fire the bottom four pins of the print head. Data for all eight of the print-head pins is now available.

g. If a negative image is requested, each of the four row data bytes will be inverted. This causes black to become white, and vice versa.

h. Finally, the four bytes of printer data corresponding to the eight horizontal image pixels being printed are sent to the printer.

i. This process is repeated for each row of the source image. This means eight horizontal pixels of the source image are printed from each row of the source image each time the function "PatternPrintCol" is called. When this process is completed, a carriage return code is sent to the printer, causing the whole line of graphics codes to be printed all at once.

The code shown in the listing should make this process clear. It is harder to describe the code than it was to implement it.

The function "DitherPrintCol" is more straightforward in its operation. It is a direct implementation of the dithering algorithm presented in the text. The steps involved can be summarized as follows:

a. The scaled intensity value for the right-most source image pixel is read from the display and looked up in "DensityTbl".

b. The scaled value is adjusted by the user-specified brightness factor, as before.

c. If the intensity of the adjusted pixel value is greater than the entry in the dither matrix to which it corresponds, the decimal value to actuate the top-most printer pin is loaded into the variable "PrtByte". After all of the other printer-pin values are merged into this variable, it will be sent to the printer. The correspondence between the image pixel and the dither matrix entry is maintained with "MatrixRow" and the hardcoded matrix column index. A new value of "MatrixRow" is calculated for each row of the source image processed. The matrix column index into the Bayer matrix is hardcoded because the relationship between source image column and matrix entry is known ahead of time.

d. Steps (a), (b), and (c) are repeated for all of the other seven source image pixels processed by a single call to the "DitherPrintCol" function.

e. If a positive image (an image in which lighter-colored regions print with lighter shades of gray and white) is required, "PrtByte" must be inverted. This is because the sense of the printer pins is backwards. For example, if the intensity of all eight of the horizontal pixels was less than the corresponding entries in the dither matrix, the pixels should print as black. As it is, they will not actuate any of the printer pins and will therefore print white. This condition is corrected by inverting "PrtByte" for positive images and not inverting it for negative images.

f. Finally, "PrtByte" is sent to the printer. It will be sent two times for 320×200 images and four times for images 640 pixels wide. This helps maintain a correct aspect ratio for 320×200 images at the cost of having a very small image printout. "PrtByte" can be sent to the printer multiple times because the printer's resolution in the horizontal direction is higher than in the vertical direction.

g. This process is repeated for each row of the source image. This means eight horizontal pixels of the source image are printed from each row of the source image each time the function "DitherPrintCol" is called. When this process is completed, a carriage return code is sent to the printer, causing the whole line of graphics codes to be printed all at once.

The final portion of the example program yet to be discussed is the user interface code. This code is contained in the "main()" and "ShowHelp" functions. This general approach to parsing user-specified parameters was discussed in detail in Chapter 5. Specifically, the color-image acquisition program in Chapter 5 (Listing 5.4) utilized this same type of user interface code. What needs to be discussed here is not how the user interface code works but what the user is allowed to do with the print example program from the command line.

Four different command line switches are recognized by this example program. First, if the switch "-v" is specified, a verbose listing of PCX file information will be provided to the user. This option is exactly the same as that for the "view" program discussed in Chapter 6. If the "-m" switch is specified, it should be followed by either "b/B" or "r/R" to specify which kind of printing algorithm should be used. Bayer dithering is used by default unless specifically overridden by the switch "-mR", which will cause the Rylander method to be used instead. Brightness of the printed image can be altered by specifying a "-b" switch followed by a number in the range "−9" to "+9". The more positive the number, the lighter the image prints. The final command line switch is "-n", which if included on the command line causes the image to be printed as a negative. The print example program will remind the user of valid command line parameters if any invalid parameters are specified or if the program is executed with a "?" as a parameter, as follows:

> print ? <Enter>

Image Sequence 7.2 shows two different images printed using both patterning and dithering. Dithering definitely results in a better-looking image whenever text is involved. Patterning, with its accompanying loss of resolution, distorts text in any image it is used to print. In general, you see a rougher texture in the pattern printed images along with the loss of image detail. Dithered images, in contrast, retain most of the detail from the source image. Which hardcopy technique to use really depends on the subject matter of the image and the effect you would like to obtain. Use experimentation to decide.

Conclusions

This concludes the discussion of hardcopy production methods. We have learned how to use photography to produce hardcopy of computer-generated images, how halftoning techniques work for the production of pictures in books and magazines, how halftoning can be simulated on a printer by patterning or dithering, and finally, how these algorithms can be utilized in an example program.

This chapter also concludes Part One. Chapter 1 discussed the background information necessary to fully understand (and appreciate) all of the information to be presented in the remainder of the book. Chapter 2 taught the fundamentals of video that had to be mastered before discussing the digitizer presented in Chapter 3. Chapters 4 and 5 described the software required to make the digitizer work. In Chapter 6, graphics image file formats were discussed, and code was given to save acquired images in two popular graphics image file formats. Finally, Chapter 7 showed how displayed images could be converted to hardcopy on a graphics printer.

With all of these techniques behind us, we are now prepared for Part Two, where image processing algorithms will be discussed. Many of the techniques learned in Part One will be of use in Part Two. Part Two will also explore many new ideas. Please, sit back and relax. The journey into the realms of image processing is about to begin.

PART TWO

CLASSICAL IMAGE PROCESSING

Introduction to Part Two

Welcome to Part Two. Here we leave the discussion of the digitizer behind and concentrate on the science of image processing. In a certain sense, the two parts of this book are unrelated. Part One shows how image data can be acquired and stored, while the Part Two focuses on how image data can be processed. The image data processed in this part of the book can come from a variety of sources. It does not have to be provided by the digitizer of Part One. The image processing functions provided will work with any image data available in the PCX file format.

In an attempt to provide as much organization as possible, the chapters in Part Two follow a set format. Each chapter consists of:

a. Textual information pertaining to the class of image processing algorithms being discussed, along with the problems involved with utilizing the algorithms.

b. A series of image sequences that show the effect of the application of the algorithms discussed.

c. A summary of C functions that pertain to the algorithms under discussion. The C functions in each chapter are collectively referred to as the *function library*. Each C function in the function library is described in detail.

d. A listing of the code that makes up the function library. This is usually the first code listing in a chapter.

e. An example program that shows not only how the image processing library functions are utilized but also how each of the image sequences included in the chapter was generated.

All code listings in these chapters are available on the companion disks (see Part Three for details of the contents of the companion disks). All of the code together forms what is referred to as the *image processing function library*. Each chapter in this section of the book adds new functions to this library.

With this function library and your personal computer, you can experiment with techniques that were previously available only in a photography darkroom or in the image processing labs of major corporations. These techniques are more convenient than a darkroom because you don't have chemicals to bother with, you don't waste materials, and you don't have to wait for the images to dry.

Experimentation with the techniques and code provided is encouraged. With a customized user interface, the code provided in the image processing function library could be made into a very capable image-manipulation program. Executing the image processing algorithms interactively in this manner would allow lots of experimentation with image processing functions and combinations of functions. When you produce an image you would like to retain, the PCX or TIFF library functions provided in Chapter 6 can be used to save your image. Alternatively, the hardcopy functions provided in Chapter 7 can be used to print a gray-scale version of your image.

All of the image processing in Part Two will be performed using 320×200 resolution images. This resolution was selected because of the number (256) of colors available while using this resolution. Continuous-tone images are used exclusively. They are assumed to have 64 levels of gray available for each pixel. That is, the pixel values are at least six bits in size. All images were digitized using the digitizer of Part One along with the program "acquire.c" presented in Chapter 12.

Color images can be processed by some of the image processing algorithms provided, but the results will usually be surprising. The reasons for the surprising results will become clear as the information in the next five chapters is read and understood.

Higher-resolution images can also be processed with only minor changes to the image processing code. The required changes are discussed in Chapter 8. It is hoped the discussion is complete enough to allow changes in resolution or number of colors with a minimal amount of effort.

Most of the algorithms presented in Part Two are somewhat processor intensive. The reasons for this are:

a. The algorithms are all coded in C. No assembly language was used in an attempt to increase performance.
b. No C tricks were used. The code is very straightforward and is written more in the style of Pascal. Code clarity was considered more important than speed.
c. Floating-point numbers are used. Some of the algorithms require the use of real or floating-point numbers. The floating-point software libraries provided with many of the common MSDOS C compilers are known to be slow. A numeric coprocessor could help quite a bit in this area.

For these reasons, the more powerful the computer you have at your disposal the better. If performance becomes an issue, invest in a numeric coprocessor and then try rewriting some of the C image processing support functions in assembly language. It should be possible to gain at least an order-of-magnitude improvement in performance with some relatively minor modifications.

Introduction to Image Processing

Image processing is a science that deals with images and image data. It covers a broad spectrum of techniques that are applicable to a wide range of applications. Image processing can be thought of as a special form of two-dimensional signal processing used to uncover information about images. In general, image processing techniques are applied to images or image data when:

    a. Enhancement or modification of an image is necessary to improve appearance or to highlight some aspect of the information contained in the image.

    b. Elements within an image need to be categorized, classified, matched, or measured.

    c. Portions of images need to be combined or image elements need to be reorganized.

The techniques of image processing can be applied to data even if the data is not in a visible form. The manipulation of visible image data is just one of the many uses of image processing—probably the predominant one. Image processing can be used to produce a visible image of purely numeric data enhanced in some manner to highlight some aspect of the data. Examples of this kind of image processing can be found in magnetic resonant medical imaging equipment, sonar, radar, ultrasound equipment, heat-sensing equipment, fractals, and so on.

Applying an image processing algorithm to an image is not always done with the appearance of the image in mind. Actually, the result might not be pleasing to look at. Aesthetics are not the only criterion by which to judge the effectiveness of the applied transformation. If the transformation is designed to bring out additional information and/or details not visible in the original image, the result can be considered successful even if it is not pleasing to look at.

Four different classes of image processing algorithms are discussed in Part Two:

    a. **Point Processes**. These are processes that alter pixel values in an image based only upon the original value of the pixel and possibly its location within an image.

    b. **Area Processes**. These are processes that alter pixel values based upon the original pixel value and the values of the pixels that surround it.

    c. **Frame Processes**. These processes alter pixel values within an image based on the pixel values present in one or more additional images.

    d. **Geometric Processes**. These processes alter the arrangement or placement of pixels in an image based upon some geometric transformation.

Many different image processing functions are provided in each of the above categories. These functions can be applied to an image individually or in conjunction with other functions, either within the same class or within different classes. Please note that the application of these algorithms is not commutative in nature. That is, the order of application is very important in achieving the effect you desire.

Not all possible image processing algorithms in each category are provided in this book. Because of their usefulness, basic algorithms are given good coverage, while the more esoteric algorithms are left out of the discussion. Many of the image processing books listed in "References and Additional Reading" in Part Three can provide details of the more obscure algorithms. Few, however, will provide you with code to experiment with.

The image processing algorithms that are provided are discussed in detail. These discussions are slanted toward the implementation and usage issues and away from the rigorous math upon which the algorithms are based. The result of this approach is that the image processing algorithms can be utilized in a "cookbook" manner without having to understand completely their mathematical underpinnings. Of course, the results obtained will be more controllable if the mathematics behind the transformations is fully understood. For this reason, some mathematical treatment is provided, and pointers to other texts where more details can be found are also provided. A basic understanding of algebra and trigonometry is assumed throughout.

Before the discussion can begin, it is necessary to define a few terms that will be used throughout this half of the book. The definition of these and other terms pertinent to image processing can be found in the glossary located in Part Three.

Spatial resolution is the number of samples used to define an image. In the image processing context, *spatial*, refers to space. The higher the spatial resolution, the higher the quality of the image. Spatial resolution is usually thought of as a two-dimensional quantity organized into columns and rows. The intersection of each column and row contains a digitized sample taken from an image. Images with spatial resolutions of 320×200, 640×200, and 640×480 can be acquired with the digitizer described in Part One.

Spatial frequency is the rate of change of image pixel intensity. Spatial frequency is a two-dimensional quantity because pixel intensity can and does change simultaneously in both the horizontal and vertical directions. Portions of images that have constant or nearly constant intensity pixel values are said to contain low spatial frequency content. Images with wildly fluctuating pixel-intensity values have high spatial-frequency content.

Brightness resolution is the total number of unique values used to express pixel-intensity values in an image. Brightness resolution is related to the number of bits used to store each image sample. For example, with 6 bits for each image sample, there are a total of 64 unique brightness levels possible.

With these terms defined, we can now enter the exciting world of image processing.

Image Processing
Support Functions

In this chapter you will learn about:

- **The general organization of the image processing software presented in this book**
- **The functions contained in the support function library**

Introduction

Before we can begin the discussion of the image processing algorithms themselves, we must first spend a moment discussing the support functions on which the algorithms are based. These functions form the interface between the image data in a buffer and the image processing algorithms. Every byte of image data manipulated by the image processing algorithms passes through these support functions. These functions provide image data manipulation only: they are not involved with reading or writing image data to or from disk files. In other words, these functions are not concerned with where the image data came from or where it goes, just its manipulation.

Where does the image data that these support functions manipulate come from? It can come from a variety of sources. For our image processing applications in Part Two, all image data will come from PCX files. (See Chapter 6 for a discussion of the PCX functions that provide the image I/O capability.) The data could also come directly from the digitizer, a scanner, a paint program, or other graphics files.

To keep things as uncomplicated as possible and to remain focused on image processing, we will use PCX files exclusively for all image data I/O. The block diagram shown in Figure 8.1 illustrates the hierarchy of software we will use for all image processing.

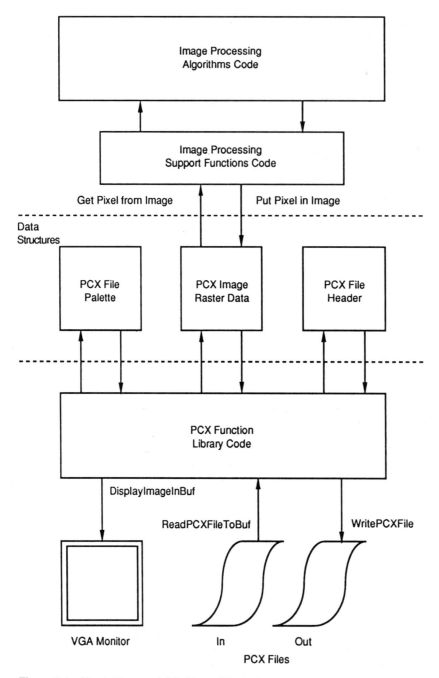

Figure 8.1   Block Diagram of Software Hierarchy

These image processing support functions are very general in their design and operation. They were designed specifically for 320×200 resolution images utilizing 64 levels of gray or 256 colors but will work with any resolution image. Performance is key in the design of the support functions. These routines can be called 64,000 times in a single image transformation, so it is important they run quickly. In a professional image processing application these routines would probably be rewritten in assembly language to squeeze every possible bit of performance out of them. For our use here, the performance of the C code will be adequate.

To utilize these support functions it is necessary to include the file "imagesup.h" in the application code and to link the file "imagesup.c" to the application. Both files are shown in Listing 8.1. By convention, the header file contains the function prototypes of the support functions. For this reason the application code, which includes the header file, does not have to declare the support functions external before they are used. The image processing support functions do not have a project make file because they do not form a stand-alone application. The make instructions for these support functions will be included in the application's project make file. See the point processing project make file "pttest.prj" in Chapter 9 for example usage.

Note that although the image processing support functions are general enough to work with images of any resolution, some of the image processing algorithm code is not. Two defines in the "imagesup.h" file will need modification if images other than 320×200 are manipulated: "MAXCOLS" and "MAXROWS".

Listing 8.1   Image Processing Support Functions

The following is the contents of the file, "imagesup.h":

```
/****************************************/
/*      Image Processing Header File    */
/*         written in Turbo C 2.0       */
/*                 by                   */
/*          Craig A. Lindley            */
/*                                      */
/*    Vers: 1.0  Last Update: 11/14/89  */
/****************************************/


/*
This file includes the general equates used for all of the
image processing code in part two of this book. Throughout
these equates, a 320x200 256 color image is assumed. If the
resolution of the processed pictures change, the equates
MAXCOLS and MAXROWS must change accordingly.
*/
```

(continued)

Listing 8.1 *(continued)*

```
/* Pixel Sample Information and Equates */
#define MAXSAMPLEBITS    6          /* 6 bits from digitizer */
#define MINSAMPLEVAL     0          /* Min sample value = 0 */

/* Max num of sample values */
#define MAXQUANTLEVELS (1<<MAXSAMPLEBITS)
/* Max sample value = 63 */
#define MAXSAMPLEVAL    (MAXQUANTLEVELS-1)

/* Image Resolution Equates */
#define MINCOLNUM        0          /* Column 0 */
#define MAXCOLS          LRMAXCOLS  /* 320 total columns */
#define MAXCOLNUM        (MAXCOLS-1) /* Last column is 319 */
#define MINROWNUM        0          /* Row 0 */
#define MAXROWS          LRMAXROWS  /* 200 total rows */
#define MAXROWNUM        (MAXROWS-1) /* Last row is 199 */

#define RASTERSIZE ((long)MAXCOLS * MAXROWS)
#define MAXNUMGRAYCOLORS MAXQUANTLEVELS

/* histogram equates */
#define HISTOCOL         0
#define HISTOROW         0
#define HISTOWIDTH       134
#define HISTOHEIGHT      84

#define BLACK            0
#define WHITE            63

#define AXISCOL          (HISTOCOL+3)
#define AXISROW          (HISTOROW+HISTOHEIGHT-5)
#define AXISLENGTH       MAXQUANTLEVELS*2-1
#define DATACOL          AXISCOL
#define DATAROW          AXISROW-1
#define MAXDEFLECTION    (HISTOHEIGHT-10)

/* External Function Declarations and Prototypes */

void CopyImage(BYTE huge *SourceBuf, BYTE huge *DestBuf);

BYTE GetPixelFromImage(BYTE huge *Image, unsigned Col, unsigned Row);

CompletionCode PutPixelInImage(BYTE huge *Image, unsigned Col,
                                 unsigned Row, unsigned Color);
```

```
CompletionCode DrawHLine(BYTE huge *Image, unsigned Col, unsigned Row,
                                   unsigned Length, unsigned Color);

CompletionCode DrawVLine(BYTE huge *Image, unsigned Col, unsigned Row,
                                   unsigned Length, unsigned Color);

void ReadImageAreaToBuf (BYTE huge *Image, unsigned Col, unsigned Row,
                                   unsigned Width, unsigned Height,
                                   BYTE huge *Buffer);

void WriteImageAreaFromBuf (BYTE huge *Buffer, unsigned BufWidth,
                                   unsigned BufHeight, BYTE huge *Image,
                                   unsigned ImageCol, unsigned ImageRow);

void ClearImageArea(BYTE huge *Image,unsigned Col, unsigned Row,
                              unsigned Width, unsigned Height,
                              unsigned PixelValue);

CompletionCode ParameterCheckOK(unsigned Col, unsigned Row,
                           unsigned ColExtent, unsigned RowExtent,
                           char *ErrorStr);
```

The following is the contents of the file, "imagesup.c":

```
/**************************************/
/* Image Processing Support Functions */
/*        written in Turbo C 2.0       */
/*                by                   */
/*        Craig A. Lindley             */
/*                                     */
/*   Vers: 1.0  Last Update: 11/14/89  */
/**************************************/

#include <stdio.h>
#include <process.h>
#include <conio.h>
#include <dos.h>
#include <alloc.h>
#include <mem.h>
#include <graphics.h>
#include "misc.h"
#include "pcx.h"
#include "vga.h"
#include "imagesup.h"
```

(continued)

Listing 8.1 *(continued)*

```
extern struct PCX_File PCXData;
extern unsigned ImageWidth;
extern unsigned ImageHeight;

/*
Image Processing Support Functions - See text for details.
*/

/*
Copy a complete image from source buffer to destination buffer
*/

void CopyImage(BYTE huge *SourceBuf, BYTE huge *DestBuf)
{
   movedata(FP_SEG(SourceBuf),FP_OFF(SourceBuf),
               FP_SEG(DestBuf),FP_OFF(DestBuf),
               (unsigned) RASTERSIZE);
}

/*
NOTE: to index into the image memory like an array, the index
value must be a long variable type, NOT just cast to long.
*/
BYTE GetPixelFromImage(BYTE huge *Image, unsigned Col, unsigned Row)
{
  unsigned long PixelBufOffset;

  if((Col < ImageWidth) && (Row < ImageHeight))
  {
     PixelBufOffset  = Row;            /* done to prevent overflow */
     PixelBufOffset *= ImageWidth;
     PixelBufOffset += Col;
     return(Image[PixelBufOffset]);
  }
  printf("GetPixelFromImage Error: Coordinate out of range\n");
  printf("  Col = %d  Row = %d\n",Col,Row);
  return(FALSE);
}

CompletionCode PutPixelInImage(BYTE huge *Image, unsigned Col,
                                          unsigned Row, unsigned Color)
{
  unsigned long PixelBufOffset;
```

```
  if((Col < ImageWidth) && (Row < ImageHeight))
  {
     PixelBufOffset  = Row;              /* done to prevent overflow */
     PixelBufOffset *= ImageWidth;
     PixelBufOffset += Col;
     Image[PixelBufOffset] = Color;
     return(TRUE);
  }
  else
  {
     printf("PutPixelInImage Error: Coordinate out of range\n");
     printf("  Col = %d  Row = %d\n",Col,Row);
     return(FALSE);
  }
}


/*
NOTE: A length of 0 is one pixel on. A length of 1 is two pixels
on. That is why length is incremented before being used.
*/
CompletionCode DrawHLine(BYTE huge *Image, unsigned Col, unsigned Row,
                                   unsigned Length, unsigned Color)
{
   if ((Col < ImageWidth) && ((Col+Length) <= ImageWidth) &&
      (Row < ImageHeight))
   {
     Length++;
     while(Length--)
             PutPixelInImage(Image,Col++,Row,Color);
     return(TRUE);
   }
   else
   {
     printf("DrawHLine Error: Coordinate out of range\n");
     printf("  Col = %d  Row = %d  Length = %d\n",Col,Row,Length);
     return(FALSE);
   }
}


CompletionCode DrawVLine(BYTE huge *Image, unsigned Col, unsigned Row,
                                   unsigned Length, unsigned Color)
{
   if ((Row < ImageHeight) && ((Row+Length) <= ImageHeight) &&
      (Col < ImageWidth))
```

(continued)

Listing 8.1 *(continued)*

```
{
   Length++;
   while(Length--)
           PutPixelInImage(Image,Col,Row++,Color);
   return(TRUE);
}
else
{
   printf("DrawVLine Error: Coordinate out of range\n");
   printf("  Col = %d  Row = %d  Length = %d\n",Col,Row,Length);
   return(FALSE);
}
}


void ReadImageAreaToBuf (BYTE huge *Image, unsigned Col, unsigned Row,
                                     unsigned Width, unsigned Height, BYTE huge *Buffer)
{
   unsigned long PixelBufOffset = 0L;
   register unsigned ImageCol, ImageRow;
   for (ImageRow=Row; ImageRow < Row+Height; ImageRow++)
      for (ImageCol=Col; ImageCol < Col+Width; ImageCol++)
        Buffer[PixelBufOffset++] =
                 GetPixelFromImage(Image,ImageCol,ImageRow);
}


void WriteImageAreaFromBuf (BYTE huge *Buffer, unsigned BufWidth,
                                     unsigned BufHeight, BYTE huge *Image,
                                     unsigned ImageCol, unsigned ImageRow)
{
   unsigned long PixelBufOffset;
   register unsigned BufCol, BufRow, CurrentImageCol;

   for (BufRow = 0; BufRow < BufHeight; BufRow++)
   {
      CurrentImageCol = ImageCol;
      for (BufCol = 0; BufCol < BufWidth; BufCol++)
      {
              PixelBufOffset = (unsigned long)BufRow*BufWidth+BufCol;
              PutPixelInImage(Image,CurrentImageCol,ImageRow,Buffer[PixelBufOffset]);
              CurrentImageCol++;
      }
      ImageRow++;
   }
}
```

```
void ClearImageArea(BYTE huge *Image,unsigned Col, unsigned Row,
                                unsigned Width, unsigned Height,
                                unsigned PixelValue)
{
   register unsigned BufCol, BufRow;

   for (BufRow = 0; BufRow < Height; BufRow++)
      for (BufCol = 0; BufCol < Width; BufCol++)
            PutPixelInImage(Image,BufCol+Col,BufRow+Row,PixelValue);
}


/*
This function checks to make sure the parameters passed to
the image processing functions are all within range. If so
a TRUE is returned. If not, an error message is output and
the calling program is terminated.
*/


CompletionCode ParameterCheckOK(unsigned Col, unsigned Row,
                                  unsigned ColExtent, unsigned RowExtent,
                                  char *FunctionName)
{
   if ((Col > MAXCOLNUM) || (Row > MAXROWNUM) ||
       (ColExtent > MAXCOLS) || (RowExtent > MAXROWS))
   {
      restorecrtmode();
      printf("Parameter(s) out of range in function: %s\n",FunctionName);
      printf("  Col = %d  Row = %d  ColExtent = %d  RowExtent = %d\n",
                        Col, Row, ColExtent, RowExtent);

      exit(EBadParms);
   }
   return(TRUE);
}
```

Nine functions make up the image processing support functions. They are described in Figure 8.2, and the code is shown in Listing 8.1. "GetPixelFromImage" and "PutPixelIn-Image" deserve special discussion.

The functions "GetPixelFromImage" and "PutPixelInImage" are the basis for all of the support functions and all of the image processing algorithms that will be described later. They manipulate the image data as a huge array of bytes. A huge array is used because an image buffer can be greater than 64KB in length. As discussed in Chapter 1, a long integer index must be used to manipulate a huge array. For this reason, an index of type unsigned long called "PixelBufOffset" is introduced to access the image data array. Casting the index

1. Copy an image from one buffer to another.

   Prototype
   void CopyImage (BYTE huge *SourceBuf, BYTE huge *DestBuf);

   Where "SourceBuf" and "DestBuf" are both huge pointers to image buffers.

   ## Operation
   This function does exactly what its name implies. It copies a complete 320×200 resolution image from one buffer to another. This function is used for saving a copy of an image while the original image is subjected to some image processing transformation. This way, the original and the transformed images can be displayed for comparison.

2. Read a specified pixel from an image buffer.

   Prototype
   BYTE GetPixelFromImage (BYTE huge *Image,unsigned Col, unsigned Row);

   Where:

   "Image" is a huge pointer to an image buffer.
   "Col" and "Row" determine where in the image buffer the byte of image data is to be extracted
       from.

   ## Operation
   This function will read a byte of image data from the image buffer pointed at by "Image" with location specified by the "Col" (column) and "Row". This function does a validity check on the specified "Col" and "Row" parameters to ensure they are contained in the "Image" buffer. If either parameter is out of range, an error message will be displayed, and a byte of zero will be returned. In a well-behaved, thoroughly tested application program, the range checking of the input parameters could be removed to increase performance. Until an image processing application is completely debugged, however, it is best to leave the checking intact.
       The byte value returned by a call to "GetPixelFromImage" will be the index into the VGA palette with which the pixel would be displayed (see below for additional details).
       This function is used whenever image data needs to be read from an image buffer.

3. Write a specified pixel to an image buffer.

   Prototype
   CompletionCode PutPixelInImage(BYTE huge *Image, unsigned Col, unsigned Row, unsigned Color);

   Where all parameters are as specified above except:

   "Color" determines the pixel intensity value to be assigned to the specified pixel in an image.

   ## Operation
   This function will write a byte of image data, "Color", into the image buffer pointed at by "Image" with location specified by the "Col" and "Row". This function does a validity check on the specified "Col" and "Row" parameters to ensure they are contained in the "Image" buffer. If either parameter is out of range, an error message will be displayed and FALSE will be returned. As mentioned previously, the parameter checking could be removed to increase performance in a well-tested applications program.

Figure 8.2 Image Processing Support Functions

"Color" is an index into the VGA palette of the color with which the pixel will be displayed. For 64-level gray-scale images, "Color" would be in the range 0 to 63 inclusive. "Color" equal to 0 is usually black, whereas "Color" equal to 63 is usually white. For 256-color images, "Color" will range from 0 to 255 inclusive. To produce an image buffer that contains all possible colors, "PutPixelInImage" could be called 256 times, incrementing the value of "Color" each time.

This function is used whenever image data must be written to an image buffer.

4. Write a horizontal line into an image buffer.

Prototype

CompletionCode DrawHLine(BYTE huge *Image, unsigned Col, unsigned Row, unsigned Length, unsigned Color);

Where all parameters are as specified.

Operation

This function places a horizontal line of pixels starting at "Col" and "Row" of length "Length" and color "Color" into the image buffer pointed to by "Image". A "Length" of 0 is a single pixel on. A "Length" of 1 is two pixels on, and so on. This function also performs parameter checking and will output an error message and return a value of FALSE if any of the parameters are found to be out of range. TRUE will be returned from this function if all is well.

This function is used whenever horizontal lines must be drawn into an image buffer. This function in conjunction with "DrawVLine" (which follows) can be used to draw a grid over the top of an image. Both functions are also used for the display of histograms, as discussed later in this chapter.

5. Write a vertical line into an image buffer.

Prototype

CompletionCode DrawVLine(BYTE huge *Image, unsigned Col, unsigned Row, unsigned Length, unsigned Color);

Where all parameters are as specified.

Operation

The operation of this function is analogous to that of "DrawHLine", just described in detail.

6. Copy an area of an image buffer into a new destination buffer.

Prototype

void ReadImageAreaToBuf(BYTE huge *Image, unsigned Col, unsigned Row, unsigned Width, unsigned Height, BYTE huge *Buf);

Where all parameters are as specified except:

"Buf", which is a pointer to the buffer into which the portion of the image specified should be read.

Operation

This function is used to copy a portion (or all) of an image contained in an image buffer to a destination buffer pointed to by "Buf". The dimensions of the portion of the image to copy are described by "Col", "Row", "Width", and "Height". The copied image data is formated as packed

Figure 8.2   *(continued)*

(continued)

bytes in the destination buffer with no relation to the columns or rows of the original image. Manipulation of the image data in the destination buffer is possible as long as the new column/row relationships of the data are kept in mind.

This function is used whenever a portion of an image buffer must be saved (for later restoration) because it is going to be overlaid. It is used later to allow a histogram to be popped up over the top of an image without losing the image data under the histogram. The function described next is used to bring the data that was saved back into the image buffer.

7. Copy a source buffer into an image buffer.

Prototype

void WriteImageAreaFromBuf(BYTE huge *Buffer,unsigned BufWidth, unsigned BufHeight, BYTE huge *Image, unsigned ImageCol,unsigned ImageRow);

Where all parameters are as specified except:

"BufWidth" and "BufHeight" determine the area of the temporary buffer, pointed to by "Buffer", that is going to be written into the image buffer pointed to by "Image".
"ImageCol" and "ImageRow" determine where in the destination image the buffer contents will be written.

Operation

"WriteImageAreaFromBuf" performs a complementary operation to the "ReadImageAreaToBuf" function discussed above. It is used to copy a source buffer, pointed to by "Buffer", to a destination image buffer pointed to by "Image". "BufWidth" and "BufHeight" describe the dimensions of the source buffer. The source buffer is copied into the image buffer starting at the location specified by "ImageCol" and "ImageRow". Because the location in the destination image buffer to which the source buffer is copied is specified by parameters, the same source buffer can be copied to the destination image buffer more than once. In other words, any portion of an image buffer (which was acquired with a call to "ReadImageAreaToBuf") can be pasted back into the image buffer at any desired position.

This function is used to restore an area of an image buffer previously saved with "ReadImageAreaToBuf". As mentioned, the histogram display function uses "WriteImageAreaFromBuf" to put back the image overlaid by the display of the histogram when the histogram is finished being viewed. Another use for this function is to make multiple copies of an object in an image buffer.

8. Set a specified area of an image buffer to a specified value.

Prototype

void ClearImageArea(BYTE huge *Image, unsigned Col, unsigned Row, unsigned Width, unsigned Height, unsigned PixelValue);

Where all parameters are as specified except:

"PixelValue", which determines the byte value written into each location of the buffer being cleared.

Operation

This function sets an area of an image buffer pointed to by "Image" and specified by "Col", "Row", "Width", and "Height" to the pixel value specified. The function of "PixelValue" is analogous to that of the parameter "Color" described for "PutPixelInImage". If "PixelValue" is specified as 0 or black, the specified image area will become black.

Figure 8.2 *(continued)*

This function is used mainly in the preparation of newly allocated image buffers. It initializes the data in the image buffer to a constant value instead of allowing the buffer to contain random data. By initializing the image buffer to a known value, the extent of any image processing done on an image placed into the initialized buffer is immediately obvious. This function can also be used as part of a frame process—discussed later in this chapter—to clear a portion of an image for subsequent overlay by another image.

9. Perform a validity check on specified parameters.

Prototype
CompletionCode ParameterCheckOK(unsigned Col, unsigned Row, unsigned ColExtent, unsigned RowExtent, char *FunctionName);

Operation
This function verifies that the image area specified by "Col", "Row", "ColExtent" (width), and "RowExtent" (height) fits completely within a 320 × 200 image buffer. If it does, this function returns TRUE. If it does not, a programming error has occurred, and the application program is terminated after an error message detailing the out-of-range parameter is displayed. Termination is necessary because a write to memory outside of an image buffer could result in a computer crash at some point. This function is used extensively in the image processing code to be described later.

Figure 8.2 *(continued)*

to type long before using it does not always work correctly. For this reason an actual type long is used in the code instead of a cast.

"ImageWidth" and "ImageHeight" are limits used to check the parameters passed to the "GetPixelFromImage" and "PutPixelInImage" functions. Any attempt to pass parameters outside these limits is considered an error and will be reported. "ImageWidth" and "ImageHeight" are variables that are updated whenever a PCX file is read into memory or displayed. "GetPixelFromImage" and "PutPixelInImage" dynamically determine the validity of the parameters they are passed from the resolution of the image just read. They will, therefore, automatically cope with images of 320 × 200, 640 × 200, or 640 × 480 resolution. The validity checking of parameters is performed at this low level to alleviate the need for this type of error checking at each level in the code.

Conclusions

It is said you cannot erect a building without first laying a firm foundation. The same principle applies to image processing. The image processing algorithms themselves do not do much good if there is not a solid software foundation on which to build them. That is what we have given in this chapter. These support functions provide all of the low-level capabilities required for the image processing performed in the remainder of this book. Like any good foundation, their presence will soon be forgotten. You must understand, however, that without them the higher-level processing would not be possible.

Point Processes

In this chapter you will learn about:

- **What point processes are**
- **What a histogram is and what it can tell you about an image**
- **How look-up tables can be used to perform point processes**
- **How to apply various point process functions to image data and what the resultant images look like**

Introduction

Point processes are fundamental image processing operations. They are the simplest and yet probably the most frequently used of the image processing algorithms. They are useful by themselves or in conjunction with the other classes of algorithms. Being less complex than other image processing algorithms, they are a natural starting place for our discussion.

Point processes are algorithms that modify a pixel's value in an image based solely upon that pixel's value (and sometimes its location). No other pixel values are involved in the transformation. Individual pixels are replaced with new values that are algorithmically related to the pixel's original value. As a result of the algorithmic relationship between the original and the new pixel value, point processes can generally be reversed. Point process algorithms scan through an image pixel by pixel, performing the pixel transformation. If the transformation depends only upon the original pixel value, the transformation process can be performed with the help of a look-up table (LUT). LUTs will be discussed in detail shortly. If the point process transformation also takes into consideration the location of a pixel, a formula or a formula in conjunction with a LUT can be used to transform the pixel values. In general, point processes do not modify the spatial relationships within an image. For this reason, point processes cannot modify the detail contained in an image.

Please note that the application of point process algorithms to an image makes sense only for continuous-tone images, whose brightness values are directly represented by the pixel values. To manipulate color images in this manner, the algorithms would need to be applied to each color plane separately instead of to the pixel values directly. Recall that for 320×200, 256-color images, the pixel value is an index into the VGA palette and not a true brightness or RGB value. Applying a transform to the index value will probably result in some rather spectacular colors in your image but not much of practical use other than the novelty. Certainly, the results will not be what was anticipated.

The point processes discussed in this chapter are

a. Image brightening
b. Negative images
c. Image thresholding
d. Image contrast stretching
e. Image pseudocoloring

All of the code for the point processing algorithms is contained in the file "ptprocess.c" on the companion disk and is shown in Listing 9.1. All function prototypes for the point process functions are contained in the file "ptprocess.h" and shown in Figures 9.2 and 9.4. This file will need to be included in any application code that utilizes the point process functions. The files "pttest.c" and "pttest.prj", shown in Listing 9.2, contain a sample application program used for testing the point processing functions. This example program can be used as a model for the structure of a typical application program utilizing the point processing functions. This example program generates all of the image sequences found in this chapter.

Listing 9.1   The Point Process Function Library

The following is the contents of the file, "ptprocess.h":

```
/****************************************/
/*    Image Processing Header File    */
/*     Point Processing Functions     */
/*        written in Turbo C 2.0       */
/*                by                   */
/*         Craig A. Lindley            */
/*                                     */
/*  Vers: 1.0  Last Update: 11/07/89   */
/****************************************/

extern unsigned Histogram[MAXQUANTLEVELS];

/* Function Prototypes for support and histogram functions */
void InitializeLUT(BYTE *LookUpTable);
```

(continued)

Listing 9.1 *(continued)*

```c
void PtTransform(BYTE huge *ImageData, unsigned Col,
                                unsigned Row, unsigned Width,
                                unsigned Height, BYTE *LookUpTable);

void GenHistogram(BYTE huge *ImageData, unsigned Col,
                                unsigned Row, unsigned Width,
                                unsigned Height);

void DisplayHist(BYTE huge *ImageData,unsigned Col,
                                unsigned Row, unsigned Width,
                                unsigned Height);

/* Point transform functions */
void AdjImageBrightness(BYTE huge *ImageData, short BrightnessFactor,
                                        unsigned Col, unsigned Row,
                                        unsigned Width, unsigned Height);

void NegateImage(BYTE huge *ImageData, unsigned Threshold,
                                unsigned Col, unsigned Row,
                                unsigned Width, unsigned Height);

void ThresholdImage(BYTE huge *ImageData, unsigned Threshold,
                                 unsigned Col, unsigned Row,
                                 unsigned Width, unsigned Height);

void StretchImageContrast(BYTE huge *ImageData, unsigned *HistoData,
                                        unsigned Threshold,
                                        unsigned Col, unsigned Row,
                                        unsigned Width, unsigned Height);
```

The following is the contents of the file, "ptprocess.c":

```
/****************************************/
/*        Image Processing Code         */
/*        Point Process Functions       */
/*        written in Turbo C 2.0        */
/*                 by                   */
/*          Craig A. Lindley            */
/*                                      */
/*    Vers: 1.0  Last Update: 11/07/89  */
/****************************************/
```

```
#include <stdio.h>
#include <stdlib.h>
#include <conio.h>
#include <dos.h>
#include <alloc.h>
#include <process.h>
#include <graphics.h>
#include "misc.h"
#include "pcx.h"
#include "vga.h"
#include "imagesup.h"

/* Histogram storage location */
unsigned Histogram[MAXQUANTLEVELS];

/*
Look Up Table (LUT) Functions

Initialize the Look Up Table (LUT) for straight through
mapping. If a point transform is performed on an initialized
LUT, output data will equal input data. This function is
usually called in preparation for modification to a LUT.
*/
void InitializeLUT(BYTE *LookUpTable)
{
  register unsigned Index;

  for (Index = 0; Index < MAXQUANTLEVELS; Index++)
    LookUpTable[Index] = Index;
}


/*
This function performs a point transform on the portion of the
image specified by Col, Row, Width and Height. The actual
transform is contained in the Look Up Table who address
is passed as a parameter.
*/
void PtTransform(BYTE huge *ImageData, unsigned Col, unsigned Row,
                          unsigned Width, unsigned Height, BYTE *LookUpTable)
{
  register unsigned ImageCol, ImageRow;
  register unsigned ColExtent, RowExtent;
```

(continued)

Listing 9.1   *(continued)*

```
   ColExtent = Col+Width;
   RowExtent = Row+Height;

   if (ParameterCheckOK(Col,Row,ColExtent,RowExtent,"PtTransform"))
      for (ImageRow=Row; ImageRow < RowExtent; ImageRow++)
            for (ImageCol=Col; ImageCol < ColExtent; ImageCol++)
               PutPixelInImage(ImageData,ImageCol,ImageRow,
                     LookUpTable[GetPixelFromImage(ImageData,ImageCol,ImageRow)]);
}


/* start of histogram functions

This function calculates the histogram of any portion of an image.
*/
void GenHistogram(BYTE huge *ImageData, unsigned Col, unsigned Row,
                              unsigned Width, unsigned Height)
{
   register unsigned ImageRow, ImageCol, RowExtent, ColExtent;
   register unsigned Index;

   /* clear the histogram array */
   for (Index=0; Index < MAXQUANTLEVELS; Index++)
      Histogram[Index] = 0;

   RowExtent = Row+Height;
   ColExtent = Col+Width;

   if (ParameterCheckOK(Col,Row,ColExtent,RowExtent,"GenHistogram"))
   {
      /* calculate the histogram */
      for (ImageRow = Row; ImageRow < RowExtent; ImageRow++)
            for (ImageCol = Col; ImageCol < ColExtent; ImageCol++)
               Histogram[GetPixelFromImage(ImageData,ImageCol,ImageRow)] += 1;
   }
}


/*
This function calculates and displays the histogram of an image
or partial image. When called it assumes the VGA is already
in mode 13 hex.
*/
void DisplayHist(BYTE huge *ImageData, unsigned Col, unsigned Row,
                           unsigned Width, unsigned Height)
```

```
{
   BYTE huge *Buffer;
   register unsigned Index, LineLength, XPos, YPos;
   unsigned MaxRepeat;

   /* Allocate enough memory to save image under histogram */
   Buffer = (BYTE huge *) farcalloc((long)HISTOWIDTH*HISTOHEIGHT,sizeof(BYTE));
   if (Buffer == NULL)
   {
      printf("No buffer memory\n");
      exit(ENoMemory);
   }
   /* Save a copy of the image */
   ReadImageAreaToBuf(ImageData,HISTOCOL,HISTOROW,HISTOWIDTH,HISTOHEIGHT,
                              Buffer);
   /*
   Set VGA color register 65 to red, 66 to green and 67 to
   blue so the histogram can be visually separated from
   the continuous tone image.
   */

   SetAColorReg(65,63,0,0);
   SetAColorReg(66,0,63,0);
   SetAColorReg(67,0,0,63);

   /* Calculate the histogram for the image */
   GenHistogram(ImageData, Col, Row, Width, Height);

   MaxRepeat = 0;

   /*
   Find the pixel value repeated the most. It will be used for
   scaling.
   */
   for (Index=0; Index < MAXQUANTLEVELS; Index++)
     MaxRepeat = (Histogram[Index] > MaxRepeat) ?
                  Histogram[Index]:MaxRepeat;


   /* Fill background area of histogram graph */
   ClearImageArea(ImageData,HISTOCOL,HISTOROW,HISTOWIDTH,HISTOHEIGHT,67);

   /* Draw the bounding box for the histogram */
   DrawVLine(ImageData,HISTOCOL,HISTOROW,HISTOHEIGHT-1,BLACK);
```

(continued)

Listing 9.1   *(continued)*

```
    DrawVLine(ImageData,HISTOCOL+HISTOWIDTH-1,HISTOROW,HISTOHEIGHT-1,BLACK);
    DrawHLine(ImageData,HISTOCOL,HISTOROW+HISTOHEIGHT-1,HISTOWIDTH-1,BLACK);
    DrawHLine(ImageData,HISTOCOL,HISTOROW,HISTOWIDTH-1,BLACK);

    /* Data base line */
    DrawHLine(ImageData,AXISCOL,AXISROW,AXISLENGTH,WHITE);
    DrawHLine(ImageData,AXISCOL,AXISROW+1,AXISLENGTH,WHITE);
    /*
    Now do the actual histogram rendering into the
    image buffer.
    */
    for (Index=0; Index < MAXQUANTLEVELS; Index++)
    {
        LineLength = (unsigned)(((long) Histogram[Index] * MAXDEFLECTION) /
                                                 (long) MaxRepeat);
        XPos = DATACOL + Index*2;
        YPos = DATAROW - LineLength;
        DrawVLine(ImageData,XPos,YPos,LineLength,66);
    }


    /*
    Display the image overlayed with the histogram
    */
    DisplayImageInBuf(ImageData,NOVGAINIT,WAITFORKEY);

    /* After display, restore image data under histogram */
    WriteImageAreaFromBuf(Buffer,HISTOWIDTH,HISTOHEIGHT,ImageData,
                                     HISTOCOL,HISTOROW);
    farfree((BYTE far *)Buffer);
}



/* Various Point Transformation Functions */

void AdjImageBrightness(BYTE huge *ImageData, short BrightnessFactor,
                                     unsigned Col, unsigned Row,
                                     unsigned Width, unsigned Height)
{
    register unsigned Index;
    register short NewLevel;
    BYTE      LookUpTable[MAXQUANTLEVELS];

    for (Index = MINSAMPLEVAL; Index < MAXQUANTLEVELS; Index++)
```

```
    {
      NewLevel = Index + BrightnessFactor;
      NewLevel = (NewLevel < MINSAMPLEVAL) ? MINSAMPLEVAL:NewLevel;
      NewLevel = (NewLevel > MAXSAMPLEVAL) ? MAXSAMPLEVAL:NewLevel;
      LookUpTable[Index] = NewLevel;
    }
    PtTransform(ImageData,Col,Row,Width,Height,LookUpTable);
}


/*
This function will negate an image pixel by pixel. Threshold is
the value of image data where the negation begins. If
threshold is 0, all pixel values are negated. That is, pixel value 0
becomes 63 and pixel value 63 becomes 0. If threshold is greater
than 0, the pixel values in the range 0..Threshold-1 are left
alone while pixel values between Threshold..63 are negated.
*/
void NegateImage(BYTE huge *ImageData, unsigned Threshold,
                 unsigned Col, unsigned Row,
                           unsigned Width, unsigned Height)
{
    register unsigned Index;
    BYTE     LookUpTable[MAXQUANTLEVELS];

    /* Straight through mapping initially */
    InitializeLUT(LookUpTable);

    /* from Threshold onward, negate entry in LUT */
    for (Index = Threshold; Index < MAXQUANTLEVELS; Index++)
            LookUpTable[Index] = MAXSAMPLEVAL - Index;

    PtTransform(ImageData,Col,Row,Width,Height,LookUpTable);
}


/*
This function converts a gray scale image to a binary image with each
pixel either on (WHITE) or off (BLACK). The pixel level at
which the cut off is made is controlled by Threshold. Pixels
in the range 0..Threshold-1 become black while pixel values
between Threshold..63 become white.
*/
void ThresholdImage(BYTE huge *ImageData, unsigned Threshold,
                    unsigned Col, unsigned Row,
                              unsigned Width, unsigned Height)
```

(continued)

Listing 9.1 *(continued)*

```
{
    register unsigned Index;
    BYTE      LookUpTable[MAXQUANTLEVELS];

    for (Index = MINSAMPLEVAL; Index < Threshold; Index++)
            LookUpTable[Index] = BLACK;

    for (Index = Threshold; Index < MAXQUANTLEVELS; Index++)
            LookUpTable[Index] = WHITE;

    PtTransform(ImageData,Col,Row,Width,Height,LookUpTable);
}


void StretchImageContrast(BYTE huge *ImageData, unsigned *HistoData,
                                       unsigned Threshold,
                          unsigned Col, unsigned Row,
                                       unsigned Width, unsigned Height)
{
    register unsigned Index, NewMin, NewMax;
    double    StepSiz, StepVal;
    BYTE      LookUpTable[MAXQUANTLEVELS];
    /*
    Search from the low bin towards the high bin for the first one that
    exceeds the threshold
    */

    for (Index=0; Index < MAXQUANTLEVELS; Index++)
       if (HistoData[Index] > Threshold)
          break;

    NewMin = Index;

    /*
    Search from the high bin towards the low bin for the first one that
    exceeds the threshold
    */

    for (Index=MAXSAMPLEVAL; Index > NewMin; Index--)
       if (HistoData[Index] > Threshold)
          break;

    NewMax = Index;
```

```
    StepSiz = (double)MAXQUANTLEVELS/(double)(NewMax-NewMin+1);
    StepVal = 0.0;

    /* values below new minimum are assigned zero in the LUT */
    for (Index=0; Index < NewMin; Index++)
       LookUpTable[Index] = MINSAMPLEVAL;

    /* values above new maximum are assigned the max sample value */
    for (Index=NewMax+1; Index < MAXQUANTLEVELS; Index++)
       LookUpTable[Index] = MAXSAMPLEVAL;

    /* values between the new minimum and new maximum are stretched */
    for (Index=NewMin; Index <= NewMax; Index++)
    {
       LookUpTable[Index] = StepVal;
       StepVal += StepSiz;
    }
    /*
    Look Up Table is now prepared to point transform the image data.
    */
    PtTransform(ImageData,Col,Row,Width,Height,LookUpTable);
}
```

Listing 9.2   The Point Process Example Program

```
The following is the contents of the file, "pttest.prj":

graphics.lib
vgagraph.obj
egavga.obj
pcx        (misc.h pcx.h)
vga        (misc.h vga.h pcx.h)
imagesup   (misc.h vga.h pcx.h imagesup.h)
ptprocess  (misc.h vga.h pcx.h imagesup.h ptprocess.h)
pttest     (misc.h vga.h pcx.h imagesup.h ptprocess.h)


The following is the contents of the file, "pttest.c":
```

(continued)

Listing 9.2 *(continued)*

```
/***************************************/
/*        Image Processing Code        */
/*        Point Process Functions      */
/*        written in Turbo C 2.0       */
/*                 by                  */
/*          Craig A. Lindley           */
/*                                     */
/*   Vers: 1.0  Last Update: 12/26/89  */
/***************************************/

#include <stdio.h>
#include <alloc.h>
#include <process.h>
#include <graphics.h>
#include "misc.h"
#include "pcx.h"
#include "vga.h"
#include "imagesup.h"
#include "ptprocess.h"

/* main point process program */

void main(void)
{
   char *InFileName1  = "p2ch9i1a";
   char *InFileName2  = "p2ch9i2a";
   char *InFileName3  = "p2ch9i3a";
   char *InFileName4a = "p2ch9i4a";
   char *InFileName4b = "p2ch9i4c";
   char *InFileName4c = "p2ch9i4e";
   char *InFileName5  = "p2ch9i5a";
   char *InFileName6  = "p2ch9i6a";

   BYTE huge *TheImage;
   unsigned GenPCXFiles = FALSE;  /* controls generation of output files */
   BYTE PseudoColorLUT[MAXQUANTLEVELS];
   InitGraphics();

   printf("Point Transform Example Program\n\n");
   printf("Reading the Image PCX File into memory\n");

   /* generate image sequence 9.1 - Image brightening */
   /* load the PCX file into memory */
```

```
if (ReadPCXFileToBuf (InFileName1,&TheImage) != NoError)
   exit(1);


/* display the image pointed at by TheImage */
DisplayImageInBuf(TheImage,INITVGALOADPALETTE,WAITFORKEY);
DisplayHist(TheImage,MINCOLNUM,MINROWNUM,130,MAXROWS);
if (GenPCXFiles)
   WritePCXFile("p2ch9i1b",8,320,200,1,320);
AdjImageBrightness(TheImage,+17,MINCOLNUM,MINROWNUM,130,MAXROWS);
DisplayImageInBuf(TheImage,NOVGAINIT,WAITFORKEY);
if (GenPCXFiles)
   WritePCXFile("p2ch9i1c",8,320,200,1,320);
DisplayHist(TheImage,MINCOLNUM,MINROWNUM,130,MAXROWS);
if (GenPCXFiles)
   WritePCXFile("p2ch9i1d",8,320,200,1,320);


farfree((BYTE far *)TheImage);



/* generate image sequence 9.2 - Image negation */
/* load the PCX file into memory */
if (ReadPCXFileToBuf (InFileName2,&TheImage) != NoError)
   exit(1);


/* display the image pointed at by TheImage */
DisplayImageInBuf(TheImage,NOVGAINIT,WAITFORKEY);
NegateImage(TheImage,0,MINCOLNUM,MINROWNUM,MAXCOLS,MAXROWS);
DisplayImageInBuf(TheImage,NOVGAINIT,WAITFORKEY);
if (GenPCXFiles)
   WritePCXFile("p2ch9i2b",8,320,200,1,320);


farfree((BYTE far *)TheImage);

/* reload the PCX file into memory */
if (ReadPCXFileToBuf (InFileName2,&TheImage) != NoError)
   exit(1);

/* display the image pointed at by TheImage */
DisplayImageInBuf(TheImage,NOVGAINIT,WAITFORKEY);
NegateImage(TheImage,50,MINCOLNUM,MINROWNUM,MAXCOLS,MAXROWS);
DisplayImageInBuf(TheImage,NOVGAINIT,WAITFORKEY);
if (GenPCXFiles)
   WritePCXFile("p2ch9i2c",8,320,200,1,320);
```

(continued)

Listing 9.2   *(continued)*

```
farfree((BYTE far *)TheImage);

/* generate image sequence 9.3 - Image thresholding */
/* load the PCX file into memory */
if (ReadPCXFileToBuf (InFileName3,&TheImage) != NoError)
   exit(1);
/* display the image pointed at by TheImage */
DisplayImageInBuf(TheImage,NOVGAINIT,WAITFORKEY);
ThresholdImage(TheImage,35,110,50,105,105);
DisplayImageInBuf(TheImage,NOVGAINIT,WAITFORKEY);
if (GenPCXFiles)
   WritePCXFile("p2ch9i3b",8,320,200,1,320);

farfree((BYTE far *)TheImage);

/* generate image sequence 9.4 - A Study of Contrasts */
/* load the PCX file into memory */
if (ReadPCXFileToBuf (InFileName4a,&TheImage) != NoError)
   exit(1);

/* display the image pointed at by TheImage */
DisplayImageInBuf(TheImage,NOVGAINIT,WAITFORKEY);
DisplayHist(TheImage,MINCOLNUM,MINROWNUM,MAXCOLS,MAXROWS);
if (GenPCXFiles)
   WritePCXFile("p2ch9i4b",8,320,200,1,320);

farfree((BYTE far *)TheImage);

/* load the PCX file into memory */
if (ReadPCXFileToBuf (InFileName4b,&TheImage) != NoError)
   exit(1);

/* display the image pointed at by TheImage */
DisplayImageInBuf(TheImage,NOVGAINIT,WAITFORKEY);
DisplayHist(TheImage,MINCOLNUM,MINROWNUM,MAXCOLS,MAXROWS);
if (GenPCXFiles)
   WritePCXFile("p2ch9i4d",8,320,200,1,320);

farfree((BYTE far *)TheImage);

/* load the PCX file into memory */
if (ReadPCXFileToBuf (InFileName4c,&TheImage) != NoError)
   exit(1);
```

```
/* display the image pointed at by TheImage */
DisplayImageInBuf(TheImage,NOVGAINIT,WAITFORKEY);
DisplayHist(TheImage,MINCOLNUM,MINROWNUM,MAXCOLS,MAXROWS);
if (GenPCXFiles)
   WritePCXFile("p2ch9i4f",8,320,200,1,320);


farfree((BYTE far *)TheImage);

/* generate image sequence 9.5 - Contrast Stretching */
/* load the PCX file into memory */
if (ReadPCXFileToBuf (InFileName5,&TheImage) != NoError)
   exit(1);


/* display the image pointed at by TheImage */
DisplayImageInBuf(TheImage,NOVGAINIT,WAITFORKEY);
DisplayHist(TheImage,MINCOLNUM,MINROWNUM,MAXCOLS,MAXROWS);
if (GenPCXFiles)
   WritePCXFile("p2ch9i5b",8,320,200,1,320);
StretchImageContrast(TheImage,Histogram,475,MINCOLNUM,MINROWNUM,MAXCOLS,MAXROWS);
DisplayImageInBuf(TheImage,NOVGAINIT,WAITFORKEY);
if (GenPCXFiles)
   WritePCXFile("p2ch9i5c",8,320,200,1,320);
DisplayHist(TheImage,MINCOLNUM,MINROWNUM,MAXCOLS,MAXROWS);
if (GenPCXFiles)
   WritePCXFile("p2ch9i5d",8,320,200,1,320);
farfree((BYTE far *)TheImage);

/* generate image sequence 9.6 - Pseudo Coloring */
/* load the PCX file into memory */
if (ReadPCXFileToBuf (InFileName6,&TheImage) != NoError)
   exit(1);

/* display the image pointed at by TheImage */
DisplayImageInBuf(TheImage,NOVGAINIT,WAITFORKEY);

/* Set color reg 64 to red, 65 to green and 66 to blue */
SetAColorReg(64,63,0,0);
SetAColorReg(65,0,63,0);
SetAColorReg(66,0,0,63);

/*
Calling InitializeLUT establishes straight through
mapping for the LUT. Only the values that need to
be changed from their default will be changed.
```

(continued)

Listing 9.2 *(continued)*

```
*/
InitializeLUT(PseudoColorLUT);
/*
Assign color register 64 to pixel values
60 - 63
*/
PseudoColorLUT[63] = 64;
PseudoColorLUT[62] = 64;
PseudoColorLUT[61] = 64;
PseudoColorLUT[60] = 64;
/*
Assign color register 65 to pixel values
56 - 59
*/
PseudoColorLUT[59] = 65;
PseudoColorLUT[58] = 65;
PseudoColorLUT[57] = 65;
PseudoColorLUT[56] = 65;
/*
Assign color register 66 to pixel values
52 - 55
*/
PseudoColorLUT[55] = 66;
PseudoColorLUT[54] = 66;
PseudoColorLUT[53] = 66;
PseudoColorLUT[52] = 66;
/*
At this point the LUT is initialized
completely. Next, apply the transform to
the image data.
*/
PtTransform(TheImage,MINCOLNUM,MINROWNUM,MAXCOLS,MAXROWS,PseudoColorLUT);

/* display the pseudo colored image */
DisplayImageInBuf(TheImage,NOVGAINIT,WAITFORKEY);
if (GenPCXFiles)
   WritePCXFile("p2ch9i6b",8,320,200,1,320);
farfree((BYTE far *)TheImage);

restorecrtmode();
closegraph();
}
```

Histograms

A histogram is a graph of the distribution of pixel-intensity values for an image or portion of an image. Histograms can indicate a lot about the overall brightness and contrast of an image. The dynamic range of the pixel values that make up an image is readily apparent. As such, histograms are valuable tools for image processing work both qualitatively and quantitatively.

A typical histogram is a two-dimensional plot of the number of occurrences of a pixel value versus pixel values. Figure 9.1 shows a typical histogram plot. This is the format of the histograms that will be used throughout this book. Although the histogram shown in the figure was fabricated for purposes of discussion, it shows the kind of information that can be conveyed about an image. For example, it shows that the whole range of possible pixel values

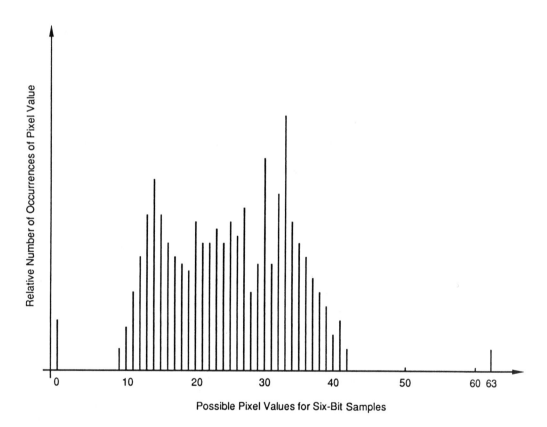

Notes
1. The vertical axis is scaled to fit the tallest vertical bar (pixel value = 33). All other vertical bars are relative to the tallest vertical bar.
2. The summation of pixel intensity values • occurrences = 64,000 for 320 × 200 resolution image.
3. This histogram was fabricated. It does not represent a real image.

Figure 9.1   Pixel-Intensity Histogram

1. Histogram data structure

   Prototype
   unsigned Histogram[MAXQUANTLEVELS];

   ## Operation
   This data structure is used to keep a count of the number of occurrences of each possible pixel value. In our case (continuous-tone gray-scale images), there are 64 possible pixel values that range from 0 to 63. An unsigned integer array is used to keep track of the count because it allows the count value to be as large as 65,535. The array type needs to be long if histograms are to be performed on images with resolutions of greater than 320 × 200. As it is, if a histogram is performed on a completely black 320 × 200 image (all pixel values are equal to 0), the 0 count bin (entry in the histogram array) would have a value of 64,000. All other bins in the histogram would, of course, have a value of 0.

2. Generate the histogram data.

   Prototype
   void GenHistogram(BYTE huge *ImageData, unsigned Col, unsigned Row, unsigned Width, unsigned Height);

   ## Operation
   This function first clears each entry or bin in the histogram array. This is necessary so that all pixel value counts start with an initial count of 0. Next, this function traverses through the portion of the image pointed to by "ImageData" and specified by the parameters "Col", "Row", "Width", and "Height". Each pixel value is examined during this traversal, and its value is used as an index into the histogram array for the count that needs to be incremented. This function returns when each pixel of the specified image area has been tabulated.

   This function is separately callable because certain point process operations require histogram data but do not require the display of a histogram. The function described next should be called directly when the generation and display of a histogram are required. (*Note:* this function modifies the global "Histogram" array during the course of its operation.)

3. Generate and display a histogram.

   Prototype
   void DisplayHist(BYTE huge *ImageData,unsigned Col,unsigned Row, unsigned Width, unsigned Height);

   ## Operation
   This function calculates and displays a histogram for the image or portion of the image specified by its parameters. This function uses almost all of the image processing support functions described previously and provides a good example of how the support functions can be used.

   The histogram plot is scaled to fit into a fixed image area. The bounds of this area are controlled by the defines in the file "imagesup.h". The histogram plot is overlaid onto the image buffer, over whatever portion of the image was there. For this reason, the image area under the histogram is saved out to another buffer while the histogram is being displayed and is subsequently restored to the image buffer when the histogram display is terminated. That way the image content remains intact. The code contained in this function, which is used to display the histogram, could be modified to display the histogram directly to the VGA screen instead of to the image buffer. Implementation of this change is left to the reader.

   This function also modifies the global "Histogram" array during the course of its operation.

Figure 9.2 Histogram Functions

are not being fully utilized. Pixel values between 42 to 62 are nonexistent. If this were a histogram of a real image, the appearance of that real image might be improved by a point process called *contrast stretching*. This would transform the image so that it would occupy the complete range of pixel values. This usually results in a more pleasing displayed image.

Histograms fall outside of the four image processing algorithm categories described in the introduction to this part of the book. Histograms are placed in this chapter because they are a very useful tool for applying and monitoring the results of point processes. The code that generates and displays histograms is included in the point process code file "ptprocess.c" on the companion disk.

Two functions and a data structure are used to provide histogram support for our image processing library. They are described in Figure 9.2. Many histogram plots can be seen throughout this section of the book. They all look a lot like Figure 9.1.

Look-Up Tables

Look-up tables (LUTs) are a convenient implementation method for point processing algorithms—so convenient, in fact, that many manufacturers of image-acquisition equipment provide LUTs in hardware for use with image processing software. Providing LUTs in hardware maximizes the speed of the image processing algorithms. We do not have hardware LUTs to toy with but we can emulate them using arrays in software. The idea is the same. The performance penalty we pay for software emulation of LUTs depends upon the speed of array operations provided by the compiler being used. Fortunately, array operations are fast with most MSDOS-based C compilers.

A software LUT uses an input pixel's value as an index into an array in order to return a new value to be used in place of the original pixel's value. The array will, of course, have been filled previously with values that represent the transformation to be performed on the image data run through the LUT. In hardware, separate RAM locations for each possible pixel value would be utilized for the LUT. An input pixel's value would be used as an address into the RAM, causing the RAM content to be returned. The RAM would also be filled with the transforming data.

For our applications, we will declare a LUT as follows:

```
BYTE LookUpTable[MAXQUANTLEVELS];
```

As stated, the array has a byte location for each possible pixel value. Using the pixel's value as an index, the output value is the value stored at that index in the LUT.

All LUTs must be initialized before being used to perform a point transform. Otherwise, the data coming out of the LUT will not have a definite relationship to the data going in. The simplest initialization that can be performed to a LUT, which will be used as an example, is storing the value of its index into each LUT location. That is, location 0 is loaded with 0, location 1 with 1, up to location 63, which is loaded with 63. This type of initialization is performed by the LUT support function "InitializeLUT". See Figure 9.3 for details.

LUT Location   LUT Content

LUT Location	LUT Content
0	0
1	1
2	2
3	3
4	4
5	5
6	6
7	7
8	8
55	55
56	56
57	57
58	58
59	59
60	60
61	61
62	62
63	63

Byte Wide

When a pixel's value is used as an index into an initialized LUT, the value fetched from the array is the same value as the index.

if PixelValue = 56 then
LUT[PixelValue] = 56.

Figure 9.3   LUT Initialization

With the LUT initialized in this manner data coming out of the LUT is the same as the data going in. In other words, the transformation applied to the data is linear, or one to one. Another LUT function, "PtTransform", actually applies the transformation contained in a LUT to an image or portion of an image specified. If "PtTransform" were used to transform an image using the LUT just initialized, the result would be exactly nil, nothing, zip. The image would not be changed. This is because what went in came out exactly the same. Of course, LUTs are not usually used to perform nil transforms. Instead, a LUT would be initialized with a transfer function to be applied to the image data. The various transforms and transfer functions are the topic of the discussion to follow.

Image Brightening

Sometimes the appearance of an image can be visually enhanced by adjusting its brightness. Brightening is a point process that adds (or subtracts) a constant value to (or

1. Initialize a look-up table (LUT) array.

Prototype
void InitializeLUT(BYTE *LookUpTable);

Operation
This function initializes a look-up table for straight-through mapping of input data to output data. That is, the value stored in a location in the look-up table is the index of that location. (See Figure 9.3 for details.)

2. Perform a point transform on an image using a look-up table.

Prototype
void PtTransform(BYTE huge *ImageData, unsigned Col, unsigned Row, unsigned Width, unsigned Height, BYTE *LookUpTable);

Operation
This function applies the transform previously programmed into "LookUpTable" to the image or portion of image pointed to by "ImageData" and specified by "Col", "Row", "Width", and "Height". This function is utilized in all of the point process algorithms described in this chapter.

3. Calculate a histogram for an image.

Prototype
void GenHistogram(BYTE huge *ImageData, unsigned Col, unsigned Row, unsigned Width, unsigned Height);

Operation
This function traverses through an image or portion of an image pointed to by "ImageData" and specified by "Col", "Row", "Width", and "Height" and counts the occurrences of each pixel value. Upon completion the global array "Histogram" contains the frequency distribution histogram data.

4. Calculate and display a histogram for an image.

Prototype
void DisplayHist(BYTE huge *ImageData, unsigned Col, unsigned Row, unsigned Width, unsigned Height);

Operation
This function is similiar to "GenHistogram" except the resultant histogram data is plotted in the "ImageData" buffer. This function assumes the VGA display is in mode 13 hex before it is called. See the code in Listing 9.2 and the text for additional details.

5. Adjust the brightness of an image.

Prototype
void AdjImageBrightness(BYTE huge *ImageData, short BrightnessFactor, unsigned Col, unsigned Row, unsigned Width, unsigned Height);

Figure 9.4   Point Process Function Library   *(continued)*

Operation

This function traverses through an image or portion of an image pointed to by "ImageData" and specified by "Col", "Row", "Width", and "Height" and adds "BrightnessFactor" to each pixel it encounters. "BrightnessFactor" can be positive or negative. Positive values lighten the image whereas negative values darken it.

6. Negate an image.

Prototype

void NegateImage(BYTE huge *ImageData, unsigned Threshold, unsigned Col, unsigned Row, unsigned Width, unsigned Height);

Operation

This function traverses through an image or portion of an image pointed to by "ImageData" and specified by "Col", "Row", "Width", and "Height" and negates any pixel value above the specified threshold. To negate a pixel means to subtract its value from the maximum sample value of "MAXSAMPLEVAL" (63). The application of this algorithm creates images that resemble a photograph negative, hence the name.

7. Threshold an image.

Prototype

void ThresholdImage(BYTE huge *ImageData, unsigned Threshold, unsigned Col, unsigned Row, unsigned Width, unsigned Height);

Operation

This function traverses through an image or portion of an image pointed to by "ImageData" and specified by "Col", "Row", "Width", and "Height" and sets to black any pixel with a value between 0 and "Threshold − 1" and sets to white all pixels with values greater than or equal to the "Threshold". The net effect of the application of this algorithm is to convert a continuous-tone gray-scale image into a black and white image. This thresholding point process algorithm has many uses (see text).

8. Stretch an image's contrast.

Prototype

void StretchImageContrast(BYTE huge *ImageData, unsigned *HistoData, unsigned Threshold, unsigned Col, unsigned Row, unsigned Width, unsigned Height);

Operation

Using the histogram data (previously generated from "ImageData") contained in array "HistoData", this function attempts to stretch the contrast of the image pointed to by "ImageData" and specified by "Col", "Row", "Width", and "Height". The algorithm used to perform the contrast stretching is discussed in detail in the text. Threshold is the search parameter used to locate the portion of the histogram to be stretched.

Figure 9.4 *(continued)*

from) pixels in an image. Expressed algebraically, a pixel with intensity value V is transformed as follows:

$$V = V + b$$

where b is the brightness constant, which can be positive or negative. If b is positive, the brightness of the pixels increases. If b is negative, the brightness decreases. Image Sequence 9.1 shows the effect of brightening the left portion of an image by a constant factor of $+17$. The histograms of the original image and the brightened image are also shown in this image sequence.

Notice how the histogram for the brightened image shown in Image 9.1(d) is related to that shown in (b). The effect of brightening the image by a constant factor of 17 causes the histogram to slide to the right toward higher pixel values. The distance of the slide is equal to the brightness factor used to brighten the image—in this case 17. You can now understand why adjusting image brightness is also called histogram sliding in some image processing textbooks.

Applying a brightness correction to an image can be as easy as applying the formula shown directly to each affected pixel. A more elegant way to implement the brightness correction is to use a LUT and the "PtTransform" function discussed earlier. The brightness transformation is computed and stored in the LUT, and then "PtTransform" is called upon to alter the image data. A function in the point processing code (Listing 9.1), "AdjImage-Brightness", uses just this tack in its operation. One complication that must be taken into consideration is pixel-value overflow or underflow. If, for example, a positive brightness correction factor is added to a pixel's value and the result exceeds the maximum value of 63 ("MAXSAMPLEVAL") the overflow condition has just been experienced. Further, if a negative brightness factor is added to a small pixel value, the result may in fact become negative. This is pixel-value underflow. For these reasons, code is in place in the "AdjImage-Brightness" function to clamp values placed in the LUT to the range 0 to 63. If a LUT entry after brightness correction would exceed the maximum value of 63, it is set equal to 63. If a LUT entry would be negative, it is set equal to 0. Setting up the LUT in this manner guarantees that all pixels transformed with this LUT will be within legal limits.

You might be telling yourself at this point that using a LUT for such a simple transform is overkill. You would probably be correct. In terms of performance, it is obviously much faster to fetch a byte of data directly from an image, add the brightness factor to it, and store it back than it is to initialize the LUT array with the transfer function and then pass each pixel value through it. The elegance of LUT-based transforms become obvious only with more complex transfer functions. Performance of LUT-based transforms can be increased substantially by precomputing the LUTs and storing them in memory until required. The performance of the precomputed LUT transform when later applied to an image will be constant regardless of the complexity of the transfer function. This is because all the time-consuming math went into initializing the LUT. Application of the LUT is thus a direct array lookup.

Another advantage of using LUTs for point process transforms is the consistent structure of the resultant algorithms. Examine the functions "NegateImage", "Thresh-

Image Sequence 9.1   Brightening-Point Process

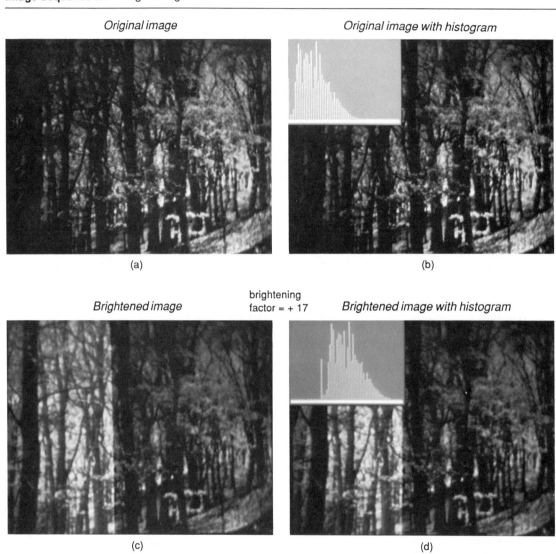

Original image

(a)

Original image with histogram

(b)

Brightened image

brightening
factor = + 17

Brightened image with histogram

(c)

(d)

oldImage'', and ''StretchImageContrast'' in addition to ''AdjImageBrightness''. Do you see
how similar they are? Once you understand how LUTs operate and have coded an algorithm,
you'll never want to go back to the other, brute force techniques.

Negative Images

Negative images, resembling photographic negatives, are easy to produce with a point
process. The idea is to make the portion of an image that was once light, dark and what was

once dark, light. Of course it's all a matter of degree. If an area of an image was just a little dark, it is transformed into an area that is just a little light, and so on. Image negation is accomplished by subtracting the value of a pixel from the maximum possible pixel value of 63. The darkest areas of an image, which had pixel values of 0 (or black), are then transformed into the brightest white pixel value of 63. Conversely, the brightest white pixels are converted to black.

This transfer function, performed by the function "NegateImage", also utilizes a LUT for its operation. To make this function a little more versatile, a threshold value is required that indicates to the code at what pixel value image negation should begin. If the threshold is 0, all pixel values are negated as just described. If the threshold is nonnegative, it indicates at which pixel value the negation will begin. This can be useful, for example, to remove the brighter aspects of an image (converting them to the darker aspects) so that other detail in an image can become apparent.

Negation of a full image is useful when looking for detail in bright portions of an image. The human eye is much more capable of discerning detail in a dark area of an image than in a light area. Image Sequence 9.2 shows the effect of image negation. Image (a) is the original image before alteration. Image (b) is a full negative image. Image (c) shows the effect of negating only the brighter pixel values. The threshold for this image is set at 50.

Thresholding Images

Image thresholding is a technique for converting a continuous-tone image into a black and white image. Pixel values below a specified threshold are all converted to black, whereas pixel values at or above the threshold are converted to white. This technique has applications ranging from art to machine vision. For artistic application, continuous-tone images that are correctly thresholded produce what is referred to as *line art*. Line art can then be used effectively in desktop publishing applications and in sign and banner production. Thresholding is also used as a crude method of obtaining hardcopy printout of continuous-tone images on a dot matrix printer. (See Chapter 7 for details.)

In the field of machine vision, images are typically thresholded before an attempt is made at edge detection. In this case, thresholding eliminates from an image extraneous information that might upset the edge-detection process. It is very important to select the threshold value correctly, however, to ensure that not too much information is lost during the thresholding process.

As seen in Listing 9.1, the function "ThresholdImage" also uses a LUT for its operation. Are you really surprised? In this function, the entries in the LUT that are less than the threshold are loaded with the value of 0 or black. LUT entries greater than or equal to the threshold are set to white, or 63. The "PtTransform" function is again used to apply the initialized LUT to the image data.

As with all the point processing functions discussed in this section, thresholding can be applied to all or just a portion of the specified image. The area of an image affected by the thresholding transformation is specified by "Col", "Row", "Width", and "Height". Unusual special effects can be produced by thresholding only a portion of an image. In effect, a portion of a continuous-tone image can be made into black and white. Other special effects

Image Sequence 9.2   Image Negation

Original image

(a)

Full image negation

(b)

*Partial image negation
threshold = 50*

(c)

Image Sequence 9.3   Image Thresholding Production of Line Art

Original continuous-time image   *Thresholded image*

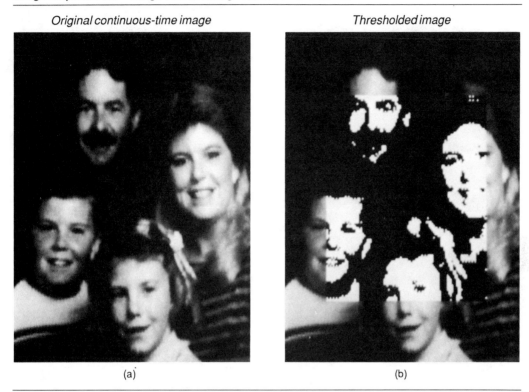

(a)   (b)

can be generated by changing the black and white thresholded image colors to orange and purple, for example. It's totally up to you.

The production of line art from a continuous-tone image is shown in Image Sequence 9.3.

Contrast Stretching

We all have an intuitive feeling for the concept of contrast. It is the distribution of lightness and darkness in an image. Images of low contrast are characterized as being either mostly all light or mostly all dark in composition. High-contrast images, on the other hand, have regions of darkness along with regions of light. In other words, high-contrast images seem to utilize the full range of gray tones available in a continuous-tone image.

Histograms are an ideal tool for examining the contrast of an image. In conjunction with a contrast-stretching point process, histograms can in some cases be used to increase the contrast of an image. As the contrast of an image is increased, the apparent detail of the image also increases. This, however, is a human eye/brain phenomenon. The amount of image detail is not really changed.

Images can be grouped, somewhat subjectively, into one of three contrast categories: low-contrast images, good-contrast images, and high-contrast images. As mentioned earlier,

Image   *Image with histogram*

Low-contrast
image

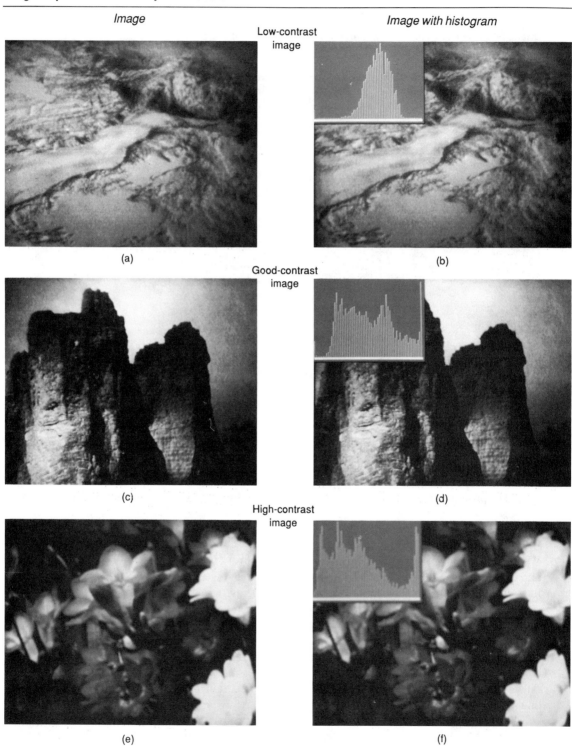

(a)   (b)

Good-contrast
image

(c)   (d)

High-contrast
image

(e)   (f)

we all have an intuitive feeling about image contrast, and if given images to view could probably sort them into these three categories. What are the characteristics of these three contrast categories that allow us to distinguish the images, and what would a histogram of each of these image categories reveal?

We have already stated what qualities low-contrast images share. They are composed of a limited range of tones (shades of gray) and are usually much too light or too dark (somewhat like an over- or underexposed photograph). On a histogram, this condition is detectible when all the image samples are tightly clustered together and occupy only a small portion of the possible pixel sample values. If this grouping of pixel values is toward the left side of the histogram (toward the lower sample values), the image tends to be dark. If the grouping is toward the larger pixel values, the image will be bright. Note that it is possible to have a low-contrast image that is neither too dark nor too light when all of the image samples cluster at the middle of the histogram, with few pixel values used outside this center cluster. Images with low contrast have a small dynamic range because only a few of the possible pixel values (brightness values) are contained in the image. See Image Sequence 9.4 for examples of images that fall into the various contrast categories.

Good-contrast images exhibit a wide range of gray shades without any single shade or range of shades dominating. Images with good contrast are generally the most pleasing to look at. They have a wide dynamic range, with most of the possible pixel values being used. This equates back to a wide range of gray shades in the original image. A histogram of an image with good contrast will show a relatively uniform distribution of pixel values without any major peaks or troughs.

Like good-contrast images, high-contrast images contain a wide range of gray shades. However, high-contrast images have large areas that are dominated by dark coloring and large areas that have bright coloring. A picture with a bright sky and a dark foreground is an example of a high-contrast image. On a histogram, this results in a bimodal plot (i.e., one having two peaks: one in the lower pixel-value area and one in the higher pixel-value area). A high-contrast image might have good utilization of gray shades between the two peaks, but these are visually overwhelmed by dominant dark and light areas.

Images that exhibit low contrast can sometimes be visually enhanced by contrast stretching. Contrast stretching uses a histogram to determine where the cluster of pixel values in the low-contrast image occurs. Typically the cluster will be surrounded on the histogram with pixel values that are never used. To stretch the contrast, we scan the histogram from the lowest pixel value upward (0 toward 63) and from the highest pixel value downward (63 toward 0) to find the first pixel value that exceeds a specified threshold. Pixel values below the lower threshold are set equal to 0. Those above the upper threshold are set to the maximum pixel value of 63. Pixel values between the two thresholds are scaled to fill the complete range of pixels (0 to 63). The result of this process is an image that better utilizes the gray scales, resulting in a more balanced appearance. Image Sequence 9.5 shows the result of a contrast stretched image. If you compare the before (a) and after (b) images the usage of the full gray scale is apparent.

The function "StretchImageContrast" in the point processing image processing library (see Listing 9.1) performs the contrast stretching operation. Note that a histogram must be generated before this algorithm can be applied. This can be done by calling "GenHistogram" directly or by calling "DisplayHist". As might have been expected, a LUT is utilized

Image Sequence 9.5   Contrast Stretching

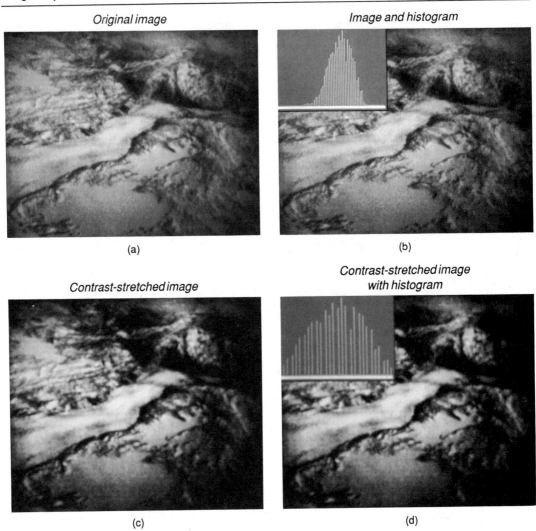

Original image

(a)

Image and histogram

(b)

Contrast-stretched image

(c)

*Contrast-stretched image
with histogram*

(d)

to perform the contrast-stretching transformation. The transfer function is loaded into the LUT, and "PtTransform" is called to actually apply the contrast stretch to an image.

Other types of transformations can be applied to images with good or high contrast. By properly selecting the values in the LUT it is possible to change good-contrast images to high-contrast images and vice versa. Not all transformed images are going to be visually appealing. Some may be visually enhanced, while others will be corrupted. As mentioned previously, the end result is not always attractive. Important unseen information might be extracted from an image with the proper transformations applied.

Pseudocoloring

Pseudocoloring is a technique that replaces a gray pixel value or values with color in an image. This technique is used to identify pixels in a certain range for various purposes. For example, if a picture of a light-bulb filament is taken and it is known that certain values of pixels represent certain temperatures, pseudocoloring might be used to better distinguish the temperatures. The highest temperature might be rendered in red, lower temperatures in shades of green, and the lowest temperatures in blue. The resultant image will contain the same amount of information, but the temperature information will be much easier to comprehend.

Using pseudocoloring in this manner requires detailed information about the images and about the imaging equipment used to acquire the images. Identifying image content is well beyond the scope of this book. Once a correlation is established, however, between pixel values and the informational content of an image, pseudocoloring can be applied with good results.

Because of the highly variable nature of pseudocoloring requirements, no algorithm is given to perform this operation. A few guidelines and an example image are provided to help in the preparation of any algorithm you might require.

The first step in the pseudocoloring process is to select the number of colors and the color values you want to use. Remember, while in VGA mode 13 hex (the mode in which all image processing in this book is performed) a total of 256 colors are available for use. The display of continuous-tone images utilizes only 64 of the 256 colors available. That means up to 192 colors are available for pseudocoloring. As you will recall, each color is controlled by a VGA color register. Again, 192 registers are available for our use (numbers 64 through 255), because the first 64 are already utilized (0 through 63). Say, for example, your pseudocoloring application requires three colors. For these three colors we will utilize color registers 64, 65, and 66. To assign the color we want to these three color registers, we will call a function contained in the VGA function library (and discussed previously in Chapter 1) called "SetAColorReg". This function assigns a red, green, and blue color component to the specified color register. Each color component is six bits in size. This means your pseudocolors can be picked from a range of 256,000 possible colors. Getting back to the example, suppose you require bright red, bright green, and bright blue pseudocolors. The three calls to "SetAColorReg" shown here will make color register 64 bright red, register 65 bright green, and register 66 bright blue.

```
SetAColorReg(64,63,0,0);
SetAColorReg(65,0,63,0);
SetAColorReg(66,0,0,63);
```

See the "DisplayHist" function for an identical example usage.

Once the color registers are assigned, it is then necessary to establish a mapping between pixels of a certain value and the pseudocolors. This is done via a LUT. For purposes of this example, suppose it is necessary to assign pseudocolor red to the pixel values between 60 and 63, green to the range 56 through 59, and blue to the range 52 through 55. All other pixel values should retain their normal value and therefore gray-scale representation. The code fragment that follows will establish the mapping and perform the transformation upon the image data.

```
BYTE PseudoColorLUT[MAXQUANTLEVELS];
/*
Calling InitializeLUT establishes straight through
mapping for the LUT. Only the values that need to
be changed from their default will be changed.
*/
InitializeLUT(PseudoColorLUT);
/*
Assign color register 64 to pixel values
60 - 63
*/
PseudoColorLUT[63] = 64;
PseudoColorLUT[62] = 64;
PseudoColorLUT[61] = 64;
PseudoColorLUT[60] = 64;
/*
Assign color register 65 to pixel values
56 - 59
*/
PseudoColorLUT[59] = 65;
PseudoColorLUT[58] = 65;
PseudoColorLUT[57] = 65;
PseudoColorLUT[56] = 65;
/*
Assign color register 66 to pixel values
52 - 55
*/
PseudoColorLUT[55] = 66;
PseudoColorLUT[54] = 66;
PseudoColorLUT[53] = 66;
PseudoColorLUT[52] = 66;
/*
At this point the whole LUT is initialized
completely. Next, apply the transform to
the image data.
*/
PtTransform(.....);
```

A pseudocolored image of Martian rocks is shown in Image Sequence 9.6.

(a) *Original image*

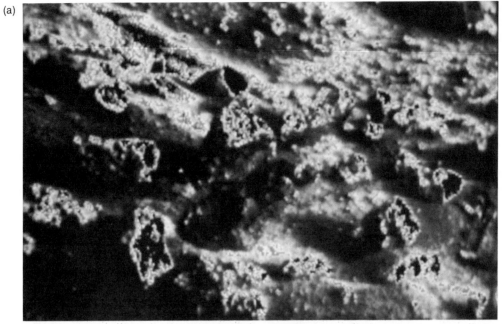

(b) *Pseudocolored image*

Pixel Range	Color
0–51	normal
52–55	blue
56–59	green
60–63	red

Conclusions

This completes our discussion of point processes. Not only were numerous varieties of point processes demonstrated in this chapter, we also saw how valuable a tool a histogram can be for image processing. A look-up table was shown to be an efficient and structured method for applying point processes to image data. The functions provided in the point process function library utilized the look-up-table method exclusively.

With the understanding of point processes provided in this chapter, we can proceed into the discussion of area processes in Chapter 10. We shall find that most real image processing applications utilize multiple transforms to arrive at the desired result. In the chapters to follow, we shall see how the application of point processes in conjunction with other image processing algorithms dramatically increases the investigative and manipulative power we have over images.

10

Area Processes

In this chapter you will learn about:

- What area processes are, how they differ from point processes, and what they can be used for
- Convolution, spatial filtering, and edge detection

Introduction

Area processes, also referred to in some texts as *group processes*, use groups of pixels to derive information about an image. This is different from point processes, which use only a single pixel's information for performing the point process. The group of pixels used in area processes is referred to as the *neighborhood*. The neighborhood is generally a two-dimensional matrix of pixel values with each dimension having an odd number of elements. The pixel of interest (the pixel whose old value is being replaced by its new value as a result of an algorithmic computation) resides at the center of the neighborhood. Having a cluster of pixels in the neighborhood around the pixel of interest furnishes brightness trend information (in two dimensions) that is utilized by most area processes. Another, more proper, term for brightness trend information is *spatial frequency*.

Spatial frequency is defined as the rate of change of pixel brightness or intensity divided by the distance over which the change occurred. Spatial frequency has components in both the horizontal and vertical directions in an image. An image with high spatial-frequency content contains large, closely spaced changes in pixel values. An image of a black and white checkerboard would contain a high spatial-frequency content. The smaller the squares, the higher the frequency content. An image with low spatial frequency contains large areas of constant or slowly changing pixel values. Images of clouds generally have a low spatial-frequency content.

Having access to the spatial-frequency information allows area processes to act as filters for removing or enhancing selective frequency components found in an image. Many area processes thus fall into the general category of spatial filters. Like their cousins in electronic engineering, spatial filters have a firm basis in mathematics. This section gives examples of how spatial filters are used without delving into the mathematics involved. The reader is encouraged to consult any good book on digital signal processing (some are listed in "References and Additional Reading") if the mathematical proofs of these algorithms are of interest or are necessary. It is interesting to note that the complex mathematical underpinnings of the algorithms presented in this section have remarkably intuitive explanations, which will be provided accordingly.

Spatial filtering has many applications in image processing. It can be used, for example, for extraction of image features (edge enhancement and detection), for sharpening an image, for smoothing an image, for blurring an image, and for removal of random noise present in an image. These aspects of spatial filtering will be demonstrated in this section. Images will be used to show the effect of various area processes in action.

In this section, three area process algorithms are provided: *convolution*, *median filtering*, and *Sobel edge detection*. The median filter algorithm has a single specific use, whereas the convolution algorithm, being more general in nature, has many uses. The operation of each of these algorithms is similar to that utilized for point processes. That is:

  a. A single pass is made over the input image on a pixel-by-pixel basis.
  b. Each pixel in the input image is processed via a transformation into a new value.
  c. The new value for the pixel is placed into the output image buffer at the same location as it was taken from in the input image buffer.

The difference between a point process and an area process is item (b). A point process utilizes only the value (and sometimes the location) of the input pixel in generating the output pixel. An area process utilizes the value of each pixel in the neighborhood of the input pixel to generate the output pixel.

From the preceding discussion, it should be apparent that more pixels are involved in the transformation calculation for an area process than are involved for a point process. In a three by three pixel neighborhood with nine total pixels, you might expect an area process to require roughly nine times more processing than a point process. In actuality, the processing time can be much worse, as we shall see. The net result is that area processes take a relatively long period of time to complete, and the time increases dramatically with the size of the neighborhood. Area processes involving floating-point numbers can take even longer. For example, a low-pass filter convolution running on an IBM PS/2 Model 70 (386 CPU) at 20 MHz can take up to three minutes to complete. Point processes running on the same machine require just seconds. A math coprocessor in your computer can substantially reduce the processing times for the execution of these area process algorithms.

The code for all of the area processes discussed in the chapter is shown in Listing 10.1 and is contained in the files "arprocess.h" and "arprocess.c". Additionally, the example

Listing 10.1   The Area Process Function Library

The following is the contents of the file, "arprocess.h":

```
/****************************************/
/*      Image Processing Header File     */
/*        Area Processing Functions      */
/*          written in Turbo C 2.0       */
/*                  by                   */
/*            Craig A. Lindley           */
/*                                       */
/*   Vers: 1.0  Last Update: 11/14/89    */
/****************************************/


/* Area Process Function Prototypes */
CompletionCode Convolution(BYTE huge *InImage, unsigned Col,
                  unsigned Row,
                                  unsigned Width, unsigned Height,
                                  short *Kernel, unsigned KernelCols,
                                  unsigned KernelRows, unsigned Scale,
                                  unsigned Absolute,
                  BYTE huge * *OutImageBufPtr);


CompletionCode RealConvolution(BYTE huge *InImage,
                                  unsigned Col, unsigned Row,
                                  unsigned Width, unsigned Height,
                                  double *Kernel, unsigned KernelCols,
                                  unsigned KernelRows, unsigned Scale,
                                  unsigned Absolute,
                      BYTE huge * *OutImageBufPtr);


CompletionCode MedianFilter(BYTE huge *InImage, unsigned Col,
                  unsigned Row,
                                  unsigned Width, unsigned Height,
                                  unsigned NeighborhoodCols,
                  unsigned NeighborhoodRows,
                                  BYTE huge * *OutImageBufPtr);


CompletionCode SobelEdgeDet(BYTE huge *InImage,
                                  unsigned Col, unsigned Row,
                                  unsigned Width, unsigned Height,
                                  unsigned Threshold, unsigned Overlay,
                                  BYTE huge * *OutImageBufPtr);
```

(continued)

Listing 10.1   *(continued)*

The following is the contents of the file, "arprocess.c":

```c
/****************************************/
/*        Image Processing Code      */
/*        Area Processing Functions  */
/*        written in Turbo C 2.0     */
/*                by                 */
/*        Craig A. Lindley           */
/*                                   */
/*   Vers: 1.0  Last Update: 11/13/89   */
/****************************************/

#include <stdio.h>
#include <stdlib.h>
#include <conio.h>
#include <dos.h>
#include <alloc.h>
#include <process.h>
#include <math.h>
#include <graphics.h>
#include "misc.h"
#include "pcx.h"
#include "vga.h"
#include "imagesup.h"
#include "arprocess.h"

/*
Integer Convolution Function
*/
CompletionCode Convolution(BYTE huge *InImage, unsigned Col, unsigned Row,
                                  unsigned Width, unsigned Height,
                                  short *Kernel, unsigned KernelCols,
                                  unsigned KernelRows, unsigned Scale,
                                  unsigned Absolute, BYTE huge * *OutImageBufPtr)
{
    register unsigned ColExtent, RowExtent;
    register unsigned ImageCol, ImageRow, KernCol, KernRow;
    unsigned ColOffset, RowOffset, TempCol, TempRow;
    BYTE huge *OutputImageBuffer;
    long Sum;
    short *KernelPtr;
```

```
if (ParameterCheckOK(Col,Row,Col+Width,Row+Height,"Convolution"))
{
   /* Image must be at least the same size as the kernel */
   if (Width >= KernelCols && Height >= KernelRows)
   {
        /* allocate far memory buffer for output image */
        OutputImageBuffer = (BYTE huge *)
                                    farcalloc(RASTERSIZE,(unsigned long)sizeof(BYTE));

        if (OutputImageBuffer == NULL)
        {
           restorecrtmode();
           printf("Error Not enough memory for convolution output buffer\n");
           return (ENoMemory);
        }

        /* Store address of output image buffer */
        *OutImageBufPtr = OutputImageBuffer;

        /*
        Clearing the output buffer to white will show the
        boarder areas not touched by the convolution. It also
        provides a nice white frame for the output image.
        */

        ClearImageArea(OutputImageBuffer,MINCOLNUM,MINROWNUM,
                                MAXCOLS,MAXROWS,WHITE);

        ColOffset = KernelCols/2;
        RowOffset = KernelRows/2;
        /* Compensate for edge effects */
        Col += ColOffset;
        Row += RowOffset;
        Width  -= (KernelCols - 1);
        Height -= (KernelRows - 1);

        /* Calculate new range of pixels to act upon */
        ColExtent = Col + Width;
        RowExtent = Row + Height;

        for (ImageRow = Row; ImageRow < RowExtent; ImageRow++)
        {
           TempRow = ImageRow - RowOffset;
```

(continued)

Listing 10.1 *(continued)*

```
                for (ImageCol = Col; ImageCol < ColExtent; ImageCol++)
                {
                   TempCol = ImageCol - ColOffset;
                   Sum = 0L;
                   KernelPtr = Kernel;
                   for (KernCol = 0; KernCol < KernelCols; KernCol++)
                           for (KernRow = 0; KernRow < KernelRows; KernRow++)
                              Sum += (GetPixelFromImage(InImage,
                                            TempCol+KernCol, TempRow+KernRow) *
                                            (*KernelPtr++));

                   /* If absolute value is requested */
                   if (Absolute)
                           Sum = labs(Sum);

                   /* Summation performed. Scale and range Sum*/
                   Sum >>= (long) Scale;

                   Sum = (Sum < MINSAMPLEVAL) ? MINSAMPLEVAL:Sum;
                   Sum = (Sum > MAXSAMPLEVAL) ? MAXSAMPLEVAL:Sum;
                   PutPixelInImage(OutputImageBuffer,ImageCol,ImageRow,(BYTE)Sum);
                }
             }
       }
       else
             return(EKernelSize);
   }
   return(NoError);
}

/*
Real Number Convolution Function. This convolution function is
only used when the kernel entries are floating point numbers
instead of integers. Because of the floating point operations
envolved, this function is substantially slower than the already
slow integer version above.
*/
CompletionCode RealConvolution(BYTE huge *InImage,
                                    unsigned Col, unsigned Row,
                                    unsigned Width, unsigned Height,
                                    double *Kernel, unsigned KernelCols,
                                    unsigned KernelRows, unsigned Scale,
                                    unsigned Absolute, BYTE huge * *OutImageBufPtr)
```

```
{
   register unsigned ColExtent, RowExtent;
   register unsigned ImageCol, ImageRow, KernCol, KernRow;
   unsigned ColOffset, RowOffset, TempCol, TempRow;
   BYTE huge *OutputImageBuffer;
   double Sum;
   double *KernelPtr;


   if (ParameterCheckOK(Col,Row,Col+Width,Row+Height,"Convolution"))
   {
      /* Image must be at least the same size as the kernel */
      if (Width >= KernelCols && Height >= KernelRows)
      {
            /* allocate far memory buffer for output image */
            OutputImageBuffer = (BYTE huge *)
                                          farcalloc(RASTERSIZE,(unsigned long)sizeof(BYTE));

            if (OutputImageBuffer == NULL)
            {
               restorecrtmode();
               printf("Error Not enough memory for convolution output buffer\n");
               return (ENoMemory);
            }

            /* Store address of output image buffer */
            *OutImageBufPtr = OutputImageBuffer;

            /*
            Clearing the output buffer to white will show the
            boarder areas not touched by the convolution. It also
            provides a nice white frame for the output image.
            */

            ClearImageArea(OutputImageBuffer,MINCOLNUM,MINROWNUM,
                              MAXCOLS,MAXROWS,WHITE);

            ColOffset = KernelCols/2;
            RowOffset = KernelRows/2;
            /* Compensate for edge effects */
            Col += ColOffset;
            Row += RowOffset;
            Width  -= (KernelCols - 1);
            Height -= (KernelRows - 1);
```

(continued)

Listing 10.1 *(continued)*

```
                /* Calculate new range of pixels to act upon */
                ColExtent = Col + Width;
                RowExtent = Row + Height;
                for (ImageRow = Row; ImageRow < RowExtent; ImageRow++)
                {
                    TempRow = ImageRow - RowOffset;
                    for (ImageCol = Col; ImageCol < ColExtent; ImageCol++)
                    {
                        TempCol = ImageCol - ColOffset;
                        Sum = 0.0;
                        KernelPtr = Kernel;
                        for (KernCol = 0; KernCol < KernelCols; KernCol++)
                                for (KernRow = 0; KernRow < KernelRows; KernRow++)
                                    Sum += (GetPixelFromImage(InImage,
                                                TempCol+KernCol, TempRow+KernRow) *
                                                (*KernelPtr++));

                        /* If absolute value is requested */
                        if (Absolute)
                                Sum = fabs(Sum);

                        /* Summation performed. Scale and range Sum */
                        Sum /= (double)(1<<Scale);

                        Sum = (Sum < MINSAMPLEVAL) ? MINSAMPLEVAL:Sum;
                        Sum = (Sum > MAXSAMPLEVAL) ? MAXSAMPLEVAL:Sum;
                        PutPixelInImage(OutputImageBuffer,ImageCol,ImageRow,(BYTE)Sum);
                    }
                }
        }
        else
                return(EKernelSize);
    }
    return(NoError);
}
/*
Byte compare for use with the qsort library function call
in the Median filter function.
*/
int ByteCompare(BYTE *Entry1, BYTE *Entry2)
{
    if (*Entry1 < *Entry2)
        return(-1);
```

```
      else if (*Entry1 > *Entry2)
         return(1);
      else
         return(0);
}
CompletionCode MedianFilter(BYTE huge *InImage, unsigned Col, unsigned Row,
                            unsigned Width, unsigned Height,
                            unsigned NeighborhoodCols,
                            unsigned NeighborhoodRows,
                            BYTE huge * *OutImageBufPtr)
{
    register unsigned ColExtent, RowExtent;
    register unsigned ImageCol, ImageRow, NeighborCol, NeighborRow;
    unsigned ColOffset, RowOffset, TempCol, TempRow, PixelIndex;
    unsigned TotalPixels, MedianIndex;
    BYTE huge *OutputImageBuffer;
    BYTE *PixelValues;

    if (ParameterCheckOK(Col,Row,Col+Width,Row+Height,"Median Filter"))
    {
       /* Image must be at least the same size as the neighborhood */
       if (Width >= NeighborhoodCols && Height >= NeighborhoodRows)
       {
             /* allocate far memory buffer for output image */
             OutputImageBuffer = (BYTE huge *)
                                          farcalloc(RASTERSIZE,(unsigned long)sizeof(BYTE));

             if (OutputImageBuffer == NULL)
             {
                restorecrtmode();
                printf("Error Not enough memory for median filter output buffer\n");
                return (ENoMemory);
             }

             /* Store address of output image buffer */
             *OutImageBufPtr = OutputImageBuffer;

             /*
             Clearing the output buffer to white will show the
             boarder areas not touched by the median filter. It also
             provides a nice white frame for the output image.
             */
             ClearImageArea(OutputImageBuffer,MINCOLNUM,MINROWNUM,
                                     MAXCOLS,MAXROWS,WHITE);
```

(continued)

Listing 10.1 *(continued)*

```
/* Calculate border pixel to miss */
ColOffset = NeighborhoodCols/2;
RowOffset = NeighborhoodRows/2;

/* Compensate for edge effects */
Col += ColOffset;
Row += RowOffset;
Width  -= (NeighborhoodCols - 1);
Height -= (NeighborhoodRows - 1);

/* Calculate new range of pixels to act upon */
ColExtent = Col + Width;
RowExtent = Row + Height;

TotalPixels = (NeighborhoodCols*NeighborhoodRows);
MedianIndex = (NeighborhoodCols*NeighborhoodRows)/2;

/* allocate memory for pixel buffer */
PixelValues = (BYTE *) calloc(TotalPixels,(unsigned)sizeof(BYTE));

if (PixelValues == NULL)
{
   restorecrtmode();
   printf("Error Not enough memory for median filter pixel buffer\n");
   return (ENoMemory);
}

for (ImageRow = Row; ImageRow < RowExtent; ImageRow++)
{
   TempRow = ImageRow - RowOffset;
   for (ImageCol = Col; ImageCol < ColExtent; ImageCol++)
   {
      TempCol = ImageCol - ColOffset;
      PixelIndex = 0;
      for (NeighborCol=0;NeighborCol < NeighborhoodCols;NeighborCol++)
    for (NeighborRow=0;NeighborRow < NeighborhoodRows;NeighborRow++)
             PixelValues[PixelIndex++] =
                GetPixelFromImage(InImage,TempCol+NeighborCol,
                    TempRow+NeighborRow);

      /*
      Quick sort the brightness values into ascending order
```

```
                   and then pick out the median or middle value as
                   that for the pixel.
                   */
                   qsort(PixelValues,TotalPixels,sizeof(BYTE),ByteCompare);
                   PutPixelInImage(OutputImageBuffer,ImageCol,ImageRow,
                                            PixelValues[MedianIndex]);
              }
           }
      }
      else
           return(EKernelSize);
   }
   free(PixelValues);          /* give up the pixel value buffer */
   return(NoError);
}

/*
Sobel Edge Detection Function
*/
CompletionCode SobelEdgeDet(BYTE huge *InImage,
                                  unsigned Col, unsigned Row,
                                  unsigned Width, unsigned Height,
                                  unsigned Threshold, unsigned Overlay,
                                  BYTE huge * *OutImageBufPtr)
{
   register unsigned ColExtent, RowExtent;
   register unsigned ImageCol, ImageRow;
   unsigned PtA, PtB, PtC, PtD, PtE, PtF, PtG, PtH, PtI;
   unsigned LineAEIAveAbove, LineAEIAveBelow, LineAEIMaxDif;
   unsigned LineBEHAveAbove, LineBEHAveBelow, LineBEHMaxDif;
   unsigned LineCEGAveAbove, LineCEGAveBelow, LineCEGMaxDif;
   unsigned LineDEFAveAbove, LineDEFAveBelow, LineDEFMaxDif;
   unsigned MaxDif;
   BYTE huge *OutputImageBuffer;


   if (ParameterCheckOK(Col,Row,Col+Width,Row+Height,"Sobel Edge Detector"))
   {
      /* allocate far memory buffer for output image */
      OutputImageBuffer = (BYTE huge *)
                                    farcalloc(RASTERSIZE,(unsigned long)sizeof(BYTE));

      if (OutputImageBuffer == NULL)
```

(continued)

Listing 10.1 *(continued)*

```
{
        restorecrtmode();
        printf("Error Not enough memory for Sobel output buffer\n");
        return (ENoMemory);
}

/* Store address of output image buffer */
*OutImageBufPtr = OutputImageBuffer;

/*
Clearing the output buffer
*/
ClearImageArea(OutputImageBuffer,MINCOLNUM,MINROWNUM,
                        MAXCOLS,MAXROWS,BLACK);

/* Compensate for edge effects of 3x3 pixel neighborhood */
Col += 1;
Row += 1;
Width  -= 2;
Height -= 2;

/* Calculate new range of pixels to act upon */
ColExtent = Col + Width;
RowExtent = Row + Height;

for (ImageRow = Row; ImageRow < RowExtent; ImageRow++)
        for (ImageCol = Col; ImageCol < ColExtent; ImageCol++)
        {
            /* Get each pixel in 3x3 neighborhood */
            PtA = GetPixelFromImage(InImage,ImageCol-1,ImageRow-1);
            PtB = GetPixelFromImage(InImage,ImageCol  ,ImageRow-1);
            PtC = GetPixelFromImage(InImage,ImageCol+1,ImageRow-1);
            PtD = GetPixelFromImage(InImage,ImageCol-1,ImageRow  );
            PtE = GetPixelFromImage(InImage,ImageCol  ,ImageRow  );
            PtF = GetPixelFromImage(InImage,ImageCol+1,ImageRow  );
            PtG = GetPixelFromImage(InImage,ImageCol-1,ImageRow+1);
            PtH = GetPixelFromImage(InImage,ImageCol  ,ImageRow+1);
            PtI = GetPixelFromImage(InImage,ImageCol+1,ImageRow+1);

            /*
            Calculate average above and below the line.
            Take the absolute value of the difference.
            */
```

```
                LineAEIAveBelow = (PtD+PtG+PtH)/3;
                LineAEIAveAbove = (PtB+PtC+PtF)/3;
                LineAEIMaxDif = abs(LineAEIAveBelow-LineAEIAveAbove);

                LineBEHAveBelow = (PtA+PtD+PtG)/3;
                LineBEHAveAbove = (PtC+PtF+PtI)/3;
                LineBEHMaxDif = abs(LineBEHAveBelow-LineBEHAveAbove);

                LineCEGAveBelow = (PtF+PtH+PtI)/3;
                LineCEGAveAbove = (PtA+PtB+PtD)/3;
                LineCEGMaxDif = abs(LineCEGAveBelow-LineCEGAveAbove);

                LineDEFAveBelow = (PtG+PtH+PtI)/3;
                LineDEFAveAbove = (PtA+PtB+PtC)/3;
                LineDEFMaxDif = abs(LineDEFAveBelow-LineDEFAveAbove);
                /*
                Find the maximum value of the absolute differences
                from the four possibilities.
                */
                MaxDif = MAX(LineAEIMaxDif,LineBEHMaxDif);
                MaxDif = MAX(LineCEGMaxDif,MaxDif);
                MaxDif = MAX(LineDEFMaxDif,MaxDif);
                /*
                If maximum difference is above the threshold, set
                the pixel of interest (center pixel) to white. If
                below the threshold optionally copy the input image
                to the output image. This copying is controlled by
                the parameter Overlay.
                */
                if (MaxDif >= Threshold)
                  PutPixelInImage(OutputImageBuffer,ImageCol,ImageRow,WHITE);
                else if (Overlay)
                  PutPixelInImage(OutputImageBuffer,ImageCol,ImageRow,PtE);
             }
      }
   return(NoError);
}
```

program (Listing 10.2) used to create all of the image sequences in this section is comprised of the files "artest.c" and "artest.prj" on the companion disk. An application program designed to utilize the area process function library must include the file "arprocess.h" in its code and must subsequently be linked with "arprocess.c". Use "artest.c" as a model for a typical application program. The function prototypes and descriptions for all of the area processes contained in the area process function library are shown in Figure 10.1.

Listing 10.2   The Area Process Example Program

The following is the contents of the file, "artest.prj":

```
graphics.lib
vgagraph.obj
egavga.obj
pcx        (misc.h pcx.h)
vga        (misc.h vga.h pcx.h)
imagesup   (misc.h vga.h pcx.h imagesup.h)
arprocess  (misc.h vga.h pcx.h imagesup.h)
artest     (misc.h vga.h pcx.h imagesup.h arprocess.h)
```

The following is the contents of the file, "artest.c":

```
/***************************************/
/*       Area Process Demo Program     */
/*         written in Turbo C 2.0      */
/*                  by                 */
/*           Craig A. Lindley          */
/*                                     */
/*   Vers: 1.0  Last Update: 12/26/89  */
/***************************************/

#include <stdio.h>
/* #include <stdlib.h> */
#include <conio.h>
#include <dos.h>
#include <alloc.h>
#include <process.h>
#include <graphics.h>
#include "misc.h"
#include "pcx.h"
#include "vga.h"
#include "imagesup.h"
#include "arprocess.h"

static double LP1[]=
{ 0.11111111, 0.11111111, 0.11111111,
  0.11111111, 0.11111111, 0.11111111,
  0.11111111, 0.11111111, 0.11111111 };
```

```
static short HP1[]=
{  -1, -1, -1,
   -1,  9, -1,
   -1, -1, -1 };

static short LAP2[]=
{  -1, -1, -1,
   -1,  8, -1,
   -1, -1, -1 };

static short GN[]=
{   1,  1,  1,
    1, -2,  1,
   -1, -1, -1 };

static short GE[]=
{  -1,  1,  1,
   -1, -2,  1,
   -1,  1,  1 };

static short BLUR[]=
{   1,  1,  1,  1,  1,
    1,  1,  1,  1,  1,
    1,  1,  1,  1,  1,
    1,  1,  1,  1,  1,
    1,  1,  1,  1,  1 };


/* main area process demo program */

void main(void)
{
   char *InFileName1 = "p2c10i1a";
   char *InFileName2 = "p2c10i2a";
   char *InFileName3 = "p2c10i3a";
   BYTE huge *TheInImage;
   BYTE huge *TheOutImage;
   unsigned GenPCXFiles = FALSE; /* controls the generation of output files */


   InitGraphics();
```

(continued)

Listing 10.2 *(continued)*

```
printf("Area Process Demonstration Program\n\n");
printf("Reading the Image PCX File into memory\n");

/* generate image sequence 10.1 - Various Convolutions */
if (ReadPCXFileToBuf (InFileName1,&TheInImage) != NoError)
   exit(1);

DisplayImageInBuf(TheInImage,INITVGALOADPALETTE,NOWAITFORKEY);

if (RealConvolution(TheInImage,MINCOLNUM,MINROWNUM,MAXCOLS,MAXROWS,
                         LP1,3,3,0,FALSE,&TheOutImage) == NoError)
{
   DisplayImageInBuf(TheOutImage,NOVGAINIT,WAITFORKEY);
   if (GenPCXFiles)
         WritePCXFile("p2c10i1b",8,320,200,1,320);
   farfree((BYTE far *)TheOutImage);
}
DisplayImageInBuf(TheInImage,NOVGAINIT,NOWAITFORKEY);
if (Convolution(TheInImage,MINCOLNUM,MINROWNUM,MAXCOLS,MAXROWS,
                         HP1,3,3,0,FALSE,&TheOutImage) == NoError)
{
   DisplayImageInBuf(TheOutImage,NOVGAINIT,WAITFORKEY);
   if (GenPCXFiles)
         WritePCXFile("p2c10i1c",8,320,200,1,320);
   farfree((BYTE far *)TheOutImage);
}

DisplayImageInBuf(TheInImage,NOVGAINIT,NOWAITFORKEY);
if (Convolution(TheInImage,MINCOLNUM,MINROWNUM,MAXCOLS,MAXROWS,
                         LAP2,3,3,0,FALSE,&TheOutImage) == NoError)
{
   DisplayImageInBuf(TheOutImage,NOVGAINIT,WAITFORKEY);
   if (GenPCXFiles)
         WritePCXFile("p2c10i1d",8,320,200,1,320);
   farfree((BYTE far *)TheOutImage);
}

DisplayImageInBuf(TheInImage,NOVGAINIT,NOWAITFORKEY);
if (Convolution(TheInImage,MINCOLNUM,MINROWNUM,MAXCOLS,MAXROWS,
                         GN,3,3,0,FALSE,&TheOutImage) == NoError)
{
   DisplayImageInBuf(TheOutImage,NOVGAINIT,WAITFORKEY);
```

```
if (GenPCXFiles)
        WritePCXFile("p2c10i1e",8,320,200,1,320);
   farfree((BYTE far *)TheOutImage);
}


DisplayImageInBuf(TheInImage,NOVGAINIT,NOWAITFORKEY);
if (Convolution(TheInImage,MINCOLNUM,MINROWNUM,MAXCOLS,MAXROWS,
                        GE,3,3,0,FALSE,&TheOutImage) == NoError)
{
   DisplayImageInBuf(TheOutImage,NOVGAINIT,WAITFORKEY);
   if (GenPCXFiles)
        WritePCXFile("p2c10i1f",8,320,200,1,320);
   farfree((BYTE far *)TheOutImage);
}


DisplayImageInBuf(TheInImage,NOVGAINIT,NOWAITFORKEY);
if (Convolution(TheInImage,MINCOLNUM,MINROWNUM,MAXCOLS,MAXROWS,
                        BLUR,5,5,4,FALSE,&TheOutImage) == NoError)
{
   DisplayImageInBuf(TheOutImage,NOVGAINIT,WAITFORKEY);
   if (GenPCXFiles)
        WritePCXFile("p2c10i1g",8,320,200,1,320);
   farfree((BYTE far *)TheOutImage);
}


/* generate image sequence 10.2 - Sobel Edge Detection */
if (ReadPCXFileToBuf (InFileName2,&TheInImage) != NoError)
   exit(1);

DisplayImageInBuf(TheInImage,NOVGAINIT,NOWAITFORKEY);
if (SobelEdgeDet(TheInImage,MINCOLNUM,MINROWNUM,MAXCOLS,MAXROWS,
                        10,FALSE,&TheOutImage) == NoError)
{
   DisplayImageInBuf(TheOutImage,NOVGAINIT,WAITFORKEY);
   if (GenPCXFiles)
        WritePCXFile("p2c10i2b",8,320,200,1,320);
   farfree((BYTE far *)TheOutImage);
}
/* Do detection again this time with overlaying */
DisplayImageInBuf(TheInImage,NOVGAINIT,NOWAITFORKEY);
if (SobelEdgeDet(TheInImage,MINCOLNUM,MINROWNUM,MAXCOLS,MAXROWS,
                        10,TRUE,&TheOutImage) == NoError)
```

(continued)

Listing 10.2 *(continued)*

```
{
    DisplayImageInBuf(TheOutImage,NOVGAINIT,WAITFORKEY);
    if (GenPCXFiles)
            WritePCXFile("p2c10i2c",8,320,200,1,320);
    farfree((BYTE far *)TheOutImage);
}


/* generate image sequence 10.3 - Median Filtering */
if (ReadPCXFileToBuf (InFileName3,&TheInImage) != NoError)
    exit(1);

DisplayImageInBuf(TheInImage,NOVGAINIT,NOWAITFORKEY);
if (MedianFilter(TheInImage,MINCOLNUM,MINROWNUM,MAXCOLS,MAXROWS,
                          3,3,&TheOutImage) == NoError)
{
    DisplayImageInBuf(TheOutImage,NOVGAINIT,WAITFORKEY);
    if (GenPCXFiles)
            WritePCXFile("p2c10i3b",8,320,200,1,320);
    CopyImage(TheOutImage,TheInImage);
    farfree((BYTE far *)TheOutImage);
}


/* apply filtering twice for effect */
if (MedianFilter(TheInImage,MINCOLNUM,MINROWNUM,MAXCOLS,MAXROWS,
                          3,3,&TheOutImage) == NoError)
{
    DisplayImageInBuf(TheOutImage,NOVGAINIT,WAITFORKEY);
    if (GenPCXFiles)
            WritePCXFile("p2c10i3c",8,320,200,1,320);
    CopyImage(TheOutImage,TheInImage);
    farfree((BYTE far *)TheOutImage);
}

farfree((BYTE far *)TheInImage);
restorecrtmode();
closegraph();
}
```

1. Integer Convolution Function

Prototype

CompletionCode Convolution(BYTE huge *InImage, unsigned Col, unsigned Row, unsigned Width, unsigned Height, short *Kernel, unsigned KernelCols, unsigned KernelRows, unsigned Scale, unsigned Absolute, BYTE huge **OutImageBufPtr);

Where:

"InImage" is a pointer to an input image buffer.
"Col", "Row", "Width", and "Height" are parameters describing the portion of the input image over which the convolution transformation will be applied.
"Kernel" is a pointer to a convolution kernel consisting of unsigned integers.
"KernelCols" and "KernelRows" are the dimensions of the convolution kernel. Typically the values would be 3 and 3 for a 3 × 3 convolution kernel.
"Scale" is the power of 2 by which the convolution sum should be divided to scale the result into the usable range of 0 to 63. A scale value of 0 results in no scaling of the convolution sum.
"Absolute" is a flag that, if TRUE, forces the convolution sum to its absolute value. If FALSE, negative convolution summations will be set equal to 0.
"OutImageBufPtr" is a pointer to the storage location of a pointer to the output image buffer area.

Operation

The convolution function begins by checking the parameters it is passed to make sure they are valid. If out-of-range parameters are detected, the program is terminated and an error message is displayed. Next, an image buffer is allocated for the output image. If insufficient memory is detected, this function returns with a return code of "ENoMemory". On successful allocation of the image buffer from the far heap, the address of the buffer is stored at the location pointed to by "OutImageBufPtr". This effectively returns the address of the output image buffer to the calling code. The newly allocated output image buffer is cleared to white so the effects of the convolution function will be visually obvious when the output image is displayed. The border areas that are not processed by the convolution function will retain the white color when the image is displayed. (Due to cropping of the image for book production, these white borders are not always visible.) The parameters that determine the area of the image to be convoluted are then modified to compensate for the edge effects of the convolution kernel. The "Col" and "Row" must both be advanced by half the kernel size, and the "Width" and "Height" are reduced by the kernel size minus 1. After these adjustments are made, nested loops are entered that perform the weighted sum convolution calculation on each pixel in the specified image area. When the sum is completed for each pixel of interest, the absolute value may be taken, and the sum may be scaled depending upon parameters passed to the convolution function. Finally, the new pixel value is checked to make sure it is in the valid range of pixel values. The new pixel value is then placed into the output image at the same spot it was taken from the input image.

2. The Real Number Convolution Function

Prototype

CompletionCode RealConvolution(BYTE huge *InImage, unsigned Col, unsigned Row, unsigned Width, unsigned Height, double *Kernel, unsigned KernelCols, unsigned KernelRows, unsigned Scale, unsigned Absolute, BYTE huge **OutImageBufPtr);

Figure 10.1 Area Processing Functions   *(continued)*

Where all parameters are identical to those described above except for "Kernel", which is now a pointer to a convolution kernel consisting of double numbers instead of unsigned integers.

Operation
See the description just given. The operation is exactly the same except the sum and kernels utilize real floating-point numbers instead of integers.

3. Sobel Edge Detection Function

Prototype
CompletionCode SobelEdgeDet(BYTE huge *InImage, unsigned Col, unsigned Row, unsigned Width, unsigned Height, unsigned Threshold, unsigned Overlay, BYTE huge **Out-ImageBufPtr);

Where:

"Threshold" is the value that determines if the largest absolute difference detected should produce a black or a white pixel. Absolute differences at the threshold and above result in a white pixel being output.
"Overlay" is a flag that determines whether the value of the source pixel should be used as the output pixel of interest. Copying will occur only when the absolute difference is less than the specified threshold. If the absolute difference is at the threshold or greater, the output pixel is automatically set to white. If "Overlay" is FALSE, no copying of the source image occurs, so the pixel retains a black color.

Operation
The initialization for the execution of this function is the same as that used for convolution and will not therefore be repeated. The pixel-by-pixel process differs greatly, however, and is discussed below. This function (and this description) assumes a 3 × 3 pixel neighborhood. Any changes in the size of this neighborhood will require changes in this function's code.

At each pixel location to be processed, the 9 pixel values that make up its neighborhood are fetched. The averages of the 3 pixel intensities above and below the 4 possible dividing lines (see text) are then calculated. Next, the absolute value of the intensity differences are calculated. The maximum difference from the 4 line calculations is compared to the threshold parameter. If the difference exceeds that of the threshold, the output pixel is set to white (given a value of 63). If the difference is less than the threshold, the output pixel is either left black (the color to which the output image buffer was initialized) or the source pixel is copied to the output image. The copying is dependent upon the "Overlay" parameter, as discussed.

This function returns the value of "NoError" if it completes successfully.

4. Median Filter Function

Prototype
CompletionCode MedianFilter(BYTE huge *InImage, unsigned Col, unsigned Row, unsigned Width, unsigned Height, unsigned NeighborhoodCols, unsigned NeighborhoodRows, BYTE huge **OutImageBufPtr);

Where:

"InImage", "Col", "Row", "Width", "Height", and "OutImageBufPtr" are as previously discussed.
"NeighborhoodCols" and "NeighborhoodRows" determine the size of the pixel neighborhood to utilize during the filtering process. A 3 × 3 neighborhood is generally used.

Figure 10.1 *(continued)*

Operation

This function operates in a manner very close to that of convolution. All initialization and edge adjustments that are performed in the convolution function are also performed in this function. The difference with median filtering is that instead of performing the summation process used in convolution, the values of the pixels in the neighborhood are sorted with a quick sort into ascending order. The value of the median or middle pixel is then assigned to the pixel of interest, and this pixel is placed into the output image.

This function returns the value of "NoError" if it completes successfully.

Figure 10.1 *(continued)*

Convolution

As mentioned, convolution is a very general-purpose algorithm that can be used in performing a variety of area process transformations. Complex as convolution might sound, it is actually quite easy to understand and implement. Various examples of the visual effects of convolution are shown throughout this section. Figure 10.2 illustrates the convolution process.

The best way to understand a convolution is to think of it as a weighted summation process. Each pixel in the neighborhood (assumed in Figure 10.2 to be three by three) is multiplied by a similarly dimensioned *convolution kernel*; the sum that results replaces the value of the center pixel of interest. Each element of the convolution kernel is a weighting factor (also called a *convolution coefficient*). The size and the arrangement of the weighting factors contained in a convolution kernel determine the type of area transform that will be applied to the image data. Changing a weighting factor within a convolution kernel influences the magnitude and possibly the sign of the overall sum and therefore affects the value given to the pixel of interest. Figure 10.3 shows various convolution kernels and the transfer functions they represent. As you can see from this figure, most kernels are three by three, and all have odd numbers of rows and columns. This format of convolution coefficients within the kernel has been accepted by the industry as a standard. A larger kernel size increases the flexibility of the convolution process. Although some rather complex mathematics went into the design of these convolution kernels (see the references given in the figure), feel free to experiment with kernels of your own making. The results you produce may surprise you.

Unfortunately, the simple weighted sum convolution calculation has some implementation details that complicate its realization. The first and foremost has to do with the edges of an image. As we move the convolution kernel (with the pixel of interest under the center of the kernel) across an image a pixel at a time, we will have problems with our calculations whenever we come to the borders of an image. That is because the weighting coefficients in the kernel are no longer positioned over nine pixels of the source image. In other words, the convolution kernel is, in effect, "hanging" over the edge of the image buffer. This perturbance happens at the top, left, right, and bottom borders of an image. Several methods may be used to cope with this situation. The two most straightforward solutions are (1) the data at the edges of the image can be ignored, or (2) image data can be replicated to "synthesize" additional border data. Method (1) was utilized in the code provided in the area processing function library.

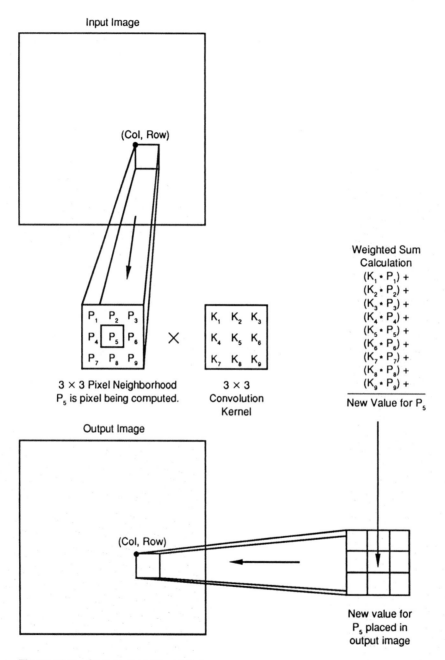

Input Image

(Col, Row)

P_1 P_2 P_3
P_4 P_5 P_6
P_7 P_8 P_9

×

K_1 K_2 K_3
K_4 K_5 K_6
K_7 K_8 K_9

3 × 3 Pixel Neighborhood
P_5 is pixel being computed.

3 × 3
Convolution
Kernel

Weighted Sum
Calculation
$(K_1 * P_1) +$
$(K_2 * P_2) +$
$(K_3 * P_3) +$
$(K_4 * P_4) +$
$(K_5 * P_5) +$
$(K_6 * P_6) +$
$(K_7 * P_7) +$
$(K_8 * P_8) +$
$(K_9 * P_9) +$
_____
New Value for P_5

Output Image

(Col, Row)

New value for
P_5 placed in
output image

Figure 10.2 Convolution Illustrated

Low-Pass Spatial Filters

$$
\begin{array}{ccc}
\frac{1}{9} & \frac{1}{9} & \frac{1}{9} \\
\frac{1}{9} & \frac{1}{9} & \frac{1}{9} \\
\frac{1}{9} & \frac{1}{9} & \frac{1}{9}
\end{array}
\qquad
\begin{array}{ccc}
\frac{1}{10} & \frac{1}{10} & \frac{1}{10} \\
\frac{1}{10} & \frac{5}{10} & \frac{1}{10} \\
\frac{1}{10} & \frac{1}{10} & \frac{1}{10}
\end{array}
\qquad
\begin{array}{ccc}
\frac{1}{16} & \frac{1}{8} & \frac{1}{16} \\
\frac{1}{8} & \frac{4}{8} & \frac{1}{8} \\
\frac{1}{16} & \frac{1}{8} & \frac{1}{16}
\end{array}
$$

LP1   LP2   LP3

$\Sigma = 1$

High-Pass Spatial Filters

$$
\begin{array}{ccc}
-1 & -1 & -1 \\
-1 & 9 & -1 \\
-1 & -1 & -1
\end{array}
\qquad
\begin{array}{ccc}
0 & -1 & 0 \\
-1 & 5 & -1 \\
0 & -1 & 0
\end{array}
\qquad
\begin{array}{ccc}
1 & -2 & 1 \\
-2 & 5 & -2 \\
1 & -2 & 1
\end{array}
$$

HP1   HP2   HP3

$\Sigma = 1$

Shift and Difference Edge Enhancements

$$
\begin{array}{ccc}
0 & 0 & 0 \\
-1 & 1 & 0 \\
0 & 0 & 0
\end{array}
\qquad
\begin{array}{ccc}
0 & -1 & 0 \\
0 & 1 & 0 \\
0 & 0 & 0
\end{array}
\qquad
\begin{array}{ccc}
-1 & 0 & 0 \\
0 & 1 & 0 \\
0 & 0 & 0
\end{array}
$$

Vertical Edges   Horizontal Edges   Horizontal and Vertical Edges

$\Sigma = 0$

Matched Filter Edge Enhancements[1]

$$
\begin{array}{ccc}
-1 & 0 & 1 \\
-1 & 0 & 1 \\
-1 & 0 & 1 \\
-1 & 0 & 1 \\
-1 & 0 & 1
\end{array}
\qquad
\begin{array}{ccccc}
-1 & -1 & -1 & -1 & -1 \\
0 & 0 & 0 & 0 & 0 \\
1 & 1 & 1 & 1 & 1
\end{array}
$$

Vertical Edges   Horizontal Edges

$\Sigma = 0$

Gradient Directional Edge Enhancements

$$
\begin{array}{ccc}
1 & 1 & 1 \\
1 & -2 & 1 \\
-1 & -1 & -1
\end{array}
\qquad
\begin{array}{ccc}
1 & 1 & 1 \\
-1 & -2 & 1 \\
-1 & -1 & 1
\end{array}
\qquad
\begin{array}{ccc}
-1 & 1 & 1 \\
-1 & -2 & 1 \\
-1 & 1 & 1
\end{array}
\qquad
\begin{array}{ccc}
-1 & -1 & 1 \\
-1 & -2 & 1 \\
1 & 1 & 1
\end{array}
$$

North   Northeast   East   Southeast

$$
\begin{array}{ccc}
-1 & -1 & -1 \\
1 & -2 & 1 \\
1 & 1 & 1
\end{array}
\qquad
\begin{array}{ccc}
1 & -1 & -1 \\
1 & -2 & -1 \\
1 & 1 & 1
\end{array}
\qquad
\begin{array}{ccc}
1 & 1 & -1 \\
1 & -2 & -1 \\
1 & 1 & -1
\end{array}
\qquad
\begin{array}{ccc}
1 & 1 & 1 \\
1 & -2 & 1 \\
-1 & -1 & -1
\end{array}
$$

South   Southwest   West   Northwest

$\Sigma = 0$

Blurring Kernel

$$
\begin{array}{ccccc}
1 & 1 & 1 & 1 & 1 \\
1 & 1 & 1 & 1 & 1 \\
1 & 1 & 1 & 1 & 1 \\
1 & 1 & 1 & 1 & 1 \\
1 & 1 & 1 & 1 & 1
\end{array}
$$

$\Sigma = 25$

Laplace Edge Enhancements

$$
\begin{array}{ccc}
0 & 1 & 0 \\
1 & -4 & 1 \\
0 & 1 & 0
\end{array}
\qquad
\begin{array}{ccc}
-1 & -1 & -1 \\
-1 & 8 & -1 \\
-1 & -1 & -1
\end{array}
\qquad
\begin{array}{ccc}
-1 & -1 & -1 \\
-1 & 9 & -1 \\
-1 & -1 & -1
\end{array}
\qquad
\begin{array}{ccc}
1 & -2 & 1 \\
-2 & 4 & -2 \\
1 & -2 & 1
\end{array}
$$

LAP1[3]   LAP2   LAP3[2]   LAP4

Σ normally = 0 except LAP3

Notes
1. All kernels from Baxes except these from Dawson.
2. Equivalent to adding original image to output of convolution using kernel LAP2.
3. Proof can be found in Gonzalez and Wintz.

Figure 10.3 Various Convolution Kernels

The second implementation complication has to do with the dynamic range of the new value calculated for the pixel of interest. For most kernels, the new value calculated for the pixel of interest is within the range of valid pixel values: 0 to 63. The blurring kernel, unfortunately, produces values well out of the valid range of pixel values. For this reason, the concept of scaling had to be introduced into the convolution algorithm. The parameter "Scale", passed to the convolution functions, determines how many times the calculated weighted sum will be divided by two before being assigned to the pixel of interest. If "Scale" is 0, the weighted sum will not be altered.

Under close inspection, it is easy to understand why the blurring kernel produces such large values while the other kernels listed in Figure 10.3 are so well behaved. Notice that in all kernels except the blurring kernel the sum of all weighting coefficients is either 0 or 1. The sum of the coefficients for the blurring kernel is 25. This means the weighted sum calculation will be the sum of the 25 pixel values in the five by five neighborhood. If, for example, each of the 25 pixels had a value equal to one half of the maximum value, or 32, the sum would equal $25 \cdot 32$, or 800. To bring this sum back into the appropriate range, a "Scale" value of 4 or 5 would be applied. This would reduce the value of the weighted sum to 50 or 25, respectively. The final choice of "Scale" is somewhat subjective and will depend upon image appearance.

The final consideration that must be taken into account in the implementation of a convolution algorithm is the sign of the calculated pixel values. When a convolution kernel contains negative-weighting coefficients, as most do, it is possible to produce negative pixel-intensity values. Even though negative-intensity values are interesting, we cannot display them. For this reason, our convolution implementation sets negative pixel-intensity values to 0. Other methods could be used to deal with negative intensity values. For instance, the absolute value of the intensity could be used instead of setting the value to 0. Another tack would be to scale all calculated pixel values upward so the most negative value would become 0. Any of these other treatments of negative pixel values could easily be added to the convolution code provided.

The convolution code provided in this section is in two parts: integer convolution code, which utilizes convolution kernels with integer coefficients, and real number convolution code, which is used with kernels with real number coefficients. Two algorithms were provided for performance reasons. As might be expected, the integer realization runs much faster than the floating-point or real version. Integer convolution is used for all area processes except the low-pass filters. These spatial filters require a kernel with fractional coefficients and therefore the use of real numbers in the convolution calculations. Both functions are shown in Listing 10.1.

Low-Pass Spatial Filters

Low-pass spatial filters leave the low-frequency content of an image intact while attenuating the high-frequency content. Low-pass filters are good at reducing the visual noise contained in an image. They are also used to remove the high-frequency content of an image so that the low-frequency content can be examined more closely. With the high frequencies gone, more subtle low-frequency changes can be identified. The cutoff frequency of a low-pass filter is determined by the size of the kernel and the kernel coefficients. Three different low-pass frequency kernels are given in Figure 10.3. Notice that the sum of the kernel values for all of the low-pass filters is 1. This fact is important for understanding how low-pass filters operate.

Consider a portion of an image without high-frequency content. This means that the pixel values are of constant value or that they are changing slowly. As a low-pass kernel is passed over this portion of the image, the new value for the pixel of interest (the pixel centered under the kernel) is calculated as the sum of the kernel coefficients times the neighborhood pixel values. If all the neighborhood pixel values are the same (constant), the new pixel value is the same as the old value. This is the reason the sum of the coefficients is chosen to be 1. Low-frequency content has been preserved. As the kernel is moved over a portion of the image with high-frequency content, any rapid changes in intensity get averaged out with the remaining pixels in the neighborhood, thereby lowering the high-frequency content. The visual result of low-pass filtering is a slight blur of the image. This blur results because any sharp pixel transitions are averaged with their surroundings as the high-frequency content is attenuated. Image Sequence 10.1(a) shows the original image and 10.1(b) the low-pass filtered image.

Because of the use of floating-point numbers in the convolution calculation for low-pass filters, these transformations can take a very long time to execute in software. Approximately three minutes was required to generate image (b) on an IBM PS/2 Model 70. Again, the availability of a numeric coprocessor would greatly speed these calculations.

Contrary as it sounds, low-pass filtering can be used to sharpen the appearance of an image. If a low-pass filtered image is subtracted from the original image, the result is a relative increase in high-frequency informational content without an increase in image noise. Subjectively, the resultant image appears sharper than the original. This could be used to highlight portions of an image that are obscured by haze or clouds. This technique might even be able to make an image of Los Angeles look good on a smoggy day.

High-Pass Spatial Filters

High-pass filters accentuate the high-frequency details of an image while leaving the low-frequency content intact. Relative to the high-frequency content, the low-frequency content is attenuated. High-pass filtering is used whenever objects with high spatial-frequency content need to be examined. The higher-frequency portions of an image will be highlighted (become brighter), while the lower-frequency portions become black. Image sharpness is sometimes enhanced with high-pass filtering at the expense of accentuated image noise. Edge enhancement of an image is also possible with the application of high-pass filtering. Again, Figure 10.3 shows three high-pass filter kernels, and (c) in Image Sequence 10.1 shows the visual result of the application of high-pass filtering.

The large center kernel coefficient holds the key to the operation of high-pass filters. As the large center coefficient moves across a portion of an image with high spatial-frequency content (meaning a large-step change in pixel intensity) the new value of the pixel of interest

Image Sequence 10.1   Area Processes in Action

Original image

(a)

Low-pass
filtered
image

High-pass
filtered
image

(b)   (c)

is multiplied many times in value. The smaller negative coefficients in the kernel clustered around the large center value work to reduce the effect of the large weighting factor. The net effect is that large changes in pixel intensity are intensified, while areas of constant pixel intensity are left alone. In other words, areas of constant pixel intensity (areas of low spatial frequencies) are not affected by this transformation.

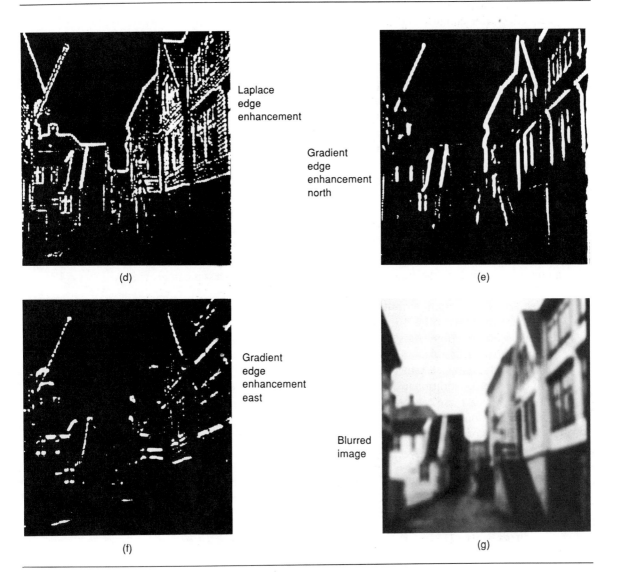

Laplace
edge
enhancement

Gradient
edge
enhancement
north

(d)

(e)

Gradient
edge
enhancement
east

Blurred
image

(f)

(g)

Edge Enhancement

Another area process that can be performed using convolution is edge enhancement. Edge enhancement is used as a preliminary step in image feature extraction and is typically followed by a thresholding point process. Edge-enhancement algorithms reduce an image into just edges; the image content is reduced and in many cases completely eliminated. For this reason, the processed image may not closely resemble the original image. The brightness of an edge after enhancement is proportional to the change in brightness surrounding the edge in the original image.

Although edge enhancement is used mainly for machine vision, it does have other uses as well. For example, the edge information provided by an edge-enhancement process can be added back into the original image to sharpen it. Edge enhancement can also be used as an artistic tool to produce striking outlined images. These images can then be touched up with a paint program to produce real works of art.

In this section, we will present three different edge-enhancement methods and one method of edge detection. All of these methods work by analyzing the intensity of pixels contained in the pixel of interest's neighborhood. Again, the brightness trends in a pixel's neighborhood are used to find and accent the edges contained in an image. By its very definition, an edge is a large change in intensity. It should be noted that all edge-enhancement algorithms that use convolution are linear. That is, they are made up of the sum of first-degree products. The Sobel edge-detection algorithm, however, uses first derivatives to detect edges. This nonlinear method does a better job of detecting edges with much less computation. The visual appearance of images processed using the Sobel algorithm gives one an intuitive feeling for the greater accuracy that nonlinear processes can provide.

Laplacian Edge Enhancement. Laplacian edge enhancement differs from the other enhancement methods to be discussed in being omnidirectional. That is, it highlights edges regardless of direction. It is called *Laplacian enhancement* because this transformation approximates the Laplacian operator utilized throughout mathematics and electronics. Laplacian edge enhancement generates sharper edge definition than do most other enhancement operations. Additionally, it highlights edges having both positive and negative brightness slopes. For these reasons, Laplacian edge enhancement finds use in many machine vision applications.

For the more mathematically oriented reader, the Laplacian of an function $f(x, y)$ is

$$L(f(x,y)) = d^2f/dx^2 + d^2f/dy^2$$

where d^2f/dx^2 is the second partial derivative of f with respect to x and d^2f/dy^2 is the second partial derivative of f with respect to y. For discrete functions, the second partial derivatives can be approximated by

$$d^2f/dx^2 = f(x+1) - 2 \cdot f(x) + f(x-1)$$

and

$$d^2f/dy^2 = f(y+1) - 2 \cdot f(y) + f(y-1)$$

The Laplacian can therefore be approximated by

$$L(f(x,y)) = f(x+1,y) + f(x-1,y) + f(x,y+1) + f(x,y-1) - 4 \cdot f(x,y)$$

This can be expressed as a a convolution kernel that is convolved with $f(x,y)$. The kernel becomes:

$$p(x,y) = \begin{vmatrix} 0 & 1 & 0 \\ 1 & -4 & 1 \\ 0 & 1 & 0 \end{vmatrix}$$

This kernel is given as LAP1 in Figure 10.3.

All edge-enhancement operations, Laplacian included, attenuate the low spatial frequencies of an image. Regions of constant intensity or linearly increasing intensity become black as a result of these transformations, whereas regions of rapidly changing intensity values are highlighted. Convolution kernels that attenuate low frequencies have coefficients that sum to 0.

Some interesting effects can be produced by applying the Laplacian convolution kernel to various images. For example, try convolving an image with kernel LAP3. This has the effect of directly adding the convoluted image back to the original image, which adds striking details to otherwise uninteresting images.

The Shift and Difference Edge Enhancement. As the name implies, this algorithm enhances image edges by shifting an image by a pixel and then subtracting the shifted image from the original. The result of the subtraction is a measure of the slope of the brightness trend. In an area of constant pixel intensity, the subtraction will yield a slope of zero. Zero slope results in black pixel values. In an area with large changes in intensity, an edge, for example, the subtraction will yield a large value for the slope, which will become a light-colored pixel. The larger the difference in intensities, the "whiter" the resultant pixel. Care must be taken when implementing this technique, as negative slope values will occur with transitions from white to black. An absolute value function should be employed so the shift and difference algorithm can detect both black to white and white to black pixel transition edges.

When this approach is used to enhance vertical edges, an image is shifted left one pixel and then subtracted from the original. To enhance horizontal edges, an image is shifted up one pixel and subtracted. To enhance both vertical and horizontal edges the image is first shifted left one pixel and then shifted up one pixel before the subtraction is performed.

Simple as this approach sounds, its implementation is somewhat complex. For this reason, instead of actually shifting the images around, a convolution will be used to obtain the same effect. The convolution kernels that provide shift and difference edge enhancements are shown in Figure 10.3. These kernels resemble visually the shift and difference algorithm. Take, for example, the vertical edge enhancement. We said earlier that to enhance vertical edges the image is shifted to the left one pixel and subtracted. The vertical kernel performs the same process. It compares two horizontally adjacent pixels in an image in an attempt to find the slope of the brightness. If it passes over constant-intensity areas, the result of the convolution will be 0, because

$$-1 \cdot \text{Intensity} + 1 \cdot \text{Intensity} = 0$$

If there is a large intensity change, however, the result will be either a large positive number (for a black to white transition) or a large negative number (for a white to black transition). The intensity of the resultant pixel will be directly proportional to the intensity slope. When using this edge-enhancement method with the convolution code provided, be sure to set the "Absolute" parameter to TRUE so that white to black transitions as well as black to white transitions will be enhanced.

Gradient Directional Edge Enhancement. The shift and difference edge enhancement detailed earlier showed how vertical and horizontal edges in an image can be enhanced. In actual practical application, most edge-enhancement algorithms utilizing only a three by three kernel will enhance more than just completely vertical and horizontal lines. A larger kernel may be used to enforce the vertical and horizontal edge requirements.

Sometimes it is necessary to highlight edges in an image other than strictly vertical or horizontal edges. Diagonal edges of parts during a machine inspection operation may also be important. Selectively highlighting edges in different directions can be used to give a computer an overall idea of what it is looking at. The gradient directional edge-enhancement method can be used for just this purpose. It provides eight different convolution kernels to highlight edges in eight different directions. The directions are called out as points on a compass: "North", "NorthEast", "East", "SouthEast", "South", "SouthWest", "West", and "NorthWest". These kernels are shown in Figure 10.3.

If a positive slope in the direction of the kernel exists, a light-colored pixel will be placed in the output image. The intensity of the output pixel will depend upon the slope of the brightness. The larger the slope, the brighter the pixel. For example, the "East" gradient kernel will enhance edges that transition from black to white from left to right. The application of a "North" and "East" gradient operation is shown in Image Sequence 10.1.

We now know that since the summation of the kernel coefficients equals 0, regions of constant brightness (low spatial frequency) will be attenuated. In other words, areas of constant brightness will result in black pixels being output.

Many special convolution kernels exist for enhancing and detecting image edges. Two such kernels, referred to as *matched filter kernels*, are shown in Figure 10.3. They are called matched filters because they resemble the attributes of the edges they are designed to enhance. They are examples of larger convolution kernels, which guarantee more accurate edge detection at a price of decreased performance. Still larger kernels are possible. These contain *templates*, or shape definitions of the object(s) being searched for in an image. When a shape matches that of the template, the edges are highlighted and all other portions of the image become black.

Image Blurring

Intentionally blurring an image might seem contrary to the philosophy of image enhancement with image processing. True, image blurring does not bring to mind any industrial applications, although there may be some. However, as an artistic tool, blurring can sometimes be put to good use. It can be used to provide a blurred background over which a foreground object is to be placed. We have all seen the wedding pictures with the bride and groom in sharp focus and the background blurred. The contrast of sharpness and blurriness can have a pleasing, eye-catching effect. Photographic filters that provide a blurring effect are available for just this reason.

Blurring can be produced using convolution. A kernel used to blur an image is shown in Figure 10.3. It is a five by five kernel containing all 1's. The larger the kernel dimensions, the more blurred the image. In essence, convolution with the blur kernel averages all pixel values in the pixel neighborhood. Averaging causes the details of an image to be reduced, resulting in the blurring effect.

As mentioned previously, judicious use of the "Scale" parameter passed to the convolution function is required to prevent output image saturation. This is because there are no negative convolution coefficients to reduce the effect of the convolution sum. The value chosen for "Scale" can be subjectively determined by visual inspection of the resulting image.

Edge Detection with Sobel's Algorithm

Sobel's algorithm is the only nonlinear edge-enhancement/detection method discussed in this book. It is described here because of its wide use and because of its efficacy. It is another example of an algorithm with complex mathematical underpinnings that is rather simple to implement.

Actually, there are two distinctly different methods for the implementation of Sobel's algorithm. The first method calculates two different convolutions:

$$X \text{ using kernel} \quad \begin{vmatrix} -1 & 0 & 1 \\ -2 & 0 & -2 \\ -1 & 0 & 1 \end{vmatrix}$$

$$Y \text{ using kernel} \quad \begin{vmatrix} 1 & 2 & 1 \\ 0 & 0 & 0 \\ -1 & -2 & -1 \end{vmatrix}$$

and from these convolutions calculates the magnitude and direction of the detected edges from

Magnitude = SquareRoot $(X^2 + Y^2)$
Direction = arctan (Y/X)

As you can probably tell, this is a very computationally expensive process to perform at each pixel location. For this reason, a different method was chosen for the implementation of Sobel's algorithm. Because of the amount of computation involved, numerous shortcuts, described in the literature, are available to speed up the calculation of Sobel edges. The method chosen is just one of them.

The method we will use is very simple to understand. First, consider a 3- by 3-pixel neighborhood with the pixels labeled as follows:

a   b   c
d   e   f
g   h   i

Exactly four unique lines can be drawn through this neighborhood to pass through the middle pixel (e). These lines are:

Line 1: a-e-i
Line 2: b-e-h
Line 3: c-e-g
Line 4: d-e-f

Each line drawn through the pixel neighborhood subdivides the pixel space into two three-pixel neighborhoods. For example, line 1 subdivides the pixel space into neighborhood d, g, and h and neighborhood b, c, and f.

For each of the four lines the absolute value of the difference in the averages of the two subneighborhoods is calculated. Thus, four total difference calculations are performed. The pixel of interest is given the value of the largest of the four absolute differences.

After the application of Sobel's algorithm to each pixel in an image, the output image is usually subjected to a thresholding point process operation. Whenever the new value of the pixel of interest (the largest absolute difference just calculated) meets or exceeds the specified threshold, the color of the output pixel is set to white. If the value is less than the threshold, the pixel is set to black. The net result of applying Sobel's algorithm followed by a point thresholding process is a black and white image that contains none of the original image information except edge information. Image Sequence 10.2 shows the visual effect of this processing.

The implementation of Sobel's algorithm provided in this chapter and in the area process function library slightly departs from the description just given. Essentially, the thresholding point process is built directly into the Sobel function instead of being a separate transformation. This results in better performance, as the image data does not have to be fetched from the image buffer so many times. Also, a mode of operation was built into the Sobel realization that allows the original image information to be copied to the output buffer if and only if the threshold is not exceeded. That is, if the calculated maximum absolute difference for the pixel of interest is above the specified threshold, the pixel color is set to white unconditionally. If, however, the difference is less than the threshold, the original pixel value can optionally be copied to the output buffer. If that option, which is controlled by the "Overlay" parameter passed to the Sobel function (see Figure 10.1) is not exercised, the value of the output pixel is set to black.

The value chosen for the threshold makes a difference in the appearance of the output image. Image Sequence 10.2 shows Sobel's edge detection in operation.

Median Filtering

Median filtering is an area process that does not fall under the category of convolution. Some people consider median filtering to be more a point process than an area process because of the way in which it works. For our purposes, median filtering is considered an area process.

Median filtering uses the values of the pixels contained in the pixel neighborhood to determine the new value given to the pixel of interest. However, it does not algorithmically

Image Sequence 10.2   Sobel Edge Detection

(a)

Original image

(b)

Edge-detected image

Threshold = 10
Overlay = False

(c)

Edge-detected image

Threshold = 10
Overlay = True

Image Sequence 10.3   Median Filtering

(a)

*Original image
corrupted with
random noise*

(b)

*Median -filtered image.
Notice absences
of noise.*

(c)

*Median-filtered image
2nd application*

calculate the new pixel value from the pixels in the neighborhood. Instead, it sorts the pixels in the neighborhood into ascending order and picks the middle or median pixel value as the new value for the pixel of interest. The median filter algorithm is illustrated in Figure 10.4. Median-filtered images are shown in Image Sequence 10.3.

The result of median filtering is that any random noise contained in an image will be effectively eliminated. This is because any random, abrupt change in pixel intensity within a pixel neighborhood will be sorted out. That is, it will be placed at either the top or the bottom of the sorted neighborhood values and will be ignored because the median value is always picked for the new pixel value. The sorting out of random pixel values is shown in Figure 10.4.

Multiple applications of median filtering to an image can result in rather pleasing visual effects. See Image Sequence 10.3(c) for an example.

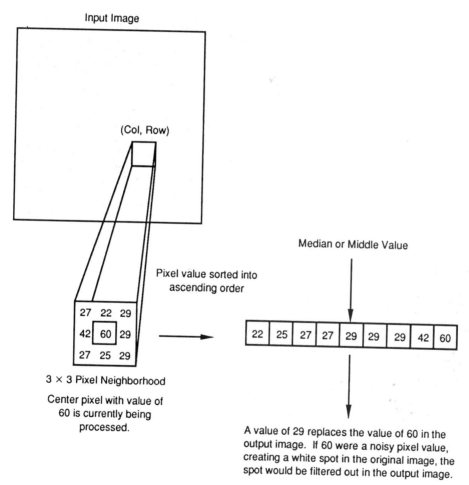

Figure 10.4 Median Filter Operation

Conclusions

In this chapter we have discussed various image processing algorithms that fall into the category of area processes. A large number of these area processes utilize the concept of convolution. The area process or transformation performed on an image is controlled by a convolution kernel. Numerous kernels for various transformations were given. Applications, both industrial and artistic, were suggested for many of the area processes. Example images were given to show the visual result of the application of many of the area processes. Applying the point processes discussed in Chapter 9 and the area processes discussed in this chapter further expand our image processing capabilities.

11

Frame Processes

In this chapter you will learn about:

- **What frame processes are and how they differ from point and area processes**
- **How frame processes are used for inspection and image modification**
- **What things to be careful about when applying frame processes to image data**

Introduction

The discussion in the previous two chapters has centered around point and area image processing algorithms. Both of these classes of algorithms (and the geometric process class yet to be discussed) use information contained in an image in conjunction with a transformation function to generate a new image. Frame processes break with that tradition. Instead, they use information from two (or more) images together with a combination function to produce a brand-new image. This new image depends not only upon the content of each input image but also upon the type of function used to combine them. These processes are called *frame processes* because a complete video image is called a *frame*. They work on two complete video images.

Frame processes have many practical applications. They are being used in industry today for security, quality control, and image-quality-enhancement applications. They have artistic uses as well, as we shall see. We shall investigate some of these applications in the discussion that follows.

For security applications, frame processing can be used to detect motion and therefore intruders. Assume a video camera is positioned within the lobby of a building in such a manner that its field of view covers the complete lobby. If each frame from the video camera is digitized and compared to the previous frame, any movement within the field of view of the camera can be detected. The comparison of the video images is actually the subtraction of the images followed by a thresholding process and finally a pixel difference tally. If the number of pixels that differ in two sequential video images crosses a predetermined threshold, it is time to set off the alarms. Not only is motion detected, but the direction and speed of the motion can also be measured. This is possible as long as three things are known:

1. The time between sequential video frames
2. The distance from the camera to the moving object
3. The total displacement of the object in pixels

Armed with this information and some trigonometry, speed and direction can be approximated.

It is important that the comparison always be performed between sequential video frames instead of between a reference image of the lobby and the incoming video. This is because changes in the light-intensity level of the monitored area over the course of a day could be enough to set off the alarms. The use of sequential video frames for comparison will eliminate the problems caused by slowly changing light levels. If, however, an intruder were to step into the field of view and switch the lights on if they were previously off or off if they were on, the alarms would go off as a result of the drastic change in light level.

Subtraction of video images has practical applications other than security. Consider Image Sequence 11.1. In this sequence, the ability to subtract out a busy background from an image is illustrated. This would be useful, for example, if the study of a foreground object needed to be performed and the busyness of the background was distracting (visually and/or numerically). As long as two images are available, one of only the background and one of the foreground object obscuring the same background, subtraction can be used to remove almost all traces of the background. Note that the subtraction process will not leave the foreground object totally unscathed. If the portion of the background obscured by the foreground object contains bright pixels, the foreground object left after the subtraction process will be mottled in the pattern of those bright pixels. However, if the background in the proximity of the foreground object is dark, the subtraction of the foreground and background images will have very little impact on the foreground object. If the background does pose a problem, a better study of the foreground object might be possible using a mask (discussed later in this chapter). A properly positioned mask can remove all of the background surrounding the foreground object without impacting the foreground object.

One more use of the subtraction frame process is for quality control inspections. Consider a flow of newly manufactured printed circuit boards (PCBs) down a conveyor on the way to being tested. Anyone who has been involved with visual inspection of PCBs knows how tedious the job is and how easy it is to miss something—that is, to let a PCB pass with an obvious flaw: missing part, parts in backwards, and so on.

If an image of a perfectly assembled PCB is available and a video image is digitized for each PCB going down the conveyor, subtraction can be used to locate missing or improperly positioned parts on the board. Manufacturing costs can be kept down if this automated inspection process can return the substandard PCBs to manufacturing for touch-up before a test technician wastes time locating the missing parts. If PCBs with all common manufacturing mistakes are also digitized, it is possible for other frame processes to be used to print out

Image Sequence 11.1 Background Removal

(a)

Original image

(b)

*Original image,
background only*

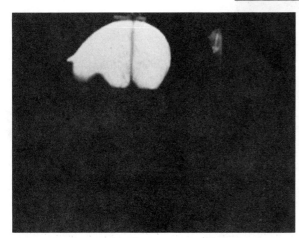

(c)

*Original image with
background subtracted out*

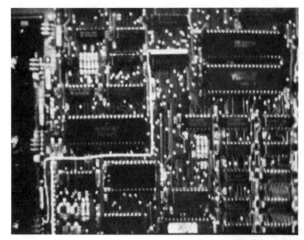

(a)

*Complete circuit board.
Note white jumper wire.*

(b)

*Complete circuit board
without jumper*

(c)

*Subtracted image
Missing jumper wire
is obvious.*

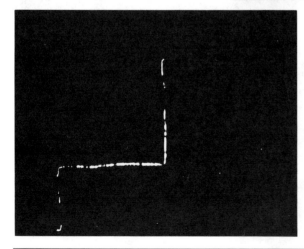

exactly which parts (by part numbers) are affected. This would make the manufacturing touch-up process very efficient indeed. Image Sequence 11.2 gives a demonstration of PCB inspection in operation. The white jumper wire missing from the PCB under inspection is immediately obvious in the subtracted image.

Many image-combination functions other than subtraction are possible. The code provided in the frame process function library (actually, only the single function "CombineImages") provides each of the following combination functions: "And", "Or", "Xor", "Add", "Subtract", "Multiply", "Divide", "Average", "Maximum value", "Minimum value", and "Overlay". See Figure 11.1 for the details. Some of these combination functions make intuitive sense while others (multiplying images, for example) make very little sense. Each combination function will be discussed.

| Combine Function | Image Source Data | | Dest Image | Data |
	SImage @SCol,SRow	DImage @DCol,DRow	Combine Function Description	@DCol,DRow
1. And	SData	DData	DData &= SData	DData
2. Or	SData	DData	DData |= SData	DData
3. Xor	SData	DData	DData ^= SData	DData
4. Add	SData	DData	DData += SData	DData
5. Sub	SData	DData	DData − = SData	DData
6. Mult	SData	DData	DData * = SData	DData
7. Div	SData	DData	DData /= SData if SData != 0	DData
8. Min	SData	DData	DData = MIN(SData,DData)	DData
9. Max	SData	DData	DData = MAX(SData,DData)	DData
10. Ave	SData	DData	DData = (SData+DData)/2	DData
11. Ovrly	SData	DData	DData = SData	DData

Notes
1. "SData" is data fetched from the source image. "DData" is data fetched from the destination image and eventually stored back into the destination image.
2. The destination image is modified by all of these combine operations.
3. Overlay performs a copy operation from the source to the destination image.

Truth Table for Basic Logic Functions

| Inputs | | Outputs | | | | | |
A	B	And	Nand	Or	Nor	Xor	XNor
0	0	0	1	0	1	0	1
0	1	0	1	1	0	1	0
1	0	0	1	1	0	1	0
1	1	1	0	1	0	0	1

This table gives the rules for the basic combination functions (and then some). With this table it is possible to predict the result of combining overlapping image data using the simple logic functions.

Figure 11.1 Image Combination Functions Provided by the Frame Process Function Library

(a)

Original image

(b)

Image mask

(c)

Masked image

The bitwise "And" combination function is used mainly to mask out portions of an image. First, a mask image is produced that contains a 1 in every pixel location that is to be retained and a 0 in each pixel location to be masked out (changed to black). When an image and the mask image are combined using the "And" function, the output image will be the same as the source image wherever the mask image contained 1's and will be black everywhere the mask contained 0's. Image Sequence 11.3 shows the effect of image masking.

The use of the "And" function with a mask having values other than 0 or 1 is of questionable value. The effect would be selectively to remove bits from each pixel's value, thereby changing its displayed color. A practical application of this technique is unknown, although artistic uses can probably be imagined. Also, using the "And" function to combine actual images may have interesting visual impact but otherwise is of dubious value. The same is true when combining images with any of the logical operators: "And", "Or", and "Xor".

The "Or" function can be used under certain conditions to combine two images quite effectively. If two images are available that have bright foreground objects on dark (black) backgrounds and that do not overlap, the "Or" function can be used to merge both foreground objects into a single image. The foreground object of one image overlays the other image's black background and vice versa. The "Or" function will cause the bits that are set in the foreground objects to be assimilated into output image, because any bit set in the foreground object "Or"ed with the 0 bit of the background will become set. "Or"ing follows exactly the same rules for image combination as it does in logic gates in electronics.

Problems arise, however, if the foreground objects of the two images being combined overlap. The "Or"ing of the two nonzero pixel values in the foreground objects will result in a new pixel value that is the combination of the two. The color used for the display (gray-scale tone) of the overlapping pixels will then be unrelated to either image. The results are not very pleasing to look at and there is no known practical use. Image Sequence 11.4 shows the effect of image "Or"ing with overlapping objects.

The exclusive "Or", "Xor", is another combination function available. From elementary logic you'll remember that with an "Xor" operation any bits that are the same become 0 and bits that are different become 1's (see Figure 11.1). With this combining function it is possible to detect all pixels of an image with a specified value. To do this, an image buffer is prepared by clearing it to the specified pixel value, say 32. If this image is then "Xor"ed with a real image, every pixel in the real image that was exactly equal to 32 will be set to black, with all other pixels becoming some other nonblack color (gray tone). To make the effect more noticeable, a point process can follow the "Xor" operation that sets all black pixels to white and all other pixels to black. Image Sequence 11.5 shows this effect. The code to perform this operation is contained in the file "frtest.c" on the companion disk and is shown in Listing 11.2. Note that a point process alone can be used to provide the same transformation in a one-step process. This would be accomplished by storing the color for white (63) into a LUT at location 32 and putting zeros at every other location. When an image was point transformed using this LUT, all pixels from the original image with a value of 32 would be displayed as white and all other pixels would be black.

Arithmetic "add"ing is another way to combine images, one that works much better than the "Or" operation discussed previously. This method can be used to combine images that overlap each other without the bizarre (bit-filling) effects created by the "Or" opera-

Image Sequence 11.4   Combining Images

Original image one

(a)

Original image two

(b)

One + two

(c)

One or two

(d)

tion. When pixels from two images are ''add''ed together, no intensity information is lost or artificially created (as long as arithmetic overflow does not occur). The resultant pixel intensity will be the sum of the two pixels used to create it.

Pixel-value overflow is a problem that must be considered when ''add''ing images together. This overflow is possible because the intensity sum of two pixels can easily exceed the maximum permissible pixel value: in our case the value 63. To prevent this overflow, our ''CombineImages'' function can scale the intensity of the generated images so as not to

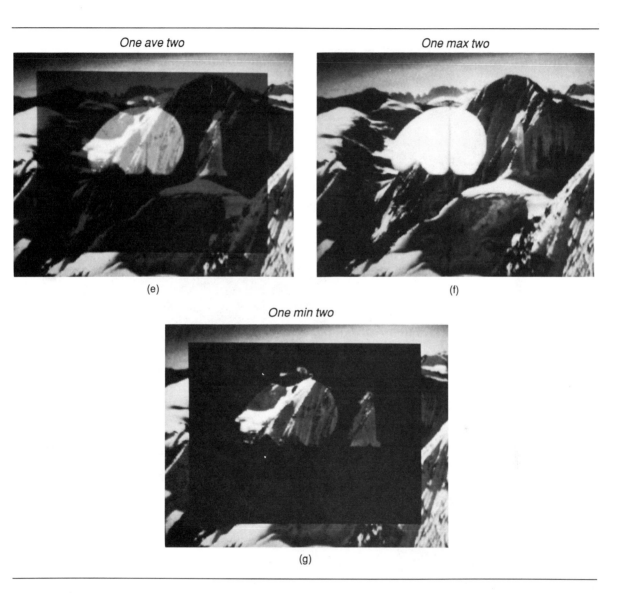

One ave two

(e)

One max two

(f)

One min two

(g)

saturate the display. The parameter "Scale" passed to this function controls the amount of scaling applied to the generated image. See Figure 11.2 for more information on "Scale".

The subtraction combination has been discussed at length. This is because image subtraction is one of the most useful of the image-combination functions. A note of caution must be given about using the subtraction function. Image subtraction often results in negative pixel values. Negative pixel intensities cannot be displayed and are therefore converted to a value of 0 in the code provided. If your application involves negative pixel

Image Sequence 11.5   Image Pixel Intensities

(a)

Original image

(b)

*This image was
cleared to a pixel
value of 32.*

(c)

*All pixels in original
image equal to 32*

Combine Images Function

Prototype
void CombineImages(BYTE huge *SImage, unsigned SCol, unsigned SRow, unsigned SWidth, unsigned SHeight, BYTE huge *DImage, unsigned DCol, unsigned DRow, enum BitFunction CombineType, short Scale);

Where:

"SImage" is a pointer to the source image. This source image will be combined with the destination image, but the source image will never be corrupted.

"SCol", "SRow", "SWidth", and "SHeight" are parameters controlling the portion of the source image that will be used in transforming the destination image. "SWidth" and "SHeight" describe a square area with its upper left corner situated at "SCol", "SRow". The same-size area in the destination image will be transformed.

"DImage" is a pointer to the destination image. The source image (or a portion of it) along with the specified combining function will transform this destination image. The destination image is always overwritten by the transformation process.

"DCol" and "DRow" are parameters controlling the portion of the destination image that will be affected by the transformation process. The square area that will be transformed is controlled by "SWidth" and "SHeight", but the location in the destination buffer is controlled by "DCol" and "DRow".

"CombineType" is an enumeration type that controls which of the combining functions to apply to the image data. Currently supported types are "And", "Or", "Xor", "Add", "Sub(tract)", "Mult(iply)", "Div(ide)", "Ave(rage)", "Max(imum value)", "Min(imum value)", and "Overlay". (See the text for a description of the operation of each of these combining functions.)

"Scale" controls whether and by how much the pixel value that results from the combination function should be scaled before being placed in the destination image. A scale value of 0 performs no scaling. The calculated pixel value is stored directly in the destination buffer. A positive or negative "Scale" value determines which direction (right or left respectively) and how many shifts should be applied to the data before storage in the destination image. The following table illustrates the operation of the "Scale" parameter.

Given a pixel value of I,

Scale Value	Number of Right Shifts	Number of Left Shifts	Resultant Value
-5	0	5	$I * 32$
-4	0	4	$I * 16$
-3	0	3	$I * 8$
-2	0	2	$I * 4$
-1	0	1	$I * 2$
0	0	0	I
$+1$	1	0	$I / 2$
$+2$	2	0	$I / 4$
$+3$	3	0	$I / 8$
$+4$	4	0	$I / 16$
$+5$	5	0	$I / 32$

Thus, quite a bit of control exists for keeping the calculated pixel values within the valid range.

Figure 11.2 Frame Process Library Functions   *(continued)*

Operation
The operation of "CombineImages" is very straightforward. As usual, two nested loops control the movement through the image buffers. Inside the two loops, a byte of source and destination image are fetched and then combined according to the type of combining function currently in effect. The new pixel value that results from the combining is optionally scaled and then forced into the valid pixel intensity range of 0 to 63. This new pixel value is subsequently placed in the destination image at the specified locations.

Figure 11.2 *(continued)*

intensities, an absolute value function can be used to force the values positive and thereby make them displayable.

Multiplication and division of images are interesting concepts that can produce some rather unusual results when applied to the proper type of image; however, no practical application of these combining functions is known. Multiplication of two images would result in a contrast stretch of one image based upon the intensity content of the other. The multiplication and division combining functions are included here for completeness only.

Again, scaling is very important when utilizing these functions. The value of multiplied or divided pixels can easily get out of range. Use scaling to bring the values back into a usable range for display.

The minimum and maximum combining functions work exactly as one would expect. The minimum function places the smaller pixel value from the two source images into the destination image, whereas the maximum function places the larger value. Images produced with these functions seem to melt overlapping areas of the source images together. Industrial uses for these combining functions are unknown.

The average combining function sums the pixel values from the two source images and divides the result by two before placing it in the destination image. When used with images of differing composition, the average function performs a smooth merge of the image content. Again, this function probably has more artistic uses than industrial ones.

When the average function is used to average two identical images, the result is an image with less noise. In fact, the signal to noise ratio of any image (a measure of its quality) goes up by a factor square root of N when averaged with N identical frames. This is because over the long run any random noise in the images being averaged is diluted by being averaged with good pixel data. Noise produced by video cameras is a prime candidate for reduction using averaging techniques. Constant, nonrandom aberrations in a series of images will not be improved by averaging. The average combining function provided by "CombineImages" works on two images only. If multiple images need to be averaged, a new function will have to be developed.

The final combining function is "Overlay". It essentially provides a direct copy of pixel data from the source image to the destination image without other transformation. This function can be used to copy an object from one image to another or from one image to another portion of the same image. When the source and destination images are the same, care must be taken, because no checks are made in the code to detect and prevent overlap. The "Translation" function from the geometric process function library described in Chapter 12 can also be used to move objects around within a single image.

The code for the frame processes discussed in this chapter is shown in Listing 11.1 and

Listing 11.1 The Frame Process Function Library

The following is the contents of the file, "frprocess.h":

```
/***************************************/
/*      Image Processing Header File    */
/*      Frame Processing Functions      */
/*         written in Turbo C 2.0       */
/*                 by                   */
/*          Craig A. Lindley            */
/*                                      */
/*   Vers: 1.0  Last Update: 11/14/89   */
/***************************************/


/* User defined image combination type */
typedef enum {And,Or,Xor,Add,Sub,Mult,Div,Min,Max,Ave,Overlay} BitFunction;


/* Frame Process Function Prototypes */

void CombineImages(BYTE huge *SImage,
                   unsigned SCol, unsigned SRow,
                   unsigned SWidth, unsigned SHeight,
                   BYTE huge *DImage,
                   unsigned DCol, unsigned DRow,
                   enum BitFunction CombineType,
                   short Scale);
```

The following is the contents of the file, "frprocess.c":

```
/***************************************/
/*       Image Processing Code          */
/*       Frame Process Functions        */
/*         written in Turbo C 2.0       */
/*                 by                   */
/*          Craig A. Lindley            */
/*                                      */
/*   Vers: 1.0  Last Update: 11/14/89   */
/***************************************/


#include <stdio.h>
#include <stdlib.h>
#include <conio.h>
#include <dos.h>
```

(continued)

Listing 11.1 *(continued)*

```c
#include <alloc.h>
#include <process.h>
#include <graphics.h>
#include "misc.h"
#include "pcx.h"
#include "vga.h"
#include "imagesup.h"
#include "frprocess.h"


/* Single function performs all image combinations */

void CombineImages(BYTE huge *SImage,
                        unsigned SCol, unsigned SRow,
                        unsigned SWidth, unsigned SHeight,
                        BYTE huge *DImage,
                        unsigned DCol, unsigned DRow,
                        enum BitFunction CombineType,
                        short Scale)
{
    register unsigned SImageCol, SImageRow, DestCol;
    short SData, DData;
    unsigned SColExtent, SRowExtent;

    if (ParameterCheckOK(SCol,SRow,SCol+SWidth,SRow+SHeight,"CombineImages") &&
        ParameterCheckOK(DCol,DRow,DCol+SWidth,DRow+SHeight,"CombineImages"))
    {
        SColExtent = SCol+SWidth;
        SRowExtent = SRow+SHeight;

        for (SImageRow = SRow; SImageRow < SRowExtent; SImageRow++)
        {
                /* Reset the destination Column count every row */
                DestCol = DCol;
                for (SImageCol = SCol; SImageCol < SColExtent; SImageCol++)
                {
                    /* Get a byte of the source and dest image data */
                    SData = GetPixelFromImage(SImage,SImageCol,SImageRow);
                    DData = GetPixelFromImage(DImage,DestCol,DRow);

                    /* Combine source and dest data according to parameter */
                    switch(CombineType)
                    {
                        case And:
```

```
                    DData &= SData;
                    break;
            case Or:
                    DData |= SData;
                    break;
            case Xor:
                    DData ^= SData;
                    break;
            case Add:
                    DData += SData;
                    break;
            case Sub:
                    DData -= SData;
                    break;
            case Mult:
                    DData *= SData;
                    break;
            case Div:
                    if (SData != 0)
                        DData /= SData;
                    break;
            case Min:
                    DData = MIN(SData,DData);
                    break;
            case Max:
                    DData = MAX(SData,DData);
                    break;
            case Ave:
                    DData = (SData+DData)/2;
                    break;
            case Overlay:
                    DData = SData;
                    break;
    }
    /*
Scale the resultant data if requested to. A positive
Scale value shifts the destination data to the right
thereby dividing it by a power of two. A zero Scale
value leaves the data untouched. A negative Scale
value shifts the data left thereby multiplying it by
a power of two.
    */
```

(continued)

Listing 11.1 *(continued)*

```
                    if (Scale < 0)
                       DData <<= abs(Scale);
                    else if (Scale > 0)
                       DData >>= Scale;

                    /* Don't let the pixel data get out of range */
                    DData = (DData < MINSAMPLEVAL) ? MINSAMPLEVAL:DData;
                    DData = (DData > MAXSAMPLEVAL) ? MAXSAMPLEVAL:DData;
                    PutPixelInImage(DImage,DestCol++,DRow,DData);
                 }
                 /* Bump to next row in the destination image */
                 DRow++;
              }
           }
        }
```

is contained in the files "frprocess.h" and "frprocess.c". Additionally, the example program used to create all of the image sequences in this section is comprised of the files "frtest.c" and "frtest.prj" (Listing 11.2) on the companion disk. An application program that wishes to utilize the frame process function library must include the file "frprocess.h" in its code and be subsequently linked with "frprocess.c". Use "frtest.c" and "frtest.prj" as models for a typical application program. The function prototypes and descriptions of the frame process functions contained in the frame process function library are shown in Figure 11.2.

Listing 11.2   The Frame Process Example Program

The following is the contents of the file, "frtest.prj":

```
graphics.lib
vgagraph.obj
egavga.obj
pcx        (misc.h pcx.h)
vga        (misc.h vga.h pcx.h)
imagesup   (misc.h vga.h pcx.h imagesup.h)
ptprocess  (misc.h vga.h pcx.h imagesup.h ptprocess.h)
frprocess  (misc.h vga.h pcx.h imagesup.h frprocess.h)
frtest     (misc.h vga.h pcx.h imagesup.h ptprocess.h frprocess.h)
```

The following is the contents of the file, "frtest.c":

```
/****************************************/
/*        Image Processing Code         */
/*       Frame Process Functions        */
/*              Demo Program            */
/*         written in Turbo C 2.0       */
/*                 by                   */
/*          Craig A. Lindley            */
/*                                      */
/*   Vers: 1.0  Last Update: 12/26/89   */
/****************************************/

#include <stdio.h>
#include <conio.h>
#include <dos.h>
#include <alloc.h>
#include <process.h>
#include <graphics.h>
#include "misc.h"
#include "pcx.h"
#include "vga.h"
#include "imagesup.h"
#include "ptprocess.h"
#include "frprocess.h"

/* main frame process demonstration program */

void main(void)
{
    char *InFileName1 = "p2c11i1a";
    char *InFileName2 = "p2c11i1b";
    char *InFileName3 = "p2c11i2a";
    char *InFileName4 = "p2c11i2b";
    char *InFileName5 = "p2c11i3a";
    char *InFileName6 = "p2c11i4a";
    char *InFileName7 = "p2c11i4b";
    char *InFileName8 = "p2c11i5a";

    BYTE huge *InImage1;
    BYTE huge *InImage2;
    BYTE huge *Buffer;

    unsigned GenPCXFiles = FALSE;   /* controls output file generation */
    BYTE LUT[MAXQUANTLEVELS];
    unsigned Index;
```

(continued)

Listing 11.2   *(continued)*

```
/* Initialize graphic subsystem */
InitGraphics();

printf("Frame Transform Example Program Program\n\n");
printf("Reading the Image PCX Files into memory\n");

/*
Allocate enough memory to save destination image
as it will be written over during each transform.
*/

Buffer = (BYTE huge *) farcalloc(RASTERSIZE,sizeof(BYTE));
if (Buffer == NULL)
{
    printf("FRTEST Error: No memory for buffer\n");
    exit(ENoMemory);
}

/*
Image Sequence 11.1 - Background substraction
*/

/*
Read source and destination images into memory. The
image read into InImage2 is considered the destination
image.
*/
if (ReadPCXFileToBuf (InFileName1,&InImage1) != NoError)
    exit(1);
DisplayImageInBuf(InImage1,INITVGALOADPALETTE,WAITFORKEY);

if (ReadPCXFileToBuf (InFileName2,&InImage2) != NoError)
    exit(1);
DisplayImageInBuf(InImage2,NOVGAINIT,WAITFORKEY);
/*
Combine source image with destination image by the subtraction
process. The destination image is overwritten.
*/
CombineImages(InImage2,MINCOLNUM,MINROWNUM,MAXCOLS,MAXROWS,
                      InImage1,MINCOLNUM,MINROWNUM,Sub,0);

/*
Display image with background removed
```

```
*/
DisplayImageInBuf(InImage1,NOVGAINIT,WAITFORKEY);
if (GenPCXFiles)
   WritePCXFile("p2c11i1c",8,320,200,1,320);
/*
Return memory taken up by the image buffers
*/
farfree((BYTE far *) InImage1);
farfree((BYTE far *) InImage2);


/*
Image Sequence 11.2 - Circuit board inspection
*/


/*
Read source and destination images into memory. The
image read into InImage2 is considered the destination
image.
*/
if (ReadPCXFileToBuf (InFileName3,&InImage1) != NoError)
   exit(1);
DisplayImageInBuf(InImage1,NOVGAINIT,WAITFORKEY);

if (ReadPCXFileToBuf (InFileName4,&InImage2) != NoError)
   exit(1);
DisplayImageInBuf(InImage2,NOVGAINIT,WAITFORKEY);


/*
Combine source image with destination image by the subtraction
process. The destination image is overwritten.
*/
CombineImages(InImage2,MINCOLNUM,MINROWNUM,MAXCOLS,MAXROWS,
                       InImage1,MINCOLNUM,MINROWNUM,Sub,0);


/*
Display the differences between the circuit board images
*/
DisplayImageInBuf(InImage1,NOVGAINIT,WAITFORKEY);
if (GenPCXFiles)
   WritePCXFile("p2c11i2c",8,320,200,1,320);

/*
Image Sequence 11.3 - Image Masking
*/
```

(continued)

Listing 11.2 *(continued)*

```
/* Read in the image to be masked */
if (ReadPCXFileToBuf (InFileName5,&InImage1) != NoError)
   exit(1);
DisplayImageInBuf(InImage1,NOVGAINIT,WAITFORKEY);


/* Prepare the image mask */
ClearImageArea(Buffer,MINCOLNUM,MINROWNUM,MAXCOLS,MAXROWS,WHITE);
ClearImageArea(Buffer,200,10,80,180,BLACK);

/* Display mask */
DisplayImageInBuf(Buffer,NOVGAINIT,WAITFORKEY);
if (GenPCXFiles)
   WritePCXFile("p2c11i3b",8,320,200,1,320);


/* Preform masking operation */
CombineImages(Buffer,MINCOLNUM,MINROWNUM,MAXCOLS,MAXROWS,
                          InImage1,MINCOLNUM,MINROWNUM,And,0);
DisplayImageInBuf(InImage1,NOVGAINIT,WAITFORKEY);
if (GenPCXFiles)
   WritePCXFile("p2c11i3c",8,320,200,1,320);


/*
Return memory taken up by the image buffers
*/
farfree((BYTE far *) InImage1);
farfree((BYTE far *) InImage2);


/*
Image Sequence 11.4 - Various frame processes
*/
/*
Read source and destination images into memory. The
image read into InImage2 is considered the destination
image.
*/

if (ReadPCXFileToBuf (InFileName6,&InImage1) != NoError)
   exit(1);
DisplayImageInBuf(InImage1,NOVGAINIT,WAITFORKEY);


if (ReadPCXFileToBuf (InFileName7,&InImage2) != NoError)
   exit(1);
DisplayImageInBuf(InImage2,NOVGAINIT,WAITFORKEY);
```

```
/*
Make a copy of the destination image so it can be
restored after each frame process without having
to reload it from disk.
*/
CopyImage(InImage2,Buffer);


/*
Combine source image with destination image by addition
process. The destination image is overwritten.
*/
CombineImages(InImage1,32,20,256,160,
                        InImage2,32,20,Add,1);


DisplayImageInBuf(InImage2,NOVGAINIT,WAITFORKEY);
if (GenPCXFiles)
   WritePCXFile("p2c11i4c",8,320,200,1,320);


/*
Restore InImage2 the destination buffer for use with the
next frame process transformation. Now we are back in our
original state with the source image in InImage1 and the
destination image in InImage2.
*/
CopyImage(Buffer,InImage2);


/*
Combine source image with destination image by bitwise OR
process. The destination image is overwritten.
*/
CombineImages(InImage1,32,20,256,160,
                        InImage2,32,20,Or,0);


DisplayImageInBuf(InImage2,NOVGAINIT,WAITFORKEY);
if (GenPCXFiles)
   WritePCXFile("p2c11i4d",8,320,200,1,320);


CopyImage(Buffer,InImage2);


/*
Combine source image with destination image by average
process. The destination image is overwritten.
*/
```

(continued)

Listing 11.2   *(continued)*

```
CombineImages(InImage1,32,20,256,160,
                            InImage2,32,20,Ave,0);


DisplayImageInBuf(InImage2,NOVGAINIT,WAITFORKEY);
if (GenPCXFiles)
   WritePCXFile("p2c11i4e",8,320,200,1,320);


CopyImage(Buffer,InImage2);

/*
Combine source image with destination image by maximum
process. The destination image is overwritten.
*/
CombineImages(InImage1,32,20,256,160,
                            InImage2,32,20,Max,0);


DisplayImageInBuf(InImage2,NOVGAINIT,WAITFORKEY);
if (GenPCXFiles)
   WritePCXFile("p2c11i4f",8,320,200,1,320);
CopyImage(Buffer,InImage2);


/*
Combine source image with destination image by minimum
process. The destination image is overwritten.
*/
CombineImages(InImage1,32,20,256,160,
                            InImage2,32,20,Min,0);


DisplayImageInBuf(InImage2,NOVGAINIT,WAITFORKEY);
if (GenPCXFiles)
   WritePCXFile("p2c11i4g",8,320,200,1,320);


CopyImage(Buffer,InImage2);
/*
Return memory taken up by the image buffers
*/
farfree((BYTE far *) InImage1);
farfree((BYTE far *) InImage2);


/*
Image Sequence 11.5 - Determining Image Pixel Intensities
*/
```

```
if (ReadPCXFileToBuf (InFileName8,&InImage1) != NoError)
   exit(1);
DisplayImageInBuf(InImage1,NOVGAINIT,WAITFORKEY);
/*
Set all bytes of InImage2 buffer to a value of 32
*/
ClearImageArea(Buffer,MINCOLNUM,MINROWNUM,MAXCOLS,MAXROWS,32);
DisplayImageInBuf(Buffer,NOVGAINIT,WAITFORKEY);
if (GenPCXFiles)
   WritePCXFile("p2c11i5b",8,320,200,1,320);


/*
Combine source image with destination image using the Xor
process. The destination image is overwritten.
*/
CombineImages(InImage1,MINCOLNUM,MINROWNUM,MAXCOLS,MAXROWS,
                      Buffer,MINCOLNUM,MINROWNUM,Xor,0);


/*
After Xor operation all pixels which had the value of 32 black
and all other pixels are some other color. We will now use a
point process to convert black pixels to white and all others
to black.
*/
for (Index=0; Index < MAXQUANTLEVELS; Index++)
   LUT[Index] = 0;

LUT[0] = MAXSAMPLEVAL;

PtTransform(Buffer,MINCOLNUM,MINROWNUM,MAXCOLS,MAXROWS,LUT);
DisplayImageInBuf(Buffer,NOVGAINIT,WAITFORKEY);
if (GenPCXFiles)
   WritePCXFile("p2c11i5c",8,320,200,1,320);

/*
Free all allocated memory
*/
farfree((BYTE far *) InImage1);
farfree((BYTE far *) Buffer);

restorecrtmode();
closegraph();
}
```

Conclusions

In this chapter we have seen the effect of frame processes applied to image data and discussed many practical applications of the frame processes. Where necessary, the drawbacks of using certain of the frame combination processes have been pointed out. An example program is provided that shows the frame processes functions in operation.

12

Geometric Processes

In this chapter you will learn about:

- **What geometric processes are and how they differ from the point, area, and frame processes discussed in the previous chapters**
- **What geometric processes are used for**
- **What pixel interpolation is and why it is necessary**
- **Aspect ratio problems and corrective techniques**
- **Image scaling, rotation, translation, and mirroring**

Introduction

Geometric processes are the final class of image processing algorithm to be discussed. Geometric processes change the spatial positioning and/or arrangement of pixels within an image based upon some geometric transformation. Geometric transformations do not necessarily alter pixel-intensity values. Instead, they alter the position of the pixels. In other words, the intensity value for a given pixel (the information contained in the pixel) is moved to a new location. This makes geometric processes quite different from the point, area, and frame processes we have discussed up to this point. Each of these other classes of image processing algorithms intentionally altered the intensity value of pixels based upon a specified transformation.

Geometric transformations have many uses, both industrial and artistic. They can be used

   a. To correct for some defect inherent in an imaging system (spatial aberrations in an image sensor, aspect ratio problems, and so on)

   b. As a preprocessing step to prepare an image for subsequent point, area, or frame processing

   c. To provide precise image registration between images that will be compared

   d. As tools for image composition in preparation of display or hardcopy output (for example, the production of collage images)

   e. To provide a variety of special effects with images

This list is by no means exhaustive. Many more applications of geometric processes exist.

Like the other forms of image processing already discussed, geometric processing is not without its own set of particular implementation difficulties. When images are altered in a geometric fashion the result might not turn out as expected unless pixel positioning, aspect ratios, and buffer overlap are taken into consideration. Pixel positioning and aspect ratios are so important to accurate geometric transformations that they will each be given a detailed discussion. Image sequences will be provided that illustrate how important accurate pixel positioning and aspect ratios really are. The problems caused by source and destination buffer overlap are well understood and can easily be avoided.

The geometric process function library discussed in this chapter provides image scaling, sizing, rotation, translation, and mirror imaging. The geometric transformations provided by these functions should be somewhat self-evident from their names. The image-manipulation capabilities provided here in conjunction with those provided in Chapters 9 through 11 form a very well-rounded image processing function library. With these functions and a powerful personal computer, you'll be able to apply image processing techniques to many imaging disciplines—from astronomy to desktop publishing.

The code for the geometric processes discussed in this chapter is shown in Listing 12.1 and is contained in the files "geprocess.h" and "geprocess.c". The example program used to create all of the image sequences is comprised of the files "getest.c" and "getest.prj" on the companion disk. The example program is also shown in Listing 12.2. An application program that wishes to utilize the geometric process function library must include the file "geprocess.h" in its code and must be subsequently linked with "geprocess.c". Use "getest.c" and "getest.prj" as models for a typical application program. The function prototypes and descriptions of each of the geometric processes are shown in Figure 12.2.

Pixel Positioning and Interpolation

Applying geometric processes to images sometimes results in losing the one-to-one pixel correspondence between the source and destination images that we have enjoyed until this point. In our previous image processing, it has always been possible to identify how a pixel of the destination image was derived from the source image, that is, which of the source pixel(s) were involved. This one-to-one correspondence or mapping has always been taken for granted.

Listing 12.1   The Geometric Process Function Library

The following is the contents of the file, "geprocess.h":

```
/****************************************/
/*      Image Processing Header File    */
/*      Geometric Processing Functions  */
/*          written in Turbo C 2.0      */
/*                  by                  */
/*           Craig A. Lindley           */
/*                                      */
/*    Vers: 1.0  Last Update: 11/14/89  */
/****************************************/


/* Misc user defined types */
typedef enum {HorizMirror,VertMirror} MirrorType;

/* Geometric processes function prototypes */
void ScaleImage(BYTE huge *InImage, unsigned SCol, unsigned SRow,
                        unsigned SWidth, unsigned SHeight,
                        double ScaleH, double ScaleV,
                        BYTE huge *OutImage,
                        unsigned DCol, unsigned DRow,
                        unsigned Interpolate);

void SizeImage(BYTE huge *InImage, unsigned SCol, unsigned SRow,
                        unsigned SWidth, unsigned SHeight,
                        BYTE huge *OutImage,
                        unsigned DCol, unsigned DRow,
                        unsigned DWidth, unsigned DHeight,
                        unsigned Interpolate);

void RotateImage(BYTE huge *InImage, unsigned Col, unsigned Row,
                        unsigned Width, unsigned Height, double Angle,
                        BYTE huge *OutImage, unsigned Interpolate);

void TranslateImage(BYTE huge *InImage,
                        unsigned SCol, unsigned SRow,
                        unsigned SWidth, unsigned SHeight,
                        BYTE huge *OutImage,
                        unsigned DCol, unsigned DRow,
                        unsigned EraseFlag);
```

(continued)

Listing 12.1 *(continued)*

```
void MirrorImage(BYTE huge *InImage,
                          unsigned SCol, unsigned SRow,
                          unsigned SWidth, unsigned SHeight,
                          enum MirrorType WhichMirror,
                          BYTE huge *OutImage,
                          unsigned DCol, unsigned DRow);
```

The following is the contents of the file, "geprocess.c":

```
/***************************************/
/*        Image Processing Code        */
/*    Geometric Processing Functions   */
/*        written in Turbo C 2.0       */
/*                by                   */
/*          Craig A. Lindley           */
/*                                     */
/*    Vers: 1.0  Last Update: 11/16/89 */
/***************************************/

#include <stdio.h>
#include <conio.h>
#include <dos.h>
#include <alloc.h>
#include <process.h>
#include <math.h>
#include <graphics.h>
#include "misc.h"
#include "pcx.h"
#include "vga.h"
#include "imagesup.h"


void ScaleImage(BYTE huge *InImage, unsigned SCol, unsigned SRow,
                          unsigned SWidth, unsigned SHeight,
                          double ScaleH, double ScaleV,
                          BYTE huge *OutImage,
                          unsigned DCol, unsigned DRow,
                          unsigned Interpolate)
{
   unsigned DestWidth, DestHeight;
   unsigned PtA, PtB, PtC, PtD, PixelValue;
   register unsigned SPixelColNum, SPixelRowNum, DestCol, DestRow;
```

```
double SPixelColAddr, SPixelRowAddr;
double ColDelta, RowDelta;
double ContribFromAandB, ContribFromCandD;

DestWidth =  ScaleH * SWidth + 0.5;
DestHeight = ScaleV * SHeight+ 0.5;

if (ParameterCheckOK(SCol,SRow,SCol+SWidth,SRow+SHeight,"ScaleImage") &&
    ParameterCheckOK(DCol,DRow,DCol+DestWidth,DRow+DestHeight,"ScaleImage"))
{
    /* Calculations from destination perspective */
    for (DestRow = 0; DestRow < DestHeight; DestRow++)
    {
            SPixelRowAddr = DestRow/ScaleV;
            SPixelRowNum  = (unsigned) SPixelRowAddr;
            RowDelta      = SPixelRowAddr - SPixelRowNum;
            SPixelRowNum += SRow;

            for (DestCol = 0; DestCol < DestWidth; DestCol++)
            {
                SPixelColAddr = DestCol/ScaleH;
                SPixelColNum  = (unsigned) SPixelColAddr;
                ColDelta      = SPixelColAddr - SPixelColNum;
                SPixelColNum += SCol;

                if (Interpolate)
                {
                    /*
                    SPixelColNum and SPixelRowNum now contain the pixel
                    coordinates of the upper left pixel of the targetted
                    pixel's (point X) neighborhood. This is point A below:
                                    A       B
                                        X
                                    C       D
                    We must retrieve the brightness level of each of the
                    four pixels to calculate the value of the pixel put into
                    the destination image.

                    Get point A brightness as it will always lie within the
                    input image area. Check to make sure the other points are
                    within also. If so use their values for the calculations.
                    If not, set them all equal to point A's value. This induces
                    an error but only at the edges on an image.
                    */
```

(continued)

Listing 12.1 *(continued)*

```
                        PtA = GetPixelFromImage(InImage,SPixelColNum,SPixelRowNum);
                        if (((SPixelColNum+1) < MAXCOLS) && ((SPixelRowNum+1) < MAXROWS))
                        {
                                PtB = GetPixelFromImage(InImage,SPixelColNum+1,SPixelRowNum);
                                PtC = GetPixelFromImage(InImage,SPixelColNum,SPixelRowNum+1);
                                PtD = GetPixelFromImage(InImage,SPixelColNum+1,SPixelRowNum+1);
                        }
                        else
                        {
                                /* All points have equal brightness */
                                PtB=PtC=PtD=PtA;
                        }
                        /*
                        Interpolate to find brightness contribution of each pixel
                        in neighborhood. Done in both the horizontal and vertical
                        directions.
                        */
                        ContribFromAandB = ColDelta*((double)PtB - PtA) + PtA;
                        ContribFromCandD = ColDelta*((double)PtD - PtC) + PtC;
                        PixelValue = 0.5 + ContribFromAandB +
                                        (ContribFromCandD - ContribFromAandB)*RowDelta;
                }
                else
                    PixelValue=GetPixelFromImage(InImage,SPixelColNum,SPixelRowNum);

                /* Put the pixel into the destination buffer */
                PutPixelInImage(OutImage,DestCol+DCol,DestRow+DRow,PixelValue);
            }
        }
    }
}


void SizeImage(BYTE huge *InImage, unsigned SCol, unsigned SRow,
                        unsigned SWidth, unsigned SHeight,
                        BYTE huge *OutImage,
                        unsigned DCol, unsigned DRow,
                        unsigned DWidth, unsigned DHeight,
                        unsigned Interpolate)
{
    double HScale, VScale;

    /* Check for parameters out of range */
```

```
    if (ParameterCheckOK(SCol,SRow,SCol+SWidth,SRow+SHeight,"SizeImage") &&
        ParameterCheckOK(DCol,DRow,DCol+DWidth,DRow+DHeight,"SizeImage"))
    {
        /*
        Calculate horizontal and vertical scale factors required
        to fit specified portion of input image into specified portion
        of output image.
        */
        HScale = (double)DWidth/(double)SWidth;
        VScale = (double)DHeight/(double)SHeight;

        /* Call ScaleImage to do the actual work */
        ScaleImage(InImage,SCol,SRow,SWidth,SHeight,HScale,VScale,
                            OutImage,DCol,DRow,Interpolate);
    }
}


void RotateImage(BYTE huge *InImage, unsigned Col, unsigned Row,
                        unsigned Width, unsigned Height, double Angle,
                        BYTE huge *OutImage, unsigned Interpolate)
{
    register unsigned ImageCol, ImageRow;
    unsigned CenterCol, CenterRow, SPixelColNum, SPixelRowNum;
    unsigned ColExtent, RowExtent, PixelValue;
    unsigned PtA, PtB, PtC, PtD;
    double   DPixelRelativeColNum, DPixelRelativeRowNum;
    double   CosAngle, SinAngle, SPixelColAddr, SPixelRowAddr;
    double   ColDelta, RowDelta;
    double   ContribFromAandB, ContribFromCandD;

    if (ParameterCheckOK(Col,Row,Col+Width,Row+Height,"RotateImage"))
    {
        /* Angle must be in 0..359.9 */
        while (Angle >= 360.0)
                Angle -= 360.0;

        /* Convert angle from degrees to radians */
        Angle *= ((double) 3.14159/(double) 180.0);

        /* Calculate angle values for rotation */
        CosAngle = cos(Angle);
        SinAngle = sin(Angle);
```

(continued)

Listing 12.1 *(continued)*

```
/* Center of rotation */
CenterCol = Col + Width/2;
CenterRow = Row + Height/2;

ColExtent = Col + Width;
RowExtent = Row + Height;

/*
All calculations are performed from the destination image
perspective. Absolute pixel values must be converted into
inches of display distance to keep the aspect value
correct when image is rotated. After rotation, the calculated
display distance is converted back to real pixel values.
*/

for (ImageRow = Row; ImageRow < RowExtent; ImageRow++)
{
        DPixelRelativeRowNum = (double)ImageRow - CenterRow;
        /* Convert row value to display distance from image center */
        DPixelRelativeRowNum *= LRINCHESPERPIXELVERT;

        for (ImageCol = Col; ImageCol < ColExtent; ImageCol++)
        {
           DPixelRelativeColNum = (double)ImageCol - CenterCol;
           /* Convert col value to display distance from image center */
           DPixelRelativeColNum *= LRINCHESPERPIXELHORIZ;
           /*
           Calculate source pixel address from destination
           pixels position.
           */
           SPixelColAddr = DPixelRelativeColNum*CosAngle-
                                     DPixelRelativeRowNum*SinAngle;
           SPixelRowAddr = DPixelRelativeColNum*SinAngle+
                                     DPixelRelativeRowNum*CosAngle;

           /*
           Convert from coordinates relative to image
           center back into absolute coordinates.
           */
           /* Convert display distance to pixel location */
           SPixelColAddr *= LRPIXELSPERINCHHORIZ;
           SPixelColAddr += CenterCol;
           SPixelRowAddr *= LRPIXELSPERINCHVERT;
           SPixelRowAddr += CenterRow;
```

```
SPixelColNum = (unsigned) SPixelColAddr;
SPixelRowNum = (unsigned) SPixelRowAddr;
ColDelta = SPixelColAddr - SPixelColNum;
RowDelta = SPixelRowAddr - SPixelRowNum;

if (Interpolate)
{
   /*
   SPixelColNum and SPixelRowNum now contain the pixel
   coordinates of the upper left pixel of the targetted
   pixel's (point X) neighborhood. This is point A below:
                     A          B

                          X
                     C          D
   We must retrieve the brightness level of each of the
   four pixels to calculate the value of the pixel put into
   the destination image.

   Get point A brightness as it will always lie within the
   input image area. Check to make sure the other points are
   within also. If so use their values for the calculations.
   If not, set them all equal to point A's value. This induces
   an error but only at the edges on an image.
   */

   PtA = GetPixelFromImage(InImage,SPixelColNum,SPixelRowNum);
   if (((SPixelColNum+1) < MAXCOLS) && ((SPixelRowNum+1) < MAXROWS))
   {
           PtB = GetPixelFromImage(InImage,SPixelColNum+1,SPixelRowNum);
           PtC = GetPixelFromImage(InImage,SPixelColNum,SPixelRowNum+1);
           PtD = GetPixelFromImage(InImage,SPixelColNum+1,SPixelRowNum+1);
   }
   else
   {
           /* All points have equal brightness */
           PtB=PtC=PtD=PtA;
   }
   /*
   Interpolate to find brightness contribution of each pixel
   in neighborhood. Done in both the horizontal and vertical
   directions.
   */
   ContribFromAandB = ColDelta*((double)PtB - PtA) + PtA;
   ContribFromCandD = ColDelta*((double)PtD - PtC) + PtC;
```

(continued)

Listing 12.1 *(continued)*

```
                    PixelValue = 0.5 + ContribFromAandB +
                                    (ContribFromCandD - ContribFromAandB)*RowDelta;
                }
                else
                    PixelValue=GetPixelFromImage(InImage,SPixelColNum,SPixelRowNum);

                /* Put the pixel into the destination buffer */
                PutPixelInImage(OutImage,ImageCol,ImageRow,PixelValue);
            }
        }
    }
}


/*
Caution: images must not overlap
*/
void TranslateImage(BYTE huge *InImage,
                        unsigned SCol, unsigned SRow,
                        unsigned SWidth, unsigned SHeight,
                        BYTE huge *OutImage,
                        unsigned DCol, unsigned DRow,
                        unsigned EraseFlag)
{
    register unsigned SImageCol, SImageRow, DestCol;
    unsigned SColExtent, SRowExtent;

    /* Check for parameters out of range */
    if (ParameterCheckOK(SCol,SRow,SCol+SWidth,SRow+SHeight,"TranslateImage") &&
        ParameterCheckOK(DCol,DRow,DCol+SWidth,DRow+SHeight,"TranslateImage"))
    {
        SColExtent = SCol+SWidth;
        SRowExtent = SRow+SHeight;

        for (SImageRow = SRow; SImageRow < SRowExtent; SImageRow++)
        {
                /* Reset the destination Column count every row */
                DestCol = DCol;
                for (SImageCol = SCol; SImageCol < SColExtent; SImageCol++)
                {
                    /* Transfer byte of the image data between buffers */
                    PutPixelInImage(OutImage,DestCol++,DRow,
                                        GetPixelFromImage(InImage,SImageCol,SImageRow));
                }
```

```
                    /* Bump to next row in the destination image */
                    DRow++;
        }
        /* If erasure specified, blot out original image */
        if (EraseFlag)
                ClearImageArea(InImage,SCol,SRow,SWidth,SHeight,BLACK);
    }
}


void MirrorImage(BYTE huge *InImage,
                            unsigned SCol, unsigned SRow,
                            unsigned SWidth, unsigned SHeight,
                            enum MirrorType WhichMirror,
                            BYTE huge *OutImage,
                            unsigned DCol, unsigned DRow)
{
    register unsigned SImageCol, SImageRow, DestCol;
    unsigned SColExtent, SRowExtent;

    /* Check for parameters out of range */
    if (ParameterCheckOK(SCol,SRow,SCol+SWidth,SRow+SHeight,"MirrorImage") &&
        ParameterCheckOK(DCol,DRow,DCol+SWidth,DRow+SHeight,"MirrorImage"))
    {
        SColExtent = SCol+SWidth;
        SRowExtent = SRow+SHeight;

        switch(WhichMirror)
        {
                case HorizMirror:
                    for (SImageRow = SRow; SImageRow < SRowExtent; SImageRow++)
                    {
                        /* Reset the destination Column count every row */
                        DestCol = DCol + SWidth;
                        for (SImageCol = SCol; SImageCol < SColExtent; SImageCol++)
                        {
                                /* Transfer byte of the image data between buffers */
                                PutPixelInImage(OutImage,--DestCol,DRow,
                                            GetPixelFromImage(InImage,SImageCol,SImageRow));
                        }
                        /* Bump to next row in the destination image */
                        DRow++;
                    }
                    break;
```

(continued)

Listing 12.1 *(continued)*

```
        case VertMirror:
          DRow += (SHeight-1);
          for (SImageRow = SRow; SImageRow < SRowExtent; SImageRow++)
          {
            /* Reset the destination Column count every row */
            DestCol = DCol;
            for (SImageCol = SCol; SImageCol < SColExtent; SImageCol++)
            {
                /* Transfer byte of the image data between buffers */
                PutPixelInImage(OutImage,DestCol++,DRow,
                            GetPixelFromImage(InImage,SImageCol,SImageRow));
            }
            /* Bump to next row in the destination image */
            DRow--;
          }
          break;
      }
   }
}
```

With geometric processes, one-to-one mapping of source to destination pixels is not guaranteed. Take image scaling, for instance. If an image is magnified, one pixel in the source image may be mapped to many pixels in the destination image. Conversely, if a source image is reduced in size, many pixels of the source may map to just one pixel of the destination. Taking image magnification one step further, what if it is required to magnify an image by some noninteger scale factor, say 1.3. How can one pixel of the source image be correctly mapped into 1.3 pixels of the destination image?

Source to destination pixel mapping is further complicated because it must generally be performed from the destination image's perspective instead of from the source image perspective. Although seemingly backward, reverse mapping is required to guarantee that every pixel in the destination image is given a value. Without the one-to-one correspondence between source and destination pixels it cannot be guaranteed that a source pixel will be mapped into each and every destination pixel. Destination pixels that do not get assigned a value produce voids in the output image. As you might expect, these voids do not enhance the appearance of the produced image. In fact, the destination image is generally unusable.

To prevent the occurrence of these voids, geometric transformations generally employ reverse mapping. Reverse mapping traverses the destination image space a pixel at a time and calculates via the designated transformation which pixels of the source image would be involved in producing the destination pixel. When the value of the destination pixel is calculated in this manner and placed into the destination image, complete coverage of the destination image is guaranteed.

Listing 12.2 The Geometric Function Example Program

The following is the contents of the file, "getest.prj":

```
graphics.lib
vgagraph.obj
egavga.obj
pcx       (misc.h pcx.h)
vga       (misc.h vga.h pcx.h)
imagesup  (misc.h vga.h pcx.h imagesup.h)
geprocess (misc.h vga.h pcx.h imagesup.h geprocess.h)
getest    (misc.h vga.h pcx.h imagesup.h geprocess.h)
```

The following is the contents of the file, "getest.c":

```
/*****************************************/
/*    Geometric Process Demo Program     */
/*        written in Turbo C 2.0         */
/*                by                     */
/*          Craig A. Lindley             */
/*                                       */
/*   Vers: 1.0  Last Update: 12/26/89    */
/*****************************************/

#include <stdio.h>
#include <conio.h>
#include <dos.h>
#include <alloc.h>
#include <process.h>
#include <graphics.h>
#include "misc.h"
#include "pcx.h"
#include "vga.h"
#include "imagesup.h"
#include "geprocess.h"

/* main geometric process program */

void main(void)
{
   char *InFileName1 = "p2c12i1a";
   char *InFileName2 = "p2c12i2a";
   char *InFileName3 = "p2c12i3a";
```

(continued)

Listing 12.2 *(continued)*

```c
char *InFileName4 = "p2c12i4a";
char *InFileName5 = "p2c12i5a";

BYTE huge *InImage;
BYTE huge *Buffer;
unsigned GenPCXFiles = FALSE; /* controls output file generation */


InitGraphics();

printf("Geometric Transform Example Program\n\n");
printf("Reading the Image PCX File into memory\n");

/* allocate far memory buffer for images */
Buffer = (BYTE huge *)farcalloc(RASTERSIZE,(long)sizeof(BYTE));

if (Buffer == NULL)
{
   restorecrtmode();
   printf("Error Not enough memory for geometric operation\n");
   exit(ENoMemory);
}

/*
Prepare image sequence 12.1 - Image Magnification
*/
if (ReadPCXFileToBuf (InFileName1,&InImage) != NoError)
   exit(ENoMemory);

DisplayImageInBuf(InImage,INITVGALOADPALETTE,WAITFORKEY);

/* Clear the output buffer to black. */
ClearImageArea(Buffer,MINCOLNUM,MINROWNUM,MAXCOLS,MAXROWS,WHITE);

ScaleImage(InImage,119,13,83,111,1.3,1.3,Buffer,100,25,FALSE);
DisplayImageInBuf(Buffer,NOVGAINIT,WAITFORKEY);
if (GenPCXFiles)
   WritePCXFile("p2c12i1b",8,320,200,1,320);

/* Clear the output buffer to black. */
ClearImageArea(Buffer,MINCOLNUM,MINROWNUM,MAXCOLS,MAXROWS,BLACK);

ScaleImage(InImage,119,13,83,111,1.3,1.3,Buffer,100,25,TRUE);
DisplayImageInBuf(Buffer,NOVGAINIT,WAITFORKEY);
```

```
if (GenPCXFiles)
   WritePCXFile("p2c12i1c",8,320,200,1,320);

farfree((BYTE far *)InImage); /* free memory */

/*
Prepare image sequence 12.2 - Image Reduction
*/
if (ReadPCXFileToBuf (InFileName2,&InImage) != NoError)
   exit(ENoMemory);

DisplayImageInBuf(InImage,NOVGAINIT,WAITFORKEY);

/* Clear the output buffer to black. */
ClearImageArea(Buffer,MINCOLNUM,MINROWNUM,MAXCOLS,MAXROWS,WHITE);

ScaleImage(InImage,9,76,291,105,0.5,0.5,Buffer,80,74,FALSE);
DisplayImageInBuf(Buffer,NOVGAINIT,WAITFORKEY);
if (GenPCXFiles)
   WritePCXFile("p2c12i2b",8,320,200,1,320);

/* Clear the output buffer to black. */
ClearImageArea(Buffer,MINCOLNUM,MINROWNUM,MAXCOLS,MAXROWS,WHITE);

ScaleImage(InImage,9,76,291,105,0.5,0.5,Buffer,80,74,TRUE);
DisplayImageInBuf(Buffer,NOVGAINIT,WAITFORKEY);
if (GenPCXFiles)
   WritePCXFile("p2c12i2c",8,320,200,1,320);

farfree((BYTE far *)InImage); /* free memory */

/* Prepare image sequence 12.3 Various Sized Images */

if (ReadPCXFileToBuf (InFileName3,&InImage) != NoError)
   exit(ENoMemory);

DisplayImageInBuf(InImage,NOVGAINIT,WAITFORKEY);

/*
Clearing the output buffer to white will show the
boarder areas not touched by the scaling process. It also
provides a nice white frame for the output image.
*/
ClearImageArea(Buffer,MINCOLNUM,MINROWNUM,MAXCOLS,MAXROWS,WHITE);
```

(continued)

Listing 12.2 *(continued)*

```
/* Image 1 is scaled .5 x .5 and occupies lower right corner */
ScaleImage(InImage,MINCOLNUM,MINROWNUM,MAXCOLS,MAXROWS,
                0.5,0.5,Buffer,155,95,TRUE);


/* Image 2 is scaled .45 x .67 and occupies upper left corner */
ScaleImage(InImage,MINCOLNUM,MINROWNUM,MAXCOLS,MAXROWS,
                0.45,0.67,Buffer,4,4,TRUE);


/* Image 3 is scaled .5 x .42 and occupies upper right corner */
ScaleImage(InImage,MINCOLNUM,MINROWNUM,MAXCOLS,MAXROWS,
                0.5,0.42,Buffer,155,4,TRUE);


/* Image 4 is scaled .25 x .25 and occupies lower left corner */
ScaleImage(InImage,MINCOLNUM,MINROWNUM,MAXCOLS,MAXROWS,
                0.25,0.25,Buffer,38,145,TRUE);


DisplayImageInBuf(Buffer,NOVGAINIT,WAITFORKEY);
if (GenPCXFiles)
    WritePCXFile("p2c12i3b",8,320,200,1,320);


farfree((BYTE far *)InImage); /* free memory */


/* Prepare image sequence 12.4 - Rotated Images */
if (ReadPCXFileToBuf (InFileName4,&InImage) != NoError)
    exit(ENoMemory);


DisplayImageInBuf(InImage,NOVGAINIT,WAITFORKEY);


/*
Clearing the output buffer to black.
*/

ClearImageArea(Buffer,MINCOLNUM,MINROWNUM,MAXCOLS,MAXROWS,BLACK);


RotateImage(InImage,105,43,117,107,37.5,Buffer,FALSE);
DisplayImageInBuf(Buffer,NOVGAINIT,WAITFORKEY);
if (GenPCXFiles)
    WritePCXFile("p2c12i4b",8,320,200,1,320);


ClearImageArea(Buffer,MINCOLNUM,MINROWNUM,MAXCOLS,MAXROWS,BLACK);


RotateImage(InImage,105,43,117,107,37.5,Buffer,TRUE);
DisplayImageInBuf(Buffer,NOVGAINIT,WAITFORKEY);
```

```
        if (GenPCXFiles)
            WritePCXFile("p2c12i4c",8,320,200,1,320);


        ClearImageArea(Buffer,MINCOLNUM,MINROWNUM,MAXCOLS,MAXROWS,BLACK);

        RotateImage(InImage,105,43,117,107,300.0,Buffer,FALSE);
        DisplayImageInBuf(Buffer,NOVGAINIT,WAITFORKEY);
        if (GenPCXFiles)
            WritePCXFile("p2c12i4d",8,320,200,1,320);


        ClearImageArea(Buffer,MINCOLNUM,MINROWNUM,MAXCOLS,MAXROWS,BLACK);

        RotateImage(InImage,105,43,117,107,300.0,Buffer,TRUE);
        DisplayImageInBuf(Buffer,NOVGAINIT,WAITFORKEY);
        if (GenPCXFiles)
            WritePCXFile("p2c12i4e",8,320,200,1,320);


        farfree((BYTE far *)InImage); /* free memory */

        /* Prepare image sequence 12.5 - Mirrored Images */

        if (ReadPCXFileToBuf (InFileName5,&InImage) != NoError)
            exit(ENoMemory);


        DisplayImageInBuf(InImage,NOVGAINIT,WAITFORKEY);

        /*
        Clearing the output buffer to black.
        */
        ClearImageArea(Buffer,MINCOLNUM,MINROWNUM,MAXCOLS,MAXROWS,BLACK);
        TranslateImage(InImage,82,76,166,48,Buffer,82,10,FALSE);
        MirrorImage(InImage,82,76,166,48,HorizMirror,Buffer,82,76);
        MirrorImage(InImage,82,76,166,48,VertMirror,Buffer,82,142);
        DisplayImageInBuf(Buffer,NOVGAINIT,WAITFORKEY);
        if (GenPCXFiles)
            WritePCXFile("p2c12i5b",8,320,200,1,320);


        farfree((BYTE far *)InImage); /* free memory */
        farfree((BYTE far *)Buffer);
        restorecrtmode();
        closegraph();
}
```

Reverse pixel mapping creates another problem—namely, that of fractional pixel addresses. These occur when the source image pixel that contributes to a destination pixel's value is calculated. The lack of one-to-one pixel mapping results in the calculated source image pixel lying somewhere between four valid pixel locations in the source image. Fractional addresses are a mathematical contrivance that do not have a physical analog. Pixel addresses in the real world must have integer addresses that correspond to the rows and columns of a display. There is no such thing as fractional rows and columns.

To deal with these calculated fractional addresses, the concept of interpolation can be employed. Other methods for assigning integer pixel addresses to fractional addresses also exist. The one discussed in this text is called the *nearest neighborhood approximation*. This technique will be discussed later in this section. For now, our discussion will continue with the concept of linear interpolation.

The interpolation process applied to pixel locations is the same interpolation process used to calculate values between entries in log tables. The only difference is that image pixel interpolation must be applied in two dimensions, horizontal and vertical, to be effective.

In both cases, interpolation is used to calculate a new value for some point that is situated between other points of known value and at a known distance from the point being calculated. The points of known value that surround the point being calculated (the pixel of interest, or "Px") are referred to as the *neighborhood*. Points in the neighborhood that are closer to Px have a larger impact on the value of the calculated point. Points further away have less effect. Linear interpolation assumes that the contribution of a pixel in the neighborhood varies directly (linearly) with its distance. The need for interpolation is illustrated in Figure 12.1.

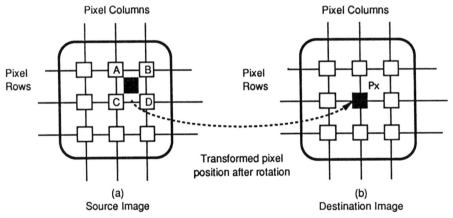

(a)
Source Image

(b)
Destination Image

Notes
1. Image (b): A black pixel is being transformed by a geometric process. As a result of the transformation, the pixel is given a noninteger address, as shown in (a). Reverse mapping is being used.
2. If interpolation is not used, the intensity value of the black pixel in (b) is given to pixel A in (a).
3. If interpolation is used, the intensity of the transformed black pixel is derived from pixels A, B, C, and D according to their relative distances from the calculated address of the transformed pixel. Two-dimensional interpolation is performed.

Figure 12.1   Pixel-Value Interpolation

In this figure, assume the destination image area is shown in (b). The black pixel, "Px", is the pixel being transformed. The reverse mapping of the black pixel places it into the source image (a) at a fractional address that lies somewhere in the neighborhood defined by pixels A, B, C, and D. The position of the black pixel in the source image is shown as if the geometric process applied was rotation, although almost any geometric process can be assumed for this discussion.

If the nearest neighbor approximation is being utilized, the fractional address of the black pixel in (a) would be truncated to the nearest integer pixel address. In this case, the destination image would be given the value of pixel A, as pixel A has the nearest integer address. Think about it.

The use of this approximation results in less than perfect geometric image transformations. Image Sequences 12.1 and 12.2 show the effect of an image processed using this approximation. Notice the blocky and jagged nature of the transformed image. The distortion in the image is apparent. Compare this result to that obtained using interpolation in the same image sequence. There really is no comparison—the interpolated images are superior, although computationally more expensive to produce.

To obtain an interpolated value for the pixel of interest in the destination image, three interpolations must actually be performed. They are the intensity contribution to the pixel of interest (Px) from pixels A and B, the contribution for pixels C and D, and the contribution from AB and CD. (Three interpolations must be performed because we are interpolating in two dimensions.)

As mentioned, the distance from each of the pixels in the neighborhood must be known in order to interpolate correctly. In practice, only the distance from the pixel in the upper left-hand corner of the neighborhood (pixel A on the diagram) to the pixel of interest must be known. For the purposes of our discussion, these distances will be referred to respectively as the column and row deltas. In other words, the column delta is the fractional column address of pixel Px minus the integer column address of pixel A. The row delta is defined the same way. Algebraically, the formulas become

```
ColDelta = Fractional Column Address of Px -
                     integer Column address of pixel A.
RowDelta = Fractional Row Address of Px -
                     integer Row address of pixel A.

With these distances calculated, the three interpolations follow:

ContribAB = ColDelta*(Pixel B intensity - Pixel A intensity) +
                     Pixel A intensity
ContribCD = ColDelta*(Pixel D intensity - Pixel C intensity) +
                     Pixel C intensity
Therefore:

     Px = RowDelta*(ContribCD - ContribAB) +
              ContribAB
```

The value calculated for Px and placed into the destination image is therefore proportional to the intensities of and the distance of Px from each pixel in its surrounding neighborhood. When interpolation is used in this manner in conjunction with reverse mapping, the resulting geometrically transformed images are of higher quality—that is, they more accurately reflect the original image after the desired transformation is performed.

Of course, there is a downside to the use of interpolation—performance. The number of calculations that must be performed utilizing floating-point numbers slows the geometric transformation down considerably. A classic trade-off exists between the amount of processing time that can be spent and the required quality of the resultant image. Since this trade-off must be made on an image-by-image basis, the functions contained in the geometric processes function library support both interpolation and the nearest neighbor approximation. Which is used depends on the application and the time available. Further information on the use of interpolation may be found in Figure 12.2.

As with the area processes described in Chapter 10, interpolation also suffers from "border effects" that must be taken into consideration during algorithm implementation. In actuality, any image processing algorithm that utilizes the concept of pixel neighborhoods will suffer from the same kinds of problems when edges of images are processed. The solution used for interpolation differs from that used for area processes. In this case, pixel neighbor data is synthesized at image edges. For area processes, edges were not processed at all. See Listing 12.1 for the details of how this works.

Interpolation is important when images are scaled, sized, and/or rotated. All other processes included in the geometric process function library maintain the one-for-one pixel mapping and therefore do not require the use of interpolation.

Aspect Ratio Considerations

For our purposes, aspect ratio can be defined as the proportionally correct ratio of height to width of an image displayed on a video monitor. A circle displayed with correct aspect ratio will appear round. An imperfect aspect ratio will distort the circle so that it looks more like an ellipse (see the "Gallery of Images" for an example). Distortions in the aspect ratio of images are usually the result of displaying an image using "nonsquare" pixels or trying to display an image scaled to an aspect ratio other than that of the video source. The latter distortion can easily be avoided. See the section later in this chapter on image scaling for more information. Nonsquare pixels, on the other hand, are much harder to deal with.

To understand the importance of aspect ratio, we start with the known aspect ratio of typical video devices (television sets, computer monitors, and cameras), which is 4:3. This means the display width of a monitor's screen is approximately 1.333 times the height of the screen. When a live video image is displayed on a video monitor, the aspect ratio appears correct because both devices have a 4:3 aspect ratio. When viewed through a camera/monitor combination a circular object will therefore appear round, as would be expected.

The 640×480 VGA mode has square pixels because the ratio of pixel width to height matches that of standard video (640/480 equals exactly 4/3). In other words, a displacement of one pixel in the horizontal direction represents the exact same distance in an image scene as the displacement of one pixel in the vertical direction. Consider an IBM 8512 monitor, for

Note

Many of the parameters required by the geometric processing functions are similar or identical. To prevent continual repetition of information, unless otherwise specified the parameters listed have the following functions:

"InImage" is a pointer to the source image. The source image is the image that will be subjected to the geometric transformation. The source image is never modified by the geometric process, as is the destination image ("OutImage").

"SCol", "SRow", "SWidth", and "SHeight" are parameters controlling the portion of the source image that will be geometrically transformed to become the destination image. "SWidth" and "SHeight" describe a square image area with the left corner positioned at "SCol", "SRow". This area will be transformed by the geometric process specified, and the result will be placed in the destination image.

"OutImage" is a pointer to the destination image. The source image (or a portion of it) will be transformed and placed into this image buffer. The destination image buffer is always overwritten by the geometric process.

"DCol" and "DRow" are parameters that control where in the destination image the transformed source image (or portion of it) will be placed. The use of these parameters in effect provides image translation in addition to geometric processing of the source image.

1. Scale an Image Function

Prototype

void ScaleImage(BYTE huge *InImage, unsigned SCol, unsigned SRow, unsigned SWidth, unsigned SHeight, double ScaleH, double ScaleV, BYTE huge *OutImage, unsigned DCol, unsigned DRow, unsigned Interpolate);

Where all parameters are as discussed except:

"ScaleH" and "ScaleV" parameters are the horizontal and vertical scaling factors respectively. They control the extent to which the source image (or portion of it) will be scaled in each of two directions. Scale factors larger than 1 cause the source image to be magnified, whereas numbers greater than 0 but less than 1 cause the image to be reduced in size. (See the discussion of aspect ratios for more information and application cautions.)

"Interpolate" is a boolean that controls whether interpolation should be used or not. If TRUE, interpolation will be used. If FALSE, the closest neighbor technique will be used instead. The use of interpolation requires much more processing time but always results in a higher-quality output image. (See text for details.)

Operation

The scaling function begins operation by calculating how big the scaled image would be. It then checks to see if the scaled image is able to fit within the confines of the destination image buffer. If it cannot, program operation terminates at this point. If the size of the scaled image fits within the destination image buffer, the scaling function continues. At this point, two nested loops are entered that traverse the destination image area (which will eventually be occupied by the scaled source image) on a pixel-by-pixel basis. For each pixel of the destination image, a reverse mapping is made to find out the address the destination pixel would correspond to in the source image. More often than not, the calculated pixel's address would lie somewhere between valid integer pixel addresses. In other words, the calculated address would have fractional components instead of purely integer ones.

A branch in the code for the scaling function then takes place based upon whether or not

Figure 12.2 Geometric Process Function Library   *(continued)*

interpolation is utilized. If interpolation is not being used, the fractional address calculated for the destination pixel in the source image is truncated to the nearest valid pixel address, and the value of that pixel in the source image is copied into the destination image. This is referred to in the text as the *nearest-neighbor technique*. If interpolation is being used, the four pixels that surround the calculated position of the destination pixel in the source image are all fetched. The value given the destination pixel depends upon the intensity of and the distance from each of the four surrounding pixels. Linear interpolation is used to calculate the effect each of the four surrounding pixels has on the pixel placed into the destination image. (See text for details of interpolation.)

2. Size an Image Function

   Prototype
   void SizeImage(BYTE huge *InImage, unsigned SCol, unsigned SRow, unsigned SWidth, unsigned SHeight, BYTE huge *OutImage, unsigned DCol, unsigned DRow, unsigned DWidth, unsigned DHeight, unsigned Interpolate);

   Where all parameters are as discussed except:

   "DWidth" and "DHeight" are parameters that delimit the area in the destination image into which the scaled version of the source image will be placed.

   ## Operation
   This function is almost identical to the "ScaleImage" function just described. The difference is that instead of supplying scale factors in the horizontal and vertical directions as we just did, we instead provide the area into which the scaled image should be placed. Scale factors are calculated internal to this function so the resultant image will fit into the prescribed area. (*Note:* if ratio of width to height of the specified destination image area is different from that of the source image area, the aspect ratio of the scaled image will be changed.)

3. Rotate an Image Function

   Prototype
   void RotateImage(BYTE huge *InImage, unsigned Col, unsigned Row, unsigned Width, unsigned Height, double Angle, BYTE huge *OutImage, unsigned Interpolate);

   Where all parameters are as described except:

   "Angle", the counter clockwise angle, in degrees, through which the source image should be rotated through its center.

   ## Operation
   This function applies the laws of trigonometry to rotate an image around its center point by the angle specified. The equations that govern the transformation of the location of a pixel of the source image ("Xold,Yold") into its new rotated location in the destination image ("Xnew,Ynew") are as follows:

   ```
   Xnew = Xold * Cos(Angle) + Yold * Sin(Angle)
   Ynew = Yold * Cos(Angle) - Xold * Sin(Angle)
   ```

   This function also operates from the destination image perspective in order to prevent voids in the destination image. In many respects image rotation is a process similar to image scaling. Image rotation, unfortunately, is complicated by both aspect ratio considerations and interpolation considerations. (See those respective discussions for more information.)

Figure 12.2 *(continued)*

4. Translate an Image Function

Prototype
void TranslateImage(BYTE huge *InImage, unsigned SCol, unsigned SRow, unsigned SWidth, unsigned SHeight, BYTE huge *OutImage, unsigned DCol, unsigned DRow, unsigned Erase-Flag);

Where all parameters are as described except:

"EraseFlag" is a boolean flag that determines if the source image (or portion of it) which is translated in location by means of this function should be cleared (set to black). If FALSE, the source image is copied to the destination image, and the source image is left intact. If TRUE, the image is still copied, but the specified portion of the source image is cleared. If the source and destination image buffers overlap, specifying TRUE for "EraseFlag" results in a movement of an image or object within the buffer. "EraseFlag" equal to FALSE results in an image copy within the buffer.

Operation
This function is used to copy or move images (or objects within images) to other image buffers or within the same buffer. The term *translation* signifies movement in computer graphics. The parameters passed to this function determine not only the portion of the source image to translate but also where to translate it to. Two nested loops are used to traverse the source image a pixel at a time. Each time, a pixel of the source image is moved to the destination image. This transformation is performed from the source image's perspective instead of from that of the destination image. This is contrary to all of the other geometric processes described up to this point. The transformation can be done in this manner because there exists a one-for-one mapping between source and destination pixels that prevents voids in the destination image. As mentioned, if "EraseFlag" is set TRUE, the source image (or portion of it specified) will be cleared to black.

5. Mirror an Image Function

Prototype
void MirrorImage(BYTE huge *InImage, unsigned SCol, unsigned SRow, unsigned SWidth, unsigned SHeight, enum MirrorType WhichMirror, BYTE huge *OutImage, unsigned DCol, unsigned DRow);

Where all parameters are as described except:

"WhichMirror" is an enumerated-type parameter that determines which type of mirror function is performed. The two valid types are "HorizMirror" and "VertMirror". "HorizMirror" generates a mirror of the source image in the horizontal direction. That is, source image left becomes destination image right, and source image right becomes destination image left. "VertMirror" generates a vertical mirror. Source image top is destination image bottom, and vice versa.

Operation
This function very simply rearranges the pixels of the source image to generate the destination image. No complications are encountered because of the one-for-one mapping between source and destination pixels. (See Listing 12.1 for additional information.)

Figure 12.2 *(continued)*

example. Its display width is approximately 9.5 inches whereas its display height is approximately 7.125 inches—a perfect 4:3 ratio. To find the resolution of the display in inches, we perform the following calculations.

```
PixelsPerInchHoriz = 640 pixels/9.5 inches   = 67.37 pixels/inch
PixelsPerInchVert  = 480 pixels/7.125 inches = 67.37 pixels/inch
```

As you can see, the distance in inches represented by a displacement of a single pixel in both the horizontal and vertical directions is the same. (A generally accepted value for computer monitor resolution is 71 dots or pixels/inch. As you can see, our calculated numbers come pretty close.) Additionally, the pixel can be shown to be square, as follows:

```
InchesPerPixelHoriz = 1 / PixelsPerInchHoriz = .0015 inches
InchesPerPixelVert  = 1 / PixelsPerInchVert  = .0015 inches
```

Therefore, each pixel on a 640×480 screen is approximately 0.0015 by 0.0015 inches square.

Unfortunately, the 320×200 resolution video mode utilized for all image processing in this book suffers from nonsquare pixel syndrome. The displayed pixels are actually taller than they are wide. Repeating the calculations above yields

```
PixelsPerInchHoriz = 320 pixels/9.5 inches   = 33.68 pixels/inch
PixelsPerInchVert  = 200 pixels/7.125 inches = 28.07 pixels/inch
```

therefore:

```
InchesPerPixelHoriz = 1 / PixelsPerInchHoriz = .0296 inches
InchesPerPixelVert  = 1 / PixelsPerInchVert  = .0356 inches
```

Thus, each pixel on a 320×200 screen is approximately 0.0296 inches wide by 0.0356 inches tall, definitely not square.

A similiar calculation could be performed for the 640×200 resolution mode. The result is that each pixel is half as wide as in the 320×200 mode but the same height. Again, the pixels are not square.

When the geometric process of rotation is applied to an image, aspect ratio considerations become important. If square pixels are available (i.e., the 640×480 mode is being used) image rotation is a trivial operation because the aspect ratio of a rotated image does not change with its orientation. Rotation with nonsquare pixels (the mode we utilize), however, requires close attention to aspect ratio considerations so the rotated image is not distorted by the rotation process. Additional computations are required to maintain an object's aspect ratio during rotation. These additional computations slow down the image rotation operation but results in a better image. The utilization of both aspect ratio correction and interpolation results in the production of the best possible rotated images.

An object's aspect ratio is kept intact during the rotation process by converting all pixel displacements from the center of the image (the center of image rotation) to the pixel being rotated to absolute inches of display distance. This is done by multiplying the pixel column number by the "InchesPerPixelHoriz" value to get the number of horizontal inches of display distance. A similar calculation is done to find the number of vertical inches of display distance. These absolute display distance numbers are then used in the transformation calculations. Finally, the transformed display distance numbers (which represent the absolute display distance from the center of the image to the new pixel's position) are converted back into screen pixel coordinates. Since the absolute distance from image center is maintained for each rotated pixel, the aspect ratio is kept intact. This process can be seen in Listing 12.1 in the rotation function's code.

Aspect ratio considerations are also important in using the digitizer developed in Part One of this book. From the earlier discussion, it should be obvious that whenever a 320×200 or a 640×200 digitized image is displayed, the aspect ratio will be incorrect. Only the 640×480 high-resolution images will have the same aspect ratio as that of the object being digitized and therefore display correctly. The spatial aberration caused by the incorrect aspect ratio of the lower-resolution display modes has been successfully ignored until this point. Ignoring the aspect ratio issue was possible because it didn't have a drastic effect on the appearance of the digitized images and because the tools necessary to correct the problem were not introduced until this chapter. Also, the discussion of aspect ratio correction earlier would have unnecessarily complicated the image-acquisition discussion. The problem was apparent only when a large circular object was digitized. Then, as anticipated, the circle looked more like an ellipse when it was displayed.

We now have the tools necessary to correct the aspect ratio problem of the 320×200 resolution display. These tools are interpolation and aspect ratio correction. It should be noted that adding the aspect ratio correction code to image acquisition will result in better images requiring extra time to acquire and display. The appropriateness of aspect ratio correction depends upon the application. The code fragments shown in Listing 12.3 illustrate how aspect ratio corrections can be incorporated into the basic image-acquisition code. This code is excerpted from the program "acquire.c" on the companion disk. This program (along with the digitizer presented in Part One of this book) digitizes and optionally saves 320×200 resolution images that have had aspect ratio correction. The "acquire.c" program was used to digitize all images used in Part Two.

Briefly, two modifications are required to the basic image-acquisition code to incorporate aspect ratio correction in 320×200 resolution images.

a. Instead of acquiring a 320×200 pixel image with the digitizer, a 320×240 pixel image is acquired instead. (*Note:* 320×240 is an aspect ratio of exactly 4:3.)

b. With this larger image acquired, the code that displays the digitized image is modified to display 240 lines of video information utilizing just 200 vertical display pixels. In other words, the content of the 240 lines is spread among the 200 possible vertical display pixels. Interpolation is used to calculate accurately the intensity values of the 200 vertical pixels. The net effect of compressing 240 lines of digitized video into 200 display pixels is to compensate for nonsquare pixels. Essentially, we are synthesizing square pixels.

Listing 12.3 Aspect Ratio Correction Code Fragment

As mentioned in the text, the pixels in 320 × 200 resolution are nonsquare. This results in aspect ratio problems when the acquired images are displayed. For a correct 4:3 aspect ratio yielding square pixels, the resolution would have to be boosted to 320 × 240. Square pixels can be approximated by having the digitizer acquire a 240-line image and by displaying the 240 lines of video information in the 200 vertical display pixels—in other words, by compressing the 240 lines of video into just 200 lines. This is accomplished by interpolating pixel values on the fly during the display process. The complete process is described in the following series of steps.

First, since a 320 × 240 image must be acquired by the digitizer, a larger image buffer is required. 320 × 200 requires 64,000 bytes of memory, whereas 320 × 240 requires 76,800 bytes. The "RasterSize" variable must be set appropriately, as follows:

```
RasterSize = 76800L;    /* big enough for 320x240 image */
```

Next, the digitizer must be told to acquire the larger image. This is done by making a change to the "ImageReq" structure, as follows:

```
Req.HMode       = LowRes;
Req.VMode       = NonInterlace;
Req.FirstLine   = 0;
Req.FirstPixel  = 0;
Req.LastLine    = 240;    /* do a 320x240 image */
Req.LastPixel   = 320;
```

The digitizer is now completely prepped for the acquisition of the larger image. Once the 320 × 240 image is acquired the remainder of the aspect ratio correction work is performed in the function that displays the acquired data.

The define below is the conversion factor that causes the traversal through the video image buffer to proceed at a rate of 1.2 rows of video per display row instead of the original one for one. The factor of 1.2 is produced by dividing the 240 lines of video to be compressed by the 200 vertical pixels of display resolution available.

```
#define RowAspectCorrection (double) 1.2
#define NumberOfVideoLines 240
```

Finally, the code to display the digitized image must be modified to correct for the aspect ratio problem. The comments in the code below describe how this is done.

```
/*
Display  the  digitized image in VGA mode 13h with 64  levels  of
gray. Correct the aspect ratio of the 320x200 image.
*/
void DisplayPictData (char huge *PictData)
{
    register unsigned Col, Row, Color, LowerColor, UpperColor;
```

```
unsigned LowerBufferRow, UpperBufferRow;
unsigned long PixelBufOffset;
double   FractionalRowAddr, RowDelta;

/* For each column of the display. 320 total */
for (Col=0; Col < LRMAXCOLS; Col++)
{
    /*
    Calculate the start of the digitized video information
    in the image buffer for this row.
    */
    PixelBufOffset = (long) NumberOfVideoLines * Col;
    /*
    For each of the 200 rows available in this display
    mode ...
    */
    for (Row=0; Row < LRMAXROWS; Row++)
    {
            /*
            Which actual digitized video row out of the
            total of 240 should we accessed? The calculated
            address will reside between two actual addresses.
            The address will be fractional.
            */
            FractionalRowAddr = RowAspectCorrection * (double) Row;
            /*
            Get the address of the row bytes just below and just
            above the calculated fractional address. Fetch the
            intensity values of each.
            */
            LowerBufferRow = (unsigned) FractionalRowAddr;
            UpperBufferRow = LowerBufferRow + 1;
            LowerColor = PictData[PixelBufOffset + LowerBufferRow];
            UpperColor = PictData[PixelBufOffset + UpperBufferRow];

            /*
            Calculate the distance the fractional address is off
            from the lower real address. This distance is required
            for the interpolation process.
            */
            RowDelta = FractionalRowAddr - LowerBufferRow;
            /*
            Interpolate for the value of the intensity to assign
            to the pixel at this row.
```

(continued)

Listing 12.3 *(continued)*

```
            */
            Color = RowDelta*((double) UpperColor - LowerColor) +
                                        LowerColor;

            /*
            Display this calculated intensity on the display
            */
            PutPixel256(Col,Row,Color);
        }
    }
}
```

When a PCX file is generated for a displayed image, the data written to the PCX file is read from the monitor's screen (the video memory). For this reason, any images displayed with aspect ratio correction will be saved with that correction also.

A similar technique could be employed to correct the aspect ratio problem with 640×200 resolution images. To do this, we would need to acquire a 640×480 resolution image (instead of 640×200) and then display the informational content of the 480 lines of digitized video with just 200 vertical display pixels. The process is the same as the one just described. The implementation is left to the reader.

Scaling and Sizing Images

The geometric process of scaling allows an image or portion of an image to be changed in size. The resulting image may be a magnified or reduced version of the original image. The goal of scaling is to produce the transformed image with as little spatial aberration as possible. The technique of interpolation discussed previously helps keep the aberration of a scaled image to a minimum.

Two functions are included in the geometric function library for changing the size of an image: "ScaleImage" and "SizeImage". Both operate in a similar manner. "ScaleImage" allows a separate specification for scaling in the horizontal and the vertical directions. "SizeImage" calculates the horizontal and vertical scale factors required to make an image fit within a specified area. Both functions will change the aspect ratio of a scaled image if the scale factors applied in both directions are not equal. Modification of an image's aspect ratio is sometimes desired and sometimes not, depending upon the application. It is important to keep aspect ratio considerations in mind when using these geometric transformation functions. Various scaling operations are illustrated in Image Sequences 12.1 through 12.3. The operational details of these functions can be found in Figure 12.2.

The scaling processes are performed from the point of view of the destination image.

Image Sequence 12.1 Image Magnification

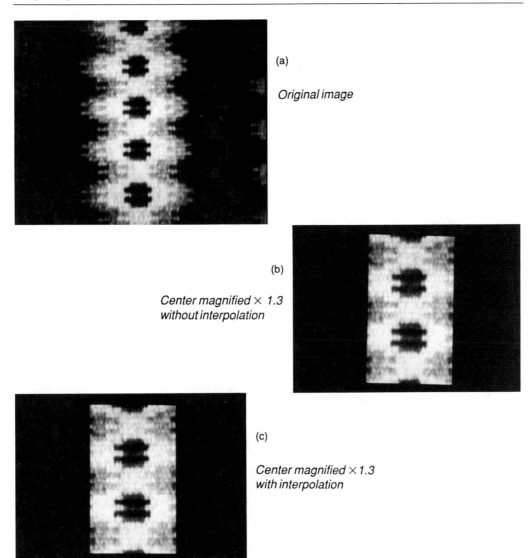

(a)

Original image

(b)

Center magnified × 1.3 without interpolation

(c)

Center magnified × 1.3 with interpolation

That is, for each pixel in the destination image, a reverse mapping is performed to calculate which pixel or pixels in the source image correspond to the destination pixel. The use of reverse mapping guarantees that each and every pixel in the destination image will have a defined value. If reverse mapping were not used and the destination pixels were calculated from the source image, voids could exist in the destination image. Voids result because there

Image Sequence 12.2   Image Reduction

(a)

Original image

(b)

Image reduced × 0.5 without interpolation

(c)

Image reduced × 0.5 with interpolation

Original image

(a)

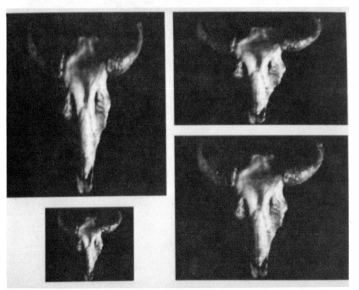

(b)

A single image scaled into various areas. Note aspect ratio distortions.

is not necessarily a one-for-one mapping between source and destination image pixels when images are scaled by arbitrary values. Reverse mapping will also automatically perform pixel replication as required for image magnification.

The majority of the complexity involved with image scaling and sizing lies in the use of interpolation for the calculation of transformed pixel-intensity values. See the earlier section on interpolation for details of this process.

Please note that the geometric process of scaling can change the spatial organization of image data to such a degree that the original image data is not recoverable. In other words, spatial information is permanently lost. Image size reduction illustrates this informational loss. As an image is reduced in size, one pixel of the destination (reduced) image is derived from four unique pixels of the source image. If the reduced image is subsequently magnified, the one pixel of the reduced image may be mapped into many pixels of the destination (magnified) image. If the image is magnified by the same amount as it was previously reduced, the four unique pixels become one during the reduction process, and subsequently the one pixel gets duplicated four times in the magnification process. Obviously, information has been lost in these two transformation processes.

A limitation of the scaling functions provided in the geometric process function library is that the scaled image must reside completely within an image buffer. Both scaling functions provided will terminate operation if a transformed image is found to exceed the size of the image buffer. This, of course, is a problem only when images are magnified in size, not when they are reduced. To correct this problem if and when it arises, the portion of an image being magnified must be reduced in area so the magnified version will fit entirely within the constraints of the image buffer.

Image scaling has too many applications to mention here. Suffice it to say that it is a very useful geometric transformation process when used by itself or in conjunction with other image processing operations. Image Sequence 12.3 shows an image that has been scaled to various sizes.

Rotation

The rotation geometric process allows an image to be rotated about its center point through any arbitrary angle specified. A complete image is rotated by separately rotating each pixel that makes up the image. The equations which govern the transformation of the location of a pixel of the source image ("Xold,Yold") into its new rotated location in the destination image ("Xnew,Ynew") are as follows:

```
Xnew = Xold * Cos(Angle) + Yold * Sin(Angle)
Ynew = Yold * Cos(Angle) - Xold * Sin(Angle)
```

These equations and their proofs can be found in many elementary trigonometry or computergraphics books under the topic of vector rotations. Please consult one of these books if a proof is required.

As discussed previously, aspect ratio considerations are very important when image rotation is to be performed. Image rotation reduces to an almost trivial process when working with square pixels on a display. Nonsquare pixels complicate image rotation considerably because of their impact on aspect ratio. Unfortunately, the 320×200 resolution mode, in which all image processing in this book is done, suffers from nonsquare pixels. See the discussion on aspect ratio consideration for detailed information on this topic.

Rotation of a 320×200 resolution image without aspect ratio correction results in an almost unusable image. For this reason aspect ratio corrections are built into the code in the geometric process function library and cannot be turned off. The use of aspect ratio correction along with interpolation results in a very accurate depiction of a source image regardless of the angle through which it is rotated.

Image Sequence 12.4 shows an image rotated with and without interpolation. The enhancement provided by the use of the interpolation process is unmistakable. All images shown in this image sequence utilize aspect ratio correction.

Translation

Translation is a geometric transformation that allows an image or a portion of an image to be changed in position. In the case of image processing and computergraphics, translation means movement. Image movement can be either between image buffers or internal to a single image buffer.

This transformation is performed from the source image's perspective instead of from that of the destination image. This is contrary to all of the other geometric processes described thus far. The transformation can be done in this manner because a one-for-one mapping between source and destination pixels prevents voids in the destination image. Because translation does not upset this mapping, the mapping does not suffer from aspect ratio distortions and does not need to utilize interpolation. This makes the translation transformations relatively quick compared to image scaling and/or rotation.

The code for the "TranslateImage" function is shown in Listing 12.1. Please refer to the listing for details about the implementation of this function. Since image translation has been illustrated (indirectly) in many of the image sequences in this book, no new image-translation sequence is provided.

Mirror Images

Mirror imaging simply rearranges the pixels of a source image (or portion thereof) to generate a mirror image of the source as the destination image. The resulting image transformation appears as if a mirror were used to produce it. Two types of mirror images are supported with the geometric process function library: horizontal mirroring, which generates a mirror of the source image in the horizontal direction, and vertical mirroring, which works in the vertical direction. With horizontal mirroring, source image left becomes destination image right and source image right becomes destination image left. With vertical mirroring, source image top becomes destination image bottom and vice versa.

No complications are encountered in the application of the mirror function because of the maintenance of the one-for-one mapping between source and destination pixels. For this reason neither aspect ratio nor interpolation issues need be considered. The code for the

Image Sequence 12.4   Image Rotation

Original image

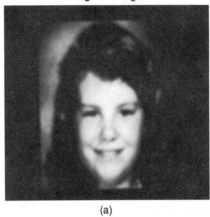

(a)

Without interpolation   *With interpolation*

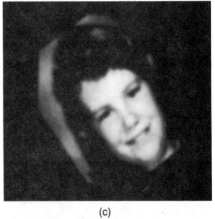

Images rotated
37.5°

(b)   (c)

Images rotated
300°

(d)   (e)

Image Sequence 12.5 Mirrored Images

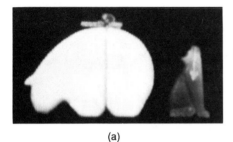

(a)

Original image

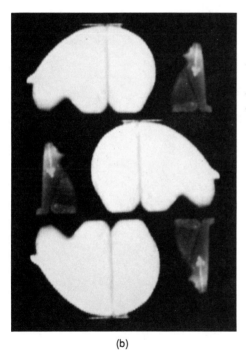

(b)

Mirrored image
Top—original image
Middle—horizontal mirror
Bottom—vertical mirror

''MirrorImage'' function is shown in Listing 12.1. Please refer to the listing for details about the implementation of this function. Image Sequence 12.5 shows both horizontal and vertical mirroring applied to an image.

Conclusions

In this chapter we have discussed a series of basic geometric transformations that can be applied to image data. Like all other classes of image processing transformations, these geometric transformations have their own set of implementation and usage problems. These problems can be minimized and/or overcome by using aspect ratio corrections and linear interpolation. Many image sequences were provided to illustrate the operation of the geometric processes.

An addition to the digitizer's image-acquisition code that corrects for aspect ratio problems with 320×200 resolution digitized images was also presented. Using these techniques, 320×200 resolution images can be acquired with no aspect ratio aberrations.

THE GALLERY OF IMAGES

[1]
Low-resolution
gray-scale image

320 × 200 RESOLUTION
64 LEVELS OF GRAY

[2]
High-resolution
gray-scale image

640 × 480 RESOLUTION
16 LEVELS OF GRAY

vide access to the I/O ports. These instructions place the port
cified by the instruction on the eight low order address lines. A
t the desired I/O device can be identified. The CPU issues an I/O
nal with either a read or a write signal to read or write data to t
d port. The port numbers, or addresses, are completely separate
mory addresses and do not use up any memory address space. A
e of a port mapped I/O device on the TRS-80 is the cassette reco
    A memory mapped device doesn't use the port mechanism for
ange with the CPU. Instead, a memory mapped I/O device appea
PU as a normal memory location. Data is transferred to the devi
0, using any of the load instructions normally used for storing
gular memory. Similarly, data is read from the I/O device by re
ading from, the same location. The advantages of this method
re than 256 devices can be accessed by the CPU at one time. The
tructions can also be used to read or write data to the device.
a can be transferred to a device by either direct or indirect instr
nces. The disadvantage of this method is that for each memory
a added to the system, one real memory location is removed.
disadvantage of memory mapped I/O is that the electronics

[3]
High-resolution text digitized.
Digitizer could be used to
experiment with optical character
recognition techniques.

640 × 480 RESOLUTION
16 LEVELS OF GRAY

[4]
A demonstration of why
objects must remain still during
the digitization process

640 × 480 RESOLUTION
16 LEVELS OF GRAY

[5]
Image displayed
with 16 total colors

320 × 200 RESOLUTION

[6]
Image displayed
with 64 total colors

320 × 200 RESOLUTION

[7]
Image displayed
with 128 total colors

320 × 200 RESOLUTION

[8]
Image displayed
with 256 total colors

320 × 200 RESOLUTION

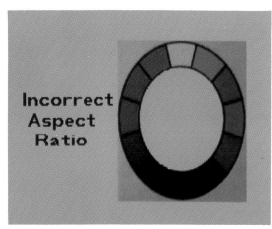

[9]
Image without
aspect ratio correction

Notice how the circle
appears as an ellipse.

320 × 200 RESOLUTION
256 COLORS

[10]
Image with aspect
ratio correction

The circle
is now a circle.

320 × 200 RESOLUTION
256 COLORS

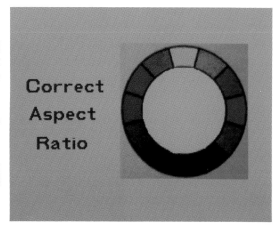

Various scaling factors
applied to the same image

Collage of image
processing algorithms

Random coloring of
a continuous-tone image

High-contrast
color image

PART THREE

ADDITIONAL INFORMATION

Glossary

Amplitude resolution. The accuracy with which an A-to-D converter converts an analog signal into its digital representation. The greater the number of bits used by the converter, the higher its resolution.

Analog-to-digital (A-to-D) converter. A device that senses an analog signal and converts it into a proportional representation in digital form.

Animation. The creation of a motion picture using a computer with a graphics device. Quickly changing the image displayed on the graphics device gives the appearance of motion.

Antialiasing. Smoothing out the jagged appearance of edges in an image on a raster display.

APA. All Points Addressable. The expression is used with raster displays and printers. It implies graphics capabilities in which every element is individually controllable.

Argument. Data passed to a function or a program.

Aspect ratio. The ratio of width to height of a single pixel on a display. If a display has an aspect ratio of 1, it is said to have square pixels.

Assembler language. The mnemonic codes that are converted into machine language by an assembler program. Assembler language is the only language a computer can execute directly.

Bilevel image. Synonym for binary image.

Binary image. Image that uses only one bit per pixel for display. Binary images are displayed in black and white. If a pixel is a 1, it is white (usually). If a pixel is 0, it is displayed as black (usually).

BIOS. A set of ROM-based firmware functions that control the resources of an IBM-compatible computer system. BIOS stands for Basic Input Output System.

Bit map. A memory image of a portion of a display area. The size of a bit map depends upon display resolution and the number of supported colors.

Byte map. A type of image in which each pixel is defined by one byte of storage (eight bits). The byte is capable of storing up to 256 levels of gray with 0 as black (typically) and 255 as white. A color image that utilizes a palette for display can also be considered to be byte-mapped.

Casting or type casting. A method for forcing a compiler to convert a variable's value from one type to another.

CCD camera. A video camera containing a Charged-Coupled Device, which is a transistorized light sensor on an integrated circuit. CCDs are smaller and more rugged than older video cameras, which utilize a vidicon tube as the light sensor.

CCITT. The CCITT (International Telegraph and Telephone Consultative Committee) is an international organization that develops and promotes standards in the communication industry.

Chrominance. The color portion of a video signal.

Clip. To eliminate a portion of the image outside a specified boundary.

Color filter. A sheet of colored glass or plastic used in photography to absorb certain colors and permit better rendition of others. The primary color filters (red, green, and blue) can be used with monochrome image scanners to create color images.

Color separation. The process of separating color images into the three primary color components: red, green, and blue.

Command line arguments or switches. Arguments passed into a program when it is run from the DOS command line; the string of arguments that follow a DOS command, including the command to initiate the execution of an application program.

Compression. Various techniques used by imaging devices and software to reduce image-storage requirements without drastically affecting the appearance of the image.

Continuous-tone images. Images that contain gradient tones from black through gray to white.

CRT. Cathode Ray Tube; the display device for a computer monitor or TV.

Default. An assumed value that exists if no other value is assigned.

Digital image processing. Digital image processing deals with arrays of numbers (samples) that represent an image. Various algorithms are used to manipulate the image samples to obtain some desired result. After processing is completed, the modified samples are used to reconstruct a continuous-tone image for viewing.

Display or graphics adapter. Electronic circuitry designed to interface a display (monitor) to a computer system. Usually but not always located on a printed circuit card.

Dithering. A technique for displaying gray-scale images on a monochrome monitor by carefully distributing the location of OFF and ON pixels.

Dot. The smallest controllable element on an APA device. Often referred to as a *pixel* or a *pel*.

Dynamic range. The ratio between the brightest and dimmest light level (pixel-intensity values).

Electron beam. A moving beam of electrons that creates an image on a display screen.

Facsimile, or FAX. A system for the transmission of textual and pictorial images. The image is digitized at the transmitter, sent across some medium, reconstructed at the receiver, and subsequently printed.

Filter. A device, method, or program that separates data, signals, or material based upon specified criteria.

Frame grabber. An input device that picks up an image from a video camera and subsequently digitizes it (the analog signal) into a defined number of bits per sample. A frame grabber usually digitizes both fields of a video frame for higher resolution. A field grabber digitizes just one of the two video fields that make up a video frame.

Graphics mode. A mode of the display adapter in which all pixels are independently controllable. This is opposed to text modes, where only predefined characters and symbols can be displayed.

Gray level. When an analog video signal is digitized (sampled), the numerical values obtained must be mapped into a range of integers (which represent the gray levels) for display. Because gray-level images contain information about the gray tones in the image, more than one bit per pixel is required. One byte per pixel is typical. The number of gray levels used has to do with the amplitude resolution of the digitizing equipment and the display equipment available. Sixty-four to 256 levels of gray are enough for realistic display of monochrome images.

Gray scale. See gray level.

Halftoning. The process of converting continuous-tone images to binary (black and white) images for display or printing. Various levels of gray are simulated by adjusting the size of a black dot within a white picture element.

Horizontal retrace. The time interval when the electron beam returns from the right to the left side of the display screen. The electron beam is turned off during retrace.

Hue. Hue refers to the name of a color, such as red, green, or blue. The hue of a color is its dominant wavelength.

Image. A physical likeness; a two-dimensional representation of a document (photograph, drawing, text, and so on) or natural scene as a numeric table; a two-dimensional function, obtained with a sensing device, that records the value of an image feature at all points. Values might be binary for black and white images, gray level (i.e., intensity) for halftone images. Images are converted into a digital form for processing with a computer.

Include files. Files that are temporarily inserted into a source code file during the compilation process, usually containing identifiers that are referenced in the source file. Used to ensure consistency of identifiers across an application program.

Interpolation. The determination of the value of a pixel that is located between known pixels on a desired path or contour defined by a mathematical function.

Latch. A type of memory device that captures and holds several bits of digital data.

Luminance. The black and white or brightness portion of a video signal.

Machine dependent code. Code that relies on some feature of a particular computer.

Machine independent code. Code that can be made to work on any computer because it does not rely on any particular features of any one computer.

Mapping. The mathematical conversion of one set of numbers into a different set based upon some transformation.

Mask. A technique for eliminating certain bits within a number, leaving only the bits of interest.

Memory model. A designation that tells a compiler where code and data are located and how they are to be referenced.

Monitor. Another term for CRT or display.

Monochrome image. Images that are displayed in shades of gray; single-color images with gray being the single color.

NTSC. The video standard used in North America, Central America, and Japan. It stands for the National Television Standard Committee. This standard specifies an interlaced picture of 525 lines scanning every 1/30 second.

PAL. Another video standard, like NTSC, used in Europe, Australia, and New Zealand. PAL video broadcasts 625 lines every 1/25 second.

Palette. A set or collection of colors available simultaneously for display of an image.

Patterning. Simulation of gray areas by a fixed set of patterns, each of which reproduces a gray tone of the gray scale.

Pel. *P*icture *el*ement. The smallest area of an image display device capable of being addressed and switched between the visible and the invisible states.

Picture. A collection of pels that form a recognizable image when visually represented together.

Pixel. Element of an image on a logical and conceptual level.

Quantization. The process of mapping the brightness and/or color values into integers. An A-to-D converter performs the quantizing process.

Raster. A predetermined pattern of lines that provides uniform coverage of a display space.

RGB. An additive color model that forms colors by mixing various ratios of red, green, and blue.

Resolution. The number of discernible points in a given field of view. The density of the sampling points affects the amount of detail visible in an image. The greater the image detail, the higher the resolution.

Sampling. The selection of a set of points over the field of observation. Only the values at those points will be used in further processing. All values in between are discarded.

Saturation. Designates the purity of a color or how much the color is diluted by white. Red is a highly saturated color. Pink has the same hue but a lower saturation.

Scaling. Translation of pixel coordinates to manipulate the size of an image. Performed by multiplication of pixel coordinates by a scaling factor, which can be different for the x and y directions.

Scanline. A single row of display data.

Scanner. A device capable of capturing image data. A scanner converts a continuous-tone picture into a discrete form.

SECAM. A video standard used in Iran, Poland, Russia, and Saudi Arabia, which broadcasts 625 lines every 1/25 second, and in France, which broadcasts 819.

Signal-to-noise ratio. The ratio between the level of signal (or significant information) and the level of noise.

Spatial frequency. The rate of change of pixel intensity in an image. Generally regarded as a two-dimensional quantity with both horizontal and vertical components.

Spatial resolution. In quantization, the density of sample points.

Thresholding. The simplest process for converting a gray-level image to a binary image. This process is performed by comparing each pixel value which makes up an image to a constant threshold value. Those pixels that exceed the threshold become white, while all others become black. The result is a high-contrast, black and white image.

Vector. A directed line segment.

Vertical retrace. The time interval between the display of video fields. During this time, the electron beam is returned to the top left side of the CRT from the bottom right. The electron beam is off during retrace. Vertical retrace occurs between 50 and 70 times per second, depending upon the CRT.

References and Additional Reading

Books: Image Processing and Graphics

Baxes, Gregory A., *Digital Image Processing, A Practical Primer*, Prentice Hall, Englewood Cliffs, NJ, 1984.

Castleman, Kenneth R., *Digital Image Processing*, Prentice Hall, Englewood Cliffs, NJ, 1979.

CONRAC Division, CONRAC Corp., *Raster Graphics Handbook*, CA, 1980.

Gonzalez and Wintz, *Digital Image Processing*, Addison-Wesley, Reading, MA, 1977.

Holzmann, Gerald J., and AT&T Bell Labs Staff, *Beyond Photography: The Digital Darkroom*, Prentice Hall, Englewood Cliffs, NJ, 1988.

Newman, W. M., and Sproull, R. F., *Principles of Interactive Computer Graphics*, McGraw-Hill, New York, 1979.

Rosenfeld, A., and Kak, A. C., *Digital Picture Processing*, 2d ed., Vols. 1 and 2, Academic Press, New York, 1982.

Schacter, Bruce J. (ed.), *Computer Image Generation*, Wiley, New York, 1983.

Sugiyama, Marc B., and Metcalf, Christopher D., *Learning C—Programming Graphics on the Amiga and the Atari ST*, Compute Publications, Inc., Greensboro, NC, 1987.

VanDam, A., and Foley, J. D., *Fundamentals of Interactive Computer Graphics*, Addison-Wesley, Reading, MA, 1983.

Books: Programming Reference

Borland International Inc., *Turbo C Reference Guide* and *Turbo C User's Guide*, Scotts Valley, CA, 1987.

Morgan, Christopher L., and Waite, Mitchell, *8086/8088 16-Bit Microprocessor Primer*, BYTE/McGraw-Hill, Peterborough, NH, 1982.

Willen, David C., and Krantz, Jeffrey I., *8088 Assembler Language Programming: The IBM PC*, Howard W. Sams, Indianapolis, 1983.

Books: Digital Signal Processing

Oppenheim, A., and Schafer, R., *Digital Signal Processing*, Prentice Hall, Englewood Cliffs, NJ, 1975.

Oppenheim, A. (ed.), *Applications of Digital Signal Processing*, Prentice Hall, Englewood Cliffs, NJ, 1978.

Rabiner, L., and Gold, B., *Theory and Application of Digital Signal Processing*, Prentice Hall, Englewood Cliffs, NJ, 1975.

Books: Computers and Mircoprocessors

IBM Corp., *Personal System/2 and Personal Computer BIOS Interface Technical Reference*, 68X2341, S68X-2341–00, May 1988.

IBM Corp., *Personal System/2 Hardware Interface Technical Reference*, 68X2330, S68X-2330–00, 1988.

Intel Corp., *iAPX 86/88, 186/188 User's Manual, Programmer's Reference*, CA, 1986.

Intel Corp., *Microprocessor and Peripheral Handbook, Volume 1—Microprocessor*, CA, 1987.

Articles

Ciarcia, Steven A., "Building the ImageWise Video Digitizer," part 1 and part 2, *BYTE* magazine, May and June 1987.

Ciarcia, Steven A., "Using the ImageWise Video Digitizer," *BYTE* magazine, August 1987.

Dawson, Benjamin M., "Introduction to Image Processing Algorithms," *BYTE* magazine, March 1987.

Heckbert, Paul, "Color Image Quantization for Frame Buffer Display," *ACM Computer Graphics Journal*, Vol. 16, No. 3, July 1982.

McManis, Charles, "Low-Cost Image Processing," *BYTE* magazine, March 1987.

Nelson, Mark R., "LZW Data Compression," *Dr. Dobb's Journal*, October 1989.

Rylander, Richard, "Solid Shape Drawing on the Commodore 64," *Dr. Dobb's Journal*, May 1985.

Star, Jeffrey L., "Introduction to Image Processing," *BYTE* magazine, February 1985.

White, Ronald G., "Compressing Image Data with Quadtrees," *Dr. Dobb's Journal*, March 1987.

Wilton, Richard, "Programming the Enhanced Graphics Adapter," *BYTE* magazine, Fall 1985.

Wilton, Richard, "PS/2 Video Programming," *BYTE* magazine, Fall 1987.

Wilton, Richard, "VGA Video Modes," *BYTE* magazine, Fall 1988.

The Companion Disk

The companion disk contains all of the code described and listed in this book along with a selection of digitized images for your viewing and image processing pleasure. They are available directly from the publisher. Please send in the tear-out form provided along with $49.95 to receive your copy of the companion disk. Using the disk will save hours of typing and program debugging caused by typing errors.

All files on the companion disk are in archive format. This was necessary because of the large amount of source code, executable files, and images provided. To use these files, they must be "de-arced." This is accomplished using the "XARC" utility program provided on the disk. To de-arc the files contained in the "GALLERY.ARC" file, for example, the following command would be used:

```
xarc gallery.arc enter
```

This command would be typed at the DOS command prompt. Because the disk is tightly packed, you may have to copy the file you wish to de-arc onto a different disk before de-arcing.

Two types of image files are included on the companion disk in the "GALLERY.ARC" file. These are PCX files and autodisplay (".COM") files. PCX files require the use of the "view.exe" program to display. Autodisplay files will display themselves on a VGA-equipped computer when their filename is typed at the DOS command prompt.

All C code is directly compilable by Turbo C version 2.0. Some code changes will be required for use with other C compilers. The following table describes the types of files to be found on the companion disk. The file "readme.doc" on the companion disk describes last-minute changes to the code, if any, that did not make it into the printing of this book. Please read this file carefully.

Note: not all image files necessary to recreate the image sequences in the book are included on this disk. For this reason, the filenames used in the example programs must be changed to those of your images before the programs are compiled.

Filename Extension	Type/Content of file
".C"	C source code files
".H"	C header (include) files
".PRJ"	Turbo C's "project make" files
".ASM"	assembler language source code files
".EXE"	directly executable program files
".COM"	directly executable autodisplay image files
".PCX"	PCX format image files

Companion Disk Contents

File: README.DOC   Last-minute information file

File: C1.ARC
VGAGRAPH.ASM   small-memory-model version of the video mode 13H assembler
                language support
VGA.H   VGA Function Library header file
VGA.C   VGA Function Library

File: C4.ARC
DIGITIZER.ASM   The low-level digitizer driver code
DIGITIZER.H   The low-level digitizer driver header file
TEST1.C   Digitizer test program one
TEST1.PRJ   Digitizer test program one project make file
TEST1.EXE   Executable test program one
TEST2.PRJ   Digitizer test program two project make file
TEST2.C   Digitizer test program two
TEST2.EXE   Executable test program two

File: C5GVIDEO.ARC
GVIDEO.PRJ   Generic image example program project make file
GVIDEO.C   Generic image example program
PVIDEO.PRJ   Focus window example program project make file
PVIDEO.C   Focus window example program
ALLVIDEO.PRJ   All-resolution example program project make file
ALLVIDEO.C   All-resolution example program
ALLVIDEO.EXE   Executable example program
ACQUIRE.PRJ   320 × 200 image-aspect-ratio corrected program project make file
ACQUIRE.C   See above

File: C5CVIDEO.ARC
CVIDEO.PRJ   Full-color example program project make file
CVIDEO.C   Full-color example program
IMAGECOM.ASM   Autodisplay program

File: C6PCX.ARC
PCX.H   PCX function library header file
PCX.C   PCX function library
COMPRESS.ASM   Assembler language RLL encoder program

File: C6TIFF.ARC
TIFFINFO.DOC   Additional details about the TIFF library functions.
TIFF.H   TIFF header file one
TIFFIO.H   TIFF header file two
TIFFINTF.H   TIFF interface header file
CCITT.C   Stubs for CCITT compression code
COMPRESS.C   Compression algorithm selector code
DIR.C   Directory parsing and building code
DUMPMODE.C   Uncompressed image functions
ERROR.C   Error and warning functions
IO.C   File I/O functions
LZW.C   Lempel-Ziv & Welch compression/expansion functions
PACKBITS.C   PackBits compression/expansion functions
PRINT.C   TIFF directory listing functions
TIFF.C   TIFF function library code
SWAB.C   Byte swapping code

File: C6VIEW.ARC
VGAGRAPH.ASM   Medium-memory-model version of mode 13H graphics functions
VIEW.PRJ   The view program project make file
VIEW.C   The view program (medium-memory model)
VIEW.EXE   An executable version of the view program

File: C7.ARC
PRTSIMP.C   A bonus threshold printing program
PRINTER.H   Print program header file
PRINT.PRJ   Print program project make file
PRINT.C   Print program

File: C8.ARC
IMAGESUP.H   Image processing support function header file
IMAGESUP.C   Image processing support functions

File: C9.ARC
PTPROCESS.H   Point process header file
PTPROCESS.C   Point process function library
PTTEST.PRJ   Point process example program project make file
PTTEST.C   Point process example program

File: C10.ARC
ARPROCESS.H   Area process header file
ARPROCESS.C   Area process function library
ARTEST.PRJ   Area process example program project make file
ARTEST.C   Area process example program

File: C11.ARC
FRPROCESS.H   Frame process header file

FRPROCESS.C	Frame process function library
FRTEST.PRJ	Frame process example program project make file
FRTEST.C	Frame process example program
File: C12.ARC	
GEPROCESS.H	Geometric process header files
GEPROCESS.C	Geometric process function library
GETEST.PRJ	Geometric process example program project make file
GETEST.C	Geometric process example program
P2CH12L3.C	Aspect-ratio-correction code fragment
File: GALLERY.ARC	

This archived file contains a miscellaneous collection of images, some from the book, others not. Remember, any files with the ".PCX" extension must be viewed with the "view.exe" program. Any files with the ".COM" extension will automatically display themselves when their filename is typed at the DOS command line.

APPENDIX 1

PC BIOS Function Summary

Function—00H Set mode
           01H Set cursor type
           02H Set cursor position
           03H Read cursor position
           04H Read light pen position
           05H Select active display page
           06H Scroll active page up
           07H Scroll active page down
           08H Read attribute/character at current cursor position
           09H Write attribute/character at current cursor position
           0AH Write character at current cursor position
           0BH Set color palette
           0CH Write dot
           0DH Read dot
           0EH Write teletype to active page
           0FH Read current video state
           10H Set palatte register
                 Sub Function 00H Set individual palette register
                              01H Set overscan register
                              02H Set all palette registers and overscan
                              03H Toggle intensity/blinking bit
                              07H Read individual palette register
                              08H Read overscan register
                              09H Get all palette registers and overscan
                              10H Set individual color register
                              12H Set block of color registers
                              13H Select color page
                              15H Read individual color register

17H Read block of color registers
1AH Read color page state
1BH Sum color values to gray shades

11H Character Generator
Sub Function 00H and 10H User alpha load
01H and 11H ROM 8x14 monochrome set
02H and 12H ROM 8x8 double dot
03H Set block specifier
04H and 14H ROM 8x16 font
20H Set interrupt 1FH font pointer
21H Set interrupt 43H user font
22H Set interrupt 43H for ROM 8x14 font
23H Set interrupt 43H for ROM 8x8 font
24H Set interrupt 43H for ROM 8x16 font
30H Get font information

12H Alternate Select
Sub Function 10H Return EGA information
20H Select alternate print screen

12H Alternate Select
Sub Function 30H Select scan lines for text modes
31H Enable/Disable palette loading
32H Enable/Disable video
33H Enable/Disable gray-scale summing
34H Enable/Disable cursor emulation
35H Switch active display
36H Video screen On/Off

13H Write string
14H Load LCD character font/Set LCD high-intensity substitute
15H Return physical display parameters for active display
1AH Read/Write display combination code
1BH Get functionality/state information
1CH Save/Restore video state

Interrupt Number 11H—Equipment Determination
Interrupt Number 12H—Memory Size Determination
Interrupt Number 13H—Diskette and Fixed Disk

Function—00H Reset diskette system
01H Read status of last operation
02H Read desired sectors into memory
03H Write desired sectors from memory
04H Verify desired sector
05H Format desired track
08H Read drive parameters
09H Initialize fixed disk characteristics
0AH Read sector long
0BH Write sector long
0CH Seek
0DH Reset fixed-disk system

0EH Read sector buffer
0FH Write sector buffer
10H Get drive status
11H Recalibrate drive
12H Controller RAM diagnostics
13H Controller drive diagnostics
14H Controller internal diagnostics
15H Read DASD type
16H Diskette change line status
17H Set DASD type for format
18H Set media type for format
19H Park heads
1AH Format ESDI drive

Interrupt Number 14H—Asynchronous Communications

Function—00H Initialize COM port
01H Send character
02H Receive character
03H Read status
04H Extended initialize
05H Extended COM port control

Interrupt Number 15H—System Services

Function—00H Turn on cassette motor
01H Turn off cassette motor
02H Read cassette
03H Write cassette
0FH Format unit periodic interrupt
21H Sub Function—00H Read POST error log
                  01H Write POST error log
40H Read/Modify profiles
41H Wait for external event
42H Request system power off
43H Read system status
44H Activate/Deactivate internal modem power
4FH Keyboard intercept
80H Device open
81H Device close
83H Process termination
84H Joystick support
85H System Request key pressed
86H Wait
87H Move (extended memory) block
88H Extended memory size determination
89H Switch processor to protected mode
90H Device busy
91H Interrupt complete

C0H Return system configuration parameters
C1H Return extended BIOS data area segment address
C2H Pointing Device BIOS Interface
Sub Function 00H Enable/Disable pointing device
01H Reset pointing device
02H Set sample rate
03H Set resolution
04H Read device type
05H Initialize pointing device interface
06H Extended commands
07H Device driver far call initialization
C3H Enable/Disable watchdog time-out
C4H Programmable option select (POS)

Interrupt Number 16H—Keyboard

Function—00H Keyboard read
01H Keystroke status
02H Shift status
03H Set typematic rate
04H Keyboard click adjustment
05H Keyboard write
10H Extended keyboard read
11H Extended keystroke status
12H Extended shift status

Interrupt Number 17H—Printer

Function—00H Print character
01H Initialize the printer port
02H Read status

Interrupt Number 18H—ROM BASIC
Interrupt Number 19H—Bootstrap Loader
Interrupt Number 1AH—System Timer and Real-Time Clock Services

Function—00H Read system timer time counter
01H Set system timer time counter
02H Read real-time clock time
03H Set Set real-time clock time
04H Read real-time clock date
05H Set real-time clock date
06H Set real-time clock alarm
07H Reset real-time clock alarm
08H Set real-time clock activated power on mode
09H Read real-time clock alarm time and status
0AH Read system timer day counter
0BH Set system timer day counter
80H Set up sound multiplexer

APPENDIX 2

Tag Image File Format (TIFF) Specification Revision 5.0

The following is the complete TIFF specification. It is included here as a reference for those programmers who wish to delve deeply into TIFF internals. Be sure to look closely at the appendices of this specification. They contain a lot of important information about imaging in general as well as TIFF in particular. This specification is reprinted here with the permission of Aldus Corporation. I would like to thank Aldus Corporation for allowing me to publish this specification. © Aldus Corporation 1990. Used with the express permission of Aldus Corporation. Aldus®, PageMaker®, and Persuasion® are registered trademarks of Aldus Corporation. Aldus FreeHand™ is a trademark of Aldus Corporation. All rights reserved.

Preface

This memorandum has been prepared jointly by Aldus and Microsoft in conjunction with leading scanner vendors and other interested parties. This document does not represent a commitment on the part of either Microsoft or Aldus to provide support for this file format in any application. When responding to specific issues raised in this memo, or when requesting additional tag or field assignments, please address your correspondence to either:

Developers' Desk	Windows Marketing Group
Aldus Corporation	Microsoft Corporation
411 First Ave. South	16011 NE 36th Way
Suite 200	Box 97017
Seattle, WA 98104	Redmond, WA 98073-9717
(206) 622-5500	(206) 882-8080

Revision Notes

This revision replaces "TIFF Revision 4." Sections in italics are new or substantially changed in this revision. Also new, but not in italics, are Appendices F, G, and H.

The major enhancements in TIFF 5.0 are:

1. *Compression of grayscale and color images, for better disk space utilization. See Appendix F.*

2. *TIFF Classes—restricted TIFF subsets that can simplify the job of the TIFF implementor. You may wish to scan Appendix G before reading the rest of this document. In fact, you may want to use Appendix G as your main guide, and refer back to the main body of the specification as needed for details concerning TIFF structures and field definitions.*

3. *Support for "palette color" images. See the TIFF Class P description in Appendix G, and the new ColorMap field description.*

4. *Two new tags that can be used to more fully define the characteristics of full color RGB data, and thereby potentially improve the quality of color image reproduction. See Appendix H.*

The organization of the document has also changed slightly. In particular, the tags are listed in alphabetical order, within several categories, in the main body of the specification.

As always, every attempt has been made to add functionality in such a way as to minimize incompatibility problems with older TIFF software. In particular, many TIFF 5.0 files will be readable even by older applications that assume TIFF 4.0 or an earlier version of the specification. One exception is with files that use the new TIFF 5.0 LZW compression scheme. Old applications will have to give up in this case, of course, and will do so "gracefully" if they have been following the rules.

We are grateful to all of the draft reviewers for their suggestions. Especially helpful were Herb Weiner of Kitchen Wisdom Publishing Company, Brad Pillow of TrueVision, and engineers from Hewlett Packard and Quark. Chris Sears of Magenta Graphics provided information which is included as Appendix H.

Abstract

This document describes TIFF, a tag based file format that is designed to promote the interchange of digital image data.

The fields were defined primarily with desktop publishing and related applications in mind, although it is possible that other sorts of imaging applications may find TIFF to be useful.

The general scenario for which TIFF was invented assumes that applications software for scanning or painting creates a TIFF file, which can then be read and incorporated into a "document" or "publication" by an application such as a desktop publishing package.

TIFF is not a printer language or page description language, nor is it intended to be a general document interchange standard. The primary design goal was to provide a rich environment within which the exchange of image data between application programs can be accomplished. This richness is required in order to take advantage of the varying capabilities of scanners and similar devices. TIFF is therefore designed to be a superset of existing image file formats for "desktop" scanners (and paint programs and anything else that produces images with pixels in them) and will be enhanced on a continuing basis as new capabilities arise. A high priority has been given to structuring the data in such a way as to minimize the pain of future additions. TIFF was designed to be an extensible interchange format.

Although TIFF is claimed to be in some sense a rich format, it can easily be used for simple scanners and applications as well, since the application developer need only be concerned with the capabilities that he requires.

TIFF is intended to be independent of specific operating systems, filing systems, compilers, and processors. The only significant assumption is that the storage medium supports something like a "file," defined as a sequence of 8-bit bytes, where the bytes are numbered from 0 to N. The largest possible TIFF file is 2**32 bytes in length. Since TIFF uses pointers (byte offsets) quite liberally, a TIFF file is most easily read from a random access device such as a hard disk or flexible diskette, although it should be possible to read and write TIFF files on magnetic tape.

The recommended MS-DOS, UNIX, and OS/2 file extension for TIFF files is ".TIF." The recommended Macintosh filetype is "TIFF". Suggestions for conventions in other computing environments are welcome.

1) Structure

In TIFF, individual fields are identified with a unique tag. This allows particular fields to be present or absent from the file as required by the application. For an explanation of the rationale behind using a tag structure format, see Appendix A.

A TIFF file begins with an 8-byte "image file header" that points to one or more "image file directories." The image file directories contain information about the images, as well as pointers to the actual image data.

See Figure 1.

Figure 1

Header		
0		Byte Order
2		Version
4	A	Offset of 0th IFD
6		

IFD		
A	B	Entry Count
A+2		Directory Entry 0
A+14		Directory Entry 1
A+26		Directory Entry 2
A+2+B*12	C	Offset of next IFD

Directory Entry		
X		Tag
X+2		Type
X+4		Length
X+8	Y	Value O
Y		Value

We will now describe these structures in more detail.

Image file header

A TIFF file begins with an 8-byte image file header, containing the following information:

Bytes 0-1: The first word of the file specifies the byte order used within the file. Legal values are:

> "II" (hex 4949)
> "MM" (hex 4D4D)

In the "II" format, byte order is always from least significant to most significant, for both 16-bit and 32-bit integers. In the "MM" format, byte order is always from most significant to least significant, for both 16-bit and 32-bit integers. In both formats, character strings are stored into sequential byte locations.

All TIFF readers should support both byte orders—see Appendix G.

Bytes 2-3 The second word of the file is the TIFF "version number." *This number, 42 (2A in hex), is not to be equated with the current Revision of the TIFF specification. In fact, the TIFF version number (42) has never changed, and probably never will. If it ever does, it means that TIFF has changed in some way so radical that a TIFF reader should give up immediately. The number 42 was chosen for its deep philosophical significance. It can and should be used as additional verification that this is indeed a TIFF file.*

A TIFF file does not have a real version/revision number. This was an explicit, conscious design decision. In many file formats, fields take on different meanings depending on a single version number. The problem is that as the file format "ages," it becomes increasingly difficult to document which fields mean what in a given version, and older software usually has to give up if it encounters a file with a newer version number. We wanted TIFF fields to have a permanent and well-defined meaning, so that "older" software can usually read "newer" TIFF files. The bottom line is lower software release costs and more reliable software.

Bytes 4-7 This long word contains the offset (in bytes) of the first Image File Directory. The directory may be at any location in the file after the header but must begin on a word boundary. *In particular, an Image File Directory may follow the image data it describes. Readers must simply follow the pointers, wherever they may lead.*

(The term "byte offset" is always used in this document to refer to a location with respect to the beginning of the file. The first byte of the file has an offset of 0.)

Image file directory

An **Image File Directory (IFD)** consists of a 2-byte count of the number of entries (i.e., the number of fields), followed by a sequence of 12-byte field entries, followed by a 4-byte offset of the next Image File Directory (or 0 if none). *Do not forget to write the 4 bytes of 0 after the last IFD.*

Each 12-byte IFD entry has the following format:

Bytes 0-1	contain the Tag for the field.
Bytes 2-3	contain the field Type.
Bytes 4-7	contain the Length ("Count" might have been a better term) of the field.
Bytes 8-11	contain the Value Offset, the file offset (in bytes) of the Value for the field. The Value is expected to begin on a word boundary; the corresponding Value Offset will thus be an even number. *This file offset may point to anywhere in the file, including after the image data.*

The entries in an IFD must be sorted in ascending order by Tag. Note that this is not the order in which the fields are described in this document. *For a numerically ordered list of tags, see Appendix E.* The Values to which directory entries point need not be in any particular order in the file.

In order to save time and space, the Value Offset is interpreted to contain the Value instead of pointing to the Value if the Value fits into 4 bytes. If the Value is less than 4 bytes, it is left-justified within the 4-byte Value Offset, i.e., stored in the lower-numbered bytes. Whether or not the Value fits within 4 bytes is determined by looking at the Type and Length of the field.

The Length is specified in terms of the data type, not the total number of bytes. A single 16-bit word (SHORT) has a Length of 1, not 2, for example. The data types and their lengths are described below:

1 = BYTE	An 8-bit unsigned integer.
2 = ASCII	8-bit bytes that store ASCII codes; the last byte must be null.
3 = SHORT	A 16-bit (2-byte) unsigned integer.
4 = LONG	A 32-bit (4-byte) unsigned integer.
5 = RATIONAL	Two LONG's: the first represents the numerator of a fraction, the second the denominator.

The value of the Length part of an ASCII field entry includes the null. If padding is necessary, the Length does not include the pad byte. *Note that there is no "count byte," as there is in Pascal-type strings. The Length part of the field takes care of that. The null is not strictly necessary, but may make things slightly simpler for C programmers.*

The reader should check the type to ensure that it is what he expects. TIFF currently allows more than 1 valid type for some fields. For example, ImageWidth and ImageLength were specified as having type SHORT. Very large images with more than 64K rows or columns are possible with some devices even now. Rather than add parallel LONG tags for these fields, it is cleaner to allow both SHORT and LONG for ImageWidth and similar fields. *See Appendix G for specific recommendations.*

Note that there may be more than one IFD. Each IFD is said to define a "subfile." One potential use of subsequent subfiles is to describe a "sub-image" that is somehow related to the main image, such as a reduced resolution version of the image.

If you have not already done so, you may wish to turn to Appendix G to study the sample TIFF images.

2) Definitions

Note that the TIFF structure as described in the previous section is not specific to imaging applications in any way. It is only the definitions of the fields themselves that jointly describe an image.

Before we begin defining the fields, we will define some basic concepts. An **image** is defined to be a rectangular array of "**pixels**," each of which consists of one or more "**samples**." With monochromatic data, we have one sample per pixel, and "sample" and "pixel" can be used interchangeably. RGB color data contains three samples per pixel.

3) The Fields

This section describes the fields defined in this version of TIFF. More fields may be added in future versions—if possible they will be added in such a way so as not to break old software that encounters a newer TIFF file.

The documentation for each field contains the name of the field (quite arbitrary, but convenient), the Tag value, the field Type, the Number of Values (N) expected, comments describing the field, and the default, if any. Readers must assume the default value if the field does not exist.

"No default" does not mean that a TIFF writer should not pay attention to the tag. It simply means that there is no default. If the writer has reason to believe that readers will care about the value of this field, the writer should write the field with the appropriate value. TIFF readers can do whatever they want if they encounter a missing "no default" field that they care about, short of refusing to import the file. For example, if a writer does not write out a PhotometricInterpretation field, some applications will interpret the image "correctly," and others will display the image inverted. This is not a good situation, and writers should be careful not to let it happen.

The fields are grouped into several categories: basic, informational, facsimile, document storage and retrieval, and no longer recommended. A future version of the specification may pull some of these categories into separate companion documents.

Many fields are described in this document, but most are not "required." See Appendix G for a list of required fields, as well as examples of how to combine fields into valid and useful TIFF files.

Basic fields are fields that are fundamental to the pixel architecture or visual characteristics of an image.

BitsPerSample

    Tag   = 258 (102)
    Type   = SHORT
    N   = SamplesPerPixel

Number of bits per sample. Note that this tag allows a different number of bits per sample for each sample corresponding to a pixel. For example, RGB color data could use a different number of bits per sample for each of the three color planes. *Most RGB files will have the same number of BitsPerSample for each sample. Even in this case, be sure to include all three entries. Writing "8" when you mean "8,8,8" sets a bad precedent for other fields.*

Default = 1. See also SamplesPerPixel.

ColorMap

    Tag   = 320 (140)
    Type   = SHORT
    *N   = 3 * (2**BitsPerSample)*

This tag defines a Red-Green-Blue color map for palette color images. The palette color pixel value is used to index into all 3 subcurves. For example, a Palette color pixel having a value of 0 would be displayed according to the 0th entry of the Red, Green, and Blue subcurves.

*The subcurves are stored sequentially. The Red entries come first, followed by the Green entries, followed by the Blue entries. The length of each subcurve is 2**BitsPerSample. A ColorMap entry for an 8-bit Palette color image would therefore have 3 * 256 entries. The width of each entry is 16 bits, as implied by the type of SHORT. 0 represents the minimum intensity, and 65535 represents the maximum intensity. Black is represented by 0,0,0, and white by 65535, 65535, 65535. The purpose of the color map is to act as a "lookup" table mapping pixel values from 0 to 2**BitsPerSample-1 into RGB triplets.*

The ColorResponseCurves field may be used in conjunction with ColorMap to further refine the meaning of the RGB triplets in the ColorMap. However, the ColorResponseCurves default should be sufficient in most cases.

See also PhotometricInterpretation—palette color.

No default. ColorMap must be included in all palette color images.

ColorResponseCurves
Tag   = 301 (12D)
Type = SHORT
N   = 3 * (2**BitsPerSample)

This tag defines three color response curves, one each for Red, Green and Blue color information. *The Red entries come first, followed by the Green entries, followed by the Blue entries.* The length of each subcurve is 2**BitsPerSample, using the BitsPerSample value corresponding to the respective primary. *The width of each entry is 16 bits, as implied by the type of SHORT. 0 represents the minimum intensity, and 65535 represents the maximum intensity. Black is represented by 0,0,0, and white by 65535, 65535, 65535. Therefore, a ColorResponseCurve entry for RGB data where each of the samples is 8 bits deep would have 3 * 256 entries, each consisting of a SHORT.*

The purpose of the color response curves is to refine the content of RGB color images.

See Appendix H, section VII, for further information.

Default: curves based on the NTSC recommended gamma of 2.2.

Compression
Tag   = 259 (103)
Type = SHORT
N   = 1

1 = No compression, but pack data into bytes as tightly as possible, with no unused bits except at the end of a row. The bytes are stored as an array of type BYTE, for BitsPerSample <= 8, SHORT if BitsPerSample > 8 and <= 16, and LONG if BitsPerSample > 16 and <= 32. The byte ordering of data >8 bits must be consistent with that specified in the TIFF file header (bytes 0 and 1). "II" format files will have the least significant bytes preceeding the most significant bytes while "MM" format files will have the opposite.

If the number of bits per sample is not a power of 2, and you are willing to give up some space for better performance, you may wish to use the next higher power of 2. For example, if your data can be represented in 6 bits, you may wish to specify that it is 8 bits deep.

Rows are required to begin on byte boundaries. *The number of bytes per row is therefore (ImageWidth * SamplesPerPixel * BitsPerSample + 7) / 8, assuming integer arithmetic, for PlanarConfiguration=1. Bytes per row is (ImageWidth * BitsPerSample + 7) / 8 for PlanarConfiguration=2.*

Some graphics systems want rows to be word- or double-word-aligned. Uncompressed TIFF rows will need to be copied into word- or double-word-padded row buffers before being passed to the graphics routines in these environments.

2 = CCITT Group 3 1-Dimensional Modified Huffman run length encoding. See Appendix B: "Data Compression -- Scheme 2." BitsPerSample must be 1, since this type of compression is defined only for bilevel images.

When you decompress data that has been compressed by Compression=2, you must translate white runs into 0's and black runs into 1's. Therefore, the normal PhotometricInterpretation for those compression types is 0 (WhiteIsZero). If a reader encounters a PhotometricInterpretation of 1 (BlackIsZero) for such an image, the image should be displayed and printed with black and white reversed.

5 = LZW Compression, for grayscale, mapped color, and full color images. See Appendix F.

32773 = PackBits compression, a simple byte oriented run length scheme for 1-bit images. See Appendix C.

Data compression only applies to raster image data, as pointed to by StripOffsets. All other TIFF information is unaffected.

Default = 1.

GrayResponseCurve
   Tag   = 291 (123)
   Type = SHORT
   N   = 2**BitsPerSample

The purpose of the gray response curve and the gray units is to provide more exact photometric interpretation information for gray scale image data, in terms of optical density.

The GrayScaleResponseUnits specifies the accuracy of the information contained in the curve. Since optical density is specified in terms of fractional numbers, this tag is necessary to know how to interpret the stored integer information. For example, if GrayScaleResponseUnits is set to 4 (ten-thousandths of a unit), and a GrayScaleResponseCurve number for gray level 4 is 3455, then the resulting actual value is 0.3455. *Optical densitometers typically measure densities within the range of 0.0 to 2.0.*

If the gray scale response curve is known for the data in the TIFF file, and if the gray scale response of the output device is known, then an intelligent conversion can be made between the input data and the output device. For example, the output can be made to look just like the input. In addition, if the input image lacks contrast (as can be seen from the response curve), then appropriate contrast enhancements can be made.

The purpose of the gray scale response curve is to act as a "lookup" table mapping values from 0 to 2**BitsPerSample-1 into specific density values. *The 0th element of the GrayResponseCurve array is used to define the gray value for all pixels having a value of 0, the 1st element of the GrayResponseCurve array is used to define the gray value for all pixels having a value of 1, and so on, up to 2**BitsPerSample-1. If your data is "really," say, 7-bit data, but you are adding a 1-bit pad to each pixel to turn it into 8-bit data, everything still works: If the data is high-order justified, half of your GrayResponseCurve entries (the odd ones, probably) will never be used, but that doesn't hurt anything. If the data is low-order justified, your pixel values will be between 0 and 127, so make your GrayResponseCurve accordingly. What your curve does from 128 to 255 doesn't matter. Note that low-order justification is probably not a good idea, however, since not all applications look at GrayResponseCurve. Note also that LZW compression yields the same compression ratio regardless of whether the data is high-order or low-order justified.*

It is permissable to have a GrayResponseCurve even for bilevel (1-bit) images. The GrayResponseCurve will have 2 values. It should be noted, however, that TIFF B readers are not required to pay attention to GrayResponseCurves in TIFF B files. See Appendix G.

If both GrayResponseCurve and PhotometricInterpretation fields exist in the IFD, GrayResponseCurve values override the PhotometricInterpretation value. But it is a good idea to write out both, since some applications do not yet pay attention to the GrayResponseCurve.

Writers may wish to purchase a Kodak Reflection Density Guide, catalog number 146 5947, available for $10 or so at prepress supply houses, to help them figure out reasonable density values for their scanner or frame grabber. If that sounds like too much work, we recommend a curve that is linear in intensity/reflectance. To compute reflectance from density: R = 1 / pow(10,D). To compute density from reflectance: D = log10 (1/R). A typical 4-bit GrayResponseCurve may look therefore something like: 2000, 1177, 875, 699, 574, 477, 398,

331, 273, 222, 176, 135, 97, 62, 30, 0, assuming GrayResponseUnit=3. Such a curve would be consistent with PhotometricInterpretation=1.

See also GrayResponseUnit, PhotometricInterpretation, ColorMap.

GrayResponseUnit

Tag   = 290 (122)

Type = SHORT

N   = 1

1 = Number represents tenths of a unit.

2 = Number represents hundredths of a unit.

3 = Number represents thousandths of a unit.

4 = Number represents ten-thousandths of a unit.

5 = Number represents hundred-thousandths of a unit.

Modifies GrayResponseCurve.

See also GrayResponseCurve.

For historical reasons, the default is 2. However, for greater accuracy, we recommend using 3.

ImageLength

Tag   = 257 (101)

Type = SHORT *or LONG*

N   = 1

The image's length (height) in pixels (Y: vertical). The number of rows (sometimes described as "scan lines") in the image. See also ImageWidth.

No default.

ImageWidth

Tag   = 256 (100)

Type = SHORT *or LONG*

N   = 1

The image's width, in pixels (X: horizontal). The number of columns in the image. See also ImageLength.

No default.

NewSubfileType
   Tag = 254 (FE)
   Type = LONG
   N = 1

Replaces the old SubfileType field, due to limitations in the definition of that field.

A general indication of the kind of data that is contained in this subfile. This field is made up of a set of 32 flag bits. Unused bits are expected to be 0. Bit 0 is the low-order bit.

Currently defined values are:

   Bit 0   *is 1 if the image is a reduced resolution version of another image in this TIFF file; else the bit is 0.*
   Bit 1   *is 1 if the image is a single page of a multi-page image (see the PageNumber tag description); else the bit is 0.*
   Bit 2   *is 1 if the image defines a transparency mask for another image in this TIFF file. The PhotometricInterpretation value must be 4, designating a transparency mask.*

These values have been defined as bit flags because they are pretty much independent of each other. For example, it be useful to have four images in a single TIFF file: a full resolution image, a reduced resolution image, a transparency mask for the full resolution image, and a transparency mask for the reduced resolution image. Each of the four images would have a different value for the NewSubfileType field.

Default is 0.

PhotometricInterpretation
   Tag   = 262 (106)
   Type = SHORT
   N   = 1

   0 = For bilevel and grayscale images: 0 is imaged as white. 2**BitsPerSample-1 is imaged as black. If GrayResponseCurve exists, it overrides the PhotometricInterpretation value, *although it is safer to make them match, since some old applications may still be ignoring GrayResponseCurve. This is the normal value for Compression=2.*

1 = For bilevel and grayscale images: 0 is imaged as black. 2**BitsPerSample-1 is imaged as white. If GrayResponseCurve exists, it overrides the PhotometricInterpretation value, although it is safer to make them match, since some old applications may still be ignoring GrayResponseCurve. If this value is specified for Compression=2, the image should display and print reversed.

2 = RGB. In the RGB model, a color is described as a combination of the three primary colors of light (red, green, and blue) in particular concentrations. For each of the three samples, 0 represents minimum intensity, and 2**BitsPerSample - 1 represents maximum intensity. Thus an RGB value of (0,0,0) represents black, and (255,255,255) represents white, assuming 8-bit samples. For PlanarConfiguration = 1, the samples are stored in the indicated order: first Red, then Green, then Blue. For PlanarConfiguration = 2, the StripOffsets for the sample planes are stored in the indicated order: first the Red sample plane StripOffsets, then the Green plane StripOffsets, then the Blue plane StripOffsets.

The ColorResponseCurves field may be used to globally refine or alter the color balance of an RGB image without having to change the values of the pixels themselves.

3="Palette color." In this mode, a color is described with a single sample. The sample is used as an index into ColorMap. The sample is used to index into each of the red, green and blue curve tables to retrieve an RGB triplet defining an actual color. When this PhotometricInterpretation value is used, the color response curves must also be supplied. SamplesPerPixel must be 1.

4 = Transparency Mask. This means that the image is used to define an irregularly shaped region of another image in the same TIFF file. SamplesPerPixel and BitsPerSample must be 1. PackBits compression is recommended. The 1-bits define the interior of the region; the 0-bits define the exterior of the region. The Transparency Mask must have the same ImageLength and ImageWidth as the main image.

A reader application can use the mask to determine which parts of the image to display. Main image pixels that correspond to 1-bits in the transparency mask are imaged to the screen or printer, but main image pixels that correspond to 0-bits in the mask are not displayed or printed.

It is possible to generalize the notion of a transparency mask to include partial transparency, but it is not clear that such information would be useful to a desktop publishing program.

No default. *That means that if you care if your image is displayed and printed as "normal" vs "inverted," you must write out this field. Do not rely on applications defaulting to what you want! PhotometricInterpretation = 1 is recommended for bilevel (except for Compression=2) and grayscale images, due to popular user interfaces for changing the brightness and contrast of images.*

PlanarConfiguration

Tag   = 284 (11C)
Type = SHORT
N   = 1

1 = The sample values for each pixel are stored contiguously, so that there is a single image plane. See PhotometricInterpretation to determine the order of the samples within the pixel data. *So, for RGB data, the data is stored RGBRGBRGB...and so on.*

2 = The samples are stored in separate "sample planes." The values in StripOffsets and StripByteCounts are then arranged as a 2-dimensional array, with SamplesPerPixel rows and StripsPerImage columns.   (All of the columns for row 0 are stored first, followed by the columns of row 1, and so on.) PhotometricInterpretation describes the type of data that is stored in each sample plane. *For example, RGB data is stored with the Red samples in one sample plane, the Green in another, and the Blue in another.*

If SamplesPerPixel is 1, PlanarConfiguration is irrelevant, and should not be included. *Default is 1.* See also BitsPerSample, SamplesPerPixel.

Predictor

Tag   = 317 (13D)
Type = SHORT
N   = 1

To be used when Compression=5 (LZW). See Appendix F.

1 = No prediction scheme used before coding.

Default is 1.

ResolutionUnit
>   Tag   = 296 (128)
>   Type = SHORT
>   N   = 1

To be used with XResolution and YResolution.

> 1 = No absolute unit of measurement. Used for images that may have a non-square aspect
>   ratio, but no meaningful absolute dimensions. *The drawback of ResolutionUnit=1 is that*
>   *different applications will import the image at different sizes. Even if the decision is*
>   *quite arbitrary, it might be better to use dots per inch or dots per centimeter, and pick*
>   *XResolution and YResolution such that the aspect ratio is correct and the maximum*
>   *dimension of the image is about four inches (the "four" is quite arbitrary.)*
> 2 = Inch.
> 3 = Centimeter.

Default is 2. *See also XResolution, YResolution.*

RowsPerStrip
>   Tag   = 278 (116)
>   Type = SHORT or LONG
>   N   = 1

The number of rows per strip. The image data is organized into strips for fast access to individual rows when the data is compressed—though this field is valid even if the data is not compressed.

RowsPerStrip and ImageLength together tell us the number of strips in the entire image. The equation is **StripsPerImage** = (ImageLength + RowsPerStrip - 1) / RowsPerStrip, assuming integer arithmetic.

Note that either SHORT or LONG values can be used to specify RowsPerStrip. SHORT values may be used for small TIFF files. It should be noted, however, that earlier TIFF specification revisions required LONG values and that some software may not expect SHORT values. *See Appendix G for further recommendations.*

Default is 2**32 - 1, which is effectively infinity. That is, the entire image is one strip. *We do not recommend a single strip, however. Choose RowsPerStrip such that each strip is about 8K bytes, even if the data is not compressed, since it makes buffering simpler for readers. The "8K" part is pretty arbitrary, but seems to work well.*

See also ImageLength, StripOffsets, StripByteCounts.

SamplesPerPixel

    Tag   = 277 (115)
    Type = SHORT
    N   = 1

The number of samples per pixel. *SamplesPerPixel is 1 for bilevel, grayscale, and palette color images. SamplesPerPixel is 3 for RGB images.*

Default = 1. See also BitsPerSample, PhotometricInterpretation.

StripByteCounts

    Tag   = 279 (117)
    Type = *SHORT or* LONG
    N   = StripsPerImage for PlanarConfiguration equal to 1.
          = SamplesPerPixel * StripsPerImage for PlanarConfiguration equal to 2

For each strip, the number of bytes in that strip. *The existence of this field greatly simplifies the chore of buffering compressed data, if the strip size is reasonable.*

No default. See also StripOffsets, RowsPerStrip.

StripOffsets

    Tag   = 273 (111)
    Type = SHORT or LONG
    N   = StripsPerImage for PlanarConfiguration equal to 1.
          = SamplesPerPixel * StripsPerImage for PlanarConfiguration equal to 2

For each strip, the byte offset of that strip. The offset is specified with respect to the beginning of the TIFF file. Note that this implies that each strip has a location independent of the locations of other strips. This feature may be useful for editing applications. This field is the only way for a reader to find the image data, and hence must exist.

Note that either SHORT or LONG values can be used to specify the strip offsets. SHORT values may be used for small TIFF files. It should be noted, however, that earlier TIFF specifications required LONG strip offsets and that some software may not expect SHORT values. *See Appendix G for further recommendations.*

No default. See also StripByteCounts, RowsPerStrip.

XResolution
    Tag   = 282 (11A)
    Type   = RATIONAL
    N   = 1

The number of pixels per ResolutionUnit in the X direction, i.e., in the ImageWidth direction. It is, of course, not mandatory that the image be actually printed at the size implied by this parameter. It is up to the application to use this information as it wishes.

No default. *See also YResolution, ResolutionUnit.*

YResolution
    Tag   = 283 (11B)
    Type   = RATIONAL
    N   = 1

The number of pixels per ResolutionUnit in the Y direction, i.e., in the ImageLength direction.

No default. *See also XResolution, ResolutionUnit.*

Informational fields are fields that can provide useful information to a user, such as where the image came from. Most are ASCII fields. An application could have some sort of "More Info..." dialog box to display such information.

Artist

>   Tag   = 315 (13B)
>   Type   = ASCII

Person who created the image.

If you need to attach a Copyright notice to an image, this is the place to do it. In fact, you may wish to write out the contents of the field immediately after the 8-byte TIFF header. Just make sure your IFD and field pointers are set accordingly, and you're all set.

DateTime

>   Tag   = 306 (132)
>   Type   = ASCII
>   N   = 20

Date and time of image creation. Use the format "YYYY:MM:DD HH:MM:SS", with hours on a 24-hour clock, and one space character between the date and the time. The length of the string, including the null, is 20 bytes.

HostComputer

>   Tag   = 316 (13C)
>   Type   = ASCII

"ENIAC", or whatever.

See also Make, Model, Software.

ImageDescription

Tag   = 270 (10E)
Type = ASCII

For example, a user may wish to attach a comment such as "1988 company picnic" to an image.

It has been suggested that this is what the newspaper and magazine industry calls a "slug."

Make

Tag   = 271 (10F)
Type = ASCII

Manufacturer of the scanner, video digitizer, or whatever.

See also Model, Software.

Model

Tag   = 272 (110)
Type = ASCII

The model name/number of the scanner, video digitizer, or whatever.

This tag is intended for user information only.

See also Make, Software.

Software

Tag   = 305 (131)
Type = ASCII

Name and release number of the software package that created the image.

This tag is intended for user information only.

See also Make, Model.

Facsimile Fields

Facsimile fields may be useful if you are using TIFF to store facsimile messages in "raw" form. They are not recommended for use in interchange with desktop publishing applications.

Compression (a basic tag)
```
Tag   = 259  (103)
Type  = SHORT
N     = 1
```

3 = Facsimile-compatible CCITT Group 3, exactly as specified in "Standardization of Group 3 facsimile apparatus for document transmission," Recommendation T.4, Volume VII, Fascicle VII.3, Terminal Equipment and Protocols for Telematic Services, The International Telegraph and Telephone Consultative Committee (CCITT), Geneva, 1985, pages 16 through 31. Each strip must begin on a byte boundary. (But recall that an image can be a single strip.) Rows that are not the first row of a strip are not required to begin on a byte boundary. The data is stored as bytes, not words—byte-reversal is not allowed. See the Group3Options field for Group 3 options such as 1D vs 2D coding.

4 = Facsimile-compatible CCITT Group 4, exactly as specified in "Facsimile Coding Schemes and Coding Control Functions for Group 4 Facsimile Apparatus," Recommendation T.6, Volume VII, Fascicle VII.3, Terminal Equipment and Protocols for Telematic Services, The International Telegraph and Telephone Consultative Committee (CCITT), Geneva, 1985, pages 40 through 48. Each strip must begin on a byte boundary. Rows that are not the first row of a strip are not required to begin on a byte boundary. The data is stored as bytes, not words. See the Group4Options field for Group 4 options.

Group3Options
```
Tag   = 292  (124)
Type  = LONG
N     = 1
```

See Compression=3. This field is made up of a set of 32 flag bits. Unused bits are expected to be 0. Bit 0 is the low-order bit. It is probably not safe to try to read the file if any bit of this field is set that you don't know the meaning of.

Bit 0   is 1 for 2-dimensional coding (else 1-dimensional is assumed). For 2-D coding, if more than one strip is specified, each strip must begin with a 1-dimensionally coded line. That is, RowsPerStrip should be a multiple of "Parameter K" as documented in the CCITT specification.

Bit 1   is 1 if uncompressed mode is used.

Bit 2   is 1 if fill bits have been added as necessary before EOL codes such that EOL always ends on a byte boundary, thus ensuring an eol-sequence of a 1 byte preceded by a zero nibble: xxxx-0000 0000-0001.

Default is 0, for basic 1-dimensional coding. See also Compression.

Group4Options
     Tag   = 293 (125)
     Type = LONG
     N   = 1

See Compression=4. This field is made up of a set of 32 flag bits. Unused bits are expected to be 0. Bit 0 is the low-order bit. It is probably not safe to try to read the file if any bit of this field is set that you don't know the meaning of. Gray scale and color coding schemes are under study, and will be added when finalized.

For 2-D coding, each strip is encoded as if it were a separate image. In particular, each strip begins on a byte boundary; and the coding for the first row of a strip is encoded independently of the previous row, using horizontal codes, as if the previous row is entirely white. Each strip ends with the 24-bit end-of-facsimile block (EOFB).

Bit 0   is unused.
Bit 1   is 1 if uncompressed mode is used.

Default is 0, for basic 2-dimensional binary compression. See also Compression.

Document Storage and Retrieval Fields

These fields may be useful for document storage and retrieval applications. They are not recommended for use in interchange with desktop publishing applications.

DocumentName
    Tag   = 269 (10D)
    Type = ASCII

The name of the document from which this image was scanned.

See also PageName.

PageName
    Tag   = 285 (11D)
    Type = ASCII

The name of the page from which this image was scanned.

See also DocumentName.

No default.

PageNumber
    Tag   = 297 (129)
    Type = SHORT
    N   = 2

This tag is used to specify page numbers of a multiple page (e.g. facsimile) document. Two SHORT values are specified. The first value is the page number; the second value is the total number of pages in the document.

Note that pages need not appear in numerical order. *The first page is 0 (zero).*

No default.

XPosition
> Tag   = 286 (11E)
> Type = RATIONAL

The X offset of the left side of the image, with respect to the left side of the page, *in ResolutionUnits.*

No default. See also YPosition.

YPosition
> Tag   = 287 (11F)
> Type = RATIONAL

The Y offset of the top of the image, with respect to the top of the page, *in ResolutionUnits.* In the TIFF coordinate scheme, the positive Y direction is down, so that YPosition is always positive.

No default. See also XPosition.

No Longer Recommended

These fields are not recommended except perhaps for local use. They should not be used for image interchange. They have either been superseded by other fields, have been found to have serious drawbacks, or are simply not as useful as once thought. They may be dropped entirely from a future revision of the specification.

CellLength
        Tag   = 265 (109)
        Type = SHORT
        N   = 1

The length, in 1-bit samples, of the dithering/halftoning matrix. Assumes that Threshholding = 2.

This field, plus CellWidth and Threshholding, are problematic because they cannot safely be used to reverse-engineer grayscale image data out of dithered/halftoned black-and-white data, which is their only plausible purpose. The only "right" way to do it is to not bother with anything like these fields, and instead write some sophisticated pattern-matching software that can handle screen angles that are not multiples of 45 degrees, and other such challenging dithered/halftoned data.

So we do not recommend trying to convert dithered or halftoned data into grayscale data. Dithered and halftoned data require careful treatment to avoid "stretch marks," but it can be done. If you want grayscale images, get them directly from the scanner or frame grabber or whatever.

No default. See also Threshholding.

CellWidth
        Tag   = 264 (108)
        Type = SHORT
        N   = 1

The width, in 1-bit samples, of the dithering/halftoning matrix.

No default. See also Threshholding. See the comments for CellLength.

FillOrder
        Tag   = 266 (10A)
        Type = SHORT
        N   = 1

The order of data values within a byte.

1 = most significant bits of the byte are filled first. That is, data values (or code words) are ordered from high order bit to low order bit within a byte.

2 = least significant bits are filled first. *Since little interest has been expressed in least-significant fill order to date, and since it is easy and inexpensive for writers to reverse bit order (use a 256-byte lookup table), we recommend FillOrder=2 for private (non-interchange) use only.*

Default is FillOrder = 1.

FreeByteCounts
    Tag   = 289 (121)
    Type = LONG

For each "free block" in the file, the number of bytes in the block.

TIFF readers can ignore FreeOffsets and FreeByteCounts if present.

FreeOffsets and FreeByteCounts do not constitute a remapping of the logical address space of the file.

Since this information can be generated by scanning the IFDs, StripOffsets, and StripByteCounts, FreeByteCounts and FreeOffsets are not needed.

In addition, it is not clear what should happen if FreeByteCounts and FreeOffsets exist in more than one IFD.

See also FreeOffsets.

FreeOffsets
    Tag   = 288 (120)
    Type = LONG

For each "free block" in the file, its byte offset.

See also FreeByteCounts.

MaxSampleValue
    Tag   = 281 (119)
    Type = SHORT
    N   = SamplesPerPixel

The maximum used sample value. *For example, if the image consists of 6-bit data low-order-justified into 8-bit bytes, MaxSampleValue will be no greater than 63. This is field is not to be used to affect the visual appearance of the image when displayed. Nor should the values of this field affect the interpretation of any other field. Use it for statistical purposes only.*

Default is 2**(BitsPerSample) - 1.

MinSampleValue
    Tag   = 280 (118)
    Type = SHORT
    N   = SamplesPerPixel

The minimum used sample value. *This field is not to be used to affect the visual appearance of the image when displayed. See the comments for MaxSampleValue.*

Default is 0.

SubfileType
    Tag   = 255 (FF)
    Type = SHORT
    N   = 1

A general indication of the kind of data that is contained in this subfile. Currently defined values are:

   1 = full resolution image data—ImageWidth, ImageLength, and StripOffsets are required fields; and

   2 = reduced resolution image data—ImageWidth, ImageLength, and StripOffsets are required fields. It is further assumed that a reduced resolution image is a reduced version of the entire extent of the corresponding full resolution data.

   3 = single page of a multi-page image (see the PageNumber tag description).

Note that several image types can be found in a single TIFF file, with each subfile described by its own IFD.

No default.

Continued use of this field is not recommended. Writers should instead use the new and more general NewSubfileType field.

Orientation

Tag   = 274 (112)
Type = SHORT
N   = 1

1 = The 0th row represents the visual top of the image, and the 0th column represents the
    visual left hand side.
2 = The 0th row represents the visual top of the image, and the 0th column represents the
    visual right hand side.
3 = The 0th row represents the visual bottom of the image, and the 0th column represents the
    visual right hand side.
4 = The 0th row represents the visual bottom of the image, and the 0th column represents the
    visual left hand side.
5 = The 0th row represents the visual left hand side of the image, and the 0th column
    represents the visual top.
6 = The 0th row represents the visual right hand side of the image, and the 0th column
    represents the visual top.
7 = The 0th row represents the visual right hand side of the image, and the 0th column
    represents the visual bottom.
8 = The 0th row represents the visual left hand side of the image, and the 0th column
    represents the visual bottom.

Default is 1.

*This field is recommended for private (non-interchange) use only. It is extremely costly for most
readers to perform image rotation "on the fly," i.e., when importing and printing; and users of
most desktop publishing applications do not expect a file imported by the application to be altered
permanently in any way.*

Threshholding

Tag   = 263 (107)
Type = SHORT
N   = 1

1 = a bilevel "line art" scan. BitsPerSample must be 1.
2 = a "dithered" scan, usually of continuous tone data such as photographs. BitsPerSample
    must be 1.
3 = Error Diffused.

Default is Threshholding = 1. See also CellWidth, CellLength.

4) Private Fields

An organization may wish to store information that is meaningful to only that organization in a TIFF file. Tags numbered 32768 or higher are reserved for that purpose. Upon request, the administrator will allocate and register a block of private tags for an organization, to avoid possible conflicts with other organizations. *Tags are normally allocated in blocks of five. If that is not enough, feel free to ask for more. You do not need to tell the TIFF administrator or anyone else what you are going to use them for.*

Private enumerated values can be accommodated in a similar fashion. For example, you may wish to experiment with a new compression scheme within TIFF. Enumeration constants numbered 32768 or higher are reserved for private usage. Upon request, the administrator will allocate and register a block of enumerated values for a particular field (Compression, in our example), to avoid possible conflicts.

Tags and values which are allocated in the private number range are not prohibited from being included in a future revision of this specification. Several such instances can be found in the TIFF specification.

Do not choose your own tag numbers. If you do, it could cause serious problems some day.

5) Image File Format Issues

In the quest to give users no reason NOT to buy a product, some scanning and image editing applications overwhelm users with an incredible number of "Save As..." options. Let's get rid of as many of these as we possibly can. For example, a single TIFF choice should suffice once most major readers are supporting the three TIFF compression schemes; then writers can always compress. And given TIFF's flexibility, including private tag and image editing support features, there does not seem to be any legitimate reason for continuing to write image files using proprietary formats.

Along the same lines, there is no excuse for making a user have to know the file format of a file that is to be read by an application program. TIFF files, as well as most other file formats, contain sufficient information to enable software to automatically and reliably distinguish one type of file from another.

6) For Further Information

Contact the Aldus Developers' Desk for sample TIFF files, source code fragments, and a list of features that are currently supported in Aldus products. *The Aldus Developers' Desk is the current "TIFF administrator."*

Various TIFF related aids are found in Microsoft's Windows Developers Tookit for developers writing Windows applications.

Finally, a number of scanner vendors are providing various TIFF services, such as helping to distribute the TIFF specification and answering TIFF questions. Contact the appropriate product manager or developer support service group.

Appendix A: Tag Structure Rationale

A file format is defined by both form (structure) and content. The content of TIFF consists of definitions of individual fields. It is therefore the content that we are ultimately interested in. The structure merely tells us how to find the fields. Yet the structure deserves serious consideration for a number of reasons that are not at all obvious at first glance. Since the structure described herein departs significantly from several other approaches, it may be useful to discuss the rationale behind it.

The simplest, most straightforward structure for something like an image file is a positional format. In a positional scheme, the location of the data defines what the data means. For example, the field for "number of rows" might begin at byte offset 30 in the image file.

This approach is simple and easy to implement and is perfect for static environments. But if a significant amount of ongoing change must be accommodated, subtle problems begin to appear. For example, suppose that a field must be superseded by a new, more general field. You could bump a version number to flag the change. Then new software has no problem doing something sensible with old data, and all old software will reject the new data, even software that didn't care about the old field. This may seem like no more than a minor annoyance at first glance, but causing old software to break more often than it would really need to can be very costly and, inevitably, causes much gnashing of teeth among customers.

Furthermore, it can be avoided. One approach is to store a "valid" flag bit for each field. Now you don't have to bump the version number, as long as you can put the new field somewhere that doesn't disturb any of the old fields. Old software that didn't care about that old field anyway can continue to function. (Old software that did care will of course have to give up, but this is an unavoidable price to be paid for the sake of progress, barring total omniscience.)

Another problem that crops up frequently is that certain fields are likely to make sense only if other fields have certain values. This is not such a serious problem in practice; it just makes things more confusing. Nevertheless, we note that the "valid" flag bits described in the previous paragraph can help to clarify the situation.

Field-dumping programs can be very helpful for diagnostic purposes. A desirable characteristic of such a program is that it doesn't have to know much about what it is dumping. In particular, it would be nice if the program could dump ASCII data in ASCII format, integer data in integer format, and so on, without having to teach the program about new fields all the time. So maybe we should add a "data type" component to our fields, plus information on how long the field is, so that our dump program can walk through the fields without knowing what the fields "mean."

But note that if we add one more component to each field, namely a tag that tells what the field means, we can dispense with the "valid" flag bits, and we can also avoid wasting space on the non-valid fields in the file. Simple image creation applications can write out several fields and be done.

We have now derived the essentials of a tag-based image file format.

Finally, a caveat. A tag based scheme cannot guarantee painless growth. But is does provide a useful tool to assist in the process.

Appendix B: Data Compression—Scheme 2

Abstract

This document describes a method for compressing bilevel data that is based on the CCITT Group 3 1D facsimile compression scheme.

References

1. "Standardization of Group 3 facsimile apparatus for document transmission," Recommendation T.4, Volume VII, Fascicle VII.3, Terminal Equipment and Protocols for Telematic Services, The International Telegraph and Telephone Consultative Committee (CCITT), Geneva, 1985, pages 16 through 31.
2. "Facsimile Coding Schemes and Coding Control Functions for Group 4 Facsimile Apparatus," Recommendation T.6, Volume VII, Fascicle VII.3, Terminal Equipment and Protocols for Telematic Services, The International Telegraph and Telephone Consultative Committee (CCITT), Geneva, 1985, pages 40 through 48.

We do not believe that these documents are necessary in order to implement Compression=2. We have included (verbatim in most places) all the pertinent information in this Appendix. However, if you wish to order the documents, you can write to ANSI, Attention: Sales, 1430 Broadway, New York, N.Y., 10018. Ask for the publication listed above—it contains both Recommendation T.4 and T.6.

Relationship to the CCITT Specifications

The CCITT Group 3 and Group 4 specifications describe communications protocols for a particular class of devices. They are not by themselves sufficient to describe a disk data format. Fortunately, however, the CCITT coding schemes can be readily adapted to this different environment. The following is one such adaptation. *Most of the language is copied directly from the CCITT specifications.*

Coding Scheme

A line (row) of data is composed of a series of variable length code words. Each code word represents a run length of either all white or all black. (Actually, more than one code word may be required to code a given run, in a manner described below.) White runs and black runs alternate.

In order to ensure that the receiver (decompressor) maintains color synchronization, all data lines will begin with a white run length code word set. If the actual scan line begins with a black run, a white run length of zero will be sent (written). Black or white run lengths are defined by the code words in Tables 1 and 2. The code words are of two types: Terminating code words and Make-up code words. Each run length is represented by zero or more Make-up code words followed by exactly one Terminating code word.

Run lengths in the range of 0 to 63 pels (pixels) are encoded with their appropriate Terminating code word. Note that there is a different list of code words for black and white run lengths.

Run lengths in the range of 64 to 2623 (2560+63) pels are encoded first by the Make-up code word representing the run length that is nearest to, not longer than, that required. This is then followed by the Terminating code word representing the difference between the required run length and the run length represented by the Make-up code.

Run lengths in the range of lengths longer than or equal to 2624 pels are coded first by the Make-up code of 2560. If the remaining part of the run (after the first Make-up code of 2560) is 2560 pels or greater, additional Make-up code(s) of 2560 are issued until the remaining part of the run becomes less than 2560 pels. Then the remaining part of the run is encoded by Terminating code or by Make-up code plus Terminating code, according to the range mentioned above.

It is considered an unrecoverable error if the sum of the run lengths for a line does not equal the value of the ImageWidth field.

New rows always begin on the next available byte boundary.

No EOL code words are used. No fill bits are used, except for the ignored bits at the end of the last byte of a row. RTC is not used.

Table 1/T.4   Terminating codes

White run length	Code word	Black run length	Code word
0	00110101	0	0000110111
1	000111	1	010
2	0111	2	11
3	1000	3	10
4	1011	4	011
5	1100	5	0011
6	1110	6	0010
7	1111	7	00011
8	10011	8	000101
9	10100	9	000100
10	00111	10	0000100
11	01000	11	0000101
12	001000	12	0000111
13	000011	13	00000100
14	110100	14	00000111
15	110101	15	000011000
16	101010	16	0000010111
17	101011	17	0000011000
18	0100111	18	0000001000
19	0001100	19	00001100111
20	0001000	20	00001101000
21	0010111	21	00001101100
22	0000011	22	00000110111
23	0000100	23	00000101000
24	0101000	24	00000010111
25	0101011	25	00000011000
26	0010011	26	000011001010
27	0100100	27	000011001011
28	0011000	28	000011001100
29	00000010	29	000011001101
30	00000011	30	000001101000
31	00011010	31	000001101001
32	00011011	32	000001101010
33	00010010	33	000001101011

34	00010011		34	000011010010
35	00010100		35	000011010011
36	00010101		36	000011010100
37	00010110		37	000011010101
38	00010111		38	000011010110
39	00101000		39	000011010111
40	00101001		40	000000101100
41	00101010		41	000000101101
42	00101011		42	000011011010
43	00101100		43	000011011011
44	00101101		44	000001010100
45	00000100		45	000001010101
46	00000101		46	000001010110
47	00001010		47	000001010111
48	00001011		48	000001100100
49	01010010		49	000001100101
50	01010011		50	000001010010
51	01010100		51	000001010011
52	01010101		52	000000100100
53	00100100		53	000000110111
54	00100101		54	000000111000
55	01011000		55	000000100111
56	01011001		56	000000101000
57	01011010		57	000001011000
58	01011011		58	000001011001
59	01001010		59	000000101011
60	01001011		60	000000101100
61	00110010		61	000001011010
62	00110011		62	000001100110
63	00110100		63	000001100111

Table 2/T.4   Make-up codes

White run length	Code word		Black run length	Code word
64	11011		64	0000001111
128	10010		128	000011001000
192	010111		192	000011001001
256	0110111		256	000001011011

320	00110110	320	000000110011
384	00110111	384	000000110100
448	01100100	448	000000110101
512	01100101	512	0000001101100
576	01101000	576	0000001101101
640	01100111	640	0000001001010
704	011001100	704	0000001001011
768	011001101	768	0000001001100
832	011010010	832	0000001001101
896	011010011	896	0000001110010
960	011010100	960	0000001110011
1024	011010101	1024	0000001110100
1088	011010110	1088	0000001110101
1152	011010111	1152	0000001110110
1216	011011000	1216	0000001110111
1280	011011001	1280	0000001010010
1344	011011010	1344	0000001010011
1408	011011011	1408	0000001010100
1472	010011000	1472	0000001010101
1536	010011001	1536	0000001011010
1600	010011010	1600	0000001011011
1664	011000	1664	0000001100100
1728	010011011	1728	0000001100101
EOL	000000000001	EOL	000000000001

Additional make-up codes

White and Black run length	Make-up code word
------	----
1792	00000001000
1856	00000001100
1920	00000001101
1984	000000010010
2048	000000010011
2112	000000010100
2176	000000010101
2240	000000010110
2304	000000010111
2368	000000011100
2432	000000011101
2496	000000011110
2560	000000011111

Appendix C: Data Compression—Scheme 32773— "PackBits"

Abstract

This document describes a simple compression scheme for bilevel scanned and paint type files.

Motivation

The TIFF specification defines a number of compression schemes. Compression type 1 is really no compression, other than basic pixel packing. Compression type 2, based on CCITT 1D compression, is powerful, but not trivial to implement. *Compression type 5 is typically very effective for most bilevel images, as well as many deeper images such as palette color and grayscale images, but is also not trivial to implement.* PackBits is a simple but often effective alternative.

Description

Several good schemes were already in use in various settings. We somewhat arbitrarily picked the Macintosh PackBits scheme. It is byte oriented, so there is no problem with word alignment. And it has a good worst case behavior (at most 1 extra byte for every 128 input bytes). For Macintosh users, there are toolbox utilities PackBits and UnPackBits that will do the work for you, but it is easy to implement your own routines.

A pseudo code fragment to unpack might look like this:

```
Loop until you get the number of unpacked bytes you are expecting:
        Read the next source byte into n.
        If n is between 0 and 127 inclusive, copy the next n+1 bytes literally.
        Else if n is between -127 and -1 inclusive, copy the next byte -n+1 times.
        Else if n is 128, noop.
Endloop
```

In the inverse routine, it's best to encode a 2-byte repeat run as a replicate run except when preceded and followed by a literal run, in which case it's best to merge the three into one literal run. Always encode 3-byte repeats as replicate runs.
So that's the algorithm. Here are some other rules:

- Each row must be packed separately. Do not compress across row boundaries.
- The number of uncompressed bytes per row is defined to be (ImageWidth + 7) / 8. If the uncompressed bitmap is required to have an even number of bytes per row, decompress into word-aligned buffers.
- If a run is larger than 128 bytes, simply encode the remainder of the run as one or more additional replicate runs.

When PackBits data is uncompressed, the result should be interpreted as per compression type 1 (no compression).

Appendix D

Appendix D has been deleted. It formerly contained guidelines for passing TIFF files on the Microsoft Windows Clipboard. This was judged to not be a good idea, in light of the ever-increasing size of scanned images. Applications are instead encouraged to employ file-based mechanisms to exchange TIFF data. Aldus' PageMaker, for example, implements a "File Place" command to allow TIFF files to be imported.

Appendix E: Numerical List of TIFF Tags

NewSubfileType
Tag = *254 (FE)*
Type = *LONG*
N = *1*

SubfileType
Tag = 255 (FF)
Type = SHORT
N = 1

ImageWidth
Tag = 256 (100)
Type = SHORT *or LONG*
N = 1

ImageLength
Tag = 257 (101)
Type = SHORT *or LONG*
N = 1

BitsPerSample
Tag = 258 (102)
Type = SHORT
N = SamplesPerPixel

Compression
Tag = 259 (103)
Type = SHORT
N = 1

PhotometricInterpretation
Tag = 262 (106)
Type = SHORT
N = 1

Threshholding
Tag = 263 (107)
Type = SHORT
N = 1

CellWidth
Tag = 264 (108)
Type = SHORT
N = 1

CellLength
Tag = 265 (109)
Type = SHORT
N = 1

FillOrder
Tag = 266 (10A)
Type = SHORT
N = 1

DocumentName
Tag = 269 (10D)
Type = ASCII

ImageDescription
Tag = 270 (10E)
Type = ASCII

Make
Tag = 271 (10F)
Type = ASCII

Model
Tag = 272 (110)
Type = ASCII

StripOffsets
Tag = 273 (111)
Type = SHORT or LONG
N = StripsPerImage for PlanarConfiguration
equal to 1.
= SamplesPerPixel * StripsPerImage for
PlanarConfiguration equal to 2

Orientation
Tag   = 274 (112)
Type = SHORT
N   = 1

SamplesPerPixel
Tag   = 277 (115)
Type = SHORT
N   = 1

RowsPerStrip
Tag   = 278 (116)
Type = SHORT or LONG
N   = 1

StripByteCounts
Tag   = 279 (117)
Type = LONG *or SHORT*
N   = StripsPerImage for PlanarConfiguration
        equal to 1.
      = SamplesPerPixel * StripsPerImage for
        PlanarConfiguration equal to 2.

MinSampleValue
Tag   = 280 (118)
Type = SHORT
N   = SamplesPerPixel

MaxSampleValue
Tag   = 281 (119)
Type = SHORT
N   = SamplesPerPixel

XResolution
Tag   = 282 (11A)
Type = RATIONAL
N   = 1

YResolution
Tag   = 283 (11B)
Type = RATIONAL
N   = 1

PlanarConfiguration
Tag   = 284 (11C)
Type = SHORT
N   = 1

PageName
Tag   = 285 (11D)
Type = ASCII

XPosition
Tag   = 286 (11E)
Type = RATIONAL

YPosition
Tag   = 287 (11F)
Type = RATIONAL

FreeOffsets
Tag   = 288 (120)
Type = LONG

FreeByteCounts
Tag   = 289 (121)
Type = LONG

GrayResponseUnit
Tag   = 290 (122)
Type = SHORT
N   = 1

GrayResponseCurve
Tag   = 291 (123)
Type = SHORT
N   = 2**BitsPerSample

Group3Options
Tag   = 292 (124)
Type = LONG
N   = 1

Group4Options
Tag   = 293 (125)
Type = LONG
N   = 1

ResolutionUnit
>   Tag = 296 (128)
>   Type = SHORT
>   N   = 1

PageNumber
>   Tag = 297 (129)
>   Type = SHORT
>   N   = 2

ColorResponseCurves
>   Tag = 301 (12D)
>   Type = SHORT
>   N   = 3 * (2**BitsPerSample)

Software
>   *Tag = 305 (131)*
>   *Type = ASCII*

DateTime
>   *Tag = 306 (132)*
>   *Type = ASCII*
>   *N   = 20*

Artist
>   *Tag = 315 (13B)*
>   *Type = ASCII*

HostComputer
>   *Tag = 316 (13C)*
>   *Type = ASCII*

Predictor
>   *Tag = 317 (13D)*
>   *Type = SHORT*
>   *N   = 1*

WhitePoint
>   *Tag = 318 (13E)*
>   *Type = RATIONAL*
>   *N   = 2*

PrimaryChromaticities
>   *Tag = 319 (13F)*
>   *Type = RATIONAL*
>   *N   = 6*

ColorMap
>   *Tag = 320 (140)*
>   *Type = SHORT*
>   *N   = 3 * (2**BitsPerSample)*

Appendix F: Data Compression—Scheme 5— LZW Compression

Abstract

This document describes an adaptive compression scheme for raster images.

Reference

Terry A. Welch, "A Technique for High Performance Data Compression", IEEE Computer, vol. 17 no. 6 (June 1984). Describes the basic Lempel-Ziv & Welch (LZW) algorithm. The author's goal in the article is to describe a hardware-based compressor that could be built into a disk controller or database engine, and used on all types of data. There is no specific discussion of raster images. We intend to give sufficient information in this Appendix so that the article is not required reading.

Requirements

A compression scheme with the following characteristics should work well in a desktop publishing environment:

- Must work well for images of any bit depth, including images deeper than 8 bits per sample.
- Must be effective: an average compression ratio of at least 2:1 or better. And it must have a reasonable worst-case behavior, in case something really strange is thrown at it.
- Should not depend on small variations between pixels. Palette color images tend to contain abrupt changes in index values, due to common patterning and dithering techniques. These abrupt changes do tend to be repetitive, however, and the scheme should make use of this fact.
- For images generated by paint programs, the scheme should not depend on a particular pattern width. 8x8 pixel patterns are common now, but we should not assume that this situation will not change.
- Must be fast. It should not take more than 5 seconds to decompress a 100K byte grayscale image on a 68020- or 386-based computer. Compression can be slower, but probably not by more than a factor of 2 or 3.

- The level of implementation complexity must be reasonable. We would like something that can be implemented in no more than a couple of weeks by a competent software engineer with some experience in image processing. The compiled code for compression and decompression combined should be no more than about 10K.
- Does not require floating point software or hardware.

The following sections describe an algorithm based on the "LZW" (Lempel-Ziv & Welch) technique that meets the above requirements. In addition meeting our requirements, LZW has the following characteristics:

- LZW is fully reversible. All information is preserved. But if noise or information is removed from an image, perhaps by smoothing or zeroing some low-order bitplanes, LZW compresses images to a smaller size. Thus, 5-bit, 6-bit, or 7-bit data masquerading as 8-bit data compresses better than true 8-bit data. Smooth images also compress better than noisy images, and simple images compress better than complex images.
- On a 68082- or 386-based computer, LZW software can be written to compress at between 30K and 80K bytes per second, depending on image characteristics. LZW decompression speeds are typically about 50K bytes per second.
- LZW works well on bilevel images, too. It always beats PackBits, and generally ties CCITT 1D (Modified Huffman) compression, on our test images. Tying CCITT 1D is impressive in that LZW seems to be considerably faster than CCITT 1D, at least in our implementation.
- Our implementation is written in C, and compiles to about 2K bytes of object code each for the compressor and decompressor.
- One of the nice things about LZW is that it is used quite widely in other applications such as archival programs, and is therefore more of a known quantity.

The Algorithm

Each strip is compressed independently. We strongly recommend that RowsPerStrip be chosen such that each strip contains about 8K bytes before compression. We want to keep the strips small enough so that the compressed and uncompressed versions of the strip can be kept entirely in memory even on small machines, but large enough to maintain nearly optimal compression ratios.

The LZW algorithm is based on a translation table, or string table, that maps strings of input characters into codes. The TIFF implementation uses variable-length codes, with a maximum code length of 12 bits. This string table is different for every strip, and, remarkably, does not need to be kept around for the decompressor. The trick is to make the decompressor automatically build the same table as is built when compressing the data. We use a C-like pseudocode to describe the coding scheme:

```
InitializeStringTable();
WriteCode(ClearCode);
Ω = the empty string;
for each character in the strip {
        K = GetNextCharacter();
        if Ω+K is in the string table {
                Ω = Ω+K;    /* string concatenation */
        } else {
                WriteCode (CodeFromString(Ω));
                AddTableEntry(Ω+K);
                Ω = K;
        }
} /* end of for loop */
WriteCode (CodeFromString(Ω));
WriteCode (EndOfInformation);
```

That's it. The scheme is simple, although it is fairly challenging to implement efficiently. But we need a few explanations before we go on to decompression.

The "characters" that make up the LZW strings are bytes containing TIFF uncompressed (Compression=1) image data, in our implementation. For example, if BitsPerSample is 4, each 8-bit LZW character will contain two 4-bit pixels. If BitsPerSample is 16, each 16-bit pixel will span two 8-bit LZW characters.

(It is also possible to implement a version of LZW where the LZW character depth equals BitsPerSample, as was described by Draft 2 of Revision 5.0. But there is a major problem with this approach. If BitsPerSample is greater than 11, we can not use 12-bit-maximum codes, so that the resulting LZW table is unacceptably large. Fortunately, due to the adaptive nature of LZW, we do not pay a significant compression ratio penalty for combining several pixels into one byte before compressing. For example, our 4-bit sample images compressed about 3 percent worse, and our 1-bit images compressed about 5 percent better. And it is easier to write an LZW compressor that always uses the same character depth than it is to write one which can handle varying depths.)

We can now describe some of the routine and variable references in our pseudocode:

InitializeStringTable() initializes the string table to contain all possible single-character strings. There are 256 of them, numbered 0 through 255, since our characters are bytes.

WriteCode() writes a code to the output stream. The first code written is a Clear code, which is defined to be code #256.

Ω is our "prefix string."

GetNextCharacter() retrieves the next character value from the input stream. This will be number between 0 and 255, since our characters are bytes.

The "+" signs indicate string concatenation.

AddTableEntry() adds a table entry. (InitializeStringTable() has already put 256 entries in our table. Each entry consists of a single-character string, and its associated code value, which is, in our application, identical to the character itself. That is, the 0th entry in our table consists of the string <0>, with corresponding code value of <0>, the 1st entry in the table consists of the string <1>, with corresponding code value of <1>, ..., and the 255th entry in our table consists of the string <255>, with corresponding code value of <255>.) So the first entry that we add to our string table will be at position 256, right? Well, not quite, since we will reserve code #256 for a special "Clear" code, and code #257 for a special "EndOfInformation" code that we will write out at the end of the strip. So the first multiple-character entry added to the string table will be at position 258.

Let's try an example. Suppose we have input data that looks like:

Pixel 0:	<7>
Pixel 1:	<7>
Pixel 2:	<7>
Pixel 3:	<8>
Pixel 4:	<8>
Pixel 5:	<7>
Pixel 6:	<7>
Pixel 7:	<6>
Pixel 8:	<6>

First, we read Pixel 0 into K. ΩK is then simply <7>, since Ω is the empty string at this point. Is the string <7> already in the string table? Of course, since all single character strings were put in the table by InitializeStringTable(). So set Ω equal to <7>, and go to the top of the loop. Read Pixel 1 into K. Does ΩK (<7><7>) exist in the string table? No, so we get to do some real work. We write the code associated with Ω to output (write <7> to output), and add ΩK (<7><7>) to the table as entry 258. Store K (<7>) into Ω. Note that although we have added the string consisting of Pixel 0 and Pixel 1 to the table, we "re-use" Pixel 1 as the beginning of the next string.

Back at the top of the loop. We read Pixel 2 into K. Does ΩK (<7><7>) exist in the string table? Yes, the entry we just added, entry 258, contains exactly <7><7>. So we just add K onto the end of Ω, so that Ω is now <7><7>.

Back at the top of the loop. We read Pixel 3 into K. Does ΩK (<7><7><8>) exist in the string table? No, so write the code associated with Ω (<258>) to output, and add ΩK to the table as entry 259. Store K (<8>) into Ω.

Back at the top of the loop. We read Pixel 4 into K. Does ΩK (<8><8>) exist in the string table? No, so write the code associated with Ω (<8>) to output, and add ΩK to the table as entry 260. Store K (<8>) into Ω.

Continuing, we get the following results:

After reading:	We write to output:	And add table entry:
Pixel 0		
Pixel 1	<7>	258: <7><7>
Pixel 2		
Pixel 3	<258>	259: <7><7><8>
Pixel 4	<8>	260: <8><8>
Pixel 5	<8>	261: <8><7>
Pixel 6		
Pixel 7	<258>	262: <7><7><6>
Pixel 8	<6>	263: <6><6>

WriteCode() also requires some explanation. The output code stream, <7><258><8><8><258><6>... in our example, should be written using as few bits as possible. When we are just starting out, we can use 9-bit codes, since our new string table entries are greater than 255 but less than 512. But when we add table entry 512, we must switch to 10-bit codes. Likewise, we switch to 11-bit codes at 1024, and 12-bit codes at 2048. We will somewhat arbitrarily limit ourselves to 12-bit codes, so that our table can have at most 4096 entries. If we push it any farther, tables tend to get too large.

What happens if we run out of room in our string table? This is where the afore-mentioned Clear code comes in. As soon as we use entry 4094, we write out a (12-bit) Clear code. (If we wait any longer to write the Clear code, the decompressor might try to interpret the Clear code as a 13-bit code.) At this point, the compressor re-initializes the string table and starts writing out 9-bit codes again.
Note that whenever you write a code and add a table entry, Ω is not left empty. It contains exactly one character. Be careful not to lose it when you write an end-of-table Clear code. You can either write it out as a 12-bit code before writing the Clear code, in which case you will want to do it right after adding table entry 4093, or after the clear code as a 9-bit code. Decompression gives the same result in either case.

To make things a little simpler for the decompressor, we will require that each strip begins with a Clear code, and ends with an EndOfInformation code.

Every LZW-compressed strip must begin on a byte boundary. It need not begin on a word boundary. LZW compression codes are stored into bytes in high-to-low-order fashion, i.e., FillOrder is assumed to be 1. The compressed codes are written as bytes, not words, so that the compressed data will be identical regardless of whether it is an 'II' or 'MM' file.

Note that the LZW string table is a continuously updated history of the strings that have been encountered in the data. It thus reflects the characteristics of the data, providing a high degree of adaptability.

LZW Decoding

The procedure for decompression is a little more complicated, but still not too bad:

```
while ((Code = GetNextCode()) != EoiCode) {
        if (Code == ClearCode) {
                InitializeTable();
                Code = GetNextCode();
                if (Code == EoiCode)
                   break;
                WriteString(StringFromCode(Code));
                OldCode = Code;
        } /* end of ClearCode case */

        else {
                if (IsInTable(Code)) {
                        WriteString(StringFromCode(Code));

AddStringToTable(StringFromCode(OldCode)+FirstChar(StringFromCode(Code)));
                        OldCode = Code;
                } else {
                        OutString = StringFromCode(OldCode) +
FirstChar(StringFromCode(OldCode));
                        WriteString(OutString);
                        AddStringToTable(OutString);
                        OldCode = Code;
                }
        } /* end of not-ClearCode case */
} /* end of while loop */
```

The function GetNextCode() retrieves the next code from the LZW-coded data. It must keep track of bit boundaries. It knows that the first code that it gets will be a 9-bit code. We add a table entry each time we get a code, so GetNextCode() must switch over to 10-bit codes as soon as string #511 is stored into the table.

The function StringFromCode() gets the string associated with a particular code from the string table.

The function AddStringToTable() adds a string to the string table. The "+" sign joining the two parts of the argument to AddStringToTable indicate string concatenation.

StringFromCode() looks up the string associated with a given code.

WriteString() adds a string to the output stream.

When SamplesPerPixel Is Greater Than 1

We have so far described the compression scheme as if SamplesPerPixel were always 1, as will be be the case with palette color and grayscale images. But what do we do with RGB image data?

Tests on our sample images indicate that the LZW compression ratio is nearly identical regardless of whether PlanarConfiguration=1 or PlanarConfiguration=2, for RGB images. So use whichever configuration you prefer, and simply compress the bytes in the strip.

It is worth cautioning that compression ratios on our test RGB images were disappointing low: somewhere between 1.1 to 1 and 1.5 to 1, depending on the image. Vendors are urged to do what they can to remove as much noise from their images as possible. Preliminary tests indicate that significantly better compression ratios are possible with less noisy images. Even something as simple as zeroing out one or two least-significant bitplanes may be quite effective, with little or no perceptible image degradation.

Implementation

The exact structure of the string table and the method used to determine if a string is already in the table are probably the most significant design decisions in the implementation of a LZW compressor and decompressor. Hashing has been suggested as a useful technique for the compressor. We have chosen a tree based approach, with good results. The decompressor is actually more straightforward, as well as faster, since no search is involved—strings can be accessed directly by code value.

Performance

Many people do not realize that the performance of any compression scheme depends greatly on the type of data to which it is applied. A scheme that works well on one data set may do poorly on the next.

But since we do not want to burden the world with too many compression schemes, an adaptive scheme such as LZW that performs quite well on a wide range of images is very desirable. LZW may not always give optimal compression ratios, but its adaptive nature and relative simplicity seem to make it a good choice.

Experiments thus far indicate that we can expect compression ratios of between 1.5 and 3.0 to 1 from LZW, with no loss of data, on continuous tone grayscale scanned images. If we zero the least significant one or two bitplanes of 8-bit data, higher ratios can be achieved. These bitplanes often consist chiefly of noise, in which case little or no loss in image quality will be perceived. Palette color images created in a paint program generally compress much better than continuous tone scanned images, since paint images tend to be more repetitive. It is not unusual to achieve compression ratios of 10 to 1 or better when using LZW on palette color paint images.

By way of comparison, PackBits, used in TIFF for black and white bilevel images, does not do well on color paint images, much less continuous tone grayscale and color images. 1.2 to 1 seemed to be about average for 4-bit images, and 8-bit images are worse.

It has been suggested that the CCITT 1D scheme could be used for continuous tone images, by compressing each bitplane separately. No doubt some compression could be achieved, but it seems unlikely that a scheme based on a fixed table that is optimized for short black runs separated by longer white runs would be a very good choice on any of the bitplanes. It would do quite well on the high-order bitplanes (but so would a simpler scheme like PackBits), and would do quite poorly on the low-order bitplanes. We believe that the compression ratios would generally not be very impressive, and the process would in addition be quite slow. Splitting the pixels into bitplanes and putting them back together is somewhat expensive, and the coding is also fairly slow when implemented in software.

Another approach that has been suggested uses uses a 2D differencing step following by coding the differences using a fixed table of variable-length codes. This type of scheme works quite well on many 8-bit grayscale images, and is probably simpler to implement than LZW. But it has a number of disadvantages when used on a wide variety of images. First, it is not adaptive. This makes a big difference when compressing data such as 8-bit images that have been "sharpened" using one of the standard techniques. Such images tend to get larger instead of smaller when compressed. Another disadvantage of these schemes is that they do not do well with a wide range of bit depths. The built-in code table has to be optimized for a particular bit depth in order to be effective.

Finally, we should mention "lossy" compression schemes. Extensive research has been done in the area of lossy, or non-information-preserving image compression. These techniques generally yield much higher compression ratios than can be achieved by fully-reversible, information-preserving image compression techniques such as PackBits and LZW. Some disadvantages: many of the lossy techniques are so computationally expensive that hardware assists are required. Others are so complicated that most microcomputer software vendors could not afford either the expense of implementation or the increase in application object code size. Yet others sacrifice enough image quality to make them unsuitable for publishing use.

In spite of these difficulties, we believe that there will one day be a standardized lossy compression scheme for full color images that will be usable for publishing applications on microcomputers. An International Standards Organization group, ISO/IEC/JTC1/SC2/WG8, in cooperation with CCITT Study Group VIII, is hard at work on a scheme that might be appropriate. We expect that a future revision of TIFF will incorporate this scheme once it is finalized, if it turns out to satisfy the needs of desktop publishers and others in the microcomputer community. This will augment, not replace, LZW as an approved TIFF compression scheme. LZW will very likely remain the scheme of choice for Palette color images, and perhaps 4-bit grayscale images, and may well overtake CCITT 1D and PackBits for bilevel images.

Future LZW Extensions

Some images compress better using LZW coding if they are first subjected to a process wherein each pixel value is replaced by the difference between the pixel and the preceding pixel. Performing this differencing in two dimensions helps some images even more. However, many images do not compress better with this extra preprocessing, and for a significant number of images, the compression ratio is actually worse. We are therefore not making differencing an integral part of the TIFF LZW compression scheme.

However, it is possible that a "prediction" stage like differencing may exist which is effective over a broad range of images. If such a scheme is found, it may be incorporated in the next major TIFF revision. If so, a new value will be defined for the new "Predictor" TIFF tag. Therefore, all TIFF readers that read LZW files <u>must</u> pay attention to the Predictor tag. If it is 1, which is the default case, LZW decompression may proceed safely. If it is not 1, and the reader does not recognize the specified prediction scheme, the reader should give up.

Acknowledgements

The original LZW reference has already been given. The use of ClearCode as a technique to handle overflow was borrowed from the compression scheme used by the Graphics Interchange Format (GIF), a small-color-paint-image-file format used by CompuServe that also is an adaptation of the LZW technique. Joff Morgan and Eric Robinson of Aldus were each instrumental in their own way in getting LZW off the ground.

Appendix G: TIFF Classes

Rationale

TIFF was designed to make life easier for scanner vendors, desktop publishing software developers, and users of these two classes of products, by reducing the proliferation of proprietary scanned image formats. It has succeeded far beyond our expectations in this respect. But we had expected that TIFF would be of interest to only a dozen or so scanner vendors (there weren't any more than that in 1985), and another dozen or so desktop publishing software vendors. This turned out to be a gross underestimate. The only problem with this sort of success is that TIFF was designed to be powerful and flexible, at the expense of simplicity. It takes a fair amount of effort to handle all the options currently defined in this specification (probably no application does a complete job), and that is currently the only way you can be <u>sure</u> that you will be able to import any TIFF image, since there are so many image-generating applications out there now.

So here is an attempt to channel some of the flexibility of TIFF into more restrictive paths, using what we have learned in the past two years about which options are the most useful. Such an undertaking is of course filled with fairly arbitrary decisions. But the result is that writers can more easily write files that will be successfully read by a wide variety of applications, and readers can know when they can stop adding TIFF features.

The price we pay for TIFF Classes is some loss in the ability to adapt. Once we establish the requirements for a TIFF Class, we can never add new requirements, since old software would not know about these new requirements. (The best we can do at that point is establish new TIFF Classes. But the problem with that is that we could quickly have too many TIFF Classes.) So we must believe that we know what we are doing in establishing these Classes. If we do not, any mistakes will be expensive.

Overview

Four TIFF Classes have been defined:

- Class B for bilevel (1-bit) images
- Class G for grayscale images
- Class P for palette color images
- Class R for RGB full color images

To save time and space, we will usually say "TIFF B", "TIFF G", "TIFF P," and "TIFF R." If we are talking about all four types, we may write "TIFF X."

(Note to fax people: if you are interested in a fax TIFF F Class, please get together and decide what should be in TIFF Class F files. Let us know if we can help in any way. When you have decided, send us your results, so that we can include the information here.)

Core Requirements

This section describes requirements that are common to all TIFF Class X images.

General Requirements

The following are required characteristics of all TIFF Class X files.

Where there are options, TIFF X writers can do whichever one they want, though we will often recommend a particular choice, but TIFF X readers must be able to handle all of them. Please pay close attention to the recommendations. It is possible that at some point in the future, new and even-simpler TIFF classes will be defined that include only recommended features.

You will need to read at least the first three sections of the main specification in order to fully understand the following discussion.

Defaults. TIFF X writers may, but are not required, to write out a field that has a default value, if the default value is the one desired. TIFF X readers must be prepared to handle either situation.

Other fields. TIFF X readers must be prepared to encounter fields other than the required fields in TIFF X files. TIFF X writers are allowed to write fields such as Make, Model, DateTime, and so on, and TIFF X readers can certainly make use of such fields if they exist. TIFF X readers must not, however, refuse to read the file if such optional fields do not exist.

'MM' and 'II' byte order. TIFF X readers must be able to handle both byte orders. TIFF writers can do whichever is most convenient or efficient. Images are crossing the IBM PC/Macintosh boundary (and others as well) with a surprisingly high frequency. We could force writers to all use the same byte order, but preliminary evidence indicates that this will cause problems when we start seeing greater-than-8-bit images. Reversing bytes while scanning could well slow down the scanning process enough to cause the scanning mechanism to stop, which tends to create image quality problems.

Multiple subfiles. TIFF X readers must be prepared for multiple images (i.e., subfiles) per TIFF file, although they are not required to do anything with any image after the first one. TIFF X writers must be sure to write a long word of 0 after the last IFD (this is the standard way of signalling that this IFD was the last one) as indicated in the TIFF structure discussion. If a TIFF X writer writes multiple subfiles, the first one must be the full resolution image. Subsequent subimages, such as reduced resolution images and transparency masks, may be in any order in the TIFF file. If a reader wants to make use of such subimages, it will have to scan the IFD's before deciding how to proceed.

TIFF X Editors. Editors, applications that modify TIFF files, have a few additional requirements.

TIFF editors must be especially careful about subfiles. If a TIFF editor edits a full-resolution subfile, but does not update an accompanying reduced-resolution subfile, a reader that uses the reduced-resolution subfile for screen display will display the wrong thing. So TIFF editors must either create a new reduced-resolution subfile when they alter a full-resolution subfile, or else they must simply delete any subfiles that they aren't prepared to deal with.

A similar situation arises with the fields themselves. A TIFF X editor need only worry about the TIFF X required fields. In particular, it is unnecessary, and probably dangerous, for an editor to copy fields that it does not understand. It may have altered the file in a way that is incompatible with the unknown fields.

Required Fields

NewSubfileType. LONG. Recommended but not required.

ImageWidth. SHORT or LONG. (That is, both "SHORT" and "LONG" TIFF data types are allowed, and must be handled properly by readers. TIFF writers can use either.) TIFF X readers are not required to read arbitrarily large files however. Some readers will give up if the entire image cannot fit in available memory. (In such cases the reader should inform the user of the nature of the problem.) Others will probably not be able to handle ImageWidth greater than 65535. Recommendation: use LONG, since resolutions seem to keep going up.

ImageLength. SHORT or LONG. Recommendation: use LONG.

RowsPerStrip. SHORT or LONG. Readers must be able to handle any value between 1 and $2**32-1$. However, some readers may try to read an entire strip into memory at one time, so that if the entire image is one strip, the application may run out of memory. Recommendation 1: Set RowsPerStrip such that the size of each strip is about 8K bytes. Do this even for uncompressed data, since it is easy for a writer and makes things simpler for readers. (Note: extremely wide, high-resolution images may have rows larger than 8K bytes; in this case, RowsPerStrip should be 1, and the strip will just have to be larger than 8K. Recommendation 2: use LONG.

StripOffsets. SHORT or LONG. As explained in the main part of the specification, the number of StripOffsets depends on RowsPerStrip and ImageLength. Recommendation: always use LONG. (LONG must, of course, be used if the file is more than 64K bytes in length.)

StripByteCounts. SHORT or LONG. Many existing TIFF images do not contain StripByteCounts, because, in a strict sense, they are unnecessary. It is possible to write an efficient TIFF reader that does not need to know in advance the exact size of a compressed strip. But it does make things considerably more complicated, so we will require StripByteCounts in TIFF X files. Recommendation: use SHORT, since strips are not supposed to be very large.

XResolution, YResolution. RATIONAL. Note that the X and Y resolutions may be unequal. A TIFF X reader must be able to handle this case. TIFF X pixel-editors will typically not care about the resolution, but applications such as page layout programs will.

ResolutionUnit. SHORT. TIFF X readers must be prepared to handle all three values for ResolutionUnit.

TIFF Class B - Bilevel

Required (in addition to the above core requirements)

The following fields and values are required for TIFF B files, in addition to the fields required for all TIFF X images (see above).

SamplesPerPixel = 1. SHORT. (Since this is the default, the field need not be present. The same thing holds for other required TIFF X fields that have defaults.)

BitsPerSample = 1. SHORT.

Compression = 1, 2 (CCITT 1D), or 32773 (PackBits). SHORT. TIFF B readers must handle all three. Recommendation: use PackBits. It is simple, effective, fast, and has a good worst-case behavior. CCITT 1D is definitely more effective in some situations, such as scanning a page of body text, but is tough to implement and test, fairly slow, and has a poor worst-case behavior. Besides, scanning a page of 12 point text is not very useful for publishing applications, unless the image data is turned into ASCII text via OCR software, which is outside the scope of TIFF.

PhotometricInterpretation = 0 or 1. SHORT.

A Sample TIFF B Image

Offset (hex)	Name	Value (mostly hex)			

Header:

0000	Byte Order	4D4D			
0002	Version	002A			
0004	1st IFD pointer	00000014			

IFD:

0014	Entry Count	000D			
0016	NewSubfileType	00FE	0004	00000001	00000000
0022	ImageWidth	0100	0004	00000001	000007D0
002E	ImageLength	0101	0004	00000001	00000BB8
003A	Compression	0103	0003	00000001	8005 0000
0046	PhotometricInterpretation	0106	0003	00000001	0001 0000
0052	StripOffsets	0111	0004	000000BC	000000B6
005E	RowsPerStrip	0116	0004	00000001	00000010
006A	StripByteCounts	0117	0003	000000BC	000003A6
0076	XResolution	011A	0005	00000001	00000696
0082	YResolution	011B	0005	00000001	0000069E
008E	Software	0131	0002	0000000E	000006A6
009A	DateTime	0132	0002	00000014	000006B6
00A6	Next IFD pointer	00000000			

Fields pointed to by the tags:

00B6	StripOffsets	Offset0, Offset1, ... Offset187
03A6	StripByteCounts	Count0, Count1, ... Count187
0696	XResolution	0000012C 00000001
069E	YResolution	0000012C 00000001
06A6	Software	"PageMaker 3.0"
06B6	DateTime	"1988:02:18 13:59:59"

Image Data:

00000700	Compressed data for strip 10
xxxxxxxx	Compressed data for strip 179
xxxxxxxx	Compressed data for strip 53
xxxxxxxx	Compressed data for strip 160

.

.

.

End of example

Comments on the TIFF B example

1. The IFD in our example starts at position hex 14. It could have been anywhere in the file as long as the position is even and greater than or equal to 8, since the TIFF header is 8 bytes long and must be the first thing in a TIFF file.

2. With 16 rows per strip, we have 188 strips in all.

3. The example uses a number of optional fields, such as DateTime. TIFF X readers must safely skip over these fields if they do not want to use the information. And TIFF X readers must not require that such fields be present.

4. Just for fun, our example has highly fragmented image data; the strips of our image are not even in sequential order. The point is that strip offsets must not be ignored. Never assume that strip N+1 follows strip N. Incidentally, there is no requirement that the image data follows the IFD information. Just the follow the pointers, whether they be IFD pointers, field pointers, or Strip Offsets.

TIFF Class G - Grayscale

Required (in addition to the above core requirements)

SamplesPerPixel = 1. SHORT.

BitsPerSample = 4, 8. SHORT. There seems to be little justification for working with grayscale images shallower than 4 bits, and 5-bit , 6-bit, and 7-bit images can easily be stored as 8-bit images, as long as you can compress the "unused" bit planes without penalty. And we can do just that with LZW (Compression = 5.)
Compression = 1 or 5 (LZW). SHORT. Recommendation: use 5, since LZW decompression is turning out to be quite fast.

PhotometricInterpretation = 0 or 1. SHORT. Recommendation: use 1, due to popular user interfaces for adjusting brightness and contrast.

TIFF Class P - Palette Color

Required (in addition to the above core requirements)

SamplesPerPixel = 1. SHORT. We use each pixel value as an index into all three color tables in ColorMap.

BitsPerSample = 1,2,3,4,5,6,7, or 8. SHORT. 1,2,3,4, and 8 are probably the most common, but as long as we are doing that, the rest come pretty much for free.

Compression = 1 or 5. SHORT.

PhotometricInterpretation = 3 (Palette Color). SHORT.

ColorMap. SHORT.

Note that bilevel and grayscale images can be represented as special cases of palette color images. As soon as enough major applications support palette color images, we may want to start getting rid of distinctions between bilevel, grayscale, and palette color images.

TIFF Class R - RGB Full Color

Required (in addition to the above Core Requirements)

SamplesPerPixel = 3. SHORT. One sample each for Red, Green, and Blue.

BitsPerSample = 8,8,8. SHORT. Shallower samples can easily be stored as 8-bit samples with no penalty if the data is compressed with LZW. And evidence to date indicates that images deeper than 8 bits per sample are not worth the extra work, even in the most demanding publishing applications.

PlanarConfiguration = 1 or 2. SHORT. Recommendation: use 1.
Compression = 1 or 5. SHORT.

PhotometricInterpretation = 2 (RGB). SHORT.

Recommended

Recommended for TIFF Class R, but not required, are the new (as of Revision 5.0) colorimetric information tags. See Appendix H.

Conformance and User Interface

Applications that write valid TIFF X files should include "TIFF B" and/or "TIFF G" and/or "TIFF P" and/or "TIFF R" and/or in their product spec sheets, if they can write the respective TIFF Class X files. If your application writes all four of these types, you may wish to write it as "TIFF B,G,P,R." Of course, a term like "TIFF B," while fine for communicating with other vendors, will not convey much information to a typical user. In this case, a phrase such as "Standard TIFF Black-and-White Scanned Images" might be better.

The same terminology guidelines apply to applications that read TIFF Class X files.

If your application reads more kinds of files than it writes, or vice versa, it would be a good idea to make that clear to the buyer. For example, if your application reads TIFF B and TIFF G files, but writes only TIFF G files, you should write it that way in the spec sheet.

Appendix H: Image Colorimetry Information

Chris Sears
210 Lake Street
San Francisco, CA 94118

June 4, 1988
Revised August 8, 1988

I. Introduction

Our goal is to accurately reproduce a color image using different devices. Accuracy requires techniques of measurement and a standard of comparison. Different devices imply device independence. Colorimetry provides the framework to solve these problems. When an image has a complete colorimetric description, in principle it can be reproduced identically on different monitors and using different media, such as offset lithography.

The colorimetry data is specified when the image is created or changed. A scanned image has colorimetry data derived from the filters and light sources of the scanner and a synthetic image has colorimetry data corresponding to the monitor used to create it or the monitor model of the rendering environment. This data is used to map an input image to the markings or colors of a particular output device.

Section II describes various standards organizations and their work in color.
Section III describes our motivation for seeking these tags.
Section IV describes our goals of reproduction.
Sections V, VI and VII introduce the colorimetry tags.
Section VIII specifies the tags themselves.
Section IX describes the defaults.
Section X discusses the limitations and some of the other issues.
Section XI provides a few references.

II. Related Standards

TIFF is a general standard for describing image data. It would be foolish for us to change TIFF in a way that did not match existing industry and international standards. Therefore, we have taken pains to note in the discussion below the efforts of various standards organizations and select defaults from the work of these organizations.

CIE   *(Commission Internationale de l'Eclairage)* The basis of the colorimetry information is the CIE 1931 Standard Observer [3]. While other color models could be supported [1]

[4], CIE 1931 XYZ is the international standard accepted across industries for specifying color and CIE xyY is the chromaticity diagram associated with CIE 1931 XYZ tristimulus values.

NTSC   *(National Television System Committee)* NTSC is of interest primarily for historical reasons and its use in encoding television data. Manufacturing standards for monitors have for some time drifted significantly from the 1953 NTSC colorimetry specification.

SMPTE   *(Society of Motion Picture and Television Engineers)* Most of the work by NTSC has been largely subsumed by SMPTE. This organization has a set of standards called "Recommended Practices" that apply to various technical aspects of film and television production [5] [6].

ISO   *(International Standards Organization)* ISO has become involved in color standards through work on a color addendum to "Office Document Architecture (ODA) and Interchange Format" [7].

ANSI   *(American National Standards Institute)* ANSI is the American representative to ISO .

III. Motivation

Our motivation for defining these tags stems from our research and development in color separation technology. With the information described here and the RGB pixel data, we have all of the information necessary for generating high-quality color separations. We could supply the colorimetry information outside of the image file. But since TIFF provides a convenient mechanism for bundling all of the relevant information in a single place, tags are defined to describe this information in color TIFF files.

A color image rendered with incorrect colorimetry information looks different from the original. One of our early test images has an artifact in it where the image was scanned with one set of primaries and color ramps were overlaid on top of it with different primaries. The blue ramp looked purple when we printed it. Using incorrect gamma tables or white points can also lead to distorted images. The best way to avoid these kinds of errors is to allow the creator of an image to supply the colorimetry information along with the RGB values [1] [2].

The purpose of the colorimetry data is to allow a projective transformation from the primaries and white point of the image to the primaries and white point of the rendering media. Gamma reflects the non-linear transfer gradient of real media.

IV. Colorimetric Color Reproduction

Earlier we said that given the proper colorimetric data an image could be rendered identically using two different calibrated devices. By identical, we mean colorimetric reproduction [9]. Specifically, the chromaticities match and the luminance is scaled to correspond to the luminance range of the output device. Because of this, we only need the chromaticity coordinates of the white point and primaries. The absolute luminance is arbitrary and unnecessary.

V. White Point

In TIFF 4.0, the white point was specified as D_{65}. This appendix allocates a separate tag for describing the white point and D_{65} is the logical default since it is the SMPTE standard [6].

The white point is defined colorimetrically in the CIE xyY chromaticity diagram. While it is rare for monitors to differ from D_{65}, scanned images often have different white points. Rendered images can have arbitrary white points. The graphic arts use D_{50} as the standard viewing light source [8].

VI. Primary Chromaticities

In TIFF 4.0, the primary color chromaticities matched the NTSC specification. With the wide variety of color scanners, monitors and renderers, TIFF needs a mechanism for accurately describing the chromaticities of the primary colors. We use SMPTE as the default chromaticity since conventional monitors are closer to SMPTE and some monitors (Conrac 6545) are manufactured to the SMPTE specifications. We don't use the NTSC chromaticities and white point because present day monitors don't use them and must be 'matrixed' to approximate them.

As an example, the primary color chromaticities used by the Sony Trinatron differ from those recommended by SMPTE. In general, since real monitors vary from the industry standards, the chromaticities of primaries are described in the CIE xyY system. This allows a reproduction system to compensate for the differences.

VII. Color Response Curves

This tag defines three color response curves, one each for red, green, and blue color information. The width of each entry is 16 bits, as implied by the type SHORT. The minimum intensity is represented by 0 and the maximum by 65535. For example, black is represented by 0,0,0 and white by 65535, 65535, 65535. The length of each curve is 2**BitsPerSample. A ColorResponseCurves field for RGB data where each of the samples is 8 bits deep would have 3*256 entries. The 256 red entries would come first, followed by 256 green entries, followed by 256 blue entries.

The purpose of the ColorResponseCurves field is to act as a lookup table mapping sample values to specific intensity values, so that an image created on one system can be displayed on another with minimal loss of color fidelity. The ColorResponseCurves field thus describes the "gamma" of an image, so that a TIFF reader on another system can compensate for both the image gamma and the gamma of the reading system.

Gamma is a term that relates to the typically nonlinear response of most display devices, including monitors. In most display systems, the voltage applied to the CRT is directly proportional to the value of the red, green, or blue sample. However, the resulting luminance emitted by the phosphor is not directly proportional to the voltage. This relationship is approximated in most displays by

luminance = voltage ** gamma

The NTSC standard gamma of 2.2 adequately describes most common video systems. The standard gamma of 2.2 implies a dim viewing surround. (We know of no SMPTE recommended practice for gamma.) The following example uses an 8 bit sample with value of 127.

voltage = 127 / 255 = 0.4980
luminance = 0.4980 ** 2.2 = 0.2157

In the examples below, we only consider a single primary and therefore only a single curve. The same analysis applies to each of the red, green, and blue primaries and curves. Also, and without loss of generality, we assume that there is no hardware color map, so that we must alter the pixel values themselves. If there is a color map, the manipulations can be done on the map instead of on the pixels.

If no ColorResponseCurves field exists in a color image, the reader should assume a gamma of 2.2 for each of the primaries. This default curve can be generated with the following C code:

```
ValuesPerSample = 1 << BitsPerSample;
for (curve[0] = 0, i = 1; i < ValuesPerSample; i++)
    curve[i] = floor (pow (i / (ValuesPerSample - 1.0), 2.2) * 65535.0 + .5);
```

The displaying or rendering application can know its own gamma, which we will call the "destination gamma." (An uncalibrated system can usually assume that its gamma is 2.2 without going too far wrong.) Using this information the application can compensate for the gamma of the image, as we shall see below.

If the source and destination systems are both adequately described by a gamma of 2.2, the writer would omit the ColorResponseCurves field, and the reader can simply read the image directly into the frame buffer. If a writer writes out the ColorResponseCurves field, then a reader must assume that the gammas differ. A reader must then perform the following computation on each sample in the image:

NewSampleValue = floor (pow (curve[OldSampleValue] / 65535.0, 1.0 / DestinationGamma) *
     (ValuesPerSample - 1.0) + .5);

Of course, if the "gamma" of the destination system is not well-approximated with an exponential function, an arbitrary table lookup may be used in place of raising the value to 1.0 / DestinationGamma.

Leave out ColorResponseCurves if using the default gamma. This saves about 1.5K in the most common case, and, after all, omission is the better part of compression.

Do not use this field to store frame buffer color maps. Use instead the ColorMap field. Note, however, that ColorResponseCurves may be used to refine the information in a ColorMap if desired.

The above examples assume that a single parameter gamma system adequately approximates the response characteristics of the image source and destination systems. This will usually be true, but our use of a table instead of a single gamma parameter gives the flexibility to describe more complex relationships, without requiring additional computation or complexity.

VIII. New Tags and Changes

The following tags should be placed in the "Basic Fields" section of the TIFF specification:

White Point
Tag   = 318 (13E)
Type = RATIONAL
N   = 2

The white point of the image. Note that this value is described using the 1931 CIE xyY chromaticity diagram and only the chromaticity is specified. The luminance component is arbitrary and not specified. This can correspond to the white point of a monitor that the image was painted on, the filter set/light source combination of a scanner, or to the white point of the illumination model of a rendering package.

Default is the SMPTE white point, D65: x = 0.313, y = 0.329.

The ordering is x, y.

PrimaryChromaticities
Tag   = 319 (13F)
Type = RATIONAL
N   = 6

The primary color chromaticities. Note that these values are described using the 1931 CIE xyY chromaticity diagram and only the chromaticities are specified. For paint images, these represent the chromaticities of the monitor and for scanned images they are derived from the filter set/light source combination of a scanner.

Default is the SMPTE primary color chromaticities:

Red:	x = 0.635	y = 0.340
Green:	x = 0.305	y = 0.595
Blue:	x = 0.155	y = 0.070

The ordering is red x, red y, green x, green y, blue x, blue y.

Color Response Curves

Default for ColorResponseCurves represents curves corresponding to the NTSC standard gamma of 2.2.

IX. Defaults

The defaults used by TIFF reflect industry standards. Both the WhitePoint and PrimaryChromaticities tags have defaults that are promoted by SMPTE . In addition, the default for the ColorResponseCurves tag matches the NTSC specification of a gamma of 2.2.

The purpose of these defaults is to allow reasonable results in the absence of accurate colorimetry data. An uncalibrated scanner or paint system produces an image that be displayed identically, though probably incorrectly on two different but calibrated systems. This is better then the uncertain situation where the image might be rendered differently on two different but calibrated systems.

X. Limitations and Issues

This section discusses several of the limitations and issues involved in colorimetric reproduction.

Scope of Usefulness

For many purposes the data recommended here is unnecessary and can be omitted. For presentation graphics where there are only a few colors, being able to tell red from green is probably good enough. In this case the tags can be ignored and there is no overhead. In more demanding color reproduction environments, this data allows images to be described device independently and at small cost.

User Burdens

The data we recommend isn't a user burden; it is really a systems issue. It allows a systems solution but doesn't require user intercession. Calibration however is a separate issue. It is likely to involve the user.

Resolution Versus Fidelity

Some manufacturers supply greater than 24 bits of resolution for color specification. The purpose of this is either to avoid artifacts such as contouring in the shadows or in some cases to be more specific or device independent about the color. Both reasons can be misguided. Other, less expensive techniques can be used to prevent artifacts, such as deeper color maps. As for accuracy, fidelity is more important than precision.

Colorimetric Color Reproduction

There are other choices for objectives of color reproduction [9]. Spectral color reproduction is a stronger condition and most are weaker, such as preferred color reproduction. While device independent spectral color reproduction is impossible, device independent colorimetric reproduction is possible, within a tolerance and within the limits of the gamuts of the devices. By choosing a strong criteria we allow the important objectives of weaker criteria, such as preferred color reproduction, to be part of design packages.

Metamerism

If two patches of color are identical under one light and different under another, they are said to be metameric pairs. Colorimetric color reproduction is a weaker condition than spectral color reproduction and hence allows metamerism problems. By standardizing the viewing conditions we can largely finesse the metamerism problem for print. Because television is self-luminous and doesn't use spectral absorption, metamerism isn't so much a problem.

Color Models - xyY Versus Luv, etc.

We choose xyY over Luv [1] because XYZ is the international standard for color specification and xyY is the chromaticity diagram associated with XYZ. Luv is meant for color difference measurement.

Ambient Environment And Viewing Surrounds

The viewing environment affects how the eye perceives color. The eye adapts to a dark room and it adapts to a colored surround. While these problems can be compensated for within the colorimetric framework [4], it is much better to finesse them by standardizing. The design environment should match the intended viewing environment. Specifically it should not be a pitch dark room and, on average, it should be of a neutral color. For print, ANSI recommends a Munsell N-8 surface [8].

XI. References

In particular, we would like to mention the work of Stuart Ring of the Copy Products Division of the Eastman Kodak Company. He and his colleagues are promoting a color data interchange paradigm. They are working closely with the ISO 8613 Working Group [7].

[1]   *Color Data Interchange Paradigm*, Eastman Kodak, Rochester, New York, 7 December 1987.

[2]   *Color Reproduction and Illumination Models*, Roy Hall, International Summer Institute: State of the Art in Computer Graphics, 1986.

[3]   *CIE Colorimetry: Official Recommendations of the International Commission on Illumination*, Publication 15-2, 1986.

[4]   *Color Science: Concepts and Methods, Quantitative Data and Formulae*, Gunter Wyszecki, W.S. Stiles, John Wiley and Sons, Inc., New York, New York, 1982.

[5]   *Color Monitor Colorimetry*, SMPTE Recommended Practice RP 145-1987.

[6]   *Color Temperature for Color Television Studio Monitors*, SMPTE Recommended Practice RP 37.

[7]   *Office Document Architecture (ODA) and Interchange Format—Addendum on Colour*, ISO 8613 Working Draft.

[8]   ANSI Standard PH 2.30-1985.

[9]   *The Reproduction of Colour in Photography, Printing and Television*, R. W. G. Hunt, Fountain Press, Tolworth, England, 1987.

[10]   *Raster Graphics Handbook*, The Conrac Corporation, Van Nostrand Reinhold Company, New York, New York, 1985. Good description of gamma.

APPENDIX 3

Conversion Guide to Other C Compilers

Introduction

The purpose of this appendix is to discuss the conversion of the example programs presented in this book to a C compiler other than Turbo C. This discussion assumes the conversion will be to Microsoft C (because of its ubiquity), although the same processes can be applied when converting to any C compiler. Conversion of the Turbo C code to another ANSI standard compiler (like Microsoft C) is fairly straightforward. Conversion to a non-ANSI standard C compiler will require more effort. Because so few changes are required to convert the Turbo C code to Microsoft C, and because the changes that are required are documented in this appendix, a typical conversion should take approximately 30 minutes. The term "port" is commonly used in industry to describe the software conversion process.

Because both Turbo C and Microsoft C are ANSI standard compilers, all features of the C language are identical. Language differences occur when using features outside of the specification—namely, graphics extensions and certain memory allocation extensions. Luckily, the example programs in this book do not use many of the non-ANSI extensions of the C language. Where extensions were used in the Turbo C code, they must be carefully ported to the environment of the new compiler.

Both Turbo C and Microsoft C are good compilers in which to develop image processing code. Both compilers have their strengths and weaknesses. Turbo C with its integrated environment and rich graphics capabilities makes programming easy and fun. The executable code produced by Turbo C for a typical program in this book is also smaller than that produced by Microsoft C. Microsoft C, while less convenient to use than Turbo C, consistently produced code that ran slightly faster than the equivalent Turbo C code. I'll gladly trade a little execution speed for ease of program development. This, however, is just the opinion of the author. You probably have your own thoughts on this topic. You'll probably develop your code in whichever environment you are most comfortable in.

As mentioned, few differences exist between the Turbo C and the equivalent Microsoft C code for the example programs given in this book. Most of these differences could have been taken care of using conditional compilation in the source code files. This was not done because it complicates the code and can make reading it confusing for beginning C programmers. In those few cases where the Turbo C and the Microsoft C code vary substantially (as you will see), conditional compilation would have complicated matters unacceptably.

As you will recall from the discussion in Chapter 1, the purpose of the VGA function library was to provide support of VGA mode 13 hex (320 × 200 256 colors) because Turbo C did not provide such support. Microsoft C, however, does provide support for this VGA mode. When porting the code to Microsoft C, you have the option of using the functions in the VGA function library or using the functions provided by Microsoft C. The choice is yours. Along the same vein, Microsoft C does not require the video graphics device to be initialized prior to being used, as Turbo C does. For this reason, the call to the function "InitGraph" in the Turbo C code can be completely removed when the code is ported to Microsoft C.

Microsoft C program development is assisted with a utility program called *make*. The make utility program automates the process of building (assembling, compiling, and linking) software, just as the "project make" facility does within the Turbo C environment. The make program (like project make) examines the dates of all of the files that make up a complete software project. When a component file is updated, the make utility issues the correct sequence of assembler, compiler, and/or linker commands to bring the executable code for the project up to date. Please consult either the Turbo C or the Microsoft C documentation for a complete discussion of the make program and how it works. For our purpose here, it is enough to realize that the project make files for each example program presented in this book must be converted into a make file for most other software development environments. To show the similarities and differences between a project make file and a make file as required by Microsoft C, the "All-Resolution Imaging Program" of Chapter 5 is used as an example.

The following is the contents of the file "allvideo.prj". This is the project make file for the example program of Chapter 5.

```
graphics.lib
vgagraph.obj
digitize.obj
egavga.obj
pcx        (misc.h pcx.h)
vga        (misc.h pcx.h vga.h)
allvideo   (misc.h pcx.h vga.h digitize.h)
```

The make file required by Microsoft C for the same example program is shown below. It would be named "allvideo.mak" for use with the make utility program.

```
CSwitch = /c /Zpil /G2 /Ox
LnkSwitch = /CO /MAP
```

```
pcx.obj : pcx.c pcx.h misc.h
          cl $(CSwitch) pcx.c

vga.obj : vga.c vga.h pcx.h misc.h
          cl $(CSwitch) vga.c

allvideo.obj : allvideo.c pcx.h vga.h misc.h
          cl $(CSwitch) allvideo.c

vgagraph.obj : vgagraph.asm
          masm vgagraph.asm,,,,

digitize.obj : digitize.asm
          masm digitize.asm,,,,

allvideo.exe : allvideo.obj pcx.obj vga.obj vgagraph.obj digitize.obj
          link $(LnkSwitch) allvideo+pcx+vga+vgagraph+digitize,\
allvideo,allvideo,graphics.lib+slibce.lib;
```

To execute the make program from the Dos command line, the command

```
make allvideo.mak
```

would be issued.

The Conversion Process

The conversion of Turbo C code to a different C compiler can be performed in the three distinct steps listed below. The amount of effort required at each step increases with the step. That is, the effort required for step 1 is generally trivial, while that required for step 3 is much greater. You might want to perform these steps in order as you convert the Turbo C code for use with your compiler.

1. Conversion of C language features: These are the features that are specified by whichever standard (K&R or ANSI) your compiler (also referred to as the target compiler) follows. In general, little effort is required during this conversion step as long as your compiler follows the same standard as Turbo C. If your compiler is non-ANSI standard, you will have some work to do. Specifically, you'll have to edit the source files to remove all parameter-type checking for function calls and remove references to void. Use the warning messages produced by your compiler to guide you through this step of the conversion. If possible, make whatever changes are necessary to the source code to stop the production of all warning messages.

2. Directly replaceable statements can sometimes be used to convert many of the nonstandard C language extensions (graphics extensions, for example) utilized by Turbo C to those required by the target compiler. This type of conversion also requires very little effort once the one-for-one language replacement is identified.

3. Code rewrites are required whenever the functionality offered by the Turbo C compiler (and its accompanying libraries) does not have an equivalent in the target compiler for which the code is being converted. Depending upon how different the compilers are, a lot of effort can be expended in the performance of this step.

To continue with our example of converting the Turbo C code to Microsoft C, we find that no effort is required in the first conversion step because the compilers are both ANSI standard and therefore very compatible. As expected, however, the language extensions offered by these compilers are quite different. These differences must be taken into consideration in conversion steps 2 and 3 discussed next.

Directly Replaceable Statements

Direct replacements are those items (functions, parameters, include files, and so on) in the Turbo environment that have a one-for-one correspondence to equivalent items in the target environment. In other words, the same functionality exists in the target environment, with possibly a different name or parameter passing convention. These types of changes could be taken care of using conditional compilation. These are generally items that are not controlled by either the ANSI or K&R C standard and therefore vary from compiler to compiler. When porting to the Microsoft C environment, replace the code specified for Turbo C with that specified for Microsoft C (MSC) in the list that follows.

    1. Selection of a VGA video mode

```
Turbo C: setgraphmode();
 in MSC: setvideomode();
```

The parameters passed to these functions to select the various graphics modes must also be changed. The correspondence is shown below:

Graphics Mode	Turbo C Parameter	Microsoft C Parameter
320 × 200 256 color	unsupported mode	_MRES256COLOR
640 × 200 16 color	VGALO	_HRES16COLOR
640 × 350 16 color	VGAMED	_ERESCOLOR
640 × 480 16 color	VGAHI	_VRES16COLOR

For example, selecting the 640 × 480 graphics mode

```
Turbo C: setgraphmode(VGAHI);
 in MSC: setvideomode(_VRES16COLOR);
```

    2. Placing the VGA back into the text mode from a graphics mode

```
Turbo C: restorecrtmode();
 in MSC: setvideomode(_DEFAULTMODE);
```

3. Setting a pixel on the graphics screen

```
Turbo C: putpixel(x,y,color);
 in MSC: _setcolor(color); followed by
         _setpixel(x,y);
```

4. Reading a pixel from the graphics screen

```
Turbo C: getpixel(x,y);
 in MSC: _getpixel(x,y);
```

5. Clearing the text screen

```
Turbo C: clrscr();
 in MSC: _clearscreen(_GCLEARSCREEN);
```

6. Suspending program execution for a specified period of time

```
Turbo C: delay();
 in MSC: no equivalent
```

7. Determining the amount of free space on the far heap

```
Turbo C: farcoreleft();
 in MSC: no equivalent
```

8. Allocating a block of memory from the far heap

```
Turbo C: farcalloc();
 in MSC: halloc();
```

The parameters to both functions are the same.

9. Freeing a block of memory allocated from the far heap

```
Turbo C: farfree();
 in MSC: hfree();
```

The parameters to both functions are the same.

10. Include filenames

```
Turbo C: "graphics.h"
 in MSC: "graph.h"
```

```
Turbo C: "alloc.h"
 in MSC: "malloc.h"
```

Code Rewrites

The final step in the software conversion process is to identify the functionality available in Turbo C that is not available from the target compiler. This functionality delta will have to be written into the converted C code to allow the example programs to run successfully. In converting the Turbo C code to Microsoft C, we have found that only the palette manipulation functions are lacking with Microsoft C. For this reason, the parts of the example programs that manipulate palettes must be rewritten for Microsoft C as follows:

```
Turbo C code to read and save the currently displayed palette


This  code is extracted from the "pcx.c" file where most  of  the
palette manipulation takes place.

    /*
    Read the current VGA palette into the palette
    data structure.
    */
    getpalette(&palette);
    /*
    For each entry in the palette data structure, find the RGB
    values of the color register associated with the palette entry.
    Store those values in the palette portion of the PCXData
    file structure.
    */
    for (Index = 0; Index < palette.size; Index++)
    {
        regs.h.ah = 0x10;  /* Get color reg RGB components function code */
        regs.h.al = 0x15;
        ColorRegisterNum = palette.colors[Index];
        regs.x.bx = ColorRegisterNum;

        int86(VIDEO,&regs,&regs);
        /* RGB values must be scaled by 4 before storing in file */
        PCXData.Palette[Index].Red   = regs.h.dh <<= 2;
        PCXData.Palette[Index].Green = regs.h.ch <<= 2;
        PCXData.Palette[Index].Blue  = regs.h.cl <<= 2;
    }


Microsoft C code to read and save the currently displayed palette

    for (Index = 0; Index < MAXPALETTECOLORS; Index++)
```

```
{
    regs.h.ah = 0x10;  /* Get palette reg entry function code */
    regs.h.al = 0x07;
    regs.h.bl = Index; /* for entry number Index */
    int86(VIDEO,&regs,&regs);
    ColorRegisterNum = regs.h.bl; /* Color reg number is in bl reg */

    regs.h.ah = 0x10;  /* Get color reg RGB components function code */
    regs.h.al = 0x15;
    regs.x.bx = ColorRegisterNum;

    int86(VIDEO,&regs,&regs);
    /* RGB values must be scaled by 4 before storing in file */
    PCXData.Palette[Index].Red   = regs.h.dh <<= 2;
    PCXData.Palette[Index].Green = regs.h.ch <<= 2;
    PCXData.Palette[Index].Blue  = regs.h.cl <<= 2;
}
```

Turbo C code for building and installing a VGA palette

This code is extracted from the "vga.c" file.

```
/* load the gray palette */
void LoadGray16Palette(void)
{
    struct palettetype palette;
    unsigned Index;
    union REGS regs;

    /*
    With a graphics mode set, we can proceed to load our palette and
    color registers in the DAC. The palette is set up in sequential
    order and the color register are set to gray scale values.
    */

    palette.size = MAXPALETTECOLORS;  /* 16 colors */
    /*
    Palette is mapped straight through. Palette entry zero
    is color register zero, one is one etc.
    */
    for (Index = 0; Index < MAXPALETTECOLORS; Index++)
        palette.colors[Index] = Index;
```

```
        /* set a block of Color Registers */
        regs.h.ah = 0x10;
        regs.h.al = 0x12;
        regs.x.bx = 0;
        regs.x.cx = MAXPALETTECOLORS;
        _ES = FP_SEG(Gray16ColorPalette);
        regs.x.dx =FP_OFF(Gray16ColorPalette);
        int86(VIDEO,&regs,&regs);

        /* install the newly created palette */
        setallpalette(&palette);
}


Microsoft C code for building and installing a VGA palette

/* load the gray palette */
void LoadGray16Palette(void)
{
        union REGS regs;
        struct SREGS segregs;

        /*
        With a graphics mode set, we can proceed to load our palette and
        color registers in the DAC. The palette is set up in sequential
        order and the color register are set to gray scale values.
        */

        /*
        Palette is mapped straight through. Palette entry zero
        is color register zero, one is one etc.
        */
        for (Index = 0; Index < MAXPALETTECOLORS; Index++)
        {
            regs.h.ah = 0x10;
            regs.h.al = 0x00;    /* Set palette register function code */
            regs.h.bh = Index;   /* Color reg number */
            regs.h.bl = Index;   /* Palette entry number */
            int86(VIDEO,&regs,&regs); /* Set palette entry to color reg number */
        }

        segread(&segregs);       /* read the values of the segment regs */

        /* set a block of Color Registers */
        regs.h.ah = 0x10;
```

```
        regs.h.al = 0x12;
        regs.x.bx = 0;
        regs.x.cx = MAXPALETTECOLORS; /* set all 16 entries at once */
        segregs.es = segregs.ds;      /* es:dx pts at palette array */
        regs.x.dx = Gray64ColorPalette;
        int86x(VIDEO,&regs,&regs,&segregs);
    }
```

Once all three of the steps just listed are performed, the following sequence of steps can be used to finish the conversion process.

1. Build a make file, using as an example the "project make" file that Turbo C uses.
2. Edit the C source files to incorporate the changes required in the C code.
3. Run the make program on the make file you built in step 1 to compile the new code. Pay close attention to any error or warning messages produced by the compiler and/or linker. All error and most warning messages must be cleared up before your port will be successful.
4. If error and warning messages were produced, go back to step 2 and correct the source(s) of the problem(s).
5. Once the errors and warning messages are gone, run the program.
6. If the program does not execute correctly, go back to step 2 and correct the problem(s).

When you arrive at this point, the conversion process should be complete. Although Microsoft C was used as the target for the conversion process illustrated here, similiar steps can be used for converting the example programs written in Turbo C and furnished in this book to any other C compiler.

Index